Who Killed Abraham Lincoln?

An investigation of North America's most
famous ex-priest's assertion that the Roman
Catholic Church was behind the assassination
of America's greatest President

Paul Serup

SALMOVA
PRESS

Canadian Cataloguing in Publication Data
Serup, Paul
Who killed Abraham Lincoln?

Includes bibliographical references and index.

ISBN 978-0-9811685-0-0
1. Lincoln, Abraham, 1809-1865--Assassination
2. Chiniquy, Charles, 1809-1899. Fifty years in the Church of Rome
3. United States--Foreign relations-- Catholic Church
4. Catholic Church--Foreign relations-- United States
5. Catholic Church--Political activity-- History--19th century
6. Conspiracies--United States-- History--19th century
I. Title.
E457.5 S43 2009   973.7092   0903

Salmova Press, 230 – 1126 3rd Ave, Prince George, B.C., Canada, V2L 3E5
www.salmovapress.com

Printed and bound in Canada
First Edition

Contributors

Cover design by Candice Rosenbaum and Paul Serup
Editorial assistance by Amelia Gilliland
Layout by ArtiFax Publishing & Design

Acknowledgements

Thanks is extended to the many staff members of libraries, archives, museums and other like institutions which assisted in the research needed to finish this work, in particular, Michele McNabb, formerly of the Champaign County Historical Archives, The Urbana Free Library. Thanks is also is tendered to Jane Ehrenhart and Kathryn Harris of the Abraham Lincoln Presidential Library, Springfield, Illinois, Jorie A. Walters, Research Assistant ,of Kankakee County Museum , and numerous interlibrary loans specialist of the Prince George area libraries, particularly Mickie Sexsmith of the Prince George Public Library.

The encouragement and advice of the few friends and relatives who knew that this book was being published, is also greatly appreciated.

DEDICATION

To the American people, especially the Yankees of yesterday,
and their descendants living today, who are still willing to
lay down their lives for the nation they love and for freedom.

Contents

Introduction

On February 12th, 1809, on a farm in poor, rural Kentucky, a baby boy was born to Thomas and Nancy Lincoln. They named their second child, Abraham, after his grandfather. More than five months later, on July 30th, in Kamouraska, Québec, another baby boy appeared. He was born to Charles and Reine Chiniquy and they named him Charles. Though they were not born in the same nation and grew up in separate countries and cultures, the two boys were destined to meet decades later and become very good friends.

Abraham Lincoln, despite his humble beginnings and lack of formal education, went on to become America's most beloved President and to gain enduring fame as one of the greatest men of all time. The other, Charles Chiniquy, although relatively unknown today, gained a national and international reputation during his lifetime, first as a Roman Catholic priest and then as a Protestant orator, writer and evangelist of his former co-religionists.

Among Chiniquy's numerous achievements were his efforts as a young French Canadian priest to persuade a reported 200,000 people in Québec to give up alcohol. According to one historical account, this resulted in the closing of all distilleries in the province except two, an accomplishment for which he received an award from the Canadian Parliament. Concerning his remarkable eloquence, one source reported that "He traveled more miles and delivered more public addresses and addressed more people and larger audiences than any other person in the nineteenth century."[1] He was painted by important Canadian artists: Hamel and Plamondon. Canadian Prime Minister Wilfred Laurier commented on him at his passing. Chiniquy was also referred to in books by well known Canadian writers such as Pierre Berton and Lucy Maud Montgomery, author of *Anne of Green Gables*.[2] The news of his passing made the front page of the *New York Times* and was reported in newspapers as diverse as the *Atlanta Constitution*, *Washington Post* and the *Times* of London.[3] One obituary described him as one of the most notable man in United States and Canada's national magazine, *Maclean's*, listed Charles Chiniquy as one of the one hundred most important Canadians in history.[4]

Although Abraham Lincoln achieved much greater and lasting fame, the *Kankakee Daily Gazette* stated that Kankakee County, Illinois, had not "conferred citizenship on so picturesque and notable a figure as Father Chiniquy" whose life was "full of adventures".[5] Chiniquy's experiences seem to have been amazingly varied and fascinating and they included establishing a large Roman Catholic colony in Illinois.

Although he tried to remain a faithful Catholic, changing the religious order he served in and the location where he ministered: the gulf between what the Church preached and what it practiced, the divide between the doctrines of Catholic theologians and what God's Word taught, finally caused him the leave the religion of his childhood and become a Protestant. Before he left, a struggle with a tyrannical Church superior led him to meet and make friends with the popular Springfield attorney, Abraham Lincoln, whom Charles Chiniquy hired to successfully defend him in a high profile law-suit.

One of the former priest's successes was his autobiography, *Fifty Years in the Church of Rome*. Commenting on the work, even a relatively hostile reviewer of the book stated that Chiniquy's account:

> met with amazing success. In 1892 translations of the French version into nine languages were circulating. By 1898 it had reached 70 editions. All over the world bishops were seeking information from their colleagues in Quebec so that they could counter the influence of Chiniquy's memoirs.[6]

As a priest and ex-priest, Charles Chiniquy was a controversial figure and many statements in *Fifty Years* about Catholicism caused a stir, especially amongst his former co-religionists. The most striking allegation he made about the Church of his youth was that its officials were behind the assassination of President Lincoln.

He stated that it was after Abraham Lincoln had masterfully represented him in court that he first began to fear for his defender's life. After the murder of his famous friend, Chiniquy began his own investigation into the crime, undoubtedly helped by his own background as a priest. In 1885, he declared in his autobiography, "after twenty years of constant and most difficult researches, I come fearlessly, to-day, before the American people, to say and prove that the President, Abraham Lincoln, was assassinated by the priests and the Jesuits of Rome."[7]

The question that can be asked is: was he correct? This volume is the result of in-depth research on the subject over a period of more than 22 years. It looks mainly at the life of the colourful ex-priest and his friendship with President Lincoln and whether historical fact supports his account, particularly his stunning allegation of the Catholic Church's culpability in the murder of the great Civil War leader.

The life of a man of international reputation like Charles Chiniquy's is a significant field of study. In addition, the teachings and actions of the Roman Catholic Church throughout history, particularly at the time of the Civil War, as well as the assassination of Abraham Lincoln, are two other large areas of investigation. For instance, an attorney of John Surratt, one of those accused of participating in the Lincoln murder conspiracy, called his 1867 prosecution, "an enormous case". Discussion of this particular legal saga, found mainly in the two volume court record, form just a small part of this work. Old newspaper accounts, books, journals, letters and other resources, including court, church and cemetery records, as well as manuscripts and other documents, have been explored to complete the research for this volume.

These matters have been examined from a vantage point of well over a century after the events. The individuals involved are all dead and some pieces of evidence have proved to be very difficult to find, if not lost forever. Although Charles Chiniquy maintained an extensive personal library and kept many important personal letters, newspaper clippings and other papers relevant to his life, his collection suffered loss due to at least one fire, deliberately set according to him.

Providentially, in 1999, a large part of these documents were released by Charles Chiniquy's family to become available for public research for the first time in more than a century since his death.[8] They make up the Chiniquy Collection, held in the province of Ontario, Canada. After careful review of essentially all of the relevant documentation available, it does not seem possible to find any part of the ex-priest's book where it appears certain that he made a significant error regarding historical fact. Information as to the whereabouts of further evidence that may shed more light on the subject is welcome.

It is not the author's contention that there is a conspiracy lurking around every corner or that the Church of Rome is to blame for every crime that has been committed since the beginning of its existence. When however, a man with the stature of the United States Secretary of War, Edwin Stanton, who *headed* the official U.S. government investigation into the assassination of Abraham Lincoln, believed that the President's death was the result of a Catholic plot, it certainly justifies further investigation.[9] As this work will demonstrate, from its beginning in the fourth century A.D., at the time of Constantine the Great, the evidence points to the fact that the hierarchy of the Roman Catholic Church and members of its flock have been involved in much more than their fair share of crime, including the assassination of the 16th President of the United States.

As shrouded in the mists of time as the Civil War appears to be today, the conflict and its main character, Abraham Lincoln, continue to hold immense interest for Americans and people around the world. Since his death, there have been some 15,000 imprints produced on the subject of the Great Emancipator. Although the cruel murder of this great man seems far removed from modern times, many people alive today are unaware that they have lived contemporaneously with a man who actually was in Ford's Theatre that night and personally witnessed the President's murder, Samuel J. Seymour, who died in 1956. In addition, a woman believed to be the last widow of a U.S. Civil War veteran, just passed away in 2004.[10]

In addition to being a brilliant speaker, Charles Chiniquy was also a prolific writer. Although the other works he produced were well received, his most popular book was *Fifty Years in the Church of Rome*. His fascinating autobiography is the basis for this volume, detailing his life from the year of his birth which he shared with another special person. Born in the same annum, separated by seasons, two young boys growing toward greatness to become like brilliant lights of varied intensity in the sky of humanity, drawn together by a common love of freedom, justice and truth. This is their story.

Chapter 1
Chiniquy's Early Life

Born in Kamouraska, into the Catholic faith of his French Canadian parents, Charles Chiniquy's first teacher was his mother as there was no school for him to go to as a child. His father had studied to be a priest but after learning of clergy scandal, he changed his mind. Before leaving the Seminary of Quebec, he was given a Bible by one of his superiors as a token of his esteem.

It was from this French Bible that young Charles was taught to read by his mother and he spent many hours at her side, fascinated by its words. He memorized many of the stories, as well as other portions. Even as a young boy, he felt Christ touch his heart as he learned the Scriptures. As he went through life, he found that the Word of God, hidden in his young heart while at his mother's side, was his spiritual shield and strength.

When he was eight years old, the parish priest came to their house and tried to take their Bible, telling his father that according to the law of the Church, he had to take it from them, if their son had been reading it. Charles had been given the Bible the previous Christmas and he was relieved when his father refused to hand it over, ordering the priest to leave their home instead.

Later that year, he was sent to attend a school with an excellent reputation in St. Thomas, run by a Protestant teacher. He stayed with his aunt and uncle and enjoyed his time there, fishing in the local rivers or playing with his friends when he was not in school.

When he was ten, Charles heard that he and the other Catholic children in St. Thomas would need to go to confessional for the first time. The youngsters were told that confessing all their sins to the priest would be one of the most important things they would ever do, the priest being in the place of God himself. Concealing any wrongdoing and lying to their father confessor would in many cases be an irreparable sin. Filled with dread, Charles worried about whether he would forget some sin and make a bad confession. He went to speak to the priest at confessional and felt ashamed after confessing all the sins he could remember to the man. What made it worse was the fact that after he was finished, his father confessor began to ask questions on a different kind. Thought he didn't state exactly what the priest said, it was clearly of a sexual nature which he felt was so disgusting, he couldn't repeat it.

Shortly after this, he heard that this priest had been beaten by some men of the village one night after he had visited the home of two sisters, evidently for immoral reasons. After all he had seen and heard, Charles wanted to go home and he was able to do so a few weeks later, in July of 1821. He spent a wonderful afternoon and evening with his parents. Early the next morning however, he woke to the cries of his mother, telling him that his beloved father was dead. His passing left them destitute and what made this terrible blow worse was the visit of the priest, a few days later. He demanded and took their only source of food, the family milk cow, as payment for the funeral service.

Wondering what to do, Charles and his mother knelt down and prayed. God heard their cry and a few days later, his mother received a letter from each of her two sisters, telling her to sell what they had and come and live with them. His mother and his two younger brothers went to live with her sister's family in St. Thomas, where Charles had formerly boarded, and Charles went to live in Kamouraska with his other aunt and uncle.

Charles expressed his wish to become a priest and was given the opportunity to study Latin under the vicar of Kamouraska, Rev. Morin. Morin had been a priest in a parish in Montreal but he was discovered to be in a sexual relationship with a female member of his congregation so he was transferred to Kamouraska where his sin was not as well known. The vicar was very kind to his students and Chiniquy felt sincere affection for him.

It was at this time that Charles experienced yet another struggle in his mind, caused by his first communion. He was pleased to know that through this sacrament, he would be in full possession of Christ but at the same time was also disturbed by the absurdity of it. His intellect rebelled at the idea that by eating the communion wafer, he was consuming the actual flesh of Jesus Christ. He found it very difficult to believe that Almighty God could be eaten by him, as he would eat a common piece of bread. Like the other children however, distracted by the pomp and ceremony of the occasion, he ignored his intellect and blindly accepted what his senses told him couldn't be true.

Charles completed his studies for the priesthood at the college of Nicolet, stating that what he could have learned in three or four years was spread out to seven. He again struggled, feeling that instead of stimulating the pupil's intelligence, Roman Catholic education institutions tried to prove that each student's own intellect was actually his greatest enemy.

They were taught fables as gospel truth and the moral education they received was from pagan writers such as Homer, Socrates, Virgil, etc. The students were not allowed to read the Bible to provide balance with the pagan sources. He also had trouble accepting the teaching that said he had to obey his superiors without question, no matter what they might command him to do.

In addition, he and his fellow classmates had great difficulty accepting the doctrine of celibacy which their college instructor, Rev Leprohon, admitted was not taught by God's Word but only by Catholic tradition. Though defeated by Chiniquy, Leprohon rebuked him and the other students for listening to their reason, instead of the Church. He warned them if they continued down that path they would be lost, becoming heretics, apostates and Protestants. Although some students quit their studies over it and though Charles knew that his logic was correct, he wished to remain a sincere Catholic, so he suppressed the voice of his conscience and reason, and in May of 1832, made a vow, as a priest, not to marry.

After the vow, in order to prepare for his duties in the confessional, Charles was stunned to find himself studying the most debauched forms of sin which he and other students were convinced would pollute their minds. According Roman Catholic theologians, they would have to question their female penitents in detail and listen to their confession on sins of a sexual nature, something that he and others were sure would degrade and irresistibly tempt them. Led again by Charles, the students protested but they were told to put reason aside and obey the Church's teaching without question. It was explained to them that despite these pollutions and temptations, the hearts of priests could remain pure. Charles again obeyed, though confused as to the practical application of this by the constant parade of priests sent to the seminary of Nicolet to do penance for siring children out of wedlock.

Despite the conflict between what the doctrines of the Catholic Church taught, and what God's Word and his reason told him, Charles Chiniquy completed his studies with honors and was ordained a priest in Montreal on September 21st, 1833. The numerous biographical accounts of his life, generally agree with Chiniquy's statements about his youth. According to the *Dictionary of Canadian Biography*, he was an " 'excellent pupil', gifted in public speaking and praised for his piety."[1]

Another account stated that he was:

> sent to the Seminary of St. Nicholet to be educated for the Romish priesthood. He entered this institution in 1822, and continued under its care till 1833, becoming one of the best linguists and mathematicians of the period. In short, his scholarship in every branch of the sciences was thorough, and he was without a rival in his university, carrying off all the first prizes of his classes. He had also become a most zealous son of the church, and was dubbed by his companions, 'the little saint.'[2]

His initial postings were in Québec, first as curate, or assistant, to the priest at St. Charles parish, then Charlesbourgh, and St. Roch after that. Mainly through the influence of a Protestant doctor he met while ministering to sick soldiers at the Québec Marine Hospital, in St. Roch, Father Chiniquy became thoroughly convinced of the damage alcohol does to individuals and society as a whole.

When he was appointed curate of Beauport in 1838, he organized a temperance society. Initially opposed in this work by his ecclesiastical superiors and fellow priests, he pressed on, convinced of the righteousness of the cause. In the time he was there, the customer base of the seven taverns in the community dwindled to the point that they had to close and seven schools were established when there had been none before, the people filled with gratefulness to their priest for the change.

Transferred to Kamouraska, Father Chiniquy's work of temperance continued. In 1846, greatly discouraged by scandals of the secular priesthood, he decided to join the religious order of the Oblates of Mary Immaculate, moving into their monastery at Longueuil, Quebec. He found however, that the priests of this order were even more corrupt than the ones he had left. Late in 1847, he departed from the monastery to preach temperance full time, mainly in the province of Québec, until 1851. Of this period, he reported:

During the four years, I gave 1800 public addresses, in 200 parishes, with the same fruits, and enrolled more than 200,000 people under the banners of temperance. Everywhere, the taverns, the distilleries and breweries were shut, and their owners forced to take other trades to make a living; not on account of any stringent law, but by the simple fact that the whole people had ceased drinking their beverages[3]

Chiniquy stated that he received the gift of a gold medal and $400.00 from the city of Montreal as a token of appreciation for his work. In addition, he helped frame legislation for the Canadian House of Commons which made liquor sellers responsible for the damage their wares caused and was honored by Parliament, by among other things, a gift of 500 pounds sterling. He received the title of "Apostle of Temperance" from the bishop of Montreal, as well as the benediction of the Pope for his efforts to stop drunkenness.[4]

According to Rev. Chiniquy, his independent thought, high moral standards and reliance on the Bible brought him into conflict with his superiors in the Church at times. He had been the father confessor of a rich single woman from his time as Longueuil. The bishop of Montreal attempted to get Chiniquy to persuade her to join a nunnery, partially so her fortune could be transferred to the Church. He refused, angering the bishop.[5]

A short time later, when he was hearing confessions in a church in Montreal, an attractive girl he didn't know came to confess. She detailed the orgies she had participated in with other priests in such a way that Chiniquy felt she had been sent by someone to tempt him. He told her to stop, ordering her never to come to confess to him again. She left the church, furious. Several weeks later, he received a letter from the bishop of Montreal, telling him that for a criminal action the bishop would not disclose, he had withdrawn all of Chiniquy's authority as a priest and suspended him.

The day he received the letter, Chiniquy went to see Bishop Bourget to find out what crime he had been charged with. He also asked that he be allowed to confront his accusers but the prelate refused his requests, disdainfully ordering him out of his palace. Chiniquy felt that what had happened to him was connected to the girl in the confessional. He decided to spend the next eight days in prayer at the Jesuit college in Montreal where he also hoped get assistance from members of the Society of Jesus to get to the bottom of the accusation against him.

With the help of a priest at the college, he found out the girl's identity. They confronted her and she confessed to bringing a false accusation against Chiniquy to the bishop. Four copies of her sworn confession were made and one sent to Bishop Bourget, who ended Chiniquy's suspension. The other copies would be used later to defend him when the same bishop, after destroying his own copy, tried to press this charge against him years later.[6]

While successfully toiling for the cause of temperance and for his Church, doubts continued to be sown in Chiniquy's mind however, by the public and private scandals involving fellow priests, the misdeeds of high officials, as well as the opposition of the teachings of the Catholic Church to the Bible and reason. He tried to ignore them, along with the protesting voice of his conscience, and in 1851, he accepted an invitation from Bishop Vandeveld of Chicago to establish a Roman Catholic settlement on the untamed prairie of Illinois.

Charles Chiniquy wrote an open letter which was published in the Canadian press, urging Canadians who were already leaving the country, to immigrate to Illinois. It was very effective and in the fall of 1851, the Apostle of Temperance, along with 40 families, founded the town of St. Anne in the eastern part of the state. As the community grew, mainly through French Canadian immigration, nearby towns of L'Erable and St. Mary were established. Though the colony increased and prospered, the change of scenery didn't help Chiniquy's belief in his religion as the scandals involving fellow priests in the area were as troubling as those in Canada.

On a visit to the colony in the spring of 1853, the kindly Bishop Vandeveld informed Chiniquy he felt he had to resign his bishopric. Vandeveld told him that if he obeyed the laws of the Church, he would have to remove all of the priests except Chiniquy and two or three others because most of them were drunkards or living publicly or secretly in common-law relationships.

Charles Chiniquy's faith in his Church was further shaken when he went to call the bishop for breakfast the next morning and discovered him drunk on wine reserved for the mass. After some delay, Bishop Vandeveld's resignation was accepted by Church authorities and he was appointed bishop of Natchez, Mississippi.[7] In 1854, Vandeveld was replaced by Anthony O'Regan. Bishop O'Regan proved to be a tyrannical administrator with whom Chiniquy clashed with almost immediately.

Rev. M. A. Lebel was the pastor of the French Canadian congregation in Chicago at this time of Catholic colonization of central Illinois. When he learned of Chiniquy's plan to establish a colony, he became jealous and opposed his efforts. Lebel later paid a drunken visit to Chiniquy along with another neighboring priest, a former owner of a Chicago brothel. Arriving at the colony one afternoon, they were politely received by him and they left after dinner. The next day however, Chiniquy wrote to them and told them never to come back. Bishop O'Regan complained about this and ordered Chiniquy to fellowship with his fellow priests, which he refused to do. He describes how this caused the celebrated court battles he would fight against Peter Spink, which would eventually involve Abraham Lincoln:

> The bishop felt insulted by my letter, and was furious against me. It came to be a public fact that he had said before many people: 'I would give anything to the one who would help me to get rid of that unmanageable Chiniquy.'

> Among those who heard the bishop, was a land speculator, a real land-shark, against whom a bill for perjury had been found by the jury of Iroquois county, the 27th of April, 1854. That man was very angry against me for protecting my poor countrymen against his too sharp speculations. He said to the bishop, 'if you pay the expense of the suit, I pledge myself to have Chiniquy put in gaol.' The bishop had publicly answered him:

'No sum of money will be too great to be delivered from a priest, who alone gives me more trouble than the rest of my clergy.'

To comply with the desires of the bishop, this speculator dragged me before the criminal court of Kankakee, on the 16th day of May, 1855, but he lost his action, and was condemned to pay the cost.[8]

A prominent Catholic resident of the area, Peter Spink was the man who prosecuted Charles Chiniquy, in an attempt to have him put in jail. Several weeks after the drunken visit of Lebel, Bishop O'Regan visited St. Anne with Rev. Lebel and another priest, Rev. Carthuval, sparking an argument with Chiniquy about their presence in his pastorate. Father Chiniquy finally agreed to fellowship with them for the sake of peace but refused to comply when O'Regan demanded to be given the title to Chiniquy's own home in St. Anne. The bishop left, angry with him again.

Later in August of that year, Charles Chiniquy was told he would have to participate in a spiritual retreat for priests in Chicago. While he was at the function, he was distressed by the immoral behavior he witnessed on the part of many of the Catholic clergy who attended. One of the reasons the priests had been called together was to pledge to raise money for an extravagant new palace the bishop wanted to build in Chicago.

Hardly a month went by after this before a chorus of complaints began to circulate in Illinois about the misdeeds of Bishop O'Regan. The French Canadians in Chicago said he had stolen vestments they had purchased for their religious services, the German Catholics said he had swindled them out of the land they planned to build their church on and so forth. After going to Chicago to investigate, Chiniquy found these reports to be accurate and protested to the bishop. There was yet another argument, O'Regan pointing out that as bishop, he legally had the right to personally possess all the church property of the Catholics in his diocese. [9]

According to *Fifty Years*, Peter Spink continued to pursue him in the courts, at the urging of Bishop O'Regan:

My Lord O'Regan had determined to interdict me; but not being able to find any cause in my private or public life as a priest, to found such a sentence, he had pressed that land speculator, Spink, to prosecute me again; promising to base his interdict on the condemnation which, he had been told, would be passed against me by the Criminal Court of Kankakee.

But the bishop and Peter Spink were again to be disappointed; for the verdict of the court, given on the 13th of November, 1855, was again in my favour.[10]

It was here that events brought Charles Chiniquy, bright light that he was, into the orbit of another that would shine so much brighter.

Chapter 2
Lincoln: Childhood to Spink vs. Chiniquy

Though he was to rise to become the greatest U.S. President, Abraham Lincoln was born in humble circumstances in a log cabin in Kentucky in 1809. He grew up on America's western frontier and received less than a year of formal schooling. In 1816, his father, Thomas, moved the family to Indiana. Lincoln's mother died when he was nine and the year after her death was the most difficult of his childhood. On December 2nd, 1819, however, his father married a widow, Sarah Bush Johnson. She became very fond of Abraham, as he became of her. As a youth, Lincoln had to help his father carve productive land out of their wild forested property and then work the resulting useful farmland. At night he would study by firelight. In order to borrow a book, he sometimes had to walk great distances. Probably the only book his family owned was the Bible and like Charles Chiniquy, Abraham Lincoln became very well acquainted with it.

Well before the age of 20, Lincoln reached the height of 6'4" and although he was lanky, he was very strong and skilled with an axe. He could cut firewood, split rails, as well as plow, harvest corn and thresh wheat. His speaking and story-telling ability also made him popular among his neighbors. When he was nineteen, he helped transport a flatboat loaded with produce down the Ohio River to New Orleans, exposing him to the world beyond his immediate surroundings.

In 1830, the family moved to Illinois. After another flatboat trip to New Orleans in 1831, Lincoln was hired by the boat owner to be a clerk in his new store in New Salem, a village some 20 miles from Springfield. The business failed within several months. When the Black Hawk War began in 1832, Lincoln volunteered and was elected captain of the militiamen of his community. He re-enlisted several times. After he had finished serving, he was encouraged by his friends to run for a seat in the state legislature. He was not successful though and instead, he worked as a postmaster and a land surveyor in New Salem. In 1833, he bought a store, on credit, in partnership with William F. Berry. The store also failed short afterwards. Berry died a couple of years later, leaving the debts to Lincoln. He paid them off years later, earning himself the nickname, "Honest Abe". In 1834, he again ran and won a seat in the lower house of the Illinois General Assembly, as a member of the Whig Party. He won three more consecutive elections, serving eight years in the General Assembly.

Lincoln began to study law and in 1836, he received his license to practice law. In 1837, he moved to the state capital, Springfield, and met Mary Todd, whom he married five years later. They had four boys, only one of which survived to adulthood. In the same year, in his first public statement on slavery, Lincoln and another legislator asserted that slavery was, "founded on both injustice and bad policy."

Abraham Lincoln began his legal career as the junior partner of older, more experienced lawyers and he was involved in a variety of legal work. He also "rode the circuit" for six months of the year, following the court as it made its way from county to county around Springfield. In 1844, Lincoln asked William Herndon to be his law partner and by 1856, twenty years after he became an attorney, Lincoln was the senior partner of Lincoln Herndon and according to one biographical source, he "had made himself one of the most distinguished and successful lawyers in Illinois."

According to *Fifty Years*, it was legal need that occasioned Charles Chiniquy's first meeting with the tall prairie lawyer whose honesty and ability were well-known in Illinois, despite his humble beginnings. The celebrated Apostle of Temperance's fame in 1856, however, was such that the slander suit, in which Abraham Lincoln defended him, attracted large crowds of people who attended because Chiniquy was involved, not Lincoln. Spink vs. Chiniquy was the most high profile case of this type in Abraham Lincoln's legal career.

Although Charles Chiniquy had been initially victorious over Peter Spink through two court battles in Kankakee, his opponent applied for a change of venue to Urbana, stating he had no confidence in the Kankakee court (see Figure 1). Chiniquy said he almost fainted when he heard that he would be faced with the enormous cost of continuing the legal struggle at a distant court, not to mention the risk of being tried in a community where he was not known, and though innocent, possibly found guilty.

Outside the Kankakee courthouse, a stranger approached the priest and said that he had been following the legal battle from the beginning. He explained to Chiniquy that his struggle was more formidable than he realized. He said that Bishop O'Regan was the one really behind the prosecution, Spink being merely a tool the bishop was using to try to destroy him. As he was the only one of his priests that dared to oppose him, the prelate was determined to get rid of him and though they hated O'Regan, bishops the world over would help him to neutralize the priest that challenged his authority and by extension, theirs as well.

The stranger strongly suggested he hire Abraham Lincoln to defend him, describing him as the "best lawyer and most honest man", in Illinois. With the enthusiastic approval of his other lawyers, Chiniquy telegraphed Mr. Lincoln to ask if he would defend him at the next spring court session at Urbana. A short time later he received an affirmative answer.

On May 19th, 1856, Charles Chiniquy had to deliver himself into the custody of the Sheriff of Kankakee, who was required to bring him, like a criminal, to the Sheriff of Champagne County, Illinois. There the priest made the acquaintance of Abraham Lincoln. Chiniquy described the occasion:

> It was then that I met Abraham Lincoln for the first time. He was a giant in stature; but I found him still more a giant in the noble qualities of his mind and heart. It was impossible to converse five minutes with him without loving him. There was such an expression of kindness and honesty in that face, and such an attractive magnetism in the man; that, after a few moments' conversation, one felt as tied to him by all the noblest affections of the heart.

Figure 1

Letter and sworn statement from P. Spink with transcriptions

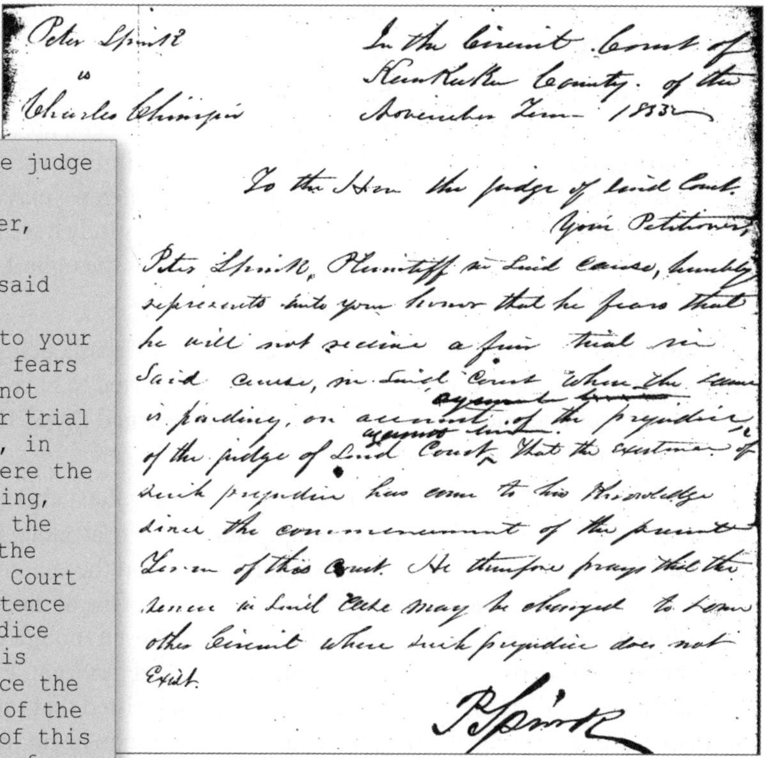

Peter Spink vs Charles Chinipin — In the Circuit Court of KenKaKee County. of the November Term / 1855

To the Hon the judge of said Court

Your Petitioner,

Peter Spink, Plaintiff in said cause, humbly represents unto your honor that he fears that he will not receive a fair trial in said cause, in said court where the cause is pending, on account of the prejudice of the judge of said Court that the existence of such prejudice has come to his knowledge since the commencement of the present Term of this Court. He therefore prays that the venue in said cause may be changed to some other Circuit where such prejudice does not exist.

P Spink

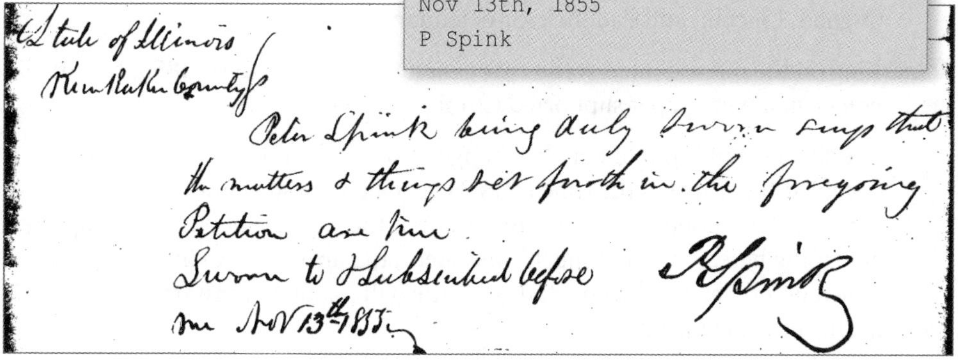

State of Illinois, KenKaKee County

Peter Spink being duly sworn says that the matters & things set forth in the foregoing Petition are true.

Sworn to & Subscribed before me.

Nov 13th, 1855

P Spink

Archival Collections, Kankakee County Museum

Abraham Lincoln greeted Charles Chiniquy warmly, telling him that he already knew the priest by reputation as the protector of his fellow French Canadians and opponent of the tyrannical bishop of Chicago. He asked Chiniquy why he had requested his services. Chiniquy stated:

> I answered by giving him the story of that unknown friend who had advised me to have Mr. Abraham Lincoln for one of my lawyers, for the reason that "he was the best lawyer and the most honest man in Illinois." He smiled at my answer, with that inimitable and unique smile, which we may call the "Lincoln smile," and replied: "That unknown friend would surely have been more correct had he told you that Abraham Lincoln was the ugliest lawyer of the country!" And he laughed outright.

Chiniquy stated that although he spent six long days at Urbana being treated as a criminal and enduring a variety of abuse, he was comforted to have the eloquent Abraham Lincoln defending him and his judge, the learned David Davis, who was to go on to become U.S. Vice-President.

Lincoln demolished the testimony of two Catholic priests, Rev Lebel and Rev Carthuval, who had testified against Chiniquy during the trial, along with a number of other false witnesses. After Lincoln's outstanding work and the charge of Judge Davis, Chiniquy felt sure he would have been declared innocent. One of the jurors however, was an Irish Catholic. He wanted Chiniquy condemned even though the other eleven jurors, who were Protestants, wanted him declared innocent. Unable to come to a unanimous verdict, the jury was dismissed. Spink insisted that the sheriff keep Chiniquy prisoner, having obtained the court's permission to begin the prosecution again at the fall court term.[1] Although he doesn't expressly say so, Chiniquy evidently gained his freedom by making a bail arrangement, perhaps a day or two later.

Along with the surviving court documents of the 1856 spring and fall court actions of Spink vs. Chiniquy, there are some newspaper reports and historical accounts of the legal struggle. *Lincoln Day by Day* reported for May 20, 1856:

> Trial of Spink v. Chiniquy, from Kankakee on change of venue, commences. Spink, layman in Catholic Church, has charged Chiniquy, his priest, with slander from pulpit. Case has aroused much interest, and many of Chiniquy's parishioners attend. Norton, Davis, and Starr are counsel for plaintiff, Osgood, Lincoln, and Paddock for defendant.

Remarking on the intense interest the case generated, the May 29th, 1856, edition of the *Urbana Union* newspaper supported Chiniquy's account:

> The slander suit brought here by change of venue from Kankakee county occupied the whole of the time from 3 o'clock on Tuesday until adjournment, completely monopolizing the whole affair at the expense of business properly belonging here. After that much time spent, the jury failed to find a verdict, which unless the parties conclude to settle will make it necessary to try it again at the next term.

This suit by the way involved of a good deal of interest to all who attended Court.

Reporting that the lawsuit involved a priest being accused by a layman of slander, the *Union* declared that, "The plaintiff brought up among his witnesses another priest who was impeached by the opposite party, whose witnesses swore they would not believe him under oath"[2] (see Figure 2). *Fifty Years* reported that Lincoln had demolished the testimony of the perjured priest, Rev Lebel. Was Lebel the priest on Spink's side who was impeached by defence witnesses, who swore they wouldn't believe him on his oath, as the Urbana newspaper reported? It seems very likely as he and Rev Carthuval were the only priests mentioned in court documents, which confirm their involvement in the case on the plaintiff's side.[3]

According to *Fifty Years*, when the fall term arrived, the Sheriff of Kankakee took Chiniquy into custody again and transported him, again as a criminal to Urbana. He, along with his lawyers, Uri Osgood, John Paddock and a dozen witnesses, joined Abraham Lincoln and Judge Davis there on October 20th, 1856.

The first witness called to testify at the trial was Rev. Lebel. Over the objections of Abraham Lincoln, he was allowed to say what he wanted about Chiniquy's character. He began by stating, "Chiniquy was one of the vilest men of the day—that every kind of bad rumors were constantly circulating against him." In testimony that lasted almost an hour, he reported a good number of them, although he could not tell if they were true or not, having not substantiated them. Expressing regret at having to reveal such a shameful thing, Lebel said he did know the truth about one charge because he had thoroughly investigated it:

> "*Mr. Chiniquy*," he said, "*had attempted to do the most infamous things with my own sister, Madame Bosse*. She herself has told me the whole story under oath, and she would be here to unmask the wicked man to-day before the whole world, if she were not forced to silence at home from a severe illness". (italics in original)

Chiniquy stated that even though the story of the attempted seduction, or rape, was a complete lie, the priest appeared to be so sincere that Chiniquy wished the floor would open up to swallow him. Mercifully, Abraham Lincoln soon diminished the effect of Lebel's testimony by a vigorous cross-examination of him and by introducing the testimony of 12 reputable former parishioners of the priest who declared that he was such a drunkard, so vicious and so clearly Chiniquy's enemy, that they wouldn't believe his testimony, even on his oath. According to *Fifty Years*, there evidently was another priest beside Lebel who also gave false testimony against Chiniquy.

Meeting with Mr. Lincoln and his other lawyers that night, Charles Chiniquy told them how discouraged he was by the day's events. Lincoln also expressed his concerns. He said that although he had no doubts that Rev. Lebel's testimony was all lies, he felt that the jury believed him.

He said that the only way to destroy Lebel's testimony would be to have direct testimony contradicting what he said, or showing that he perjured himself, something that seemed impossible because the plaintiff's side had been careful not

Figure 2
Article in the *Urbana Union*, May 29, 1856

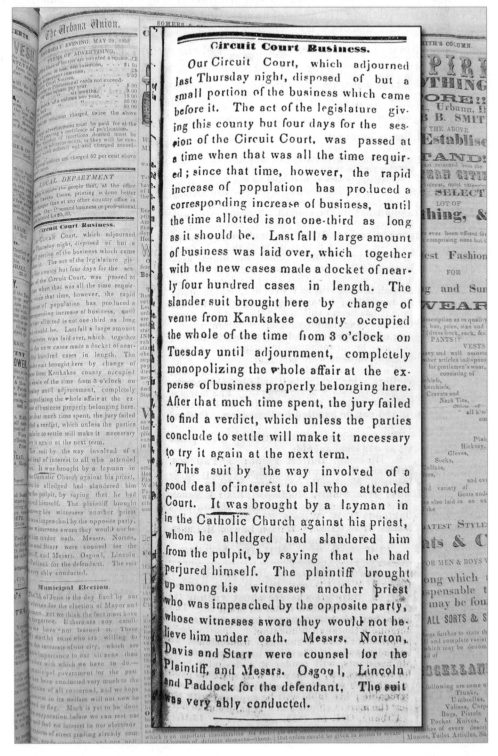

Circuit Court Business.

Our Circuit Court, which adjourned last Thursday night, disposed of but a small portion of the business which came before it. The act of the legislature giving this county but four days for the session of the Circuit Court, was passed at a time when that was all the time required; since that time, however, the rapid increase of population has produced a corresponding increase of business, until the time allotted is not one-third as long as it should be. Last fall a large amount of business was laid over, which together with the new cases made a docket of nearly four hundred cases in length. The slander suit brought here by change of venue from Kankakee county occupied the whole of the time from 3 o'clock on Tuesday until adjournment, completely monopolizing the whole affair at the expense of business properly belonging here. After that much time spent, the jury failed to find a verdict, which unless the parties conclude to settle will make it necessary to try it again at the next term.

This suit by the way involved of a good deal of interest to all who attended Court. It was brought by a layman in in the Catholic Church against his priest, whom he alledged had slandered him from the pulpit, by saying that he had perjured himself. The plaintiff brought up among his witnesses another priest who was impeached by the opposite party, whose witnesses swore they would not believe him under oath. Messrs. Norton, Davis and Starr were counsel for the Plaintiff, and Messrs. Osgood, Lincoln and Paddock for the defendant. The suit was very ably conducted.

to fix the date when the alleged crime was committed. Saying that only Almighty God could save him, Lincoln ended their meeting by urging Chiniquy to seek help through prayer. Chiniquy wrote:

> I have often been asked if Abraham Lincoln had any religion; but I have never had any doubt about his profound confidence in God, since I heard those words falling from his lips in that hour of anxiety. I had not been able to conceal my deep distress. Burning tears were rolling on my cheeks when he was speaking, and there was on his face the expression of friendly sympathy which I shall not forget.

Charles Chiniquy stated that he went back in his room and although he tried to pray, his troubles seemed so overwhelming that he could not do so. Eventually though, in tears, he was able to call upon the Almighty for help. He spent hours in supplication to God until three in the morning, when he heard a knock at his hotel room door.

It was Abraham Lincoln, telling him that the court battle was over and that the plot of Lebel had been completely revealed. Lincoln explained that right after Lebel had given his testimony, a journalist had telegraphed some of the major newspapers in Chicago, reporting that Father Chiniquy would surely be condemned. This was published in the city and a friend of Chiniquy's, named Narcisse Terrien, happened to buy one of the papers containing the news. He informed his wife of this and she told him that she knew that Charles Chiniquy was innocent.

She explained that she had overheard Lebel when he made an agreement with his sister to give her 160 acres of land in exchange for her false testimony against Chiniquy. Terrien asked his wife to go with him to Urbana to expose Lebel but she said she couldn't go because she was too ill to travel. She instead suggested that her husband take Philomene Moffat, a friend of hers who had also been there and had heard the scheme as well.

Miss Moffat was willing to go, so she and Terrien started for Urbana immediately, arriving by train in the early hours of the next day. As soon as she got there, she went to see Abraham Lincoln and told him what she knew. According to *Fifty Years*, Lebel had been unable to sleep after the numerous lies he had told in court. Looking in the guest register of the hotel he was staying in, he was stunned to see Philomene Moffat's name there. He remembered that some time previously, she had told him, in the confessional, that she had heard the plot from his own lips.

He sent for her, exclaiming, "Ah! wretched girl! you come to destroy me?" Learning she planned to be a witness against him the next day, he tried to bribe her to go back to Chicago on the morning train. She refused his offer and Lebel rushed off to tell Spink to withdraw the suit and to pack his belongings before fleeing Urbana.[4]

According to Illinois state marriage records, Philomene Moffat married Jules Schwartz on April 25th, 1857, in Cook County (Chicago is in Cook County). The marriage changed her last name to Schwartz. In the section on Spink vs. Chiniquy, *Fifty Years* reproduced an affidavit made by her, made at the request of Charles Chiniquy. It details in her own words what part she had played in this court case

Figure 3

Affidavit sworn by Mrs. Schwartz before Stephen R. Moore.
Dated October 21st, 1881, with transcription

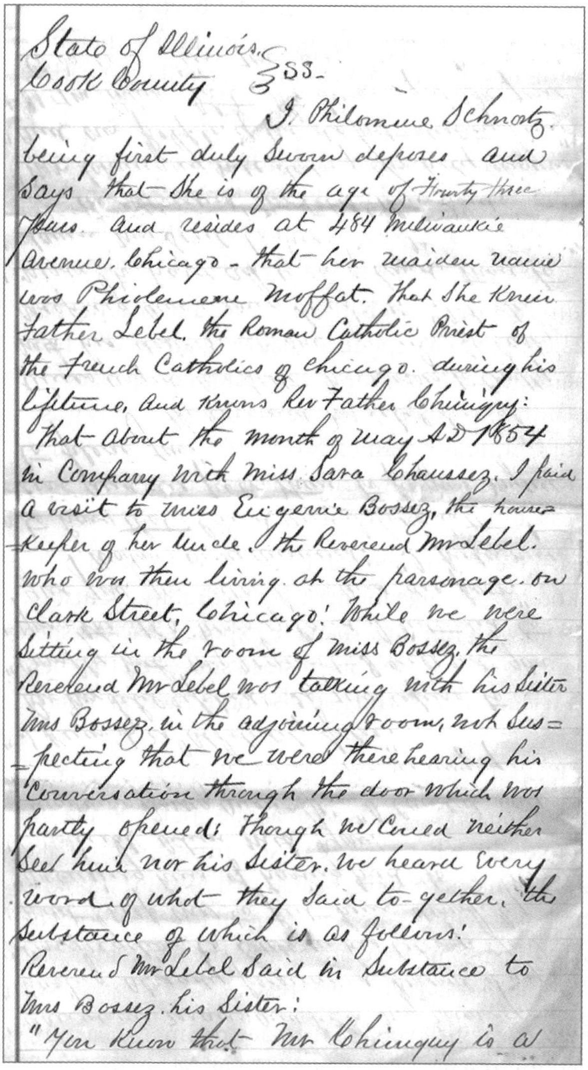

State of Illinois
Cook County } SS-
I Philomine Schwartz
being first duly sworn deposes and
says that she is of the age of forty three
years. and resides at 484 Milwaukie
avenue. Chicago - that her maiden name
was Philomene Moffat. that she knew
Father Lebel. the Roman Catholic Priest of
the French Catholics of Chicago. during his
lifetime, and knows Rev Father Chiniquy:
that about the month of May AD 1854
in Company with Miss Sara Chaussey. I paid
a visit to Miss Eugenie Bossey, the house
keeper of her uncle. the Reverend Mr Lebel.
who was then living at the parsonage. on
Clark Street, Chicago: While we were
sitting in the room of Miss Bossey, the
Reverend Mr Lebel was talking with his sister
Mrs Bossey, in the adjoining room, not sus=
pecting that we were there hearing his
conversation through the door which was
partly opened: Though we could neither
see him nor his sister, we heard every
word of what they said to-gether. the
substance of which is as follows:
Reverend Mr Lebel said in Substance to
Mrs Bossey. his sister:
"You know that Mr Chiniquy is a

The Chiniquy Collection

STATE OF ILLINOIS)
Cook County,) SS.

I, Philomine Schwartz, being first duly sworn deposes and says that she is of the age of forty three years and resides at 484 Milwaukie avenue, Chicago - that her maiden name was Philomine Moffat, that she knew Father Lebel, the Roman Catholic Priest of the French Catholics of Chicago during his lifetime, and knows Rev Father Chiniquy: that about the month of May AD 1854 in company with Miss Sara Chaussey, I paid a visit to Miss Eugenie Bossey, the house keeper of her uncle, the Reverend Mr Lebel, who was then living at the parsonage on Clark Street, Chicago: While we were sitting in the room of Miss Bossey, the Reverend Mr. Lebel was talking with his sister Mrs Bossey, in the adjoining room, not suspecting that we were there hearing his conversation through the door which was partly opened: Though we could neither see him nor his sister, we heard every word of what they said to together, the substance of which is as follows:

Reverend Mr Lebel said in substance to Mrs Bossey, his sister: "you know that Mr Chiniquy is a and it closely supports Chiniquy's version of what happened. Held in the Chiniquy Collection, the original affidavit was sworn by Mrs. Schwartz before Stephen R. Moore, the well-known and respected Kankakee lawyer, notary public, and reportedly, judge. Dated October 21st, 1881, the wording is essentially the same as was reproduced in *Fifty Years*.[5] It is shown in part in Figure 3. The full document is reproduced in the Appendix 3, Part 1.

Historical accounts indeed show that Rev. Lebel was the pastor of the French-Canadian congregation in Chicago, as Chiniquy reported. For instance, *The Chicago Directory*, 1855-1857, listed Rev. Antony Isadore Lebel as living at 237 Clark Street. This evidently was the address of the parsonage of St. Louis Catholic church, where he was residing when Philomene Schwartz overheard his conversation with his sister.[6]

Several of the surviving court documents from the Spink vs. Chiniquy, October, 1856, court action also support what Charles Chiniquy and Philomene Moffat / Schwartz stated. Two accounts of Chiniquy's legal costs from the October term lists both a Miss Maffit and a N. Therrien as witnesses. They are shown in Figures 4 and 5. Both names appear to be misspelled but this was not unusual. Rev. Lebel's name,

Figure 4

List of defence witnesses, Spink vs. Chiniquy, October, 1856

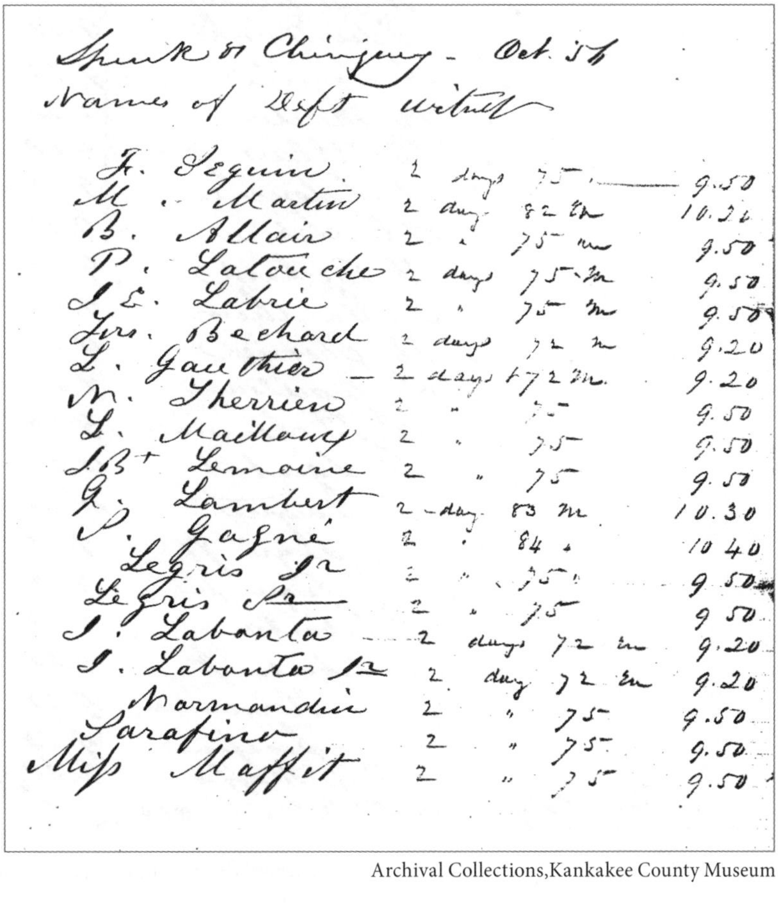

Spink vs Chiniquy – Oct. 56

Names of Deft witnesses

F. Seguin	2	days	75	9.50
M. Martin	2	days	82 m	10.20
B. Allain	2	"	75 m	9.50
P. Latouche	2	days	75 m	9.50
J. E. Labrie	2	"	75 m	9.50
Frs. Bechard	2	days	72 m	9.20
L. Gauthier	2	days	72 m	9.20
N. Therrien	2	"	75	9.50
L. Mailloux	2	"	75	9.50
J. Bt Lemoine	2	"	75	9.50
G. Lambert	2	days	83 m	10.30
P. Gagné	2	"	84	10.40
Legris Jr	2	"	75	9.50
Legris Sr	2	"	75	9.50
J. Labonta	2	days	72 m	9.20
J. Labonta Jr	2	days	72 m	9.20
Narmandie	2	"	75	9.50
Sarafine	2	"	75	9.50
Miss Maffit	2	"	75	9.50

Archival Collections,Kankakee County Museum

Figure 5

Defence costs, Spink vs. Chiniquy, October, 1856

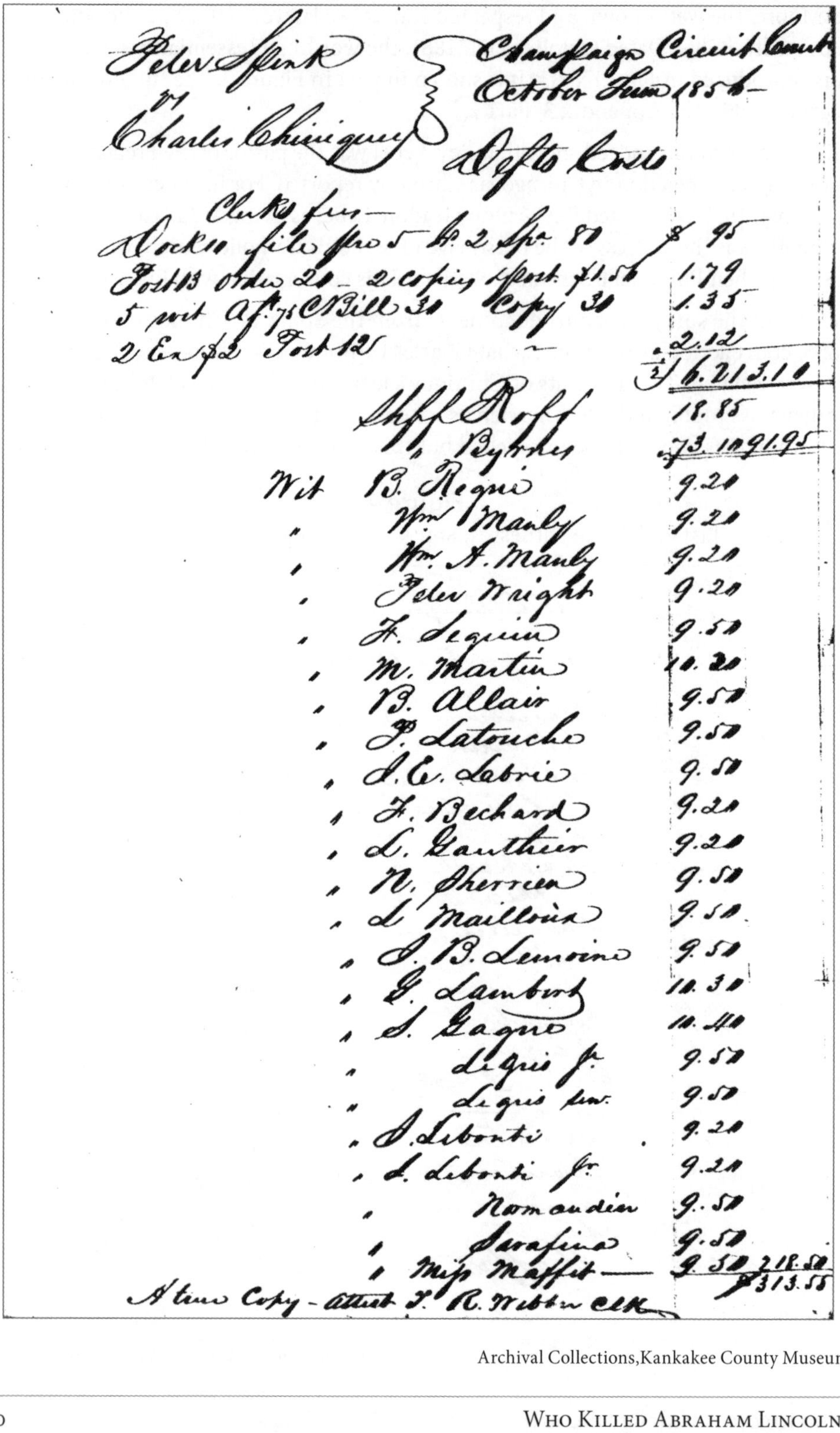

Peter Spink vs Charles Chiniquy } Champaign Circuit Court October Term 1856

Defts Costs

Clerks fees—

Dock 10 file pro 5 Ap. 2 Spr. 80	$ .95	
Post 13 Order 20 – 2 copies Spost. $1.50	1.79	
5 wit Af. 75 C Bill 30 Copy 30	1.35	
2 Ex $2 Post 12	2.12	
½	6.21	3.10
Shff Roff	18.85	
" Byrnes	73.10	91.95
Wit B. Regnie	9.20	
" Wm Manly	9.20	
" Wm. A. Manly	9.20	
" Peter Wright	9.20	
" F. Seguin	9.50	
" M. Martin	10.20	
" B. Allair	9.50	
" P. Latouche	9.50	
" J. C. Labrie	9.50	
" F. Bechard	9.20	
" L. Gauthier	9.20	
" N. Sherrien	9.50	
" L. Maillour	9.50	
" J. B. Lemoine	9.50	
" G. Lambert	10.30	
" S. Gagne	10.40	
" Legris Jr.	9.50	
" Legris Sen.	9.50	
" J. Libonti	9.20	
" L. Libonti Jr.	9.20	
" Normandin	9.50	
" Sarafina	9.50	
" Miss Maffit	9.50	218.50
		$313.55

A true Copy – attest J. R. Webber Clk

Archival Collections,Kankakee County Museum

for instance, was given in court documents as Revrd I. A. Lebel, Rev Antoine LeBel, and I. A. LeBell. [7]

According to death records and her own statements in the affidavit, Philomene Schwartz was about 18 years old in October, 1856, young enough to be called a girl, yet old enough to leave on the spur of the moment without a family member accompanying her, just Narcisse Terrien, as she traveled on an evening train to Urbana.

It was not easy to further check her story because of a lack of information. Two of her descendants found living in United States unfortunately knew of no oral or written record that has been passed down from her regarding these events. Other descendants who may have had such records were not located at the time of writing.

At the end of her affidavit, Stephen R. Moore certified that Philomene Schwartz had personally appeared before him and had sworn to the truth of her affidavit. There was no reason for this distinguished lawyer and judge to not have told the truth regarding this matter, or Philomene Schwartz either. She evidently remained a Catholic until her death and her funeral service was held in Notre Dame church in Chicago. As well, as noted earlier, court documents that listed her as one of the witnesses for Chiniquy's side, confirmed her statement that she was in Urbana when she said she was. [8]

According to *Fifty Years*, there was a large crowd both inside and outside the court-room the next morning when Spink withdrew his lawsuit and declared in court that he now did not believe that Charles Chiniquy was guilty of what he had been charged with. Abraham Lincoln received the statement on behalf of Chiniquy. He then made a brief and eloquent speech on the cruel persecution that his client had suffered at the hands of his merciless enemies and the corruption and hypocrisy of the priests that had perjured themselves in an attempt to destroy him.

Chiniquy's story is supported by other accounts. Both the October 25 issue of *Our Constitution* and the October 23rd *Urbana Union* stated that the lawsuit was settled with each side paying their own costs (see Figure 6 for the *Urbana Union* report). [9]

The Library of Congress holds a letter written by Abraham Lincoln from Urbana, dated Tuesday, October 21st, 1856. Writing to an A. Jonas, Mr. Lincoln explained that he wouldn't be able to meet with his correspondent because he is was "so 'hobbled' with a particular case" (see Figure 7). [10] He didn't mention what case it was but because of its high profile and length, Spink vs. Chiniquy would likely be the only one that could have been tying up Lincoln.

Two orders dismissing the case were written, mostly in Lincoln's hand. One is held at the Herndon-Weik collection of the Library of Congress (see Figure 8). It reads:

> Peter Spink vs. Charles Chiniquy
>
> This day came the parties, and the defendant denies that he has ever charged, or believed the plaintiff to be guilty of Perjury; that whatsoever he has said, from which a charge could be inferred, he said on the information of others, protesting his own disbelief in the charge; and that he now disclaims any belief in the truth of such charge against said plaintiff- It is therefore, by agreement of the parties, ordered that this suit be dismissed, each party

Figure 6
Urbana Union, October 23, 1856

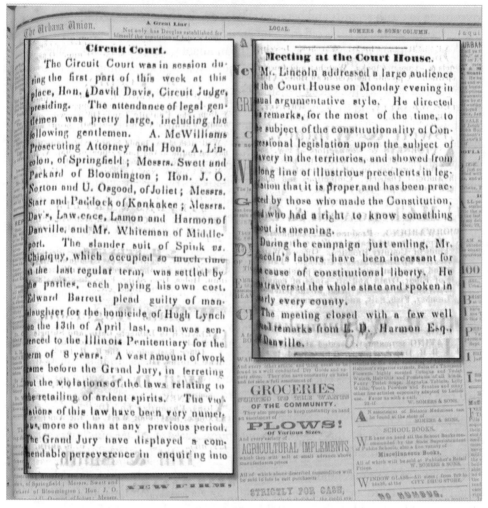

paying his own cost- the defendant to pay his part of the cost heretofore ordered to be paid by said Pltiff-. [11]

Lincoln biographers also discussed the case and their statements do not show Charles Chiniquy's account to be in error. Lincoln legal scholar Albert Woldman supported Chiniquy's account. In his book, *Lawyer Lincoln*, Woldman acknowledged how high profile Spink vs. Chiniquy was, saying it had "attracted wide attention" and was "undoubtedly the most exciting slander suit in which Lincoln ever participated." He agreed with Chiniquy's assertion that a change of venue had brought the case to Urbana, as the court record also showed, and that the first jury in Urbana couldn't agree on a verdict. He disagreed with Charles Chiniquy when he reported that Chiniquy, at the time, had not denied calling Spink a perjurer.[12] He cited Henry Clay Whitney's, *Life on the Circuit with Lincoln* as his source. Whitney did report that in a sermon, Chiniquy had said that Spink had committed perjury and was prepared

Figure 7

Letter by Abraham Lincoln to A. Jonas, October 21, 1856

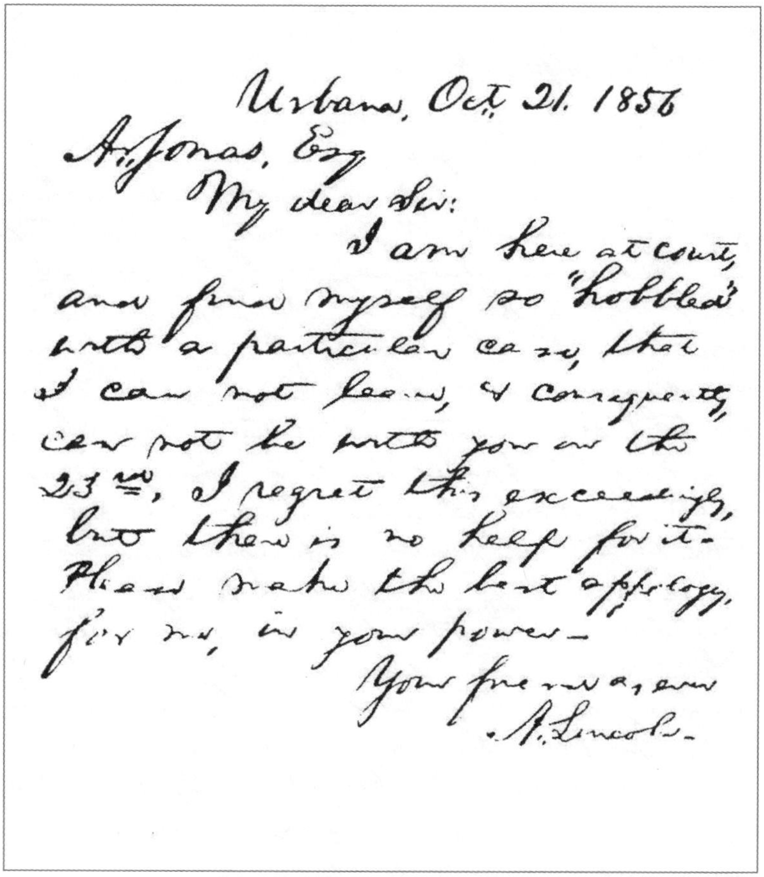

Urbana, Oct. 21. 1856

A. Jonas, Esq

My dear Sir:

I am here at court, and find myself so "hobbled" with a particular case, that I can not leave, & consequently, can not be with you on the 23rd. I regret this exceedingly, but there is no help for it. Please make the best apology, for me, in your power—

Your friend, as ever

A. Lincoln

photostatic reproduction, Library of Congress,
Lincoln Series 4, Box 2, Folder 1856

to contest a lawsuit, "Father Chiniquy was plucky, and plead justification; and preparations were made for a 'fight to the finish' " Whitney did not disclose what the source was for this information.[13]

In the order dismissing the case however, Chiniquy clearly denied ever charging the plaintiff with perjury. If this were not true, it is hard to believe that honest Abe Lincoln, as well as Spink and the others would have accepted this statement in the agreement ending the suit.

Charles Chiniquy was correct however, in stating that a bill for perjury had been found against Peter Spink by a jury in Iroquois County. As he reported in *Fifty Years*, Spink was indicted for this crime. The bill, presented by a grand jury before the Iroquois circuit court on April 27th, 1855 is reproduced in Figure 9. It could be asked, why in 1856 did Chiniquy deny saying that Spink had committed perjury and then in 1885, some 29 years later, say he had been indicted for this? One explanation is that before the lawsuit, Chiniquy may have heard something of this allegation, made a remark relating to it that was misunderstood but did not have the

Figure 8
Order dismissing Spink vs. Chiniquy

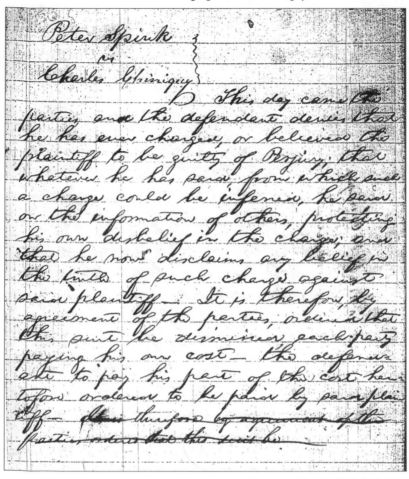

Figure 11
Chiniquy promissory note, Urbana, May 23, 1856

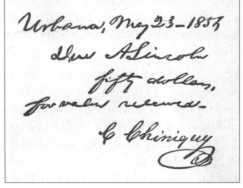

Fifty Years in the Church of Rome

WHO KILLED ABRAHAM LINCOLN?

Figure 9
Bill for perjury found against Peter Spink, Iroquois County, Illinois, with transcription

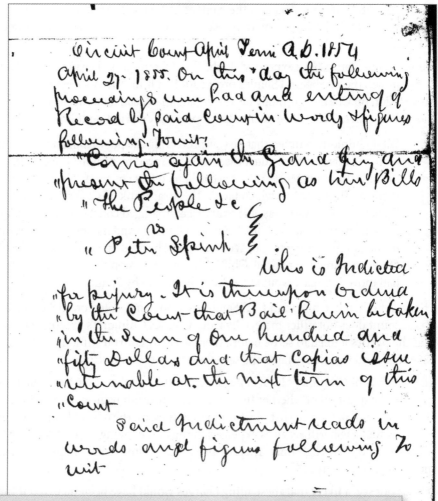

Circuit Court April Term A.D. 1854

April 27 1855. On this day the following proceedings were had and entering of Record by said Court in words & figures following. To wit:

"Comes again the Grand Jury and "presents the following as true Bills

"the People & c
 vs.
"Peter Spink

Who is Indicted "for perjury. It is thereupon ordered "by the Court that Bail herein be taken "in the sum of one hundred and "fifty Dollars and that capias issue "returnable at the next term of this "Court

Said Indictment reads in words and figures following To wit

Archival Collections, Kankakee County Museum

proof that Spink had been charged with the crime. After he began research on his autobiography in 1865, he uncovered the evidence and therefore, 29 years later, he reported it. The indictment for perjury, People vs. Peter Spink, one day before, on April 26th, 1855, is reproduced in the Appendix 3, Part 2. Another court document that gives more detailed information relating to this is reproduced in the Appendix 3, Part 3.

Some commentators have expressed doubt about Chiniquy's allegation that Bishop O'Regan was the one behind Spink's prosecution of him.[14] In his 1993 Ph.D. dissertation on Charles Chiniquy however, Canadian academic Richard Lougheed showed that there was good evidence to support the ex-priest on this point. He stated:

> Later Chiniquy claimed that he was protecting the poor from an unscrupulous land speculator, whose court cases were financed by Bishop O'Regan, in order to ruin Chiniquy. Most critics have ridiculed this conspiracy idea. Nevertheless there are strong points which favour the idea: Spink was a very committed French Catholic who was able to afford a prolonged court case, employing the same lawyers as the Catholic Diocese of Chicago and having a priest testify on his behalf According to four witnesses, sent by St. Anne parish to the bishop, O'Regan wanted to relocate Chiniquy, in part, to stop the court case. If the priest had moved the case would likely have been won by Spink.[15]

The well-known late historian Carl Sandburg also commented on the legal battle. His account does not differ materially from Charles Chiniquy's except he maintained that the parties agreed to settle before there was any court testimony at the October, 1856 term and Chiniquy stated the settlement came after testimony.[16]

The two lists of Chiniquy's legal expenses from the October, 1856 term shed some light on the question of whether there was court testimony given at the fall session (Figures 4 and 5). One is a list of Chiniquy's witnesses, the cost of bringing them to court, as well as Sheriff services expenses, filing and copying costs. The other lists the witnesses and their costs only. There is also a short summation of Spink's expenses, including filing charges.[17]

It does not seem likely that these filing charges would have been incurred if these two parties had not met in court, nor does it seem probable that the cost of a large number of witnesses who did not testify would have been recorded by the court. The existence of these lists of expenses infers that services had been rendered, including the witnesses giving testimony. Would the court take the word of the litigants as to the witness they had planned to call and give their accounts the court's legal stamp, even if there had been no court testimony?

According to *Fifty Years*, Spink suffered a heavy financial loss. Bishop O'Regan had refused to pay his legal costs because Chiniquy had not been found guilty. When taking stock of his own legal expenses, Chiniquy reflected that not only had Abraham Lincoln been the finest lawyer he had ever known but also had been his best friend. He told Lincoln that he believed that he owed him a very large amount of money, as he had been engaged in his defence for more than a year and had acted for him through two sessions at the Champaign Circuit Court, without having been paid anything. His other two lawyers had billed him a thousand dollars each, which he felt was not unreasonable and they had not done half the work that Lincoln had done. After thanking him for his great service, Chiniquy asked for his bill, telling his friend that although he couldn't pay it all immediately, he would pay it completely if he would kindly wait a little time. In answer, Abraham Lincoln stated:

> My dear Mr. Chiniquy, I feel proud and honored to have been called to defend you. But I have done it less as a lawyer than as a friend. The money I should receive from you would take away the pleasure I feel at having fought your battle. Your case is unique in my whole practice. I have never met a man so cruelly persecuted as you have been, and who deserves it so little.

He expressed amazement that Philomene Moffat had come to the rescue that night, when everything looked so bleak. Regarding the bill, he said:

> Now let us speak of what you owe me. Well! -- Well! --how much do you owe me? You owe me nothing! for I suppose you are quite ruined. The expense of such as suit, I know, must be enormous. Your enemies want to ruin you. Will I help them to finish your ruin, when I hope to have the right to be put among the most sincere and devoted of your friends?

There is indeed powerful evidence that Abraham Lincoln and Charles Chiniquy became very close friends. For example, in September, 1885, no less an authority than President Lincoln's oldest son, Robert Todd Lincoln, sent Chiniquy a letter. Robert Todd was, at the time, the only surviving member of the 16th President's immediate family. In it, he thanked him for "the expression you use in your note in regards to my father", and for "sending your book" which undoubtedly was *Fifty Years*, (*Fifty Years* was first published in 1885). Robert Lincoln also declared that his father had "made many friend(s) in his life but plainly none were more than yourself" (see figure 10).

Chiniquy disagreed about the bill, saying that his friend couldn't receive nothing for the travel and hotel expenses he had incurred, not to mention all the time he had put in defending him. At the priest's insistence, Lincoln agreed to give him a promissory note to sign. It read: "Urbana, May 23- 1856, I owe A Lincoln fifty dollars for value received"[18] (see Figure 11). Although Chiniquy protested that the services rendered were worth at least $2,000.00, Abraham Lincoln laughed and said he would pinch some rich clients for the rest.

Chiniquy was greatly moved by the kindness of his defender in reducing the charges so much. This, along with the relaxation of the stress he was under and the dreadful premonition that Lincoln would pay with his life for what he had done, reduced him to tears. Mr. Lincoln asked him why he was crying. He also asked why Chiniquy shouldn't be extremely happy. The priest, however, told Lincoln that he had noticed at least ten or twelve Jesuits in court when the suit was dismissed who had been there to see him condemned. Instead, they heard the courthouse walls tremble with the eloquence of the tall prairie lawyer as he condemned the malice and lack of principles, Christian or otherwise, of those who had tried to destroy an innocent

Figure 10

Letter from Robert Todd Lincoln to Charles Chiniquy,
September 10, 1885, with transcription

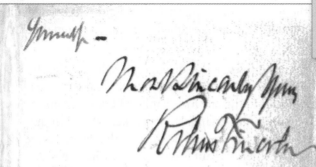

ISHAM & LINCOLN
HONORE BUILDINGS
CHICAGO

My Dear Sir

I beg you to accept
my thanks for
sending your book
and especially for
the expression you
use in your note in
regards to my father.
He made many friend
in his life but
plainly
none were more
than yourself.

Most Sincerely Yours
Robert Lincoln

The Chiniquy Collection

man. Chiniquy said he felt he could see Abraham Lincoln's sentence of death in their eyes. According to the priest, the tall prairie lawyer:

> tried to divert my mind, at first, with a joke, 'Sign this,' said he, 'It will be my warrant of death.'

> But after I had signed, he became more solemn, and said, 'I know that Jesuits never forget nor forsake. But man must not care how and where he dies, provided he dies at the post of honour and duty,' and he left me.[19]

It can be seen therefore, although there are a few missing pieces of evidence that would help make the story fuller, legal documents, newspapers, and other accounts of the day support Chiniquy's account. His autobiography enjoyed amazing success from the time it was first published in 1885. With its allegations of the Catholic Church's involvement in Lincoln's murder, it undoubtedly did much harm to the cause of Catholicism, especially in the United States. It therefore was in the interest of the Roman Catholic Church to show Chiniquy was wrong in what he claimed. In numerous editions of *Fifty Years*, Charles Chiniquy stated that Philomene Schwartz was alive, living in Chicago and he gave her address. She did indeed live in Chicago and evidently remained a Romanist until her death in 1893.

The Roman Catholic Church however, did not persuade her to publish a denial of Chiniquy's account. Catholic apologists did not find the register in Urbana that *Fifty Years* spoke about, to show that Philomene Moffat/Schwartz had not signed it. The American House and Pennsylvania House were the two main hotels in the community at the time of the trial.[20]

Neither Narcisse Terrien or his wife were found and presented to the public to deny playing the part Chiniquy said they played. No material evidence was produced to show the account of Spink vs. Chiniquy in *Fifty Years* was in error.

John Surratt was prosecuted for his part in the conspiracy to murder Lincoln. In his argument at Surratt's 1867 trial, District Attorney E.C. Carrington asserted that because the defence had not brought anyone to contradict a particular government witness, the rule of law gave him the right to infer it was because they couldn't do it, "*expressio unius est exclusio alterius*".[21] Although the Catholic Church would certainly have been interested in showing Chiniquy to be wrong regarding Spink vs. Chiniquy, it didn't do so. Wasn't this because it couldn't do so, because what Charles Chiniquy said was correct?

Chapter 3

Charles Chiniquy: A Remarkable Life

The Spink vs. Chiniquy legal battle was fought against the backdrop of a wider dispute between the bishop of Chicago and Illinois Catholics. It was a struggle which often involved Charles Chiniquy, especially when his own countrymen were involved.

Chiniquy alleged that Bishop O'Regan wanted to destroy the French Canadian Catholic congregations in Chicago and St. Anne. He reported that in the spring of 1856, the Catholic priest of the St. Louis church of Chicago, Rev. Lemaire, was dismissed and sent from the diocese of Chicago for no reason, leaving the French Canadians without a pastor. Shortly afterwards, the parsonage they had built on Clark Street was sold. As well, the small attractive church they had sacrificed to build was moved blocks away and rented to Irish Romanists. No notice was given to the outraged French and the rent money was evidently pocketed by Bishop O'Regan.[1]

The French Catholics of the city asked Father Chiniquy for advice and he suggested sending a delegation to protest to the bishop. They dispatching eight men, which included a man named Fanchere and another named Roffinot. The group was to be disappointed though. The prelate told them they didn't know their religion because he had the right to sell their church along with other church properties and do what he liked with the money.

According to *Fifty Years*, O'Regan sent for Charles Chiniquy on August 19th, 1856. The bishop blamed him for the rebelliousness of his countrymen and told Chiniquy that he wanted him transferred to Kahokia, (apparently what is now Kahoka, Missouri). He informed the priest that if he did not report to this post by September 15th, he would be interdicted and excommunicated. Chiniquy resisted, later arguing in a letter that in doing this, O'Regan would be helping Peter Spink because if he was transferred, it would be much more difficult for him to fight his court battle with him.

Leaving O'Regan, Father Chiniquy reached St. Anne where he heard rumors that he had been suspended from his duties as a priest. Chiniquy wrote to O'Regan, protesting the planned reassignment and a delegation of four men went from the colony to deliver his letter to the bishop. The men asked about the alleged suspension but the bishop gave them no satisfaction, ordering Charles Chiniquy to Chicago for his new assignment.[2]

On September 3rd, three intoxicated priests from Chicago arrived at the St. Anne colony. They nailed a writ of excommunication from O'Regan to the door of the chapel and fled. It was not signed by the bishop or by any of his deputies, though. Chiniquy paid no attention to it and continued his duties as pastor because it was not signed by the proper authorities, as it should have been according to Church law. These and subsequent events, reported in *Fifty Years*, are detailed in a letter by Charles Chiniquy published in the *Chicago Daily Democrat* (see Figure 12). The newspaper is dated May 1, 1856 but in all likelihood, the correct date is actually May 1, 1857.

On October 11, 1856, in an article entitled, "Schism in the Roman Catholic Church of Chicago; Excommunication of Father Chiniquy, The Great Apostle of Temperance", the *New York Times* published a pastoral letter from Bishop O'Regan. In the letter, dated September 3, 1856, O'Regan stated that he had suspended Charles Chiniquy and since the priest had continued in his normal duties as a priest, the bishop therefore excommunicated him by his letter. In a later article, dated November 1st however, the *Times* also reported that Chiniquy and his flock had met at the court-house at Kankakee, where the priest made a speech and the people resolved to support him in his struggle with the bishop. They stated "That we, French Canadians of the County of Kankakee, do hereby decide to give our moral support to Rev. C. CHINIQUY, in the persecution now exerted against him by the Bishop of Chicago, in violation of the laws of the Church, expressed and sanctioned by the Councils." The *New York Times* article backs up what *Fifty Years* stated about this part of Chiniquy's life. As well, in his letter printed in the May 1, 1857 *Chicago Daily Democrat*, while he acknowledged that O'Regan had published that he had suspended him, Chiniquy vigorously disputed this, saying that the Bishop was mistaken.

With Chiniquy and his people having seemed to have made a public break with the Church of Rome because of their disregard for the sham excommunication of O'Regan, Church officials made a final effort to show Chiniquy and his people their error and bring them back to the fold. According to *Fifty Years*, in November, 1856, a couple of Charles Chiniquy's old friends came to see him. Together they worked out a compromise to bring about reconciliation but it was later rejected by Bishop O'Regan.[3]

Believing that O'Regan would increase his efforts to crush them, the French Canadian Catholics of Chicago met together and decided to make a public appeal. The meeting was officiated by two men who had been part of the eight-man delegation originally sent to O'Regan: P.F. Rofinot, who presided over the gathering, and David Franchere, who acted as secretary. Their lengthy protest against the bishop's actions was published in the January 26th, 1857 edition of the *Chicago Daily Tribune*, (see Figure 13). O'Regan was described as a savage enemy, a revengeful foe, a tyrant who had lied to the French and swindled them out of their church, the home for their priest, essentially everything. The French Catholics also expressed their gratitude and support for Charles Chiniquy in his struggle with the Bishop of Chicago.[4] The *Chicago Tribune* also commented on this the next day (see Figure 14).

There didn't appear to be much in the way of answers coming from O'Regan's side in reply to the many accusations leveled against him. The *Chicago Tribune* noted this in the March 31, 1857 issue, stating that the bishop was "represented as grasping, avaricious and tyrannical, by his enemies, and but feebly defended by his friends" (see Figure 15).[5]

Figure 12 a
Chicago Daily Democrat, May 1, (probably 1857)

DAILY DEMOCRAT.

NO. 45 LA SALLE STREET.

Friday Morning, May 1, 1856.

[advertisement.]

To the Editor of the Montreal Herald.

St. Ann's, Kankakee Co., Ill., Feb. 2, '57.

Mr. Editor,—He whom ages agree to call the wisest of men, said that, "There is a time to keep silence, and a time to speak."

Since more than four months, those who wished to speak and write against me, have had full freedom to do so, and have done so, most unscrupulously. From our Bishops who have cursed me, and called me a sacrilegious Priest, even to the good Curate, of the District of Quebec, who announced to his parishioners that I was excommunicated because I had eloped with an Irishwoman, and even to dear Mr. Desaulnier, who announced lately to the people of Bourbonnais that the Devil was preparing a place for the people and the missionary of St. Ann's, there has been, around me, I must say, a concert which has not been very agreeable.

With the exception of my letter to the Bishop of Chicago, dated 25th of Oct., and of a few private letters, I have kept the most profound silence, leaving to the good sense of the people, to the zeal of my friends, and above all to my God, to make known that which I believe to be my innocence.

If I am mistaken, let it be known to me, but let it not be with those harsh words of sacrilegious, of excommunicated, and of seducer; they will not convince me thus,—such expressions are not proofs, nor arguments, and do not frighten me, since I have read in a book which is but too little known and meditated upon by men: "Blessed are ye, when men shall revile you, and persecute you, for my name's sake: rejoice ye therefore."—Mathew vii. I therefore believe that, for the interests of religion, the time has come for me to speak, and since your paper has not refused the writings of the attack, I expect your honesty will permit me to speak to my friends by the medium of your columns. I will then say:

1. That the Bishop of Chicago did not suspend me on the 19th of August. I left him with all my powers. He has published the contrary, I know; but it is a mistake on his part. I leave to God to judge if that error comes from the mind, the heart, or the memory.

2. The Bishop of Chicago having let me return with my powers of Priesthood, I again leave it to God to make known the motives which led him to publish, three days after, in the neighboring churches, that I had been suspended, when such a sentence had never been signified by him to me, neither by writing, nor verbally.

3. I am ready to prove, by the most irrefutable witnesses, and by writings signed by his own hand, that it is nothing uncommon with the Bishop of Chicago to say things contrary to what they are. Leaving always to God to judge if those errors are wilful or not.

4. I did not at all revolt against the Bishop of Chicago, when on the 19th of August he signified that he would suspend me in a fortnight, if I did not accept of another mission. I spoke to him with firmness, most undoubtedly; but I take God to witness that I said nothing against the respect due to my Bishop. I asked him for my exeat, he refused it to me; I then told him that, the Church allowed me to remain where I was, in the sanctuary of private life, he could not suspend me but at the expiration of a fortnight. I meant to enjoy this privilege. On bended knees, at his feet, I then entreated him to grant me eight weeks, instead of a fortnight, that I might have time to finish my lawsuit; all was useless. I then told him that I preferred going to the world's end, rather than to be interdicted. These were my last words, and this is as true as there is a God in heaven.

5. I had then the power of offering the Holy Sacrifice, and enjoy the privileges of a Priest, during the ensuing fortnight, which followed my interview of the 19th with the Bishop of Chicago. It is important that no one should forget that fact.

6. Having learnt that the neighboring curates were publishing that I was struck with suspension, I sent four persons of the highest respectability to know from the Bishop, the cause of these publications. The names of these deputies are J. B. Lemoine, advocate, A. Allaire, merchant, Leon alloux, cultivator, Francois Bochard, student at law.

7. Those gentlemen were the bearers of the letter here below written, which I addressed to the Bishop, and of which I made them take a copy, for fear that the Bishop, through want of memory or for another reason of which I leave the secret to God, might sooner or later, deny the reception of that letter and its contents.

St. Ann's Kankakee Co., Ill., Aug. 25, '56.
To the Rt. Rev. O'Regan, Bishop of Chicago.

My Lord—The more I consider your design to turn me out of the settlement which I have created, and of which I am the father here, the more I believe it a duty which I owe to myself, my friends and my dear countrymen, to protest before God and his angels, against what you intend to do.

Not one of your priests stands higher than I do in the public opinion and not a single one is more respected by his people, than I am here. I defy my bitterest enemies to say to the contrary. And that public good character, which is my most precious treasure, you intend to despoil me of, by ignominiously turning me out from among my people.

Certainly I have enemies, and I am proud of it. My chief ones are well known in the community as the most depraved of men. And the cordial reception they say they have received from you, has not effaced the many stains they have on their foreheads.

By this letter, I again request you to make a public and a most minute inquest on my conduct. My conscience gives me the assurance that nothing can be found against me, and that such a public and fair dealing with me, would confound my accusers. But I speak of accusers, though I do not really know if I have any.

Where are they? What are their names? Of what iniquity do they accuse me?

All these questions, which I put to you last Tuesday, were left without a single word of answer! And would to God that you would answer me now with the names of my accusers. I would be ready to meet them before any tribunal.

Before you strike the last blow to the victim of the most hellish plot, I request you in the name of God, to give a moment of attention to the consequences of my removal from here at this period.

1. You know I have a suit with Mr. Spink for the beginning of October. My lawyers and witnesses are all here and in Iroquois county. And, the very moment that I am most needed to be here to protect my honor and innocence, you order me to go more than 300 miles! Did you ever consider that by such strange conduct, you seem to help Spink against your own Priest?

When at Kahokia, I will have to bear the heavy expense of travelling more than 300 miles, often, to consult my friends, or to be deprived of their valuable help. It is possible that you thus try to tie my hands and feet and deliver me into the hands of my most cruel and merciless enemy.

Since the beginning of that suit Mr. Spink is proclaiming that you are in his favor, that with the perjured Priest, you have promised him to do all in your power to help him to crush me. For the sake of your sacred character, then, do not show so publicly your hands and your heart to the heartless speculator of l'Erable. Let us then live in peace here till that suit is ended.

2. By turning me out of my settlement, you destroy it, ... than the nine-tenths of the ... me you strike ... Where will you find a Priest who will ... do as much as I have,—to give ... every year $1000 or $2000 as I have done! ... at the price of so many sacrifices that with ... poorer class of emigrants from Canada I ... formed here, in four years, a settlement wh ... annot be surpassed, for its progress, and now ... I have expended my last

cent to form that ... my you turn me out of it! Our fine college, where 150 boys are receiving so good an education, will be closed the very day I start. You know well that the good teachers I got from Montreal will go away the same day that I leave this place! And our female Academy is also destroyed by my departure. Ah! if you are merciless for the Priest of St. Ann, have mercy at least on the poor, dear little children. I would rather die than see them running again through the streets destroying their intelligence. Let me, then, finish my work here and give me time to strengthen those young institutions, which will fall to the ground with me.

3. If you turn me out or interdict me, as you say you will do if I disobey your orders, my enemies will proclaim that you are treating me with such rigor because you found me guilty of some black crime; and that impression will naturally find ground in the minds of my judges, and will induce them to look upon me as a miserable criminal! For who will suppose in this free country, that there is a class of men, who can judge a man and condemn him, as our Bishop of Chicago is doing now, without telling him of what he is accused, and without giving the names of his accusers. No, they cannot suppose it; and I hope the American people will never come to the knowledge of that sad truth!

In the name of God, then, I request again not to bid me to leave this place before I will have proved my innocence, and the iniquity of Spink before the honest people of Urbana. But if you are deaf to my voice, and if nothing can deter you from your resolution, I do not wish the union victim position of a suspended Priest among my countrymen. Send me by the next mail my letters of mission for the new place you intend to trust to my care. The sooner I get these, the better for me and my people. I am ready. I will pray the God of Abraham to give me the fortitude he gave to Isaac, when laying on the altar, he willingly presented his throat to the sword, and I will pray my Saviour, bearing the heavy Cross on Calvary, to direct and help my steps to that land of exile you have prepared for me.

Your devoted Priest,
C. Chiniquy, Prt.

8. All those who will read this letter with attention will see that there is not even a shadow of revolt in my heart against my Bishop, and that which he wrote himself to the Bishop-Coadjutor of Montreal on the subject against me, was not; most certainly inspired to him by the God of truth.

9. The only answer to this letter a few days later, was that the Bishop of Chicago sent three Priests half intoxicated to put on the walls of my Chapel a paper (not signed by him) saying that I was excommunicated for having despised the orders and the censures of my Bishop.

10. The greatest Catholic Theologians tell us that a Priest unjustly struck with excommunication can continue to exercise his ministry among the people who know the injustice of the sentence.

11. Those who know what dreadful and scandalous abuse a number of Popes and Bishops have made of the power of excommunicating, know that the Church was inspired by the Holy Ghost, when she said to the Priest and to the people thus oppressed; to despise the sentence of those who have the word of the gospel on their lips, but other things at the bottom of their hearts.

12. The Saviour of the world said to his Apostles, "Go teach all truth;" "Be ye like lambs in the midst of wolves, carry neither purse nor shoes; whatsoever house ye shall enter eat that which will be presented to you; in whatsoever house ye shall enter, say 'Peace be with you.' He that heareth you, heareth me; he that despiseth you despiseth me, and he that despiseth me, despiseth Him that sent me."

13. But Jesus Christ never said, "I send you to lie and to thieve; and those who shall despise your lying words, and shall be exposed to your extortions, you shall curse them and they shall be cursed of me; and that those who despise you for this shall despise me."

14. Jesus Christ never said to his Apostles,

Figure 12 b

Continuation of article

8. All those who will read this letter with attention will see that there was not even a shadow of revolt in my heart against my Bishop, and that which he wrote himself to the Bishop Coadjutor of Montreal on this subject against me, was not, most certainly inspired to him by the *God of truth*.

9. The only answer to this letter a few days later, was that the Bishop of Chicago sent three Priests half intoxicated, to put on the walls of my Chapel a paper (not signed by him) saying that I was excommunicated for having despised the orders and the censures of my Bishop.

10. The greatest Catholic Theologians tell us that a Priest unjustly struck with excommunication can continue to exercise his ministry among the people who know the injustice of the sentence.

11. Those who know what dreadful and scandalous abuse a number of Popes and Bishops have made of the power of excommunicating, know that the Church was inspired by the Holy Ghost, when she said to the Priest and to the people thus oppressed, to despise the sentence of those who have the word of the gospel on their lips, *but other things* at the bottom of their hearts.

12. The Saviour of the world said to his Apostles, "Go teach all truth;" "Be ye like lambs in the midst of wolves, carry neither purse nor shoes; whatsoever house ye shall enter eat that which will be presented to you; in whatsoever house ye shall enter, say 'Peace be with you.' He that heareth you, heareth me; he that despiseth you despiseth me, and he that despiseth me, despiseth Him that sent me."

13. But Jesus Christ never said, "I send you to lie and to thieve; and those who shall despise your lying words, and shall be exposed to your extortions, you shall curse them and they shall be cursed of me; and that those who despise you for this shall despise me."

14. Jesus Christ never said to his Apostles, "I send you to preach my gospel to the poor; and the first thing you shall do will be to build a fine Marble Palace; and when you have not sufficient money to do this, you will sell the Churches which the poor have built; you will carry off their property which they had gained by the sweat of their brows; you will drive the priests from their humble dwellings, and you will sell those houses, and if the priest and the people murmur, you will excommunicate them, and to convince them that they are wrong you will quote this text of my gospel, 'he who despiseth you despiseth me.'"

15. No, Jesus Christ never said to his Apostles, "When you have torn away the poor people's property, honestly acquired; when you have hunted from the foot of the altars those who have elevated them to the glory of my name, if they ask you by what right you act so, you will answer them with haughtiness, "I have the right to sell the churches, the altars, and the lands which you have consecrated to God; I can put the money in my pocket and go where I please with it. (See the Address of the French Canadians of Chicago.)

16. Who are the greatest enemies of the Church of Jesus Christ?

Answer: They, who being sent to preach humility, justice, and truth, become proud, thieves, and liars in the name of Jesus Christ.

17. Who are the priests and the people who betray the cause of Christ, and do not deserve to belong to the great family of Catholics?

Answer: Those who bow down to a liar, a thief, and a murderer of souls, and call him Holy, Venerable, High, because he holds a place of dignity in the Church.

18. The Catholic religion is imperishable: and God will grant that there will always be in her men to unmask hypocrisy, tell the truth and throw down the idols of their thrones.

19. Last summer I had told my brethren of St. Ann's that "Bishop Baillargeon, coadjutor to the Archbishop of Quebec, had the goodness to send me a chalice and an ornament for the altar." A few weeks after, a few drunkards assembled in a tavern, were reading a letter which the Archbishop's secretary had addressed them, they published that I was a liar and a thief, and gave for proof the words of the Archbishop of Quebec, which was in the public papers of Canada: "It is true that the Bishop of Troa sent, in the beginning of last spring, by Mr. Chiniquy's request, a few church ornaments for the chapel of his mission, but *this gift was not made to Mr. Chiniquy, but to the chapel of his mission.*

20. Here is the letter that was written by the hands of the Bishop of Troa himself:

Archbishopric of Qubec,
9th ay, 1856

Miss Caroline Deslormier,

I send you, *for Mr. Chiniquy*, some church ornaments, with vestments necessary to say mass, a missal, cloth for a hassock, and a chalice, all of which are rather badly packed up, as I suppose you will be able to find room for these in your trunks; and I pray God to bless you, and to conduct you safe to your journey's end.

Your devoted servant,
† C. F., Bishop of Troa.

21. I leave the people to judge between my accusers and me.

22. The Bishop of Chicago, in his letter to the coadjutor of Montreal, Bishop Larocque, says, among other words, "Mr. Chiniquy persuaded a person of Martino not to transmit to the Bishop of the Diocese the title of a small lot of ground, *on which* they proposed to building a Church, and in consequence of this they have not as yet any Church."

23. Here is what the Syndics write to me on the subject:

Martino, Kankakee Co., Ill.,
1st February, 1857.

Rev. Mr. Chiniquy:

We have read with sentiments of surprise and profound confusion, the letter which the Bishop of Chicago addressed to the Bishop of Cydonia, dated Nov. last. We believe it a duty on our part to say that the contents of that letter, with regard to the ground and the church of Martino, is a tissue of falsehoods. It is true that we refused to give the title of the ground to the Bishop of Chicago, but it was solely because we had no confidence whatever in the honesty of Bishop O'Regan, that we took this determination, without having a word on your part beforehand, either directly or indirectly. The calumny which the Bishop invented on this subject, is still greater, as we had already informed him of the truth on this subject. It is not you, Rev. Mr. Chiniquy, who are the cause of our not having a church, this misfortune is entirely due to the bad administration of the Bishop of Chicago, and to the public immorality of the priest who wished to serve us here.

We have the honor to be, Rev. Mr. Chiniquy,
Your devoted servants,
Alfred Deslauriers,
Proprietor of the ground.
Medord Martin,
J. E. Labrie,
Louis Betourne,
Antoine Langlois,
Pierre Lounotin,
Syndics of the Church of Martino.

The Bishop of Cydonia, coadjutor of Montreal, in his letter against me, dated 27th Nov. last, is in extacy on reading the Bishop of Chicago's letter; he admires that voice so calm and benignant of Bishop O'Regan, and contrasts it with the blustering pomp of that which resounded in the papers for my defence. Bishop Larocque has reason to fall into extacy. It is really admirable how a Bishop can lie with so much dignity, and publish with so much calm the dreams of a troubled and sick imagination.

25. The good Coadjutor of Montreal does not like those noisy voices; nor I either. But he is ignorant of the laws of custom, that when the robber is in search of his prey on the high way, and seizes his victim, he makes the least noise possible. It is always the poor victim who screams, with all his might, Murder! Thief! It is not always polite, but what is to be done? Custom wills it thus.

26. Mr. Desaulnier publicly said to my people assembled in the chapel of St. Ann's:—"It is impossible to condemn you and to find you guilty in the position you have taken in following the advice of your pastor in your debates with the Bishop of Chicago."

27. Mr. Desaulnier having heard the Bishop of Chicago's reasonings and then hearing mine, said: "Mr. Chiniquy is right, but we must not tell him so; for he is already sufficiently stubborn."

said: "Mr. Chiniquy is right, but we must not tell him so; for he is already sufficiently stubborn."

28. Messrs. Brassard and Desaulnier assured me that the Bishop of Chicago had confessed to them that there was no canonical accusations proved before him against me. He declared the same truth to the four gentlemen whom I had sent to him, to inquire into the reasons of my pretended suspension. And, I take God to witness, that the Bishop of Chicago never gave me any canonical admonition, neither by mouth nor by writing, and that, that which he said on this subject, in the sentence of excommunication, as well as in his letter in the public papers sometime afterwards, is entirely contrary to the truth.

29. The Bishop of Chicago in his letter to the Coadjutor of Montreal, gave to understand that it was I, and not him who engaged the press of Chicago to print the sentence of excommunication launched against the Pastor and the people of St Ann's. By writing to the Editors of these papers you will know more from them, than my words can utter, and then you will judge of the veracity of my Bishop.

30. My letter against the Bishop of Chicago which appeared last fall, was published a long time after the Bishop had received it, and it was because being fully convinced that the only means of obtaining justice, for me, and my brethren, was to meet him on the same ground he had imprudently chosen himself, against me: "The appeal to the sentiments of the public, through the medium of the press." There is not a single word in the letter that I cannot prove when it is necessary. The brutality of the attack against us explains the strength, and perhaps also the roughness of the defence.

31. Many of my friends have blamed me for having appealed to my rights of an American citizen to tell the Bishop that he could not make me leave my house, especially as the laws of the Catholic Church allowed me to remain. They must then also blame St. Paul, for having appealed to his title of Roman citizen to frighten his executioners.

32. Let every one listen with an attentive ear to the cries of despair from their unhappy brethren of Chicago, and they will understand that our patience has been of as long duration as was possible for us to bear, and that it was high time to defend ourselves.

33. It appears to me that the Bishops of Canada, instead of having so much zeal, and eagerness to throw the seeds of eternal discord among their brethren of Illinois, would have done better to serve the interests of the Catholic Faith by obliging the Bishop of Chicago to be just, true and humane towards his fellow-creatures. For supposing that they succeed in destroying me, they will have done nothing to re-establish the peace so long desired by all, as long as the administration of the Diocese is not changed.

34. The awful exactions which weigh on the Catholics of Illinois, will soon bring, if there is not a prompt remedy, a crisis more terrible than that of which St. Ann's is the theatre. Do not imagine that the French Canadians are the only ones who groan and are oppressed. Amongst the Irish and German Catholics of the State of Illinois there is but one cry of indignation and of unspeakable confusion at the sight of the public actions of the Bishop of Chicago.

35. One of the greatest writers in France said lately: "When we study the laws that the Catholic Church has passed in her councils, in all centuries, to regulate the relation of the Bishops, with their Priests, and when we see how the Bishops observe these laws, we are tempted to ask ourselves: Where is the Catholic Church?"

36. I would wish to know in what council the Church passed a law to oblige a Priest to submit to a sentence which *he knows* to have never been pronounced.

37. St. Jerome, writing to his Bishop, said to him: "If you come to me as a Bishop and a Father, I will obey you: but if you come to me as a Paster, I will despise your tyranny. These were noble words: that old Priest of the desert knew his dignity and his rights, and his eloquent letters are an unimpeachable proof that he knew how to defend them. But we are be-

Figure 12 c
Continuation of article

come so servile and so cowardly that these words of his frighten us.

38. In the month of May, 1855, the Bishop of Chicago came to visit my colony. Seeing a poor little house of 30 by 24, that I got built at some short distance from the Chapel, the following conversation began between the Bishop and me:

Bishop—Whose house is this?

Answer—It is mine, my Lord.

B—And whose ground is it?

A—That ground is mine.

B—With what money did you purchase this lot?

A—With my money.

B—You must give me this house.

A—It is impossible, my Lord.

B—I see that you are a bad Priest, as I was told, Mr. Chiniquy, since you resist your Bishop and refuse to obey the orders he gives you to give him this property.

A—I believe I have a right to keep this property without being a bad Priest.

B—But the church forbids you to own property.

A—Do tell me in what council and in what epoch the church passed such a law, and I will give you this house instantly.

B—But if such a law is not passed, I shall soon make it pass.

A—Notwithstanding the great idea you have of your power, you are yet too young and too weak to pass such a Law for the Catholic Church.

39. Some historians wish to make us believe that Henry VIII. destroyed Catholicity in England. This assertion is not correct. The Apostacy of England was more the work of English Catholic Bishops than of the tyrant who then governed Great Britain. It was the English Bishops who sold the Church and delivered it to the tyrant, for money and worldly honors.

"The 18th September, 1535 the Archbishop sent circulars to all the Bishops, informing them that the King proposing to visit his kingdom had suspended all the Bishops of their powers; and the Bishops submitted with all humility to this sentence during a month. They then presented a petition to be reinstated in their powers."—Lingard, vol. 6, page 251.

40. "There is a vice so common among the Bishops, that if you avoid it, you will be the only one who will be exempt, and you will elevate yourself above yourself. . . . credulity! I never saw any one who was exempt of it. From thence arise dreadful passions for nothing and the ruin of the absent." It is not I who utter this harsh truth—it is St. Bernard.—Lib. de consideratione, 41.

"A Bishop cannot, without cause, and without being obliged to declare it, and even without a sentence, interdict a Priest, his Diocessan, and hinder him from saying Mass, nor to perform the other functions for which he has no need of permission, nor a special power; because no one can be deprived, without a sentence, of that which is proper and essential to his state, (Apostolical Notary, book 2d chapter 6th.")

41. You would be greatly mistaken if you thought that there is but the priest of St. Ann's in the world who suffer, because some bishops put their passions in the places of equity, justice, and the laws.

42. The learned author of the biography of the cotemporary clergy, affirms, without fear of being contradicted, in the face of the French Episcopacy, "Mr. Peltier, de la croix, to be a man of great valor, ought to incur the disgrace of some authority; sad thing to say; but a reality, which is experienced every day, . . could affirm that not one of the best priests of our days has avoided, either to be interdicted, or of being threatened to be so. I readily mention M. M. DeGehoud, Guilton, Cœur, Marlot, Peltier."

43. 'Migne. There has not been one Council which has not complained of the strange abuses which numbers of bishops make of their powers and has not sought to put a restraint to it.

44. By what rule of justice and equity have the venerable Bishops of Canada allowed themselves to condemn me, on a question of facts without hearing me and without telling me a word of it before hand.

45. The Bishop of Chicago says that, on the 19th of August, I left him suspended of my ecclesiastical powers. And I say, I am certain to the contrary, and as certain of it as I am certain of my existence, I left him possessed of all my powers; and that he gave me a fortnight at the expiration of which time I was threatened with suspension, if I did not go to a distance of three hundred miles to take a new mission.

Supposing that the Bishops naturally tend to believe that their confrere of Chicago says the truth, and that I disguise it, is there not a sufficient matter of reflection to examine and to suspend a judgment; above all, when the question is to hunt from the midst of the Church 500 families.

46. It is said that the position I have taken gives scandal in Canada. But would this scandal exist if the Bishops and Priests had said directly, that which I believe, and that which God knows to be the truth, that the sentence of suspension not having been pronounced, I could, and can still, exercise all the holy functions of my ministry, for which I became a Priest.

Would there have been any scandal if they had told the people the truth: *That an unjust excommunication is null and of no effect?*

47. The Bishops, in general, do not sufficiently consider what it is to suspend a priest. To suspend a priest is to take away his honor—his character. It is making him the dregs of society; it is worse than branding him with a hot iron; it is worse than taking his life; for who would not prefer losing his life to losing his honor.

The assassination of the Archbishop of Paris, by a Priest, is a frightful crime.

But there is, in a manner a still greater crime. It is the degradation, the moral assassination of a good priest, by the hands of a proud and ambitious Bishop.

The Archbishop of Paris, falling at the foot of the altar, under the steel of an assassin, descends into the tomb honored, his soul united to Jesus Christ, ascends to Heaven; his fate is, in a manner, worthy of envy.

But the poor priest, struck with suspension! Ah! What will become of him! The laughing stock of the impious, the children's jest, the scandal of the people!! He has no more place in society; death, for him, would be a favor; he

This gift of the priesthood, so great, so sublime, for the possession of which he had joyfully renounced the holy felicities of a family, and for which he has sacrificed all, not only escapes from him, but is changed into a bitter deception and becomes a priesthood of shame and infamy. The Bishop, at whose feet he made his awful vows, instead of remaining his father, his friend, his support and his comfort has become his executioner. Frightful despair is always at the door of his heart; the rays of the sun fatigues him; the darkness of night is not sufficiently profound to hide his shame and conceal him from the eyes of his friends. But what am I saying! Where will the Priest, struck with suspension, find friends!

And when we think that numbers of excellent Priests are thus struck every year, on empty suspicions, accusations without proof, and still more often for having spoken with dignity the truth to a Bishop?

Some will say; perhaps the Priest thus struck with suspension, has he not the right to appeal to his Archbishop?

Ah! for God's sake do not force me to say what I know of these appeals to the Archbishop. To the one even!

"I know that this Priest has been unjustly stricken," said a Bishop lately, "but it would give too great a blow to the administration of my predecessor if I re-establish this Priest." And the Priest is left with the stroke of the interdict, and this Bishop is still living—passes for a great Saint in his Diocese.

I would name him, if I did not take pity on him.

48. I believe that the Episcopacy is a Divine institution, but I do not believe that this Divine institution gives to whomsoever the power to put himself above Justice, truth and God; and how many worthy Priests do say in secret what I do say here publicly!

49. O Holy Catholic Church! It is on the threshold of thy Temple, that God adopted me for his child; it is thee, who opened unto me the gates of Heaven; it is at the foot of thy altars that I received, for the first time, the bread of life; it was again at the foot of thy altars that I had the honor to be devoted to the dignity of minister of the gospel—rather die a thousand times than be unfaithful to thy faith! and where would I go, if I forsook thee? Thou alone hast the words of eternal life. Thou art the spotless Spouse of Christ. The faults of thy children cannot be imputed to thee; thy infallible voice has in all ages protested against all errors; and thy laws, full of wisdom and equity, are there to guide the pastor and the people. I love thee, and bless thee, O immaculate Daughter of Heaven! It is to enlighten, to save the souls of thy most weak children that I consecrated the most beautiful years of my life! Oh! leave me consecrated, to my last days, to defend the weak and the poor, whom they seek to oppress in thy bosom.

Holy Catholic Church! even if my strayed and deceived brethren, should say the contrary, it is in thy arms that I wish to live, it is in thy bosom that I wish to die; it is under the shadow of thy Temples that I wish to wait, in the tomb, the Great day of thy God!

C. Chiniquy, Prt.

Figure 13 a
Chicago Daily Tribune, January 26, 1857

At a public meeting of French Canadian Catholics of Chicago held in the Hall of Mr. Bandins, on the 2d of January, 1857. Mr. Remiot, being called to preside, and Mr. D. Franchere, acting as Secretary, the following address and resolutions, being read, have been unanimously approved:

Editors of the Tribune:—Will you allow a thousand voices from the dead to speak to the public, through your valuable paper.

Everybody in Chicago knows that a few years ago there was a flourishing congregation of French people coming from France and Canada. They had their Priest, their church, their religious meetings. All that is now dispersed and destroyed. The present Bishop of Chicago has breathed his deadly breath on us, he has killed us. Instead of coming to us as a father he came as a savage enemy—instead of helping us as a friend, he has put us down as a revengeful foe. He has done the very contrary to which was commanded him by the Gospel, "The bruised reed he shall not break;" and the "smoking flash he shall not extinguish." Instead of guiding us with the Cross of the meek Jesus, he has ruled over us with an iron rod.

Every Sunday the warm-hearted and generous Irish goes to his church to hear the voice of his Priest, in his English language. The intelligent Germans have their Pastors to address them in their mother tongue.

The French people are the only ones now, who have a Priest, and no Church. They are the only ones whose beautiful language is prohibited, and, which is not heard from any pulpit in Chicago, and is it from lack of zeal and liberality? Ah! no, we take the whole city of Chicago as a witness of what we have done. There was not in Chicago a better looking little church than the French and Canadian Church called St. Louis. But, alas! we have been turned out of our church by our very Bishop! Loud as he is now publishing many stories to contradict that fact, we owe to ourselves and to our children to rise from the tomb where Bishop O'Regan has buried us, a voice to tell the truth the whole truth, and nothing but the truth

As soon as Bishop O'Regan came to Chicago he was told that the French Priest was too popular, that his Church was attended not only by his French and Canadian people, but that many Irish or Germans were going daily to him for their religious duties. It was whispered in the ears of his Rt. Reverence that, on account of this, many dollars and cents were going to the French Priest which would be better stored in his Rt. Reverence's purse.

Till that time, the Bishop was not in appearance, taking much trouble about us, but as soon as he saw that there were dollars and cents at stake, we had the honor to occupy his thoughts day and night. Though our *good* Bishop was born in Ireland, you would swear he was a real Yankee, if you talked to him of dollars and cents. The trick played by him to take from us our priest, our church revenues, and finally our church, proves him to be a skillful man and not a green horn. These are the facts, the undeniable public facts. He (the Bishop,) began by sending for our priest and telling him that he had to prepare himself to be removed from Chicago to some other place. As soon as we knew that determination, a deputation was sent to his Rt. Reverence to get the promise that he would give us another French priest, and received from him the assurance that our just request would be granted. But the next Sunday an Irish priest having been sent to officiate instead of a French one, we sent a deputation to ask him where the French priest was that he had promised us? He answered, "That we ought to take the priest we could get and be satisfied." This short and sharp answer raised our French blood, and we began to speak more boldly to his Reverence, who got up and walked through the room in a rage, saying some half-dozen times during a short conversation, "You insult me?" But seeing we were a fearless people, and determined to have no other priest but one whom we could understand, he at last promised us again, a French priest if we were ready to pay the debts of our church and house. We said we would pay them, but our verbal promise was nothing to his Reverence. He immediately wrote an agreement, though it was Sunday, and we signed it. But to obtain sooner or later his object, he imposed upon that unfortunate priest, a condition that he knew no Christian could obey. This condition was that he should not receive in his church or countenance any one but the French. This was utterly impossible, as many Irish, Germans, and American Catholics had been in the habit for years past, of coming to our church for any thing they wanted in spiritual matters, and it was impossible to turn them out at once.

We did everything in our power to help our priest in the matter, by taking all the seats of the church against the will of all the other respectable people of different nations who had occupied those seats for years. Finding themselves turned out of the church, and unable to conceive the reason of so gross an insult from a fellow Christian people, they said to us, "Have we not paid for our seats in your church till this day? Double the rent if you like; we are ready to pay for it; but, for God's sake, permit us to come and pray with you at the foot of the same altars." We explained to them the tyrannical orders of the Bishop, and they, too, commenced cursing the Bishop and "the ship that brought him over."

They continued, however, to come to our church, though they had no seat. They attended Divine Service in the aisles of the

Figure 13 b
Continuation of article

church, and we did not like to disturb them; but our feelings were too Christian for our Bishop. He kept a watch over our priest, and, of course, found out that he was receiving many who were forbidden to attend our religious meetings.

The Bishop then thought once more of his dear French priest; so he came in person to his house and asked him if he had kept his orders. The priest answered that "it was quite impossible to obey such orders and remain a Christian; that in many instances he had been obliged by the laws of charity to give religious help to some who were not French people."

"Well then," answered the Bishop, "from this very moment I silence you, and I forbid you the functions of priest in my Diocese."

The poor, trembling priest, thunderstruck, could not say a word.

He went to some friends to relate what had just happened him, and he was advised by them to go back to the Bishop immediately to beg the privilege to remain at the head of his congregation till Lent was over. The Bishop said "I will consent to your request if you will pay me one hundred dollars." "I will give you the sum as soon as I can collect it, and will give you my note for thirty days," answered the priest. "I want the money cash down," said the Bishop; "go to some of your friends, and you can easily collect that amount." The poor priest went away in search of the almighty dollars; but he could not find them as soon as he wished, and did not return to his lordship that day. The Bishop started that night for St. Louis, but he did not forget his dear French people in his long journey. As soon as he arrived in St. Louis he wrote to his Grand Vicar, Rev. Mr. Dunn that the French priest pay him $100 or remain suspended.

This good will of our Bishop for our spiritual welfare, and his paternal love for our purses, did not fail to strike us. Our priest made a new effort that very day; he went to see an old friend who had been absent from town for some time, related to him his sad position. This friend (his name is P. F. Rofinot) seeing that he could redeem a priest for so little a sum, (for the priest had collected part of it himself,) immediately proceeded with the priest to the house of the very Rev. Dun, with the money in hand to satisfy the Bishop.

But alas! that bargain did not last very long; for as soon as the Bishop returned the watch that he had left behind him, performed his duty well and told him that the French priest was going on the same as before. So the poor priest had to go again to the Bishop to explain his conduct. But this time, he would not bear the idea of buying again the right of officiating under such a tyrant. He left us to fight the hardest battles ourselves, against our Bishop.

As the church and the house of our priest were on leased ground, the lease had to be renewed or the buildings removed. We went to the Bishop, who advised us to buy a lot and move the church on it, and sell the house to help pay for the lot. Suspecting nothing wrong in that advice, we followed it. We bargained for a lot, agreed to sell the house and went to report our progress.

But we were going too fast. The Bishop must stop us, or he would be frustrated in his calculations, for he had a lot himself, to put the church on, and opposed our removing our church, by telling us that there was another lot adjoining the one we had bargained for; and that we must buy it also. We went immediately and bought the lot on ninety days time. But he objected to this again, saying that he would not allow us to touch the church, unless we had the whole lot paid for, and put the deed in his hands, and that the deed should be made to him privately.

This had the effect desired by the Bishop. We had collected all the money that could be collected then in our small congregation; it was impossible for us to do any more at once, so we concluded to give up the battle. The Bishop then went on, took the money we had sold the house for ($1,200). A Catholic lady whose husband had bought the house, had subscribed $100 for removing the church, provided the Bishop would promise that it would remain in the hands of the French and attended by a French priest. The Bishop proffered again to that lady the lie, which he had so often uttered to us, every where even from the altar, that upon his word of Bishop, it would remain a French church, and that they should have a French priest. (This we shall call lie No. 1.) He then moved the church to another lot of his own, sent an Irish priest to officiate in it, put the money in his pocket, and made the congregation, which is now Irish, pay for the lot, the moving and repairing of the church, and he takes quarterly the revenues which are not less than $2,000 a year.

This is the way we have been swindled of our church, of the house of our priest, and of our all, by the tyrant Bishop O'Regan; and when a French priest visits our city he forbids him to address us in our cherished mother tongue. And this is also the way that we, French Catholics, as a society, have been blotted out of the book of the living!

And when Rev. Father Chiniqui has publicly accused Bishop O'Regan to have deprived us most unjustly of our church, he has preferred a truth which has as many witnesses as there are Catholics and Protestants in Chicago.

We know well that Bishop O'Regan is proclaiming that he has not deprived us of our church, that if it is in the hands of the Irish, it is because the Irish and not the French built it. This is lie No. 2, which can be easily proven by more than ten thousand witnesses.

We would like to know if he has forgotten the agreement (mentioned above) which he made

Figure 13 c
Continuation of article

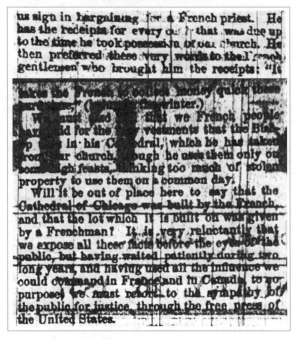

Chiniquy's report of what happened to the French Catholic church of Chicago is supported by Catholic sources, as well as independent accounts. According to *Fifty Years*, when P. F. Roffinot and a group of French Canadians went to see Bishop O'Regan about the loss of their church in Chicago, he said, "French Canadians: You do not know your religion! Were you a little better acquainted with it, you would know that I have the right to sell your churches and church properties, pocket the money, and go eat and drink it where I please." *A History of Chicago from the Earliest Period to the Present Time*, published in 1884, reported on the response when P. F Rofinot and the other French Canadian Catholics informed O'Regan that they could not bring the deed for the lot in the bishop's name, as he wished, because they could only afford the down payment, "To this the Bishop excitedly, and with a plentitude of energetic gesticulation, replied: 'I want you to understand, Mr. Rofinot, that I can sell all the churches in my diocese, put the money in my pocket, and spend it wherever I please.'"

This sentiment of the Bishop was also reported in an article entitled, "The Church Property Question" in the April 13th, 1857 edition of *Chicago Tribune*. In the piece, the *Tribune* noted a Rev. Matthew Dillon was engaged in defending Bishop O'Regan (see Figure 16). Dillon is mentioned in *Fifty Years* as O'Regan's "pro secretary".[6]

Another account that confirmed, albeit unwittingly what Chiniquy said, is a letter published in the June 11th, 1857, *Chicago Tribune* (see Figure 17). Another example of one of the rare efforts to publicize O'Regan's side of the story, the unsigned letter, though plainly written by an apologist for the prelate, supported Charles Chiniquy in several areas. It reported on a religious celebration, designed as a public statement

Figure 13 d
Continuation of article

RESOLUTIONS.

Resolved, That the Right Rev. O'Regan, Bishop of Chicago, has entirely lost the confidence of the French and Canadian population of Illinois, and particularly of Chicago, since he has taken away from us our church.

Resolved, That the Right Rev. O'Regan has published a base slander against the French and Canadian population of Chicago, when he said he took our church from our hands on the pretence that we could not pay for it.

Resolved, That the Right Rev. Bishop O'Regan, having said to our deputies who went to inquire from him by what right he was taking our church from us to give it to another congregation, " I have the right to do what I like with your church and your church properties; I can sell them and put the money in my pocket, and go where I please with it," has assumed a power too tyrannical to be obeyed by a Christian and a free people.

Resolved, That the nature of the different suits which the Right Rev. Bishop O'Regan has had before the civil courts of this State, and which he has almost invariably lost, have proved to the whole people of Illinois that he is quite unworthy of the position he holds in the Catholic Church.

Resolved, That the Rt. Rev. O'Regan is here publicly accused of being guilty of Simony for having extorted $100 from a priest to give him permission to officiate and administer the sacraments among us.

Resolved, That the Rt. Rev. O'Regan, in forbidding the Irish and German Catholics to communicate with the French Catholic Church, and allowing the French and Canadians to communicate with the Irish and German churches, has acted with a view to deprive the French church of religious fees and other donations, which acts we consider unjust and against the spirit of the church, and more resembling a mercantile transaction than a Christian charity.

Resolved, That the French and Canadian people of Illinois have seen with feelings of grief and surprise that the Rev. Mr. Desaulnier has made himself the humble valet of the merciless and shameless persecutor of his countrymen.

Resolved, That the Rev. Mr. Chiniquy, pastor of St. Anne deserves the gratitude of every Catholic of Illinois for having the first put a stop to the rapacious tyranny of the Bishop of Chicago.

Resolved, That the French Catholics of Chicago are determined to give all support in their power to the Rev. Mr. Chiniquy in his struggle against the Bishop of Chicago.

Resolved, That a printed copy of these resolutions be sent to every Bishop and Arch-Bishops of the United States and Canadas, that they may see the necessity of giving to the Church of Illinois a Bishop more worthy of that high position.

Resolved, That a copy of these resolutions may be sent to His Holiness Pius IX, that he may be incited to make inquiries about the humble condition of the Church in Illinois since the present bishop is among us.

Resolved, That the independence and liberty loving press of the United States may be requested to publish the above address and resolutions all over the country.

P. F. ROFINOT, President.

DAVID FRANCHERE, Secretary.

Figure 14

Chicago Daily Tribune, January 27, 1857

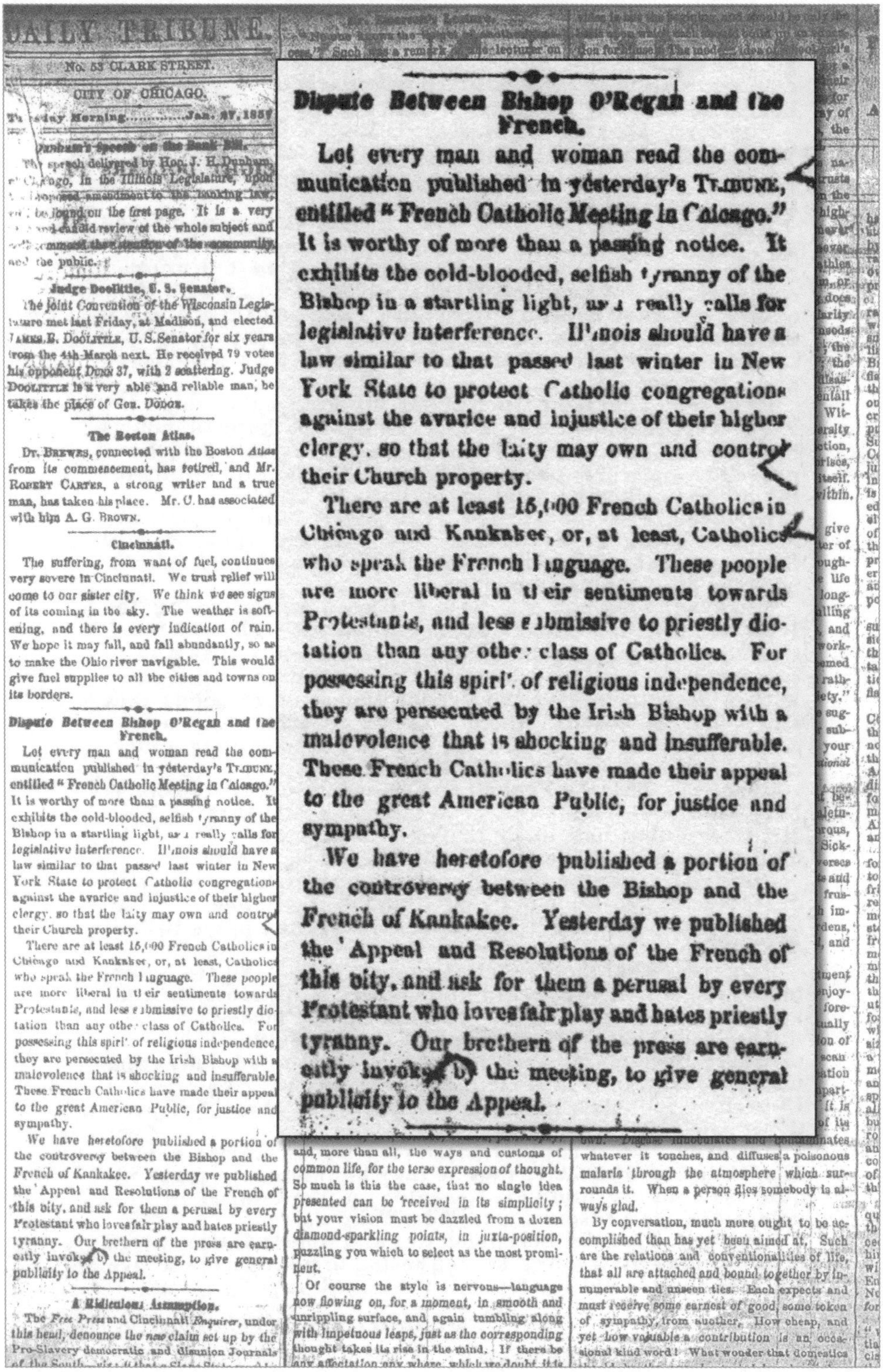

DAILY TRIBUNE.

No. 53 CLARK STREET.

CITY OF CHICAGO.

Tuesday Morning..............Jan. 27, 1857

Dispute Between Bishop O'Regan and the French.

Let every man and woman read the communication published in yesterday's TRIBUNE, entitled "French Catholic Meeting in Chicago." It is worthy of more than a passing notice. It exhibits the cold-blooded, selfish tyranny of the Bishop in a startling light, and really calls for legislative interference. Illinois should have a law similar to that passed last winter in New York State to protect Catholic congregations against the avarice and injustice of their higher clergy, so that the laity may own and control their Church property.

There are at least 15,000 French Catholics in Chicago and Kankakee, or, at least, Catholics who speak the French language. These people are more liberal in their sentiments towards Protestants, and less submissive to priestly dictation than any other class of Catholics. For possessing this spirit of religious independence, they are persecuted by the Irish Bishop with a malevolence that is shocking and insufferable. These French Catholics have made their appeal to the great American Public, for justice and sympathy.

We have heretofore published a portion of the controversy between the Bishop and the French of Kankakee. Yesterday we published the Appeal and Resolutions of the French of this city, and ask for them a perusal by every Protestant who loves fair play and hates priestly tyranny. Our brethern of the press are earnestly invoked by the meeting, to give general publicity to the Appeal.

Figure 15
Chicago Daily Tribune, March 31, 1857

DAILY TRIBUNE.

No. 53 CLARK STREET.

CITY OF CHICAGO.

Tuesday Morning........March 31, 1857.

Our readers are doubtless somewhat confused by the contradictory communications, which have from time to time appeared in our columns, in relation to the matter in difference between Father CHINIQUY, the head and spiritual director of the French colonists of Kankakee county, and † ANTHONY, Catholic Bishop of this Diocese. The controversy has arisen naturally and unavoidably out of the well established policy of the Church, which invests its ecclesiastics with the control of its temporal possessions, as well as its ghostly affairs, and the spirit of resistance which has been growing up among laymen, to what they regard as an infringement of their well defined rights of property. It is, in fact, the revival, in Illinois, of the Buffalo agitation by which the Church has been long convulsed. In this case, there is another element which gives a tinge of bitterness and personality to the contest. Between the French Catholics and the Irish of the same faith, there is anything but a fraternal feeling. Father CHINIQUY represents the one nationality, and † ANTHONY the other; and when the reader remembers that in the present dispute, the contending parties are animated by the spirit which makes all religious quarrels so intensely rancorous, as well as by the mutual antipathies growing out of differences of race, language, manners and hereditary methods of thought, they will readily agree with us that the struggle between them has but just commenced.

Father CHINIQUY, whose name, in connection with this imbroglio, our readers will often see, came to Illinois as the friend and protector of of his people. In Canada he was known as the Apostle of Temperance among his countrymen; and to this day, he is remembered there with the affection and reverence that characterise the feeling of the Irish, in Ireland, for THEOBALD MATHEW. He left Canada some years ago, after a succession of failures in the wheat crop, which had reduced his parishioners among others to extreme want, in search of a more genial climate and a more fertile soil. He was

accompanied by a large number of his friends, and though the colonists boasted of little wealth and claimed but an humble social position, they were rich in industry, frugality, contentment, love of their faith and of each other. In their new homes they have for years given full play to those virtues; and there is not now in all Illinois a happier or more prosperous people. While they have been building their homes and gathering together such of the comforts and luxuries as are within reach of those in their condition, Father CHINIQUY has been industriously engaged in promoting their spiritual welfare, in strictest accordance with doctrines and practices of their Church. He has built a house for their accommodation, has founded a school, has watched, with the solicitude of a father and the patience of good priest, over their welfare. But their little church and their school have been until now, though both loyally Catholic, under their own control, and so they still desire them to remain. But that does not suit the Bishop; and here the quarrel begins. That dignitary—represented as grasping, avaricious and tyrannical, by his enemies, and but feebly defended by his friends—demands the title to their ecclesiastical property, the control of their educational institutions, and their unqualified submission to such priests as he shall send them as the representatives of his will. Father CHINIQUY refuses to obey; his people cling to him with the affection of children, and beg that their affairs, heretofore so happily guided, may be under his management still. The Bishop threatens them with the terrors of excommunication; but they are independent in spite of his wrath. Thus the contest stands.

This case, thus briefly related, will call the attention of the people of the State to the necessity which exists for some legislation, like that of New York, for the protection of the laity of all religious sects against the rapacity of those, who, in the name of our Maker, rule over them. Without that protection, Father CHINIQUY will, sooner or later, be forced to submit; and thus add another to the thousands of instances in which priestly tyranny has been relentlessly exercised for oppression, even in this country, where we boast of perfect religious freedom.

Figure 16

Chicago Tribune, June 11th, 1857

The Church Property Question.

We have at last, in a very brief but plain statement of the difficulty between the French Catholics at St. Anne's, and † ANTHONY, his lordship the Bishop of Chicago, the means of confounding Rev. Matthew DILLON, who came forward voluntarily as the Bishop's defender and in flat contradiction of the TRIBUNE's statement of the origin and progress of this interesting affair. We freely forgive the Reverend gentleman for calling us hard names; but at the same time will take the liberty to advise him not to rush into a newspaper controversy until he has read up both sides of the question. Having given you absolution without conditional penance, we commend you, Brother DILLON, to the following letter from Father CHINIQUY himself:

STE. ANNE, KANKAKEE CO., ILL.,
6th April, 1857.

R'D MR. DILLON—R'd Sir: You are correct when you say that the French Catholics of Ste. Anne had given the deed of the land on which their chapel is erected, to the Rt. Revd. Bishop Vandevelde; but that deed contains this most heretical and schismatical clause: "for the use and benefit of the Catholics of Ste. Anne."

That deed was received with a blessing hand by His Lordship Bishop Vandevelde. But you are not yet aware, that, as soon as Bishop O'Regan saw that damnable clause—"for the use and benefit of the Catholics of Ste. Anne,"—which took away from him his dear divine right to sell our property, and go and eat it where he likes (as he has done with the French of Chicago), that he ordered me, three times, under the threat of suspense, interdict and excommunication, to oblige my people to give another deed whereby the clause "for the use," &c. should be blotted out.

Three times I have refused to obey the Bishop of Chicago, in this matter; and I believe that neither you, my dear Mr. Dillon, nor any other Christian in Chicago, can blame me for having refused to submit myself and my people to such orders.

I am, R'd Sir and dear Friend, yours,
C. CHINIQUY.

Here is the case in a nut-shell. † ANTHONY wants that most "heretical and schismatical clause," "for the use and benefit of the Catholics of St. Anne," stricken out of the deeds which he holds in his hands—why, let our readers judge. The Catholics of St. Anne are willing that the deed should repose in his strong box; but they will not give him unconditional control over their property — why? Father CHINIQUY tells. There, Father DILLON, tell your beads, read your breviary, and let the newspapers alone.

---

against the Chiniquy schism, which was allegedly attended by more than 4,000 people. The letter confirmed Chiniquy's statement about the numerous public complaints about the bishop. The letter's effectiveness is questionable however because not only did this correspondence not agree with *Fifty Years* and other sources, it appeared not to agree with itself.[7]

Shortly afterwards, the letter was answered in the *Tribune* by a writer who did give his name. P. Gendron, who was also at this gathering, stated that there were less than the reported 4,000 people there and many were present because pressure had been applied to ensure their attendance. He also stated that a gift publicly presented to Rev. Desaulniers, had been paid for by his fellow priests, not the people of Bourbonnais, who evidently didn't support him, (it is reproduced in the Appendix 3, Part 4). Regarding the anonymity of the letter writer, Gendron wrote,

> Come forward, Mr," An Eye Witness," and give us your name, so that we may know if you are a Christian, the only exception to the rule, who supports by his pen, a man like Bishop O'Regan who has insulted your countrymen, when he said that they could not pay even for the *potatoes and salt* to support their priest; and also Mr. Desaulniers who addressed you this graceful compliment: that you Canadians were all ignorant and unable to sign you own names![8]

Another example of the criticism that O'Regan faced in the *Chicago Tribune*

WHO KILLED ABRAHAM LINCOLN?

Figure 17
Chicago Tribune, June 11th, 1857

The Chiniquy Calumnies.

To the Editor of the Tribune

SIR:—The facility with which a portion of the Chicago press opens its pages to unauthorized correspondence, has become the subject of just and very general complaint. Of this, there have been many and very shameless instances in connection with the Chiniquy schism, and its Chicago adherents. Notorious calumnies have been published in this city against the Bishop of Chicago, and from the circumstance that these are admitted into the local papers, it is expected to give them, in distant places, the air of truthfulness. A recent occurrence will still more illustrate this.

On the fourth of the month, a religious celebration took place at Bourbonnais Grove, in Kankakee county. It was designed as a public demonstration by the Canadians, in this State, against the schism of Chiniquy, as a compliment to the Bishop of Chicago, and to the Very Rev. W. Desaulniers, whose zeal and success in putting down that schism, won for him, in union with the Bishop, the love of all good men, and the ire of every friend to irreligion.

At this celebration, there were present not less than four thousand persons, from Bourbonnais, Kankakee, L'Erable, Beaver, Petites Iales, St. Anne, and the other Canadian settlements. The Bishop, who left Chicago in the morning, attended by many of his clergymen, was received at the R. R. depot, at Kankakee, by this immense assemblage. At this place an address was presented to him in the name of all those Catholics conjointly, by P. Spink, Esq., of L'Erable, after which a procession was formed, and moved on to Bourbonnais, with the American flag in advance, a band of music and other numerous and appropriate emblems of joy, honor and festivity. I was present at this scene, and a more magnificent and enthusiastic one I never beheld. Carriages and horsemen, and persons on foot, filled the filled the entire space, two miles and a half, between Kankakee and Bourbonnai's Grove.— The houses were decorated. The inhabitants were all abroad, in their gayest festive dresses, either with the Bishop in procession, or on bended knees in front of their houses to receive his benediction. On approaching the Church, we found the young and old arrayed in two lines in front of it, and extending to a great distance. The procession stopped here, dividing to the right and left and filling the immense area; then on bended knees, and with hearts overflowing with joy, this vast assemblage received the benediction of their devoted Bishop. The large church was soon crowded. In the Sanctuary there was a throne for the Bishop, and on the corresponding side, a very elevated seat for the very Rev. Mr. Desaulniere, the distinguished Canadian Missionary,

who so very effectually crushed Chiniquy and his schism. On a table, within the sanctuary, was the beautiful present of plate designed for this gentleman, by the Canadians of Illinois, and on the Altar was placed a magnificent copy of the Bible, the gift of the Bishop of Chicago to the same Ecclesiastic.

After the usual acts of thanksgiving, addresses were presented to the Rt. Rev. Bishop, by the Canadian congregations of the Diocese, while the very Rev. Desaulniers, in a long and very powerful address, represented the sentiment and respect of Catholic Canada, towards this eminent Prelate. Numerous, and most complimentary addresses were also presented to the very Rev. Mr. Desaulniers. V. G.

The reply of the Bishop was much admired. Now, for the first time, he publicly denounced this miserable noisy schism, and exposed its character and manifold calumnies. This was done with force and eloquence, bringing joy and conviction (were this needed) to every person in that vast assembly. We trust that this beautiful address, of which we believe a report has been taken, will be soon published. We regard this of immense value to the interests of religion in this country, which have been outraged by the wanton and wicked assaults on truth, decency, and the personal character of this most worthy Prelate.

The reply of the Bishop was much admired. Now, for the first time, he publicly denounced this miserable noisy schism, and exposed its character and manifold calumnies. This was done with force and eloquence, bringing joy and conviction (were this needed) to every person in that vast assembly. We trust that this beautiful address, of which we believe a report has been taken, will be soon published. We regard this of immense value to the interests of religion in this country, which have been outraged by the wanton and wicked assaults on truth, decency, and the personal character of this most worthy Prelate.

The festivities of the day terminated with a banquet, of which not less than two thousand persons partook, in the course of the afternoon. This was served up with much taste and elegance, in a beautiful grove. The Bishop was accompanied to the grounds, by the entire assembly, preceded by a band of music, whose performance contributed much to enliven this delightful scene. Late that evening, the Bishop, with Rev. Mr. Desaulniers and his other clergymen, returned to Chicago, being escorted to Kankakee Station, by the same band of music, and by the morning's numerous and joyous retinue. At the Depot, a scene occurred calculated to excite the indignation of all, but more particularly of those who understand the artifices of the notorious Chiniquy. A solitary man, neither a Canadian nor a Catholic, but an Irish Orangeman, stood not far from the railway station, holding in one hand a revolver and in the other a black flag, surmounted with a dark

Figure 17
Continuation of article

figure. On the flag this inscription, in white letters, was legible: "The departure of Judas, the traitor." It was designed as an insult to the Very Rev. Mr. Desaulniers, then returning to Canada, from his mission in Kankakee.

In your paper of Tuesday, all reference to the magnificent demonstration at Bourbonnais, is studiously omitted, whilst the disgraceful incident at Kankakee, the act of an abandoned desperado, is not only put forward as the action of the Canadian population, but it is, moreover, incorrectly and offensively represented, as an insult to the person of the Bishop of Chicago.

We know Bishop O'Regan, and are aware, that any disrespect to the humblest of his clergemen, is sensitively felt by him, as if offered to himself. We also know, that for him external pressure has no peril, when that pressure would assume unduly to control the faithful discharge of his sacred duties. His difficulties are numerous and fearful, but for all these he clearly foresaw, and for all these he has been fully prepared. His success is certain, for his course is firm and wise, and guarded. He sought not the dangers with which he has had to contend, for he accepted his exalted office with great reluctance, and only in obedience to the obedience to the positive command of the Holy Father.

For him we do not, therefore, deprecate trouble, and insult and fearful calumnies. They are a portion of his inheritance, but rendered sweet by the example of his Divine Master.—They are inseparable from the work of reform and correction, which the condition of some portions of his diocese has made his most necessary and painful duty. For him, therefore, trials are a portion of his daily life, which we will not regret, for these he knows how to accept, and bear and turn to good account; but we condemn and denounce, in connection with all this, the action of a portion of the secular press of this city. We condemn and denounce it, as interfering, most unduly, with the ministry of our Prelate. We condemn and denounce it as calculated to lead many astray, and confirm others in their errors. With every upright man, we condemn and denounce it, for its shameless suppressions, omissions, distortions and misrepresentations in reference to the entire of this miserable Chiniquy affair, in St. Anne's and in Chicago.

Let us select, as an illustration, what has recently occurred at Kankakee. The Bishop is invited to a great celebration at Bourbonnais Grove, designed as an honor for himself and one of his distinguished clergymen—designed as a great and solemn profession of affection to his person and office, by the Canadian population of his Diocese. The Bishop attends, accompanied by about twenty of his clergymen.

A vast assemblage meets him at Kankakee, and forms into procession, covering miles in extent. Flags, banners, music, addresses, and a public banquet, and all the adjuncts of a festive celebration—all these are there in the most appropriate fashion. The Canadian people—the young and old, men and women—from the most distant settlements, all these assemble to honor their Bishop and their excellent missionary, to share in the blessings of this day of religious joy, all these, without exception, on bended knees, and with deep reverence implore the benediction of their Bishop, and implore for him the protection of Heaven. Such was the fourth of June in Bourbonnais Grove, and all this is but an imperfect sketch of this great scene. The entire day is passed without the slightest interruption, as to time or incident, in this continuous flow of festive joy. At the close of the day, and in the village of Kankakee, one miserable man—one only—a low-looking, solitary being, neither a Catholic nor a Canadian, as we have been assured—this one man, whom all confess to be the meanest creature in the community, whose condition and character will explain his motives—this man attempts a wanton insult against one of the Bishop's retinue. The object of the outrage is seen by all. It is most legibly, distinctly inscribed on the banner, which this wretch bore in his hands, yet, the press of Kankakee and Chicago is silent as to this circumstance.

It publishes not one word about the proceedings of that festive day and scene. It is silent with regard to this great solemnity. Not a word of the triumphs for the interests of religion; not a word of the honors paid to the Bishop; not a word of the sacred joy that filled his soul and the souls of his people. All this is suppressed, entirely suppressed, and in its place a dark picture only is presented to the public, the purchased ruffianism of one wretch, who owes his life to the mercy of those whom he would offend—this is put forward as the action of a devoted, faithful people; and the entire scene of that day is placed before the people in this brief form of calumny:

"On the 4th inst., the Bishop of Chicago was burned in effigy, at Kankakee, by the Canadian Catholics of his Diocese."

We will not now further enlarge on this most disreputable mode of suppressing truth, and of disseminating calumny. We trust that, that portion of the Press, from which this grievance is so repeatedly suffered, will soon awaken to a better perception of its real duties, of its high and useful and honorable functions, and to some consciousness that truth, and justice, and decency are due even to Catholic Priests and Bishops, and to Catholic interests and principles.   AN EYE WITNESS.

Chicago, June 9th, 1857.

is a letter from a priest, other than Chiniquy, in the August 25th, 1857 edition. The *Tribune* introduced the man, who did not give his name, in a separate article on the front page of this edition and declared that he was a priest in good standing with the Catholic Church.[9] A reproduction of the letter and the introduction are in the Appendix 3, Parts 5 and 6.

According to Chiniquy, other bishops became alarmed by the continued conflict and tried to end it by helping O'Regan. In a letter to the people of Bourbonnais, Bishop Bourget of Montreal again unsuccessfully tried to discredit Chiniquy by making public, the 1851 accusation of the young woman.[10] This incident is also considered further in Appendix 1.

Fifty Years reported that Rev. M. Dunn, grand victor of Chicago, visited Chiniquy on March 11th, 1858. He relayed the news that O'Regan had been relieved of his position and Bishop Smith of Dubuque was appointed in his place. According to Chiniquy, O'Regan then left Chicago with all the money he had stolen over the years.[11]

Rev. Dunn informed Chiniquy of Bishop Smith's view that in many distant places, those not knowing the facts, thought he was a rebel against the Church and not just O'Regan. Dunn told him that Smith considered it advisable that Chiniquy give the bishop a canonical declaration of submission in writing, so he could show the world that the Apostle of Temperance was still a good Catholic priest. Chiniquy agreed to do so. As he sat down to pen the submission, the thought struck him:

> 'Is not this a providential opportunity to silence those mysterious voices which are troubling me almost every hour? That, in the church of Rome, we do not follow the Word of God, but the lying traditions of men?'

> I determined then to frame my act of submission in such a way that I would silence those voices, and be, more than ever, sure that my faith, the faith of my dear church, which had just given me such a glorious victory at Rome, was based upon the Holy Word of God, on the divine doctrines of the gospel. I then wrote down, in my own name and in the name of my people:

>> 'My lord Bishop Smith, bishop of Dubuque and administrator of the diocese of Chicago: ---We want to live and die in the holy Catholic, apostolic and Roman church, out of which there is no salvation, and to prove this to your lordship, we promise to obey the authority of the church according to the word and commandments of God as we find them expressed in the gospel of Christ.

> 'C. CHINIQUY'

Dunn and Chiniquy traveled to Dubuque, Iowa on March 25th, 1858. The submission was cordially accepted by Bishop Smith, who insisted that after the stress of the past months, Chiniquy spend 15 days of relaxation and meditation at a Catholic institution of his choice.

On Palm Sunday, at St. Anne, a representative of the bishop proclaimed that peace between the prelate and Father Chiniquy had been achieved. The following day,

Figure 18

Chicago Daily Democrat, March 31, 1858

RESTORATION OF FATHER CHINIQUY.—We are glad to learn that Father Chiniquy, the celebrated French Canadian Priest, of St. Ann's Parish, Iroquois Co., in this State, who was deposed and excommunicated by Bishop O'Regan, has been restored by Bishop Smith of Du Buque. Father Dunn, of St. Patrick's Church, West Chicago, officiated in St. Ann's Parish on Sunday last, and announced the restoration to Father Chiniquy's flock.

Chiniquy traveled to the University of St. Joseph, Indiana for his retreat. An article on the front page of the *Chicago Daily Democrat*, published a few days later on March 31, 1858, confirmed Chiniquy's account and also showed the high profile he enjoyed (see Figure 18).[12]

A few days later however, Chiniquy received word that Bishop Smith had ordered him to return to Dubuque. On the way there, he learned from Rev. Dunn that the Jesuits of Chicago were responsible for the early end of his rest. After learning of his submission to Bishop Smith, they protested the wording. They said that the authority of the Church and the bishop would be lost if this submission was accepted. This was because Chiniquy and his people had not submitted to the bishop unconditionally but to him only if the bishop's orders to them were in accordance with the Word of God.

Arriving at Dubuque, Rev. Chiniquy went immediately to the bishop's palace. There, Bishop Smith told him he needed to change his declaration of submission, saying it had to be unconditional and not include any reference to the Word of God, Gospel of Christ, etc. According to *Fifty Years*, Chiniquy answered his superior:

> 'What you ask me is not an act of submission, it is an act of adoration. I do absolutely refuse to give it.'
>
> 'If it be so, sir,' he answered, 'you can no longer be a Roman Catholic priest.'
>
> I raised my hands to heaven, and cried with a loud voice: 'May God Almighty be forever blessed.'

During the next couple of hours, Chiniquy's mind was in turmoil: knowing that he had left the only Church he had ever been part of, the organization that had been his life. He realized then that the voice that had been troubling him had been the voice of God, calling him to leave the Catholic Church and to join those who, by simple faith, were followers of Christ.

After praying and reading his Bible, he felt the Spirit of God speak to him, telling him that he could not be saved from his sins by such things as: penances, confessions, indulgences, prayers to Mary and the saints, practiced by those in the Church of Rome. He felt God show him that he could only be saved by simple, child-like faith in Christ and by believing that the Son of God's shed blood on the Cross was a sufficient and final payment for his sins. Feeling transformed and emboldened by his new faith, he returned to his colony.

Arriving home in St. Anne, Chiniquy was met by his countrymen who were confused by a telegram from the Bishop of Dubuque, telling them to turn away from their rebellious priest. Gathering the people in the chapel, he told them how their conditional declaration of submission to the bishop had been rejected. He told them that unconditional submission had been requested instead, which he refused to give, necessitating his leaving the priesthood.

Speaking for more than two hours, he told of his desolation, his internal struggle and how God showed him that by faith, Christ could and would take away his sins forever by his substitutionary death on the cross. He believed he would have to leave

St. Anne as he expected most, if not all of his congregation would not break their allegiance to the Church of Rome, as he had. Stating that he wanted the people, instead of himself, to sever the precious ties between them, he asked them to tell him to go away by standing. With great emotion, the congregation surprised him by refusing to do so.

Realizing that the people wanted to be intelligent followers of the Gospel instead of slaves of the Pope, he asked them if they wanted him to stay and preach only the Word of God to them. Requesting them to stand if they wanted him to stay, he wrote, "Without a single exception, that multitude arose! More than a thousand of my countrymen had, forever, broken their fetters. They had crossed the Red Sea and exchanged the servitude of Egypt, for the blessings of the Promised Land!"

As can be expected with any change of this magnitude, there was confusion and misunderstandings. Not all the people had come to the chapel at this time. Later at home therefore, men would be explaining to wives and children why they had left the Roman Catholic Church or wives would be explaining the same to their husbands and family. Some did stay in the Church of Rome but according to Chiniquy, after a week, 405 of the 500 families in St. Anne had left the Catholic Church and accepted Christ. In two months time, it was all of the families except 15.[13]

Independent sources confirmed that Charles Chiniquy did leave the Church of his youth, along with more than a thousand people. The *London Times*, for example, reported that "in 1858 he seceded from the Church of Rome, taking a congregation, numbering over a thousand, with him".

As these evangelical Christians grew in their new faith, the remnants of Catholic worship and superstition that remained in their lives began to disappear. More and more of Charles Chiniquy's French Canadian countrymen were leaving the Church of Rome to follow Christ, something that alarmed Bishop Duggan of Chicago, who announced plans to come to St. Anne on August 3rd, 1858. He intended to speak to the people, show them their error and bring them back to the fold. He visited that day and addressed a large crowd from the raised platform that the colonist had erected for the bishop and Chiniquy to speak from. The people listened politely to Duggan's call to return to the Church of their forefathers but rejected it. There was almost a riot when the bishop tried to prevent Chiniquy from speaking but order was restored. Crushed by his defeat, the prelate and his entourage left. This account is supported by an article a week later on the front page of the *Chicago Press and Tribune*. Duggan was to spend the end of his life in an institution for the insane in St. Louis.[14]

Charles Chiniquy and his followers initially called themselves Christian Catholics. Their break from the Church of Rome caused intense interest throughout the Protestant world and they received many visitors, including ministers and laymen of different denominations. After prayerful consideration, they decided to join the Presbyterian Church of the United States. According to Chiniquy, they did so on April 15th, 1860, in a group of almost 2,000, a fact also confirmed by independent accounts.[15]

Despite difficulties, the movement grew and churches and missions were planted in other communities in Illinois with sizable French Canadian populations, the number of converts growing to some 6,500 by 1860. As the work became larger and spread out, Chiniquy and his people felt the need to build a college to educate ministers for these congregations. Later that year, Rev. Chiniquy was invited on what turned out to be a very successful speaking tour of Europe which raised his profile and as well as a large amount of money for their college. After he returned home however, he found that due to mismanagement by two men he had left in charge of the colony, the funds that were raised had been lost, an event that caused difficulties with the U. S. Presbyterian Church.

To avoid ruin, they had to ask the help of the Presbyterian Church of Canada. Representing this body, Rev. Dr. Kemp and two others investigated the difficulties between Charles Chiniquy, those he led, and the Presbyterian Church of the United States. They published their findings, which cleared Chiniquy. Kemp concluded that: "my own deliberate conviction is, in which I believe my colleagues share, that Chiniquy's Christian integrity and ministerial character come out of this fiery trial unscathed."[16]

Kemp expressed his hope that the Presbyterian Church of Canada would extend "the hand of fellowship to Pastor Chiniquy and his people" which it did, and he and his congregants joined this body on June 11th, 1863.

Charles Chiniquy spent the time after he left the Catholic Church, writing, teaching and speaking across the world. He continued to preach to and attempt to win his former co-religionist to Christ, something that was not appreciated by many in the Church of Rome.

His life story is similar to the great apostle Paul's in some ways although Chiniquy, of course, did not achieve Paul's enduring fame. Both warred against beliefs they eventually embraced. Both were very energetic men. Paul shouldered a large part of the work of establishing and expanding the early churches. Chiniquy was perpetually busy with his many evangelical activities, one account commenting on "his extraordinary energy—he seemed to be always at white heat."[17]

Both were busy writers, Paul used by God to author a significant part of the New Testament. One hostile source reported that Charles Chiniquy's works were published by the million. From the time it was first published in 1885, *Fifty Years* went through 70 editions before his death in 1899. Chiniquy biographer Richard Lougheed stated that the Apostle of Temperance is still Canada's best-selling author. Both were very influential and were good speakers. Both suffered attacks by the religious groups they formerly were part of. Rev. Chiniquy stated that in addition to numerous threats to his safety by Catholics, there were no less than 30 attempts on his life. He was beaten, shot and stoned 20 times. He and his associates were injured a number of times. The protection of British troops was needed to keep him safe from Roman Catholic mobs in Quebec, in 1859.[18] Charles Chiniquy was also known as the "Martin Luther of America," His obituary in the *Times* of London confirmed his statements regarding Catholic attacks:

Serious disorders occurred on his visiting Quebec in 1859, and Mr. Chiniquy was himself wounded. In the following year the ex-priest, now a Presbyterian Minister, spent six months in the United Kingdom, giving 182 addresses in the course of his tour--a record which he surpassed during subsequent visits in 1874 and 1882. In July, 1874, he was stoned after speaking against Roman Catholicism at Antigonish, Nova Scotia. Two years later he was struck down at Halifax, N.S., and the church in which he preached was injured. In 1879 he visited Australia, always on the same errand, and was roughly handled at Horsham, in Victoria. Relating this incident in public he said: --

'They have so often attacked me with stones, sticks, daggers, and pistols; I have been so often struck and bruised, that the idea of dying under their blows has become as my daily thought--I dare say, my daily bread. Besides that, at my age--70 years--death has absolutely lost all its terrors for me.'[19]

Newspapers such as the *New York Times* and the *Chicago Tribune* supported Chiniquy's reports of violent Catholic mobs that attempted to silence him. Charles Chiniquy also wrote about the June attack in an 1884 letter to Archbishop Lynch of Toronto. His correspondence was an answer to a letter the Archbishop had addressed to officials of the Presbyterian Church. Chiniquy's masterful two page response was apparently published for the general public. It provides real insight into the genius that made him such a magnetic speaker, as well as showing his sense of humour and the formidable strength his high moral standards gave him in debate. It is reproduced in the Appendix 3, Part 7.[20]

Not only attacked physically, Charles Chiniquy also had to combat the Roman Catholic Church in court. He stated:

Thirty-two times, my name has been called before the civil and criminal courts of Kankakee, Joliet, Chicago, Urbana, and Montreal, among the names of the vilest and most criminal of men.

I have been accused by Grand Vicar Mailloux of having killed a man and thrown his body into a river to conceal my crime. I have been accused of having set fire to the church of Bourbonnais and destroyed it. Not less than seventy-two false witnesses have been brought by the priests of Rome to support this last accusation.

But thanks be to God, at every time, from the very lips of the perjured witnesses, we got the proof that they were swearing falsely, at the instigation of their father confessors. And my innocence was proven by the very men who had been paid to destroy me. In this last suit, I thought it was my duty as a Christian and citizen, to have one of those priests punished for having so cruelly and publicly trampled under his feet the most sacred laws of society and religion. Without any vengeance on my part, God knows it, I asked the protection of my country against those incessant plots. Father Brunet, found guilty of having invented those calumnies and supported them by false witnesses, was condemned to pay $2,500 or go to gaol for fourteen years. He preferred the last punishment, having the promise from his Roman Catholic friends that they would break the doors of the prison and let him go free to some remote place. He was incarcerated at Kankakee; but on a dark and stormy night, six months later, he was rescued, and fled to Montreal (900 miles).[21]

The January 23rd, 1860 edition of the *Chicago Press and Tribune* supported Charles Chiniquy's account of this particular court victory over Brunet. Regarding Chiniquy, one biographical account stated, "Thirty-four times he has been dragged before the courts, on criminal charges preferred by Catholics. " Another account made it thirty-five times. One example of his legal struggles with the Church of Rome is the case of the Catholic Bishop of Chicago v. Charles Chiniquy et al, on appeal to the Illinois Supreme Court, (see Appendix 3, Part 8).[22]

It wasn't just Charles Chiniquy who was persecuted. Even those that went to listen to him risked incurring the displeasure of the Church of Rome. In 1879, the *New York Times* related a story of a Catholic man in Massachusetts who was put out of business because he had attended a lecture by Chiniquy and apparently refused to apologize to his priest for doing so.

Charles Chiniquy also reported that when the priests and bishops saw that he could not be easily disposed of with sticks and stones, they tried to destroy his reputation by false accusations. A March 10th, 1892 article in the *Montreal Witness* newspaper confirmed his allegation, stating that he was unsuccessfully, "pursued by carefully concocted slanders of the vilest kind, which would appear to have been furnished by some slander bureau in Canada." The paper also stated that "though he has been similarly vilified ever since he left the church of Rome, he is still, as he has been for over twenty years, a minister in good standing of the Presbyterian Church of Canada."

The vilification has continued after his death as well. After making the allegations he did about the Catholic Church, especially regarding its involvement in the murder of Abraham Lincoln, Charles Chiniquy has not been forgotten. Though he died more than a century ago and while certainly not as famous as he once was, Chiniquy is still a controversial figure today. This volume is just the latest of a string of books, articles, etc., on the man and his works. A significant amount of the criticism of him and his writings seem to have been published after his death, when he could no longer defend himself.

The same *Montreal Witness* article that reported on the slander attempts also stated, "such attacks, when publicly made where Mr. Chiniquy is, are comparatively harmless, as he is well able to shame his slanderers, and they only furnish him with a more effective text." After his death, his critics apparently hoped that so much knowledge and insight would be lost at his passing that almost anything could be said about him, which seems to have occurred. As this work will show however, the evidence still exists for those that are interested in looking for it that confirms that there is no real basis in fact for criticism of Charles Chiniquy, for his statements about his former Church.

The modern detractor that has seemed to have most influential at shaping attitudes toward Chiniquy has been Joseph George Jr., who wrote a paper on the subject of the ex-priest published in the *Journal of the Illinois State Historical Society*, when he was chair of the history department of Villanova University, a Catholic institution. The significant errors in his 1976 paper entitled, "The Lincoln Writings of Charles P. T. Chiniquy", in which he criticized the ex-priest, are analyzed in Appendix 1, along with the mistakes in the work of a number of other Chiniquy critics.

In the end, nearing the close of his most eventful and interesting life, despite the best efforts of his Catholic enemies to hurt him, Charles Chiniquy continued on well past the biblical, three score years and ten or four score, living into his 90th year. In the words of one account:

> The stir created by Chiniquy's writings did not disturb the serenity of his old age, which he spent surrounded by his family in Montreal, in enviable circumstances. Enjoying good health, he travelled, preaching here and there in the province and abroad. Following a brief illness he died peacefully on 16 Jan. 1899. [23]

Chapter 4

A Godly President in the White House

In the late 1850's, while Charles Chiniquy was doing battle with officials of the Church of Rome Abraham Lincoln was involved in a struggle in a different arena. He had won a seat in the U.S. House of Representatives in 1847. When the two year term was up, because of his opposition to President Polk in relation to the Mexican War, he considered himself too unpopular in his district to win once more and he did not run again.

Believing his political career was over, he returned to Springfield to concentrate on his law practice. In 1854 however, a political rival of Lincoln, U.S. Senator from Illinois, Stephen Douglas, introduced a bill to organize the Kansas and Nebraska territories. The Kansas-Nebraska Act effectively repealed the Missouri Compromise of 1820, which had limited slavery from most of the lands of the massive Louisiana Purchase. In 1803, the United States had bought more than 800,000 square miles of land from France, from the Mississippi River to the Rocky Mountains and the Canadian border to the Gulf of Mexico. The Kansas-Nebraska Act meant that the settlers in Kansas and Nebraska could decide for themselves whether slavery would be allowed there. This legislation fomented angry opposition, as well as violence in the North. It also aroused Abraham Lincoln, who had thought that slavery had been permanently limited in America.

Lincoln's old party, the Whig Party, was torn apart over the issue and he joined the newly formed anti-slavery Republican Party. In 1858, he was nominated to be the Republican candidate for U.S. Senator. His opponent was Stephen Douglas, the Democratic incumbent. Lincoln challenged Douglas to a series of debates, and between August 12th, and October 15th, they met in seven different communities in Illinois. Their subject was whether slavery should be allowed in United States territories. Douglas argued that people in any territory could keep slavery out by refusing to pass laws to protect it. Lincoln countered that the 1857 Dred Scott decision of the U.S. Supreme Court prevented slavery from being barred from any part of the territories. Lincoln also declared that slavery was "a moral, social, and political evil" and asserted that his opponent, Douglas, ignored the question of whether slavery was morally wrong. The debates attracted large crowds and although he ultimately did not win the seat, the election campaign made Lincoln nationally known.

Two years later, the two again faced each other but this time, they were candidates for U.S. President. Douglas had angered the proslavery section of the Democratic Party in the South however, and they nominated a different candidate for President. With the support for his opponents split, Abraham Lincoln won the presidency, although he did not receive a majority of the popular vote, or any votes from the Deep South.

In February, 1861, Lincoln bid farewell to his friends and neighbors in Springfield and began his trip by train to Washington. He was scheduled to visit most of the large Eastern cities but after hearing of an assassination plot when he was in Philadelphia, he left for in the capital earlier than planned, arriving there in secret.

Even before he was inaugurated, southern states had begun to withdraw from the America Union and by the time Abraham Lincoln took the presidential oath of office on March 4th, seven states had already seceded. Four more states were to join them to form the rebel Confederate States of America.

In his first inaugural address, the President assured the people of the South that he had no intention of interfering with slavery in the states where it existed, as he had stated on other occasions. He also pointed out that because they occupied the same immovable land mass, physical separation was actually impossible. Lincoln also stated that, as President, he had taken an oath to preserve, protect and defend the United States Constitution and the Constitution had no provision for the termination of the Union. It therefore could not be legally broken by the unilateral actions of one state, or a number of states, but only by the agreement of all, as it had been formed.

Abraham Lincoln wanted to avoid armed conflict but was determined to fulfill his duties as President, which included continuing to hold federal property in the South. Many federal forts in the seceding states had been taken over by Confederate forces. Fort Sumter, which lay in the harbor of Charleston in South Carolina, was also threatened and it became a symbol of the Union itself. Lincoln sent provisions to the garrison there, which the South considered an act of war. On April 12th, 1861, Confederate General Beauregard ordered his artillery to fire on the fort, thereby starting the Civil War.

President Lincoln called for volunteer soldiers and many came forward. The conflict did not begin well for the North however. The initial optimism vanished after early defeats, such as the first and second Battles of the Bull Run, Fredericksburg, and Chancellorsville. These losses depressed spirits in the North and some influential people urged a negotiated peace with the South. As the President and commander in chief of the army, the ultimate responsibility for the Civil War and the affairs of state fell on Abraham Lincoln's shoulders. After the Battle of Fredericksburg, he stated, "If there is a worse place than hell, I am in it".

At the time of the Civil War, the United States was the only important democracy in the world. As such, it represented the hopes of the common man for self rule, instead of rule by kings, dictators and the like. Abraham Lincoln believed this experiment in self government had to succeed. Having come from such humble origins to rise to such a high office, President Lincoln also represented the hopes of millions the world over.

The setbacks convinced Lincoln to change tactics and on September 22, 1862, he publicly declared that unless the Southern states stopped their rebellion and returned to the fold, he would proclaim the freedom of all their slaves. They refused to, so on January 1st, 1863, he issued the Emancipation Proclamation.

To win the war, Lincoln needed good generals and they took time to find. Ulysses S. Grant began to make a habit of winning victories and early in 1864, Lincoln made him commander of all Union forces. Even so, during the summer of that year, Lincoln's prospects for winning another term as President looked bleak. Victory at the Battle of Mobile Bay, the capture of Atlanta and Union victories in Virginia changed public opinion however, and he easily won the presidency again. Though the South had exceptional military leaders, such as Robert E. Lee, the Union population outnumbered the South and as the war continued, the Confederacy began to run out of men and materials to fight with. There were some prisoner exchanges earlier in the war but they tended to mainly help the South. The Union administration therefore suspended them, upsetting those on the side of the South because they knew it meant, barring a miracle, that the Confederacy was doomed.

The high water mark of the Confederacy's military campaign was the battle of Gettysburg where the Army of the Potomac, commanded by General George Meade, met the invading force of Confederate General Robert E. Lee. Some 165,000 men fought in southern Pennsylvania in the largest battle in North American history. After three days of battle, with some seven million bullets fired, Lee was defeated and never had the military strength to engage in another large scale offensive. After this setback, the Confederacy was generally in retreat. It was at the ceremony to dedicate a cemetery on the battlefield at Gettysburg that President Lincoln read his famous Gettysburg address.

It is understandable that the years in office, at such a time of national crisis, would have changed Abraham Lincoln. Even before he arrived in Washington in early 1861 however, he knew of the great task he faced. This foresight is reflected in the speech he made when he left Springfield. Along with his statement about a possible future demise, with prophetic overtones, what is also interesting is what he expressed regarding his need for God's help:

> I now leave, not knowing when, or whether ever, I may return, with a task before me greater than that which rested upon Washington. Without the assistance of that Divine Being, who ever attended him, I cannot succeed. With that assistance I cannot fail. Trusting in Him, who can go with me, and remain with you and be every where for good, let us confidently hope that all will yet be well. To His care commending you, as I hope in your prayers you will commend me, I bid you an affectionate farewell.[1]

Abraham Lincoln quoted the Bible more than any U.S. President, before or since. As he never joined any church however, the question has arisen as to what his religious views were. For some students of the 16th President, the beliefs of this great statesman have been a matter of intense interest. Charles Chiniquy stated that not long after he began his first term, it was widely reported that Lincoln had actually been a Catholic but had left the faith. As one of the President closest friends, Chiniquy could comment, with authority, on Abraham Lincoln's beliefs.

His declaration that the President was the embodiment of the most perfect kind of Christian, while not professing to be a strict member of any Protestant denomination, put him very much at odds with some of Lincoln's associates in legal and political circles.

Chiniquy spoke of the confidence Lincoln had in God, in 1856, as he urged his client to pray when things looked so dark in the lawsuit of Spink vs. Chiniquy. After the case had come to a successful conclusion, Chiniquy quoted Abraham Lincoln regarding his deliverance from his enemies:

> But the way you have been saved from their hand, the appearance of that young and intelligent Miss Moffat, who was really sent by God in the very hour of need, when, I confess it again, I thought everything was nearly lost, is one of the most extraordinary occurrences I ever saw. It makes me remember what I have too often forgotten, and what my mother often told me when young -- that our God is a prayer-hearing God. This good thought, sown into my young heart by that dear mother's hand, was just in my mind when I told you, 'Go and pray, God alone can save you.' But I confess to you that I had not faith enough to believe that your prayer would be so quickly and so marvellously answered

Charles Chiniquy stated that from the first, he had felt that not only was Abraham Lincoln a giant in size but one in mind and heart also. He asked "how such elevation of thought and childish simplicity could be found in the same man". He also wondered how this man of humble beginnings, this "rail-splitter", could have "so easily raised himself to the highest range of human thought and philosophy". He concluded that the President had reached such heights because of his personal relationship with God, declaring that Lincoln was the personification of the ideal Christian.

According to the ex-priest, at their last meeting in the White House, Abraham Lincoln compared himself with Moses, telling his friend that both he and the Old Testament leader were used by God to free millions of slaves. Chiniquy said "Never had I seen a human face so solemn and so prophet-like" as when the President declared that like Moses, it seemed to him that God would allow him to see the promised land of peace, prosperity and happiness but not enter it.[2]

As noted earlier, in his speeches and proclamations, Abraham Lincoln did quote Scripture more than any other President in history, as he led the United States through the worst crisis of its existence. The words that inspired the war-torn nation, echoed and still echo with the power and the beauty of the King James Bible.[3]

In *Fifty Years*, Chiniquy quoted a man who knew the President well and who had discussed Lincoln's faith with him shortly before he became President, Newton Bateman. Bateman was the Illinois Superintendent of Public Instruction for some 14 years and Abraham Lincoln's temporary election headquarters was next to his office in the state capitol from mid 1860 to early 1861. Lincoln would sometimes invite Bateman, his "little friend, the big schoolmaster of Illinois", over to his rooms and after locking the doors to escape the crowds, they would talk. According to Superintendent Bateman, close to the end of October, 1860, he and Lincoln went through a political survey of the Springfield citizens, before the presidential election. Abraham Lincoln was curious as to how the prominent Christians of the city were going to vote and he was disappointed with what he found. The account of Bateman in *Fifty Years* came from the artist, Francis. B. Carpenter's book, *The Inner Life of Abraham Lincoln*. It read in part:

At length he turned to Mr. Bateman, with a face full of sadness, and said: 'Here are twenty-three ministers, of different denominations, and all of them are against me but three; and here are a great many prominent members of the churches, a very large majority are against me. Mr. Bateman, I am not a Christian,--God knows I would be one,--but I have carefully read the Bible, and I do not so understand this book;' and he drew forth a pocket New Testament. 'These men well know,' he continued, 'that I am for freedom in the Territories, freedom everywhere as free as the Constitution and the laws will permit, and that my opponents are for slavery. They *know* this, and yet, with this book in their hands, in the light of which human bondage cannot live a moment, they are going to vote against me; I do not understand it at all.'

'Here Mr. Lincoln paused,--paused for long minutes,--his features surcharged with emotion. Then he rose and walked up and down the reception-room in the effort to retain or regain his self possession. Stopping at last, he said, with a trembling voice and his cheeks wet with tears: 'I know there is a God, and that He hates injustice and slavery. I see the storm coming, and I know that his hand is in it. If He has a place and work for me--and I think He has--I believe I am ready. I am nothing, but Truth is everything. I know I am right, because I know that liberty is right, for Christ teaches it, and Christ is God. I have told them that a house divided against itself cannot stand; and Christ and Reason say the same; and they will find it so.

'Douglas don't care whether slavery is voted up or down, but God cares, and humanity cares, and I care; and with God's help I shall not fail. I may not see the end; but it will come, and I shall be vindicated; and these men will find that they have not read their Bible right.' 'Much of this was uttered as if he was speaking to himself, and with a sad, earnest solemnity of manner impossible to be described. After a pause, he resumed: 'Doesn't it appear strange that men can ignore the moral aspect of this contest? A revelation could not make it plainer to me that slavery, or the Government must be destroyed. The future would be something awful, as I look at it, but for this rock on which I stand,' (alluding to the Testament which he still held in his hand,). 'especially with the knowledge of how these ministers are going to vote. It seems as if God had borne with this thing [slavery] until the very teachers of religion had come to defend it from the Bible, and to claim for it a divine character and sanction; and now the cup of iniquity is full, and the vials of wrath will be poured out.' After this the conversation was continued for a long time. Everything he said was of a peculiarly deep, tender, and religious tone, and all was tinged with a touching melancholy. He repeatedly referred to his conviction that the day

Figure 19

Letter by Newton Bateman to Josiah Holland, June 19, 1865, with transcription

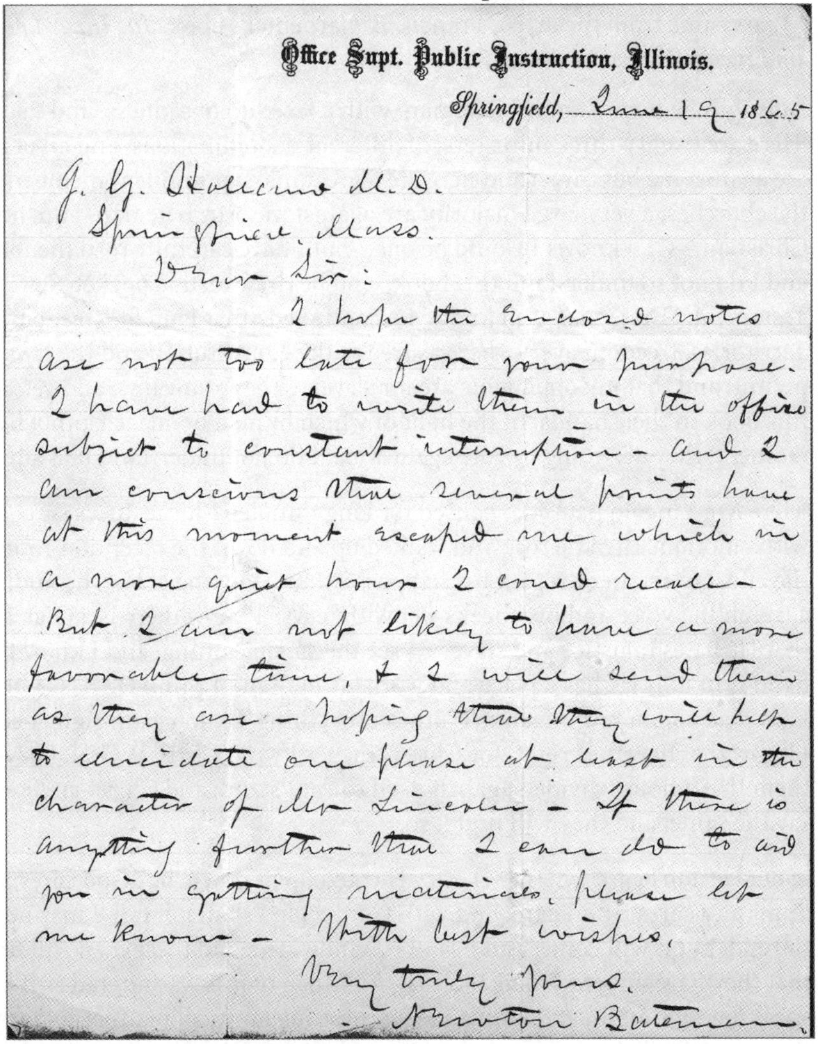

Dear Sir:

I hope the enclosed notes are not too late for your purpose. I have had to write them in the office subject to constant interruptions - and I am conscious that several points have at this moment escaped me which in a more quiet hour I could recall. But I am not likely to have a more favourable time, & I will send them as they are - hoping that they will help to illuminate one phase at least in the character of Mr. Lincoln - If there is anything further that I can aid to you in getting materials please let me know - With best wishes

Very truly Yours

Newton Bateman

WHO KILLED ABRAHAM LINCOLN?

of wrath was at hand, and that he was to be an actor in the terrible struggle which would issue in the overthrow of slavery, though he might not live to see the end.

'After further reference to a belief in Divine Providence, and the fact of God in history, the conversation turned upon prayer. He freely stated his belief in the duty, privilege, and efficacy of prayer, and he intimated, in no unmistakable terms, that he had sought in that way the Divine guidance and favor. The effect of this conversation upon the mind of Mr. Bateman, a Christian gentleman whom Mr. Lincoln profoundly respected, was to convince him that Mr. Lincoln had, in his quiet way, found a path to the Christian standpoint--that he had found God, and rested on the eternal truth of God. As the two men were about to separate, Mr. Bateman remarked: 'I had not supposed that you were accustomed to think so much upon this class of subjects; certainly your friends generally are ignorant of the sentiments you have expressed to me.' He replied quickly: 'I know they are, but I think more on these subjects than upon all others, and I have done so for years; and I am willing you should know it.' (italics in original) [4]

Chiniquy's report of Newton Bateman's account was actually third hand. He got it from Francis Carpenter and Carpenter's source was the first great comprehensive Lincoln biography ever published, Josiah G. Holland's 1866 book, *Life of Abraham Lincoln*, which had appeared earlier than Francis Carpenter's book that year.[5] Carpenter, and *Fifty Years* as well, did not precisely reproduce Josiah Holland's account of what Bateman stated. There are slight discrepancies in the wording.

When Holland's biography was published, quoting Bateman, Lincoln's former partner William Herndon was furious that the President had been portrayed as a Christian and also felt that Holland had made Lincoln look hypocritical.[6] The complete text of what Bateman said in his statement to Holland is in the Appendix 3, Part 14. Beginning his research soon after Lincoln's death, Holland, a Massachusetts journalist, traveled to Springfield, Illinois and interviewed, among others, Newton Bateman.

A month after his interview, at Holland's request, Bateman reproduced what he had told the journalist on eight pages of legal sized paper and he sent them to Holland, along with a letter. The account contained the qualifier that "Mr. Lincoln's language made a vivid impression upon me, and while I do not claim that the above quotations are absolutely verbatim, I know that they are very nearly so, and the sentiments are exactly as he uttered them" (Appendix 3, Part 14 b).[7]

Where Newton Bateman's statements could be checked with independent sources, his recollections were found to be essentially correct. According to historian William Barton, the day after the President-elect left Springfield for Washington, the *Illinois State Journal* published Lincoln's Farewell Address, almost certainly based on Bateman's recollections. When compared to Lincoln's own version, it is found to be a relatively accurate rendition of the speech [8] (See Appendix 3, Part 15, for the two versions of the speech).

The first biography that attempted to show the "real" Lincoln to the world, *The Life of Abraham Lincoln from His Birth to His Inauguration As President*, appeared in 1872. It was the product of the collaborative efforts of an Illinois lawyer friend of Lincoln's, Ward Hill Lamon, William Herndon and Chauncey Black, the son of Lamon's law partner.[9]

The biography proved to be controversial and unpopular. What disturbed the American public mostly about this portrait of the national hero was its assertion that the slain President:

> 'was never a member of any church, nor did he believe in the divinity of Christ, or the inspiration of the Scriptures'; that as a youth if 'he went to church at all, he went to mock, and came away to mimic'; that in his New Salem days he wrote a book 'deriding the gospel history of Jesus'; that in later years, though politics made him more discreet, he never changed his religious views.[10]

Included in the book were accounts of interviews Herndon had with two early associates of Abraham Lincoln and himself, who said Lincoln had been an infidel. They were John T. Stuart and James H. Matheny. They however, later denied much of what Herndon quoted them as saying. As well, in a handbill published in 1846, when he ran for Congress, Lincoln asserted that he had "never denied the truth of the Scriptures" or "spoken with intentional disrespect of religion in general, or of any denomination of Christians in particular".[11]

Was Charles Chiniquy wrong? Did the fact that his friend had not made any public profession of faith or adherence to any sect or dogma mean that he was not a Christian? Regarding Lincoln's silence, there were other times that he didn't reveal his feelings publicly on particular subjects but this did not mean he did not have any. Many men who surrounded Abraham Lincoln up to the time of his successful Presidential election campaign, although upright citizens, probably did not spend much of their spare time in Bible studies. An Abraham Lincoln who spoke about God and quoted the Scriptures freely before his election in 1860 may have seemed out of place.

Once the terrible Civil War broke upon the land however, with its torrents of bloodshed and with the fate of the American nation and the experiment of self-government and democratic freedoms themselves, hanging in the balance, it was perfectly natural for President Lincoln to speak more openly about the God he believed in, the God he increasingly depended on to guide himself and deliver the country. [12] One commentator stated, "Significantly, Lincoln's invocation of the Divinity steadily grew in frequency as the war proceeded".

Abraham Lincoln was never a member of any church although he did rent a pew in the Presbyterian Church in Springfield, as well as one in Washington, and attended regularly. A friend of the President's, Henry C. Deming, a Republican Congressman from Connecticut, shed some light on why Lincoln hadn't joined a church:

> He said, he had never united himself to any church, because he found difficulty in giving his assent, without mental reservations, to the long complicated statements of Christian doctrine which characterize their Articles

of Belief and Confessions of Faith. 'When any church,' he continued, 'will inscribe over its altar as its sole qualification for membership the Saviour's condensed statement of the substance of both the law and Gospel, Thou shalt love the Lord thy God with all thy heart, and with all thy soul, and with all thy mind, and thy neighbor as thyself,--that church will I join with all my heart and soul.' [13]

Artist Francis Carpenter spent nearly six months in the White House, working on his famous painting, "First Reading of the Emancipation Proclamation of President Lincoln". Although he said he accepted Herndon's view of Lincoln's beliefs before his first election as President, he stated, "during the last four years of his life he passed through for example, what few men could have experienced without growth and change". When considering the magnitude of the trial that Lincoln endured, the experiences of few other leaders in history can compare.

Like Charles Chiniquy, Union General James Rusling also remarked on the similarity he saw between Abraham Lincoln and Moses when he recalled a conversation between the President and General Sickles just after the battle of Gettysburg. He quoted Lincoln as saying:

> General Sickles, I had no fears of Gettysburg, and if you really want to know I will tell you why. Of course, I don't want you and Colonel Rusling here to say anything about this--at least not now. People might laugh if it got out, you know. But the fact is, in the stress and pinch of the campaign there, I went to my room, and got down on my knees, and prayed Almighty God for victory at Gettysburg. I told Him that this was His country, and the war was His war, but that we really couldn't stand another Fredericksburg or Chancellorsville. And then and there I made a solemn vow with my Maker that if He would stand by you boys at Gettysburg I would stand by Him.

> 'And He did, and I will! And after this, I don't know how it was, and it is not for me to explain, but, somehow or other, a sweet comfort crept into my soul, that God Almighty had taken the whole thing into His own hands, and we were bound to win at Gettysburg! No, General Sickles, I had no fears of Gettysburg, and that is the why!'

> Mr. Lincoln said all this with great solemnity and impressiveness, almost as Moses might have spoken when first down from Sinai[14]

Other statements by friends and associates of Abraham Lincoln, as well as the 16th President's own words, support Chiniquy's views regarding the Great Emancipator's beliefs. A man who knew the Lincoln family well, the pastor of the first Baptist church of Springfield, Rev. Dr. Miner, related a story that Mary Lincoln told him concerning the morning her husband delivered his first inaugural address. In an account published in 1873, while Mrs. Lincoln was still alive, he quoted her as saying:

> Mr. Lincoln wrote the conclusion of his inaugural address the morning it was delivered. The family being present, he read to them. He then said he wished to be left alone for a short time. The family retired to an adjoining room,

but not so far distant but that the voice a prayer could be distinctly heard. There, closeted with God alone, surrounded by the enemies who were ready to take his life, he commended his country's cause and all dear to him to God's providential care, and with a mind calmed with communion with his Father in heaven, and courage equal to the danger, he came forth from that retirement ready for duty.[15]

As he led the country though the Civil War, President Lincoln was observed reading the Bible numerous times. Mrs. Elizabeth Keckley, a servant in the Lincoln White House, affirmed that the President had obtained relief from the stresses of his office through prayer and by reading the Scriptures.

His former law partner tried to portray the President as an infidel but in his introduction to *Holland's Life of Abraham Lincoln*, historian Allen C. Guelzo stated, "not even Herndon could deny that Lincoln's state papers, from his farewell address in Springfield to the Second Inaugural, were shot through with religious references, and in ways and in sheer volume that departed markedly from Lincoln's Democratic predecessors." Another historian, David Donald, also pointed out that Herndon was forced to admit that "Lincoln made 'addresses at Bible and Sunday school societies,' used the Christian 'ideas, language, speech and forms' in his presidential proclamations, and had many Christian sentiments".

The foregoing is a sampling of the straightforward, unchallenged testimony, both from President Lincoln and others close to him, that show his Christian beliefs. This is also discussed in further detail in the Appendix 2.

When his statements concerned spiritual subjects, Abraham Lincoln's words were in step with evangelical Christianity. He said he had not denied the truth of the Bible, he spoke of God ruling the nations, of the Almighty guiding him in office. If any President of the United States, a nation founded on Protestant Christian principles, was a believer in Jesus Christ, would it not be logical to conclude that it was the one who quoted the Scripture more than all others, especially a man like Mr. Lincoln whose honesty was so widely praised?[16]

It is not unreasonable therefore to conclude from President Lincoln's own public pronouncements, his speeches, his known conversation with groups, as well as individuals, that this great statesman also was what Charles Chiniquy, Bateman, and others said he was, a Christian.

Chapter 5
The Catholic Church and the Civil War

From 1861 to 1865, as the United States was held in the throes of the terrible Civil War, the tall prairie lawyer who had been such a help to Charles Chiniquy, occupied the White House. Chiniquy said he visited his old friend there three times, first in late August, 1861, again in June, 1862 and finally in June, 1864. He did so mainly to warn the President to be on guard against assassination attempts by the Jesuits.

The Jesuits are members of an order of Roman Catholic priests called the Society of Jesus. The order was established to support the papacy and protect the Catholic faith from heresy, as well as engage in missionary work. The Society's constitution is military, autocratic and subject only to the Pope. Historically, the order has been suppressed in a number of countries because it has been seen to be constantly seeking power and influence.

Though President Lincoln was usually very busy, Chiniquy said that he always found the nation's leader glad to see him, greeting him warmly and making time for private conversation. They spent their time together mainly discussing the Civil War and the part the Catholic Church was playing in it. According to the ex-priest, the President talked about the planned attempt on his life in Baltimore that had been thwarted by a change in his travel plans. He also stated that Samuel Morse had told him of a Jesuit plot against the United States that the artist and inventor had learned of when he was in Rome.

To help find out more about the conspiracy, Lincoln offered to make Chiniquy a secretary of the American ambassador to France, a position he said that could lead to the ambassadorship. Thanking the President, the ex-priest said that he was too busy preaching to his fellow countrymen to be of help in uncovering the plot.

Chiniquy's claim that he visited Abraham Lincoln at the White House has been questioned by critics. His last visit to the White House however, was actually publicized in the August 12th, 1864 edition of the *Chicago Tribune*. The *Tribune* published a letter from Chiniquy in which he told of his visit to see the President. The visit also happened to be the occasion of Abraham Lincoln's reception of delegates of the National Union Convention, informing him of his re-nomination for the Presidency (see Figure 20). This letter closely agrees with what Chiniquy said about this meeting in *Fifty Years*.

There also is indirect proof that supports his statements of visits to the White House, such the strong evidence of his close friendship with the President, provided by Robert Lincoln who, as noted earlier, declared that of all the friends his father had "none were more than yourself" (see figure 10).[1] This is also considered in more detail in the Appendix 1.

Figure 20
Chicago Tribune, August 12, 1864

LETTER FROM FATHER CHINIQUY.

His Interview with President Lincoln.

Washington July 29,

EDITOR KANKAKEE GAZETTE:—In my last I spoke of our bleeding and wounded soldiers who are filling the hospitals of Washington; I told you something of what I felt when I had the privilege of conversing with those thousands of heroes, who, covered with wounds, unable to move, have still their hearts filled with the purest love of their country, and feel only one regret, "not to be able to fight any more for their glorious flag." No one can visit those thousands of wounded soldiers without blessing God to belong to a country which can boast of possessing millions of such men; and when one has seen and heard them, he has no more any doubt about the issue of our war; "The North must conquer; armies composed with such men, lead by a Grant, must, at the end, destroy the last vestige of slavery."

Now, permit me to say a word about our President. It was my good luck to be paying my respects to our good President, the honest Mr. Lincoln, when the delegates of the National Union Convention came to announce to him his re-nomination to the Presidency.

There is not a single thoughtful man in Europe or in America who does not recognize in Abraham Lincoln one of the most remarkable and worthy men of our age. I have read somewhere that the young men who were working with him on the shores of the Mississippi had declared him not only the best rail-splitter but *the most honest* young man; and I have no doubt the United States will pronounce him also one of the wisest, and ablest, and most honest Presidents. No doubt, also, that posterity which will study his eventful life with more calmness than we can do, will say, that from the days he was handling the axe on the shores of the great river, to the days he was holding the helm of our great Republic, *he has done remarkably well what he has done.*

Abraham Lincoln is one of the few men whose large views and profound wisdom will be better understood as the generations of men pass away to give place to new generations.

Like the few giants whom the hands of God have placed at long distance from each other, on the top of the high mountains of humanity, Abraham Lincoln will grow greater to the eyes of the generations which will cross the plains below.

It is only when I have seen Abraham Lincoln surrounded by his most devoted friends, that I have been struck with the marked furrows which these last three years have left on his forehead. It is then that I have fully understood the sublimity of the words which he framed in the darkest hours of our civil war; "If the damned in hell do suffer more than I do, I pity them. Perhaps the anxieties of a bleeding heart have never been expressed with more eloquence.

After the President had listened to the address of the deputation, he told them, in my presence, with his usual kind and jovial manner of talking:—"The convention and the league have not concluded, I know well, to decide that I am either the greatest or the best man in America. But rather they have concluded that it is not best to swap horses when crossing the river; they have further concluded that I am not so poor a horse that they might make a botch of it to swap."

A few days after I had heard those words from the President, being on my way back to Philadelphia, I heard in the cars a genuine Copperhead saying to his neighbor of the same blood and skin, "Lincoln has done more with that joke to help his election, than by all the stump speeches of the d—d abolitionists. The people will fear to swap the horse when crossing the river, and they will elect him again;" and, no doubt, that new Balaam ass prophecy will be a correct one.

In Abraham Lincoln, we have more than an able and honest man for our President; we have the personification of the most sublime and consoling words falling from the lips of Christ: "Ye are all brethren, children of the same father.

When I travel back, in imagination, to the shores of the Mississippi, some thirty years ago, and there see the young Abraham Lincoln, covered with dust and sweat, handling his axe and splitting his rails; and then a few years after I see him here to day, in our Capital, surrounded by the Ambassadors of France, England, Russia, Austria, &c, holding with a firm hand the reins of the greatest Republic of modern times, I am proud to belong to a country where such a thing can be seen. I understand that if there is a tyranny and oppression everywhere else, here there is true equality before the law; if everywhere else the poor is the slave of the rich; the weak the footstool of the strong; here in America, virtue, honesty and intelligence, make the poor a king and the weak man a giant.

As long as the American people will be true to that great and sacred principle of equality before the law, as long as the great principles which have brought step by step the honest young rail splitter to the Presidential chair of the United States, shall be carried out and respected, all the honest and intelligent poor from every part of the world will ask God in their prayers to grant them or their children the privilege to come here; all the oppressed and trampled down from every where, will look to this country, as the Israelites, in the burning deserts looked to the promised land; all who love liberty, from all parts of the world will come and help us to fight and destroy to the last vestige the demon of human servitude and slavery.

Truly yours,

C. CHINIQUY.

Regarding the content of the conversations between Chiniquy and the President, there is independent proof that corroborates the ex-priest's story. Two separate groups of detectives and policemen discovered a plot to assassinate Lincoln in Maryland's largest city, Baltimore, before his inauguration.[2] A former colony which was founded as a haven for Catholics, Maryland was rife with disloyalty. It was in Baltimore, for instance, that the first blood was shed in the Civil War. Several soldiers were killed when a number of its residents attacked the Sixth Massachusetts Volunteer Militia Regiment as the Washington-bound Union soldiers passed through the city on April 19, 1861.[3] The federal government was so concerned about rebel activities in Baltimore that federal troops occupied the city for four years, beginning in May, 1861. During this time period, the people arrested there included the mayor, the police chief and police commissioners along with the publishers and owners of several newspapers, including the *Catholic Mirror*, the official publication of the Archbishop of Baltimore.[4]

It is very possible that Samuel Morse could have told the President about a plot against America by the Catholic Church, as similar sentiments are expressed by the artist and creator of the electric telegraph and code in his 1835 book, entitled "Foreign Conspiracy Against the Liberties of the United States: the Numbers of Brutus".

Charles Chiniquy stated in *Fifty Years*, "Long before I was ordained a priest, I knew that my church was the most implacable enemy of this Republic." According to Chiniquy, his professors of history, philosophy and theology, "had been unanimous in telling me that the principles and laws of the Church of Rome were absolutely antagonistic to the laws and principles which are the foundation-stones of the Constitution of the United States."

This is supported by Pope Pius IX's Encyclical Letter, published in the *New York Times* on January 13, 1865. In this letter, the Roman pontiff showed the Church's opposition to democracy and freedom by railing against, among other things, the principle that "Liberty of conscience and of worship is the right of every man" and "that the will of the people, manifested by what is called public opinion or by other means, constitutes a supreme law superior to all divine and human right" (See figure 21). In another piece, published several months later in the *Times*, the Cardinal Vicar at Rome is quoted as denouncing, "the errors of liberty of conscience and religious worship being recognized as legal rights," adding that he also couldn't recognize, "as just the right of all to propagate through the Press erroneous principles, nor can he recognize that the will of the people is the supreme law."[5]

There were a number of factors that set the stage for the bloody U.S. Civil War. Slavery was one of them and it was a Roman Catholic judge who played a vital role in placing it there by rendering the infamous Dred Scott decision in 1857. This judgment seemed designed to rip up every bit of anti-slavery legislation enacted in the United States since the Northwest Ordinance was passed by Congress in 1787. Ruling for the majority, U. S. Supreme Court Chief Justice Roger B. Taney, a devout Catholic, decreed that blacks could not become U.S. citizens and that they "had no rights which the white man is bound to respect."[6] The judgment outraged opponents

Figure 21
New York Times, January 13, 1865

The New-York Times, Friday, January 13, 1865

ligion, unless required by considerations of public

THE POPE'S NEW BULL.—By the European mail which arrived yesterday we have the text of a Bull which has just been issued from the Vatican at Rome, under the sign and seal apostolic of His Holiness the Pope. The letter denounces the pernicious writings of those who seek to overturn the foundations of the Catholic religion. Addressing the Bishops and clergy throughout the world, His Holiness reminds them that the promulgation of evil doctrines have excited " a horrible storm." He refers to former encyclical letters and allocutions in which he felt bound to denounce " the monstrous opinions which particularly predominate in the present day ;" but as these letters and allocutions have not produced the desired effect, His Holiness makes this new appeal. Especially does he dwell with fervor on what he considers the false prevailing notions as to the relation of civil Government to the Church. Thus, he says, for example, that,

"There are many who do not hesitate to affirm 'that the best condition of society is that in which the power of the laity is not compelled to inflict the penalties of law upon violators of the Catholic religion, unless required by considerations of public safety.' Actuated by an idea of social government so absolutely false, they do not hesitate further to propagate this erroneous opinion, very hurtful to the safety of the Catholic Church and of souls, and termed delirium by our predecessor, GREGORY XVI., of excellent memory, viz.: 'Liberty of conscience and of worship is the right of every man, a right which ought to be proclaimed and established by law in every well constituted State ; and that citizens are entitled to make known and declare, with a lib-

peace at this time with us, we may be sure

erty which neither the ecclesiastical nor the civil authority can limit, their convictions, of whatever kind, either by word of mouth or through the press, or by other means.' But in making these rash assertions, they do not reflect, they do not consider that they preach the liberty of perdition, (St. Augustine, Epistle 105. al. 166,) and that ' if it is always free to human conviction to discuss, men will never be wanting who dare to struggle against the truth, and to rely upon the fecundity of human wisdom, when we know by the example of our Lord Jesus Christ how faith and Christian sagacity ought to avoid this very culpable vanity.' "

The prevalence of such beliefs as the Pope herein denounces, no one with his eyes open can doubt. It has become an exceedingly hard task, even in Italy, to "inflict the penalties of the law upon violators of the Catholic religion." It is a harder task still, we believe, on this continent, not even excluding Mexico, where the brother of the "Eldest Son of the Church" is making quite free already with what remains of the property of the Jesuists and other religious orders. A large portion of the letter is occupied with denunciations of those who dare to secularize the property of the Church ; and secular pamphlets, journals and books are promiscuously condemned. But, in spite of all the superabounding evil, the letter proceeds thus toward the conclusion :

"By these letters, emanating from our Apostolic authority, we grant to all and each of the faithful of both sexes throughout the universe, a plenary indulgence during one month, up to the end of the year 1865, and not longer."

superabounding evil, the letter proceeds thus toward the conclusion :

"By these letters, emanating from our Apostolic authority, we grant to all and each of the faithful of both sexes throughout the universe, a plenary indulgence during one month, up to the end of the year 1865, and not longer."

The Question of Negotiation.

The idea of JEFFERSON DAVIS negotiating himself out of existence, or allowing himself to be negotiated out of existence, as President of the Southern Confederacy, is one which must be hard of entertainment by those who comprehend his character, or who have studied his rebellious career as it has appeared in his speeches, proclamations and deeds during the last four years ; or who have noted the

coasting steamer, supposed to be well commanded, well manned, well provisioned, thoroughly provided with long boats, small boats, and life boats, and to be in every respect a safe conveyance.

The transport *Melville* cleared from New-York on the 5th inst., for Hilton Head, and made her way with moderate ease against strong head winds until the 7th. About 9 on the evening of that day (Saturday last) the *Melville* was struck by a heavy sea, which stove in her bows. The Captain immediately ordered a boat to be lowered. Into that boat he himself was the first to get, along with the Chief Engineer, the cook of the vessel, a seaman, and such of the more hardy of the passengers as could venture after them. This boat was swamped. Probably, the brave of slavery, including Abraham Lincoln, who effectively reversed the ruling six years later when he issued the Emancipation Proclamation.

Lincoln: a Catholic?

According to *Fifty Years*, on his first visit to the White House, the President said he had a question for Chiniquy:

> I want your views about a thing which is exceedingly puzzling to me, and you are the only one to whom I like to speak on that subject. A great number of Democratic papers have been sent to me, lately, evidently written by Roman Catholics, publishing that I was born a Roman Catholic, and baptized by a priest. They call me a renegade, an apostate, on account of that; and they heap upon my head mountains of abuse. At first, I laughed at that, for it is a lie. Thanks be to God, I have never been a Roman Catholic. No priest of Rome has ever laid his hand on my head. But the persistency of the Romish press to present this falsehood to their readers as a gospel truth, must have a meaning. Please tell me, as briefly as possible, what you think about that.'

> 'My dear President,' I answered, 'it was just this strange story published about you, which brought me here, yesterday. I wanted to say a word about it; but you were too busy.

> 'Let me tell you that I wept as a child when I read that story for the first time. For, not only my impression is, that it is your sentence of death; but I have from the lips of a converted priest, that it is in order to excite the fanaticism of the Roman Catholic murderers, whom they hope to find, sooner or later, to strike you down, they have invented that false story of your being born in the Church of Rome, and of your being baptized by a priest. They want by that to brand your face with the ignominious mark of apostasy. Do not forget that, in the Church of Rome, an apostate is an outcast, who has no place in society, and who has no right to live.

> 'The Jesuits want the Roman Catholics to believe that you are a monster, an open enemy of God and of his Church, that you are an excommunicated man. For, every apostate is, *ipso facto* (by that very fact) excommunicated. I have brought to you the theology of one of the most learned and approved of the Jesuits of his time, Bussambaum, who, with many others, say that the man who will kill you will do a good and holy work. More than that, here is a copy of a decree of Gregory VII., proclaiming that the killing of an apostate, or an heretic and an excommunicated man, as you are declared to be, is not murder; nay, that it is a good, a Christian action.[7]

In making this assertion, Charles Chiniquy really seemed to go out on a limb. As noted earlier, there has been some 15,000 different books and imprints published on the subject of Lincoln. Except for Chiniquy's book and a few others that have generally followed his theme, there has been hardly a whisper about the Great Emancipator being called a Catholic and most students of Lincoln have never heard of it.

Although generally very popular, the 16th President certainly had enemies. During his first Presidential election campaign, he was called a wide variety of derogatory names: a "beast": a "sooty" and "scoundrelly" creature; a "blood thirsty tyrant"; to name a few.[8]

Searches for what might have been termed "Democratic papers" that made the statement that Chiniquy reported did not yielded any results. Nevertheless, there is ample evidence that the allegation was made that Lincoln was a Catholic. In his book, *Myths after Lincoln*, biographer Lloyd Lewis stated:

> On account of the association of the two men in the lawsuits, the rumor arose that Lincoln, like Chiniquy, was a renegade from Catholicism; that he had been baptized by Jesuit priests in Kentucky as a boy, and that he had assisted at masses. Copperheads opposing the Republican Presidential candidate in 1860, and thereafter through the Civil War, noised these rumors about, and anti-Catholics added their mite to the jumble of prejudice by saying that the church was opposing Lincoln because of his apostasy. That the Vatican, like almost all other European organizations, spiritual or temporal, favored the South as against the North, was generally believed by Union populations, and when in April, 1865, a few of the conspirators in the Lincoln assassination plot were found to be Catholics, the tale took on fresh strength.

No admirer of Charles Chiniquy, Lewis alleged that the rumor of Lincoln's supposed Catholicism arose from his association with the priest. In his book, *The Soul Of Abraham Lincoln*, Lincoln biographer and minister, Rev. William Barton, reported "Yet, singularly, a report was current and somewhat widely believed in 1860 that Abraham Lincoln had been baptized as a Roman Catholic and was himself a renegade from that faith". As well, according to a report in a Catholic publication, *American Catholic Historical Researches*, several priests had declared that Lincoln had been a member of the Church of Rome as a youth. This particular account, which concerned the celebration of Lincoln's birthday, shows that the allegation of Lincoln's Catholicism had indeed been made, the truth of it, and how opposed Catholics had been to the President:

> 'Rev. John W. Moore, C. M., made the address of the day. He told the children what a great man Lincoln was; of the evils and miseries of slavery, and how Lincoln seemed providentially sent to preserve the integrity of the Union. Father Moore made mention of a fact not generally known, viz., that Lincoln was a Catholic, but owing no doubt to the scarcity of priests in Illinois, where Lincoln lived, and to his environments, he drifted away from the faith of his fathers. Father Moore stated that Father St. Cyr, an old pioneer priest of Illinois, and who afterwards died at the convent of the Sisters of St. Joseph in Carondelet, St. Louis, Mo., told Father James McGill, C. M., of Germantown, and Thomas J. Smith, C. M., of Perryville, Mo. who paid Father St. Cyr a visit one day for the express purpose of finding out something about Lincoln, that Lincoln was a Catholic.

'Father St. Cyr said that he often celebrated mass in Abraham Lincoln's father's house, and that young Abraham Lincoln, who was a boy then of some 10 or 12 year of age, frequently served his mass.'

That tale of Father Moore's went the rounds years ago. There is no truth in it. Even if it were true, what credit is it to Lincoln or the Church to tattle it now?

My! What 'a great man' Lincoln is to Catholics nowadays. Forty-odd years ago few Catholics condemned the 'evils and miseries of slavery,' and any who did would have fared better to have abandoned their faith.

Few thought kindly of Lincoln or that he was a 'providential' instrument to save the Union. That Lincoln was not a Catholic, and, indeed, from his surroundings could not have been, here is the very best possible authority, one who knows, perhaps, every hour of Lincoln's life, Miss Ida M. Tarbell, who writes:

New York, March 8, 1905.

My Dear Mr. Griffin: --- I am afraid the claim made in the clipping which you sent me---and which I am returning--that Mr. Lincoln was a Catholic, will scarcely bear investigation. Mr. Lincoln's father, Thomas Lincoln, was a Baptist, according to the best authorities, and Lincoln attended the church of that denomination in his early years in Indiana. In Springfield he attended the Presbyterian church, although he was never a member of any religious denomination. I believe that the fact that he attended the Presbyterian church in Springfield was due to Mrs. Lincoln's being a member.

Very sincerely yours, IDA M. TARBELL.

The foregoing, from a Catholic source, confirmed that the allegation of Lincoln's Catholicism had indeed been aired, as *Fifty Years* stated. Ida Tarbell was a writer who authored a number of books about Lincoln. Rev. Moore's statement that Lincoln had "drifted away from the faith of his fathers," meant, according to Chiniquy, that in the sight of Catholics, Lincoln had apostatized by leaving the faith of his fathers and therefore was an apostate. Official Church law at that time, as now, held that apostates should be killed if they refuse to repent, therefore Lincoln could and should have been killed, according to the Church of Rome. [9]

Papal Recognition of the Confederacy

The *American Catholic Historical Researches* account also showed the opposition Lincoln faced from Catholics as he strove to preserve the Union. Chiniquy reported that he and Abraham Lincoln also talked about the 1863 letter of Pope Pius IX to Jefferson Davis, whom the Pope had addressed as the President of the Confederate States of America. Both the ex-priest and the President agreed that this letter was recognition of the Southern Confederacy by the papacy.

Catholic apologists and historians have stated their disagreement with this. In his book however, *Americans Interpret Their Civil War*, academic Thomas Pressly dealt with this question. Pressly reported that the distinguished historian George Bancroft, "delivered the official eulogy on Lincoln (as he had done twenty-one years before at the death of Andrew Jackson) before a joint session of both Houses of Congress attended by the President with his Cabinet, the Justices of the Supreme Court, and other dignitaries." Ten days after the President's death, Bancroft also gave a speech in New York City's Union Square to part of the crowd who had previously paid their last respects to President Lincoln. According to Pressly, in his Washington and New York speeches, Bancroft declared:

> A confederacy with slavery as its cornerstone and supported by all the 'worn out aristocracies of Europe' and even by the 'Pope of Rome' had challenged the republic of the new world in a life and death struggle. But working in harmony with the moral laws of God, Abraham Lincoln and the people of the Union states had overcome the forces of evil and had won their battle for 'freedom itself.'

This eminent historian, George Bancroft, therefore clearly supported Chiniquy in his assertion that the Pope and the Catholic Church had recognized and supported the Confederacy. Pressly also discussed writer Orestes Brownson, considered by some to be Catholicism's greatest American intellectual:

> Brownson's wartime actions not only conflicted with his past, they also placed him in opposition to some of his coreligionists. Deploring the lukewarm support given the government by some members of his faith, he stated that Catholics did not understand the war. It was undeniable, he wrote,
>
> > that no religious body in the country stands so generally committed to slavery and the rebellion, or as a body have shown so little sympathy with the effort of the government to save the unity and life of the nation, as the Catholics.
>
> His stand led him into controversy with several members of the Catholic hierarchy; and, undaunted, he even challenged the views of the Pope. In an article published in 1863, he implied that the Pope expressed opinions on the war which were contrary to Catholic doctrine, and suggested that 'the Holy Father....has been induced to lend the [Southern] conspiracy his powerful aid.'[11]

Orestes Brownson changed his view at the end of the war however and he began to defend the Church's role in the struggle. Perhaps he realized how badly it needed defending. While the evidence shows that in reality, the Catholic Church was, at best, indifferent to the continuation of slavery for blacks, it was the Protestants in the North who were against it and committed to see it destroyed. For instance, in 1862, a Catholic priest in the diocese of New Orleans reportedly ended the practice of maintaining different sacramental registers for whites and colored people. This man, an exception to the rule, also preached equality of all people and an end of slavery. His reward was to be silenced by the archbishop and his parish put under ecclesiastical censure.

Why did such a prominent historian like George Bancroft believe the Confederacy was supported by the Pope? A look at the Pope's December 3rd, 1863, letter to Jefferson Davis does much to explain. It reads:

Illustrious and honorable sir, greeting:

We have lately received with all kindness, as was meet, the gentlemen sent by your Excellency to present to us your letter dated on the 23d of last September. We have received certainly no small pleasure in learning both from these gentlemen and from your letter the feelings of gratification and of very warm appreciation with which you, illustrious and honorable sir, were moved when you first had knowledge written in October of the preceding year to the venerable brethren, John, archbishop of New York, and John, archbishop of New Orleans, in which we again and again urged and exhorted those venerable brethren that because of their exemplary piety and episcopal zeal they should employ their most earnest efforts, in our name also, in order that the fatal civil war which had arisen in the States should end, and that the people of America might again enjoy mutual peace and concord, and love each other with mutual charity. And it has been very gratifying to us to recognize, illustrious and honorable sir, that you and your people are animated by the same desire for peace and tranquillity, which we had so earnestly inculcated in our aforesaid letters to the venerable brethren above named. Oh, that the other people also of the States and their rulers, considering seriously how cruel and how deplorable is this internecine war, would receive and embrace the counsels of peace and tranquillity. We indeed shall not cease with most fervent prayer to beseech God, the best and highest, and to implore Him to pour out the spirit of Christian love and peace upon all the people of America, and to rescue them from the great calamities with which they are afflicted. And we also pray the same most merciful Lord that he will illumine your Excellency with the light of His divine grace and unite you with ourselves in perfect charity.

Given at Rome at St. Peters on the 3d December, 1863, in the eighteenth year of our pontificate.

Pius P. P. IX.
Illustrious and Hon. JEFFERSON DAVIS,
President of the Confederate States of America, Richmond[12]

As well as referring to Jefferson Davis as, "Illustrious and Honorable" and "your Excellency", Pius IX called him "President of the Confederate States of America". This letter was addressed to the leader of a rebellion, the man heading a massive revolt against the United States that was resulting in the deaths of hundreds of thousands of America's finest young men. Doesn't this communication show that Chiniquy, George Bancroft and others were correct when they asserted that the Pope had recognized the Confederacy? The voice of colored Methodism in Philadelphia, *The Christian Recorder*, concurred in an 1890 piece, stating:

I would ask whether he thinks loyal Americans can soon forget the letter of the Pope to Jefferson Davis during our civil war? It was a noticeable fact that after the official recognition of the Southern Confederacy, the work of recruiting among our Roman Catholic fellow citizens was greatly hindered, and desertions were quite frequent.

In its last word on the subject, *The New York Times* also declared its agreement with Charles Chiniquy in an 1876 article entitled "How The Pope Recognized The Southern Confederacy – His Letter to Jeff Davis".

While the Pope called Jeff Davis the "President of the Confederate States of America", Davis was in fact, leading the treasonous attempt to destroy the United States. In the letter, the Pope stated he recognized that Jefferson Davis and his people were, "animated by the same desire for peace and tranquility" as himself and others at the Vatican. If so, why did the Confederates continue to shoot at U.S. forces? If Davis and company wanted peace, they could have laid down their arms anytime.

The Pontiff requested, "that the other people also of the States and their rulers, considering seriously how cruel and how deplorable is this internecine war, would receive and embrace the councils of peace and tranquility". Maybe the reason these councils had not been received was because the Lincoln administration would not accept peace until the United States had been saved and rebellion stopped on American soil.

Regarding these "councils of peace", did the Pope expect that if the North stopped fighting and asked the Confederates nicely, they would put down their guns and allow the federal government authority over the South as before? The South would only accept peace with America broken in two, with one of the resulting countries being the Confederate States of America.

In his volume, *The Catholics and Mrs. Mary Surratt*, even historian and, it appears, Catholic apologist, Kenneth Zanca, admitted that during the American Civil War, the Church of Rome "worked both sides of the street" in regards to the Union and the Confederacy and gave the South "private encouragement and support".

Further proof of the Pope's recognition of the Confederacy is provided by the response of the pontiff to the manifesto of the Confederate States, which was published in the *New York Times*, January 7th, 1865. Speaking for the Pope, Cardinal Antonelli declared that the "sentiments expressed in the manifesto, tending as they do to the cessation of the most bloody war which still rages in your countries" was entirely in accordance with the disposition and character of Pius IX. What "countries" would these be? Antonelli also stated of the Pontiff:

> Being the vicar on earth of that God who is the author of peace, he yearns to see these wraths appeased and peace restored. In proof of this he wrote to the Archbishops of New York and New Orleans, as far back as Oct. 18, 1862, inviting them to exert themselves in bringing about this holy object.

The letter ended by listing those whom it was addressed to: Messrs. A. Dudley Mann, J.M. Mason and John Blidell, Commissioners of the Confederate States of America,

Paris (See Figure 22). The United States and the "Confederate States of America" undoubtedly were the two countries that Cardinal Antonelli and the Pope were speaking about in their correspondence. These communications further confirm that Pope Pius IX indeed recognized the Confederacy as the *New York Times*, Chiniquy, George Bancroft, and others asserted.[13]

Charles Chiniquy told President Lincoln that the Pope's letter contained a message for Catholics about him, saying that the "letter is a poisoned arrow by the Pope, at you personally; and it will be more than a miracle if it is not your irrevocable warrant of death." Chiniquy also stated:

> That letter, then, tells logically the Roman Catholics that you are a bloody tyrant! a most execrable being when fighting against a government which the infallible and holy Pope of Rome recognizes as legitimate. The Pope, by this letter, tells his blind slaves that you are an infamous usuper, when considering yourself the President of the Southern States; that you are outraging the God of heaven and earth, by continuing such a bloody war to subdue a nation over whom God Almighty has declared, through his infallible pontiff, the Pope, that you have not the least right; that letter means that you will give an account to God and man for the blood and tears you cause to flow in order to satisfy your ambition.

> By this letter of the Pope to Jeff Davis you are not only an apostate, as you were thought before, whom every man had the right to kill, according to the canonical laws of Rome; but you are more vile, criminal and cruel than the horse thief, the public bandit, and the lawless brigand, robber and murderer, whom it is a duty to stop and kill, when we take them in their acts of blood, and that there is no other way to put an end to their plunders and murders.

Chiniquy also stated that what he had expressed was not just his imagination but the unanimous views of a number of Catholic priests that he had talked to on the subject.

Abraham Lincoln's Views on Catholicism

In 1924, in answer to Chiniquy's allegations, Thomas F. Meehan published an article entitled "Lincoln's Opinion of Catholics" in *Historical Records and Studies*, journal of the United States Catholic Historical Society. Meehan quoted what Lincoln said in a letter dated August 24th, 1855, to his friend Joshua Speed:

> As a Nation we began by declaring that 'All men are created equal.' We now practically read it, 'All men are created equal except negroes.' When the Know Nothings get control of this country, it will read, 'All men are created equal except negroes, foreigners and Catholics.' When it comes to this I shall prefer emigrating to some country where they make no pretense of loving liberty

Fifty Years reported that when the suit of Spink vs. Chiniquy was dismissed however, Charles Chiniquy told Abraham Lincoln, "There were, then, in the crowd, not less than ten or twelve Jesuits from Chicago and St. Louis, who came to hear my sentence of condemnation to the penitentiary." Instead, according to Chiniquy, they

Figure 22
New York Times, January 7th, 1865.

NEW-YORK, SATURDAY, JANUARY 7, 1865.

THE POPE AND THE REBELS.

ANSWER TO THE CONFEDERATE MANIFESTO.

The *Index* publishes the subjoined reply of the Pope to the manifesto of the Confederate States:

HONORABLE GENTLEMEN: Mr. SOUTTER has handed me your letter of Nov. 11, with which, in conformity to the instructions of your Government, you have sent me a copy of the manifesto issued by the Congress of the Confederate States and approved by the most honorable President, in order that the attention of the Government of the Holy See, to whom, as well as to the other Governments, you have addressed yourselves, might be called to it. The sentiments expressed in the manifesto, tending as they do to the cessation of the most bloody war which still rages in your countries, and to the putting an end to the disasters which accompany it by proceeding to negotiations for peace, being entirely in accordance with the disposition and character of the august head of the Catholic Church, I did not hesitate a moment in bringing it to the notice of the Holy Father. His Holiness, who has been deeply afflicted by the accounts of the frightful carnage of this obstinate struggle, has heard with satisfaction the expression of the same sentiments. Being the vicar on earth of that God who is the author of peace, he yearns to see these wraths appeased and peace restored. In proof of

this he wrote to the Archbishops of New-York and New-Orleans, as far back as Oct. 18, 1862, inviting them to exert themselves in bringing about this holy object. You may, then, honorable gentlemen, feel well assured that whenever a favorable occasion shall present itself, His Holiness will not fail to avail himself of it, to hasten so desirable a result, and that all nations may be united in the bonds of charity. In acquainting you with this benignant disposition of the Holy Father, I am pleased to declare myself, with sentiments of the most distinguished esteem, truly your servant,   G. Card. ANTONELLI.

ROME, Dec. 2, 1864.

Messrs. A. DUDLEY MANN, J. M. MASON and JOHN SLIDELL, Commissioners of the Confederate States of America, Paris.

heard Lincoln's," awful and superhumanly eloquent denunciation of their infamy, diabolical malice, and total want of Christian and human principle, in the plot they had formed for my destruction." After Chiniquy expressed his fears that his friend might pay with his life for rescuing him from the hands of the Jesuits, Abraham Lincoln said to him, "I know that Jesuits never forget nor forsake. But man must not care how and where he dies, provided he dies at the post of honor and duty".

Despite Meehan's protestations to the contrary, the correspondence of Abraham Lincoln to Joshua Speed doesn't prove Mr. Lincoln couldn't have said what Chiniquy said he did. It was months after his letter to Speed that Lincoln agreed to defend Chiniquy and it was almost a year after that point, at the conclusion of the trial, that he made the statement about the Jesuits. Chiniquy stated that when they first met, Abraham Lincoln told him:

> I know you, by reputation, as the stern opponent of tyranny of your bishop, and the fearless protector of your countrymen in Illinois. I have heard much of you from two priests; and, last night, your lawyers, Messrs. Osgood & Paddock, acquainted me with the fact that your bishop employs some of his tools to get rid of you.

Spink vs. Chiniquy had ended in the fall of 1856 by the exposure of the perjury of the Catholic priest, Lebel. As well, the May 29, 1856 edition of the *Urbana Union* reported that during the spring round of the case, one of Spink's witnesses, a priest, was impeached by the other party, i.e. Lincoln. Although Chiniquy didn't speak about it previously in his autobiography, he evidently had become aware that there were a group of Jesuits who had helped form, or at least were in sympathy with, the plot to destroy him.[14]

According to *Fifty Years*, when things looked black during the fall court battle, Lincoln remarked, undoubtedly referring to Lebel and Carthuval, "I have never seen two such skillful rogues as those two priests! There is really a diabolical skill in the plan they have concocted for your destruction. It is evident that the bishop is at the bottom of the plot." At the end of the court battle, Abraham Lincoln said to Chiniquy, "Your case is unique in my whole practice. I have never met a man so cruelly persecuted as you have been, and who deserves it so little. Your enemies are devils incarnate. The plot they had concocted against you is the most hellish one I ever knew."

Many people, including Catholics, have viewed the Jesuits differently from other elements of the Catholic Church. History records that the Jesuits have been expelled from a number of countries and even Pope Clement XIV banned the order in 1773, (one papal command that the Jesuits didn't obey). The ban was lifted by a later pope. Charles Chiniquy quoted a priest he knew, Rev. Dunn, saying "The Jesuits who want to rule the priests and the church with an iron rod, and who are aiming to change the Pope and the bishops into the most heartless tyrants".

Chiniquy also stated that it was the Jesuits who caused the final conflict between him and his ecclesiastical superior, Bishop Smith, resulting in him leaving the Church. If the Jesuits had been opposed to Chiniquy at time he left the Church, then it is possible they could also have been working against him earlier, at the time of the trial as well. If, as *Fifty Years* asserted, Lincoln had become increasingly aware of the role the Jesuits were playing in the attempted destruction of his client, then it is not unthinkable for him to have said what Chiniquy reported he did. Lincoln biographer William Barton stated regarding Spink vs. Chiniquy, "I think there is good reason to believe that in this trial Lincoln spoke with some severity of the ecclesiastical machinery that could be made available for the crushing of a man who had incurred the ill will of priests."

At the conclusion of his celebrated 1858 U.S. Senate race with Stephen Douglas, Lincoln summarized the differences between his position on slavery and his opponent's:

> It is the eternal struggle between…two principles--right and wrong--throughout the world. They are the two principles that have stood face to face from the beginning of time; and will ever continue to struggle. The one is the common right of humanity and the other the divine right of kings

History shows that Abraham Lincoln was clearly on the side of the rights of the common man, on the side of democracy. Its statements and actions in Civil War times on the other hand, showed the Roman Catholic Church was on the side of the divine right of kings and tyranny.

In addition, Rev. Chiniquy stated that Lincoln told him that when he entered the White House years later and began the fight to preserve the nation, his views on the Catholic Church changed even more as he learned more and realized the adversarial role it was playing in the Union war effort.

On the subject of the Civil War, while recognizing the patriotism and bravery of some Catholic soldiers, Lincoln told Chiniquy that many had deserted, according to *Fifty Years*. The President also stated that while the Catholic general, George Meade, won the battle of Gettysburg, he really couldn't have lost it with all the brave officers and soldiers surrounding him. According to Chiniquy, Lincoln added that Meade's "Romanism superseded his patriotism after the battle. He let the army of Lee escape, when it was so easy to cut his retreat and force him to surrender".[15] Historical accounts show that after the defeat of Robert E. Lee at Gettysburg, Meade made little effort to pursue the Confederates and they escaped almost completely, much to President Lincoln's thorough disgust.

Regarding Catholic desertions, U. S. Brigadier General Thomas M. Harris reported that according to the United States Pension Department, though less than 7% of the Union military were Irish Catholics, they accounted for 72% of desertions.[16]

Catholic soldiers were not the only members of the Church to be disloyal to the United States. In his biography of Confederate General Stonewall Jackson, Pulitzer Prize winning journalist and author Lenoir Chambers revealed that General Jackson was helped by Church officials. Fighting in the eastern part of what is now West Virginia, Jackson wanted to find out where the Union commander Nathaniel Banks was. Chambers wrote:

He had not been informed that Banks had gone east, but he wanted to be sure. 'I will see what can be effected through the Catholic priests in Martinsburg,' he told Johnston, thereby revealing for a moment the intelligence efforts which brought him much information.[17]

The New York Draft Riots

President Lincoln also talked with Chiniquy about the New York draft riots of 1863. According to *Fifty Years*, the President said he was sure they were the work of the Catholic bishop of the city, John Hughes, and his agents. Asserting that the Catholic Church was clearly an implacable enemy of freedom that had been energetically engaged in helping the Confederacy behind the scenes, Lincoln told Chiniquy that the danger to his own life from Jesuit assassins would surely increase as the Southern armies continued to crumble.

Regarding the Draft Riots in New York, the brutal insurrection would be more accurately termed the Catholic Draft Riots, as the rioters were essentially all of this religion. The federal government needed more soldiers to increase the strength of the northern forces and so began a conscription program in 1863. The draft began in New York on July 11th at a time when almost all of the city's military was in Pennsylvania, trying to corner the invading General Robert E. Lee and his forces.

As opposed to the misleading portrayal of these events in Martin Scorsese's 2002 motion picture, *The Gangs of New York*, historian Joel Headley provided an accurate and independent account of the horrific riots that almost destroyed the largest city in United States, thereby threatening the whole nation. In his 1873 book, *The Great Riots of New York*, Headley stated that, "Losses and defeats in the field could be and were repaired, but defeat in New York would in all probability have ended the war". Headley explained:

> Had the rioters got complete possession of the city but for a single day, their first dash would have been for the treasures piled up in its moneyed institutions. Once in possession of these, they, like the mobs of Paris, would have fired the city before yielding them up. In the crisis that was then upon us, it would not have required a long stoppage in this financial centre of the country to have effected a second revolution. With no credit abroad and no money at home, the Government would have been completely paralyzed.

As his book showed, Joel Headley had no axe to grind regarding the Roman Catholic Church. He explained that the opposition to the draft arose because it was viewed by some as being tyrannical and unfair, more fitting a dictatorship than a democracy. Beginning in the spring of 1863, able bodied men in the North between ages 20 and 45 were drafted to serve for three years. The draft was opposed because the men drafted could pay the government $300 to avoid serving or pay a substitute to take their place, meaning that the poorer members of society would tend to end up bearing the larger burden of serving in the military.

In answer to these objections however, Headley stated that the freedom loving First Congress of the United States made George Washington, in large part, a dictator, to effectively deal with the crisis the country faced at that time. As well, he pointed out that life is not always perfectly fair and war required money as well as men. The rich generally would be needed to help with the former, the poorer citizens with the latter. It was also important that the country's key businessmen stayed in position to continue to run the nation's industries. At this time of national crisis therefore, the draft was the best way to get the soldiers so badly needed to continue the fight.

Chiniquy believed that the Catholic Church was behind these riots. Headley disagreed, stating "The draft riots, as they are called, were supposed by some to be the result of a deep-laid conspiracy on the part of those opposed to the war, and that the successful issue of Lee's invasion of Pennsylvania was to be the signal for open action." In his opinion, "the manner of its commencement, the absence of proper organization, and almost total absence of leadership" showed that the riots were not the result of a "general well-understood plot."[18]

Headley confirmed that others besides Charles Chiniquy believed the insurrection was the result of a conspiracy. As well, in variance with his conclusion, his description of the beginning of the riots shows that there are very good grounds to believe the horrific insurgency was planned.

The drafting in New York began on Saturday, July 11th, with the names of men drafted published in the Sunday morning papers in the city. Those to be made soldiers would mostly be members of the Irish Catholic working-class. Those drafted, their friends and relatives had the weekend to consider their future, accompanied in many cases by cheap liquor. Headley described the start of the riot on Monday morning, July 13th:

> Meanwhile, events were assuming an alarming aspect in the western part of the city. Early in the morning men began to assemble here in separate groups, as if in accordance with a previous arrangement, and at last moved quietly north along the various avenues. Women, also, like camp followers, took the same direction in crowds. They were thus divided into separate gangs, apparently to take each avenue in their progress, and make a clean sweep. The factories and workshops were visited, and the men compelled to knock off work and join them, while the proprietors were threatened with the destruction of their property, if they made any opposition. The separate crowds were thus swelled at almost every step, and armed with sticks, and clubs, and every conceivable weapon they could lay hands on, they moved north towards some point which had evidently been selected as a place of rendezvous. This proved to be a vacant lot near Central Park, and soon the living streams began to flow into it, and a more wild, savage, and heterogeneous-looking mass could not be imagined. After a short consultation they again took up the line of march, and in two separate bodies, moved down Fifth and Sixth Avenues, until they reached Forty-sixth and Forty-seventh Streets, when they turned directly east.[19]

This does not sound like a mob gathering by random chance. The early morning is not a time that people idly meet. The only way people gather together in separate groups at one general location at an early hour to collectively engage in illegal activities has to be "in accordance with a previous arrangement." The quiet movement, each group taking an avenue on its own to "make a clean sweep", the organized gathering of more people at businesses along the way, the arming of the mob, moving to a point "selected as a place of rendezvous", doesn't speak of something happening by chance. In an editorial, the *New York Daily Tribune* asserted that the insurrection was planned and directed by leaders helping the South. The *Tribune* stated that the riots, coordinated with Confederate battlefield results, were not about the draft but about rebellion (see figure 23). The *Tribune* also reported:

> No person who carefully watched the movements of this mob, who noted their careful attention to the words of certain tacitly-acknowledged leaders, who observed the unquestionably preconcerted regularity with which they proceeded from one part of their infernal programme to the next; and the persistency with which the 'rear guard' remained and fought off all who dared attempt to check any part of the destruction that everywhere marked their work, can presume to doubt that these men are acting under leaders who have carefully elaborated their plans, who have, as they think, made all things sure for their accomplishment, and that they are resolved to carry them out through fire and blood, this day's crimson work fully attests.

The mob first attacked an office where the drafting of soldiers was being done, then began burning buildings, looting, pillaging, as well as attacking and killing policemen, soldiers, and civilians, especially black people. From Monday, July 11th to Thursday, July 14th, a vastly outnumbered body of police and soldiers courageously fought huge bloodthirsty mobs, day and night. As well, it is clearly established that these were Irish, Roman Catholic mobs. Headley describes what was happening in the city during the second day of rioting:

> Nearly four hundred citizens had been sworn in at police head-quarters as special policemen, and had been furnished with clubs and badges. All this time the fight was going on in every direction, while the fire-bells continually ringing increased the terror that every hour became more wide-spread. Especially was this true of the negro population. From the outset, they had felt they were to be objects of vengeance, and all day Monday and to-day those who could leave, fled into the country. They crowded the ferry-boats in every direction, fleeing for life. But old men and women, and poor families, were compelled to stay behind, and meet the fury of the mob, and to-day it became a regular hunt for them. A sight of one in the streets would call forth a halloo, as when a fox breaks cover, and away would dash a half a dozen men in pursuit. Sometimes a whole crowd streamed after with shouts and curses, that struck deadly terror to the heart of the fugitive. If overtaken, he was pounded to death at once; if he escaped into a negro house for safety, it was set on fire, and the inmates made to share a common fate. Deeds were done and sights witnessed that one would not have dreamed of, except among savage tribes.

Figure 23 a

New York Daily Tribune, July 14, 1863

4

NI

New-York Daily Tribune.

TUESDAY, JULY 14, 1863.

News agents on the New-York and New-Haven Railroad are not allowed to charge more than four cents for any of the Daily Papers, except on the 8 a. m. and 3:30 p. m. Express Trains, on which the price is five cents.

NEWS OF THE DAY.

THE WAR.

—Gen. Burnside has declared Martial law in Cincinnati, Covington and Newport. All business is suspended until further orders, and all citizens are required to organize, in accordance with the direction of the State and municipal authorities. There is nothing definite as to Morgan's whereabout, but it is supposed that he will endeavor to move around the city and cross the river between here and Maysville. The military is concentrating in obedience to the order of Gov. Tod.

—Yesterday arrived prize-schooner Emma captured in Mosquito Inlet, Florida, by the U. S. schooner Para, loaded with liquors, salt and muskets. The crew ran her ashore and escaped. The Emma afterward was got off.

—Yesterday was the Seventy-sixth Anniversary of the Ordinance of July 13, 1787, which gave *freedom forever* to the great North-west. That Ordinance was drawn by the hand of THOMAS JEFFERSON.

—The funeral of Brigadier-Gen. Zook took place yesterday afternoon, and notwithstanding the great excitement in regard to the draft, it was most honorably and respectably attended.

—An armed steamer was off Portland harbor on Sunday. She refused to answer any signals, and as she burnt soft coal, it is supposed she was a Confederate privateer.

GENERAL NEWS.

—The inquest on the body of the unknown man who was murdered at the Elysian Fields last week was concluded before Coroner Bohnstedt yesterday. No person appeared to identify him. The Jury rendered a verdict that deceased came to his death at the hands of some person or persons unknown, and they recommend that special policemen be appointed on the grounds, for the better protection of the public.

—The U. S. gunboat Pembina, Lieut.-Commander Jonathan Young, from Pensacola July 1, arrived at this port yesterday. She has been on blockading duty for the past year, and has captured the schooner Joe Hanner and sloop Elisha Beckwith off Mobile,

within his grasp, and that he may take what time is needful to recruit and reenforce his army.

THE RIOT.

We give in other columns the fullest details that it is possible to collect of the proceedings of the mob yesterday in various parts of the city. Relentless and cruel and cowardly as all mobs are, the actions of this at least are equal to any that have yet earned a record in history. "Pull down that d——d flag !" was their greeting to the Stars and Stripes. "Kill the d——d nigger !" was the infuriated howl raised at the sight of any unfortunate black man, woman, or child that was seen on the street, in the cars, or an omnibus. Resistance to the Draft was merely the occasion of the outbreak; absolute disloyalty and hatred to the negro were the moving cause. It was not simply a riot but the commencement of a revolution, organized by the sympathizers in the North with the Southern Rebellion. It was meant, undoubtedly, to break out on the 4th, but postponed by the defeat of Lee in Maryland. It was well known on Sunday that preparations were made for the outbreak on Monday, and the points of attack and for destruction were designated. Like incendiary fires, it broke out at different places at the same moment, and at the extreme ends of the city. While the first assault was made in the upper Wards the mob appeared in front of our office; all through the day it appeased its wrath and hate on any stray negro that was so unfortunate as to be found, and attacked the dwellings here and there of those miserable people. Reenforced at dark by ruffians from the upper part of the city, they made their assault upon this building, completely sacking its publication office. By the timely, energetic and brave efforts of a company of policemen, under Capt. Thorne, the whole structure was barely saved from destruction.

Articles continued on next page

WHO KILLED ABRAHAM LINCOLN?

Figure 23 b
Continuation of article

Joe Hanner and sloop Elisha Beckwith off Mobile, and drove the schooner Gil Blas ashore, all on the night of 24th April, when the Pembina broke down, and was towed into Pensacola.

—The Cunard screw steamer Sidon, from Liverpool at 3 p. m. on the 30th ult., and Queenstown on the 1st inst., arrived here yesterday. Her news has been fully anticipated.

Enroll!
PROCLAMATION BY THE MAYOR.
MAYOR'S OFFICE, N. Y. CITY, }
July 14, 1863. }

In view of the riot now existing in this city, I do hereby request all loyal citizens to report at the Headquarters of the Police, No. 300 Mulberry street, this day, to be sworn in and enrolled as special policemen for the restoration of law and order. All who shall not thus enroll themselves are requested to continue their usual avocations.   GEORGE OPDYKE,
                                    Mayor.

A Call to the Veteran Volunteers!

The veterans who have recently returned from the field of battle have again an opportunity of serving, not only their country, but the great emporium of New-York, from the threatened dangers of a ruthless mob.

The Commanding General of the Eastern Department trusts that those who have exhibited so much bravery in the field of battle, will not hesitate to come forward at this time, to tender their services to the Mayor, to stay the ravages of the city by men who have lost all sense of obligations to their country, as well as to the city of

structure was barely saved from destruction. But the chief devastation was up town, where private houses were sacked and burned, the Colored Orphan Asylum destroyed, and at least one child burned to death. To the efficiency of the police it is alone due that the city is not already given up to utter sack and pillage.

The city must protect itself. There are loyal citizens enough to do so, if they understand this crisis in our affairs. Let them not be deceived by the belief that this is a mere outbreak against the Draft. It has a deeper meaning, and is literally a removal of the seat of war to the banks of the Hudson. These howling mobs are hounded on by thoughtful and designing men who are at work in the interests of the Southern rebellion. Their organization is as yet incomplete and purposeless except for destruction, but it will grow, if let alone and not arrested in time, into a systematic revolution. Let us be warned in time. Courage and energy can control and suppress it, but the measures must be prompt. Support the authorities; give them strength if they need it. Make them understand, if necessary, the importance of the emergency, and aid them to put it down. It is not the city only, but the country and the cause that is at stake, and this week must decide whether we have a country to live for. The riot is formidable only in its possibilities, and is to-day manageable by the Government and the people. It is not a time to falter or hesitate at extreme measures. When to-day's sun goes down it ought to be decided that the danger is past.

MARTIAL LAW.

The plain obvious duty of the Government is to declare at once Martial Law in this city, and to place some officer in command who will enforce it. A mob, not formidable by organization, by arms, hardly even by numbers, was suffered all yesterday to work its will on lives and property. Where the po-

Articles continued on next page

Figure 23 c
Continuation of articles

New-York.   John E. Wool,
                          Major-General.

P. S.—These men are requested to report to Maj.-Gen. Sanford, corner of Elm and White streets, on Tuesday, July 14, at 10 a. m.

The police came with great promptness to the rescue of THE TRIBUNE buildings, and instantly scattered the mob, which had taken possession of the counting-room, and lighted a fire in its center. Old officers say they never saw a charge more handsomely made than that of the men of the Twenty-sixth Precinct, under Capt. Thorne. Many of the rioters went down under the heavy blows of the gallant policemen, and the rest fled in utter confusion. It is safe to presume that they will not be in a hurry to meet Capt. Thorne and his men again.

Dispatches for Maryland are to the effect that Lee is strongly intrenched on the Williamsport road, three miles south-east of Hagerstown, and resting on the Potomac. The forces under Gen. Couch are said to have joined Gen. Meade on Saturday night. The Potomac is still rising, but the rains affect the roads as well as the river, and a battle is postponed by reason of their condition. Still we interpret the protracted delay of Gen. Meade to mean that he is sure the Rebels are within his grasp, and that he may take what time is needful to recruit and reënforce his army.

lice were used, they did in the main very well, but they were not half used. The civil power was at fault; lacked capacity and lacked courage—even the poor courage to summon the military to its protection. Such military leadership as we had was no better. It presented only the spectacle of irresolution, and incompetence; was worse than useless, and must be replaced.

Let the Government take thought for this city. The mob which governed it yesterday, and may resume its lawless scepter at any moment, needs to be crushed with relentless purpose and an iron hand. Only the Government can do it, or the citizens who, failing the Government, will organize for self-defense. The Government can do it only by martial law, and by declaring that promptly, exercising it mercilessly, and maintaining it till the last vestige of treason is annihilated.

THE CONSCRIPTION—THE RIOTS.
The first man we ever heard advocate a general Conscription for the prosecution of the War for the Union was Archbishop Hughes, in his sermon directly after his last return from Europe last year. He condemned the reliance on Volunteering as hazardous and as placing too large a share of the burden on the generous and public-spirited, urging that, since the obligation to serve rested equally on all, the liability or risk should be apportioned accordingly.

> At one time there lay at the corner of Twenty-seventh Street and Seventh Avenue the dead body of a negro, stripped nearly naked, and around it a collection of Irishmen, absolutely dancing or shouting like wild Indians.[20]

Martin Scorsese's 2002 motion picture attempted to portray these cataclysmic events. What is most regrettable about the *The Gangs of New York* however, is how historically inaccurate is it. A group of Irish Catholic immigrants in the city are shown trying to survive in their new surroundings despite their supposed harassment by the "native" Americans. Undoubtedly to demonstrate their supposed tolerance, Scorsese had a black man hanging around with them. In reality however, the only hanging coloured people generally did around these Romanists was from the end of a rope when they were caught by them. The motion picture did show blacks being lynched but it is unclear which group was killing them. When the riots started in the movie, Scorsese had the army facing the rioters on the street, firing into them and killing some of them. At the same time this was happening, by Hollywood coincidence, in another part of the city, a gang of Irish men are facing a "native" gang. As they begin to fight, the federal navy opened fire on the warring groups. When the riots started though, neither the navy or the army played any real part in the events. The rioter were opposed only by a small, outnumbered force of brave police officers because essentially all of New York's regiments were in Pennsylvania, pursuing Lee, after the Catholic General Meade let him escape. Headley went on:

> It is impossible to give a detailed account of what transpired in every part of the city. If there had been a single band of rioters, no matter how large, a force of military and police, properly armed, could have been concentrated to have dispersed it. But bodies of men, larger or smaller, bent on violence and devastation, were everywhere; even out at Harlem eight buildings were burned, and the lower end of Westchester was in a state of agitation and alarm. A mob of thousands would be scattered, only to come together at other points. A body of police and military plunging through the heaving multitude, acted often only as a stone flung into the water, making but a momentary vacuum. Or, if they did not come together again, they swung off only to fall in, and be absorbed by a crowd collected in another part of the city.

In his description of one battle between the police and the rioters, Joel Headley detailed how one young leader of the Catholic mob, fighting with desperate courage despite the terrible blows he had absorbed, fell and was impaled on an iron railing. When his body was examined:

> It was found, to the surprise of all, to be that of a young man of delicate features and white, fair skin. 'Although dressed as a laborer, in dirty overalls and filthy shirt, underneath these were fine cassimere pants, handsome, rich vest, and fine linen shirt.' He was evidently a man in position far above the rough villains he led on, but had disguised himself so as not to be known [21]

If the riots had just been a spur-of-the-moment, spontaneous occurrence, why would this leader be disguised? Doesn't this also support the view that this uprising was planned?

The *New York Daily Tribune*'s news and editorial coverage of the riots on Tuesday, July 14, 1863, (shown in Figures 23), confirm what Headley described regarding mob and police actions, including the mob's attack on the Tribune's own offices on the first day.

Headley detailed the account of a young, wealthy and cultured Roman Catholic widow who, to her credit, was outraged by the carnage and felt compelled to do something about it. Finding that Catholics were the cause of it, she went to the archbishop of New York, John Hughes, and by sheer determination, forced her way in to see him. She begged him to speak to the mob to stop the bloodshed but he said he was too busy writing a letter to the *New York Tribune*. He also said that if he did speak to the crowds, he was afraid that the military might interfere and attack them. Leaving him, she rushed to see New York Governor Horatio Seymour, again insisting that she see him and she managed to persuade him to meet Hughes. After the meeting, the archbishop agreed to speak to the mob. Headley said of the prelate:

> Why Archbishop Hughes took no more active part than he did in quelling this insurrection, when there was scarcely a man in it except members of his own flock, seems strange. It is true he had published an address to them, urging them to keep the peace; but it was prefaced by a long, undignified, and angry attack on Mr. Greeley, of the Tribune, and showed that he was in sympathy with the rioters, at least in their condemnation of the draft. The pretence that it would be unsafe for him to pass through the streets, is absurd; for on three different occasions common priests had mingled with the mob, not only with impunity, but with good effect. He could not, therefore, have thought himself to be in any great danger. One thing, at any rate, is evident: had an Irish mob threatened to burn down a Roman Catholic church, or a Roman Catholic orphan asylum, or threatened any of the institutions or property of the Roman Church, he would have shown no such backwardness or fear. The mob would have been confronted with the most terrible anathemas of the church, and those lawless bands quailed before the maledictions of the representative of 'God's vicegerent on earth.' It is unjust to suppose that he wished this plunder and robbery to continue, or desired to see Irishmen shot down in the streets; it must, therefore, be left to conjecture, why he could not be moved to any interference except by outside pressure, and then show so much lukewarmness in his manner---in fact, condemning their opponents almost as much as themselves.[22]

Joel Headley made it crystal clear that these mobs destroying property and lives were, with very few exceptions, all Catholics. The planned and orchestrated rebellion, timed with the battlefield results, as the *Tribune* pointed out, was therefore a Catholic uprising, threatening the very existence of the United States. The riots would have been extremely difficult to suppress if they had been accompanied with battlefield losses to Union forces in Pennsylvania or Maryland, with the setbacks keeping federal soldiers from New York.

As the incredible carnage continued, the one person in the city who could have stopped the insurrection that threatened the city and the nation, the highest-ranking Roman Catholic official in New York, Archbishop John Hughes, refused to do so although it clearly was within his power. On Thursday, July 16th, he issued an invitation to those involved in the insurrection to hear a speech from him on Friday, beginning his invitation with the words: "To the men of New York, who are now called in many of the papers rioters"

This statement stunned the editorial staff of the *New York Times*, who undoubtedly spoke for many of the city's outraged residents when it rebuked Hughes in a stinging editorial (see figure 24). In the July 18th issue, the *Times* stated in part:

Figure 24
New York Times, July 18, 1863

The New-York Times, Saturday, July 18, 1863.

Archbishop Hughes and the Rioters.

We were surprised to learn yesterday that the call purporting to be issued by Archbishop HUGHES "to the men of New-York, who are now called in many of the papers rioters," was a genuine document. It did not seem to us possible that any person holding a position of so much dignity and responsibility could say a word which could be construed to imply that *he* did not regard as "rioters" men who had burned down public buildings, plundered private dwellings, set fire to orphan asylums, assailed with bludgeons and stones the legal defenders of the public peace, hung innocent and defenceless men, murdered, with every conceivable brutality, the officers of justice, and done everything which men could do to overthrow the law and plunge society into the very depths of anarchy and crime. If the mob had burned the Catholic Orphan Asylum next door to the Bishop's Cathedral, somebody beside "the papers" would probably have called them "rioters:"—that Archbishop HUGHES could regard the term as less applicable to the men who burned the Colored Orphan Asylum, seemed to us incredible. Nor did we dream for a moment that in a City convulsed with a bloody and raging riot, Archbishop HUGHES could pre-sume to call a meeting of the rioters, and, of his own authority, say to them, "you *shall not* be disturbed by any exhibition of municipal or military *presence*." Such an assurance implies the assumption of a power superior to that of the law: and whatever the Archbishop might feel, we did not think he would be unwise enough openly to proclaim the possession of such a personal or official supremacy.

For these reasons, when we first saw the call we pronounced it spurious. We regret to say, for the Archbishop's sake, that in this we were mistaken. The call was genuine. The meeting of "the men called rioters" was summoned and was held; and in another column will be found a report of the speech made by the Archbishop on that occasion. Its aim, as will be seen, was to dissuade the rioters from any further riotous proceedings, by showing them that in this country there is a peaceful and effective remedy for all political evils, and that it is the interest as well as the duty of every citizen to resort to that alone. Without being an able speech in any respect, it was reasonably well suited to the object it was designed to accomplish, and we trust that in this it may be successful.

If the mob had burned the Catholic Orphan Asylum next door to the Bishop's Cathedral, somebody beside "the papers" would probably have called them "rioters" - that Archbishop Hughes could regard the term as less applicable to the men who burned the Colored Orphan Asylum, seemed to us incredible.

Joel Headley described the end of the riot and Hughes' speech:

> Even if the military under General Brown and the police had not shown the mob that they were its masters, the arrival of so many regiments, occupying all the infected districts, was overwhelming evidence that the day of lawless triumph was over, and that of retribution had come. Some acts of individual hostility were witnessed, but nothing more.
>
> Archbishop Hughes had his meeting, and some five thousand assembled to hear him. They were on the whole a peaceable-looking crowd, and it was

evidently composed chiefly, if not wholly, of those who had taken no part in the riot. None of the bloody heads and gashed faces, of which there were so many at that moment in the city, appeared. The address was well enough, but it came too late to be of any service. It might have saved many lives and much destruction, had it been delivered two days before, but now it was like the bombardment of a fortress after it had surrendered--a mere waste of ammunition. The fight was over, and to use his own not very refined illustration, he 'spak" too late.' [23]

It wasn't until the Union forces were back in New York in sufficient strength to put an end to the mayhem that the archbishop finally asked his flock to stop rioting. As the accounts of Headley and the *New York Tribune* show, the Catholic insurrection clearly was organized. Those leading the mob evidently made a concerted effort to keep their identities secret. As the *Tribune* had reported, the leaders were not openly but "tacitly-acknowledged". Why would the leaders of a "spontaneous" riot be concerned about such things as keeping their identity secret, and disguises, etc?

The only acceptable excuse the Church has to explain Hughes' actions in allowing the horrific continuation of death and destruction to continue is gross incompetence. Yet Pope Pius IX did not remove this official from his position. In fact, as was noted earlier, in his letter to Jeff Davis some four and a half months later, Pius spoke highly of the "venerable" Bishop Hughes. The archbishop's "exemplary piety and episcopal zeal" however, apparently didn't extend to restraining his flock from trying to destroy New York and ultimately the United States. The pope's lack of action also supports Chiniquy's allegation of deliberate and immediate Church involvement in these horrific and barbaric crimes.

Leonard Wibberley, prolific Irish author, and Catholic apologist, it appears, commented on the insurrection in his book, *The Coming of the Green*. He alleged the reason that the Irish Catholics rioted was because of the Emancipation Proclamation and the unfairness of the draft. He declared:

> In January, 1863, however, the whole basis of the war, from the point of view of the Irish, was changed. In that month and year President Lincoln issued his proclamation freeing all slaves, and the freedom of the slaves became the war aim.

> This was something the Irish did not want. It was not what they were fighting for. Occupying the lowest rung of the economic ladder in the United States, they saw in the freeing of the slaves a massive threat to their own precarious livelihoods. If the slaves were freed, they would without a doubt come north in large numbers and compete with the Irishman for his pick and shovel. If they did not actually displace the Irish on the road gangs and on the railroads, they would still certainly force the Irishman's miserable wage down and down.

Wibberley stated as well:

> The Emancipation Proclamation was soon followed by a conscription act on which the most unbiased verdict can only be that it was monstrous. Basically it proclaimed that all within certain age limits, and of sound health, must serve

in the Union army, except that any man might escape being drafted either by paying three hundred dollars in cash or by furnishing a substitute.

In short, the rich could put up three hundred dollars while the poor put up their lives. And who were the poor? They were, of course, the immigrants, largely the Irish, most of whom had a toehold on the ladder of existence but had amassed little capital. Of them it was required that they be prepared to sacrifice their lives so that others would be freed to compete for their jobs.

He also wrote:

The Irish who now were reluctant to volunteer for the Abolition Army were to be forced to serve, while the rich non-Irish bought their way out. The Irish erupted.

They erupted on July 13, 1863, and for the next three days mobs of infuriated Irishmen (and others, but principally Irishmen) controlled large sections of the city of New York. They committed crimes for which there can be no excuse. But they committed them in white-hot anger against what they conceived to be a terrible injustice-and injustice is one thing that makes the Irish so fighting mad they forget what justice is.

July 13 was a Monday. On the previous Saturday the drawing of names under the new conscription act had begun and the Irish noted that almost all the names were Irish, fathers of large families and men with no hope whatever of securing the three hundred dollars needed to buy freedom. All Sunday the city seethed with anger. Monday the lid blew off.

Gangs of Irishmen, several thousands strong, marched into Central Park and burned down the draft office. They beat the superintendent of police and they stormed the houses of the rich on Lexington Avenue. They did worse than that in their fury. They tore down a Negro orphan asylum housing about two hundred children between the ages of two and twelve, they drove utterly innocent Negroes through the streets, and they lynched a number of them. They cut telegraph wires and raided stores and overturned carriages and horsecars, and there was a roar about the city as if some great beast was loose and lusting for blood.[24]

Regardless of what anyone thought, the ultimate war aim of Abraham Lincoln was never the end of slavery. It was to preserve, protect and defend the Constitution of the United States and therefore preserve the Union. He stated in August, 1862, that if he could save the Union by freeing none of the slaves, he would do it. In August, 1864, Lincoln declared that "My enemies say I am now carrying on this war for the sole purpose of abolition. It is & will be carried on so long as I am President for the sole purpose of restoring the Union."

Wibberley stated that emancipation was "something the Irish did not want. It was not what they were fighting for". Actually, the Catholic Irish men in New York at this time were not fighting for anything, including their adopted country. That is why they had to be conscripted.

As well, the Emancipation Proclamation did not free all the slaves. In fact, it liberated few, if any, as it freed slaves only in areas under Confederate control where the U.S. government had no power to liberate them. Wibberley explained the reason the Irish didn't want the slaves freed was because they knew they would end up having to compete with them for laboring jobs and he appears to accept this as a reasonable excuse. This statement says as much about Leonard Wibberley as it does about these Irish Catholics. According to Wibberley and these Romanists, it evidently was best that the enslaved black people stayed enslaved, so as to not inconvenience the Irish.

When Jesus observed a poor widow casting all the money she had into the treasury at the temple, he commended her, saying that she had given more than all the rich people who had donated of their excess wealth, (Mark 12:41 - 44, Luke 21:1 - 4). This lesson regarding faith and giving to others seems not to have been taught by the Catholic Church to her children. Rather than share the little they had with those who were less fortunate, like newly freed black people, these fine religious people preferred to beat them to death.

Leonard Wibberley declared that the most unbiased persons would view the conscription act as monstrous. Joel Headley's statements show that he couldn't be accused of being unfair in his assessment of these events. Introduced as it was, in a time of great national emergency, he saw nothing wrong with the government's draft policy to obtain the troops the country desperately needed.

Wibberley stated that the Irish, "committed crimes for which there can be no excuse," then promptly tried to excuse them. There was undoubtedly was much, much, more than the several thousand Catholic rioters on the street that he said went to burn the draft office. Headley wrote:

> The number composing this first mob has been so differently estimated, that it would be impossible from reports merely, to approximate the truth. A pretty accurate idea, however, can be gained of its immense size, from a statement made by Mr. King, son of President King, of Columbia College. Struck by its magnitude, he had the curiosity to get some estimate of it by timing its progress, and he found that although it filled the broad street from curbstone to curbstone, and was moving rapidly, it took between twenty and twenty-five minutes for it to pass a single point.[25]

The Catholic mob didn't just beat the police Superintendent Kennedy, as Wibberley reported. Recognizing him in plain clothes near the burning draft office at the start of the riots, they would have beaten him to death but after desperately fighting for his life, a friend who happened by helped him to escape, although he was so badly injured, he was almost unrecognizable.

Wibberley seemed to believe that the draft would ensure that poor Catholic Irishmen would do all the fighting and dying for the Union cause and the other northern citizens would stand by and watch. According to the U.S. Pension Department however, as reported by U.S. Army General Thomas M. Harris, the Irish actually only made up 6.8 percent of the number of enlisted men in the Union army (General Harris was a member of the military commission that tried the eight conspirators in the summer of 1865).

If the poor were largely the Irish, as Leonard Wibberley maintained, then there were many times more "rich" native born Americans, as well as U.S. citizens of other extraction, that fought and died when compared to these Catholics. Of course, there were many other, less than wealthy, patriots who took up arms to defend the United States. When it is considered that 72 percent of the Irish are recorded as having deserted, as opposed to five percent for native born Americans, then the percentage of Irish men that swerved in the Union army is even lower. In his book, *American Catholic: the saints and sinners who built America's most powerful church*, Catholic writer Charles R. Morris stated, " The truth is that Irish Catholic were the most underrepresented of all socioethnic groups in the Union army, with German Catholics next". [26]

The bias and lack of balance of Wibberley's point of view is clearly shown when he stated that the measure to get more badly needed soldiers for the Union forces, the draft, was monstrous because it would make the Irish shoulder what would actually be, proportionally, a tiny part of the burden in the fight for the survival of America.

He did get it right when he said that the Irish Catholics committed, "crimes for which there can be no excuse." There truly was no justification for what they did. Their actions were not those of a people so maddened that they could no longer reason. Instead there is very strong evidence that points to the riots being planned and timed to overcome the North from within, as the *New York Tribune* stated. The sympathy of the archbishop of New York also was clearly with his flock in their attempt to help destroy the city and the nation.

As it can be seen, there is ample evidence to convince the unbiased that in reality, both overtly and covertly, a more than significant portion of the Church's hierarchy and laymen were solidly behind the effort to destroy the country that since 1776 has been the citadel of human freedom, the United States.

Figure 25
Ford's Theatre, Washington D.C.

Library of Congress, Prints & Photographs Division, LC-DIG-cwpbh-03304

WHO KILLED ABRAHAM LINCOLN?

Chapter 6
Stanton Agrees with Chiniquy, the Assassination Heard of Before it Happened

The spring of 1865 arrived in Washington with the promise of new life and hope that had not been present for years. The constant strain that President Lincoln had labored under began to ebb away along with the winter's snow and cold. On the 9th of April, the North cheered the news of Confederate General Robert E. Lee's surrender to U. S. Forces commander Ulysses S. Grant at Appomattox, Virginia. This ended, for the most part, the bloody struggle between the United States government and the Southern rebel states, with the loss of over half a million young Americans. Peace seemed to have been achieved and the Union preserved, the terrible Civil War appeared to be drawing to a close.

A night out to watch the popular play, *Our American Cousin*, at Ford's Theatre was arranged by Mary Lincoln for the evening of April 14th (see Figure 25). Mrs. Lincoln and the President were to be accompanied by their invited guests, General Grant and his wife. The Grants however, abruptly changed their plans and left Washington. Miss Clara Harris, the daughter of a New York Senator and her fiancé, Major Henry Rathbone, were invited to go instead.

It was a mild evening in the capital and the Lincolns and their guests were late getting to the theatre. The play stopped and the orchestra struck up "Hail to the Chief" to honour President Lincoln, as the Presidential party entered and proceeded to their box overlooking the right hand side of the stage. It was not to be a pleasant outing for long though. During the second scene of the third act, a well known figure in the theatre, prominent actor John Wilkes Booth, gained admission to the Lincoln's box, approached the President from behind and shot him in the back of the head. Also armed with a knife, Booth stabbed Major Rathbone as the officer attempted to prevent the assassin's escape. Though he was not successful, Rathbone's effort resulted in Booth losing his balance as he jumped from the Presidential box, possibly breaking a bone in his left leg when he landed heavily on the stage. Momentarily stunned, the actor swiftly moved to the back entrance of the theatre where he mounted a waiting horse in the alley and made his escape from Washington, riding south across the Navy Yard Bridge into southern Maryland.

At approximately the same time that evening, Secretary of State William Seward was in bed recovering from a serious carriage accident, when another member of the conspiracy named Lewis Payne came to the Seward home. The powerful young man, who had fought on the side of Confederacy earlier in the Civil War, said that he had some medicine he had to give to the Secretary personally. Denied entry, Payne fought his way into William Seward's room with a knife and pistol and tried to kill him. Although badly injuring the Secretary and other members of the household, he failed in his attempt. Payne had been guided to Seward's home earlier by another young associate, a boyish former druggist clerk named David Herold.

At the same hour, another member of the conspiracy, German-born coachmaker and boatman, George Atzerodt, assisted by Herold, was to kill Vice President Andrew Johnson. Herold did not link up with him however and left alone, Atzerodt's nerve failed and he didn't act. There may have also been an attempt on the life of General Grant planned but he had left the capital earlier in the day and was not attacked.

The effort to kill so many leaders was seen an attempt to paralyze the American government, the thinking being that the United States Constitution had no provisions for the replacement of so many officials at one time. Abraham Lincoln was taken unconscious to the home of a private citizen across the street, William Peterson. He clung to life until 7:22 the next morning, when he breathed his last. Thus the cruel, fatal blow fell on the beloved head of the U.S. government that Charles Chiniquy and others had so feared would come.[1]

At 10:00 A.M., more than two and a half hours after the death of Abraham Lincoln, Andrew Johnson assumed the highest position in the land, swearing that he would faithfully execute the office of the President and preserve, protect and defend the Constitution of the United States.

While doing research for *Fifty Years*, Charles Chiniquy stated that he went to Washington and was dismayed to find how much influence the Catholic Church wielded there. He discovered that officials in the U.S. government would not talk to him about the Church's role in Lincoln's murder, except off the record.

According to Charles Chiniquy, several government men that he had confidence in told him that they hadn't the least doubt that the Jesuits were at the bottom of the assassination. They said it was out of concern for the country as a whole and not cowardice that they did not reveal to the American public what they knew. They related that at the trial of the conspirators, a large number of priests were very nearly compromised, as Mary Surratt's Washington home was both the conspirators' and the priests' common meeting place.

These men explained to Chiniquy that the Civil War had not been over long and the Confederacy was still alive in many hearts. They feared that the execution or exiling of these priests would give new life to the elements of rebellion that still lurked in the country, causing more bloodshed, destruction, and possibly a new conflict, this time between the Protestants and the Catholics in the war weary nation.[2]

Academic Roy Chamlee Jr. supported Chiniquy's statements in his 1990 book, *Lincoln's Assassins: A Complete Account of their Capture, Trial, and Punishment.* Though the evidence led Chamlee to the conclusion that Mary Surratt was one of the conspirators, he evidently had no axe to grind regarding the Catholic Church. Commenting on the five priests who were character witnesses for Mary Surratt, he stated, "The opening defense, instead of being a powerful statement in favor of the prisoner, gave the impression that she was trying to hide behind her church. The priests, however, did not fit well into the scheme." Chamlee also declared:

Several reporters criticized this tactic as an effort to introduce religious influences into court procedures. Actually, ecclesiastical questions boiled beneath the surface. Soon after the assassination, some individuals introduced a religious element. Government authorities received letters accusing the Catholic Church of involvement. As the investigation progressed, it became evident that many suspects were Catholics. Letters to newspapers occasionally asserted that John Surratt was harbored in some Catholic institution or home in Washington; some more accurately mentioned Canada.

Occasionally the Catholic Church was described in unflattering terms. Benjamin Wood, editor and proprietor of the *New York Daily News*, was paid by the Confederate Government to publish his Copperhead paper. On May 5, 1865, he wrote that the *New York Tribune* charged the Roman Catholic Church with complicity in Lincoln's assassination. While newspapers agitated religious themes, and unfounded rumors caused tensions, the Government avoided the explosive issue.

Chamlee also stated, "The Government sought to convict conspirators and keep religious tensions out of it". Who were the government officials who, according to *Fifty Years*, were sure that Lincoln's murder was the work of the Jesuits? Evidently one of them was no less than, besides the President, the most powerful member of Lincoln's cabinet, and the man who was in control of the United States in the aftermath of Abraham Lincoln's death, Secretary of War, Edwin M. Stanton.

The late Daniel Patrick Moynihan, diplomat, scholar and former U.S. Senator, (Dem. New York) stated that Stanton believed that Lincoln's murder had been a Catholic conspiracy. He wrote a piece about John F. Kennedy's assassination, entitled, "The Paranoid Style", which was published in the December 29th, 1991 edition of the *Washington Post*. In it, Moynihan stated "Let it be noted that Lincoln's secretary of war, Edwin M. Stanton, believed that the assassination had indeed been a Catholic plot."[3] Moynihan wrote the piece in response to the release of Oliver Stone's 1991 movie, JFK, which advanced the view that the murder of President John F. Kennedy was the result of a large scale conspiracy.[4]

Years before the Civil War brought these two powerful political figures together, Abraham Lincoln and Edwin Stanton, both attorneys, had been hired to defend John Manny. Manny had been sued for patent infringements, pertaining to the McCormack Reaper, by farm equipment maker Cyrus McCormack. Lincoln was hired because it was thought the case would be tried in Chicago, but in the end it was transferred to Cincinnati. On the occasion of the opening of the trial in September, 1855, the highly educated and accomplished Stanton, an Ohio native, snubbed the tall unrefined prairie lawyer, reportedly remarking, "If that giraffe [Lincoln] appeared in the case, I would throw up my brief and leave." Though he had prepared for it, Lincoln was not allowed to play any part in the legal proceeding.[5]

Despite how Stanton had treated him, Lincoln offered to appoint him Secretary of War because he knew he was the best candidate for the job. Though he retained his low opinion of Abraham Lincoln during the first part of the Civil War, Stanton, a prominent Democrat, accepted the President's offer to join the cabinet in 1862, doing so solely for the good of the country. As the war went on however, the men became close.

One Lincoln biographer reported, "When George Harding, his old partner in the Reaper trial, assumed that Stanton was the author of the 'remarkable passages' in one of Lincoln's messages, Stanton set him straight. 'Lincoln wrote it—every word of it; and he is capable of more than that, Harding, no men were ever so deceived as we were in Cincinnati.'"

After he joined the cabinet, Lincoln spent more time with his Secretary of War than with any other person, the President describing Stanton as the, "rock upon which are beating the waves of this conflict...I do not see how he survives--why he is not crushed and torn to pieces. Without him, I should be destroyed."[6] When Abraham Lincoln breathed his last on the morning of April 15th, 1865, the weeping War Secretary declared, "now he belongs to the ages."[7]

As the *Paranoid Style* shows, Daniel Patrick Moynihan was no fan of conspiracy theories or Charles Chiniquy either, stating that at one point he carried a copy of *Fifty Years* with him as proof of how gullible people are. While disclosing the Secretary of War's view of who was responsible for Lincoln's murder, Moynihan, a Catholic, didn't reveal the full significance of who Stanton was, however.

The Civil War was the terrible backdrop of nearly all of Abraham Lincoln's presidency and for the majority of Lincoln's time in office, Secretary Stanton's tremendous ability and energy was dedicated to efficiently discharging his duties as head of the all important War department. In his position, Stanton undoubtedly would have known more about the conflict and the enemies of the nation than any other man, including perhaps the President himself. For example, Stanton wouldn't even allow Lincoln to use the military cipher that the army had developed.

As well, for the time period immediately after Lincoln was shot by Booth, and before Andrew Johnson was sworn in as President, Edwin Stanton was essentially the dictator of the United States. Even for weeks after, he remained very much in control. And most importantly, this man who came to believe that the President's assassination had been the result of a Catholic plot, *headed* the investigation into Lincoln's murder, as well as the effort to prosecute of the conspirators in 1865. [8]

This truly stunning disclosure regarding Stanton's views would be like having Earl Warren, who chaired the presidential committee that investigated the assassination of John F. Kennedy, state that he believed that, for example, the Cuban government was responsible for Kennedy's murder. In Secretary Stanton's unique position, all important information concerning the President's murder flowed to him. Even without any other evidence of Catholic complicity, this is practically unanswerable proof of the Church's guilt regarding Lincoln's death. The presidential committee that Earl Warren led came to the conclusion that Kennedy's assassination was the work of a lone gunman.

Daniel Patrick Moynihan is also supported by Lloyd Lewis in his book, *Myths after Lincoln*. In this volume, Lewis stated that Stanton "had conceived the

notion that the conspiracy to kill Lincoln had been manned by Catholics."
According to Lewis, Stanton:

> had jumped to this conclusion when his detectives had brought him the
> news that, among the accused, four were members of the Catholic Church—
> Mrs. Surratt, her son John, Michael O'Laughlin and Dr. Mudd. Whether
> Stanton believed it or not, at least one of the judges, Gen. T. M. Harris,
> believed that J. Wilkes Booth had recently left the Episcopal Church to
> become a Roman Catholic.

Although Lloyd Lewis evidently didn't believe it himself, he showed that Stanton
had reason to come to the conclusion that he did. It will be shown that there is very
strong evidence that most, if not all, of the conspirators were Catholics.

It is true that a small group of writers such as Otto Eisenschiml and Theodore
Roscoe alleged that Stanton was actually part of the conspiracy to murder the
President. William Hanchett however, who wrote the book, *The Lincoln Murder
Conspiracies*, for one, appears to do an adequate job of refuting the theory and
Hanchett certainly was no admirer of Charles Chiniquy.[9]

Edwin Stanton was not without enemies and detractors. He reportedly came to
the too hasty conclusion that the assassination was the result of a Confederate
conspiracy and he was faulted for the lengths the prosecution went to prove the
connection between the South and the murder of Lincoln. *The Abraham Lincoln
Encyclopedia* reported that Stanton and Judge Advocate-General Joseph Holt,
"relied on extremely questionable witnesses in an attempt to link the conspirators to
Confederate agents in Canada."

In the Secretary's defence however, he was not alone, as many in the North also
came to the same conclusion regarding the South's culpability, including other
government officials as well. President Johnson was reportedly amongst these
officials. It is easy to understand Stanton's thinking in view of the fact that the
Confederacy had used guerrilla warfare against the Union in the past. Philip Van
Doren Stern wrote the introduction to a 1954 reproduction of the 1865 military
commission's official court report entitled *The Assassination of President Lincoln and
the Trial of the Conspirators*. Van Doren Stern commented in the introduction on the
South's unconventional military actions:

> Confederate irregular troops under the command of Lieutenant Bennett H.
> Young raided St. Albans, Vermont, on October 19, 1864, robbed three of its
> banks of more than $200,000, killed one of its townspeople, and then returned
> to Canadian territory, where they were safe from pursuit. It is also true that
> an attempt was made to seize a Federal gunboat on Lake Erie in order to use
> it to set free the Confederate prisoners of war confined on Johnson's Island. It
> is equally true that Confederate agents tried to set a number of New York City
> hotels on fire on November 25, 1864.

Confederates based in Canada also attempted to use a form of biological warfare
against the North. Witnesses at the trial of the assassination conspirators in 1865

testified that the year before, successful efforts were made to smuggle clothing in the U.S. to sell in Washington. Apparently the clothing had been contaminated with yellow fever, small-pox and other contagious diseases. A valise or small case, evidently also containing contaminated clothes, was to be sent to President Lincoln, its purpose undoubtedly to cause him to become ill or die. Montreal, Quebec, was such a center of Confederate activity that it was nicknamed "Little Richmond."

Regarding Confederate activities in Canada, Van Doren Stern concluded, "the prosecution failed to trace any connection between them and Booth's plot to assassinate the President, nor was the prosecution able to implicate Jefferson Davis or his Cabinet in the plot." He added, "And it is, of course, entirely possible that all the important documents concerning a cloak-and-dagger operation of this kind were long ago destroyed."

Calling Stanton's opinion of Roman Catholic responsibility for Lincoln's death, one of his "freaks of imagination," Lloyd Lewis also stated that the War Secretary was fanatically anti-Catholic. He provided no evidence that Edwin Stanton had been always against the Catholic Church though. Stanton biographer Frank Abial Flower however, did provide proof that the accomplished War Secretary had not been opposed to the Church of Rome before his experience in Civil War times undoubtedly opened his eyes to the role it had been playing in the conflict. Flower quoted John Mullen, who had worked for Edwin Stanton when he lived in Steubenville, Ohio, years before Secretary Stanton joined Lincoln's cabinet. Mullen reported that Stanton gave freely to all churches, "I was a Catholic and he gave money to me to spend as my own for church purposes. I recollect that he entertained Archbishop Purcell of Cincinnati in his own home and always listened to the Archbishop's sermon in Steubenville."[10]

Stanton was obviously not opposed to the Roman Catholic Church at this time. It undoubtedly was what he saw in his high position, later in life, that convinced him of the Church of Rome's hostility to the young republic and its great President. The testimony of the eminent statesman, Edwin Stanton, remains therefore a formidable witness against the Catholic Church in its role in the murder of America's greatest President.

Lincoln's Murder Heard of Before it Happened in Minnesota

In his autobiography, Charles Chiniquy also stated that one day, while searching for information regarding the assassination of President Lincoln, he met Rev. Francis F. A. Conwell in Chicago. *Fifty Years* reported what Conwell told Chiniquy:

> 'The very day of the murder,' he said, 'he was in the Roman Catholic village of St. Joseph, Minnesota State, when, at about six o'clock, in the afternoon, he was told by a Roman Catholic of the place, who was a purveyor of a great number of priests who lived in that town, where they have a monastery, that the State Secretary Seward and the President Lincoln had just been killed. This was told me,' he said, 'in the presence of a most respectable gentleman, called

Bennett, who was not less puzzled than me. As there were no railroad lines nearer than 40 miles, nor telegraph offices nearer than 80 miles, from that place, we could not see how such news was spread in that town.[11]

At Charles Chiniquy's request, Rev. Conwell made a sworn statement regarding his experience before the distinguished Kankakee lawyer and notary, Stephen R. Moore. The original affidavit is held in the Chiniquy Collection, in Ontario, Canada. It is reproduced in *Fifty Years* as follows:

State of Illinois,)
) s. s.
Cook County.)

Rev. F. A. Conwell, being sworn, deposes and says that he is seventy-one years old, that he is a resident of North Evanston, in Cook County, State of Illinois, that he has been in the ministry for fifty-six years, and is now one of the chaplains of the 'Seamen's Bethel Home,' in Chicago; that he was chaplain of the First Minnesota Regiment, in the war of the rebellion. That, on the 14th day of April, A.D., 1865, he was in St. Joseph, Minnesota, and reached there as early as six o'clock in the evening in company with Mr. Bennett, who, then and now, is a resident of St. Cloud, Minnesota. That on that date, there was no telegraph nearer than Minneapolis, about 80 miles from St. Joseph; and there was no railroad communication nearer than Avoka, Minnesota, about 40 miles distance. That when he reached St. Joseph, on the 14th day of April, 1865, one Mr. Linneman, who, then, kept the hotel of St. Joseph, told affiant that President Lincoln and Secretary Seward were assassinated, that it was not later than half-past six o'clock, on Friday, April 14th, 1865, when Mr. Linneman told me this. Shortly thereafter, Mr. Bennett came in the hotel, and I told him that Mr. Linneman said the President Lincoln and Secretary Seward were assassinated; and then the same Mr. Linneman reported the same conversation to Mr. Bennett in my presence. That during that time, Mr. Linneman told me that he had the charge of the friary or college for young men, under the priests, who were studying for the priesthood at St. Joseph. That there was a large multitude of this kind at St. Joseph, at this time. Affiant says that, on Saturday morning, April 15th, 1865, he went to St. Cloud, a distance of about 10 miles, and reached there about eight o'clock in the morning. That there was no railroad or telegraph communication to St. Cloud. When he arrived at St. Cloud he told Mr. Haworth, the hotel-keeper, that he had been told that President Lincoln and Secretary Seward had been assassinated, and asked if it was true. He further told Henry Clay, Wait, Charles Gilman, who was afterwards Lieutenant Governor of Minnesota, and Rev. Mr. Tice, the same thing, and inquired of them if they had any such views; and they replied that they had not heard anything of the kind.

Affiant says that, on Sunday morning, April 16th, 1865, he preached in St. Cloud, and on the way to the church, a copy of a telegram was handed him, stating that the President and Secretary were assassinated Friday evening, at about 9 o'clock. This telegram had been brought to St. Cloud by Mr. Gorton, who had reached St. Cloud by stage; and this was the first intelligence that had reached St. Cloud of the event.

Affiant says further that, on Monday morning, April 17th, 1865, he furnished the 'Press,' a paper of St. Paul, a statement that three hours before the event took place, he had been informed at St. Joseph, Minnesota, that the President had been assassinated, and this was published in the 'Press.'

FRANCIS ASHBURY, CONWELL

Subscribed and sworn to by Francis A. Conwell, before me, a Notary Public of Kankakee County, Illinois, at Chicago, Cook County, the 6th day of September, 1883.

STEPHEN R. MOORE, Notary Public[12]

How could the murder of Lincoln and Seward be known, three to four hours before it happened, particularly in a place like St. Joseph, with no direct telegraph or rail links to Washington? Charles Chiniquy stated that this was possible because the priests of St. Joseph had heard from their counterparts in the U.S. capital regarding what had been planned there. The priests, in turn, told their good friend, Linneman, who was a main supplier of the college.

Was Rev. Conwell telling the truth? Independent sources show that he was indeed chaplain of the 1st Minnesota regiment during the Civil War.[13] At Charles Chiniquy's request, Stephen Moore went on a trip to Minnesota in 1883 to obtain more information. Moore also got a sworn statement from Horace Bennett, a resident of St. Cloud, mentioned by Conwell in his affidavit, confirming what Rev. Conwell stated. Moore reported on his trip in an October 30, 1883 letter to Chiniquy. The letter and the original affidavits of Horace Bennett are also held in the Chiniquy Collection, (Bennett and Conwell's affidavits and the letter are reproduced in the Appendix 3, Part 9 - 11).[14]

"Deacon" Horace P. Bennett, a prominent and well-respected pioneer and businessman of Stearns County, first came to central Minnesota from Massachusetts in 1856. His bravery during the 1862 Indian insurrections in the state distinguished him amongst his fellow citizens, whom he helped save from possible harm. He operated a gun and ammunition business in central Minnesota for a quarter century and was an expert marksman into his eighties. Among other endeavors, he served as a justice of the peace.[15] In his letter to Rev Chiniquy, Moore stated, "Mr. Bennett is a very respectable man and his evidence cannot be impeached".

Moore also reported that he had seen the large Catholic institution at St. Joseph that Linneman had been supplying. The establishment he was referring to evidently was St. Benedict's monastery in St. Joseph, Minnesota, which is still in existence today. As well, Stephen Moore confirmed the religious makeup of the community of St. Joseph when he was there in 1883. He stated, "It was almost wholly settled by Roman Catholics, and at that time, (of the assassination), the community were all Roman

Catholics".[16] Some 27 years after Stephen Moore visited, the 1910 federal census reported that the vast majority of people in Stearns County were Catholic.

The men that Rev. Conwell said he spoke to in St. Cloud were indeed living there at the time. Although his name evidently was reproduced in the affidavit as Haworth, historical accounts show that J. F. Hayward was the proprietor of Central House, one of the main hotels in St. Cloud by the end of the Civil War.[17] H. C. Wait, who appeared to also go by the name Henry Chester Waite, was an early settler and prominent citizen of the community.[18] "Governor" C. A. Gilman, who settled in St. Cloud in 1861, became active in politics, serving for many years in the Minnesota Legislature and was first elected Lieutenant Governor in 1879.[19]

Local historical sources also show that at time of the President's murder, Rev. David Tice was the pastor of the Methodist church in St. Cloud.[20] Leander Gorton, who Rev. Conwell said first brought the news of Lincoln's assassination to St. Cloud, was another early settler and leading businessman of Stearns County.[21]

John H. Linneman, a devout Catholic and one of the first settlers in the St. Joseph area, was a prominent businessman who operated an inn, store and flour mill in the town. His home was the scene of the first mass said by a Catholic priest in St. Joseph. His name was also spelt Linnemann.[22] In his letter to Charles Chiniquy, Stephen Moore also reported that he had obtained a statement from Linneman regarding the President's death being reported before it happened. He said that he had "quite a time" getting it however, explaining that Linneman changed his story considerably after he found out that Moore wanted him to swear to what he said.[23]

Not only were all the people mentioned by Rev. Conwell as being residents of St. Cloud and St. Joseph, living in these communities at the time but as he stated, the *St. Paul Press* did indeed print his statement about the startling coincidence (See Figure 26).

In the April 27th, 1865 article however, the *Press* went further in its accusations of Linneman than Chiniquy, Conwell and Bennett had. The newspaper asserted that if the matter was thoroughly investigated, Linneman would be found to be part of a secret society of traitors that knew about the planned assassinations, including the day it would be carried out, although probably not knowing the method or instruments to be used.[24] Chiniquy and the others had only stated that Linneman had known about the planned murders hours before they were to occur, Chiniquy declaring that the businessman had been told about it by his friends, the priests of St. Joseph.

According to the rival of the *Press*, the *St. Paul Pioneer*, John Linneman was in the city on the day the article appeared and after reading it, he went to the *Press* office and protested. Although neither paper expressly said so, Linneman may have threatened to sue and as a businessman of some significance in St. Joseph, with connections in St. Paul, he may have threatened a boycott of the paper as well. The *St. Paul Press* evidently was the Republican newspaper of the city, the St. Paul Pioneer was the Democratic paper, and there seemed to be little love lost between the two.

The *Press* printed a partial apology the next day, clearing Linneman of playing any part in the conspiracy to kill the President. The *Press*, which according to the

Figure 26
St. Paul Press, April 27, 1865

SAINT PAUL PRE

SAINT PAUL, THURSDAY, APRIL 27, 1865.

SHERMAN'S SURRENDER.

A STRANGE COINCIDENCE.

We received, more than a week ago, the following communications from St. Cloud. They relate to a circumstance in connection with the assassination of Mr. Lincoln and the attack upon Mr. Seward, which, to say the least, is a most remarkable coincidence—so remarkable, indeed as to afford ground for some very strong suspicions:

ST. CLOUD, Minn., April 17 1865.

Editors St. Paul Press:

A strange coincidence. At 6:30 P. M., Friday April 14th, I was told, as an item of news, 8 miles west from this place, THAT LINCOLN AND SEWARD HAD BEEN ASSASSINATED. *This was true three hours after I heard the news.*

F. A. CONWELL,

At the same time we received from two private sources a confirmation of this statement, with the following facts. Mr. Linneman, a hotel keeper, at St. Joseph eight miles west of St. Cloud, made the remark in presence of Mr. Conwell on the evening of the 14th April, about three hours before the event actually took place, that news had been received that Messrs. Lincoln and Seward had been assassinated. "He spoke of it," says our correspondent, "as a piece of news as well confirmed as the surrender of Lee. Mr. Conwell argued against the probability of such an occurrence and especially against their having information from Washington City at so remote a point."

Another correspondent says that this "Linneman is one of the most prominent and influential Copperheads in that region, one very likely to be entrusted with an important political secret."

Upon this we remark that it is semi-officially given out, as the result of the secret investigation, now going on at Washington, into the details of the conspiracy, that Booth was the agent of a band of conspirators composed of Knights of the Golden Circle—a secret society of traitors—of which he was a member Booth made no secret of his purpose to kill the President, even with his professional and social companions, though his utterances upon the subject were regarded as the empty threats of a braggart. It is not at all impossible that the general purpose to assassinate the President about that time, may have been communicated to this secret society, and it was probably known by the society that that very day had been selected for the purpose, though it is hardly probable the instruments or method of assassination were revealed to any but the actual participants in the deed, and their immediate accessories.

That the event was anticipated in copperhead quarters there is said be considerable evidence, though we have seen no other indications that the details of the enterprise were known outside of the circle of assassins, than the statement that a Spanish merchant in New York had been overheard to say, on the day of the assassination, that the greatest news ever yet made known to the public would be received next morning. On the whole we are inclined to think that if the case were properly worked up, it would be found that this Mr. Linneman has been in close communication with the Knights of the Golden Circle—the Sons of Liberty—or some other secret society of traitors, to whose dark conclaves the fiendish plot was know. Upon no other hypothesis can we account for the fact that parties sixteen hundred miles West of Washington, and eighty miles beyond the reach of the telegraph, could confidently believe that Mr. Lincoln and Mr. Seward had been assassinated just three hours before the one was murdered, and the other one assaulted with a view to his murder.

Pioneer, was already being sued for slander at the time by another party, blamed Rev. Conwell for the misunderstanding, stating that Linneman had reported that he had said, "only that Mr. Lincoln had been killed" and not Seward too, as if Lincoln was a mere doorkeeper in Washington. According to the *Press*, Linneman said he heard of the President's assassination "from his wife, who got it from a neighbor, who heard it in the store of a well-known loyal gentleman at St. Cloud, who said he heard it on his way from St. Paul (see figure 27)."[25] The *St. Paul Pioneer* article is reproduced in the Appendix 3, Part 13.

The *Press* editor, probably hoping to avoid another lawsuit, embraced this flimsy and likely false account, which enabled him to back away from his earlier statements. If Seward is not included, then the explanation can be advanced, as it has been more recently, that a misunderstanding had caused someone to think that Lincoln had been killed, thereby starting the story.

In a November 9, 1998 piece in the *St. Cloud Times*, Sister Owen Lindblad, a Catholic actually connected with the Roman Catholic institution that Linneman used to supply, St. Benedict's Monastery, alleged that the "rumor" started when Linneman's wife reported that in a local store, "she had overheard a woman customer complaining about the high prices and blaming it on the Republicans. A clerk supposedly replied that she needn't worry because the President was dead. However, she meant the statement in political terms."[26]

This explanation is difficult to accept because Lincoln was most certainly not politically dead. The huge military effort that had been his Presidency was all but over and he was about to embark on a generous program of reconciliation and rebuilding. The unprecedented outpouring of grief at his death attested to his great popularity. The *New York Times* described the crowds that gathered in that city to see President Lincoln's funeral procession as "immense" as well as "almost soundless, but intensely interested and deeply sympathetic". A line of 500,000 waited to view their fallen leader and in all, more than one and a half million city residents gathered to honour the President. According to one source, as Abraham Lincoln's body was transported to Springfield, Illinois, where it was interred, "More than seven million people gathered along the city streets and country fields to pay their respect to the funeral train….One in every four Americans had come to see their president or watch his funeral train pass by."[27]

Lindblad got the information about the clerk saying Lincoln was dead, meaning in political terms, presumably from an interview John Linnemann gave in the spring of 1891 to a Catholic publication, the *Northwestern Chronicle*. The interview was also reproduced in an April 30th, 1891, *St Cloud Journal Press* article entitled "The Assassination of President Lincoln" (see Figure 28). According to the *Journal Press* piece, Linnemann stated "Seventeen days after the assassination, two weeks from Easter Monday" when he was visiting St. Paul, someone told him that there was a story about him in the papers. Linneman then said, "I looked at the Pioneer newspaper. The report in that paper was not correct."

Figure 27
St. Paul Press, April 28, 1865

THAT COINCIDENCE EXPLAINED AWAY.

Yesterday we published some correspondence from St. Cloud in which it was noted and commented upon as a curious and suspicious coincidence, that a Mr. Linneman who keeps a hotel at St. Joseph, near St. Cloud, had stated as a matter of news, on the 14th inst., at 6½ P. M., that President Lincoln and Secretary Seward had been assassinated, thus describing the tragic event of that memorable day, only two or three hours before its actual occurrence in Washington.

The coincidence would certainly have been extremely singular and suspicious if the statements of our correspondents had been wholly accurate. We are happy to say that we have the best reasons for believing that our correspondent's report of Mr. Linneman's remarks were only partially correct—and while enough remains to form a somewhat curious coincidence—what is taken away deprives it of its suspicious features, while the collateral facts, as they have been explained to us make it absurd to suppose that the remark was based on any foreknowledge of the event.

It happened curiously enough that Mr. Linneman was in the city yesterday morning when our article appeared, and he was very much astonished and shocked to find himself an object of such astounding suspicions based on a casual remark to a passer-by. His own explanation strips the circumstance of any possible ground of such suspicion. In the first place, as to the remark itself, he stated as a matter of idle current report, only that Mr. Lincoln had been killed; he did not, as reported, mention Mr. Seward's name at all. This lops off the most striking and suspicious feature of the coincidence as the case was reported. For while it was hardly strange that casual rumors should be floating about that Mr. Lincoln had been killed so soon after his visit to Richmond, the coupling of his name and Mr. Seward's in the same catastrophe, almost simultaneously with its actual occurrence, certainly looked a little suspicious.

Then as to the origin of the rumor at that time, Mr. Linneman says that, being reminded afterwards of his having reported that the President was assassinated on the very day when it occurred, he took considerable pains to trace the rumor to its source.

He got it from his wife, who got it from a neighbor, who heard it in the store of a well-known loyal gentleman at St. Cloud, who said he had heard it on his way from St. Paul.

This explanation, of course, acquits Mr Linneman of any foreknowledge of the event. Moreover, we are glad to be able to say, upon the testimony of a number of our leading citizens, who are well acquainted with Mr. Linneman, that he is the last man in the world to be a party to any treasonable conspiracy. Messrs. Mayo, Raguet, Marvin. and other good Republicans, called upon us yesterday to say that they have been acquainted with Mr. Linneman for several years, and have been in constant business intercourse with him; and they state that he is an honest, upright, straightforward man; and, although a Democrat in politics, a strictly loyal and patriotic citizen; and that his own explanation of the remark attributed to him may be entirely relied upon as the exact truth, from which they have never known him to deviate.

We have given thus much space to the exculpation of Mr. Linneman, with a view to atone to the fullest extent, for any injury which may have been done him by our publication yesterday.

Figure 28 a
St. Cloud Journal Press, April 30, 1891

St. Cloud Journal

ST. CLOUD, MINNESOTA, THURSDAY, APRIL 30, 1891.

THE ASSASSINATION OF PRESIDENT LINCOLN.

What J. H. Linnemann Says Regarding the St. Joseph Incident.

The people of this vicinity or rather those who resided here in 1865 are familiar with the report that the assassination of President Lincoln had been discussed at the little village of St. Joseph, in this county, before the event actually occurred. The Rev. J. H. Conwell, the chaplain of a colored regiment, and Mr. H. P. Bennett, of this city, are the persons to whom the statement was first made, on Friday evening, April 14, while the fact of the assassination was not known in St. Cloud until the following Sunday. The matter has been embodied in a book by Pere Chinequy, an ex-Catholic priest, in which the assassination is treated as the result of a conspiracy formed by the priests of Washington, who were supposed to be in close communication with the priests at St. Joseph. Mr. Linnemann was interviewed in St. Paul a few days since by a reporter of the Northwestern Chronicle (Catholic), which publishes the following in its last number:

"Mr. Linneman have you ever heard of the Rev. Mr. Conwell?" "Yes, I have met him. He was chaplain of one of the Minnesota regiments, I cannot recall which now." "You remember the assassination of President Lincoln and Mr. Conwell's statements in connection with it?" "Yes, that or some similar question has been often asked me since the assassination of Lincoln on Good Friday, 1865." "Please tell me as fully as you remember how the report originated that Lincoln's assassination was talked of in your neighborhood before it had taken place?"

"On the Wednesday before the assassination I was confined to my room with a bad cold. About noon my wife came into my room, brought me some soup and said the news is in the store that the President is dead. I asked her who told her. She said she did not notice, as the store was so full of people. The fact of it being near Easter accounts for the great number of people in the store. I made the remark that it might be on account of Richmond having been taken that the rumor was spread. On Thursday, while still in my sickroom, there drove up to my door two men. One of these is a Mr. Bennett, a gunsmith still living in St. Cloud, and he introduced me to the Rev. Mr. Conwell who accompanied him. Conwell asked me did I know an old Indian called Tanner, who lived out at Spunk Lake, eight miles from northwest of St. Joseph. Conwell was going to make claims for the soldiers. I learned afterwards that he got ten dollars from each soldier but the soldier never got any claims.

I asked the two men had they heard that President Lincoln was dead. Conwell said no, it might be another man by name of Lincoln. Later on I heard that Lincoln and Seward were assassinated. Seventeen days after the assassination, two weeks from Easter Monday, I was in St. Paul and on the corner of Fourth and St. Peter streets I heard my name mentioned. A man named Charles Clarke said to me: 'That is a nice story in the papers about you!' What is it, I asked? 'Oh, you killed the President,' he replied. I looked at the Pioneer newspaper. The report in that paper was not correct. It said that I mentioned assassination. I could not have used that word, for I did not know it at that time. I did not know enough of the English language to use such a word. My statement of the rumor was —Abraham Lincoln is dead.

"I also read the account in the Press. Several merchants came with me to the editor, but Mr. Wheelock would not retract in full. He did retract in some measure. The reason he would not re-

Figure 28 b
Continuation of article

St. Cloud Journal

ST. CLOUD, MINNESOTA, THURSDAY, APRIL 30, 1891.

tract in full was, because the story was calculated to reflect upon Democracy. Next day the Pioneer gave Conwell a very rough handling for his communications about the matter. I may add that the Pioneer was the Democratic paper and the Press the Republican paper. In St. Cloud and my neighborhood the people used to point me out, in fun, and say, 'There is the man who killed Abe Lincoln.'

"J. C. and H. C. Burbank had a general manager in their store, by name, A. B. Currey, a very generous man, who tells the story in this way: 'Conwell arrived in St. Cloud on Saturday night. On the following day, Easter Sunday, he went to the house of Leander Gordon to get a permit to preach in a Protestant church that day. On entering the house he took up the papers and saw that A. Lincoln and Seward had been assassinated. Then, said he, a coincidence has happened. We stopped, said he, at the house of Linnemann's, and he told the story that Lincoln was killed an hour or two before it happened. In the evening Conwell called a meeting to have the matter investigated. The meeting was held in Broker's hall. Conwell opened the meeting and told the story. When Conwell made his speech, Mr. Gordon said to some of the hearers at that meeting: 'How he lies; this morning he told a different tale; now he has improved upon it.'

"A. B. Currey asked me did I know how the story first started. On assuring him that I did not he said, 'I can tell you.' And he proceeded: You know a certain young woman from St.

Joe, mentioning her name. She is a strong Democrat. She came to this store lately and purchased some goods. She complained bitterly of the price and said this is a hard country to live in, as goods are so high and the Republican party are to blame. Our young salesman, who can put on the face of a preacher, said: 'Don't be afraid young lady, the President is dead.' He meant politically dead.

"The young lady came to my store and told my wife the story which originated in Burbank's store in St. Cloud. The girl's name was Mary Schroeder. She still lives in St. Joe. From that time until the first Cleveland campaign I heard no more about it. During that campaign two men came to my store and an oldish man said to me, 'Mr. Linnemann, do you know me yet?' He said, 'My name is Bennett. I am the gunsmith from St. Cloud. This is Mr. ———, from Boston.' I forget the latter's name. The Boston man said he came all the way from that city to get my testimony. I told Bennett and the Boston man that Conwell lied. And I added that they were going to make political capital out of it. The Boston man said no, that he was going to write a book. I told him the whole story as I tell you now. Then he wanted to make me take an oath. I refused and said: 'What do you think of me? Do you consider that I would swear for every man who comes along? I take an oath in court and only on occasions when necessary, but not at other times. My religion forbids me take an oath without necessity.'"

but a sample of the floral tributes showered upon the President in this City of Bloom. Miss B. sent from the old homestead enough white-throated red lilies to make a frieze a yard or more deep along one entire end of the Beach hotel parlors.

"In the afternoon I went with the B.s to see the parade. We went first to the Club and then for a better position to the corner of Tremont (along which street the procession passed) and Broadway. It should be called Oleander avenue, for it is lined on each side with tall oleander trees, with a double row in the centre, all just bursting into bloom; a

has never failed to destroy every squirrel in a 40 acre field, and there is no danger of other animals getting poisoned. But don't set the hired man or boys to do the business; let the farmer do it himself.   E. H. ATWOOD.

ST. CLOUD PERSONALS.

Wat Cooper, of St. Cloud, a former resident of this place, is circulating among friends here for a day or two.

Mrs. C. W. Cooper, who has been visiting her daughter, Mrs. L. S. Thomas, returned to her home in St. Cloud yesterday.

Mrs. A. Rosenbush, of St. Cloud,

Thursday, while still in my sickroom, there drove up to my door two men. One of these is a Mr. Bennett, a gunsmith still living in St. Cloud, and he introduced me to the Rev. Mr. Conwell who accompanied him. Conwell asked me did I know an old Indian called Tanner, who lived out at Spunk Lake, eight miles from northwest of St. Joseph. Conwell was going to make claims for the soldiers. I learned afterwards that he got ten dollars from each soldier but the soldier never got any claims.

I asked the two men had they heard that President Lincoln was dead. Conwell said no, it might be another man by name of Lincoln. Later on I heard that Lincoln and Seward were assassinated. Seventeen days after the assassination, two weeks from Easter Mon-

Actually, what he is quoted as saying is not correct. The paper he would have looked at would have been the *St Paul Press*, not the *Pioneer* and it would have been the April 27th edition, thirteen days after the assassination, not seventeen days, as the next day, the 28th, the *Press* reported that Linneman had come and talked to the paper about the story.

The introduction to "The Assassination of President Lincoln" read:

> The people of this vicinity or rather those who resided here in 1865 are familiar with the report that the assassination of President Lincoln had been discussed at the little village of St. Joseph, in this county, before the event actually occurred. The Rev. J. H. Conwell, the chaplain of a colored regiment, and Mr. H. P. Bennett, of this city, are the persons to whom the statement was first made, on Friday evening, April 14, while the fact of the assassination was not known in St. Cloud until the following Sunday.

Later in the *St Cloud Journal Press* piece however, Linneman was quoted as saying that the news of the President's death was first spoken about on Wednesday, April 12th, not Friday, as the introduction stated. Another obvious mistake is the statement in the article that Linneman spoke to Conwell and Bennett on Thursday, not on the Friday.

According to *Journal Press* piece, Linneman also stated that he couldn't have used the word, assassination, when he spoke to Conwell and Bennett because at the time he did not understand what it meant. Linneman had spent his childhood in Germany and had immigrated to America in 1848. He said "My statement of the rumor was - Abraham Lincoln is dead."

However, neither Rev. Conwell, nor Horace Bennett stated that they had reported what Linnemann had said, word for word. Linneman certainly was able to communicate in English and by this time, he had been in the United States for 17 years. He was able to speak to these men and he could have said to them in his own words that Lincoln had been murdered. Even if he hadn't known this word, they could have used the words, assassination or assassinated, in place of the words he did, therefore conveying the same meaning.

Stephen Moore also supported Bennett and Conwell, reporting that when he interviewed John Linneman for Charles Chiniquy in 1883, Linneman told him that he remembered well that he had told Bennett and Conwell that President Lincoln and the Secretary of State Seward were assassinated. This is contained in an affidavit made by Moore in 1892. As well, even when printing the partial apology on April 28th, the *St. Paul Press* reported that Linneman said Lincoln had been killed, not that he was dead.[28]

The *Press* was correct the first time when it stated that the news of the assassinations of Lincoln and Seward, reported before the deed had occurred, was so remarkable as to afford grounds for some very strong suspicions. There is substantial agreement between the accounts of Linneman and those of Conwell, Bennett and Moore. Where there is disagreement, it comes down to Linneman's word against theirs. Aside from being outnumbered, he was unwilling to swear to what happened, unlike the other three. Their statements, under oath, are down in black and white so there is no disputing what they said, whereas Linneman's version did not come first hand to the public in his own words but through the press or through persons such as Stephen Moore. For instance, did Linneman make the mistakes in the *Journal Press* article regarding when had he heard about the story concerning him, and which newspaper it was in, or was it the *Journal Press* and / or the *Chronicle* that made the mistakes?

In his letter to Charles Chiniquy, Moore commented on how difficult was to get a statement from John Linneman and the fact that he changed his story, first saying, according to Horace Bennett, that he heard the news of Lincoln's murder from a soldier and then telling Moore that he heard it from a woman whose identity he couldn't remember.[29] The *St. Paul Press*, as well as the *Journal Press*, reported that he heard it from his wife. *Fifty Years* quoted from a written declaration of Linneman in which he said he couldn't remember from whom he had heard of the assassination. Linneman had refused to swear to this declaration and had just signed it. Chiniquy stated that the reason Linneman could remember hearing this stunning news, yet not be able to say who told him about it, was that the priests who gave him the information cautioned him not to tell where it came from.

According to the 1891 *Journal Press* account, John Linneman quoted store manager, A. B. Currey, who reported that Leander Gordon had said that Rev. Conwell had lied about what had happened. According to this account, Linneman also stated that his wife had told him the news of the President's death but said she did not know who had told her because Linneman's store, where she evidently heard it, was so crowded at the time. A. B. Currey however, explained that in the store he managed, a young lady named Mary Schroeder had been told by a salesman in jest, that Lincoln was dead. According to the account, Ms. Schroeder then came to Linneman's store and told his wife this.

A question arises. Where did this piece of information: that Ms. Schroeder told this news to Linneman's wife, come from? Linneman wasn't there; he was home sick in bed. His wife didn't know who had told her the news. Presumably A. B. Currey wasn't in Linneman's store, as he had his own to run. Linneman took over the narrative at the point that Ms. Schroeder came to his store. Mary Schroeder would logically be the one to have given this information but Linneman did not say she had, although for example, he went to the trouble of making it clear what information Currey had supplied.

John Linneman's account contained the accusation that Rev. Conwell had lied. It also attempted to explain how the news of Lincoln's death was innocently started. Yet Linneman's statements are third hand, going through the *Chronicle* and the *Journal Press*. It is easy to deny things, call people liars and explain things away when it is done through newspapers. This is why court cases are not decided in the media but by having witnesses testify, under oath, as to what they saw and heard. Linneman's statement regarding when he heard the story about himself and what newspaper he read it in is clearly wrong. What other possible untruths were made in his statement, such as who he heard the news of Lincoln's murder from?

Charles Chiniquy's autobiography enjoyed immediate success when it was published in 1885 and it reported that Linneman had talked about Lincoln's murder before it had occurred. The Roman Catholic Church undoubtedly wished to cast doubt on the ex-priest's account. Like the case of Spink vs. Chiniquy and the role that Philomene Schwartz and Narcisse Terrien played in it, the Roman Catholic Church, as well as John Linneman, needed to ask the people who had played a part in Linneman's account to make a public statement about what had happened, preferably in the form of an affidavit. It was in the Church's interest, and Linneman's, to find Leander Gordon, Mary Schroeder, A. B. Currey and if possible, get them to comment if they had anything pertinent to say regarding Lincoln's death being heard of before it happened. At least two of the three, Gordon and Ms. Schroeder were still alive in 1885.

Chiniquy got sworn statements from Rev. Conwell, Horace Bennett and Stephen Moore regarding the suspiciously early news of Lincoln and Seward's assassinations in St. Joseph. If Gordon, Schroeder and Currey were not produced to publicly dispute what Conwell, Bennett and Moore said, as with the case of Spink vs. Chiniquy, it can be concluded that they couldn't have done so.

It could be asked, if the plan was to kill Vice President Johnson and General Grant, as well as Lincoln and Seward, why wasn't it rumoured in St. Joseph that all four had been killed? This actually shows the accuracy of the information that Linneman possessed in St. Joseph. It demonstrates that those that furnished the news, the priests, had a very good grasp of what was going to happen in Washington. The plan was for Johnson and Grant to be killed but the people in the know undoubtedly were aware that the Vice President's would-be assassins, George Atzerodt, and the person, or persons, who were to kill Grant, for various reasons, were probably not going to be as successful as the other two. If Grant and Johnson were killed, all the better but in the end, Booth and Payne were the ones that would be most likely to succeed. The killings would have to essentially be done simultaneously and the would-be assassins could only be at one place at a time. Though he almost succeeded in murdering Secretary of State William Seward, even the powerful young giant, Lewis Payne, ultimately failed in his task.

As Charles Chiniquy concluded in *Fifty Years*, there remains therefore clear and irrefutable evidence that some three to four hours before the attacks on Lincoln and Seward, their deaths were talked about by people, including one of the most prominent Catholics, in the solidly Roman Catholic town of St. Joseph. It is more evidence of Catholic involvement in the assassination of President Lincoln and the planned attempts on the lives of other high government officials.[30]

THE CONSPIRATORS

Mrs. SURRATT's witnesses were the first called on the part of the defence, and in two instances gave evidence damaging to her. In one instance the defendant's counsel appears to have been picked up by a witness, who alleges that the attorney, Mr. AIKEN, made corrupt proposals to him, under the impression that he could be bought up. This announcement created quite a stir in the assembly, and completely nonplussed the counsel.

New York Times May 26,1865 Page 1

The WITNESS. If the Court will allow me, I should like to tell the whole conversation. I met Mr Aiken at the Metropolitan Hotel on Saturday evening last, I think. He asked me to take a drink. I went up and drank with him. He then said, "I am going to have you as a witness in this case." He asked me to sit down on a sofa and have some conversation. I said no, it would not look well for me to be sitting there, but I would go outside and take a walk. When we went outside, the first question Mr. Aiken put to me was whether I was a Catholic. I said I was not. We walked along, and he

National Intelligencer May 27,1865 Page3

Chapter 7
Mary Surratt

While Abraham Lincoln was fighting for his life that fateful April evening, his assailant was on horseback, riding for his. John Wilkes Booth headed south toward Maryland across the Navy Yard bridge, giving his correct name to the sentry, who hadn't yet heard what he had done and therefore let him pass, (see Figure 29). Thus the most important man-hunt in U.S. history began. The men initially wanted were Booth and David Herold but this number quickly grew. Almost immediately, government agents also began searching for John Surratt. After Booth, his name was the second one listed on federal government wanted posters but he had fled north to Canada (see figure 30). The investigation soon led to the home he shared with his mother Mary, his sister and others. They were arrested a few days later, along with Lewis Payne, who happened to come to their door just as they were about to be taken to jail. John Surratt, initially hidden by officials of the Roman Catholic Church in Quebec, was finally captured in Egypt more than a year and a half after Lincoln's murder.[1]

After witnessing the carnage caused by Payne at the Seward household, Herold, evidently having lost his nerve, did not try to join Atzerodt in the planned attack on the Vice-President. Crossing the Navy Yard Bridge, he rode after Booth instead. Linking up on the road, they continued on horseback to Surrattsville, an establishment consisting of a tavern and farm that the owner, Mary Surratt, had rented out. There they picked up provisions that had been made ready for them, including a gun and whiskey. Booth, whose left leg may have been broken from his jump to the stage at the

Figure 29
Navy Yard Bridge

Library of Congress Prints and Photographs Division, LC-USZ62-124280

Figure 30
Lincoln assassination wanted poster, U.S. War Department

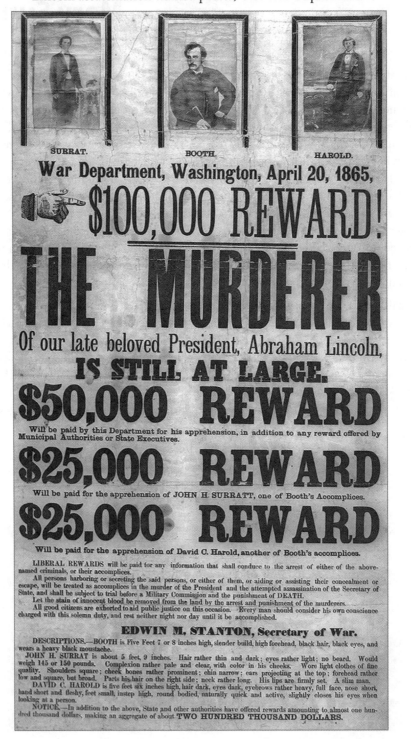

Library of Congress, Prints & Photographs Division, LC-USZ62-11193

theater, was in great pain. Seeking medical aid, they proceeded to Dr. Samuel Mudd's home, northeast of Bryantown, Maryland, arriving around dawn. After Dr. Mudd set his leg, Booth and Herold stayed at the doctor's house until the afternoon.

Helped by Confederate sympathizers to keep a low profile, they continued southward, finally crossing the Potomac River into Virginia on April 21st. The U.S. forces that had been relentlessly combing the countryside finally picked up their trail and found the pair on the farm of Richard Garrett, a few miles from Port Royal, Virginia, on April 26. Cornered in a barn, Herold surrendered, but Booth refused to give himself up. The President's killer was shot by a soldier, disobeying a government order to take him alive. Booth died a few hours later.[2]

Thus Herold was one of the last conspirators to be arrested and brought back to Washington to face trial in 1865. He joined seven others who were tried that summer for conspiring to murder Abraham Lincoln and other high-ranking government officials. The eight were: Herold, Lewis Payne, George Atzerodt, Mary Surratt, Michael O'Laughlin, Samuel Arnold, Samuel Mudd and Edward Spangler. At the conclusion of their trial they were all found guilty. Herold, Payne, Atzerodt and Mary Surratt were hung. O'Laughlin, Arnold, Mudd and Spangler received various prison terms. The official court reporter, Benn Pitman, helped to record the testimony given before the military commission and he later published it in book form.

John Surratt stood trial two years later, in 1867. Despite the weight of evidence against him however, the jury couldn't agree on a verdict and the case against him was eventually dismissed.[3] Were these conspirators truly guilty? The evidence shows that all the defendants tried before the military commission, as well as John Surratt, were certainly guilty of at least conspiring in a plan to abduct Lincoln, if not murder him. Of those culpable, did any of them have any association with the Catholic Church? According to Charles Chiniquy all the conspirators were Catholics. He stated:

> There is a fact to which the American people have not yet given a sufficient attention. It is that, without a single exception, the conspirators were Roman Catholics. The learned and great patriot, General Baker, in his admirable report, struck and bewildered by that strange, mysterious and portentous fact, said: 'I mention, as an exceptional and remarkable fact, that every conspirator, in custody, is by education a Catholic.'

> But those words which, if well understood by the United States, would have thrown so much light on the true causes of their untold and unspeakable disasters, fell as if on the ears of deaf men. Very few, if any, paid attention to them. As General Baker says, all the conspirators were attending Catholic Church services and were educated Roman Catholics. It is true that some of them, as Atzeroth, Payne and Harold, asked for Protestant ministers, when they were to be hung. But they had been considered, till then, as converts to Romanism.[4]

Charles Chiniquy also stated:

> the plot of the assassination of Lincoln was matured, if not started, in the house of Mary Surratt, No. 561 H Street, Washington City, D. C. But who

were living in that house, and who were visiting that family? The legal answer says:"The most devoted Catholics in the city!" The sworn testimonies show more than that. They show that it was the common rendezvous of the priests of Washington…What does the presence of so many priests, in that house, reveal to the world? No man of common sense, who knows anything about the priests of Rome, can entertain any doubt that, not only they knew all that was going on inside those walls, but that they were the advisers, the counselors, the very soul of that infernal plot.

No one, if he is not an idiot, will think and say that those priests, who were the personal friends and the father confessors of Booth, John Surratt, Mrs. and Misses Surratt, could be constantly there without knowing what was going on, particularly when we know that every one of those priests, was a rabid rebel at heart. Every one of those priests, knowing that his infallible Pope had called Jeff Davis his dear son, and had taken the Southern Confederacy under his protection, was bound to believe that the most holy thing a man could do, was to fight for the Southern cause, by destroying those who were its enemies.

In his 1867 book, *History of the United States Secret Service*, General Lafayette C. Baker did indeed publish what Charles Chiniquy said he did. Baker however, was actually quoting what newspaper reporter George Alfred Townsend's wrote in his short volume, *The Life, Crime, And Capture Of John Wilkes Booth* (1865). General Baker acknowledged in one section of his book that he was reproducing what others had penned stating, "I shall freely quote from sketches written at the time by others" and "With this general explanation, there will be no further reference to the extracts; they will be indicated by their connection and the tone of narrative, and quite accurate in detail." As Baker did not identify the writers, it is possible to see how Charles Chiniquy could have made the mistake of thinking that General Baker himself was making the statements. Baker did however, vouch for the accuracy of those he had quoted.[5]

The U.S. government, with Andrew Johnson newly inaugurated as President, decided that the conspirators would be tried before a military tribunal, instead of a civil court, because the United States was, in reality, still at war when Abraham Lincoln was assassinated. Although a significant part of the Southern military had laid down their arms, large rebel forces remained in the field and some continued to fight. Confederate Generals Joseph Johnston and Kirby Smith, though facing powerful Union armies, were still at large with their troops in the South. The last battle of the Civil War was actually fought on May 13 at Palmito Hills, Texas by soldiers unaware of Lee's surrender more than a month earlier. The crew of the Confederate warship, Shenandoah, also uninformed of the general collapse of the Southern government, continued to attack and harass the U.S. whaling fleet along the Pacific coast through the spring and summer of 1865. It wasn't until August of 1866 that President Johnson proclaimed the insurrection to be at an end in the last of the Secessionist states, Texas.

In addition, President Lincoln, the commander-in-chief of the army and navy, had been murdered in the heavily fortified city that was his military headquarters, with a military governor and with the exception of John Surratt, who was still at large, all the conspirators had been captured by military personnel, Booth being killed by one of the soldiers that had been pursuing him.[6]

After Mary Surratt was found guilty of being part of the conspiracy to murder America's greatest President, she received the distinction of being the very first woman ever to be executed by the United States government. As Charles Chiniquy pointed out in *Fifty Years*, this female pioneer of capital crime also happened to be a very devout Catholic. Although apologists have tried to say she was innocent, or at the least not culpable enough to been given the death penalty, her guilt is as clear to unbiased persons reading the account of her trial as the need to critically examine the beliefs that governed her actions. Historians who have closely studied the evidence concerning this conspiracy have come to the same conclusion of her guilt in more recent books. As this and the next two chapters will show, she was certainly not the only Roman Catholic to be involved in the treasonous plot.

Mary Surratt had lived for years in Surrattsville, or John Surratts, named for her late husband, who had run a farm and tavern there. Surrattsville is now Clinton, Maryland. After her spouse passed away, she leased the property to John Lloyd, a former Washington police officer, in the fall of 1864. With her son John and daughter Anna, Mrs. Surratt moved into Washington, where she opened a boarding house at 541 H Street.[7]

John Lloyd was one of the witnesses the government called to testify against her at the trial of the conspirators. According to the court record, he stated that five or six weeks before the assassination, John Surratt, David Herold and George Atzerodt came to the tavern he had been renting from Mary Surratt and left some items, including two guns and some ammunition. Lloyd told them he didn't want the items stored there but John Surratt assured him that they would only be in place for a few days.

Three days before the assassination, on Tuesday, April 11th, John Lloyd stated that he met Mrs. Surratt on the road from Surrattsville to Washington at a place called Uniontown. At the time of the meeting, she asked him to get the "shooting irons" ready, as they would soon be needed.[8]

This meeting was confirmed by the main prosecution witness against Mary Surratt, another of her tenants, Louis Weichmann. Weichmann had been a school mate of John Surratt when they both attended St. Charles College, a Catholic educational institution in Maryland. At the time of the assassination, Weichmann roomed at the Surratt boarding house and worked in Washington as a clerk in the office of the General Hoffman, Commissary General of prisoners. On April 11th, he drove his landlady to Surrattsville and back again to Washington. Weichmann testified that when they met John Lloyd at Uniontown, Lloyd and Mary Surratt spoke to each other but he said he did not heard the conversation because Mrs. Surratt whispered into Lloyd's ear.[9]

John Lloyd testified that on the day of the assassination, Mrs. Surratt came to the tavern in the mid-afternoon and again asked him about the guns, saying someone would want them that night. Lloyd had been away and he didn't get back to the establishment until about 5 p.m. but Mary Surratt was still there when he arrived. He said that when he saw her there, she gave him an object wrapped in a piece of paper which he later found to be a field-glass, or set of binoculars. She also told him to get two bottles of whiskey ready for the people that would come for them.

According to Lloyd, Booth and Herold came to the tavern that evening around midnight. Herold came in and told him to get the things immediately, while Booth, whom he had never met, stayed outside. The way Herold spoke made Lloyd believe they expected that he would have had the guns and other items ready. He gave Herold a gun, whiskey and the field-glass, as Mrs. Surratt had instructed. Booth did not want a gun so Lloyd held on to the second one.[10]

In an apparent attempt to discredit Lloyd, Mary Surratt's defence lawyers called six witnesses who testified that he had been drunk on the day of the assassination. None of them testified that his being drunk would have necessarily affected his memory however, and two of them in fact, admitted to drinking that day with Lloyd.[11] No one testified that Lloyd had been drinking constantly though. As well, no one testified that Lloyd had been drinking constantly. The only period that John Lloyd testified about where it was specifically alleged that he had been drinking was the afternoon of April 14th and other witnesses corroborated his testimony for this time.

Evidence was presented to show that Mrs. Surratt had a legitimate reason to go to Surrattsville: that being an attempt to settle a land deal. 12 There was no testimony provided however, to show that she couldn't have transacted her business, for instance, the day after the one planned for the assassination. She certainly could have attempted to use this excuse to go to Surrattsville on this day, as a cover for her part in the conspiracy though.

Lloyd's sister-in-law, Emma Offutt, a witness for both the prosecution and the defence, supported John Lloyd. She testified that on the day of the assassination, she saw Mary Surratt at Surrattsville before Lloyd arrived. According to Mrs. Offutt, Mrs. Surratt gave her a package that she wished to stay at the tavern. Offutt stated:

> That was about half-past 5 o'clock, and before Mr. Lloyd came in. After that I saw the package lying on the sofa in the parlor. Shortly afterward Mr. Lloyd came in. When I saw Mrs. Surratt and Mr. Lloyd talking together at the buggy in the yard, I was in and out all the time. I did not see Mr. Lloyd go into the parlor, but I saw him on the piazza, and I think from that that he must have gone into the parlor. He had a package in his hand, but I did not see Mrs. Surratt give it to him. After the package was handed to me, it might have been taken by Mrs. Surratt and handed to Lloyd, but I did not see her give it to him.[13]

Louis Weichmann, who had driven the buggy for Mary Surratt that day as well, confirmed that she had brought two packages to Surrattsville. One was the package of papers that pertained to her land deal. He did not say what was in the other one but it undoubtedly was the package that Lloyd and Emma Offutt both testified about, the one that held the field-glass.[14] Mrs. Surratt had left the package containing the binoculars at Lloyd's place so even if she had not spoken to him, it would be there so Herold and Booth could ask for it.

No witness contradicted John Lloyd on any material point in his testimony. Thus, court testimony that was not challenged, clearly shows that Mary Surratt took an active part in providing and readying provisions to assist the escape of President Lincoln's assassin.

Another problem for Mrs. Surratt was her close association with actual and would be murderers. Besides being a major meeting place for Confederate spies and couriers, her house was a gathering place for the assassination conspirators as well. President Andrew Johnson called it "the nest that hatched the egg" (see Figure 31).[15]

The Surratts had owned the house in Washington since 1853. John Surratt Sr. died in 1862 and his widow did not move into the city until late 1864. Roy Chamlee commented, "From the standpoint of economics, there was no reason for Mary Surratt to move to Washington. Due to the scarcity of rooms in the city during the war, the house on H Street could be profitably rented." He also stated:

> John Wilkes Booth visited the Surrattsville area in the fall of 1864, ostensibly inquiring about farms. About that time Mrs. Surratt first proposed the move to Washington. During his first trip to Lower Maryland, Booth met John

Figure 31
Mary Surratt Boarding House

Library of Congress, Brady-Handy Collection, LC-USZ62-92592

Surratt and began an active enlistment of conspirators. A safe, convenient rendezvous in Washington was absolutely necessary for the operation Booth was concocting. Mrs. Surratt's house served perfectly. John Surratt later confessed that he had been a Confederate blockade-runner for more than three years when they moved to Washington and that after the move his activities increased.

It seems that one of the people Booth recruited was Mary Surratt, who moved in Washington so her home could be used as the headquarters / safe house for those involved in the conspiracy. One of the conspirators Mrs. Surratt entertained was Lewis Payne. According to Louis Weichmann, sometime in March, 1865, Payne came to the Surratt house. He gave his name as Wood and he asked for John Surratt. Surratt was not at home, so he asked for his mother. Weichmann, who had not met Payne before, introduced him to his landlady. Payne was fed supper in Weichmann's room and given a bed in the attic. Claiming to be a Baptist preacher, Payne visited the Surratt's house several times. Weichmann reported that he had heard no explanation why a Baptist preacher would be staying with the Surratt's, who were Catholics.[16] Court testimony showed that when he visited, Lewis Payne spent time with John Surratt. Payne was captured when he came to the Surratt house a few days after he attempted to kill Secretary of State Seward.

Weichmann stated that George Atzerodt had been to the Surratt house some 10 or 15 times. Other witnesses supported Weichmann regarding the numerous visits by various conspirators. [17] As well, Weichmann testified that on March 17th, 1865, a woman named Mrs. Slater came and stayed at the Surratt's house overnight. Later that month, John Surratt drove Mrs. Slater to Richmond, Virginia. Afterwards, Mary Surratt told Weichmann that the woman was either a blockade runner or a bearer of dispatches for the Confederates.

Louis Weichmann also declared that on about January 15th, 1865, while walking down Seventh Street in Washington with John Surratt, they met an old friend of Surratt's, Dr. Samuel Mudd, who was with John Wilkes Booth. After introductions, they went to Booth's room in the National Hotel. During their time there, Dr. Mudd went out into the passageway for private conversation with Booth and John Surratt. Mudd and Booth apologized afterwards, saying they had been talking about the sale of the doctor's farm to Booth. According to Weichmann, after this meeting, Booth called on the Surratt home frequently, having private conversations with John Surratt, or Mary Surratt, if her son was not in.[18]

Later that year, on the 2nd of April, Mrs. Surratt sent an invitation to Booth, via Weichmann, to see her on private business and the actor came to the Surratt home that night. On other occasions, Weichmann testified that "Mrs. Surratt would sometimes leave the parlor on being asked by Booth to spare him a word. She would then go into the passage and talk with him. These conversations would not, generally, occupy more than five or eight minutes."[19]

He testified that on the 11th of April, Mrs. Surratt sent him to Booth's hotel to get his buggy to take to Surrattsville. Saying he had sold it, Booth gave Louis Weichmann ten dollars to hire one instead. On the day of the assassination, Weichmann drove his landlady to Surrattsville in the afternoon, one of her errands being to deliver the field-glass to Lloyd, which was ultimately meant for Booth. As he approached the Surratt front door, before they left on this trip, Weichmann stated that he saw Booth in the parlor in conversation with Mrs. Surratt. Booth departed three or four minutes later and then Weichmann and Mary Surratt left.[20]

Why would Mrs. Surratt expect Booth to lend her his buggy and why did he give ten dollars to hire one, since his was sold? What did he owe her, unless she was doing something for him? Why the constant private discussions with Booth, the man who would soon be the murderer of President Lincoln, the final one taking place on the day of the assassination? Why didn't Mrs. Surratt give Booth the field-glass before she left for Surrattsville? They evidently were making final preparations for Booth's escape after his assassination of Abraham Lincoln. He had just given the binoculars to her to convey to the countryside, the last of the supplies he would need as he fled.

Booth's flight immediately after the murder would have to have be swift and he couldn't be burdened down with provisions. Once out of the city, he could afford to take more time to get away and would then need the supplies that Mrs. Surratt helped arrange for him. Is it logical to believe that having such close social intercourse with these men, Mary Surratt did not know what was going on in her house, the place where such a cruel conspiracy was "hatched"?

Another major difficulty for Mary Surratt's apologists is her actions after the assassination. Shortly before midnight on April 17th, three days after President Lincoln was shot, military personnel came to her door and arrested her and everyone in the house. According to the testimony of Major H. W. Smith, who was in charge of the force that took control of the home, Mrs. Surratt's actions were suspicious from the start.

At the door, Mrs. Surratt identified herself as the widow of John H. Surratt and mother of John H. Surratt. Smith stated that he was there to arrest her along with everyone else in the house and take them to General Auger's headquarters. He testified that, "No inquiry whatever was made as to the cause of the arrest."[21]

Detectives first came to the Surratt home in the early morning hours of April 15th, so Mary Surratt did know that she and the other inhabitants might be of interest to the authorities. [22] This still doesn't explain why Mrs. Surratt didn't ask why they were being arrested although she was supposed to an innocent Christian woman. Why she allowed herself and her household be arrested without question? She was certainly not frightened into silence by the appearance of the soldiers. The most natural thing for her to do would be to ask why the authorities were at her door and the reason she was being arrested, yet she was silent. Mary Surratt evidently knew why she was being arrested and this is why she said nothing, thereby unconsciously confirming her guilt.

While the occupants of the house were in the parlor, readying themselves to go to military headquarters, Lewis Payne, in hiding since his attempt to kill the Secretary Seward, came to the door. According to Major Smith, when he was questioned,

Payne said he had come to dig a gutter at the request of Mary Surratt. He was invited inside and immediately arrested. He was wearing workman's clothing which was different from what he normally wore. He was carrying a pick-axe and had a shirtsleeve as a make-shift hat on his head.

Smith then asked Mary Surratt to come near the door where Payne was and asked her, "Do you know this man, and did you hire him to come and dig a gutter for you?" Smith stated that Payne was standing three paces from Mrs. Surratt and in full view of her. She answered, raising her right hand, "Before God, sir, I do not know this man, and have never seen him, and I did not hire him to dig a gutter for me."[23]

He also reported that a short time afterward, apparently after Major Smith announced the carriage was ready to take Mrs. Surratt to headquarters, she asked that she be allowed to pray for a minute or so. Receiving permission, she knelt down to do so in the presence of the others.

What was Payne, the man who had attempted to murder the U. S. Secretary of State a few days earlier doing at the door of a supposedly innocent woman, asking for her? Though court testimony showed that Payne had on different clothing than normal that night, no witness testified that his facial features had been changed in any way. Mrs. Surratt's defence produced a number of witnesses who stated that she had poor eyesight. They did not however, claim that she couldn't see at all. Some stated that at times she had failed to recognize people she knew but no one claimed that she was unable to recognize people at all. She had certainly made Payne's acquaintance and had talked to him. In fact, Louis Weichmann testified that Mrs. Surratt had once remarked that Payne was a great looking Baptist preacher. [24] Clearly she knew what he looked like and could recognize him. Mary Surratt's only defence, therefore, was that she had just looked at him casually and not closely enough to correctly identify him.

This explanation is extremely hard to believe. The question of whether she knew this man, coming as it did from the very officer that had placed her and her household under arrest, should have focused her attention on telling truthfully and accurately if she knew him or not. Her actions of raising her right hand and stating, "before God, sir I do not know this man" shows that she had not glanced at him casually. Her declaration is a definite, positive statement, no glib, off the cuff answer, regarding something she said she was very sure about.

A number of witnesses, including no less than five Catholic priests, came before the military commission and testified that she was in their estimation, an honourable Christian woman. If the words "Before God" mean anything to her, she would not state this regarding something she did not know. It would be sacrilege to invoke God's name to solemnly, positively, affirm something that one was not sure of. If her words are taken at face value, as they have to be taken, the solemn affirmation of a statement of fact, especially by a person of "faith", then Mary Surratt lied about not knowing Lewis Payne. The motive, of course was simple. The statement was made to show her innocence but instead it served to confirm her guilt. Charles Chiniquy commented:

> She had received the communion just two or three days before that public perjury. Just a moment after making it, the officer ordered her to step out into

the carriage. Before doing it, she asked permission to kneel down and pray; which was granted. (page 123)

I ask it from any man of common sense, could Jeff Davis have imparted such a religious calm, and self-possession to that woman, when her hands were just reddened with the blood of the President, and she was on her way to trial!

No! such *sang froid*, such calm in that soul, in such a terrible and solemn hour, could only come from the teachings of those Jesuits who, for more than six months, were in her house, showing her a crown of eternal glory, if she would help to kill the monster apostate-- Lincoln"[25]

Mrs. Surratt did attend mass the day before the assassination and the evidence presented at the trial clearly shows that Mary Surratt, devout daughter of the Catholic Church, was part of the conspiracy that took the life of the great emancipator, Abraham Lincoln. In her 2008 book, *The Assassin's Accomplice: Mary Surratt and the Plot to Kill Abraham Lincoln*, academic Kate Clifford Larson asked a very good question,"Why did Mary willingly participate in such a vicious plot, risking her life and the lives of her children? Her strong Southern sympathies do not adequately explain her dangerous level of involvement." Charles Chiniquy provides an explanation, pointing out that her Catholic beliefs, as well as the influence of the Jesuits and other priests that met in her house, pulled her into the conspiracy.

Ignoring evidence as well as making errors of fact, her lawyers said that Mrs. Surratt was guilty of committing only innocent acts. They stated, "She may have delivered a message to Lloyd -- so have a hundred others" but the prosecution was not arguing that she was guilty because she had delivered a message of course.[26] It was the content of the communication was vital: that being to have guns and whiskey ready for the President's assassins as they fled.

Her defence asserted that the "innocent" actions of Mrs. Surratt that they listed were established "*Solely* by the testimony of Louis J. Weichmann and John M. Lloyd" but the last act they mentioned in court, the non-recognition of Payne, wasn't proven "solely" by the testimony of these two.[27] Neither of them testified about Mary Surratt not recognizing Payne because they weren't there at the time.

To discredit Weichmann's testimony, Mary Surratt's lawyers brought up the message he took to Booth. They stated:

'Do you remember,' the question was asked him, 'early in the month of April, of Mrs. Surratt having sent for you and asking you to give Mr. Booth notice that she wished to see him?' Weichmann in his reply stated that she did; that it was on the 2d of April, and that he found in Mr. Booth's room John McCullough, the actor, when he delivered the message. One of two things to which he swears in this statement can not be true: 1. That he met John McCullough in Booth's room for we have McCullough's sworn statement that at that time he was not in the city of Washington, and if, when he delivered the message to Booth, McCullough was in the room, it could not have been on the 2d of April.

The defence provided a statement made by McCullough in June, 1865 in which he swore that he had not been in the capital since March 26 of the same year and he did not recall meeting anyone named Weichmann. They contended that if Weichmann "can be so mistaken about those facts, may he not be in regard to the whole transaction?"[28]

In his book, *Lincoln's Assassins* though, Roy Chamlee declared that McCullough, a close associate of Booth, actually knew enough about the conspiracy that he could have saved Lincoln's life had he had alerted the authorities in time. The actor fled to Canada before he could be questioned but if his role had been properly investigated, Chamlee asserted that he would have probably have been given a prison term.

Weichmann did make mistakes regarding dates but defence lawyers at the trial of the conspirators and the trial of John Surratt were unable to discredit him, and other witnesses, as well as even one of the conspirators, supported his testimony on a number of points.[29]

What the defence believed discredited Lloyd testimony was that he could not swear positively to hearing Mrs. Surratt mention "shooting irons" when they met at Uniontown, Tuesday, April 11th.[30] Lloyd stated that he was confident that Mrs. Surratt spoke of the shooting irons, though he was not as positive about the first time. At the first meeting, they had a very hasty conversation so it is understandable that he was not so positive about what was said. Although the last conversation would have been fresher in Lloyd's mind, the defence complained that he was drunk at the time, forgetting that two of their witnesses who said Lloyd was intoxicated, were drunk themselves for part, if not all of the time period they testified about.

On the subject of the Friday, April 14th meeting between Lloyd and Mary Surratt however, historian Edward Steers Jr. reported that conspirator George Atzerodt provided support for Lloyd. In his 2001 book, *Blood On The Moon*, Steers reported that while in prison, Atzerodt confessed that "Booth told me that Mrs. Surratt went to Surrattsville to get out the guns (two carbines) which had been taken to that place by Herold. This was Friday."[31]

Apparently Mary Surratt's defence counsel believed that Louis Weichmann and John Lloyd were such a danger to their client that their credibility had to be destroyed. For this reason and because some of their most damaging statements couldn't be directly contradicted, they needed to show they had a motive to lie in court. The defence therefore advanced the argument that if there was a conspiracy to murder the President and others, then Weichmann and Lloyd had actually been part of it. They asserted that by putting all blame they could on Mrs. Surratt, the pair gave the prosecution a victim that could be offered up to appease the wrath of the American people and save themselves in the process.

There obviously was a conspiracy; eight people were convicted for their part in it. Were Weichmann and Lloyd part of the plot or were they just innocent people who didn't know what was going on around them? The defence claimed that Mary Surratt was an innocent person who was in the wrong place at the wrong time. Couldn't the same be said for these two?

If they had lied under oath, it would be reasonable to believe the motivation was to escape prosecution. If they were part of the conspiracy however, it doesn't make Mrs. Surratt innocent, as her guilt wasn't proven by only their testimony. Her apologists still have to explain, among other things, her delivery of the field-glass to Surrattsville and her actions on the night when Payne came to her house.

Her defence team was finally reduced to arguing that no true American woman could have been involved in this criminal conspiracy. They finally were correct when they asserted that no genuine daughter of the land of liberty could have played a part in such a crime.

Even if Mrs. Surratt could be shown to be innocent and Weichmann and Lloyd guilty, it still wouldn't help the cause of the Catholic Church because one Catholic conspirator would be exchanged for one, and possibly, two more. Weichmann was a Catholic at this time and Charles Chiniquy, for one, asserted that Lloyd was one too.[32] If they are counted amongst the plotters and Mrs. Surratt continues to be considered guilty, as the evidence shows she clearly was, then the number of conspirators that can be counted as Catholics increases by as much as two.

Regarding the Catholic priests who were character witnesses for the defendant, as noted earlier, Roy Chamlee Jr., commented on how this gave the impression that Mary Surratt was trying to hide behind her Church. This religious body was evidently trying to do more for her than this, according to Captain George Cottingham, who had held John Lloyd in custody and had successfully interrogated him. He testified that before the trial, defence lawyer Frederick Aiken took him aside and told him he wished to call him as a witness. The first question he then asked Cottingham was whether he was a Catholic (see the start of this chapter: opposite page). The *New York Times* called it a corrupt proposal and indeed, what would be the possible reason for Aiken to tell Cottingham he was thinking of calling him as a witness and then ask him if he was a Catholic, unless there was a plan to make a corrupt proposal and tamper with this potential witness, via his beliefs?

There apparently is other evidence that the Church of Rome tried to interfere with the process of justice at the trial of the conspirators. In *Lincoln's Assassins*, Chamlee stated,

> Another incident known to the War Department, but not revealed to the public, involved Father N. D. Young, pastor of St. Dominic's. The priest testified on behalf of Mrs. Surratt but also seemed concerned about John Lloyd, one of the witnesses against her. On May 12, just as the trial started, he requested permission to give spiritual comfort to Lloyd in Old Capital Prison. The Government did not allow him or any other visitor to see the prisoners at that time. But the timing of his request raised questions – it was the day before Lloyd was to testify against Mrs. Surratt. Father Young made no effort to visit Mrs. Surratt.[33]

In the end, as the evidence clearly showed, the judges ruled correctly and Mary Surratt, devoted daughter of the Church, received the due reward for her role in the conspiracy to murder the great Abraham Lincoln as part of a larger plan to resurrect the Confederacy and destroy the United States.

WASHINGTON.

Special Dispatches to the New-York Times.

WASHINGTON, Thursday, Sept. 24.

THE DISCHARGE OF SURRATT.

The discharge of SURRATT from custody through the technicalities of the law and a flaw in the indictment, the particulars of which are given elsewhere, causes much surprise and comment here to-night. The case had dragged along to such an extent that a conviction was not expected, but the formality of another trial upon the charge of conspiracy, was considered certain, which, if fruitless, was expected to be the end of the case. SURRATT, one of the conspirators in the most hellish assassination in the world's history, now walks the streets of the city where the deed was committed, as free as an innocent child, and is the special pet of those who cherish revenge and hatred against the Government.

New York Times Sept 25, 1868 Page 4

Chapter 8

John Surratt

As the search intensified for the conspirators immediately after the assassination of the President, government wanted posters appeared, featuring John Surratt prominently. The U.S. authorities very much wanted Mary Surratt's son but he couldn't be found. In the months after the President's murder, he was in Canada, hidden by Roman Catholic priests while his mother was being tried and then ultimately executed in the nation's capital.

In September, 1865, he left Canadian soil. Boarding a ship to Liverpool, England, he stayed in the Catholic Church of the Holy Cross there. From this city, he stole through Europe, reportedly being received in Roman Catholic institutions until he ended up as part of the Pontifical Zouaves in the Papal States.

A friend from his school days, Henry St. Marie, discovered him there in the Papal guard during the spring of 1866 and alerted the U.S. government. Surratt was arrested by the Papal authorities but then managed to, or was allowed to, escape.[1] He was finally captured by a U.S. government agent in Egypt and brought back to Washington to face trial in the summer of 1867 for his part in the conspiracy to murder President Lincoln.

John Surratt was a Roman Catholic who had attended the Catholic educational institution, St. Charles College, with Louis Weichmann. His sister Anna testified she believed that her brother had been in attendance there for three scholastic years but had not been training for the priesthood. Weichmann told the military commission in 1865 that they both had been divinity students. Several Catholic accounts also confirm Weichmann's statement. Neither of them finished their studies.[2]

John Surratt was tried before Judge George P. Fisher and a jury in the Supreme Court of the District of Columbia. Although she had been dead for some two years, Surratt's defence lawyers tried to put Mary Surratt on trial as well and prove her innocence in addition to her son's. Their reason for doing so apparently was to provide an explanation for their client's behavior after the assassination. His actions had been those of a guilty man, fugitively moving from one hiding place to another until he was finally caught. The defence evidently believed that if they could show Mary Surratt to be an innocent woman who had been executed to appease a public crying for blood, then they could argue that John Surratt's flight and time in hiding was reasonable and he was not seeking to avoid justice but injustice. The problem with that is that the evidence against her clearly shows her guilt and no re-presentation of it could make any difference.

John Surratt's lawyer, R.T. Merrick, commented on the military trial:

> Says the district attorney, Surratt has confessed his guilt by flight--flight from a mother over whose head was impending such a sad fate. Gentlemen of the

jury, he knew not of her condition until she was executed, or about that time; and when he got the information he was restrained by force from coming. This we were ready to prove. Fly! What else could he do? Suspicion of guilt in that day was certainty of conviction. Military commissions were organized, not to try, but to condemn. Who of you would not have fled if a reward had been offered for your head? He saw his name in the papers while in Canada, and he fled. Of course he fled. He went from a blazing country. He fled not from justice, but from lawlessness. He fled not from trial, but from conviction and oppression. Suppose he had been here, could he have had a trial? Why, guilty or innocent, he would have been hung. Law was dead in the country. The iron hand of power had suppressed judicial authority. Tyranny rode wild in the land. No man was safe with a price on his head. To tell me that to flee under such circumstances was confession is to tell me that which is too absurd to merit the dignity of reply.[3]

According to Surratt's defence team's assertions therefore, any defendant's appearance before the military commission would have guaranteed his or her death. Eight people were tried by the military commission however, and four of them, Michael O'Laughlin, Edward Spangler, Samuel Arnold and Dr Samuel Mudd, were not executed but given prison sentences. Of these, O'Laughlin died of yellow fever in prison and the rest were released after serving only four years.

In addition, others arrested were not charged. Thomas A. Jones, a member of the Confederate underground in southern Maryland, helped Booth and Herold across the Potomac River. Jones was taken into custody but after a short incarceration was set free. Samuel Cox, Jones' superior in the Confederate services, helped Booth and Herold and he was also arrested and then let go.

As well, Louis Weichmann testified that John Surratt had asked the woman who kept the Herndon House, a Washington hotel, if a woman named Miss Anne Ward had talked to her about reserving a room for a delicate gentleman. Even though the "delicate gentleman" turned out to be the hulking Louis Payne, Miss Ward was not charged.[4] In his informative 1997 book, *His Name Is Still Mudd*, Edward Steers Jr. showed that with what is now known about his activities, Samuel Mudd was fortunate to get a jail sentence instead of the death penalty.

Arrest at this time therefore did not guarantee a trial and prosecution before the military commission did not guarantee one's death. Mary Surratt assuredly was not an innocent woman, executed to appease a public howling for blood but a guilty one who got what she deserved.

The prosecution alleged that John Surratt was part of the conspiracy to murder Lincoln. His defence team denied this but admitted, amazingly, that Surratt had been part of a conspiracy to kidnap the President. Joseph Bradley Sr. declared:

> You see the prosecution have proved not only by McMillen, but by this admission of Surratt's, that he was in the former conspiracy--a conspiracy to abduct. That plan was changed, so that if he came to assist in a plan, it was a plan of which he knew nothing, and they have shown that he knew nothing of it.[5]

At this time, the penalty for conspiracy to kidnap evidently also was death and Surratt's own lawyer stated that he admitted to have conspired to kidnap Lincoln. In addition, when the scheme was changed to a plan of assassination, all involved legally became accessories to murder as each conspirator was responsible for the acts of the others. As well, whether or not murder was involved, conspiring to overthrow the American government at a time of war was also a capital offense.[6]

Successfully kidnapping Lincoln would not have been out the realm of possibility, especially since the President sometimes drove in Washington, unarmed and unescorted. If this group of conspirators had managed to seize Lincoln, there would have been a real possibility of the President being injured, perhaps fatally, to say nothing of possible harm to those who might have attempted to stop the kidnappers. What role would Surratt have played? He knew how to ride and the trial evidence showed he had the nerve to repeatedly cross the Union and Confederate lines, transporting dispatches for the Confederacy.[7]

Booth undoubtedly would have played a central role in the operation. He had no qualms about shooting the defenceless President in Ford's Theatre, so what would have stopped him from shooting Lincoln during the kidnapping attempt if he felt he had to or shooting anyone pursuing them? Surratt's role might have been to just position provisions or to wait along the escape route with fresh horses but this would not have made him less guilty legally, or morally, for the kidnapping and any loss of life that may have resulted. This is to say nothing of the difficulties the United States federal government would have faced in its struggle to save the country with its inspirational commander-in-chief in the hands of its enemies.

John Surratt's legal team argued that aside from probably being a blockade runner and Confederate agent, Surratt was part of the conspiracy to merely kidnap Lincoln but he certainly would not have stooped to conspire to assassinate him.[8] This defence though, was based in large part on the writings of the man who murdered Lincoln in cold blood, John Wilkes Booth. His diary was introduced as evidence at the trial.[9]

The defence believed that the conclusive proof showing that the plot to capture had been changed to one of murder on the day of the assassination, or the day before, lay in these words of this murderer.[10] Were Booth's statements credible though? In his diary, he wrote of Lincoln,"Our country owed all our troubles to him". Was the 16th President responsible for all the troubles of the United States? Comments like this showed how exaggerated and untrustworthy his statements were. Inferring courage, Booth also wrote of himself, that he had "walked with a firm step, through a thousand of his friends, was stopped but pushed on". The actor was well known in Ford's Theatre and before the assassination, was not seen carrying arms or perceived as a threat in the theatre that evening and there is no record of him struggling with anyone to get to the President.

Booth's wrote, "I bless the entire world. Have never hated or wronged any one. This last was not a wrong, unless God deems it so, and it's with Him to damn or bless me." The statement that the murder of the good and great President Lincoln, as well as the wounding of Major Rathbone, was no wrong unless God deemed it so, further illustrated how twisted his thinking was, especially along religious lines. As they apparently had nothing else, John Surratt's legal team based their arguments for their client's innocence largely on the words of this cold-blooded killer.

At the trial of the conspirators, a statement made by George Atzerodt was read by his lawyer, W. E. Doster, during his final argument for his client. According to Atzerodt's statement, the plan to kidnap was not changed to one to kill until the night of the 14th. Along with this statement, Surratt's defence argued that the testimony of other witnesses showed that the plot to kill Lincoln was created very late in the game. For instance, they alleged that John Surratt had owned some horses in Washington but in March or possibly April, 1865, had given up the kidnapping plan and sold them to Booth.

The conclusion to the apparent change of horse ownership is not necessarily that Surratt had withdrawn from any conspiracy though. He could simply have needed some money and sold them to Booth. Or Surratt could have lied about who owned the horses, just like he lied about what his name was on a number of occasions. According to court testimony and other sources, John Surratt used at least seven aliases.

Was there a plot afoot to murder Abraham Lincoln well before April 14th and if so, was John Surratt part of it? Even before he was inaugurated in 1861, strong evidence pointed to a conspiracy to kill the President in Baltimore, which Lincoln avoided by traveling through the city in secret.[11] As well, at the trial of John Surratt, a woman named Mrs. E. W. McClermont testified about a plan to assassinate the President that she had overheard one day in April, 1864. She stated that while waiting for streetcar in the city of Washington, she heard three men talking speaking of the President, his travels about Washington and a "telescope rifle", evidently to be used on him.[12] She identified the three men as Herold, Atzerodt and Booth.

In August, 1864, a bullet was fired through the President's hat, narrowly missing him as he traveled along a wooded road between the White House and his summer residence at the Soldier's Home, three miles north of the White House. This was no abduction attempt. Did Booth, Surratt and company have anything to do with this?[13]

In 1865, a widow named Mary Hudspeth testified for the prosecution at the trial of the conspirators. Two years later, she was also a witness at John Surratt's trial. She testified on both occasions that while traveling in a streetcar in New York City on Nov. 14th, 1864, she noticed two men sitting beside her. One was a large "common-looking" man, the other was taller and thinner than the other man. The taller man, who appeared to be disguised, called the other man "Johnson".[14]

She saw the two men exchange letters. They got off before she did and dropped an envelope. It contained two letters which she took to the authorities. The first one, introduced as evidence, was as follows:

> DEAR LOUIS: The time has at last come that we have all so wished for, and upon you everything depends. As it was decided before you left, we were to cast lots. Accordingly we did so, and you are to be the Charlotte Corday of the nineteenth century. When you remember the fearful, solemn vow that

was taken by us, you will feel there is no drawback. *Abe* must *die*, and *now*. You can choose your weapons--the cup, the *knife*, the *bullet*. The cup failed us once, and might again. Johnson, who will give you this, has been like an enraged demon since the meeting, because it has not fallen upon him to rid the world of the monster. He says the blood of his grayhaired father and his noble brother call upon him for revenge, and revenge he will have; if he cannot wreak it upon the fountain head, he will upon some of the blood-thirsty generals. Butler would suit him. As our plans were all concocted and well arranged, we separated; and as I am writing--on my way to Detroit--I will only say that all rests upon you. You know where to find your friends. Your disguises are so perfect and complete that, without *one* knew *your face*, no police telegraphic despatch would catch you. The English gentleman, *Harcourt*, must not act hastily. Remember he has *ten* days. Strike for your home, strike for your country; bide your time, but strike sure. Get introduced, congratulate him, listen to his stories--not many more will the brute tell to earthly friends. Do anything but fail, and meet us at the appointed place within the fortnight. Enclose this note, together with one of poor Leenea. I will give the reason for this when we meet. Return by Johnson. I wish I could go to you, but duty calls me to the West. You will, probably, hear from me in Washington. Sanders is doing us no good in Canada.

Believe me, your brother in love,
CHARLES SELBY. [15] (emphasis in original)

At the conspiracy trial, the lawyer who defended Michael O'Laughlin and Samuel Arnold asked why there was no attempt on the President's life within the two week time period spoken of in the letter if this was a real letter detailing the final arrangements of a plot to kill Lincoln. The obvious explanation for this is that the conspirators, realizing that these letters were lost and possibly in government hands, thought it best to change their plans. Charlotte Corday was the woman who murdered Jean Paul Marat, a leader of the French Revolution in 1793.[16]

The letter she found mentioned a previous assassination attempt, the cup or poison, stating that it "failed us once". At this time, David Herold reportedly was working as a druggist clerk for a Washington pharmacy, where the Lincolns generally bought their medicine.

A letter, dated November 12, 1864, was introduced by the prosecution at Surratt's trial. Written by John Surratt to Louis Weichmann, it read in part, "Been busy all the week taking care of and securing the crops. Next Tuesday, and the jig's up. Good by, Surrattsville. Good by, God forsaken country. Old Abe, the good old soul, may the devil take pity on him."[17]

It could be asked, why would the devil need to take pity on Abe Lincoln, if he was to be kidnapped and taken safely to the Confederate capital to be held until there was an end to hostilities or a large troop exchange? Could this letter, written about the same time period that Mary Benson found the two letters, been speaking about the same attempt of President Lincoln's life as the correspondence she found?

A cipher letter was introduced as evidence in both the conspiracy trial and the trial of John Surratt (found in North Carolina, it was dated the day after the assassination). After deciphering, it read:

'WASHINGTON, April the 15, 1865.

'DEAR JOHN: I am happy to inform you that Pet has done his work well. He is safe and Old Abe is in hell. Now, sir, all eyes are on you. You must bring Sherman. Grant is in the hands of Gray ere this. Red Shoes showed a lack of nerve in Seward's case. But he fell back in good order. Johnson must come. Old Crook has him in charge. Mind well that brother's oath and you will have no difficulty. All well. Be safe and enjoy the fruits of our labor. We had a large meeting last night. All were bent on carrying out the program to the letter. The rails are laid our safe exit. Old, always behind, lost the pass at City Point. Now I say again the lives of our brave officers and the life of the South depends upon the carrying this program into effect. No. two will give you this. Its ordered. No more letters shall be sent by mail; when you write sign no real name, and send by some of our friends w ho are coming home. We want you to write us how the news was received there. We receive great encouragement from all quarters. I hope there will be no getting weak in the knees. I was in Baltimore yesterday. Pet had not got there yet. Your folks are well and have heard from you. Don't lose your nerve.

'O'B. NO. FIVE.[18]

The man Johnson was mentioned in this letter. "Pet" was credited with killing Lincoln. Louis Weichmann testified that Pet was the nickname Mary Surratt had for Booth.[19] The letter speaks about a large meeting of people intend on carrying out a program, of which Lincoln's murderer was a part. The foregoing evidence shows that the plan to kill the President was not hatched at the last minute but was in existence long before the fateful Friday.

John Surratt's associates, his actions, as well as his whereabouts before, during and after Lincoln's assassination, were of interest to the prosecution. As noted earlier, Louis Weichmann, Surratt's classmate when they both attended the same school for training Catholic priests in Maryland, provided information on the relationship Surratt had with other conspirators.

John Surratt, who knew David Herold, introduced him to Weichmann in March, 1863. Weichmann testified that Dr. Mudd introduced himself and Surratt to Booth in late December, 1864 or January, 1865. After the introduction, Booth became a frequent visitor to the Surratt home and was often in John Surratt's company. Weichmann also stated that Atzerodt visited John Surratt very frequently.[20]

As well, Louis Weichmann testified that Louis Payne came to the Surratt house in the latter part of February, 1865, asking for John Surratt, who was not home. Payne came again and visited Surratt on March 14th, 1865. The next day Weichmann went into the attic room where Payne was staying and found John Surratt and Payne playing with various weapons. Weichmann also told of an unusual incident the next day. At about 6:30 p.m., one after another, John Surratt, Lewis Payne and Booth all came hurriedly into the room that Weichmann shared with Surratt. At least two were armed with pistols and they were all very excited.[21]

In an 1870 lecture, John Surratt stated that at about this time period, he, along with Booth and others had planned to capture Abraham Lincoln as he went to Campbell Hospital in Washington to attend a benefit show for wounded soldiers. At the last minute, President Lincoln changed his plans and did not attend, disappointing the conspirators. What Weichmann described may well have been the would-be kidnappers' return to the Surratt house.

Weichmann stated that he received a telegram from Booth dated March 23rd, 1865, containing a message for Surratt. It read:

> 'NEW YORK, March 23, 1865.
>
> 'Received, Washington, March -----1865,---- o'clock.
> 'To-------------WICKMAN, Esq., 541 H street:
> 'Tell John to telegraph number and street at once.
>
> 'J. BOOTH.'[22]

In *Lincoln's Assassins*, Roy Chamlee reported that in an 1870 lecture, John Surratt also "revealed that the conspirators seldom used their real names when sending letters to one another. A device Booth used, according to Surratt, was to send letters to him addressed to Louis Weichmann. This confirmed Weichmann's statement about letters meant for Surratt being sent to him."

Surratt refused to tell Weichmann what the telegram was about. That evening they went for a walk to Herndon House where Surratt inquired about whether a room had been engaged for a "delicate gentleman", whose meals were to be sent to his room. The gentleman was Louis Payne and the prosecution alleged that it was Payne's address that Booth wanted sent to him.

Weichmann testified that on March 25th, John Surratt, his mother and Mrs. Slater went south from Washington in a horse-drawn carriage. Mrs. Surratt returned that night.[23] The next day John Surratt had the following note sent to the Howard stable in Washington (see Figure 32):

> 'MARCH 26, 1865.
>
> 'Mr. BROOKS: As business will detain me for a few days in the country I thought I would send your team back. Mr. Bearer will deliver in safety and pay the hire on it. If Mr. Booth, my friend, should want my horses, let him have them, but no one else. If you should want any money on them, he will let you have it. I should have liked to have kept the team for several days, but it is too expensive, especially as I have women on the brain and may be away for a week or so.
>
> 'Yours, respectfully,
> 'J. HARRISON SURRATT.'

Figure 32
Howard stable, Washington, D.C.

He stayed in at least one hotel in Richmond under the name of Henry Sherman and returned to Washington on April 3rd. John Surratt left that same night for Montreal and other testimony shows he arrived there a few days later. A hotel clerk at St. Lawrence Hall in the city testified that a man registered there under the name John Harrison on April 6th and left the hotel April 12th, on the 3:00 o'clock New York train, returning on the 18th.[24]

Dr. Lewis McMillan, the surgeon of the ship that Surratt traveled to Europe on, reported that the defendant had said he was in Montreal at the beginning of the week of the assassination. While he was there, he received a letter from Booth, saying he needed to go to Washington immediately. This is one of the main areas where the defence and the prosecution parted ways. Both sides agreed that he was in Montreal on April 12th, left the city on that date and returned on April 18th. The defence alleged that he went to Elmira, New York and was there on the day of the assassination but the prosecution argued that he was in Washington at this time.

The defence called four residents of Elmira who didn't know John Surratt but said they saw him there between the 13th and the 15th of April. The prosecution called 11 witnesses who said they saw a man they positively identified, or said resembled, the defendant in Washington on the day of the assassination. This number swells to 15 when including those who saw him traveling to or from the capital at this time. Some of these witnesses knew John Surratt, including a barber named Charles Wood, who stated he shaved him that morning.[25] The defence argued that some of the prosecution witnesses were not to be trusted and the others, though honest, were simply mistaken.

In closing arguments however, the prosecution pointed out that although the defence could say where John Surratt stayed the week before April 12th and from April 18th until he left for Europe in September, they evidently couldn't show where he stayed for the crucial days between the 12th and the 18th. Surratt's defence lawyers attempted to prove that he had an alibi in order to show that he was not in Washington on the day of the assassination.

His defence team claimed that he had stayed at the Brainard House in Elmira, New York on April 14th but they could not find the hotel register. The defence therefore did not produce any admissible physical evidence, no receipt for a hotel room or meal, no record as to his whereabouts for this time. This apparently was because the real evidence would have put him in a location where they didn't want him to be found to be, namely Washington. In final arguments, district attorney E.C. Carrington stated, "That the defence of alibi being an affirmative defence, the burden proof rests upon the defendant to establish it to the satisfaction of the jury by a preponderance of the evidence."

Defence witnesses, whose truthfulness was not challenged, put him in Elmira at the time of the assassination and witnesses for the prosecution whose veracity also was not questioned, put him in Washington at this time, or on the way to the city, or the way back to Montreal. The defence argued that these prosecution witnesses were just honestly mistaken. If it could be possible however, for witnesses who knew him, or provided a personal service (like the barber), to be mistaken, then surely it would also be possible for those defence witnesses who didn't know him to also be wrong.

The defence believed what conclusively proved that Surratt couldn't have been in the capital on the day of the assassination was the fact that there was not enough time for him to travel on April 12th from Montreal to Elmira and then on to Washington in time for him to be seen there on the 14th. The prosecution showed that even if he had traveled through Elmira however, Surratt could have made it to Washington in time for an appointment with the barber, Charles Wood, the first witness to see him there. Wood gave a detailed narrative, stating he had shaved Booth and Surratt in the company of Michael O'Laughlin and another man in Washington, at about nine o'clock in the morning of April 14th. Besides the barber, the prosecution brought some 10 more witnesses that testified to seeing Surratt or someone closely resembling him in the U.S. capital on the day of April 14th. The defence did not effectively rebut this mass of testimony and among this group were people who knew the defendant, or at least knew him by sight.[26]

The last prosecution witness to see John Surratt in Washington on that fateful day was a non-commissioned officer in the U.S. Army, Joseph Dye. Sergeant Dye's testimony was supported by fellow officer, Robert Cooper. Dye was in front of Ford's theatre at about 9:30 that evening with Sergeant Cooper, sitting on a low platform in front of the theatre. While he was there, Dye noticed John Wilkes Booth, whom he knew. The actor was near the entrance of the theatre, talking to a man that Dye described as a villainous-looking person. They were joined by another man whom Dye identified as John Surratt.

A crowd of people came from the theatre and as they exited, Booth said "he would come out now" which Dye understood to mean President Lincoln. He said Booth, Surratt and the other man waited eagerly but the President did not appear. Surratt looked at the clock on the vestibule of the theatre and called the time to the other two. He then walked off in the direction of H Street, returning after a short time to look at the clock and call the time again. Again he walked in the same direction and return, calling the time for a third time. The last time he called out was ten past ten. He then hurried toward H Street and disappeared. Dye stated that time period between the first calling of the time and the second was eight to ten minutes and between the second and third was not more than five minutes.

After witnessing what he considered to be suspicious behavior by the three men, Dye and Cooper went to an oyster saloon but before they could eat, the news of Lincoln's assassination reached them. They then hurried back up H Street to their base. On the way, they told the news to an elderly lady at the window of her home. Dye said the woman resembled Mary Surratt.[27]

Regarding Surratt calling out the time, the defence brought three witnesses whose testimony, they believed, related to this very point. According to the defence, the person in charge of costumes at Ford's theatre, Louis Carland, was the man that Dye thought was Surratt. Carland testified that he and another man, James Gifford, were standing outside at the front of the theatre when actor C.B. Hess came up and asked what the time was. Carland walked over, looked in the theatre vestibule at the clock and then called the time to them, which was ten past ten.[28] This, the defence alleged, was what had happened outside the theatre that night.

Dye however, stated that the time was called three times, not just once. As well, Hess, Carland and Gifford's testimony was so contradictory and confusing that it is uncertain what could really be established by their statements. For example, Hess testified that while he was talking with Gifford and Carland, there was another man in front of the theatre dressed, he thought, as an officer. Carland said that after telling Hess the time and before the news of the assassination reached them, he couldn't remember a soul being on the street outside the theatre. Gifford stated that he saw a number of people in front of the theatre that night.

 It theoretically might have been possible for what both sets of witnesses reported, Sergeants Dye and Cooper and the other group, Carland, Gifford and Hess, to have happened, with some time discrepancies.[29]

Ultimately, Carland, Gifford and Hess were either very inaccurate in relating what transpired that evening or what is more probable, they lied, as the prosecution alleged. It is quite a coincidence that with the substantial disagreement between the three regarding what happened that night, they would all have been in complete agreement as to the time that was called and also very interesting that out of all the different times that they could have reported being called out, they just happen to state the exact same time that Dye had reported when he testified before the military commission, some two years earlier.

The three also testified before the military commission at the trial of the conspirators in 1865. Carland stated that he was interviewed by government officials before he testified and Gifford and Hess probably were interviewed also. Dye testified before the military commission on May 15th, 1865 and they testified later.[30]

It is extremely difficult to understand how Carland, Gifford and Hess didn't hear of Dye's testimony, although the trial proceedings were the talk of the day in Washington and though Lincoln was shot in the very theatre that they were intimately connected with, while they were in the immediate vicinity. As they undoubtedly must have heard how his statements mirrored their alleged experience, by the amazing coincidence of describing the same events they said they were part of, happening at the same time but with different people, it is very strange and suspicious that they apparently didn't inform the authorities at the time.

There was therefore, two witnesses, Dye and Cooper, non-commissioned officers of the United States Armed Forces against three and the three, Carland, Gifford and Hess did not agree with each other. If one group of witnesses were lying, which was it likely to be? Dye and Cooper had no reason not to tell the truth. The other three however, may have had a motive. They knew Booth and at least one of his associates who was put on trial, Edward Spangler. Carland, who was a Catholic, admitted at the trial of the conspirators that he sheltered Spangler the night after the assassination and was arrested along with him. At John Surratt's trial, he stated that he was indifferent to which side won the Civil War and did not care if the Union was preserved.[31]

In addition, James Ferguson, who kept the restaurant adjoining Ford's theatre, testified at the trial of the conspirators that Gifford had attempted to undermine his testimony. Ferguson had accurately informed the authorities about what he had seen in the theatre, stating that he had seen the flash of a pistol at the back in the President's box, as Booth shot the President. Ferguson stated, "Next morning I saw Mr. Gifford, who said, 'You made a hell of a statement about what you saw last night; how could you see the flash of the pistol when the ball was shot through the door?" Was Gifford just wrong or was he trying to create confusion as to how Lincoln was shot, and by whom, at the time Booth was desperately trying to make good his escape from U.S. authorities? James Ferguson also testified of James Gifford's lack of patriotism.

Ultimately, the contradictory and confusing testimony of these three men, whose support of the Union cause during the Civil War was questionable, cannot overcome the clear testimony of Dye and Cooper. Without being contradicted therefore, their testimony stands, putting Surratt in front of the theatre, calling the time just before Lincoln was shot.

Any successful attempt on the lives of a number of high government officials would have to be coordinated so their murders could take place simultaneously. It is clear that this occurred on the night of the assassination, as Booth and Payne struck their blows at essentially the same time. John Pettit, a resident of a building situated some 150 to 200 feet from the back of Ford's theatre, testified at the trial of John Surratt that on the evening of April 14th, he heard a series of low whistles coming from a nearby vacant lot. He found it so distracting that he actually got up from his seat where he was reading to see what was going on.[33]

Sergeant Dye testified that Surratt's role during the crime was to regulate the time of attack for the conspirators as a general commander, using one clock to synchronize their activities. They planned to strike at an agreed upon time period after the last calling of the time. The whistling undoubtedly was part of the signaling between the conspirators, coordinated by Surratt in the final stages before their murderous deeds. With Surratt playing such an important part in the plan to assassinate, it was no wonder the U.S. government was searching for him. [34]

Dr. Louis McMillan, who traveled on the same ship that Surratt took to Europe in September, 1865, testified that John Surratt told him he was in Washington on the day of the assassination. When McMillan and St. Marie are added to those who saw him traveling to the American capital or away from the city around this time, this number totals 17, more than four times the amount of witnesses who said he was in Elmira, New York.

Fleeing U. S. justice after Lincoln's murder, John Surratt headed to Canada. When he arrived back in Montreal, he went to stay for a short time with a Confederate agent by the name of Porterfield. When they learned that detectives suspected that he was there, Surratt stole away one evening and went to stay with a Catholic priest, Charles Boucher in a village outside Montreal. Boucher confirmed in court that Surratt had stayed with him and that the fugitive's presence at his home was not generally known by the people there. The priest tried to evade the question of whether he concealed Surratt. Boucher did not admit to hiding the defendant but he did say that his parishioners visited his house every day and did not see him there. He stated that within the first month of his guest's arrival, he realized that the person in his home was John Surratt, a man wanted for Lincoln's assassination. The priest did not tell the authorities however but allowed him to stay more than two more months.[35]

According to McMillan, Surratt said that when a female servant of the priest caught a fleeting glimpse of him, it was mistakenly believed by the people there that the priest had a woman secreted in his house, so again he had to leave. He returned to Montreal where he was hidden in a room, evidently in the home of the father of a Catholic priest name La Pierre.

The house was very close to the residence of the bishop of Montreal. Charles Chiniquy started that it was "under the very shadow of the Montreal bishop's palace." Boucher visited Surratt twice a week and La Pierre visited also. In September, 1865, they both escorted him onto the small steamer, Montreal, which took the fugitive from Montreal to Québec City where he boarded the Peruvian.

Charles Chiniquy said that La Pierre, the man who was so helpful to John Surratt, was the canon of Bishop Bourget of Montreal, the bishop's right hand man.[36]

Boucher stated that Surratt disguised himself and he also said that La Pierre was clothed as a civilian; a form of dress which he admitted was not customary for priests to wear. On board the Montreal, La Pierre, who had previously talked to Louis McMillan about a friend who would be making the ocean voyage, introduced Surratt to the doctor as "McCarty".

During the trip, among other things, John Surratt told Dr. McMillan that while in the South, he and a group of others had shot some unarmed Union soldiers they had come across who had probably escaped from a southern prison.[37]

After a brief stop in Londonderry, Ireland, the Peruvian docked in Liverpool. According to U.S. consulate officials there, Surratt found shelter for some days at the oratory of the Catholic Church of the Holy Cross and then he went to Paris and continued across Europe. Arriving in Rome, Surratt stayed in the English college, a Catholic institution for English students where he was given financial help from the rector at the college. In the spring of 1866, he joined the Papal guard.

He was discovered there by Henry St. Marie, who reported his presence to Rufus King, United States minister at Rome. Although the United States had no extradition treaty with the Papal states, the authorities in Rome agreed to arrest Surratt and deliver him back to face U.S. justice, undoubtedly realizing that refusing to honour the request of the powerful United States would be political suicide and focus even more attention of thinking Americans on the role the Church of Rome had played in President Lincoln's murder. Surratt was duly arrested but escaped. On the run again, he was finally captured and brought back to face trial in Washington. [38]

As his trial began in June, 1867, the district attorney protested the manner in which the jury had been selected, arguing that the jury selection had been done unlawfully. Judge George Fisher agreed, ordering the first panel of jurors to be set aside and a new jury of talesmen be summoned. Did the Catholic Church attempt to interfere in the trial of a man that its officials helped to hide for two years? Surratt's lawyer, Joseph Bradley Sr. declared:

> I think I can see where this thing is drifting. It is not delay that is sought, but they have another motive more powerful than delay. It is to get another jury in the place of an honest jury already summoned. Why, sir, the gentleman talks about the misgivings in the public prints. I do not know that he has seen what I hold in my hand, an article from this place denouncing this jury because sixteen of them are Catholics, as they say, but there it is--such an article has been written and published in the New York Herald. I know, too, that the same article, published yesterday morning, foreshadows the fact that these gentlemen were to come into court on the day they did, and make the identical motion that they have submitted here.[39]

This was confirmed by an article in the June 18th, 1867, edition of the *Springfield Daily Republican* (Springfield, Mass.), quoting the Washington correspondent of the

Boston Saturday Evening Gazette, which reported that a majority of the talesmen selected were Catholics. These jurors were supposed to be randomly selected from a pool of qualified candidates from the city of Washington, Georgetown and the county of Washington. The jury that would judge capital cases such as John Surratt's, a petit jury, would be made up of 26 men.[40]

At a time when the population of Catholics in the United States was in the neighborhood of 11 percent, was the Catholic population in the Washington area more than 61 percent, as Joseph Bradley Sr. stated the jury makeup was reported to be? As it certainly was not, how did this randomly picked jury end up with such high number of Catholics? Was there an unseen force working behind the scenes attempting to manipulate justice? Was it the Catholic Church, the same Church whose officials sheltered John Surratt after the assassination and whose members supported Surratt during his trial? United States General T.M. Harris commented on this in his book, *Assassination of Lincoln, a History of the Great Conspiracy*:

> The appeals made by the eminent counsel for the prisoner to the political and religious prejudices of jurors was ably seconded all thorough the trial by the Jesuit priesthood of Washington City and the vicinity. It will be recalled by scores of people who attended the trial that not a day passed but that some of these were in the court-room as the most interested of spectators. That they were not idle spectators may be inferred from the fact that whenever it seemed necessary to the prisoner's counsel to find witnesses to contradict any testimony that was particularly damaging to their cause they were always promptly found, and were almost uniformly Catholics in religion, as shown by their own testimony on their cross-examination....Other outside influences were brought to bear on jurors, such as these: Father John B. Menu, from St. Charles College, spent a day in the court-room, sitting beside the prisoner all day, this saying to the jury, 'You see which side I am on'. A great many of the students from the same college also visited the trial, it being vacation, and they uniformly took great pains to show their sympathy with the prisoner by shaking hands with him.[41]

General Harris was a member of the military commission that judged the conspirators in 1865. In his book, *Lincoln's Assassins: A Complete Account of their Capture, Trial, and Punishment*, Roy Chamlee supported Harris regarding overt Catholic support of John Surratt.[42]

In the end, charged with murder and conspiring to murder the President, despite the preponderance of evidence showing his guilt, the jury just couldn't agree on a verdict. Charles Chiniquy alleged that the reason John Surratt was not convicted was because the Catholics on the jury refuse to find him guilty, despite the evidence, just as years earlier, a Catholic member of a jury refused to acquit Chiniquy in a court battle with Spink. A second trial was attempted but failed. Though not acquitted, Surratt was released on $40,000 bail, an equivalent of some $500,000 today. Regarding John Surratt's trial, in her book, *The Assassin's Accomplice: Mary Surratt and the Plot to Kill Abraham Lincoln*, Kate Clifford Larson stated:

much more evidence was introduced shedding light on the extensiveness of the conspiracy, as well as new details about Mary's complicity in it. But despite the new evidence, John's case ended in a mistrial – the civilian jury was packed with Southern sympathizers. All charges were then dropped because the statute of limitations of two years on a charge of treason had passed, and, in February 1868 John was set free.[43]

Among other things, John Surratt taught afterwards at St. Joseph Catholic School in Emmetsburg, Maryland, between the years of 1870 and 1872. When he died on April 21st, 1916, a Solemn High Requiem Mass was offered at St. Pius Catholic church in Baltimore. This was an unusual honour for a man who was charged and never found innocent of conspiring to murder America's greatest President and one whose own lawyer stated he was guilty of conspiring to kidnap the President. This is to say nothing of his treasonous activities as a Confederate agent and blockade runner during the Civil War. This mass was usually reserved for the funerals of bishops, priest and nuns. When offered at the funeral of laymen, it was a token of appreciation for exceptional devotion or service to the Church.[44] What could that service have been?

WHO KILLED ABRAHAM LINCOLN?

Chapter 9
Samuel Mudd, Booth and the other conspirators

Besides Mary Surratt, seven others were put on trial in 1865 for their part in the plot to murder Abraham Lincoln and other high government officials. There are two questions to consider: were they really responsible for these crimes and how many of them were Catholics?

Dr. Samuel Mudd was found guilty of conspiring to murder the President and other leaders, according to the specification, in particular, acting to "advise, encourage, receive, entertain, harbor, and conceal, aid and assist the said John Wilkes Booth". In his book, *His Name Is Still Mudd*, Edward Steers Jr. showed that Samuel Mudd was not an innocent doctor who just happened to be in the wrong place at the wrong time who unknowingly helped the wrong person but someone deeply involved in the plan to kidnap President Lincoln and one who, while knowing who he was and what he had just done, helped Booth in his flight to escape U. S. authorities. There is no question that Dr. Mudd was a Catholic.

The evidence arrayed against the Maryland doctor was quite similar to that brought against Mary Surratt. Both of them had someone who had played a major part in the conspiracy visit their home after Lincoln's assassination. Lewis Payne came to Mrs. Surratt's house and John Wilkes Booth came to Dr. Mudd's. As opposed to those to know too much, Mary Surratt and Samuel Mudd however, knew too little. They both tried to maintain that they hadn't recognized people that they had met and talked to weeks or months earlier.

Court testimony showed that Mudd definitely knew Booth. U.S. Army officer Colonel H. H. Wells stated that Mudd told him that he had been introduced to Booth in November, 1864 at the Catholic church the doctor attended in southern Maryland. Booth had enquired if there were any good, reasonably priced horses in the neighborhood and Dr. Mudd said there was. Booth stayed at the doctor's house that night and he bought a horse from one of Mudd's neighbors the next day.[1] Defence witness John C. Thompson confirmed this, testifying that he, Booth and another man attended a service at the Catholic church at Bryantown on a Sunday "around the latter part of October last, or perhaps in November". Meeting Mudd outside the church, Thompson introduced him to Booth. Another witness, Thomas Gardiner stated that his uncle sold a horse to Booth in November, 1864.[2]

Testifying in Dr. Samuel Mudd's defence, Dr. George Mudd, a relative who lived near him, stated that the news of Lincoln's murder by Booth reached their area on the afternoon of Saturday, April 15th. He also testified that on the next day, he met Samuel Mudd in church. On their journey home, Samuel Mudd told him that two suspicious men had come to his home on Saturday morning and one of them had had a broken leg. The two Mudds agreed that George Mudd would inform the authorities, which George Mudd said he did Monday morning. [3]

Military personnel pursuing Booth and Herold reported that when they questioned Samuel Mudd, he was nervous, evasive and untruthful. Detective Simon Gavacan testified that when he was at Mudd's home on Tuesday, April 18th, "We inquired if two men passed there on the Saturday morning after the assassination, and Dr. Mudd said no. Then we inquired more particularly if two men had been there, one having his leg fractured. He said yes." Joshua Lloyd, another detective, said essentially the same thing. He reported that Mudd initially denied that he had seen Booth, Herold or Surratt. Later though, Mudd admitted that two men came to his home at four o'clock, Saturday morning but "offered no explanation of his previous denial."[4] Other military personnel who interviewed Mudd also reported his evasiveness.

Mudd's defence maintained that he had only met Booth in November of the previous year. At that time, he had seen him for just two concurrent days and then hadn't seen him again until the assassin came to his home the morning after the President's murder. According to Colonel Well, Mudd said he didn't recognize the actor because he was disguised.[5]

Dr. Mudd's wife, Sarah, evidently also said Booth was disguised. Mudd's defence for his actions then was that he didn't know it was Booth because he had changed his appearance. No proof was ever provided by any other witnesses that Booth had changed his appearance before he arrived at Mudd's house or after he left, however. The only evidence that Booth was disguised and conveniently unrecognizable therefore came just from the accused himself and his wife. John Lloyd, who gave provisions to Booth and Herold on their way, said nothing about this. Lloyd also testified that Herold told him that he was pretty sure they had assassinated the President and Secretary Seward. If they told Lloyd this, wouldn't they have told Mudd as well?

Lieutenant Alexander Lovett testified that when he was at Mudd's home on April 18th, the doctor "did not at first seem inclined to give us any satisfaction; afterwards he went on to state that on Saturday morning, at daybreak, two strangers had come to his place."[6] Mudd said one of the men had a broken leg but he did not know who the man was. Lovett reported that the colored people present told him that they recognized Booth as being the man with the broken leg who was there on Saturday, though the news that he was responsible for President Lincoln's murder hadn't yet reached them.[7]

After his trial, Captain George Dutton declared that on his way to prison after sentencing, Dr. Mudd confessed that he did recognize Booth when the murderer came to his home. Mudd also confirmed that he was in the company of Booth when they met John Surratt and Louis Weichmann on Seventh Street in Washington, as Weichmann had stated. Booth had wanted to meet John Surratt so they met and had a private conversation that evening.

Mudd heard about Dutton's statement and he denied admitting that he had known it was Booth who had come to his home. Mudd did admit to meeting John Surratt and Louis Weichmann on a Washington street in the company of Booth and then going into Booth's hotel room for drinks however. This meeting had been steadfastly denied by the conspirator's lawyers.[8]

Mudd's lawyer, Thomas Ewing, maintained that before the assassin arrived at the doctor's home with a broken leg, Mudd had met Booth only once and Colonel H. H. Wells reported that Mudd had told him that he had been introduced to Booth at church in November and hadn't seen him again until the morning after Lincoln's assassination.[9] Edward Steers however, asserted that there was evidence that showed that Samuel Mudd had actually met Booth three times before April 15th: twice in the neighborhood of Mudd's home and then in Washington. He alleged the reason Mudd did not want the government to know about a second meeting with Booth near Mudd's home in Bryantown was because it was set up by him for the purpose of introducing Booth to Thomas Harbin, a Confederate secret service agent. Steers stated:

> Mudd appears to be a principal recruiter for Booth, at least in regard to two very important members of his team: Thomas Harbin and John Surratt. Of all of the conspirators enlisted into Booth's gang, Harbin and Surratt were the most competent and experienced, and the two who were already active agents of the Confederate underground. [10]

Steers asserted that Mudd had met with Booth at least three times in the six months before Lincoln's assassination. According to Colonel Wells and Thomas Gardiner, Mudd saw the actor on three consecutive days in November, 1864 on the first occasion, and Booth stayed at the doctor's home at least one night. When Booth came to Dr. Mudd's home on the morning of April 15th, it is extremely hard to believe that there was no spark of recognition when he talked to and treated this well known public person. In all likelihood, Mudd instantly recognized Booth, if he had not already been expecting him according to a pre-arranged plan.

Edward Steers pointed out that although Samuel Mudd knew it was Booth that he had treated, and knew, or soon would know, what he had done, he did not inform the authorities, via Dr. George Mudd, until April 17th. Even then, he didn't identify the man he treated as Booth and he evidently directed the soldiers pursuing the fugitives to go the opposite way that Booth and Herold had gone. His actions caused more than a 40 hour delay in the chase for the pair, providing them with crucial time to try to make good their escape.[11]

Steers also disclosed the role that one particular Catholic church evidently played in treasonous activities:

> Booth's presence at St. Mary's Church in November, and again in December, is testified to by John F. Hardy who places him there on both occasions. St. Mary's was the church of Dr. William Queen, the senior Confederate sympathizer in Charles County, and the man who brought Booth to that church on the two occasions that Dr. Mudd was known to have been there. That Mudd attended St. Mary's Church when Booth was there, furthering his plans, suggests that it was a rendezvous for important members of the Confederate underground. [12]

Court testimony showed that Samuel Mudd's sympathies lay with the Confederacy. One witness, Milo Simms, testified that he heard Mudd agree with an acquaintance, Benjamin Gardiner, when he said Lincoln ought to have been dead long time ago. Another witness heard Dr. Mudd make no objection when Gardiner told the doctor that General Stonewall Jackson would soon capture Washington and burn Lincoln in his house.[13]

Dr. Mudd was in favor of slavery and had been the owner a number of slaves. Not surprisingly, he opposed emancipation. Although all slaves were destined for freedom by the end of the Civil War, he remained prejudiced against blacks. While several colored people who had worked for him said he treated his servants well, some of the slaves that Mudd owned reportedly had been treated harshly and the doctor had actually shot one of them, Elzee Eglent, who had been disobedient. Eglent survived the shooting.[14]

Several months after arriving in prison in Fort Jefferson, Florida, Mudd's prejudice caused him to try to escape. In letters to relatives, he stated that he had tried to get away because he hated being guarded by colored soldiers.

In the early part of the twentieth century, relatives of Samuel Mudd began what has been a long and unsuccessful campaign to clear his name and his case still appears in the news. In 1992, a moot court at the University of Richmond School of Law ruled on the question of whether the military commission that judged Dr. Mudd had the legal jurisdiction to try him. Arguing on Mudd's side was the great-great granddaughter of Brigadier General Thomas Ewing Jr., Mudd's lawyer in 1865. Also on Mudd's side was high-profile criminal lawyer F. Lee Bailey, who gained fame through his part of the 1995 defence of the murderer of Nicole Brown Simpson and Ron Goldman. In November, 2002, the U.S. Court of Appeals for the District of Columbia blocked Richard Mudd's attempt to overturn his grandfather's conviction when it dismissed his 1992 complaint against the U. S. Army. The family has vowed to fight on.

In the end however, despite the efforts of his descendents to portray Mudd as a kindly country doctor who had been convicted for merely helping an injured stranger, the evidence shows that the government was correct and this Catholic man was guilty of assisting in the conspiracy to murder Abraham Lincoln and was fortunate to escape the death penalty.[15]

John Wilkes Booth

While John Wilkes Booth was not put on trial, he clearly was one of the leaders of the conspiracy, if not the main leader. He certainly was the man who assassinated President Lincoln. The question is: to what church did he belong?

In *Fifty Years*, Charles Chiniquy alleged that the actor was a "Protestant pervert to Romanism". In her 1982 article in the *Lincoln Herald*, "Insights on John Wilkes Booth from His Sister Asia's Correspondence", historian Constance Head stated that strong evidence pointed to the fact that Booth indeed was a Catholic.[16] Booth's sister, Asia Booth Clarke, wrote a memoir of her brother which was published after her death. College history professor, Terry Alford, a leading authority on the life of John Wilkes Booth, attested to how valuable a witness Booth Clarke is regarding her brother's life.[17] He stated, "Asia Booth Clarke's memoir of her brother John Wilkes Booth has been recognized as the single most important document available for understanding the personality of the assassin of President Abraham Lincoln", adding that "no outsider could give such insights into the turbulent Booth's childhood or share such unique personal knowledge of the gifted actor". Alford edited a recent edition of the memoir.

Ms. Head agreed, declaring that "Asia should be accurate in the matter of her brother's religious preference".[18] Head quoted from a letter the actor's sister had written to a friend regarding the assassination and the conspirators. Booth Clarke wrote, "I was shocked and grieved to see the names of Michael O'Laughlin and Samuel Arnold [among the conspirators.] I am still more surprised to learn that all engaged in the plot are Roman Catholics. Wilkes was of the faith professedly and I was glad that he had fixed his faith on one religion" Head also stated:

> Although the Booth family was traditionally Episcopalian, Asia personally was very much inclined toward Catholicism as the result of her schooling at the Carmelite convent in Baltimore. Eventually she became a Catholic herself, and although the date of her conversion is unknown, it is a matter which she and Wilkes may have discussed. It is even conceivable that it was Asia who converted him. On the other hand, perhaps as an actor, he was simply attracted by the dramatic beauty of the Mass. He seems moreover to have entertained a low opinion of certain protestant clergymen who preached the sinfulness of the stage, and thus may have been drawn toward Catholicism as a faith more congenial to his vocation. In any case, it seems certain that Booth did not publicize his conversion during his lifetime. And while there is no reasonable cause to connect Booth's religious preference and his "mad act", the few who knew of his conversion must have decided after the assassination that for the good of the church, it was best never to mention it. Thus the secret remained so well guarded that even the most rabidly anti-Catholic writers who tried to depict the assassination of Lincoln as a Jesuit or Papist plot were puzzled by the seemingly accurate information that John Wilkes Booth was an Episcopalian.[19]

If any other proof is needed to show the actor was a Roman Catholic after the compelling evidence provided by his sister, several other facts point to Booth's Catholicism. Like his sister, he received education at a school established by an official of the Catholic Church, when he was a boarding student at St. Charles' College in Pikesville, Maryland. Louis Weichmann and Samuel Arnold also attended this school. The Catholic parish history that revealed this information took pains to point out that this institution was a "non-denominational school" or academy established by a priest named Father Waldron, not to be confused with St. Charles' College, a seminary for training priests at a different location, five miles west of Ellicott City, Maryland. Weichmann and John Surratt had attended the latter school.[20]

Evidence given at the trial of John Surratt showed that at his death, Booth had a small Catholic medal on his person. As well, on at least two occasions, court testimony showed him attending Roman Catholic Church services. There reportedly is also evidence that he made a donation to St. Aloysius Catholic church in Washington.[21] It would be quite unusual for someone who received education from a priest, to be carrying a Catholic medal on his person and attending Catholic Church services and even donating to the Church, yet not be a Catholic. All of this however, would naturally follow if, as his sister was undoubtedly correct in asserting, the assassin of Abraham Lincoln, John Wilkes Booth, was a Roman Catholic.

Michael O'Laughlin

Michael O'Laughlin was tried for his part in Lincoln's murder and given a life sentence by the military commission. A veteran of the Confederate armed forces during the early part of the Civil War, the evidence shows that in addition to being part of the conspiracy, he too was a Catholic. He died in an outbreak of yellow fever at the prison of Fort Jefferson in the Dry Tortugas, Florida on September 23rd, 1867.[22]

O'Laughlin was a boyhood friend of John Wilkes Booth and Samuel Arnold, living in the same neighborhood in Baltimore. Beginning in February, 1865, he and Arnold were roommates in a Washington rooming house. Their landlady testified that Booth visited them frequently there. Arnold and O'Laughlin told her that they were engaged in the oil business, a term Booth and other conspirators used as a cover for their secret plans.

O'Laughlin received a telegraph message from Booth on March 13, 1865 and another two weeks later on March 27th. Given in evidence before the commission, the March 13th communication read: "Don't fear to neglect your business. You had better come at once. [signed] J. BOOTH". The latter one read: "Get word to Sam. Come on, with or without him, Wednesday morning. We sell that day sure. Don't fail. J. WILKES BOOTH."[23] Undoubtedly, the Sam referred to was Samuel Arnold. This message, which spoke about selling, evidently referred to the same non-existent business that a letter of Booth's, found in the National Hotel, spoke about.

Discovered in an envelope bearing the initials J.W.B., the letter was also given in evidence before the military commission. The hotel clerk who found it testified that the only guest that he knew of that had those initials was John Wilkes Booth. Dated April 6th, 1865, it used the same term, "don't fail". It read:

> FRIEND WILKES: I received yours of March 12th, and reply as soon as practicable. I saw French, Brady, and others about the *oil* speculation. The subscription to the *stock* amounts to $8,000, and I add $1,000 myself, which is about all I can stand. Now, when you sink your well go DEEP enough; don't fail, every thing depends on you and your *helpers*. It you can't get through on your *trip*, after you *strike ile*, strike through Thornton Gap, and cross by Capon, Romney's, and down the Branch, and I can keep you safe from all hardships for a year. I am clear of all surveillance, now that infernal Purdy is beat. I hired that girl to charge him with an outrage, and reported him to old

Kelly, which sent him in the *shade*, but he suspects to (too) damn much now. Had he better be *silenced for good* ? I send this up by Tom, and if he don't get drunk you will get it the 9th; at all events, it can't be understood if lost. I can't half write. I have been drunk for two days. Don't write so much highfalutin next time. No more; only Jake will be at Green's with the funds. Burn this.

Truly, yours, LON.
Sue Guthrie sends much love. [24] (italics in original)

This obviously was a partially encoded letter, shown by the words "it can't be understood if lost" and "Burn this". If "Friend Wilkes", or Booth, had struck ile, or oil, why would he need to be kept safe from hardships? Wouldn't he then be wealthy? Undoubtedly meant for the President's assassin, there is no proof that Booth was directing an oil drilling operation anywhere at the time. Evidently the term "sink your well", was code for assassinating Lincoln and others. Going deep enough meant making sure that the President and other officials were killed. The letter said he had helpers. They evidently were John Surratt, Harold, O'Laughlin, Arnold and others.

The letter was explained in large part by U.S. government scout and detective, Robert Purdy. In testimony before the commission, he stated that he was the Purdy mentioned in the letter and that he resided in Marshall County, West Virginia, near the Ohio River. He reported that there was a man in the region who generally went by the name of Lon, his full name being Leonidas McAleer. Purdy stated that McAleer "had been playing both sides, loyal and disloyal". He also testified that the handwriting of the letter resembled McAleer's.

With the help of some other men, Purdy had captured a rebel spy a few miles from McAleer's home, whom he understood, "was to meet Lon McAleer that day to carry information there". A day or two later, he came across a girl near McAleer's house and found her to be carrying letters, evidently for the Confederate side. This must have upset McAleer and he apparently persuaded the girl to charge the detective with rape.[25]

Michael O'Laughlin and three other associates, James Henderson, Bernard Early, and Edward Murphy, came by train to Washington from Baltimore, on the evening of April 13th. They had allegedly come to see the fireworks scheduled for that evening and to generally enjoy themselves. O'Laughlin went to see Booth that night in the actor's room in the National Hotel. O'Laughlin was also identified as the man who twice appeared at the home of Secretary of War Stanton later that night, first asking to see General Grant, who was visiting, and then Stanton. His requests were denied.[26]

On the day of the assassination, Michael O'Laughlin left his friends in the morning to visit Booth again in his hotel room. As noted earlier, Charles Wood testified that O'Laughlin came into his barber shop that morning in the company of Booth, John Surratt and another man. Other than this two hour period in the morning, O'Laughlin's whereabouts on the day of the 14th were essentially accounted for by his associates. The next afternoon, on April 15th, O'Laughlin and company returned to Baltimore.[27]

O'Laughlin was arrested there on April 17th by an officer named William Wallace. Wallace stated that when O'Laughlin was arrested, "he seemed to understand what it was for, and did not ask any questions about it". At the time O'Laughlin, "said he knew nothing of the assassination whatever, and could account for his whereabouts during all the time of his stay in Washington by the parties who were with him". There was a two hours period on the morning of the 14th however, when no person except the prosecution's witness, Charles Wood, could account for his whereabouts. No one therefore could directly contradict Wood's testimony that O'Laughlin, Booth and John Surratt were in his shop that morning.

The defence called seven witnesses who testified that they were with or saw O'Laughlin at a time and location in Washington that the defence obviously thought would prove that he could not have been at the Secretary of War's house on the evening of the 13th.[28] Three prosecution witnesses asserted he had been at Stanton's home that night.

These defence witnesses were not independent however, in fact they were his friends and associates. At the trial of John Surratt, prosecution witness William Cleaver stated that because he was well acquainted with Surratt, he was inclined to shield him. For this reason, two years earlier, he had not told the military commission that he has seen Surratt in Washington on April 14th. Could O'Laughlin's associates have also acted to shield their friend by stating that he was with them every moment that evening when he really wasn't?[29]

O'Laughlin's lawyer, Walter Cox, declared that his client, along with two of his associates, had been invited by Henderson to go from Baltimore to Washington on "Thursday the 13th of April, the occasion of the general illumination". According to their testimony however, they never actually saw the innocent spectacle that supposedly was the reason for their trip. They stated that during the fireworks, between 9 and 10 p.m., they were inside a Washington music hall, listening to a performance instead. O'Laughlin had gone to Washington to see the fireworks but he did not see them. He also was supposed to be in a music hall that evening but was he really somewhere else instead?

Why would O'Laughlin be at the Stanton home, asking for Stanton or Grant? If he was planning to assassinate one of these men, it would helpful to meet the them, try to learn some of their habits, get to know what they looked like and gather information that could be of assistance in carrying out their murders. There was evidence that this had happened before. No less a person than the President's son, Thomas "Tad" Lincoln, testified at the trial of John Surratt that a man looking very much like Surratt had tried on two occasions to get to speak with his father in March, 1865. As well, the letter that was found by Mrs. Mary Benson, counseled the one that was to kill Lincoln to, "Get introduced, congratulate him, listen to his stories"[30]

The charge and specification against the eight conspirators included conspiring to murder President Lincoln, Vice-President Andrew Johnson, Secretary of State William Seward and the commander of the armies of the United States Army, Ulysses S. Grant. Booth, Atzerodt, Payne and Herold were to kill the President, Vice-President and the Secretary of State. This left Grant to be murdered and evidently

Michael O'Laughlin to do it. The general and his wife were scheduled to accompany the President and Mrs. Lincoln to Ford's theatre but the Grants changed their plans unexpectedly and left Washington earlier on the day of April 14th.

O'Laughlin's lawyer and most of the lawyers for the rest of the accused maintained that there indeed was a conspiracy to kidnap Lincoln but it had been abandoned well before he was killed. They argued that the conspiracy to assassinate was made just days or hours before the deed, as Atzerodt stated in a confession he made after his arrest. In argument before the military commission, O'Laughlin's counsel, Walter Cox, went over the testimony of prosecution witness Samuel Chester. Chester, an actor who knew Booth, told the commission that in late December, 1864 or January, 1865, Booth tried to enlist him in a conspiracy to capture the President and other heads of government and take them to Richmond. Chester also testified that in February, 1865, Booth told him that he was abandoning the plan to capture Lincoln and the others. Therefore between perhaps February, 1865, as Samuel Chester testified and possibly as late as eight o'clock on April 14th, 1865, as Atzerodt stated, there was no planning, no activity, no conspiracy to kidnap or kill.[31]

The evidence presented at the trial of the conspirators and the trial of John Surratt does not bear this out though. For example, the supplies brought to Surrattsville in early March, the suspicious telegrams to O'Laughlin later in the month, the trips of Mary Surratt to deliver messages to Lloyd about guns and supplies, show that the plotters were actively involved in their clandestine activities during this time.[32] It is very hard to believe that O'Laughlin was ignorant of the plans that his associates undoubtedly had in place.

Like the other conspirators considered earlier, O'Laughlin was undoubtedly guilty of participating in the conspiracy to kidnap and despite defence protestations to the contrary, there is evidence to show he was guilty of being part of the plot to kill as well. He was found guilty by the military court appointed to hear the case and received a life sentence for his part in the conspiracy.

As with the forgoing conspirators, evidence shows that he was a Catholic. In her book, *The Death of Lincoln*, (1909) author Clara Laughlin declared that O'Laughlin was a Catholic and she was certainly unconvinced of the Roman Catholic Church's role in President Lincoln's murder. Louis Weichmann and Lloyd Lewis also stated that O'Laughlin was a member of the Church of Rome.[33]

In addition, as noted earlier, Booth's sister, Asia, had expressed shock that O'Laughlin and Arnold were amongst the conspirators and stated that she was even more surprised to learn that all the conspirators were Catholics. The reason she was shocked by the news that these two were among the conspirators was undoubtedly because she knew them well, probably from childhood like her brother, John. Knowing them as she did, she would have known whether they were Catholics or not. If either one of them had not belonged to the Church of Rome, she could not have been "still more surprised" by the statement that all the conspirators were Catholics, because she would have known this to be false. Her statements therefore confirm that O'Laughlin, like Booth, was a Catholic.

Sam Arnold

Like O'Laughlin, Samuel Arnold was tried by the military commission and sentenced to life in prison. The evidence showed that Arnold, a former Confederate soldier, was part of the plot to kidnap the President and probably guilty of more.[34]

Eaton Horner, helped arrest Arnold at the federal instillation of Fortress Monroe, Virginia, on April 17th, 1865. Horner testified that at the time of his arrest, Arnold gave a statement in which he gave the names of men that he said were connected with a plot to kidnap the President. Arnold said he took the job of clerk at Fortress Monroe on April 1st, 1865. He also stated that some one to three weeks before to going there, he attended a meeting in Washington attended by Booth, O'Laughlin, Atzerodt, John Surratt and others. He admitted that he had been part of a plot to kidnap Lincoln and take him to the South in order to force the American government to exchange prisoners with the Confederacy.

He said he withdrew from the conspiracy at the time because the others refused to act the week he was in Washington and because the plan was impractical but apparently not because it was wrong. When asked if he had ever corresponded with Booth, he initially denied it but when he was told that a letter written by him to Booth had been found in the actor's hotel room, he admitted doing so.[35]

The letter that Arnold admitted writing was dated March 27th, 1865 and postmarked Hookstown, Baltimore County, Maryland. Arnold's brother, William, who resided in that community, testified that Samuel was there with him on that date. Other witnesses testified that the handwriting was Arnold's.

The letter read:

> DEAR JOHN: Was business so important that you could not remain in Balto. till I saw you? I came in as soon as I could, but found you had gone to W-n. I called also to see Mike, but learned from his mother he had gone out with you, and had not returned. I concluded, therefore, he had gone with you. How inconsiderate you have been! When I left you, you stated we would not meet in a month or so. Therefore, I made application for employment, an answer to which I shall receive during the week. I told my parents I had ceased with you. Can I, then, under existing circumstances, come as you request? You know full well that the G--t suspicions something is going on there; therefore, the undertaking is becoming more complicated. Why not, for the present, desist, for various reasons, which, if you look into, you can readily see, without my making any mention thereof. You, nor any one, can censure me for my present course. You have been its cause, for how can I now come after telling them I had left you? Suspicion rests upon me now from my whole family, and even parties in the county. I will be compelled to leave home any how, and how soon I care not. None, no not one were more in favor of the enterprise than myself, and to-day would be there, had you not done as you have---by this I mean, manner of proceeding. I am, as you well know, in need. I am, you may say, in rags, whereas to-day I ought to be well clothed. I do not feel right stalking about with means and more from appearances a beggar. I feel

my dependence; but even all this would and was forgotten, for I was one with you. Time more propitious will arrive yet. Do not act rashly or in haste. I would prefer your first query, "go and see how it will be taken at R---d, and ere long I shall be better prepared to again be with you. I dislike writing; would sooner verbally make known my views; yet your non-writing causes me thus to proceed.

Do not in anger peruse this. Weigh all I have said, and, as a rational man and friend, you can not censure or upbraid my conduct. I sincerely trust this, nor aught else that shall or may occur, will ever be an obstacle to obliterate our former friendship and attachment. Write me to Balto., as I expect to be in about Wednesday or Thursday, or, if you can possibly come on, I will Tuesday meet you in Balto., at B-----. Ever I subscribe myself,

Your friend, SAM.[36]

The letter told a very different story than the one Arnold gave to the authorities. In the correspondence, there was a future meeting between himself and Booth anticipated and it appears the group as a whole. The letter showed that Arnold had not separated from the conspiracy; he only wanted the plan delayed because of government suspicions. Was the enterprise that Arnold was talking about to kidnap or murder? Either way, the lies he told showed he was not innocent and deserved the prison sentence he received.

His religious affiliation was not as easy to discover as some of the other conspirators but as was noted earlier, the same statements by Booth's sister, Asia, which confirmed that O'Laughlin was a Catholic also showed that Arnold was one too. Arnold received at least some of his education through Catholic established institutions as well. He attended St. Charles College with Booth and Weichmann and Georgetown College in Washington D.C., now Georgetown University, a Jesuit founded education institution.[37]

Edward Spangler

Edward Spangler, an employee of Ford's theatre, was another of the conspirator. After being found guilty by the military commission, he was given a six year prison sentence. According to testimony at the trial of the conspirators, on the evening of April 14, John Wilkes Booth rode up the alley to the back door of the theatre and called for him to come and hold his horse. Spangler went out to see him and then ordered another employee, Joseph Burroughs, to hold the animal because he was too busy to do it. Burroughs also testified that during the afternoon, when he was helping him prepare the Presidential box, Spangler had cursed President Lincoln and General Grant.[38]

Jacob Ritterspaugh, a carpenter at Ford's theatre, stated that while he was standing behind the scenes during the play on the fateful evening, he heard the sound of a gun and then someone call out that the President had been shot. When he saw a man with a knife in his hand running toward the back door, he ran after him but the man struck at him with the weapon, forcing Ritterspaugh back. The knife wielding man then ran out in the alley to the horse being held by Burroughs, kicked him out of the way, mounted the horse and rode off.

When he went back into the theatre to where he had heard the shot, Ritterspaugh stated that Edward Spangler hit him "on the face with the back of his hand, and he said, 'Don't say which way he went.' I asked him what he meant by slapping me in the mouth, and he said, 'For God's sake, shut up;' and that was the last he said."

Ritterspaugh testified that when he heard the shot, Spangler was standing near him. When he left his position close to Spangler to chase the man with the knife, the carpenter did not see the assassin's face well enough to recognize who he was chasing. He said that he didn't hear it was Booth until he had again gone outside the theatre which was after Spangler had struck him. Spangler then must have known who Ritterspaugh was chasing and his attempt to hinder the pursuit of the assassin shows his involvement in the plot.[39]

John T. Ford, the proprietor of the theatre, testified that Edward Spangler seemed to have had great admiration for John Wilkes Booth and would do errands, odd jobs, and the like for him. Spangler and another man had modified the stable at the back of the theatre at Booth's request and when the actor wanted to sell his buggy, it was Spangler who sold it for him, doing so a few days before the assassination.[40]

Ritterspaugh also testified that he told theatre employees James Lamb and Louis Carland what had happened that night. Carland and James Gifford, whose questionable testimony has been discussed earlier, cast doubts on Ritterspaugh's statements, as did Lamb. They testified that Ritterspaugh told a very different story to them than what he told the military commission. It could be asked though, what reason would he have to tell one story to the commission and another one to them?

Carland certainly might have had a reason to lie however, as Spangler evidently was an associate of his and was staying with him when they were both arrested. In addition, Carland was a Catholic and the contention of this work is that Catholics were behind the conspiracy to murder Lincoln. Could Carland also have been playing a small part in the conspiracy, after the fact?[41]

Though his was a supporting role, Spangler still played an important part in the deadly plot when he arranged for Booth's horse to be held for his quick escape and when he tried to throw pursuers off his trail. Weighing the evidence, the court found him guilty, which he undoubtedly was.

What were his religious beliefs though? Edward Spangler was born in York, Pennsylvania on August 10th, 1825. He reportedly was baptized there in the First Trinity Reformed church about four months later. In 1958, he married a woman named Mary Brashears, ten years his senior, in Baltimore. After a long illness, she died in this city on July 24th, 1864. Despite extensive research, the identity of the church that they were married in or the denomination of the clergyman who conducted her funeral there could not be found.[42]

After being convicted, Edward Spangler was sent to the prison of Fort Jefferson in Florida along with the other conspirators and he was released with Mudd and Arnold in 1869. Spangler became close to Samuel Mudd during their imprisonment and he spent his last years working for him and living at the doctor's home in Maryland. Spangler died in February, 1875 and until 1983, his body was buried in an unmarked plot in the graveyard at St. Peter's church. St. Peter's is a Catholic church located about five miles west of where Mudd's farm was. Samuel Mudd, who died in 1883, was buried in the cemetery of St. Mary's Catholic church, in the neighborhood of Bryantown.[43]

Records of St. Peter's church showed that on February 7th, the day the church documented as the time of his death, Spangler was baptized. He evidently had a deathbed baptism but did he also have a deathbed conversion? It is possible that he could have converted to Catholicism years before and then with death approaching, felt he should to fulfill this sacrament.[44]

Spangler's membership in the Church of Rome therefore seems to not have been made clear until just before his passing. No direct evidence has surfaced of his Catholicism earlier in life but this doesn't mean it never will. Booth's true religion didn't become public until years after his death. Constance Head commented, regarding Booth's Catholicism, "Thus the secret remained so well guarded that even the most rabidly anti-Catholic writers who tried to depict the assassination of Lincoln as a Jesuit or Papist plot were puzzled by the seemingly accurate information that John Wilkes Booth was an Episcopalian".[45] While complimenting "rabidly anti-Catholic" writers for caring about accuracy, Ms. Head also showed that information seemingly possessed about the beliefs of such historical figures may actually be wrong.

This may be the case with Edward Spangler too. For years before Lincoln's assassination, Spangler's associates and friends were Catholics. Prior to the President's murder, he was an admirer of a main leader of the conspiracy to kill President Lincoln, John Wilkes Booth, a Catholic that he knew and did work for. He assisted Booth in his escape. After the assassination, he was sheltered by Louis Carland, another Catholic. He was put on trial and found to be part of a conspiracy dominate by Catholics. After being released from incarceration, he lived the rest of his life in close friendship with yet another Catholic, Samuel Mudd. His membership in the Church of Rome was seemingly finally revealed on his deathbed. His very close association with Romanists at the time of the assassination, as well as the fact of his Catholicism disclosed at the end of his life however, does provides some evidence that in 1865, Edward was among the conspirators who belonged to the Church of Rome.

George Atzerodt

The next conspirators to be considered is George Atzerodt, nicknamed Port Tobacco. After standing trial along with the others, he was found guilty of participating in the conspiracy to murder top officials in the United States government and executed along with Mary Surratt, Payne and Herold. Though a coach maker by profession, he was frequently ferrying spies and contraband across the Potomac River near Port Tobacco, Maryland, during the Civil War, hence his nickname. The prosecution alleged that Atzerodt's assigned role on a night of April 14th was to kill Vice-President Andrew Johnson.

He was often seen in the company of many of the conspirators in the months preceding the assassination and six weeks before, he had helped deliver guns and other provisions to Surrattsville to be picked up by Booth and Harold as they fled.[46]

Lieutenant W.R. Keim testified that a week to ten days before the assassination, he shared a multi-person room in Pennsylvania House with Atzerodt. Leaving the room one morning, Atzerodt left a large bowie knife in his bed which Keim picked up. Atzerodt asked for his knife and after receiving it back said, "I want that; if one fails, I want the other". Keim also stated that Atzerodt was always armed with a revolver.

Colonel W. R. Nevins testified that on the 12th of April, George Atzerodt entered the prestigious Washington hotel, Kirkwood House, and asked where the Vice-President was. Nevins showed him where Johnson's room was and also ushered him to the dining room where the Vice-President was having dinner. Atzerodt evidently did not try to approach Johnson. The register of the hotel showed that Atzerodt checked into a room on the morning of the 14th, before eight o'clock.[47] The Vice-President reportedly said that before the assassination, he heard footsteps in the room above him for hours. John Lee, the Washington detective, testified that Atzerodt's room was situated so that the accused would normally passed by Johnson's door to get to the lobby.

John Fletcher, foreman of Naylor's livery-stable, stated that on the day of the assassination, Atzerodt and David Herold came to his stable at one o'clock in the afternoon. Atzerodt left a mare there until later that night. Returning at ten o'clock, he took a drink with Fletcher who said he seemed to be "half-tight". Atzerodt told him, "If this thing happens to-night, you will hear of a present" or "Get a present".[48]

According to an employee of Pennsylvania House, the defendant came to the hotel between midnight and one o'clock on the night of the assassination, went into the bar and then left. Proprietor John Greenwalt stated that Atzerodt and another man came back into the hotel between two and three o'clock in the morning and asked for a room. Greenwell testified, "I had an uneasiness about the thing myself; thought there was something wrong". He also said Atzerodt hesitated when asked to register, something he had never done before. Early that morning, Atzerodt and the other man left the room.[49] That morning, Atzerodt threw his Bowie knife away on a Washington street.

On the evening of April 15th, Detective John Lee entered the room Atzerodt had rented at Kirkwood house. There he found a loaded revolver, a large bowie knife, a bank book of J. Wilkes Booth showing a credit of $455.00 at a Montreal bank, as well as a map of Virginia.[50]

Atzerodt was arrested by Sergeant L.W. Gemmill on April 20th, near Germantown, Maryland. Gemmill testified that at the time, he did not ask why he was being arrested and said he had not been in Washington recently. Among other charges,

Atzerodt was accused of lying in wait to murder Andrew Johnson and conspiring to murder Abraham Lincoln. His defence was similar to John Surratt's. While in custody, he admitted that he was part of the conspiracy to kidnap the President but he had only learned of the plot to murder Lincoln at eight o'clock on the night of the assassination. He said he was assigned by Booth to kill Johnson but he had refused to do it. According to him, Booth "told me I was a fool; that I would be hung any how, and that it was death to every man that backed out; and so we parted".[51] His defence was that he was guilty of conspiring to kidnap the United States commander-in-chief therefore, but not conspiring to kill anyone. If true, this admission is of little comfort as the kidnapping would have been a capital offence and Lincoln could still have been killed if there were problems during its commission.

As outlined earlier, there is solid evidence that a plan to kill existed long before the murder and was not created at the last moment. If the plan was only to kidnap Lincoln and not kill him and others, why did Atzerodt say to Lieutenant Keim in the Pennsylvania House, "if one fails, I want the other" regarding his knife and, apparently, his revolver. If Atzerodt was part of the conspiracy to kidnap the President and not kill the Vice-President, why did he find out what room Johnson was in? Why would he move into the unfamiliar surroundings of Kirkwood House on the morning of April 14th where the Vice-President was staying, instead of the cheaper Pennsylvania House where he usually stayed?

Atzerodt stated that the plan to kidnap was not changed until eight o'clock that night. His lawyer alleged that he rejected Booth's plan and abandoned everything to do with the conspiracy but was too afraid of Booth to tell the authorities. Four defence witnesses testified to Atzerodt's cowardice.[52]

In the end however, he either wanted to murder Johnson but was too afraid to act or wanted no part of the murder. If he wanted to murder the Vice-President but was afraid to act, he is still in agreement with the conspiracy. If he wanted no part of the murder plot, he could have warned the authorities, despite his supposed lack of courage and saved Lincoln's life. This would have been his opportunity to show by his actions at the time, not by his words later, that he really did not want to be party to the assassination.

Why did he say to John Fletcher shortly after ten o'clock on that fateful evening, "If this thing happens to-night, you will hear of a present"? He was, by his own admission, talking about murder.

The evidence shows that he was clearly guilty of plotting to kidnap Lincoln to help the Confederacy and assist in the break-up of the United States. His actions show he was also guilty of conspiring to and, at least, desiring to murder Vice-President Johnson, even if he lost his nerve at the last moment and didn't carry out the act. He was therefore rightfully convicted and executed for his treasonous acts.

Lewis Payne, David Herold

There was essentially no effort needed to prove the guilt of Lewis Payne and David Herold. Their lawyers were instead reduced to trying to explain their actions. Payne's defence called several doctors to testify in an attempt to show that he was insane and most of Herold's witnesses stated that he was really no more than an easily influenced boy than a man of 22 years of age.[53]

Were Atzerodt, Payne and Herold Roman Catholics? George Alfred Townsend asserted that all the conspirators were by education, Catholics. Charles Chiniquy alleged that all of the conspirators belonged to the Church of Rome, including these three, but they pretended to be of a different religion in order to hide the role the Catholic Church played in the terrible drama. He stated,

> It is a well authenticated fact, that Booth and Weichman, who were themselves Protestant perverts to Romanism, had proselytized a good number of semi-Protestants and infidels who, either from conviction, or from hope of the fortunes promised to the successful murderers, were themselves very zealous for the Church of Rome. Payne, Atzeroth and Harold were among those proselytes. But when those murderers were to appear before the country, and receive the just punishment of their crime, the Jesuits were too shrewd to ignore that if they were all coming on the scaffold as Roman Catholics, and accompanied by their father confessors, it would, at once, open the eyes of the American people, and clearly show that this was a Roman Catholic plot. They persuaded three of their proselytes to avail themselves of the theological principles of the Church of Rome, that a man is allowed to conceal his religion, nay, that he may say that he is an heretic, a Protestant, though he is a Roman Catholic, when it is for his own interest or the best interests of his church to conceal the truth and deceive the people. Here is the doctrine of Rome on that subject:

> > 'Soepe melius est ad dei honorem, et utiliatatem proximi, tegere fidem quam frateri, ut si latens inter herticos, plus boni facis ; vel si ex confessione fidei, plus mali sequeretur, verbi gratia turbatio, neces, exacerbotio tyrannis.'--Ligouri Theologia, b. ii., chap. iii., p. 6.

> 'It is often more to the glory of God and the good of our neighbor to conceal our religious faith, as when we live among heretics, we can more easily do them good in that way; or if by declaring our religion, we cause some disturbances, or deaths, or even the wrath of the tyrant.'

> It is evident that the Jesuits had never had better reasons to suspect that the declaration of their religion would damage them and excite the wrath of their tyrant, viz: the American people.[54]

Lewis Payne, whose name actually was Lewis Powell, was accompanied to the gallows by two Protestant clergymen, Rev. Gillette of the First Baptist church of Washington and a Rev. Stryker. Dr. A. P. Stryker was an Episcopalian clergyman from Baltimore. Payne, the son of a Baptist minister, had pretended to be a Baptist preacher by the name of Wood. His name was not Wood though. He clearly was not a Baptist clergyman either and no historian has argued he was. It has been stated though in a number of historical accounts that at the time of the assassination, he

WHO KILLED ABRAHAM LINCOLN?

was a Baptist but court testimony indicates that he was not a member of this church at this time either. Dr. James Hall, a physician who examined Payne, was called by both the prosecution and the defence to testify before the military commission. He stated that Payne had, "acknowledged to me that *at one time he had* been a member of the Baptist Church." Dr. Hall also stated that after examining Payne, he had found no evidence of insanity.[55]

Payne was accompanied to his execution by a Baptist clergyman and an Episcopal minister therefore, even though he was not a Baptist or an Episcopalian. This support Charles Chiniquy's statement that the conspirators were not of the same faith of the clergymen that went with them to their execution. If he wasn't a Baptist, what was he? Could Payne really have been a Catholic, instead of the Baptist he was mistakenly believed to be?

What about the other two? Atzerodt was accompanied to his execution by a Lutheran minister, Rev. Butler, and by a Congregationalist clergyman, Reverend W. W. Winchester. There was no evidence given showing the supposed Lutheran attending a church service of the denomination that he was allegedly belonged to. Court testimony did however show Atzerodt going to St. Aloysuis Catholic church in the nation's capital on Sunday morning, April 2nd, 1865.[56]

Herold went to the gallows in the company of an Episcopalian clergyman, Rev. Olds but as with Atzerodt, there was no evidence presented at the trial that showed him ever going to a church service of the denomination he supposedly belonged to. He had received education at Georgetown College, as had Arnold and Samuel Mudd. Court testimony also showed that this man, who received at least part of his education from this Romanist institution, attended a Catholic church service like his fellow conspirator George Atzerodt.[57]

Although he had gone to Catholic church services, Booth was mistakenly believed to be an Episcopalian. His attendance at these Catholic services was puzzling if he did not belong to the Church of Rome but his presence made perfect sense if he did. Being at these services was part of his life as a Catholic. Along with the evidence that virtually all of their close associates were Roman Catholics, doesn't the fact that Atzerodt and Herold attended these church services also show that they may very well have belonged to the Church of Rome?

For years, it was accepted that Booth was a Protestant. Constance Head commented on the Catholic interest in seeing the well guarded secret of Booth's religion remain buried. Of his membership in the Roman Church, she stated, "the few who knew of his conversion must have decided after the assassination that for the good of the church, it was best never to mention it." Charles Chiniquy alleged that Herold, Atzerodt and Payne were Roman Catholics. If so, could this same suppression of information that Head discussed regarding Booth be the reason that these three conspirators' Catholicism is not obvious today? Her statement also provided a concrete example of what Chiniquy wrote concerning the Church of Rome's counsel for her children to conceal their religion if it was not in the Church's interest to have it known.

As well, these conspirators were not plotting alone. The fact that Lincoln and Sewards's murders were talked about in the solidly Catholic community of St. Joseph, Minnesota before the deeds were carried out, points to the involvement of Catholic Church officials in the assassination plot. What connection would Booth, the Surratts, and the other conspirators have had to Minnesota? How did this information get out to this location before the assassination unless, as Charles Chiniquy asserted, the priests of St. Joseph heard it from their fellow priests in the nation's capital?

Charles Chiniquy stated that the staunch support of the Roman Catholic Church for the Southern cause, culminating in the open recognition of the Confederacy by the Pope, clearly encouraged Catholic priests to join the struggle for the South, which would have included helping in the destruction of its greatest enemies.

As *Fifty Years* asserted, the presence of so many such priests in Mary Surratt's boarding house, "the nest that hatched the egg", points to the involvement of the Church in the plot. Chiniquy commented: "Booth was nothing but the tool of the Jesuits. It was Rome who directed his arm, after corrupting his heart and damning his soul." He added:

> the Jesuits alone could select the assassins, train them, and show them a crown of glory in heaven, if they would kill the author of the bloodshed, the famous renegade and apostate—the enemy of the Pope and of the Church—Lincoln.

> Who does not see the lessons given by the Jesuits to Booth, in their daily intercourse in Mary Surratt's house, when he reads those lines written by Booth a few hours before his death: "I can never repent, God made me the instrument of his punishment!" Compare these words with the doctrines and principles taught by the councils, the decrees of the Pope, and the laws of holy inquisition, as you find them in chapter 55 of this volume, and you will find that the sentiments and belief of Booth flow from those principles, as the river flows from its source.[58]

After a review of these facts, it can be concluded that there is very strong evidence that most, if not all of the conspirators in the plot to destroy the head of America, the great Abraham Lincoln, as well as the nation and the ideals it stood for, were Catholics, aided and abetted by officials of the Church of Rome.

Chapter 10

The Roman Catholic Church: The Church of God?

A look at the history of the Roman Catholic Church: its evolution as a religious organization, the origin and development of its doctrines, as well as the deeds of its officials and lay members, can give valuable insights into whether it could be behind so great a crime as the murder of the head of the American nation and whether it is, or is not, as Charles Chiniquy concluded, the true church of God.

Through the time of its existence, the Catholic Church has amassed tremendous power and influence, at times achieving almost complete world domination. Its glittering triumphs however, have been rivaled by its defeats and scandals. Yet it has endured, claiming more than a billion adherents today: its wealth, power, prestige and size, continuing to grow.

The Church of Rome's assertion that it is the only true Church rests on its claim of unbroken apostolic succession, beginning with Saint Peter and also on its primacy, or supremacy, over the other churches of the world. On the foundation of an allegedly unbroken line of popes, leading a supreme Church, it has attempted to build the claim that it is the only true religion, with salvation only available within its embrace. The problem with the Catholic Church's assertion of apostolic succession and primacy is that there appears to be essentially no evidence for it.

According to God's Word, Simon Peter was not considered the pope or head of the Church. Jesus congratulated Peter for correctly identifying him when he asked his disciples:

> But whom say ye that I am? And Simon Peter answered and said, Thou art the Christ, the Son of the living God. And Jesus answered and said unto him, Blessed art thou, Simon Bar-jona: for flesh and blood hath not revealed it unto thee, but my Father which is in heaven. And I say also unto thee, That thou art Peter, and upon this rock I will build my church; and the gates of hell shall not prevail against it. And I will give unto thee the keys of the kingdom of heaven: and whatsoever thou shalt bind on earth shall be bound in heaven: and whatsoever thou shalt loose on earth shall be loosed in heaven. (Matthew 16:15b-19)

What praise, position, and power seem to be conferred on Peter! Jesus however then told his disciples that he would later go Jerusalem to suffer, be killed and then raised from the dead again. According to the Scriptures:

> Then Peter took him, and began to rebuke him, saying, Be it far from thee, Lord: this shall not be unto thee. But he turned, and said unto Peter, Get thee behind me, Satan: thou art an offence unto me: for thou savourest not the things that be of God, but those that be of men. (Matthew 16:22,23)

Was Jesus saying that his church would be built on Peter, a mere man whom he called Satan, when he said "upon this rock I will build my church"? In the original Greek text that the English is translated from, the word Peter comes from the Greek word petros, meaning a piece of rock, a stone and the word rock that Jesus said that he would build his church on, comes from the word petra, meaning a mass of rock.[1] A well known bible passage tells the parable of the wise man that built his house upon the rock (Matthew 7:24-27, Luke 6:48, 49). Here the word rock, which represents Christ, is translated from the word petra, not the word petros. No wise homebuilder would construct their home on a piece of rock or a stone that could shift. They would want to build on solid bedrock. In the expression "rock of offence" found in Romans 9:33, ("As it is written, Behold I lay in Sion a stumblingstone and rock of offence: and whosoever believeth on him shall not be ashamed"), the word rock, clearly a reference to Jesus Christ, also comes from the word petra. Despite Roman Catholic assertions to the contrary, this mass of rock, this bedrock that the true church is built on, is Jesus Christ, not Peter, a mere fallible man and the only one that the Bible records being calling Satan by Jesus Christ.

Chapter 16 of Matthew's gospel records Jesus appearing to give the keys of the kingdom of heaven to Peter alone. The Roman Catholic Church teaches that it was just to Peter that these keys were given. As the bishop of Rome and, in effect, the head of the Church on earth, he would decide who would enter heaven and who would not. The Catholic Church maintains that every person who desired to be accepted by God and be able to enter the Church had to submit to Peter's teaching and authority as the visible substitute, or vicar, of Jesus Christ on earth. According to the Church of Rome, these keys and the power to decide who enters heaven were passed on to all the bishops of Rome, or popes that came after Simon Peter.

A couple of chapters later in Matthew however, it is clarified that these keys were given to all the disciples of Christ. Jesus said to his disciples, "Verily I say unto you, Whatsoever ye (plural) shall bind on earth shall be bound in heaven: and whatsoever ye shall loose on earth shall be loosed in heaven" (Matthew 18:18).

God's Word teaches that all the disciples were sent out to preach the gospel or good news. They were commanded to teach that all had sinned and violated God's law and therefore were facing his wrath. They were also to teach the good news that salvation from eternal punishment in hell and the lake of fire could be obtained by repentance from sin, simple faith in Christ and acceptance of the atoning sacrifice of his shed blood on the cross. This message was the keys to the kingdom of heaven that Christ spoke of. Those that chose to continue to be enslaved by their sin on earth by refusing to accept Christ's gift of eternal life would be bound in heaven and sent to eternal punishment. Those that choose to be freed on earth by accepting Christ would be free in heaven. This, the great commission to preach the gospel, is given to all believers in Christ (Mark 16:15).

The Scriptures does show that Simon Peter distinguished himself from the other disciples and apostles at other times but not often in ways that others would want to copy. Peter was the only disciple at the mount of transfiguration that suggested making a tabernacle for Moses and Elijah as well as Jesus Christ (Luke 9:33 – Moses and Elijah appeared and spoke with Christ as he prayed apart up in a mountain with Peter and two other disciples). These two Old Testament prophets were great men of God but they were still mere men who did not deserve a place of worship for their honour or veneration. Devotion and prayers to dead "saints" is part of the teachings of this Church that calls Peter its first pope though.

When a band of men came to capture Jesus, it was Peter who drew his sword and cut off the ear of one of them. Jesus rebuked him for doing so, declaring that that they that "take the sword shall perish with the sword" (Matthew 26:52). Simon Peter didn't understand that Christ had come to earth to die on the cross, not to establish an earthly kingdom. Like Peter, the Catholic Church has apparently not understood this either and has, for example, engaged in such things as the bloody Crusades to take the Holy Land back by the sword. As well, the Holy See, situated at the Vatican, is a sovereign state, in direct contradiction of the words of Christ. He said in John 18:36," My kingdom is not of this world: if my kingdom were of this world, then would my servants fight".

This is not the only area that the doctrines of the Church of Rome are completely opposed to what the Bible teaches however. In 2006, the Roman Catholic Church restated its support for evolution after a U.S. court decision; even though the Word of God clearly declares that mankind and all living species were created by God. The book of Genesis and other scriptures teach that the world was created from nothing, thousands of years ago, not millions or billions of years in the past.

Peter was also referred to by name in the God's Word as boasting he would die with Christ and not deny him (Matthew 26:35). The scriptures also record that Peter alone, with curses, denied his Lord three times (Matthew 26:69-75).

After he repented of his denial of Christ and was converted, Peter was truly used by God. He preached a sermon at Pentecost where 3,000 people were saved (Acts 2:14-41). God also used Peter to heal people and used him to raise a woman called Tabitha from the dead, causing many to become believers in Christ (Acts 9:39-42). God also gave him the vision of a sheet coming down from heaven and it was Peter that preached to Cornelius, the centurion, and those with him, as the blessing of the Holy Spirit was poured out on this Gentile audience (Acts 10). The 15th chapter of Acts reported that Peter also played a significant role in the controversy regarding believer's circumcision that the early church had to deal with.

God's Word records that the apostles and elders met together in Jerusalem to consider this controversy but the scriptures does not show that Peter was the pope or head of the church however. Though prominent, his voice was one of many this group heard and it was James who gave judgment on what should be done, which the council agreed with.

As well, the book of Galatians disclosed that the apostle Paul had to confront Peter and publicly rebuke him for his hypocrisy regarding his association with the Gentiles (Galatians 2:11-21). So much for Peter's infallibility and headship of the church.

As for prominence, God inspired Peter to write two books of the Bible but used Paul to write 13. Much of another book, Acts, is about Paul's conversion and the journeys he made preaching the Gospel. Paul also said in 2 Corinthians 12:11, "for in nothing am I behind the very chiefest apostles" clearly stating that he was in no way inferior to any apostle, including Peter.

If Simon Peter was the first pope, he would have been a married one, since God's Word states that he had a wife (Mark 1:30, Luke 4:38). Instead of speaking of apostles and other leaders being celibate, throughout the Bible, marriage is spoken of approvingly. Hebrews 13:4 states "Marriage is honourable in all, and the bed undefiled: but whoremongers and adulterers God will judge." The current Catholic Church scandals show that many Roman Catholic priests know something about adultery, as Charles Chiniquy alleged more than a century ago, and others before him. A large 2003 poll of the priests in England and Wales reportedly showed that a stunning 60% of them believed that adultery with a married woman should not bar them from the normal ministry of the priesthood.

Was Peter the bishop of Rome, as the Catholic Church says every pope has to be? The Bible records Peter following Jesus on his earthly ministry and later journeying only to Lydia, Joppa, Caesarea and Antioch. In his letter to the church in Rome, Paul greeted some 25 people by name at the end of this epistle but didn't mention Peter, the supposed head of the church. Why would this be if Peter was the bishop? The scriptures do not say Peter went to Rome, in fact there appears to be little evidence, if any, that he ever was there.

As well, there does not seem to be any proof that the Church of Rome had the primacy among the other churches in apostolic times. There was a church in Jerusalem before one was established in Rome, as it was at Jerusalem that Christ was tried, crucified, rose from the dead and ascended to heaven. The Holy Spirit was poured out on the church on the day of Pentecost in Jerusalem, not Rome. The great commission was given to the apostles in Jerusalem, not Rome. Jesus' said "Thus it is written, and thus it behoved Christ to suffer, and to rise from the dead the third day: And that repentance and remission of sins should be preached in his name among all nations, beginning at Jerusalem", not Rome (Luke 24: 46, 47).

The Scriptures show the early church council that discussed and debated circumcision for new believers did not call for a supreme Roman church to give its sentence on what the proper teaching should be on the subject. The recorded history of the early church also shows that there was no supreme church, overseeing bishop or pope in Rome. Ignatius, bishop of Antioch, provided proof in his writings, dated near the end of the first century A.D. He did not write of Peter alone but of Peter and Paul together when referring to those with authority over the Roman church. When he wrote to other churches, he asked that they obey their own bishop. After being informed that he was to be executed, Ignatius wrote to the Roman church asking them to pray for the church of Syria since it would not have him as bishop but the Lord only for its shepherd.[2] This clearly shows that during the early church age, the bishop of Rome was not the ruler of the catholic or universal church.

Further proof of this comes from the case of Paul of Samosata, bishop of Antioch, during the third century A.D. According to Eusebius who was bishop of Caesarea, Paul, the bishop of Antioch, was tried by a church council for heresy, the charge being the denial of the divinity of Christ. At the conclusion of the trial, Paul was found guilty. The council, made up of bishops, deacons and presbyters, did not come from Rome but from Jerusalem, Tarsus, Cesarea, Pontus and Iconium. The bishop pledged to retract his error but did not honor his promise. In 270 A.D., a second council again made up of officials from those Asian churches took Paul's bishopric from him and elected a new bishop. This was all done without the Roman church playing any part in the proceedings.[3]

Among numerous other proofs of the bishop of Rome's lack of supremacy is the statement by Cyprian, an important church father of the third century. He wrote concerning a supreme bishop: "For none of us ought to make himself a bishop of bishops, or pretend to awe his brethren by a tyrannical fear, because every bishop is at liberty to do as he pleases, and can no more be judged by another than he can judge others himself".[4]

In his well researched book, *The Papacy and the Civil Power*, former U.S. Secretary of the Navy, Richard W. Thompson gave a historical outline of the early church's development:

> Before the time of Constantine, each of the several churches planted by the apostles and the early fathers exercised its own jurisdiction over its own members, and thus preserved harmony in faith and worship. The right of visitorial guardianship, exercised by the apostles while planting and watering them in infancy, existed no longer, because there was no longer any necessity for it. But while each church governed its own affairs, they all realized the necessity of preserving a spirit of unity, and such brotherhood and fellowship among the whole as would enable them to sympathize with and assist each other in the adjustment of their local disagreements, it any should arise. A harmonious and beautiful Christian system was thus created, worthy of the divine approval, and under it the Catholic Apostolic Church was able to stand up and ward off the staggering blows of the pagan emperors.
>
> The first efforts to disturb this harmony were made by the bishops of Rome. About the beginning of the third century, Victor I., with a view to establish the primacy of the Church of Rome, endeavored to compel the Asiatic churches, by threats of excommunication, to conform to its custom in keeping the festival of Easter. About half a century afterward, Stephen I. attempted to assume jurisdiction over the Church of Spain; and, still later, Dionysius made a like attempt over the Church of Alexandria. These attempts at ecclesiastical absolutism at Rome were so sternly rebuked by the great fathers, Irenaeus and Cyprian, as to demonstrate that the leading churches could not be subjugated, unless by some power they were unable to resist. The bishops of Rome soon saw that this power was political imperialism; and they availed themselves of the first opportunity of uniting Church and State at Rome, in order to obtain possession of it.

This opportunity was the arrival of Constantine, at a time when the corrupt materials necessary for such a union were abundant at Rome...

It is worthy to be repeated that, before the time of Constantine, each of the churches of Asia, Africa, and Europe had enjoyed its own independence, with no asserted or recognized principality in either over the others. Rome had no more power than Alexandria, or Alexandria than Antioch, or Antioch than Jerusalem. As the most ancient and first-established churches, those of Jerusalem and Antioch had a sort of precedence of honor, derived from the association of the names of the apostles James (the Lord's brother) and Peter and Paul, with their history. But in neither of them had there been any pretense of authority or primacy set up. They were content to adhere, in what they did and taught, to the practice of that forbearance, charity, and toleration exhibited in the apostolic assembly at Jerusalem, by which they hoped to lead the world into that condition of meekness and humility which is experienced at the genuine impress of true Christianity upon the heart, whether it be that of prince or peasant.[5]

Although gaining in privilege and wealth at the time of Constantine, the Church of Rome was still subject to him and his successors. Lacking in power but not ambition, the clergy of Rome labored continually to increase the former while not diminishing of the latter. An opportunity to achieve their objective came in the form of Pepin, the son of Charles Martel. Although in a high position in France, he wanted the French throne occupied by Childeric III. The monarch, though weak, was the rightful king of France. The monarch was the last of a line of rulers that descended from Clovis I, over a period of some 250 years, in accordance with French law.

Unwilling to attempt to directly overthrow Childeric, Pepin, who sympathized with the popes in their struggle to end their subjection to the Eastern emperors, sent a message to Pope Zachary, asking him to use his power to release the people of France from their allegiance to their rightful king and put him on the throne. It appears logical in light of subsequent events that Pope Zachary's plan was to assist Pepin to become king, in return for Pepin's help in ending the Church's subjection to the emperor. In clear violation of the laws of France, never mind what possible right the pontiff had to interfere in the affairs of this nation, Pope Zachary did what Pepin asked and with his help, Pepin became king. Keeping the Church free from machinations for raw power was apparently not a consideration.[6]

Historian George Waddington commented "This occurrence is generally related as the first instance of the temporal ambition of the Vatican, or, at least, of its interference with the rights of princes and the allegiance of subjects."[7] Zachary actually did more than was asked. Author of the masterful *History of the Decline and Fall of the Roman Empire*, Edward Gibbon stated, "The Franks were absolved from their ancient oath; but a dire anathema was thundered against them and their posterity if they should dare to renew the same freedom of choice, or to elect a king, except in the holy and meritorious race of the Carlovingian princes" (the descendants of Charles Martel).[8] The papal brief that absolved the people of France from their allegiance to Childeric III also took from them the right to pick their own king unless the pope agreed, therefore putting the government in the hands of the papacy.

Not long after, Astolphus, King of the Lombards, conquered a large part of Italy and threatened Rome. Pope Zachary asked for help from the emperor, Constantine Copronymus, but it was not immediately forthcoming. The pope, who was still a subject of the Empire, then used this alleged lack of interest, not oppression or any other wrong, to justify leading a revolt against the emperors that succeeded Constantine. Pope Zachary appealed to Pepin, who sent his army to Italy and forced the Lombards out. Pepin apparently then gave the territory, which was not his to begin with, to the Pope. He did not give Rome to the Pope because since the city had not been captured, he did not need to take it and never was in possession of it. Rome had been in the hands of the emperors until Pope Zachary, in an act of treason, simply claimed it. This marked the beginning of the temporal power of the Church of Rome, backed by French military power.[9]

The Roman Church's ambition continued through the rein of Charlemagne. Allying himself with the powerful French king, Pope Adrian I helped Charlemagne in his fight with the Duke of Bavaria by issuing an incredible bull of excommunication, published not for religious but secular reasons against the Duke and his people. According to Roman Catholic historian Louis Marie De Cormenin, Adrian I declared," the Franks were absolved in advance from all crimes they might commit in the enemy's country; and that God commanded them, through his vicar, to violate girls, murder women, children, and old men, to burn cities, and put all the inhabitants to the sword."[10] This command by the "successor" of Peter to murder and rape is totally opposite to the New Testament exhortation for Christians to love their enemies.

The natural progression in the Roman clergy's thirst for power is seen in the statements of Pope Nicolas I, claiming for the Roman Church the right to rule the world. According to Cormenin, in reply to the bishops of Lorraine he wrote:

> You affirm that you are submissive to your sovereign, in order to obey the words of the apostle Peter, who said, 'Be subject to the prince, because he is above all mortals in this world.' But you appear to forget that we, as the vicar of Christ, have the right to judge all men: thus, before obeying kings, you owe obedience to us; and if we declare a monarch guilty, you should reject him from your communion until we pardon him.

> We alone have the power to bind and to loose, to absolve Nero and to condemn him; and Christians can not, under penalty of excommunication, execute other judgment than ours, which alone is infallible. People are not the judges of their princes; they should obey without murmuring the most iniquitous orders; they should bow their foreheads under the chastisements which it pleases kings to inflict on them; for a sovereign can violate the fundamental laws of the State, and seize upon the wealth of the citizen, by imposts or by confiscations; he can even dispose of their lives, without any of his subjects having the right to address to him simple remonstrances. But if

we declare a king heretical and sacrilegious, if we drive him from the Church, clergy and laity, whatever their rank, are freed from their oaths of fidelity, and may revolt against his power.

The same pope communicated to an envoy of Constantine this way:

> Know, prince, that the vicars of Christ are above the judgment of mortals; and that the most powerful sovereigns have no right to punish the crimes of popes, how enormous soever they may be....; for no matter how scandalous or criminal may be the debaucheries of the pontiff, you should obey them, for they are seated on the chair of St. Peter.

> Again: Fear, then, our wrath and the thunders of our vengeance; for Jesus Christ has appointed us with his own mouth absolute judges of all men; and kings themselves are submitted to our authority.[11]

The King of Bulgaria allegedly become a believer and persecuted those of his people who had not turned to Christ, as he supposedly had. Pope Nicolas I wrote the following gem of Christian charity to this monarch:

> I glorify you for having maintained your authority by putting to death those wandering sheep who refuse to enter the fold; and you not only have not sinned by showing a holy rigor, but I even congratulate you upon having opened the kingdom of heaven to the people submitted to your rule. A king need not fear to command massacres, when these will retain his subjects in obedience, or cause them to submit to the faith of Christ; and God will reward him in this world, and in eternal life, for these murders.

On the subject of infallibility this pope stated:

> It is evident that the popes can neither be bound nor unbound by any earthly power, nor even by that of the apostle, if he should return upon the earth; since Constantine the Great has recognized that the pontiffs held the place of God upon earth, the divinity not being able to be judged by any living man. We are, then, infallible, and whatever may be our acts, we are not accountable for them but to ourselves.[12]

R. W. Thompson commented on this pontiff:

> The Roman Catholic Church canonizes and places in her calendar of saints those whose devotion and piety she considers worthy of imitation. In this list she has placed seventy-six of her popes; and pointing out these saints to her children, she says to them that their lives exhibit 'the most perfect maxims of the Gospel reduced to practice,' point out 'the true path,' and lead, 'as it were, by the hand into it, sweetly inviting and encouraging us to walk cheerfully in the steps of those that are gone before us.' They are called 'the greatest personages who have ever adorned the world, the brightest ornaments of the Church militant, and the shining stars and suns of the triumphant, our future companions in eternal glory.' And 'their penitential lives and holy maxims' are commended to the faithful, as furnishing 'the sublime lessons of practical

virtue.' Now, when we consider that this pope, Nicholas I., has been made a saint, and that what he did and said is held in the most sacred remembrance, we can not fail to realize the importance of scrutinizing closely the language employed by him in the foregoing decrees and encyclicals, and of knowing also their effect upon the acquisition of temporal power, and the ultimate consequences to which they led. Why was he made a saint if his pontificate was not designed as a model for imitation? Why should he be imitated, if his principles and policy are not to be made the principles and policy of all time? He was infallible, and could not err! He was in 'the place of God upon earth!' Therefore, the Church must be as obedient to him to-day as it was during his pontificate! The Encyclical and Syllabus of Pope Pius IX. sufficiently show that he so understands it.[13]

Of the time immediately after Nicholas I, prominent Catholic Church historian and apologist Baronius commented:

Never had divisions, civil wars, the persecution of pagans, heretics, and schismatics caused it to suffer so much as the monsters who installed themselves on the throne of Christ by simony and murders. The Roman Church was transformed into a shameless courtesan, covered with silks and precious stones, which publicly prostituted itself for gold; the palace of the Lateran was become a disgraceful tavern, in which ecclesiastics of all nations disputed with harlots the price of infamy.

Never did priests, and especially popes, commit so many adulteries, rapes, incests, robberies, and murders; and never was the ignorance of the clergy so great as during this deplorable period. Christ was then assuredly sleeping a profound sleep in the bottom of his vessel, while the winds buffeted it on all sides, and covered it with the waves of the sea. And, what was more unfortunate still, the disciples of the Lord slept more profoundly than he, and could not awaken him either by their cries or their clamors. Thus the tempest of abomination fastened itself on the Church, and offered to the inspection of men the most horrid spectacle! The canons of councils, the creed of the apostles, the faith of Nice, the old traditions, the sacred rites, were buried in the abyss of oblivion, and the most unbridled dissoluteness, ferocious despotism, and insatiable ambition usurped their place. Who could call legitimate pontiffs the intruders who seated themselves on the chair of the apostles, and what must have been the cardinals selected by such monsters?[14]

It is believed by historians that about this time, a body of decrees called the False Decretals, or Decretal Epistles, were created to help the Church of Rome in its bid to rule the world. They were purported to be a body of canons dating as far back as 91 A.D. Though clearly forgeries, they have helped to support the teaching that Peter was the first pope and that all bishops looked to the pope of Rome for final decisions regarding spiritual matters. Influential Catholic author Lewis Ellies Du Pin gives an example of these spurious writings:

In an epistle by Pope Victor I. he is made to confer upon himself the further title of 'Archbishop of the Universal Church,' and to speak of 'appeals to Rome.' Its falsity is shown by the fact that it is addressed to Theophilus of Alexandria, who did not live till nearly two hundred years after. There is also another letter of his, directed to Desiderius, Bishop of Vienna, when there was no bishop of that name in Vienna till near the close of the sixth century.[15]

R. W. Thompson commented:

These liberal quotations from the False Decretals---otherwise scarcely excusable---are necessary to show how the popes and the Roman Catholic hierarchy have laid the foundation of their enormous power and prerogatives. The system they have built upon this foundation would have been bad enough if what has been put into the mouths of these popes had been actually uttered by them. But when it is considered that these things are the corrupt inventions of priests of the ninth century, and that this fact is known to all intelligent Roman Catholics, and frankly admitted by many of them, it almost staggers human credulity to suppose that there are now any in the world who are willing to risk their reputation for integrity and candor by attempting to maintain a system thus originated and upheld. There is nothing else, among all the nations of earth, bearing any resemblances to it---no other system by which it has been so daringly and perseveringly proposed to erect within all the governments a foreign and antagonistic power independent of all human law, and irresponsible to human authority. By means of it emperors, kings, princes, and peoples have been brought down in abject humiliation at the feet of innumerable popes, who, claiming to be in the place of God on earth, have lorded it over them with a severity which never abated and an ambition that could never be satisfied. It is marvelous to contemplate the origin and progress of such a structure of fraud and wrong, to observe the popular degradation which it wrought out, as the means of securing the triumph of the papacy, and to see the patience with which the world now tolerates the insolent ambition which demands its reconstruction in the name of God and humanity![16]

Succeeding popes used these falsehoods to justify their assertions that they were infallible. They believed that, like God, they could set up and remove the rulers of the nations of the world and their decrees would become the law of the Church, without the councils of bishops giving their assent to them.

New doctrines were added as time went on. In the 11th century, influential Pope Gregory VII introduced the practice of celibacy so the clergy would be completely dedicated to the Church and less affected by family ties and other influences.[17]

A new set of forged writings, the Gratian Decretals, surfaced in the mid part of the 12th century. These were used to further a system of persecution based on religion. They made it not only legal but an obligation to, according to one historian, "constrain men to goodness, and therefore to faith, and to what was then reckoned matter of faith, by all means of physical compulsion, and particularly to torture and execute heretics, and confiscate their property." Those who "dared to disobey a papal command, or speak against a papal decision or doctrine" were considered heretics.[18] As papal power grew, these writings provided more justification for silencing those that criticized the sin in the lives of the Catholic clergy.

The result of the teaching that all should be forced to become Roman Catholics was the horrific large-scale persecution of those that resisted joining the Church of Rome, such as the Waldenses and the Albigenses. They were humble Christians that lived in southwest Europe in the Middle Ages. Church affairs continued in such a way that Catholic monk and historian Matthew Paris, commenting on the conduct of the popes in the 13th century, stated "Religion is dead, and the Holy City has become an infamous prostitute, whose shamelessness surpasses that of Sodom or Gomorrah."[19]

In 1215, a great Middle Age assembly of Catholic clergy convened the Fourth Lateran Council, presided over by Pope Innocent III. According to Du Pin, the canons of this council were prepared beforehand and presented by the pope to be accepted without debate. He reported:

> In the third canon they excommunicated and anathematized all the heretics who oppose the Catholic and orthodox faith, as before explained: and 'tis therein ordered that the heretics shall be delivered up, after their condemnation, to the secular powers, or to their officers, to be punished according to their demerits, the clerks being first degraded; that their goods shall be confiscated, if they be laics; and if clerks, then they shall be applied to the use of the Church; that those who lie under violent suspicions of heresy shall be likewise anathematized, if they do not give proofs of their innocence, and they shall be avoided till they have given satisfaction; and if they be in a state of excommunication during a year, they shall be condemned as heretics; that the lords shall be admonished and advised by ecclesiastical censures to take an oath that they will extirpate heretics and excommunicate persons who shall be within their territories; that if they neglect to do it after admonition, they shall be excommunicated by the metropolitan and bishops of the province; and in case they persist a year without making satisfaction, the sovereign pontiff shall be advised thereof, that so he may declare their vassals absolved from their oath of fealty, and bestow their lands upon such Catholics as will seize upon them, who shall be the lawful possessors of them, by extirpating heretics, and preserving the purity of the faith in them, but without prejudice to the right of the superior lord, provided he offer no obstruction or hinderance to the putting this ordinance in execution. The same indulgences are granted to those Catholics as shall undertake to extirpate heretics by force of arms as are granted to those who go to the Holy Land. They excommunicated those who entertained, protected, or supported heretics, and declare that those who shall be excommunicated upon that account, if they do not make satisfaction within a year, shall be declared infamous, and divested of all offices, as well as of votes in the elections; that they shall not be admitted as evidences; that they shall be deprived of the faculty of making a will, or succeeding to an estate; and, lastly, that they may

not perform the functions of any office. 'Tis likewise further ordered that those who will not avoid the company of such persons as are by the Church denounced excommunicate shall be excommunicated themselves till they have given satisfaction. But, above all, ecclesiastics are forbidden to administer the sacraments to them, to give them Christian burial, to receive their alms or oblations, upon pain of being suspended from the functions of their orders, wherein they may not be re-established without a special indulto from the pope. The same punishment is likewise inflicted on the regulars, and, besides this, that they be not any longer tolerated in the diocese wherein they shall have committed such a fact. All those are excommunicated who shall dare to preach without having received a license from the Holy See or a Catholic bishop. Lastly, the archbishops and bishops are obliged to visit in person, or by their archdeacons or by other persons, once or twice a year, the dioceses where it is reported that there are any heretics, and to put a certain number of inhabitants under their oath to discover to the bishop such heretics as may be detected. They are likewise enjoined to cause the accused to appear, and to punish them if they do not clear themselves, or if they relapse after they have been cleared. Lastly, the bishops are threatened to be deposed if they neglect to purge their dioceses from heretics.[20]

This canon became part of Church law and the commandment to extirpate, or destroy, heretics was put into practice a short time later. According to Wikipedia, part of the third canon states that secular authorities are "...to take an oath that they will strive in good faith and to the best of their ability to *exterminate* in the territories subject to their jurisdiction *all heretics* pointed out by the Church..." (emphasis added).

This canon was one of a number decided on by this ecumenical council, sometimes called the General Council of Lateran because so many attended, including 71 archbishops, 412 bishops and hundreds of abbots, as well as several representatives of monarchs. A Catholic source called it "the most important council of the Middle Ages", marking "the culminating point of ecclesiastical life and papal power." Presided over by a Pope, the decisions made by such a council, according to Catholic sources, is just as valid, infallible and permanent as the judgment by the first church council in Jerusalem, detailed in Acts 15. Therefore today, death remains a penalty for heresy according to the Church of Rome.

From this time, over a period of centuries, Bible believing Christians, Jews and others were tortured and killed in a number of horrible ways through the Inquisition. Historians give the numbers who perished in the hundreds of thousands. Others assert that it was in the tens of millions. The great 19th century Catholic historian Lord Acton commented:

> The Inquisition is peculiarly the weapon and peculiarly the work of the popes. It stands out from all those things in which they co-operated, followed or assented as the distinctive feature of papal Rome. It was set up, renewed and perfected by a long series of acts emanating from the supreme authority in

the Church. No other institution, no doctrine, no ceremony is so distinctly the individual creation of the papacy, except the dispensing power. It is the principal thing with which the papacy is identified, and by which it must be judged. The principle of the Inquisition is the Pope's sovereign power over life and death. Whoever disobeys him should be tried and tortured and burnt. If that cannot be done, formalities may be dispensed with, and the culprit may be killed like an outlaw. That is to say, the principle of the Inquisition is murderous, and a man's opinion of the papacy is regulated and determined by his opinion of religious assassination.

In England, at about the same time period of the Fourth Council of the Lateran, King John disagreed with Pope Innocent III on the matter of the pope's choice for the position of Archbishop of Canterbury. After struggling with Innocent for some time, John surrendered and was forced to give the kingdom of England and authority over Ireland to Rome and promise, along with his subjects, to pay money yearly to Rome. Though Catholic, the English barons rebelled against the loss of English liberty and independence that had been guaranteed by an earlier charter. They joined together and forced the king to sign two charters. One was the Magna Carta, an important step in the development of the freedoms now enjoyed in modern democracies. Furious, the pope annulled both charters, freed the king from his oath to observe them and commanded the barons to repent of what they had done, which they refused.

The courageous barons were eventually defeated in their long struggle with King John, and his descendents after him, who joined with the popes in the fight. Although the barons were to suffer greatly for their principled stand, the flame of liberty that they had fought for continued to burn in hearts of the people of England until it was to finally burst forth, in the new land of America and eventually in other modern democratic nations.[21]

A struggle was going on within the Roman Catholic Church in England as well, as Catholics began to demand real ecclesiastical reforms, along with as increased religious freedom. Organized persecutions of heretics, including these reformers, started in the 14th century. It began with the Lollards and their leader, John Wycliffe. In 1377, he published his reform doctrine, which was to signal the beginning tremors of the coming Reformation earthquake.

The 15th century began with two men claiming to be pope, Benedict XIII and Gregory XII. A council made up of over a hundred cardinals, archbishops, bishops, doctors of law and others met at Piza. They ruled that neither "infallible" pope was the lawful pontiff so they elected a new one, Alexander V. He was succeeded after death by John XXIII, who called together the Council of Constance to deal with the division created by Benedict and Gregory, who were still refusing to give up their claims to the papacy. This council concluded that all three should resign, even though John XXIII was the lawful pope. He resisted this and after a bishop accused him of many crimes, the council investigated. It tried John and, according to Louis Du Pin, found him guilty of:

Lewdness and disorders in his youth, the purchasing of benefices by simony; his advancement to the dignity of a cardinal by the same means; his tyranny while he was legate at Bononia; his incests and adulteries while he was in that city; his poisoning of Alexander V. and his own physician; his contempt of the divine offices after he was pope; his neglecting to recite the canonical prayers, and to practice the fasts, abstinences, and ceremonies of the Church; his denying justice, and oppressing the poor; his selling benefices and ecclesiastical dignities to those that bid most; his authorizing an infinite number of dreadful abuses in distributing of preferments, and committing a thousand and a thousand cheats; his selling bulls, indulgences, dispensations, and other spiritual graces; his wasting the patrimony of the Church of Rome, and mortgaging that of other Churches; his maladministration of the spiritual and temporal affairs of the Church; and lastly his breaking the oath and promise he had made to renounce the pontificate, by retiring shamefully from Constance, to maintain and continue the schism.'[22]

Louis Marie De Cormenin added:

The general council of Constance, after having invoked the name of Christ and examined the accusations brought against John XXIII., and established on irrefragable proof, pronounces, decrees, and declares, that Balthasar Costa [the pope] is the oppressor of the poor, the persecutor of the just, the support of knaves, the idol of simoniacs, the slave of the flesh, a sink of vices, a man destitute of every virtue, a mirror of infamy, and devil incarnate; as such it deposes him from the pontificate, prohibiting all Christians from obeying him and calling him pope. The council further reserves to itself the punishment of his crimes in accordance with the laws of secular justice; and his pursuit as an obstinate and hardened, noxious, and incorrigible sinner, whose conduct is abominable and morals infamous; as a simoniac, ravisher, incendiary, disturber of the peace and unity of the Church; as a traitor, murderer, Sodomite, poisoner, committer of incest, and corrupter of young nuns and monks![23]

The Catholic Church had sunk to new lows. For a time, it had no head as neither Benedict XIII nor Gregory XIII were lawful popes. John XXIII, a lawful, "infallible", pope was deposed by a general counsel for incredible crimes. Cormenin commented:

The fifteenth century, however, surpassed all the preceding ages in corruption; the churches became the resorts of robbers, sodomites, and assassins; popes, cardinals, bishops, and mere clerks exercised brigandage forcibly in the provinces, and employed, as was most convenient, poison, the sword, and fire, to free themselves from their enemies, and despoil their victims. The Inquisition lent its horrible ministry to popes and kings. In France, Spain, Italy, Germany, and England, it embraced in its thousand arms the victims of the cupidity of tyrants, and put them to the most frightful tortures. The country was covered with legions of priests and monks, who devoured the substance of the people, and carried off to their impure retreats young girls and handsome youths, whom they again cast out, disgraced and dishonored.

The cities became the theatres of orgies and Saturnalia, and the palaces of bishops were filled with equipages for the chase, packs of dogs, troops of courtesans, minions, jugglers, and buffoons.[24]

The Council of Constance also tried and condemned reformer John Huss of Bohemia for heresy. This forerunner of the Reformation was burned at the stake though he was promised safe-conduct if he appeared before the Council. This sparked a war between the followers of John Huss and the forces loyal to the pontiff. Elected pope by the Council in the place of John XXIII, Martin V, wrote the following nugget of Christian benevolence in a letter to the king of Poland to encourage his side:

> Know that the interests of the Holy See, and those of your crown, make it a duty to exterminate the Hussites. Remember that these impious persons dare proclaim principles of equality; they maintain that all Christians are brethren, and that God has not given to privileged men the right of ruling the nations; they hold that Christ came on earth to abolish slavery; they call the people to liberty, that is, to the annihilation of kings and priests. While there is still time, then, turn your forces against Bohemia; burn, massacre, make deserts everywhere, for nothing could be more agreeable to God, or more useful to the cause of kings, than the extermination of the Hussites.[25]

The 16th century began with the tremendous corruption of the Roman Catholic Church, particularly among the clergy, continuing unchecked despite the attempts of Catholic reformers to bring it back to its simple biblical roots. In 1517, while criticizing the sale of indulgences, Augustinian monk Martin Luther issued his famous Ninety-Five Theses in Wittenberg, Germany, thus sparking the Protestant Reformation. Within four decades, almost half of Europe was Protestant. This faith was carried by the Pilgrims and others over the Atlantic to help found the nation whose ideals of freedom and democracy would pose such a threat to the Catholic Church's lust for power, the United States of America.

As time went on, even in Catholic areas in Europe, the Papacy dealt with increased difficulties. In his 2008 book, *The Catholics and Mrs. Mary Surratt*, Catholic apologist Kenneth Zanca reported on the situation the Papacy faced on the continent during the 1800s. According to Zanca, the mid-point of the 19th century found Pope IX struggling for power with those fighting for ideals that had been part of the French revolution, such as democracy and liberalization. By 1860, after the defeat of the papal armies, much of the land mass the Catholic Church ruled over directly had been lost (property that the Church should not have had to begin with). The Pope felt surrounded, besieged by enemies. Dr. Zanca stated, "In this context, one can appreciate the publication of the controversial papal encyclical *Quanta Cura* and the *Syllabus of Errors* attached to it in December 1864, which expressed not only the pope's views but those of conservatives in the Church as well" (see Figure 21). Zanca then made the following amazing statements:

> The complete text of *Quanta Cura* and the *Syllabus* did not appear in New York papers until January 13, 1865, when America was distracted by the ongoing Civil War. Yet, the documents were noticed, and Protestant and

Catholic press commented. Characteristic of the Protestant response was the conclusion that "...this Encyclical is a covert declaration of war against the American Republic.' Anti-Catholics had a field day pulling quotations from the documents as 'proof-texts' that the Roman Church was bigoted and arrogant and bent on imposing its will and religion on everyone.

Catholics in the United States recognized that the document put them at odds with traditional principles of American democracy, and looked to Rome for clarification. What came back was a brilliant piece of selective editing and benevolent interpretation of the documents by the bishop of Orleans, Felix Dupanloup. Basically, the author explained away the obvious, and made the document mean what it did *not* say, by distinguishing between stated principles and their application in specific cases.

So, during the time of the Civil War, the pope and many in the Roman curia felt attacked, invaded, and frightened that life as they knew it was about to be violently taken from them forever. All they held dear was under assault. Their values were discounted; their intentions irrelevant. The enemies were at the gate, over the walls, and storming the keep. Is it any surprise, then, that Rome had a certain empathy with the Confederate States of America?

In Kenneth Zanca's eyes, apparently it was wrong for "anti-Catholics" to be "pulling quotations" from the papal documents as "proof-texts" of the bigotry and arrogance of the Church of Rome and its interest to impose its will on others, no matter how true this actually was. To Zanca however, the editing of the bishop of Orleans was "brilliant", by which he committed ecclesiastical fraud by making the same document "mean what it did not say", thereby deceiving honest Americans as to what the Church actually taught. As well, according to Dr. Zanca, it was understandable that the Vatican could empathize with the Southern Confederacy as both faced the loss of what was dear to them, which evidently included their right to enslave others, whether in the physically or spiritual realm.

Charles Chiniquy quoted Abraham Lincoln saying that since becoming President, he had learned that the Roman Catholic Church was the real cause of the Civil War that was reddening the land with the blood of America's finest young men. Lincoln stated that although there was a great difference of views between the North and South, it was the promises by the Jesuits of money and arms from Catholics, including the arms of France, that persuaded Jeff Davis and other Confederate leaders to start the Civil War, which the Church hoped would result in the destruction of the United States.[26]

When the bloody fratricidal war was almost won by the Union, at a tremendous cost of lives and treasure, Chiniquy asserted that the Jesuits were also behind the effort to assassinate the President. The effort to kill the leaders of the United States administration was carried out in the belief that this would paralyze the government and rally the forces of rebellion still lurking in the country but fortunately these efforts failed.

Charles Chiniquy alleged that this was all done with the American people remaining essentially unaware of the real role the Roman Catholic Church had played in these cataclysmic events. Had it not been for him, these well founded allegations of stunning wrongdoing on the part of the Church may very well have received little or no attention.[27] Since his death, public awareness of what Chiniquy and others said about the action of officials and members of the Catholic Church during this period has been steadily diminishing up to the present time, where it is largely unknown.

Does the general lack of knowledge today of the Church's malfeasance at the time of the Civil War mean that the Catholic Church has been truly reformed, its officials and lay members having been such model citizens since then that all has been forgotten? While the latest scandal of the Church of Rome to arise has been the innumerous incidents of sexual abuse and cover-ups by Catholic priests, bishops and other officials, particularly in the United States, there have been other examples of wrongdoing since the War of the Rebellion.

During World War II, when the Jews were being taken by the millions to be slaughtered, though it knew what was happening, the Vatican was silent in the face of the horrific barbarity visited upon European Jewry. In 2000, Pope John Paul II felt compelled to apologize for centuries of mistreatment of the Jewish people by the Roman Catholic Church, although the Holocaust was not mentioned.

During the Second World War however, it was not just Jewish people who were persecuted. According to Time-Life book, *Partisans and Guerillas*, after the Nazi took over in Yugoslavia, they "installed a vicious, home-grown Fascist named Ante Pavelich, a long-time advocate of Croatian independence and the founder of a pro-Catholic terrorist organization known as Ustashi, or Rebels." *Partisans And Guerillas* stated:

> As Hitler's puppet, Pavelich set about eliminating what he called 'alien elements' – Serbs, Jews and Gypsies. The Serbs comprised approximately 30 per cent of the state of Croatia's population and nearly all were members of the Eastern Orthodox Church. Pavelich's formula for dealing with the Serbs was simple and brutal: one third were to be expelled to Serbia, one third converted to Catholicism and one third exterminated.

The Time-Life volume also reported,

> The Germans, who shared local occupation duties with the Italians, were first embarrassed and then sickened by the Ustashi's indiscriminate bestiality. Their commanders threatened to replace Pavelich if he did not stop the wholesale killings. But he took the precaution of having his likely successor murdered, and the Germans, unable to find a suitable substitute, let the matter drop.

> The Ustashi massacres went on and on. By the time the killing was finally brought to an end, the Ustashi had taken an incredible toll of Serbs – variously estimated at from 350,000 to 750,000.

As well, this source disclosed that, "According to an Italian correspondent, Pavelich once put a wicker basket on his desk—filled with 40 pounds of eyes gouged from victims of the Ustashi."

During the war, Pope Pius XII met with Pavelich and most assuredly knew what was going on in Yugoslavia. If anyone would have listened to the Pope, wouldn't it have been this man who was trying to make his jurisdiction completely Catholic? Why then didn't the Pope tell him to stop the murders, the forced conversions and other crimes? Was it not because what was going on was nothing new for the Papacy and this Church?

After the war was over, with the approval of Pope Pius XII and under the direction of Giovanni Monni, who later became Pope Paul VI, the Catholic Church also knowingly helped thousands of Nazis and other war criminals escape justice, including Pavelich.

Even when Nazi leader, Adolf Hitler, killed himself, the government of officially neutral, Catholic, Ireland expressed its condolence to Germany on the death of this mass murderer. This can be compared to the time Abraham Lincoln was assassinated, eighty years earlier, when there was no expression of sympathy sent from the Holy See to America regarding his death.

In September, 1978, the death of Pope John Paul I was the cause of more distress for the Church of Rome. This man, who was planning substantial reforms in the Vatican, was discovered dead in his bed after a little more than a month as head of the Roman Catholic Church. Investigative journalists have presented strong evidence which raised the question of whether this Pope was murdered through the efforts of powerful men in the Church, who did not want reform.[28]

One of the more recent Church scandals has surfaced in Catholic Ireland. There, the discovery of hundreds of unmarked graves caused the incredible story of the Magdalene laundries to finally come to light. The laundries were part of a system of modern slavery established in Roman Catholic institutions where women considered to be "moral criminals" were essentially given life sentences to be served cleaning laundry, as well as suffering abuse. Unbelievably, the last of these Irish convents / prisons was just closed in 1996.[29]

The central bank of the Church of Rome, the Instituto per le Opere di Religione, or Vatican Bank, continues to be linked to the Mafia by criminal investigators, through such activities as money laundering and other financial wrongdoing. For years, the former head of the bank, Archbishop Paul Marcinkus was wanted by the Italian authorities for fraud, theft by deception and criminal conspiracy, relating to hundreds of millions of dollars that left an Italian bank, Banco Ambrosiano, and ended up at the Vatican Bank. According to a B.B.C. report in 2002, "The Vatican refused to admit legal responsibility for the bank's downfall but did acknowledge 'moral involvement', and paid $241m to creditors". Would the Church of Rome pay almost a quarter of a billion dollars out for no reason? These and other stunning examples of wrongdoing worldwide, including the current crisis of sexual abuse, show that this ecclesiastical leopard still has not managed to change its spots since it plotted to murder Abraham Lincoln and other high U.S. government officials in 1865.[30]

Chapter 11
America and the Catholic Church Today

This work has, so far, dealt in significant part with the Roman Catholic Church, mainly during the critical time of the U.S. Civil War and especially with its involvement in the assassination of Abraham Lincoln. It is no longer 1865 and Charles Chiniquy and Abraham Lincoln are now gone. The American Union, as well as the Catholic Church, are still in existence today of course. This begs the question, after the antagonism of its officials and laymen during the War of the Rebellion, has the Church of Rome changed? What has its relationship been with the United States? Is it still an enemy of America and the freedoms it stands for? The evidence shows that the Roman Catholic Church still is.

After coming through its great test, the Civil War, and despite more recent setbacks and difficulties, the United States remains a beacon of hope to the world and continues to be the freest and richest democracy on earth. The percentage of the American population that are Catholic however, has increased to some 25%, or about two and a half times what it was at around the beginning of the Civil War.

The increase of Roman Catholics in the United States today comes, in significant part, via illegal immigration from the nation that borders America to the south, corrupt, predominantly Catholic, Mexico. It could be asked, is the Roman Catholic Church is still proceeding with an old plan to take the U.S. over by force of numbers, as it planned and succeeded in doing in Canada, or at least try again to cause the break-up of America?

Charles Chiniquy stated that in 1852, he was invited to at a large meeting of priests in Buffalo, New York. There, he heard of a scheme to mass Roman Catholics in the large cities of the United States to take political control of the country and make way for a time when, "not a single Senator or member of Congress will be chosen, if he be not submitted to our holy father, the Pope" and when Catholics "will not only elect the President, but fill and command the armies, man the navies, and hold the keys of the public treasury"[1]

While this has not happened as yet, today Catholics are being increasingly viewed by United States politicians as an influential block of voters to be courted. In 2003, a writer for the Catholic magazine, *The Tablet*, declared that Catholics in America, "now represent the most important shifting demographic for the vote." President Barak Obama picked Senator Joe Biden, a Roman Catholic, to be his 2008 running mate in part because of Biden's connection with Catholic voters.

Among the leaders of the Roman Catholic Church, the main concern seems to be power; not doing what is right and occupying the moral high ground. Biden joins a host of Catholic politicians such as Rudy Giuliani, one-time frontrunner to be the

2008 Presidential nominee, U.S. Senator Ted Kennedy, John Kerry, 2004 Democratic candidate for President and former Canadian Prime Minister Paul Martin (2003-2006), who have all rejected moral positions of the Catholic Church on such issues as abortion and homosexuality, legislated accordingly, and faced no real censure from their Church for it.[2]

An example of the influence of Roman Catholicism in the United States today can be seen in the American Southwest. According to U.S. immigration observers, the huge influx of predominantly Catholic illegal immigrants in the region has been producing an ethnic community with a greater loyalty to Mexico than the United States. In an interview published in 2002, Glenn Spencer, president of Voices of Citizens Together, a non-profit group based in California, stated that "Unless this is shut down within two years, I believe that it will be irreversible, and that it will most certainly lead to a break-up of the United States." The number of Hispanics in America increased by 58% in the 1990s and a 2004 report states that since 1960, they have been responsible for 71% of the growth of the U.S. Catholic Church. *Time* magazine estimated that in 2004, three million illegal immigrants slipped into the U.S. via Mexico.[3]

Statements by prominent University of California professor Armando Navarro agree with Spencer's comments. In a 1995 speech, Navarro declared that the U.S. Southwest is being changed. Power is being steadily transferred into Latino hands, making possible the self-determination of the area and even "the idea of Aztlan". According to Mexican tradition, Aztlan, the mystical birthplace of the Aztecs, is made up of the land mass that includes California, Nevada, Arizona, New Mexico and portions of Texas and Colorado. In a more recent interview, Navarro indicated that if democratic and social trends remain the same in the American Southwest, the inevitable result will be secession.

Spencer maintains that the goal of the Mexican government and many Mexicans in the United States is to create a sovereign, "Republic of the North" from this part of America and northern Mexican states that would eventually merge with Mexico. In a 1997 speech, former Mexican President Ernesto Zedillo, "proudly affirmed that the Mexican nation extends beyond the territory enclosed by its borders and that Mexican immigrants are an important - a very important - part of this."[4]

The United States received Mexican lands after it had admitted Texas as the 28th state of the Union. Ten years before it became a state, Texas had been an independent nation. The change to statehood led to border conflicts between Texas and Mexico which eventually caused the Mexican War. America won the war and through the treaty of Guadalupe Hidalgo, which officially ended the conflict, Mexico gave up its claims to Texas and what now is California, Utah, Nevada and parts of Colorado, Wyoming, Arizona and New Mexico.

In March 2004, *Fox News* reported that the government of Mexico has been working with a U. S. group that it created, the Institute de los Mexicanos en el Exterior, (Institute of Mexicans Abroad):

to deploy illegals to state legislatures and city council across America. There, the illegal aliens -- Mexican nationals who have been provided a matricula consular card -- pack the gallery and seek to apply pressure against legislators who sponsor or intend to vote for bills that enhance immigration law enforcement.

Not since Americans mid-century experience with communism has there been such an organized effort at subverting our country's political institutions.[5] (emphasis added)

Aren't these Catholic individuals and groups doing exactly what Charles Chiniquy alleged the Church of Rome was trying to do to the free institutions of the United States in his day? The matricula counsular is an identification card issued by consulate offices of the Mexican government to its citizens living outside Mexico.

As well, the Institute de los Mexicanos en el Exterior has reportedly been supplying Mexicans attempting to cross the border into America with survival kits. According to the *Washington Times*, the Institute has also been cooperating with Hispanic and illegal immigration advocacy groups to agitate for access to U.S. public services for illegal aliens.

Illegal immigration has brought greater and greater numbers of Catholics into the United States, with American Protestants paying the bill in significant part. While this has been happening, princes of the American Catholic Church have shown themselves to be very willing to undermine the democratically enacted laws of the United States by siding with the Latino lawbreakers. Instead of demanding that leaders of the Roman Catholic Church in Mexico urge their flock not to violate United States law, American bishops, as well as other Church officials, have been attempting to persuade U.S. legislators to reward these illegal aliens for their criminal violations of immigration law by granting them permanent legal status.

This can be compared to what the Irish Catholics did to black people in New York, who had the right to be in country and the city during the Draft Riots. Catholic princes, as well as laymen, today strenuously argue that illegal immigrants should be welcomed, even though they take American jobs and depress wages. U.S. Catholics would assert that these Hispanic Romanists should certainly not be confronted, assaulted or worse for coming up from the south to potentially take jobs away from poorer citizens, though they do not have the legal right to do so, so how can the vicious crimes perpetrated by the Irish Catholics against colored persons during the Draft Riots possibly be justified?

His work to help Catholic illegal immigrants stay in the United States may have been a big reason why a man as immoral as Ted Kennedy was allowed to stay in the Roman Catholic Church. Kennedy sharply differed with the Church of Rome on a number of social issues that the Church says are vital but his work to help more Catholics come into America was apparently more important than, for example, the rights of the unborn. Kennedy recently received the highest honour Mexico gives to foreigners for his efforts to legislate benefits in the United States for those breaking U.S. law: illegal immigrants and those employing them.[6] There are, of course, numerous immigrants from Mexico who have entered the United States legally and have become exemplary American citizens.

Evidently, Roman Catholic officials have also openly stated the Church's intentions regarding America. In 1987, *The Wanderer*, a national Catholic newspaper, reported that Paul Marx, a priest and "one of the world's experts on contraception, sex education and abortion", addressed the International Mother's Day Walk for Life in Niagara Falls at St. John the Baptist parish in the Buffalo, New York area. Declaring the United States a dying nation, he said, "I tell the Mexicans when I am down in Mexico to keep having children, and then take back what we took from them: California, Texas, Arizona, and then to take back the rest of the country as well." In 1986, the Mexican newspaper, *La Jornada*, reported that another priest, Florencio M. Rigoni, assistant secretary for migration of the Mexican conference of bishops stated,"The march of Latin Americans to the United States shouldn't be understood as a wave of anger or revolutionary passion, but more as a peaceful conquest."[7]

What might America be like for evangelical Christians after such a "conquest"? The November 22nd, 1851 edition of *The Shepherd of the Valley*, the official journal of the bishop of St. Louis, declared, "If Catholics ever gain, - which they surely will do, though at a distant day, - an immense numerical superiority, religious freedom in this country is at an end. So say our enemies. So we believe." A taste of what this may mean has been provided not too long ago in Mexico.

While the Protestant world, Britain, Unites States, Canada, Australia, New Zealand and other nations were shouldering the fight against the mainly Catholic Axis powers, (Romanist Germany and Italy, along with Japan), to preserve basic freedoms for humanity during World War II, back in Mexico, Catholic mobs were beating, raping and murdering evangelical Christians. These incidents of vicious religious persecution through the 1940s and early 1950s were reported in the February 8, 1952 edition of the Mexican newsmagazine *Tiempo*, Mexico's equivalent of *Time* magazine.[8] The complete article and the English translation are in Appendix 3, part 17.

This persecution has continued in more recent times as well, though often unreported by the mainstream media. The number of Protestants in Latin America has increased dramatically since the 1930s in what has been called a Latin American Reformation. A 1996 *Newsweek* magazine article reported that in that year, an average of 8,000 baptized Catholics a day were becoming Protestants. The article quoted pastor Abdias Tovilla of the Mexican state of Chiapas who said, for the oppressed indigenous peasants, the Protestant faith is "the way out of a social system that does little more for them than keep them drunk and dirt poor". A *Time* magazine article, also published in 1996, reported how conversion has changed people for the better.

> "For evangelicals, progress starts at home. Church doctrine emphasizes education, hard work and frugality, and forbids vices like the consumption of liquor. Evangelicals have prospered, compared with their Catholic neighbors, and that has attracted more converts and much resentment."

This resentment has begun at the top. John Paul II has called these Protestant groups "no-account 'sects'" as well as "ravenous wolves", terms that are quite different from what he used to speak to evangelicals in the United States. Setting the tone for local Mexican Catholic officials, Girolamo Prigione, Vatican representative to Mexico, stated "Sects, like flies, should be chased out".[9] And they have been. One 1994 report stated that in the southern state of Chiapas, more than 23,000 Protestants have been forced out of their communities into internal exile. It explained that:

> The harassment, intimidation, forced exile, illegal detention, and subtle discrimination are explained in terms of indigenous tradition. Community members who converted to Protestantism are reluctant to take part in community festivals, which often involve heavy financial outlays, the purchase of icons for the local Catholic church, and consumption of large quantities of alcohol.

In 1998, the *Toronto Star* reported that government officials escorted 70 Chiapas Protestants back to their homes in the traditional Indian community of San Juan Chamula after they had been forced out by Catholics. The *Star* explained, "The expulsions were the latest in a 25-year conflict that has seen thousands of people driven from Chamula because they don't share the mix of Catholic and Maya traditions of most Indians in the region".

Evangelical Mexicans have also faced extreme violence. Believers have been attacked, stoned and worse. In June, 1992, Presbyterian preacher Melecio Gomez was brutally murdered by hit men after he refused to leave the Chiapas community of Saltillo. All of this is a far cry from the love for all that the Church of Rome preaches in America.[10]

In 1994, in language that treated both Protestants and Catholics as equal partners, an agreement was made between some well known evangelical leaders in the United States and prominent Roman Catholic Church officials to cease attempts to win converts from one another's flocks. In 2007 however, Pope Benedict XVI pulled the rug out from under these evangelical leaders when he reasserted the universal primacy of the Catholic Church by approving the release of a document which stated, in part, that Protestant churches are not true churches.

To the north, in the country of Charles Chiniquy's birth, much has changed since his time. No longer Protestant, Canada has been a predominantly Catholic country for some four decades, a transformation marked by steady decline in many areas. Since the late 1960's, despite the political stripe, Catholic-led government after Catholic-led government have moved the country further and further away from real democracy and closer to a dictatorial, banana-republic style of federal governance, continually dogged by scandal.[11]

Quebec is the most Catholic province of Canada, and for much of the history of French Canada, the Roman Catholic Church has wielded a very powerful influence in its society. After the years of Church dominance however, the 1950's found Quebec society: backwards, politically and socially insignificant, and lagging behind English Canada and other industrialized societies in many important areas, such as business and education. The Roman Catholic Church has been rightly blamed by Quebecers for holding the province back and much of its society is now very secular. Though on the surface, the Church has largely been relegated to the sidelines, it still retains sway in the province. A 2002 *National Post* article on Quebec Catholicism stated, "About 85% of Quebecers still identify themselves as Catholics, even if they rarely attend church, and they still expect to experience key rites of passage in a church. Almost without exception, they reject the idea of converting to a different religious tradition".

Regardless of how subtle the influence of Roman Catholicism appears to be, this still Catholic province has continued to cause problems for the nation as a whole. In 1995, a referendum was held in Quebec which could have resulted in a declaration of independence by the province and very possibly the break-up of Canada and / or a civil war. It failed by a very narrow margin. The political party in power in the province at the time of the referendum was the separatist Parti Quebecois.

The Parti Quebecois came from a secret Catholic group founded in the 1920s by French members of the Roman Catholic clergy. Nicknamed La Patente, or "the gimmick", the organization was anti-Semitic, anti-English, anti-Protestant, anti-foreigner and closely aligned to the leadership of the Catholic Church. In 1941, one French journalist described it as "the Ku Klux Klan of French Canada". According to Diane Francis, editor-at-large of the *National Post* and the former editor of the *Financial Post*, its original intent was the promotion of French speaking Catholics across the nation, especially in the federal civil service.

In her book, *Fighting For Canada*, she listed two of its accomplishments. One was having the red bars and maple leaf of its own flag adopted as the new Canadian flag in 1965, replacing the traditional red ensign. The other was the introduction by Prime Minister Pierre Trudeau of the divisive program of official bilingualism, which it had lobbied for.

Though the Quebec referendum failed by a margin of only 52,000 votes out of more than five million ballots cast, the provincial government did not do a general recount because as Ms Francis alleged, it would have become obvious how much election fraud had been perpetrated by the separatists to try to win.[12] In 2004, the *Montreal Gazette* reported that in the event of a positive result, the premier, Jacques Parizeau, planned to declare independence. At the time, Catholic France had made a secret agreement with the Parti Quebecois government to recognize Quebec's independence immediately after it was proclaimed and lobby other countries to do the same.

Amazingly, in 2006, an openly homosexual Catholic priest, Raymond Gravel, was elected to a seat in the Canadian Parliament as a member of the Bloc Quebecois party. The Bloc is the federal counter-part of the Parti Quebecois and has the same country destroying, "sovereignist" aims. Gravel has faced no censure from his Church for this.

Regarding the continued threat to Canada, Ms. Francis commented on a 1944 speech given by the late Canadian senator, T. D. Bouchard, which included remarks he made about his upbringing in Quebec. Bouchard stated:

> Why had I been led to believe those sillinesses?...Since my infancy I had been taught that everything the French Canadian had to suffer came from the fact that he was of French and Catholic decent.'

> Quebec Catholic textbooks even back then were, 'fictions' designed to glorify the Catholic Church and pillory the English,

Of the former senator, Ms. Francis stated "He warned back then that the Catholic-propagated myths threatened Canada as a nation. *And he's still correct.*" (emphasis added).

Although being home to less than a quarter of the nation's population, Quebec has completely dominated Canada's political culture for decades, to the detriment of the whole country. In 2005, eminent historian Jack Granatstein declared that Canadian interests, as well as national unity, have suffered because Quebecers have been dictating Canada's defence and foreign policy.[13] Current news accounts show that the lying, manipulation, racism, etc. continues as separatists in Catholic Quebec remain dedicated to their goal of breaking-up Canada, as well as using this threat to extract more power and wealth from the rest of the country.[14]

In many ways, things have not been going well in Quebec, however. Montreal, Canada's largest city until the 1970's, has been losing business in recent years as companies have moved their corporate headquarters from there to places like Calgary in booming Protestant western Canada. In the place of economic activity, it seems that Montreal has instead been attracting things like perverts. The city has been called a paradise for pedophiles in North America. It is also the one spot in Canada that the nation's most infamous convicted criminal, when freed, felt comfortable enough to live after jail. Karla Homolka, who with her then husband, Paul Bernardo, raped and murdered several young schoolgirls, resided in the city until late 2007, until she left the country.[15]

As well, in 2006, in a controversial article in one of Canada's national newspapers, *The Globe and Mail*, journalist Jan Wong pointed out that of the three shooting rampages that have occurred in postsecondary institutions in Canada, all of them have happened in Montreal. In the piece entitled "Get Under The Desk", Wong, who grew up in the city, pointed out that each of the three gunmen were not "pure laine" or "pure" francophone. While each killer was mentally disturbed, Wong said that because of the decades-long language struggle, each one "had been marginalized by a society that valued pure laine". Wong was roundly pilloried for what she wrote, especially in Quebec, despite remarks like the infamous statement of the province's highest elected official, Premier Jacques Parizeau, who, after the failed 1995 referendum, blamed "money and the ethnic vote" (the English, and foreigners).[16]

Although Quebec journalists vigorously disagreed with Jan Wong's statements, calling them prejudiced and part of a stream of insults directed against the province, both Wong and the *Globe and Mail* have never apologized for the sentiments expressed. Regarding the reaction to the article, at least one journalist, William Johnson of the *Montreal Gazette*, said that while he believed the article was ill-advised, in Quebec, "There is a flagrant double standard. Attacking Canada and English- speaking Canadians is routine." Of Wong's piece, he also stated:

> A misguided newspaper article was raised to the level of a national issue. Its provocative sentences received the widest possible publicity. Will politicians raise an equivalent hue and cry when, as happens recurrently, Quebec's journalists, novelists, poets, film-makers, playwrights, song-writers utter hostile remarks about Canadians and Canada, which is an enduring Quebec literary tradition?

The latest in the long line of the province's draconian language laws that Wong alleged alienated these gunmen is the Quebec Identity Act, which appears to provide support for her contention regarding the marginalization of minorities. Recently proposed by the Parti Quebecois, the Identity Act would require immigrants to attain an certain competency in French to be allowed to run for office, fund-raise for a political party or petition the Quebec legislature with a grievance, creating therefore an unreasonably high and undoubtedly unconstitutional barrier to political rights for immigrants in the province.[17] A prominent separatist, Jean-Francois Lisee, argues that new-comers should not even be allowed to vote unless they have the required proficiency in the language. Despite its provisions, the Act has enjoyed the support of the majority of French speakers in Quebec. Of course, there are many honorable, patriotic Canadians who are natives of "la belle province", but history shows that Romanism has ultimately done little good for citizens there.

It is evident that the more Roman Catholic the U.S. Southwest is, as with Quebec, the greater the tendency toward secession from the nation it is part of. Instead of putting all its energies into solving Mexico's problems, its Romanist government, along with Catholic leaders in the United States, has been furthering the trend of illegal immigration by assisting and encouraging more Mexico Catholics to go north to America, even if they are breaking U.S. law to do so. Can unbiased observers, watching what has been going on in Canada, the United States and Mexico, really conclude that the Church of Rome has nothing to do with these events?

Charles Chiniquy wasn't the only one concerned about a Catholic take-over in the United States. In general agreement with the sentiments found in *Fifty Years*, a *New York Times* editorial of June 6, 1892 warned of a plan hatched by priests in Canada to make New England Catholic, through immigration (see Figure 33).

As well, in an 1850 lecture, New York Archbishop John Hughes plainly said that the Roman Catholic Church planned to convert all Pagan nations and all Protestant nations, including America. His words were reported in his own New York paper, *Freeman's Journal and Catholic Register*. Hughes stated, "Everybody should know that we have for our mission to convert the world,--including the inhabitants of the United States,--the people of the cities, and the people of the country, the officers of

Figure 33
New York Times, June 6, 1892

Ŋew-Ŋork Times, Monday, June 6, 1892. ---- Ten Pag

THE FRENCH CANADIANS IN NEW-ENGLAND.

It is said that there are more French-Canadians in New-England than there are in Canada. There are 400,000 in round numbers in New-England at this time, and in five of its principal cities they have the balance of power to-day. The Irish-American population is still larger, and it probably had the balance of power in more places, but to-day the second and third generations of the Irish-Americans are so nearly assimilated to the native population in political and social life that neither their religion nor its adjunct, the parochial school, is able to keep them out of the strong currents of American life. With the French Canadians this is not the case. Mr. FRANCIS PARKMAN has ably pointed out their singular tenacity as a race and their extreme devotion to their religion, and their transplantation to the manufacturing centres and the rural districts in New-England means that Quebec is transferred bodily to Manchester and Fall River and Lowell. Not only does the French curé follow the French peasantry to their new homes, but he takes with him the parish church, the ample clerical residence, the convent for the sisters, and the parochial school for the education of the children. He also perpetuates the French ideas and aspirations through the French language, and places all the obstacles possible in the way of the assimilation of these people to our American life and thought. There is something still more important in this transplantation. These people are in New-England as an organized body, whose motto is *Notre réligion, notre langue, et nos moeurs.* This body is ruled by a principle directly opposite to that which has made New-England what it is. It depresses to the lowest point possible the idea of personal responsibility and limits the freedom which it permits.

It is next to impossible to penetrate this mass of protected and secluded humanity with modern ideas or to induce them to interest themselves in democratic institutions and methods of government. They are almost as much out of reach as if they were living in a remote part of the Province of Quebec. No other people, except the Indians, are so persistent in repeating themselves. Where they halt they stay, and where they stay they multiply and cover the earth. Dr. EGBERT O. SMYTH, in a paper just published by the American Antiquarian Society, has been at great pains to trace intelligently the extent of this immigration, and in his opinion this migration of these people is part of a priestly scheme now fervently fostered in Canada for the purpose of bringing New-England under the control of the Roman Catholic faith. He points out that this is the avowed purpose of the secret society to which every adult French Canadian belongs, and that the prayers and the earnest efforts of these people are to turn the tables in New-England by the aid of the silent forces which they control.

What will the New-Englanders do about it? There is apparently but one way in which this conquest can be arrested. That is to compel the use of the English language in all the schools by American citizens. This is a point which Archbishop IRELAND, with his intense American feeling, has had in view in the Faribault experiment in Minnesota. In that State all the European languages are constantly spoken by people who live in sections, and the placing of their children in the public instead of the parochial schools means that their children will become loyal and intelligent American citizens. One chief reason why his scheme appeals strongly to Americans is that it is likely to be more effective than anything else in destroying the race prejudices and divisions in the Nation. It is through their parochial schools, in which French is exclusively used, that the French Canadians in New-the navy and the marines, commanders of the army, the Legislatures, the Senate, the Cabinet, the President, and all" (see Figure 34).[18]

Hughes was merely stating what is official Roman Catholic Church doctrine. As in Chiniquy's time, there are, of course, Catholics who are both American citizens and true patriots. As Canada and other countries have shown however, increased Catholic population and political power generally bodes little good for the nation.

While the percentage of Catholics in the United States evidently has not been dramatically increasing, the percentage of Protestants in the U.S. has been dropping even more sharply than it did in Canada, prior to Catholics becoming the largest religious group. In just 10 years, from 1993 to 2002, the percentage of Americans who identified themselves as Protestant fell an incredible 11 percentage points, from 63% to 52%, and now for the first time in American history, Protestants may account for less than 50% of the American population.

Fortunately, evangelical Christians in the United States still remain a large and potent force. For more than two hundred years, America has successfully bucked a worldwide trend. It is the only western industrialized nation where the percentage of its citizens involved in religious participation has been going up or staying steady, currently at 60%, compared to Western Europe's 10% or less.[19] As well, because the freedoms and territorial integrity of the nation have been purchased and maintained by American blood, citizens of this great country have proven very reluctant to give them up without a fight.

It is the author's wish that this book will serve as a current and timely warning to American patriots that the Roman Catholic Church yet remains one of the most, implacable and deadly enemy of the freedoms of United States, no matter how friendly and harmless she tries appear on the surface. It is hoped that America will not be distracted from the real danger it faces by the comforts and conveniences brought by its successes, the bias and dishonesty of an often lazy, ignorant and selectively engaged mainstream news media, as well as the revisionist denials of Church officials.

It was Charles Chiniquy's heartfelt wish that like him, Roman Catholics would break free from the system of dead works that has them trying to please God through the observation of a code of religious rules that keeps these precious people slaves of the Church of Rome and, according to the Word of God, on their way to hell and the lake of fire. According to the Bible, God wants all people, including Catholics, to escape a lost eternity. John 3:16 reads, "For God so loved the world, that he gave his only begotten Son, that whosoever believeth in him should not perish, but have everlasting life."

Sin has separated mankind from God. James 4:17 provides a definition of sin, "Therefore to him that knoweth to do good and doeth it not, to him is sin". Romans 3:23 tells of all of mankind's problem with doing good, of keeping God's law, "For all have sinned and come short of the glory of God." Romans 6:23 declares the results of sin, as well as the cure, "The wages of sin is death but the gift of God is eternal life through Jesus Christ our Lord."

Figure 34

Freeman's Journal and Catholic Register, November 23, 1850

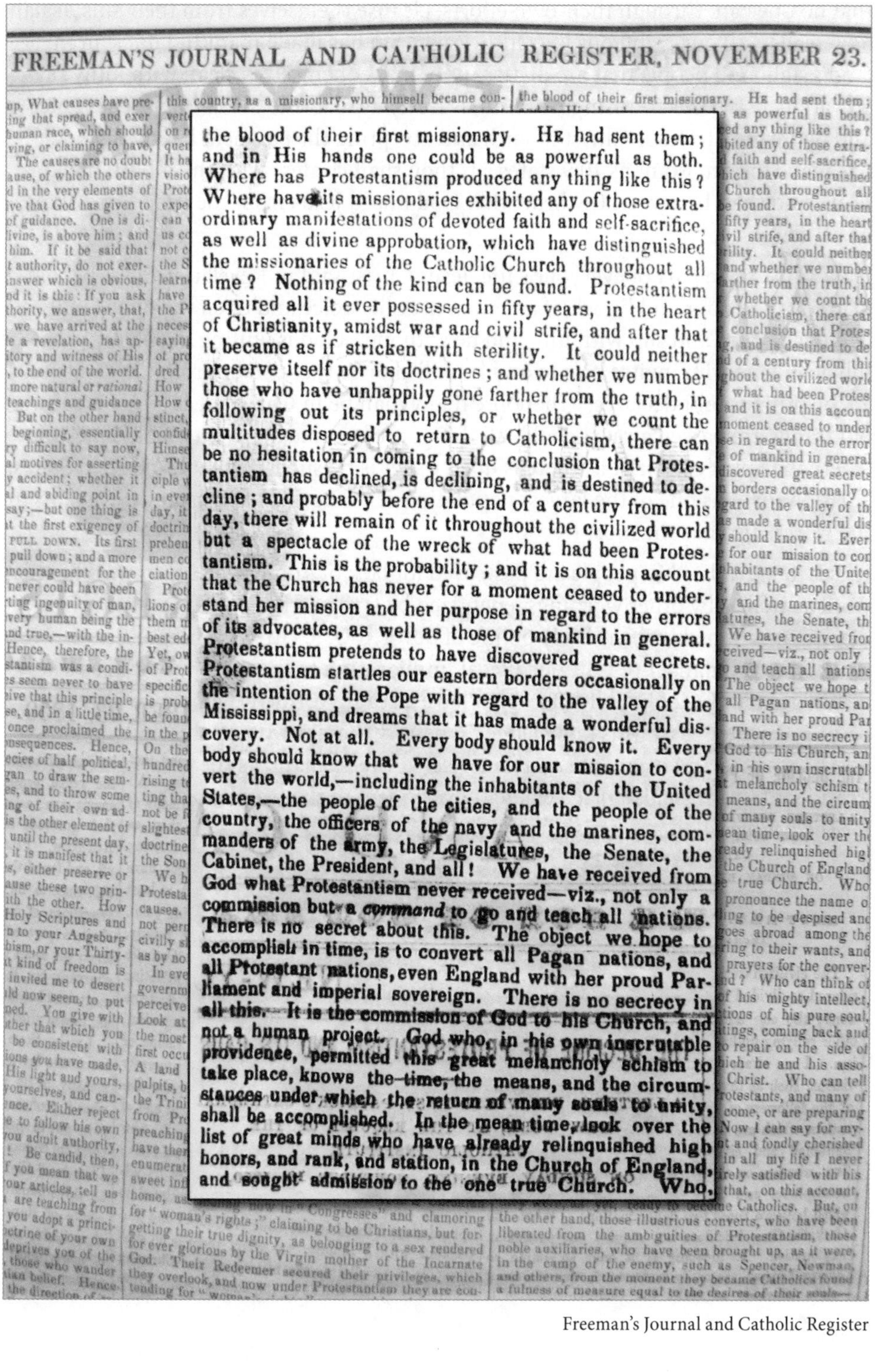

FREEMAN'S JOURNAL AND CATHOLIC REGISTER, NOVEMBER 23.

the blood of their first missionary. HE had sent them; and in His hands one could be as powerful as both. Where has Protestantism produced any thing like this? Where have its missionaries exhibited any of those extraordinary manifestations of devoted faith and self-sacrifice, as well as divine approbation, which have distinguished the missionaries of the Catholic Church throughout all time? Nothing of the kind can be found. Protestantism acquired all it ever possessed in fifty years, in the heart of Christianity, amidst war and civil strife, and after that it became as if stricken with sterility. It could neither preserve itself nor its doctrines; and whether we number those who have unhappily gone farther from the truth, in following out its principles, or whether we count the multitudes disposed to return to Catholicism, there can be no hesitation in coming to the conclusion that Protestantism has declined, is declining, and is destined to decline; and probably before the end of a century from this day, there will remain of it throughout the civilized world but a spectacle of the wreck of what had been Protestantism. This is the probability; and it is on this account that the Church has never for a moment ceased to understand her mission and her purpose in regard to the errors of its advocates, as well as those of mankind in general. Protestantism pretends to have discovered great secrets. Protestantism startles our eastern borders occasionally on the intention of the Pope with regard to the valley of the Mississippi, and dreams that it has made a wonderful discovery. Not at all. Every body should know it. Every body should know that we have for our mission to convert the world,—including the inhabitants of the United States,—the people of the cities, and the people of the country, the officers of the navy and the marines, commanders of the army, the Legislatures, the Senate, the Cabinet, the President, and all! We have received from God what Protestantism never received—viz., not only a commission but a command to go and teach all nations. There is no secret about this. The object we hope to accomplish in time, is to convert all Pagan nations, and all Protestant nations, even England with her proud Parliament and imperial sovereign. There is no secrecy in all this. It is the commission of God to his Church, and not a human project. God who, in his own inscrutable providence, permitted this great melancholy schism to take place, knows the time, the means, and the circumstances under which the return of many souls to unity, shall be accomplished. In the mean time, look over the list of great minds who have already relinquished high honors, and rank, and station, in the Church of England, and sought admission to the one true Church. Who,

According to the Scriptures, eternal life, salvation from sin, is a gift therefore, not something to be earned, as the Roman Catholic Church teaches. God's Word states that no one can, through their own efforts, cleanse themselves from their sins. Isaiah 64:6 reads, "all our righteous is as filthy rags". Sin has made mankind unclean in God's sight and people that are dirty cannot make themselves clean with filthy rags. Salvation, complete cleansing from sin, is freely available to all through repentance and by turning to Jesus Christ in faith and accepting the payment his shed blood has made for sin. Romans 10:9 states, "If thou shalt confess with thy mouth the Lord Jesus, and shalt believe in thy heart that God raised Jesus from the dead, thou shalt be saved."

God wants to be part of everyone's life. Jesus Christ said in Revelation 3:30 "behold I stand at the door and knock, if any man hear my voice and open the door I will come in to him and sup with him and he with me." God is willing to enter into the life of anyone who invites him to and he will change that person from the inside out. 2 Corinthians 5:17 declares, "Therefore if any man be in Christ, he is a new creature: old things are passed away; behold, all things are become new". The Bible states that where the Spirit of Christ is, there is liberty so it is no surprise that the United States, a nation that has one of the largest population of evangelical Protestant Christians in the world, also has the most freedom.

Hosea 4:6a reads, "My people are destroyed for lack of knowledge". Informed by this work as well as by other warnings, energized by true patriotism, and with the help of God, it is hoped that the body politic of devoted U. S. citizens and politicians will realize the full danger of Catholic illegal immigration to the nation, as well as the deadly Roman Catholic influences that have already wormed their way within and be fully warned. With this knowledge, hopefully these threats to the United States will be resisted and overcome and America will yet remain, as the great martyred President Lincoln said, a place where "government of the people, by the people and for the people, shall not perish from off the earth."

Appendix 1
Charles Chiniquy's Critics

Joseph George

Since Joseph George Jr.'s, paper, "The Lincoln Writings of Charles P. T. Chiniquy", was published in the February, 1976 issue of the *Journal of the Illinois Historical Society*, most, if not all, of those commenting negatively on Chiniquy have used his work as the basis for dismissing the ex-priest's allegations against the Catholic Church. For instance, the only source given for the entry on Charles Chiniquy in the *Abraham Lincoln Encyclopedia*, by Mark E. Neely was Professor George. Chiniquy was listed as "The principal source of allegations that Abraham Lincoln's assassination was a Jesuit plot". The sources section of the *Abraham Lincoln Encyclopedia* noted that "Joseph George, Jr.'s 'The Lincoln Writings of Charles P. T. Chiniquy,' *Journal of the Illinois State Historical Society*, LXIX (February 1976), 17-25, is a definitive and interesting refutation of Chiniquy's claims."[1] When closely examined, it is clear that whatever George accomplished, it definitely wasn't a refutation of Charles Chiniquy's allegations.

Professor George began his effort to discredit Charles Chiniquy with a correspondence between Benedict Guldner, a Jesuit priest from New York, and John G. Nicolay, President Lincoln's former private secretary. Guldner evidently had read a pamphlet alleging the assassination of Lincoln was the work of Jesuits. He wrote to Nicolay and asked if he and John Hay, another of Lincoln's secretaries, had heard of the allegation and if they believed it to be false. According to George, Nicolay conferred with Hay and then wrote:

> To [y]our first question whether in our studies on the life of Lincoln we came upon the charge that 'the assassination of President Lincoln was the work of Jesuits,' we answer that we have read such a charge in a lengthy newspaper publication.

> To your second question, viz: 'If you did come across it, did the accusation seem to you to be entirely groundless?' we answer Yes. It seemed to us so entirely groundless as not to merit any attention on our part.[2]

At first glance, this appears to be powerful evidence against Chiniquy's allegation but closer scrutiny shows otherwise. As Lincoln's former secretaries, why would they be considered authorities on who was responsible or not responsible for the President's assassination? They were not directly involved in the investigation into his murder so how would they know if the Jesuits were involved or not?

The information that Nicolay and Hay had regarding the conspiracy certainly was insignificant compared to what those that investigated Lincoln's assassination possessed and the two secretaries undoubtedly had no relevant knowledge that the authorities did not. Neither was called as a witness at the trial of the conspirators or later at the trial of John Surratt. Against these two, who really had nothing to say on the subject, can be arrayed Edwin Stanton, the great Secretary of War who *headed* the investigation into Lincoln's assassination and who believed it was the result of a Catholic plot. Between Stanton and these two, there is no contest.

In an attempt to buttress his case, George introduced someone he evidently believed was much more intimate with the 16th President than Nicolay and Hay. The Professor stated:

> In 1922 John B. Kennedy, the editor of *Columbia*, a Catholic magazine, requested information from Robert Todd Lincoln about Chiniquy's report. The reply was empathic: 'I do not know of any literature in which my father is quoted as attacking Catholics and the Catholic Church. Of course, in the years his name had been a peg on which to hang many things.'

The March, 1922 edition of *Columbia* did indeed contain this quote attributed to Robert Todd Lincoln. The original letter was not photoduplicated and the location of letter was not given though. Even if the quote is completely accurate however, Professor George did not seem to realize that instead of contradicting Chiniquy, Robert Todd Lincoln actually supported the ex-priest. Chiniquy quoted Abraham Lincoln on the subject of the allegations that he, the 16th President, had been born a Catholic and baptized by a priest. According to Chiniquy, the President said to him, "you are the only one to whom I like to speak on that subject." In another place, Chiniquy quoted Lincoln as saying to him, "There are many important things about the plots of the Jesuits that I can learn only from you", and regarding the threat of the Roman Catholic Church to freedom, especially in America, "You are almost the only one with whom I speak freely on that subject." [3] If the President's eldest son had stated that his father had talked freely about the threat that the Catholic Church posed to the institutions of the United States, that would have contradicted Chiniquy's story but he didn't.

In addition, Robert Lincoln appears to have forgotten a letter he wrote to his father's close friend, some 37 years earlier. Written in 1885, the year Charles Chiniquy's autobiography was first published, he thanked Chiniquy for "the expression you use in your note in regards to my father", and for "sending your book" which undoubtedly was *Fifty Years*, which had just been published for the first time. If he had read it, or at least the part concerning his father, which would not be unreasonable to suppose he did, then he would have known of at least one piece of literature where his father was quoted attacking the Catholic Church[4] (see Figure 10).

The area of Charles Chiniquy's account that apparently was most important to Professor George in his effort to discredit the former priest, was Chiniquy's legal struggle with Peter Spink. He evidently believed that if he could show that Chiniquy was wrong in this part of his autobiography, the rest of his story regarding Lincoln could be discounted as well. Reporting on what Charles Chiniquy said in *Fifty Years*, George began by stating that Chiniquy met Abraham Lincoln in the 1850s and hired him to defend himself against the charge of personal immorality. From this first statement, it appears that Professor George suffered from reading comprehension difficulties. Chiniquy did not say what the charges were until the last court action in October, 1856 and he stated that Lincoln began defending him at the May court term of that year. As well, Chiniquy reported that the charge of personal immorality was a departure from what he had been accused of before. Discussing Lincoln biographers that accepted Chiniquy's account, George wrote:

> The evidence is conclusive that reliance on Chiniquy was unfortunate, for his claims were baseless. Chiniquy did meet Lincoln in 1856, and he did engage Lincoln's services as an attorney. But the facts of the trial bear little resemblance to the account presented in *Fifty Years in the Church of Rome*. According to Chiniquy, the Bishop of Chicago, Chiniquy's superior, had induced a land speculator named Peter Spink to bring charges of immorality against Chiniquy in 1855[5]

Again the Professor repeated his mistake. Charles Chiniquy did not state what charges were brought against him in 1855. In fact, a more accurate thing to say would be that Joseph George's account of *Fifty Years* bears little resemblance to what Chiniquy actually said. George went on to state, "Chiniquy was then retried, he said, at Urbana. At that time Lincoln was hired as defense attorney and was influential in producing a key witness from Chicago who exposed Spink as a perjurer."

Here Professor George managed to make possibly as many as three mistakes in one sentence. First of all, *Fifty Years* did not state that Lincoln was influential in producing this key witness from Chicago. The witness in question was Philomene Moffat and it was another man, Narcisse Terrien, who independently contacted her and asked her to go to Urbana to testify. Lincoln was not aware of her existence until she showed up at his hotel door. Secondly, according to Chiniquy, she didn't publicly expose anyone as a perjurer, as she didn't end up being a witness, because Spink withdrew his charges and no more testimony was given. It appears that only Abraham Lincoln, Charles Chiniquy and his other lawyers, along with those on Spink's side of the suit, that knew of the perjury before the case ended. Thirdly, if she had testified, she would have exposed Lebel as a perjurer, not Spink.

Professor George then confidently stated, "The court records and attorneys' notes from that trial contradict almost every point in Chiniquy's autobiography. The original documents show that *Spink v. Chiniquy* involved little more than a personal feud between two embittered friends." 6

The Illinois State Historical Library (ISHL) has the originals and copies of most, if not all of the known documents relating to Spink vs. Chiniquy. There does not appear to be any attorneys' notes among the court records pertaining to this case. According to his footnote, George's statement that Spink and Chiniquy were feuding one-time friends was based on information he found in the official "Complaint of Peter Spink, Feb. 3rd, 1855" in the ISHL *Spink v. Chiniquy* file and evidently other court documents in the file. The documents in the file however, do not say anything about a former friendship between the two men.

George again repeated his mistake regarding what he thought Chiniquy said regarding what he had initially been charged with, stating "The official charge brought by Spink was slander, not immorality. The Bishop of Chicago (who was not, in any case, Chiniquy's superior) had nothing to do with the complaint."[7]

It is possible to agree that the Bishop O'Regan was not Chiniquy's superior, at least with respect to personal integrity but this is of course was not what George meant. If O'Regan was not Chiniquy's ecclesiastical superior, then why, as was noted in Chapter 3, would the official Catholic history of Notre Dame Church in Chicago state that Bishop O'Regan was involved in the Chiniquy schism? Why would he be involved if it was not his jurisdiction? Among the historians who discussed the struggles Chiniquy had with O'Regan were Richard Lougheed and Bessie Pierce. Other accounts stated that the oversight of Chiniquy's position was normally the responsibility of the bishop of Chicago (also see the *Chicago Tribune* in Figure 13, 15).[8]

How did Joseph George know that the bishop of Chicago, Anthony O'Regan, had nothing to do with Spink vs. Chiniquy? He offered no evidence to prove this statement while, as noted in Chapter 2, Professor Richard Lougheed asserted that there was good evidence to support the ex-priest's allegations that the bishop was involved.

Continuing on, George stated, "The trial was shifted, as Chiniquy said, from Kankakee to Urbana, but before, not after, the first court proceedings. There was first a mistrial, and the jury chosen for the second hearing could not agree. Lincoln then became Chiniquy's attorney."

If what Professor George asserted is correct, then the mistrial would have been the result in the spring court term of 1856 in Urbana and the second proceeding would have happened in the fall term at the same location. It would have been at the end of the second hearing in the fall that Abraham Lincoln would have been hired and not before, according to Joseph George. In the footnotes section of the same page, George stated, "The ISHL does have a photostat in its Lincoln Collection of the handwritten bill for services that Lincoln gave Chiniquy. The document reads: 'Urbana, May 23--1856 Due A. Lincoln Fifty dollars for value received,' It is signed 'C. Chiniquy' "(see Figure 8).[9]

The ISHL does indeed have a photocopy of Lincoln's bill to Chiniquy and it reads as George stated. It was also reproduced in *Fifty Years*. If, as Joseph George asserted, Mr. Lincoln was not hired until after a second trial in October, 1856, why would Lincoln present Chiniquy with a bill dated May 23rd, 1856? Lincoln wouldn't have been working for him in May if what George said was true. Why didn't Professor George notice this discrepancy in his "definitive" work?

Other sources noted earlier show that Charles Chiniquy was correct and Lincoln indeed defended him in two court actions in Urbana in 1856 during the spring and the fall terms. According to Joseph George, there were no court proceedings in Kankakee and then there were two trials in Urbana. The first was a mistrial, the second ended in a hung jury and then Mr. Lincoln arranged a compromise before a third trial. George reproduced the statement of agreement that dismissed the suit:

> This day came the parties and the defendant denies that he has ever charged, or believed the plaintiff to be guilty of Perjury; that whatever he has said, from which such a charge could be inferred, he said on the information of others, protesting his own disbelief in the charge; and that he now disclaims any belief in the truth of such charge against said plaintiff--It is therefore, by agreement of the parties, ordered that this suit be dismissed, each party paying his own cost--the defendant to pay his part of the cost heretofore ordered to be paid by said plaintiff.[10](see Figure 7)

George accurately reproduced the agreement that is held by the Library of Congress. Two copies of this agreement were made, as naturally each side would want one. The second copy is held by the University of Illinois at Urbana-Champaign. The text of the agreement was also recorded in the Champaign County's Circuit court records, which agrees with the copy held by the Library of Congress.

If Professor George is correct, then there was no judgment rendered at any time and therefore Chiniquy could not claim to have won any court victories. If George would have closely read the agreement statement however, he would have noticed the last section shows otherwise. The final part reads, "It is therefore, by agreement of the parties, ordered that this suit be dismissed, each party paying his own cost". If there had been no previous court decision between the two, the statement should have ended there but it does not. It goes on to say, "the defendant to pay his part of the cost heretofore ordered to be paid by said plaintiff."

According to this agreement, Charles Chiniquy, the defendant, was to pay his part of the cost that Peter Spink, the plaintiff, "heretofore" or previously had been ordered to pay. Who "ordered" Spink to pay Chiniquy's legal costs? His mother? His Church? The only answer that fits is a court. It is therefore reasonable to suppose that Charles Chiniquy is again correct and at least one judgment was rendered in his favor after a complete trial.

This victory would have had to have taken place in Kankakee, something that another court document supports. The document is an appeal by Peter Spink for a change of venue from Kankakee. In it, he claims that he had learned since the beginning of the November, 1855 court term that the judge there was prejudiced against him. How would Spink know that there truly was prejudice against him there, enough to ask for and successfully get a change of venue, unless some ruling had been made against him? The document, held by the Illinois State Historical Society, is dated November 13th, 1855, the day Chiniquy maintained a verdict was given in his favour (see Figure 1). In *Fifty Years*, Chiniquy said he was stunned by the news that his opponent had applied for a change of venue, as the thought of the cost involved in bringing 15 to 20 witnesses that distance overwhelmed him. The court's list of defence costs for the May term, 1856, which listed 17 witnesses, shows Chiniquy's accuracy when detailing his legal expenses (see Appendix 3, Part 16).[11]

Professor George stated, "It is difficult to believe that Chiniquy and Lincoln would have had reason or occasion at Urbana for a discussion of the evils of the Catholic church--which in any case had no connection with the trial."[12] Actually, at the conclusion of the trial, it would have been perfectly normal for Abraham Lincoln and his client to discuss the legal bill. If a couple of priests were united with Spink in the legal struggle, along with a high-ranking Church official, and Chiniquy biographer Richard Lougheed showed there is good evidence for that, then there certainly would have been the occasion and reason to discuss the evils of this religious organization.

By comparing what he mistakenly thought Chiniquy said regarding his legal struggle with Spink with independent sources of information, like court records, Joseph George wrongly believed that he had shown the ex-priest's account of Spink vs. Chiniquy to be factually incorrect in numerous points. Building on this faulty foundation, he erroneously concluded that the accuracy of what else Chiniquy said about Lincoln could be legitimately questioned as well, stating that "Chiniquy's accounts of later visits with Lincoln and discussions of religion and fears of Catholic plots against the President's life are equally unreliable."

Joseph George went on to review of this part of Chiniquy's testimony with the same level of care he gave earlier parts. He quoted David Davis saying Lincoln was a "secretive man" and the idea of the President discussing his religious views with a stranger, "absurd". According to the Professor, John G. Nicolay also stated that he never heard Lincoln explain his religious views and George concluded, "If such close associates of the President's as Davis and the Nicolay never heard Lincoln speak of his religious views, it is not likely that Chiniquy would have had long theological discussions with him".[13]

Firstly, Charles Chiniquy was not a stranger to Abraham Lincoln. The popular prairie lawyer defended him through two court terms in the most colorful and high profile slander case in Mr. Lincoln's legal career. This court case took so long and monopolized the court's time to such an extent during the 1856 spring term in Urbana that it left a huge amount of legal business waiting until the fall. How could Chiniquy and Lincoln go through all this together and not get to know each other? Lincoln only charged him $50.00 for the work he did for him. Even by Lincoln's standards, this was extremely low, 1/40th of the $2,000.00 Chiniquy said Lincoln's services was worth.

In his book *Lawyer Lincoln*, historian Albert Woldman discussed the small fees Lincoln charged his clients. Other than Charles Chiniquy, the lowest he reported Lincoln charged was a fee that was a 1/5th of what was expected.[14] Doesn't the unusually low fee he charged the priest support Chiniquy's claim of friendship with Abraham Lincoln, the great reduction in cost being Lincoln's way of further helping his client, as *Fifty Years* stated?

Instead of contradicting Charles Chiniquy, Davis and Nicolay, like Robert Lincoln, confirmed what he said. As noted earlier, Chiniquy related that Abraham Lincoln had told him that he, Chiniquy, was the only person or almost the only one he liked to speak to on the subject of faith and Catholicism. If a man is private and not generally willing to openly discuss his religious beliefs, wouldn't it would be reasonable to believe that if such a man were to ever talk about the subject, it would be with a clergyman that person knew? How many other people discussed their religious beliefs with Davis and Nicolay?

George also reproduced the comments of a historian regarding Chiniquy's statement of his conversation with Lincoln, stating" In 1924 the distinguished historian Carl Russell Fish found it necessary to use the pages of the *American Historical Review* to denounce an account titled *'An American Protestant Protest against the Defilement of True Art by Roman Catholicism.'* " According to Fish, this account repeated the claims of *Fifty Years in the Church of Rome*. What Carl Russell Fish wrote in the journal under the title of "Lincoln and Catholicism" was:

> In 'An American Protestant Protest against the Defilement of True Art by Roman Catholicism', recently circulated by the million. Abraham Lincoln is quoted as saying:
>
> > Unfortunately, I feel more and more, every day, that it is not against the Americans of the South alone I am fighting. It is more against the pope of Rome, his perfidious Jesuits, and their blind and bloodthirsty slaves…that we have to defend ourselves….It is to popery that we owe this terrible Civil War. I would have laughed at the man who would have told me that before I became President…. Now I see the mystery.
>
> Students are perfectly well aware that no such quotation is to be found in the works of Lincoln, they know that the spirit of the quotation is contrary to the whole character of Lincoln's thought and expression, they are familiar with the fact that on its face it is not less absurd to attribute such a statement to Lincoln, than it is to accuse the papacy of such a position."[15]

Abraham Lincoln certainly did not write such a thing and Chiniquy did not allege that Lincoln wrote or said anything publicly against the Catholic Church. The evidence gathered in this work however shows that it is certainly not absurd to accuse "the Pope, the Jesuits, and their slaves" of encouraging the South to start the war and trying to help them win. It is also understandable that as Chiniquy said, Abraham Lincoln's life-changing experience as President would have made him modify his attitude toward the Church of Rome as he found out how traitorously its officials and lay members often acted.

George also stated, "Moreover, there is no available documentary evidence that Chiniquy was friendly with Lincoln or visited with him privately in Washington", commenting also that, "It is safe to assert that the two men never shared long friendly conversations at any time".

Professor George is again not quite correct. To help prove his point, he introduced two letters written by Charles Chiniquy to the President, dated September 29th, 1862 and June 10th, 1864.[16] They are held by the Library of Congress.

Professor George also stated, "The Robert Todd Lincoln Collection contains a letter of June 10, 1864, from one A. Chester to the President. The letter is a request for funds for the school operated by Chiniquy in Kankakee County" (The Robert Todd Lincoln Collection is part of the Lincoln collection at the Library of Congress). George's reading comprehension problems appear again because contrary to his statement, the contents of the letter did not include any request for school funds (see Appendix 3, Part 17). George also added, "Apparently this is the same A. Chester who edited the *Kankakee Gazette* from 1853 to 1856."

As George claimed however, Chester's letter does seem to contradict Charles Chiniquy's statement regarding his friendship with Abraham Lincoln. In the correspondence, Chester appeared to introduce and recommend Chiniquy to the President. The question is: why would Chester do this if the ex-priest and the President already knew each other well? One of the two letters by Chiniquy, which did ask for help for the school, was written on the same day as Chester's. This may very well have been a coincidence as Chester wrote from Kankakee and Chiniquy wrote from Washington. As for the content of his letter, Chester didn't seem to know of Chiniquy's friendship with Lincoln but does this mean that the friendship didn't exist?

One explanation for this could be that Charles Chiniquy did not broadcast that he was good friends with the 16th President or at least did not tell Chester. It may also be possible that if Chiniquy talked to Chester about his relationship with Lincoln, he may have been misunderstood. Some years earlier Chiniquy said that his English was not very good compared to his French, (much of the testimony of Spink vs. Chiniquy was given in French and translated into English). Reporting on a speech that Chiniquy gave at the Cooper Institute in the city in 1859, the *New York Times* stated that the ex-priest had "only recently acquired the English tongue" and apologized to his audience for "his broken English". In any event, in light of all the evidence, Chester's letter does not disprove what Chiniquy said about his relationship with Lincoln.

Professor George also maintained that the two letters written by Chiniquy to the President did not show the friendship that was supposed to exist between the two. He stated:

> According to *Fifty Years in the Church of Rome*, Chiniquy visited Lincoln in August, 1861, and June, 1862. At the first interview Chiniquy claimed that the President not only spoke of the evils of Catholicism but offered his friend a secretaryship in the American legation in Paris. On September 29, 1862, three months after the second meeting was supposed to have taken place, Chiniquy wrote to Lincoln and thanked him for services rendered in Urbana in 1856. Nothing was mentioned of any meeting in Washington or any offer of a position for Chiniquy in the foreign service.[17]

George reproduced the letter:

MR. PRESIDENT,

I have the honor [and] the pleasure of forwarding to You the adress of my countrymen adopted in a meeting of our whole Colony.

Our gratitude for the good you are doing to our beloved & bleeding Country, is increased by the great services you have rendered me personally, in a very solemn circumstance, at Urbana, Ill.

I have, then, a double reason to bless the name of Abraham Lincoln, & assure you of the respect & devotedness with which I have the h[onor].

to subscribe myself, Mr. President,
Yr. Nble Ser[vant].
Charles Chiniquy

George also reproduced the second letter:

MY DEAR MR. LINCOLN

It was my privilege, yesterday, to bless you in the name of ten [?] thousand French Canadians settled in our Colony of Illinois. To day, I approach you to offer you a new opportunity of doing one of the things you like the more; and by which your life has been filled: 'a good action.'

In the Province of God I have brought some six hundred families of my countrymen from the errors of Rome; to the Knowledge of the truth as it is in Jesus Christ. Now, I am trying to give to the Children of those converts the best possible Christian & American education, and I have founded a College: 'The Saviour's College' where about 130 boys & girls are taught to serve their God & love the country.

But, alone, I can not meet all the expenses of that new Institution. Our Presbytery have advised me to make an appeal to our Freinds [sic] in Washington. The emminent services you have already rendered me, gives me, surely, the privilege of looking to you as our first & noblest Freind.

It is then to you that we go first to get some help for the education of that colony which has already sent more than 150 men to the defense of the Country, 12 of them have shed their blood on the battle fields of the West.

For God's sake, My dear Mr. Lincoln, do receive with your usual Kindness, my humble requests and Believe me

Your most devoted Servant
C. Chiniquy
My residence in Washington is 58th Missoury [sic] Ave.

George's reproductions of these letters are accurate. Chiniquy's misspelling of the words Friend and Friends shows that he still seemed to have some difficulty with English. As for the contents of the two letters, Chiniquy did not address the President as a stranger but as someone whom he knew. In the second letter, he called Lincoln, the friend of himself and his fellow colonists. When requesting help with their school, he asked the President to receive his request with his "usual kindness". This suggests a relatively regular and cordial intercourse between them. He also left his address in Washington, which would logically mean he expected the President might contact him. There was some evidence available therefore to Joseph George to show the closeness of their relationship. Since the papers of the Chiniquy Collection have become available however, there is now much better proof.

In fairness to Joseph George, this key piece of documentary evidence that shows the very strong friendship between Chiniquy and Abraham Lincoln was not available to him when he wrote his paper. It is the letter from Robert Todd Lincoln to Charles Chiniquy, noted earlier, sent on the occasion of the publishing of *Fifty Years* and held in the Chiniquy Collection. In the correspondence, dated September 10th, 1885, Robert Lincoln stated that his father had "made many friend(s) in his life but plainly none were more than yourself" (see Figure 10).[18]

By attempting to use the testimony of Robert Todd Lincoln against Chiniquy, George clearly and correctly asserted that the President's oldest son was a real authority in regards to his father's life. As Robert Todd stated that Abraham Lincoln did not have a better friend than Chiniquy, can stronger proof for their friendship possibly be found?

As well, there is the correspondence from Chiniquy entitled, "Letter From Father Chiniquy", published in the August 12, 1864 edition of the *Chicago Tribune*, regarding his visit to see the President in the White House. It showed, at the time, that Chiniquy was friendly with Lincoln and had visited with him privately in Washington. This documentary evidence certainly was available when George wrote "The Lincoln Writings" (see Figure 20).

As well, in 1894, a *New York Times* article reported that the main speaker at the annual dinner of the Republican Club of New York city called Charles Chiniquy, Lincoln's friend, and quoted what the ex-priest wrote in *Fifty Years* regarding a visit to the White House. The dinner was attended by luminaries of the party and held in honor of the birth of Abraham Lincoln. The portion quoted was a statement of Abraham Lincoln regarding the danger he faced from assassins.

Joseph George ended his paper by declaring, "Scholars, however, even when tempted to use less sensational passages from Chiniquy's book, should be wary. There is no evidence to support his claim that he was a close friend of the Sixteenth President's."[19]

This list of Professor George's errors and research shortcomings, however, should be more than enough to convince all but the truly biased that is it Joseph George's work that one should be wary of. It seems regrettably that essentially all of Charles Chiniquy's critics who wrote after George published his paper, made the mistake of quoting him.

Richard Lougheed

The most current comprehensive work, done on the ex-priest by someone who could be termed a critic of Chiniquy, has been completed by Montreal theological Professor Richard Lougheed. Lougheed stands out amongst those that commented on Charles Chiniquy by the impressive amount of research he evidently did in preparing his 1993 Ph.D. thesis, and latter book, on the celebrated French-Canadian. Professor Lougheed's doctoral dissertation entitled, "The Controversial Conversion of Charles Chiniquy", is an interesting, detailed and very informative look at the life of the Apostle of Temperance and his works. After the thesis, a book on the subject, also entitled *The Controversial Conversion of Charles Chiniquy*, has just been published. Lougheed's volume, which expands on some areas covered in the thesis, appeared this year (2009). Though organized somewhat differently, the thesis and the book generally agree together.

Lougheed is unusual among those who wrote about the ex-priest, in that he appeared to be both a detractor and an admirer of Chiniquy. He also commented on George's allegation that Chiniquy was not a close friend of Abraham Lincoln's.

Although he is in many ways an authority on Chiniquy and while his dissertation and book are important sources of information in regards to the former priest, after examination, Professor Lougheed's criticism of Charles Chiniquy is also found to be essentially without foundation. Both the thesis and the book are considered here.

He began his dissertation by giving his theological position with regard to the Catholic Church. Declaring himself to be an evangelical Protestant, he stated:

> As a post - Vatican II Christian who has lived for two years in somewhat traditional Roman Catholic communities and who has spent three years in a Catholic theological facility, I have developed a sympathy for much in Catholicism, and a greater understanding of those other practices and beliefs which I still do not share. From this background I long for greater understanding and co-operation between French evangelicals and Roman Catholics in the extremely secular Quebec culture. French Protestants have been crippled by their anti-Catholicism. In much of Quebec, evangelicals are classified as cults and face an ingrained hostility against their attempts to rend the religious uniformity in Quebec....In addition I pursue a historical goal of granting due credit to a character in Quebec history who has long been either neglected or defamed.

Continuing his thesis, he wrote:

> Chiniquy's work can be identified with by marginalized ex-Catholics. However it horrifies most of those from areas where the Catholic minority is respected as one of the many branches of the Christian faith. The militancy of Chiniquy's writings and actions eventually provided ammunition for his critics to pass resolutions rejecting proselytism. Though Chiniquy had powerfully striven for 40 years to stir up those at peace with Rome to join him in anti-Catholic battle, peacemakers made great headway after his death. H.

M. Parsons warned just after Chiniquy's death that Presbyterians of liberal theology would try to undo Chiniquy's evangelical work. In an era when home mission was declining in any event, the absence of motivating speeches by Chiniquy accelerated the process.[20]

From these statements and others he makes in *The Controversial Conversion*, it appears that Professor Lougheed would be among those that consider Catholicism, one of the many branches of Christian faith. While Professor Lougheed undoubtedly was sincere in his praise of the one he called the "Grand Old Man of Protestantism", the criticisms he leveled against Chiniquy need to be examined closely. As he came to the end of his thesis, continuing on an ecumenical theme, he summarizes the main things the ex-priest can be faulted with:

> All of the above conclusions and study would be primarily of academic interest except that it is my further contention that conflicting myths about Chiniquy have polarized relationships between Catholics and evangelicals in Quebec, ever since the 1850s. While, given his life, the polarization was almost unavoidable before Vatican II and the Quiet Revolution, it is tragic and unnecessary that this has continued in many areas since. A defusing of the propaganda is long overdue.

> There should be recognition in Catholic or secular Quebec for Chiniquy's considerable accomplishments and contributions, and also for the harassment that he and other French Protestants faced. He should take his rightful place as an important Quebec leader. This should be matched by an open evangelical admission that Chiniquy was, at times, an extremist who misjudged situations, exaggerated, used very violent language which provoked reaction, and quite possibly was involved in sexual harassment.[21]

It could be asked, what is meant by the term extremist and why would misjudging situations be considered a character flaw? Professor Lougheed mentioned the allegation of exaggeration a number of times and although he did not furnish a list of examples per se, a few instances can be gleaned from his thesis. One concerns the number of fellow Roman Catholics who followed Chiniquy out of the Catholic Church:

> There have been widely differing accounts of how many Kankakee County parishioners followed Chiniquy out of the Roman Catholic fold. I have found two detailed estimates. Chiniquy counted 886 French Canadian families or 6,200 individuals who had left the Roman Catholic Church. Mailloux provided a counter-estimate in early 1861. Excluding other French Protestants who had originally left with Chiniquy, he posited a total of 310 families or 1,553 individuals in Illinois who were Chiniquy Presbyterians. Both sets of figures are no doubt distorted in opposite directions while the time differential and the fact that different groups were tabulated add further complications.[22]

Richard Lougheed's source for the figure attributed to Chiniquy comes from the work of a man named Rev. Baird entitled, *The French Canadian Mission in Illinois*.

First of all, how does Lougheed know that the accounts on both sides are incorrect? If he does not know from another source, or sources, exactly how many people followed Rev. Chiniquy out of the Church, why does Professor Lougheed assume that the ex-priest must be wrong? Unless there is a way of proving what the correct figure is, talk of exaggeration is pure conjecture.

Another example of supposedly exaggerated numbers given by the ex-priest concerned the amount of people who reportedly left Catholicism to come to Christ through Chiniquy's preaching in Montreal:

> Astounding numbers were racked up in rosters of those abjuring Catholicism between November 1875 and June 1876. The Montreal Witness published 2,043 names in this period according to MacVicar's tabulation at Synod. Chiniquy himself claimed 7,000 converts in four years spent in Montreal.

> Naturally those statistics were disputed. It is confusing that while few were demonstrated to be frauds, there were nowhere near 7,000, nor even 2,000 new French Protestant members. Doubtless, Chiniquy did make a major impact, first with his lectures, and then as he counselled day and night. He was particularly successful with immigrants from France who felt marginalized by more conservative French Canadian Catholics. Abjuration from Catholicism did not mean conversion to Protestantism but when publicized it became a costly act. It is hard to imagine how so many francophone abjurers, even allowing for exaggeration in Chiniquy's figures, could survive without a trace in Montreal. If the abjurations were legitimate and if they were maintained, large numbers must have left the province, as many French Protestants did.[23]

If the *Montreal Witness* published the names of 2,043 people that left Catholicism in 1875 and 1876, surely census information and other sources would show whether they stayed in Montreal and what beliefs they professed, if any. If there were few frauds and there was no trace of these people in Montreal, then the natural inference would be that they had left, as Professor Lougheed indicated many did. This does not prove Chiniquy exaggerated.

Lougheed also brought up a pamphlet written by a French Protestant, W. B. Court, who criticized Chiniquy for "his authoritarianism, his inflated convert lists and his willingness to use unscrupulous means and characters." According to Lougheed, Court was the son of a pioneer of French evangelization organization with the French Canadian Missionary Society, who had worked with Chiniquy. Lougheed stated, "The one strong critique came from W.B. Court, son of James, in 1877. This critique was itself attacked by all, including his father, in part because Chiniquy's reputation was deemed so crucial to the evangelical cause."[24] What evidence does Professor Lougheed have to show that the evangelical leaders who attacked Court's statement cared more about the ex-priest's reputation than the truth? Could it be that W.B. Court's allegations suffered attack because what he said was false and not because Chiniquy's reputation had to be protected at all cost?

Another example of Rev. Chiniquy's supposed exaggerations concern his relationship with President Lincoln and conversations they had in the White House. Lougheed stated:

> Yet Chiniquy reports specific dated incidents and quotes long conversations. With obvious hyperbole he claims, 'There is no man living who had so good an opportunity of knowing Mr. Lincoln, under most trying circumstances, as I had.' Without resolving the issue, I tentatively conclude that Chiniquy's reporting of oral conversations is much more subject to embellishment. His quotation marks notwithstanding, few mortals remember long conversations from years ago with such accuracy.[25]

Professor Lougheed came to the conclusion that Chiniquy's accounts of conversations, including his talks with Lincoln, were "much more subject to embellishment" but how does he know for certain that the source of these discourses came from Chiniquy's memory? Rev. Chiniquy said he kept a journal, noting in *Fifty Years*, "I had almost lost sight of those emotional days of my young years of priesthood. Those facts were silently lying among the big piles of the daily records, which I had faithfully kept since the very days of my collegiate life at Nicolet". Regarding a question he asked Rev. Baillargeon, curate of Quebec, Chiniquy also stated, "The next day I took down in writing his answer, which I find in my old manuscripts, and I give it here in all its sad crudity"[26] In a footnote, Lougheed reported on Chiniquy's accuracy when quoting from his correspondence, "We have found all the letters quoted by Chiniquy to be accurate (except for occasional dates) when checkable." As noted earlier as well, the "Letter From Father Chiniquy" published in the *Chicago Tribune* while Abraham Lincoln was in power, gave a description of Lincoln in office and the White House reception of the National Union Convention delegates, as well as a quote of the President to them which agreed with the newspaper reports at the time.

Professor Lougheed also made the following surprising comments relating to the subject:

> From his early temperance days Chiniquy suffered from the charismatic evangelist's temptation to exaggerate his stories and actions in order to create the appropriate mood among potential converts. His success in persuasion led to a lifetime habit of stretching the truth and putting words or thoughts in others' mouth. Usually, but not always, this remained within acceptable limits.[27]

It could be asked regarding this interesting statement, what proof is there that this was true and what exactly are the acceptable limits of stretching the truth? Also, what did Richard Lougheed meant when he wrote that, Chiniquy "used very violent language that provoked reaction"? There was significant violence on the part of Catholics perpetrated against Charles Chiniquy for what he said about his former Church and hopefully Professor Lougheed was not attempting to justify it. Lougheed commented on the hostility the ex-priest had faced:

> Most of those arrested or suspected of violent opposition against his lectures, were French but many others were Irish. Strong arm tactics were transferable from politics to religion especially in Irish circles.

When municipal, often Catholic, police proved untrustworthy or slow, the Orange Order offered its services to maintain the peace. At other times a bodyguard was formed from the students of Presbyterian College. It is almost certain that without these bodyguards, Chiniquy would have been killed.

Lougheed also stated "Chiniquy never provoked a Protestant crowd to any act of violence against Catholics".[28] It could be asked, if Catholicism is just another branch of Christianity, like any other, what incidents of violence have been perpetrated against Catholics by evangelical Christians for what Catholics have said about the evangelical faith?

When Charles Chiniquy was a Catholic priest, there were no attacks made on him by evangelical Protestants for statements he made about their beliefs. Wasn't this because Protestants would not dream of physically attacking someone for making comments about their faith, no matter how offensive? Is it not correct that evangelical Christians would be only interested in answering verbal attacks on their beliefs by words, instead of by rocks or bullets? Doesn't this propensity for violence on the part of Catholics raise yet more questions about whether the Church of Rome is following the meek and mild Jesus Christ? Would Christ be considered to be guilty of using "very violent language which provoked reaction" when he said to the Pharisees, the religious leaders of his day, "Ye serpents, ye generation of vipers, how can ye escape the damnation of hell?" (Matthew 23: 33)

Finally, of the allegations summarized by Professor Lougheed, there is the question of whether or not Chiniquy was guilty of sexual immorality. In this day of post-Clinton morality, it may be asked whether it is relevant whether or not one has committed fornication or adultery. For millions of Americans and others around the world however, the truth still does matter and the breaking of a solemn pledge, whether to a church or to a spouse, says a great deal about the character of those doing so.

In his thesis, Professor Lougheed set the rules he would follow with respect to evidence, "I begin instead with the presumption, which was often confirmed in my research, that Chiniquy's own account should be given the benefit of the doubt until there is convincing evidence otherwise."[29]

Regarding allegations of sexual wrongdoings, Lougheed reported that as a teen, Chiniquy was accused of molesting a female relative but indicated the evidence did not support this allegation. He stated:

> A Chiniquy relative, Bishop Tetu, is another source followed by Catholic accounts. These claim that Chiniquy molested his own female cousin. This suggestion clashes with a letter in which the director himself took up the financing of this good prospect, after what he seems to consider a minor fault, duly confessed. This hypothesis is less likely given the existence of a continuing relationship between Chiniquy, his aunt and other Dionne relatives.

The female cousin reportedly was the daughter of his uncle Amable Dionne. Lougheed also discussed the accusation of sexual impropriety made against Chiniquy by the girl in Montreal which resulted in his suspension. First made in 1851, this same accusation was brought up again in 1857 by the Bishop of Montreal. Like Caroline Brettell, (another Chiniquy commentator whose work is critiqued next), Richard Lougheed maintained that Chiniquy was accused of sexual wrongdoing on more than one occasion.

He reported that Father Brassard went to Kamouraska in 1848 to investigate allegations of a sexual nature made against Chiniquy which, according to Lougheed, Brassard found to be false. Lougheed however, also reported that Brassard wrote to his superior, Bishop Bourget of Montreal in January, 1851, saying "sa mauvaise histoire de Kamouraska n'est connu que de ses superieurs et peut-etre de quelques pretres" or "his unfortunate story from Kamouraska is not known except by his superiors and maybe by a few priests" and that Chiniquy "a deja paye bien cherement sa faute" or "has already paid dearly for his fault". Why would Brassard say this if he had already cleared him? Professor Lougheed tried to explain, stating "Perhaps this response stemmed from a Kamouraska letter relaying news of another Chiniquy scandal there."[30] Why would there be another scandal, if Chiniquy had not been there for four years?

Could the explanation for this be the fact that the original 1851 Brassard letter seems to be lost? Lougheed reported that the archives of the archdiocese of Quebec only contained a transcript of the letter. The letter's value as evidence, already limited because of its source, is further limited because it is not an original. Couldn't this transcript have been made to say almost anything to discredit the "apostate" Chiniquy? Speaking in regard to the Rev. Chiniquy, Lougheed stated that copies of documents could have been used this way. He wrote, "Once again, I maintain that Chiniquy's printed and dated letters are reliable, although, where they are mere extracts, he could have easily distorted the picture" and "My research has not uncovered any forged letters or evidence of changes in any letters quoted by Chiniquy, which can be verified." If the ex-priest could have distorted, forged or changed letters, surely his opponents could have as well. Professor Lougheed stated further:

> In May 1851, Bishop Bourget provided guidelines for Chiniquy's trip to Chicago, including that he must avoid ostentation and respect all local priests. His first guideline was to 'take strict precautions in your relations with women.' At the time Chiniquy responded by complaining of 'calumnies' about himself relayed by Bourget to Brassard. In this letter to the bishop, he implied that he was innocent without providing an outright denial."[31]

Was Bishop Bourget's reported statement regarding precautions in relation to women necessarily an attempt to forestall wrongdoing by Chiniquy? Could the purpose of this warning have been rather to caution him against putting himself in a position where a woman could falsely accuse him? Rev. Chiniquy complained of "calumnies" passed on by Bishop Bourget about himself, evidently regarding sexual wrongdoings and Caroline Brettell disclosed at least one incident of a woman falsely accusing Charles Chiniquy.[32] If Chiniquy implied innocence instead of an outright denial, maybe he didn't feel such a denial was necessary. Professor Lougheed stated the following regarding Bourget's reintroduction of the allegation. Bishop Bourget six years later declared:

> for a long time, the guilt of Mr Chiniquy was known to me, when a certain girl came to testify against him. She expressed a repugnance to meet him. According to our regular procedure, this testimony was not recorded for canonical trial. We limit ourselves then to saying to this gentleman that in addition to all that had been reported against him, a certain girl had recently brought another complaint against him.

> No specifics are thus available for this Montreal charge. Chiniquy's autobiography claims that the reason of suspension had to remain intentionally vague and therefore impossible to refute: an unnamed criminal action with an unnamed person.

Lougheed concluded:

> Chiniquy's written response after this suspension, which is now missing, would help resolve the issue. We have Bourget's declaration that his priest confessed against Chiniquy's denial. Bourget's account is strengthened by several letters of Chiniquy which mention his exile to Illinois and his unfulfilled desire to return to Canada. I conclude, provisionally, that Chiniquy was suspended privately, after at least two unproven and virtually uninvestigated sexual allegations against him. Further, Chiniquy was allowed to go to Illinois as a concession, a decision much regretted later by Bishop Bourget.[33]

What a damning account of Bourget's administration, a bishop who apparently suspended a priest for unproven allegations, which he did not bother to investigate! Doesn't this support what Chiniquy said about the unjust actions of the bishop? If it is true that Chiniquy was allowed to go to another place as a concession to him, why Illinois? What evidence is there to show that Bishop Vandeveld couldn't have offered the Apostle of Temperance the job of helping direct French Canadian immigration into rural Illinois as the ex-priest said? There is no dispute that Charles Chiniquy ended up doing exactly that. When Professor Lougheed spoke of Chiniquy being "allowed to go to Illinois as a concession to him, a decision much regretted later by Bishop Bourget", he makes Chiniquy sound like the guilty party and the bishop the innocent one, who ended up paying for helping the erring pastor. This appears to have the situation totally reversed. It can be concluded from Lougheed's statements that if Chiniquy ended up in "exile" in Illinois, it was because of the wrong done to him by Bourget, who suspended the priest after these "unproven and virtually uninvestigated" sexual allegations were made against him.

Chiniquy did mention in *Fifty Years* that he wanted to leave Illinois and go back to Canada, when he learned of the depravity of the priests where he was. With the continued trouble regarding Catholic church officials in Illinois, he could very well have expressed this sentiment again. In his 1851 public letter calling for French Canadian immigrants to be directed to his proposed colony, he stated:

> I will then say to my young countrymen who intend emigrating from Canada:
>
> 'My friend, exile is one of the greatest calamities that can befall a man. 'Young Canadian, remain in thy country, keep thy heart to love it, thy intelligence to adorn it, and thine arms to protect it.
>
> 'Young and dear countryman, remain in thy beautiful country; there is nothing more grand and sublime in the world than the waters of the St. Lawrence. It is on those deep and majestic waters that, before long, Europe and America will meet and bind themselves to each other by the blessed bonds of an eternal peace; it is on its shores that they will exchange their incalculable treasures. Remain in the country of thy birth, my dear son. Let the sweat of thy brow continue to fertilize it, and let the perfume of thy virtues bring the blessing of God upon it.
>
> 'But, my dear son, if thou hast no more room in the valley of the St. Lawrence, and if, by the want of protection from the Government, thou canst not go to the forest without running the danger of losing thy life in a pond, or being crushed under the feet of an English or Scotch tyrant, I am not the man to invite thee to exhaust thy best days for the benefit of the insolent strangers, who are the lords of the eastern lands. I will sooner tell thee, 'go my child,' there are many extensive places still vacant on the earth, and God is everywhere....
>
> 'Go to Illinois, and the many names of Bourbonnais, Joliet, Dubuque, La Salle, St. Charles, St. Mary, etc., that you will meet everywhere, will tell you more than my words, that that country is nothing but the rich inheritance which your fathers have found for the benefit of their grandchildren.'[34]

When Charles Chiniquy spoke of exile in his letter, he meant the necessary but regrettable immigration from one's country of birth and childhood to go to a place of greater opportunity. If he mentioned exile in these other letters he reportedly wrote, could he not have meant the same thing? Professor Lougheed commented, "My study concludes that Chiniquy was invited by Van de Velde in the quoted early letter, that his visit to Illinois in early 1851 was a success, and that he was planning to return soon. The sexual allegations in Montreal complicated matters."

In any event, Chiniquy clearly stated that Bourget declared him innocent in September, 1851. He then left for Illinois at the invitation of Bishop Vandeveld, an invitation he had received in December, 1850. In this dispute between Charles Chiniquy and the Bishop of Montreal, which comes down to one man's word against another, isn't the Apostle of Temperance to be believed over the unjust bishop? (Vandeveld's name was spelt several ways)

According to Richard Lougheed, at the time Bishop O'Regan excommunicated Chiniquy or threatened to do so, "we have two accounts of horrendous charges over a broad period and involving many women." There was however, no church probe into the allegations therefore Lougheed concluded that, "Without an investigation the truth remains obscure."

Of Chiniquy's life as a Protestant, Professor Lougheed stated:

> As to sexual allegations, there is no record of any new cases during the ex-priest's Protestant years. He did marry but only six years after his final excommunication and eight years after his initial excommunication. During that time, and after, no scandals ever surfaced. Assuming as we do that some of the previous accusations were well founded, this absence is striking. If Lambert's gross accusations were true, the transformation borders on the incredible. While Catholic leaders were convinced of the depravity of Chiniquy, Protestants saw no evidence of this."[35]

By Lambert, Lougheed was evidently referring to Godefroi Lambert and his wife Marie Lambert, whose memoirs alleged the "horrendous charges over a broad period". How can Professor Lougheed assume some of these previous allegations against the priest were well founded? He stated that Chiniquy was to get the benefit of the doubt unless there was convincing proof otherwise. Where is the proof? Later he made the statement that Chiniquy, "possibly was involved in sexual harassment." He also wrote, "A few evangelists have also faced well-publicized accusations of sexual and financial offences. Chiniquy did not escape such accusations in his polemical setting but his guilt remains unproven."[36] Lougheed comments and conclusions regarding assertions of sexual wrongdoing by Charles Chiniquy therefore certainly appear to be confused.

Another area of Professor Lougheed's work where problems can be found, concern Joseph George Jr.'s piece, "The Lincoln Writings of Charles P. T. Chiniquy." He commented in his book:

> Among the most controversial chapters of Chiniquy's two autobiographies are those concerning his relationship with Lincoln. There is no dispute that the future President was his lawyer. However, virtually all Lincoln biographers have disputed the claims to an intimate relationship between the two. Neither do they credit the content of Lincoln's supposed comments to Chiniquy about faith or the Jesuits.

Lougheed also stated:

> Joseph George provides a strong argument for dismissing the Chiniquy accounts completely but he based his case on an argument from silence. The fact that other accounts do not mention the friendship can never prove that Chiniquy is a liar. Among the meagre witnesses supporting Chiniquy there appears a report that Judge Starr, an early Kankakee resident, mentioned that Lincoln consulted Chiniquy during the Civil War. Within the Chiniquy family archives we find two important letters to Chiniquy from Lincoln's son. The first states that his father had "made made many friends in his life but plainly none were more than yourself". The other requested Chiniquy not to raise the matter of his father's death any more, for the sake of social peace.

In his footnote however, he disclosed that the Chiniquy archives did not contain the second letter and only had been reported orally by Samuel Lefebvre.[37]

Lougheed's characterization of the witnesses supporting Chiniquy's assertion of a close relationship with Lincoln as meager has to be questioned. Without anyone else, the testimony of Robert Todd Lincoln, is more than enough.

When *Fifty Years* was first published in 1885, Abraham Lincoln, Mary Todd and three of their four sons, Edward, William and Thomas were dead. The only member of President Lincoln's immediate family still alive was Robert Todd Lincoln. At this time, which of his close relatives and friends would know Abraham Lincoln's better than his oldest son, Robert? How can his testimony be properly described as meagre? Joseph George used it. Robert Lincoln therefore remains a powerful witness that supports Chiniquy's statement and there is no one with direct knowledge of Abraham Lincoln's life that testified that Charles Chiniquy could not have been a close friend of the 16th President.

Regarding Lougheed's statement on the alleged disbelief of virtually all Lincoln biographers of Chiniquy's claims regarding a close friendship with the President and conversations with him on faith and Catholicism, a footnote reads, "The most comprehensive is George,' The Lincoln Writings of C. P. T. Chiniquy',"

It is not clear that Joseph George could properly be called a Lincoln biographer, as he doesn't appear to have published a biography of the Civil War President. A search of a number of sources listed no biographies by George. If by this, Professor Lougheed meant that Professor George's treatment of Chiniquy's relationship with Lincoln was the most comprehensive by any historical writer, this raises real questions about the depth of Lougheed's research, as a better description for George's work might be pathetic.

When dealing with the Spink vs. Chiniquy court struggles, Richard Lougheed also followed Joseph George. At one point in his account however, Lougheed was even unable to accurately reproduce what the blundering Professor George reported.

In one sentence, with the footnote citing George as a source, Lougheed stated that the court cases began in Illinois, "in January 1854 when the St. Anne priest evidently announced in a sermon that Peter Spink was lying to his clients about land sales". What George wrote, correct or not, was that:

> Peter Spink, the plaintiff in the case, charged in his complaint that 'on or about the 10th day of January A.D. 1854' he was accused by Chiniquy, 'in a public assembly,' of committing perjury. Apparently the public assembly was a church service, and Chiniquy, then a priest, had announced to his congregation that Spink, a land speculator, was advising clients to enter public lands on which French-Canadians had cut timber. Spink's plan, Chiniquy told his parishioners, was to make the French-Canadians pay for the wood. Spink charged that the accusation was 'false and malicious' and had caused his clients to lose confidence in him. As a result Spink was unable 'to do business as before, wherefore he was greatly injured and sustained great damage.' Spink

further charged that the priest had 'at divers times before the instituting of this suit-- slandered and defamed this deponent.'[38]

What does this have to do with lying about land sales? Lougheed reported that Chiniquy won the first Kankakee court battle with Spink in May, 1855 and that a hung jury during the May, 1856 court term in Urbana necessitated another trial in October. He then stated, "After it again resulted in deadlock, Lincoln helped to negotiate an out of court settlement where each party paid his own court costs and Chiniquy took back the original accusation as hearsay". In a footnote, Lougheed stated "Chiniquy did claim victory since he was not found guilty but, in fact, he had to retract his statements." It appears that Chiniquy did not retract any statements in the court order, however.

On numerous points, Richard Lougheed did confirm what Charles Chiniquy had said. The ex-priest alleged that agents for the Catholic Church tried to destroy his literary work, sometimes using arson. Lougheed reported, "Chiniquy produced most of his writing while in St. Anne, relying on Chicago publishers. The ex-priest attributed the remarkable string of burned proofs of his books to Catholic conspiracy."[39]

It could be asked, what else could a remarkable series of burned proofs of a book critical of the Catholic Church be attributed to? Lightning? Bad luck? Such a string would indicate arson and police always have an important question when investigating any crime. Who would have the motive to commit it?

Commenting on Charles Chiniquy's life in Illinois, Professor Lougheed also seemed to come to some questionable conclusions. He agreed with *Fifty Years* that Bishop O'Regan was forced from office. Of the prelate, he stated however "Even so, like his predecessor, he had to go directly to Rome to plead to be relieved in 1858". It could be asked what independent evidence shows that Bishop O'Regan pleaded to be relieved of his position?

In his book, Lougheed wrote regarding Bishops Vandeveld, O'Regan and Duggan:

> Could it be possible that Chiniquy played a major role in driving two bishops to request retirement after just a few years and one to go insane? That would probably be too strong a claim. The former priest of St. Anne's certainly played a major role in the demise of O'Regan. Probably all these bishops, who knew that they lacked episcopal talents, and who tried to avoid the job, were delighted to be done with Chiniquy and other independent Illinois clerics.[40]

Later Lougheed stated, "Nevertheless I find no evidence, at the time, of major problems between Chiniquy and his first bishop of Chicago." If so, it is hard to see why the first bishop of Chicago, Vandeveld, probably was delighted to be done with Chiniquy. The Apostle of Temperance stated that he had great admiration for Vandeveld which he lost only when he discovered the Bishop drunk. As well, no other historians seem to assert that there was conflict between Chiniquy and Vandeveld. As noted earlier, Bessie L. Pierce affirmed what Father Chiniquy said regarding his peaceful relationship with Bishop Vandeveld.[41] Of Chiniquy's adversarial relationship with Anthony O'Regan, Professor Lougheed stated:

> Conflict soon followed with his local Irish bishops in Chicago. Various disputes culminated in an episcopal order to move to a distant English-speaking parish. Chiniquy refused and was excommunicated in 1856.

> Chiniquy continued, however, to function as a Catholic priest with the support of virtually his whole parish. He protested that the suspension was unjust and therefore null and void.

Lougheed reported that, "Charles Chiniquy was suspended 'for canonical causes' on 19 August 1856. The interdict was read on August 24th and then he was excommunicated on September 3rd." Chiniquy however, stated that on August 19th, 1856, he was only threatened with interdiction and excommunication if he did not go to Kahokia by the 15th of the next month, (this evidently is what is now Cahokia, Illinois, located on the west side of the state). Professor Lougheed also commented:

> For two years there were various reconciliation attempts originating with the Quebec bishops or with Chiniquy himself. Several of these were effective to some extent but in the end all failed. The bishop of Chicago visited St. Anne in 1858 to announce the final excommunication of Chiniquy and all his followers.

> The dissident priest then created the Catholic Christian Church. His followers continued on in the same building, still claiming to be loyal Catholics protesting against one unjust bishop.[42]

How many times does a person need to be excommunicated? If Charles Chiniquy had been excommunicated in a proper, canonical way in 1856, would there have been a need of a final excommunication in 1858? Does not the story of the two excommunications tend to show Chiniquy was correct when he said that they were both shams? Chiniquy stated that he and his fellow colonists left the Catholic Church in the spring of 1858 and if they had done so, he and the people could not have been excommunicated later when the Bishop of Chicago visited on August 3rd, 1858. Chiniquy stated of the time immediately after he and his people left Romanism:

> A week had scarcely passed, when the Gospel cause had achieved one of the most glorious victories over its implacable enemy, the Pope. In a few days, 405 out of 500 families which were around me in St. Anne, had not only accepted the Gospel of Christ, as their only authority in religion; but had publicly given up the name of Roman Catholics, to call themselves Christian Catholics.[43]

After completing his brief summary of Chiniquy's life, Richard Lougheed discusses the two sides, those for and those against the ex-priest, including the account of French-Canadian historian, Marcel Trudel:

> These two interpretations each presuppose that the other side habitually distorts the truth. There are two detailed autobiographies by Chiniquy and

one could suppose that he knew what actually happened. The autobiographies are exciting and provide helpful details to understand the period and the man's personality. They are very accurate when a letter is quoted. It seems that Chiniquy kept a copy of every letter. His accounts show the extent of opposition against him and his evangelical beliefs but their polemical or propagandist spirit insulting the Catholic Church at every point, leaves many readers to be offended and very sceptical. Even when believed, Chiniquy's books leave out many important events in his life.

The respected Quebec historian Marcel Trudel, has produced an academic book full of research and an attempt at critical analysis. Despite his historical rigour in some respects the bias that Trudel shows prevent a balanced evaluation. He credits all Catholic accounts as reliable with even bizarre anti-Chiniquy legends as worth consideration. His starting point or at least his advice to us is 'as long as one forgets that Chiniquy lied systematically, one will be forced to accept his fantastic autobiography '. The fact that this book precedes Vatican II means that he could produce nothing else but a strong denunciation of the 'apostate'. Finally in 2004 Trudel provided backgroung to his research, explaining that he had been pressured at all points, that he had to be very careful and that he barely even managed to get the book published.

Would any fair-minded person reading *Fifty Years* agree that Chiniquy insulted the Catholic Church at every point through the polemical or propagandist spirit in his autobiography? He didn't blame the Catholic Church for all of the world's problems. In fact, he said some very complimentary things about some sons of the Church, men such as Rev. Mr. Tetu and Rev. Mr. Demars. He also discussed the bravery and selflessness of the Catholic priests as a whole during a cholera epidemic in Canada. Lougheed doesn't say who pressured Trudel but it would appear that it was the Church of Rome.[44]

As it can be seen, while the credit Professor Lougheed gave Charles Chiniquy for his accomplishments is truly commendable, there is no real grounds for his criticism of the ex-priest.

Caroline Brettell

The next of Charles Chiniquy's critics to be considered is anthropologist Caroline B. Brettell. Ms. Brettell's article "From Catholic to Presbyterians: French-Canadian Immigrants in Central Illinois" appeared in the fall, 1985 issue of the *Journal of Presbyterian History*. She seemed to approach the subject of the Apostle of Temperance in a manner much like Richard Lougheed.

Calling Chiniquy an "apostate priest", she seemed to suggest a link between nativist Know-Nothingism and the movement he headed when she stated, "In a sense, all the religious tensions of this period when Know-Nothingism was at its height were played out on the prairies of Illinois among a group whose very ethnic identity was rooted in Catholicism yet turned to Calvinism in the turmoil of the times."[45]

In the early 1850s, the American, or Know-nothing party as it was called by its opponents, emerged as a political force as native born Americans reacted to the large influx of European immigrants, especially Catholics, and the political power they were beginning to wield. A small but surprisingly powerful force nationally, the Know-nothings would not have travelled far with Charles Chiniquy and his flock however because of the nativist group's opposition to the rights of blacks and others.

Ms. Brettell alleged that as an orphaned pre-teen or teen, Chiniquy alienated his wealthy uncle who was supporting him in school by making advances on one of his daughters but she provided no proof for this.[46] As noted earlier, Richard Lougheed showed the evidence did not support this accusation.

Brettell also didn't seem to be enthusiastic about Chiniquy's efforts against liquor, calling him a "rabid advocate of total abstinence" whose approach was "overzealous", a view many at the time didn't share, including the Canadian government who handsomely rewarded the Apostle of Temperance for his labours to curtail drunkenness.

She discussed the letter from Bishop Bourget of Montreal, previously mentioned by Professor Lougheed, warning Chiniquy to "take strict precautions in your relations with persons of the opposite sex". She stated, "However, in 1846, reportedly as a result of a dalliance with a woman which was eventually communicated to the Bishop of Quebec, Chiniquy was forced to leave the diocese."

Continuing on with Chiniquy's time in Illinois she stated "He continued his outspoken preaching and, apparently, some of his philandering habits." A footnote relating to the allegations of sexual wrongdoing reads:

> It is difficult to substantiate the veracity of these stories of Chiniquy's sexual dalliances. It is probably safe to say that in some cases they were true while in others not. There is evidence that some of the accusations brought against him in Illinois were sheer fabrication. One woman, for example, in the course of one of the numerous suits brought against Chiniquy after the schism, retracted her story that Chiniquy had made suggestive remarks to her in the confessional and claimed that she had been put up to it by a local Catholic priest. In a letter to Bishop Bourget of Montreal, a Kankakee woman named Josette Michaud, who claimed to have 'resisted the schism so far,' criticized the behavior of those priests sent out as emissaries who 'say all sorts of abominations against the private character of M. Chiniquy.' 'These are not,' she continued, 'true priests of the Good Lord because they have neither the truth on their lips nor charity in their hearts.' She warned that the faith of both husbands and youths would be eroded by the words of these lying priests.' (AAM, Chicago Diocese File, Letter to Bishop Ignace Bourget Dated 30 November 1856). In the Archives of the Seminaire de Quebec there are *Memories* written by M. and Mne. Godofroi Lambert, both residents of St. Anne. While Mne. Lambert described several occasions on which Chiniquy made suggestive remarks and advances to her, M. Lambert detailed numerous instances, during his travels about the Illinois countryside with

Chiniquy, when Chiniquy remained too long in the chamber of one woman or another. These *Memoires* were taken down by a Catholic priest named Mailloux who had been sent out to Illinois to halt the progress of the schism. Although Chiniquy's biographer Marcel Trudel appears to have accepted these documents at face value, I would be extremely suspicious of their total veracity given the circumstances under which they were recorded.[47]

In a personal letter to the author in 1989, regarding a newspaper article written on a public presentation she gave on Chiniquy, she wrote:

In response to a question from the audience I was forced to mention that Chiniquy WAS ACCUSED of sexual dalliances (your reference to 'indecent comments against women and reputation as a womanizer'). I never said that these were true or could be documented. I am, however, interested in the accusations (as a form of rhetoric in a situation of social conflict) and these can indeed be documented.

....Frankly, I am rather surprised that you were sent the newspaper account rather than a copy of the article that I published in the *Journal of Presbyterian History* in 1985--a more balanced and fully documented analysis of the schism in my own words rather than in the words of a rather sloppy newspaper reporter. [48]

It appears that Ms. Brettell erred when she stated that she never said that Chiniquy was guilty of sexual dalliances. What did she mean when she said of Chiniquy, "He continued...apparently, some of his philandering habits" and her statement in the footnote that it was probably safe to say that some of the stories of sexual dalliances by Chiniquy were true?

Richard Lougheed commented on the alleged incident of 1846, noting that the allegation surfaced 38 years after its supposed occurrence:

I have not found any instance of this incident being used in Quebec Archdiocese condemnations of Chiniquy's apostasy. While this incident, according to Trudel, was supposed to have resulted in Chiniquy's banishment from the Diocese, he still maintained cordial relations with Secretary Louis Cazeau and, apparently, with Bishop Baillargeon and Turgeon. If this sexual scandal happened, then it must have been very discreetly suppressed at the time. Then, for some reason, it was rarely publicized after Chiniquy's apostasy, even when it could have destroyed his reputation.[49]

Could the reason it was rarely publicized be because there was, in essence, no evidence to support it?

Ms. Brettell also stated that Chiniquy exaggerated the numbers of people he persuaded to embrace temperance, saying he had won 900 converts in Detroit, 800 in Chicago and 1,600 in the entire community of Bourbonnais. She alleged this was in 1851, at a time when there were not 1600 residents living in the whole of Bourbonnais. According to her footnote, the information on the number of converts that were won came from the Catholic newspaper *Melanger Religueux*, July 15, 1851. The question that can be asked is, where is the proof that the figures published actually came from the Apostle of Temperance? Isn't it possible that he was misquoted by a "sloppy newspaper reporter"?

She also brought up Bishop Bourget's 1851 interdiction of Chiniquy, stating that Bishop Vandeveld was looking for French-speaking priests to help him in Illinois at the time. According to her, Chiniquy volunteered and Bourget agreed to give him an exeat to satisfy both Vandeveld and the priest.

Regarding the beginning of his life in Illinois, Professor Brettell wrote:

> As might have been expected given his past history, Chiniquy became embroiled in a series of scandals soon after his arrival in Illinois. In 1853, for example, after having assumed the pastorate of Maternity Church in Bourbonnais for several months in addition to his duties in St. Anne, he was accused of deliberately burning the Church and absconding with the funds sent to rebuild it. In a well publicized slander suit in 1855, Chiniquy was defended by no less an attorney than the future President of the United States, Abraham Lincoln.[50]

Does Ms. Brettell have proof that the famous priest was responsible for burning the church, as well as stealing funds? If she doesn't, why does she call these scandals? Wouldn't they be properly called unproven and likely libelous statements, especially in light of Chiniquy's successful lawsuit against the Catholic priest, Brunet, for making at least one of these allegations? Abraham Lincoln defended Chiniquy in 1856, not 1855. She also stated:

> In August of 1856, the Irish Bishop of Chicago, Anthony O'Regan, unable to win his battle with the renegade Chiniquy, suspended him from his duties in St. Anne. Chiniquy refused to acknowledge the suspension and for two more years continued to administer to his French Canadian parishioners as a Catholic priest despite the fact that the Bishop labeled him schismatic.

Yes, this is essentially what Charles Chiniquy reported in *Fifty Years* except Chiniquy said he was not suspended, as he also declared in his letter published in the May 1, 1857, edition of the *Chicago Daily Democrat*. She went on:

> Finally, in 1858, the new Bishop of Chicago issued a writ of excommunication which stuck. Chiniquy took to the staircase of the court house in Kankakee and announced to the French Canadian population that he was separating himself from the Roman Church forever and forming his own church to be called the Christian Catholic Church.[51]

What historical account did Ms. Brettell get this from? It wasn't anything Charles Chiniquy said. He stated that once the Bishop of Chicago rejected the colony's written submission, he left the Catholic Church. The ex-priest then went back to St. Anne, gathered the people in the chapel, and told them that he had left the Church and why he had left. Later he and the majority of the colonists who had followed him out of the Roman Catholic Church took the name Christian Catholics.

As far as any gathering at the Kankakee court-house goes, Chiniquy stated that this happened in the early part of September 1856, not 1858. On this occasion, the people gathered in the large hall of the court-house to pass a resolution supporting him, their pastor. Brettell gave part of their resolution in a letter that was evidently published in a Canadian newspaper but she stated that there were questions about its authenticity. It read:

> Resolved that we, French Canadians of Kankakee County, give our moral support to Reverend Chiniquy in the persecutions exercised against him by the Bishop of Chicago, in violation of the laws of the church, expressed and sanctioned by the council...He is persecuted because he loves us, because he does us good in making sacrifices of personal property to construct homes and a school for us.[52]

This is essentially the same as what Chiniquy stated in *Fifty Years*. Why didn't the supposed 1856 excommunication "stick"? Could it be because it was a null sentence as Chiniquy said? Can Ms. Brettell show that Chiniquy truly had been excommunicated in 1858 and had not left the Church earlier? She continued:

> He stripped the chapel he had built in St. Anne of its cross, removed the statue of the Virgin, and banished the Stations of the Cross. In this dramatic move, he was followed by roughly eighty percent of his congregation in St. Anne, having convinced them that it was a matter of defending their property from the greedy bishop of Chicago and their traditions from the assimilationist and discriminatory penchant of an essentially Irish Catholic clergy. This Irish racism clearly served to maintain loyalty and was a phenomenon not unknown at a slightly later date among the French Canadian and Irish populations of the New England factory towns.[53]

Caroline Brettell's allegations of racism on the part of French Catholics against their Irish co-religionist can be compared with the official Catholic account of the Irish Bishop O'Regan's treatment of the French congregation in Chicago, found in Chapter 3. If there was any "racism" in the struggle, (were they not all the same race, i.e., the human one?), it was the French who suffered at the hands of the Irish. As was noted earlier, a Catholic source stated that O'Regan wished to anglicize the French church and that did occur.

What evidence is there that Charles Chiniquy convinced his followers that their traditions needed to be protected from the "assimilationists"? What traditions were these? Chiniquy stated was that his people simply wanted to follow Christ instead of the Pope. In a footnote, Professor Brettell remarked:

> Chiniquy's work on Lincoln is well analyzed by Joseph George Jr., 'The Lincoln Writings of C.P.T. Chiniquy,' *Journal of the Illinois State Historical Society*, V. 69, 1976, pp. 17-34. George argues quite convincingly that the relationship between Lincoln and Chiniquy was no more than perfunctory and firmly believes that the three meetings between the two men subsequent to Lincoln's election which are described at length by Chiniquy in *Fifty Years in the Church*

of Rome probably never took place. In this volume, Chiniquy refers to anti-Catholic remarks made by Lincoln. Such sentiments have been flatly denied by Lincoln's son.[54]

As it has been shown, Chiniquy's work definitely was not well analyzed by Joseph George Jr. While Ms. Brettell does provide some interesting insights into the life and times of the colourful priest, her statement regarding George reveals her lack of care in researching the subject. It is concluded therefore that like Professor Lougheed, there is no real basis in historical fact for her criticism of the Apostle of Temperance.

William Hanchett

The next of Charles Chiniquy's critics to be considered is William Hanchett. In 1983, when his book, *The Lincoln Murder Conspiracies* was published, he was a history professor at San Diego State University. On the back cover of the book, William C. Davis of the *History Book Club Review* stated:

> Hanchett [spoils] a lot of fun for the crackpots, the paranoids, and the not-so-artful deceivers who have inhabited the Lincoln's assassination field. After years of careful, serious study, he has written a book which will stand as not only the definitive study of the several theories popularized but, more important, also a final refutation of them.

A small part of his volume deals with the allegations made by *Fifty Years*. Hanchett may do an excellent job of refuting the other theories that have been advanced regarding the President's murder but the way he handled Chiniquy's assertions raises questions as to how much careful, serious study he put into his book, at least as far as the ex-priest is concerned. Professor Hanchett began his treatment of the Apostle of Temperance by providing some historical background for Chiniquy's allegations. He stated:

> Among many staunch Unionist during the Civil War, the fact that the Irish were among the most conspicuous opponents of the war and of the policies adopted to win it--especially emancipation--contributed further to a sense that Catholics were no friends of the United States. Thus anti-Catholicism had both religious and patriotic--to say nothing of bigoted--connotations.[55]

Acknowledging that, essentially, to be Irish was to be Roman Catholic during this time period, Hanchett didn't explain why these Catholics were among the most conspicuous opponents of the war to preserve the United States or why they were against freedom for the slaves or why this is should be considered acceptable to patriotic, freedom-loving Americans. He evidently believed however that anyone who thought less of these Romanists because of this to be a bigot. He continued:

> The 'Investigation and Trial Papers' contain warnings from well-meaning citizens about Romish conspiracies against the government and institutions of the United States and about the danger of more assassinations. The newspaperman George Alfred Townsend contributed to such fears by reporting early in May 1865 that all the conspirators awaiting trial were

Catholics. He was wrong, but the error circulated as a fact; only the Surratts and Mudd were Catholics. Later it was stated that Booth himself had been a 'Protestant pervert to Catholicism'[56]

As earlier chapters regarding the conspirators shows, Hanchett was incorrect as to how many were Catholics. What George Townsend actually stated in *Life, Crime, and Capture of John Wilkes Booth*, was that "I mention it is an exceptional and remarkable fact, that every conspirator in custody is by education a Catholic".

Hanchett merely reported that it had been publicly stated that Booth had been a pervert to Rome but his footnote showed that there was good evidence to support this. It read in part, "In 'Insights on John Wilkes Booth from His Sister Asia's Correspondence,' *Lincoln Herald*, 82 (Winter 1980), 542-43, Constance Head shows that Booth may indeed have been a convert to Catholicism."[57] If Ms. Head had shown that Booth may very well have been a Catholic, why didn't William Hanchett say so instead of making the assertion that only the Surratts and Mudd were Catholics and then putting Ms. Head's information about Booth in a footnote?

A significant part of Hanchett's discussion of Chiniquy's account consisted of an inaccurate summary of *Fifty Years*, the usual treatment the ex-priest's critics gave him. He began by stating "But it was not until 1886, when Charles Chiniquy published his *Fifty Years in the Church of Rome*, that the idea of the assassination as a Catholic grand conspiracy received systematic development." *Fifty Years* was first published in 1885.

One of Hanchett's more glaring errors is his statement, "In 1860 Chiniquy left the Roman Catholic Church (if he had not already been defrocked), and with his followers affiliated with the Church of Christ". His footnote read in part:

> *New York Times*, Jan. 17, 1899; Joseph George, Jr., "The Lincoln Writings of Charles P.T. Chiniquy," *Journal of the Illinois State Historical Society*, 49 (Feb. 1976), 18. Some writers state that Chiniquy affiliated with the Presbyterian Church, but in *Fifty Years*, 571, he himself says it was with the Church of Christ.[58]

The section of *Fifty Years* he evidently got this from reads as follows:

> "The Presbytery of Chicago had the courtesy to adjourn their meeting from that city to our humble town, on the 15th of April, 1860, when I presented them with the names of nearly two thousand converts, who, with myself, were received into full communion with the Church of Christ".

If Hanchett had carefully read Charles Chiniquy's autobiography he would have realized that the priest had left the Catholic Church, not in 1860 but two years earlier, in the spring of 1858. Shortly after leaving, Chiniquy and his people gave themselves the name of Christian Catholics. In 1860 as Rev. Chiniquy and other writers reported, they joined the Presbyterian Church of the United States.[59]

When Chiniquy referred to the "Church of Christ", he was not talking about a denomination. He plainly said they were admitted into the U.S. Presbyterian Church. The Presbytery of Chicago was not an agent for the denomination named the "Church of Christ". It did not act to assist Chiniquy and others to attain full communion with it. Sincere believers in Jesus Christ: whether Baptist, Methodist, Presbyterian or the like, are all Christians. They are all part of what has been variously termed "the body of Christ", "the bride of Christ" or the "Church of Christ". All true Christians are part of this group but only God knows the complete membership list. As the U.S. Presbyterian Church was preaching and following God's Word, essentially without compromise in Chiniquy's view and since basically all of the members of this Church were believers in Christ and therefore members of the larger, Church of Christ, Chiniquy evidently felt this denomination could be called by the name of the Church at large. If asked, evangelical Christian in Professor Hanchett's own San Diego neighborhood undoubtedly would have been able to explain this to him.

Another example of Hanchett's "serious study" is his statement that "As a French-Canadian priest, Father Chiniquy in 1851 had led a group of his parishioners to Illinois, where they founded the village of St. Anne's, near Kankakee, fifty miles south of Chicago." As Rev. Chiniquy stated in his autobiography, from the years of 1847 to 1851, he was not the priest of any particular parish but worked as the Apostle of Temperance, preaching against drunkenness throughout Canada and the United States. As such, he wouldn't have had any "parishioners" to lead to St. Anne. As his account and others reported, there was a general exodus, not from one particular parish but from various parts of Canada and other countries into the colony he founded.

After his summary, Hanchett briefly reviewed other books that followed Chiniquy's theme and then spent a little more than one paragraph attempting to refute what the ex-priest alleged. He commented, "most Americans are too worldly wise to believe that the threat to their free institutions comes from Rome".[60]

Professor Hanchett then confidently stated, "Of course, there never had been any evidence of the Catholic Church's complicity in the assassination, and none that Lincoln himself feared Catholicism." Evidence presented earlier refutes the first part of Hanchett's statement. As for the second part of his statement, this was attested to by Charles Chiniquy, the most famous and accomplished priest / ex-priest in North American history. Charles Chiniquy's obituary appeared on the front page of one of America's most influential papers, the *New York Times*, and it was in close agreement with his account of his life. If the witness to what Lincoln said about the Catholic Church is such a person was Charles Chiniquy, with no less an authority than the *New York Times* attesting to his reputation and fame, along with other newspapers, why does Professor Hanchett say there is no evidence that Lincoln himself feared Catholicism? As it has been shown earlier in this work, there is strong evidence that support Chiniquy's contentions.

To further buttress his first point, Hanchett leant on Joseph George. He stated, "Professor Joseph George, Jr., has shown that in all probability Chiniquy never talked to Lincoln in the White House, and it is certain that there were no theological discussions." [61]

Here, Hanchett couldn't even quote his fellow critic correctly. As was shown earlier, George's work on Charles Chiniquy leaves much to be desired but even if everything

Professor George said about Chiniquy is accepted as accurate, he did not do what Hanchett said he did. He did not show "in all probability" that the ex-priest and the President had no conversations at the White House.

In *Fifty Years*, Chiniquy said he was a guest of the President on June 9, 1864 at the White House and also met with the President there the next day. In "The Lincoln Writings of Charles P.T. Chiniquy" George stated that Chiniquy said he was invited to "Lincoln's official notification of renomination by the Republican party." George reported that indeed Chiniquy's "descriptions of the Republican delegations conform to the newspaper reports". Regarding this renomination ceremony and meeting in the White House the next day, what George said was "Chiniquy may have attended the ceremony on June 9 and may have met with the President on June 10th".[62]

Is this showing "that in all probability Chiniquy never talked to Lincoln in the White House"? At the time when they "may have met" would they have both been struck dumb so they were not able to talk with each another?

What about Professor Hanchett's statement that George had showed that certainly there was no theological discussions between Chiniquy and Lincoln in the White House? Professor George wrote regarding June 10th, "Lincoln may have met with Chiniquy that evening, but there is no evidence of it. If such an interview did occur, the subject was probably Chiniquy's request for money". How does this show that "it is certain there were no theological discussions"?

In a footnote referred to earlier, Professor Hanchett also added, without proof, that Chiniquy's account of his trial, Spink vs. Chiniquy, "is lengthy and untrustworthy".[63] As he offers no evidence for this statement, he must expect readers to take his word for it, or believe Joseph George Jr., another bad idea. In the end, like the ex-priest's other critics, Hanchett provided no good reasons to disbelieve what Charles Chiniquy said.

Reverend Sidney Smith

The last of Charles Chiniquy's critics to be considered is Reverend Sidney F. Smith, S. J. (Society of Jesus), whose short book, *Pastor Chiniquy* is undated. Richard Lougheed gave its date of publication as 1908. *Pastor Chiniquy* began with the accusation that Chiniquy had:

> sought to gain popularity and income by wholesale misrepresentation against the personal character and beliefs of those with whom he was previously associated, and his books written for this purpose are still widely used as instruments for the persecution of poor Catholic working men and working girls in the shops and factories[64]

Aside from the fact that Rev. Smith's allegations can easily be shown to be false, if Charles Chiniquy had only wanted popularity and income, surely there would have been easier ways to get it in light of the stones that were thrown and bullets that were shot at him. As for his books being used as instruments for persecution, is hard to believe that persecution of Catholics was occasioned by Chiniquy's writings, knowing the historic tolerance of the Protestant people in America and Canada, especially when compared to the multitude of lawsuits, threats, assaults, and attempts on Chiniquy's own life that he endured at the hands of Romanists.

The Bible itself has been misused at times by the Catholic Church to maltreat people. If the persecution that Smith alleged actually happened, it was no more Chiniquy's intention to have it so than it was God's intention to have his own Word so misused. Smith stated that because of the appeals of those persecuted Catholics, he wrote his book and, "through the kindness of some American and Canadian friends we have been supplied with some materials which, if they do not enable us to check his story at every point, suffice at least to show that he was not exactly the witness of truth." [65]

To accurately report the Jesuit priest's criticisms of Charles Chiniquy and because so many points are contained, his initial accusation is reproduced:

> Before entering on the particulars of his life it will be convenient to consider the general nature of his charges against the Catholic Church and her clergy. And here at the outset we discover a very remarkable development in his allegations. In his earliest biographical effusion, published by the Religious Tract Society in 1861, he bases his conversion solely on doctrinal considerations, and so far from bringing charges against the moral character of the Catholic clergy, he says expressly that there are in the Church of Rome many most sincere and respectable men, and that 'we must surely pray God to send them His light, but we cannot go further and abuse them'; nor is there any charge against their personal character in his *Why I left the Church of Rome*, which comes next in chronological order. But it would seem that the ultra-Protestant palate required something more stimulating, for in his verbose and voluminous *Fifty Years in the Church of Rome* (1885) he tells quite a different story. There he represents himself as one whom the influences of birth, education, and social connections attached firmly to the Catholic Church, but whom a series of appalling experiences as a child, as an aspirant to the sacred ministry, as a priest, drove in spite of himself to realize that this Church was utterly unscriptural in her doctrines and corrupt in her morals. Gradually and sorrowfully he was led to realize that her rulers were perfectly well aware of this opposition between her teaching and that of the Bible, and just for this reason strove always to keep the knowledge of the sacred volumes from her people, forbidding her laity to possess copies of them, and her clergy to attach to them any meaning save such as was dictated by an unanimous consent of the Fathers, which was never obtainable. Gradually and sorrowfully he was led to realize that the practice of auricular confession meant nothing less than the systematic pollution of young minds by filthy questions, and that the vow of clerical celibacy served only to set the priests on the path of incontinence. Gradually and sorrowfully he was led to realize that the clergy practically as a whole were drunkards and infidels, whose one interest in their sacred profession was by simony and oppression to make as much money out of it as their opportunities allowed them.

Thus Bishop Panet is represented as making the acknowledgement that 'the priests [of the diocese of Quebec] with the exception of M. Perras and one or two others, were infidels and atheists,' but as finding a strange consolation in learning from M. Perras that 'the Popes themselves, at least fifty of them, had been just as bad.' Father Guignes, the Superior of the Oblate Fathers, tells him 'there are not more undefiled souls among the priests than in the days of Lot' (p. 280), that 'it is in fact morally impossible for a secular priest to keep his vow of celibacy except by a miracle of the grace of God,' but that 'the priests whom God calls to become members of any of the [religious] orders are safe.' Later he discovers that, so far from this being the case, 'the regular clergy give themselves up with more impunity to every kind of debauch and licentiousness than the secular' (p. 308). In Illinois things were quite as bad, indeed much worse. 'The drunkenness and other immoralities of the clergy there'--as pictured to him on his arrival in those parts by a M. Lebel, a Canadian priest who had charge of the Canadian colonists of Chicago-- 'surpassed all [he] had ever heard or known' (p.352), and somewhat later he made the painful discovery that Lebel himself was among the worst of them.

Nor were the bishops in the two countries any better. Bishop Lefevere, of Detroit, was a man capable of taking the teetotal pledge publicly in face of his assembled flock, and that same evening coolly disregarding it at his own private table; and his predecessor, Bishop Rese, 'during the last years he had spent in the diocese, had passed very few weeks without being picked up beastly drunk in the lowest taverns' (p. 347). Bishop Quarter, of Chicago, is fortunate in not himself coming under Chiniquy's lash, but the latter assures us that he died poisoned by his Grand Vicar, who desired thus to prevent the exposure of his own licentious conduct (p. 352). Bishop Vandevelde, who succeeded Bishop Quarter, is on the whole more leniently dealt with, but 'though he was most moderate in his drink at table' we are assured that 'at night when nobody could see him he gave himself up to the detestable habit of intoxication' (p. 389). Bishop O'Regan, the successor of Bishop Vandevelde, and the prelate who, by the force of circumstances, was brought into the sharpest conflict with Chiniquy, pays for it by being represented as the incarnation of all that can be odious in human character; and Archbishop Kenrick is represented as having agreed with Chiniquy that 'the rapacity of Bishop O'Regan, his thefts, his lies, his acts of simony, were public and intolerable,' and that 'that unprincipled dignitary is the cause that our holy religion is not only losing her prestige in the United States, but is becoming an object of contempt wherever these public crimes are known' (p. 434). Bishop Bourget, of Montreal, is another prelate whose character is aspersed by this man's allegations. In one place we are assured that this bishop, when a young priest staying with his Bishop at the Hotel Dieu, at Montreal, was one of two or three priests who so shocked the nuns that the latter said, 'unless the bishop went away and took his priests away with him, it would be far better that they themselves should leave the convent and get married' (p. 307). Also this same ecclesiastic, we are told, when Bishop of Montreal, bade Chiniquy allure into a convent a lady who confessedly had no vocation, solely in order that he might transfer her large fortune into his episcopal coffers (p. 358); and that for refusing to co-operate in this iniquitous scheme he determined to ruin him, put up an abandoned girl to make a false charge against his honour, and then suspended him without allowing him to defend himself.[66]

It didn't take long for Reverend Smith to show, like so many of Chiniquy's critics, he had difficulty quoting him correctly. Smith stated that Chiniquy's allegations changed over time. According to him, in the ex-priest's earliest biographical work, *The Life and Labours of Reverend Father Chiniquy*, Chiniquy stated he converted from Catholicism for doctrinal reasons and not because of the moral shortcomings of the Roman Catholic clergy. Smith declared that there were also no accusations against their character in his next work, *Why I Left the Church of Rome*, and asserted that it was because of a desire to cater to ultra-Protestantism that *Fifty Years in the Church of Rome* was different in this respect.

Firstly, it is not clear that *Why I Left the Church of Rome* was produced before *Fifty Years*. According to Richard Lougheed, it was published afterwards, in 1887. In any event, in defence of Chiniquy, it is possible to say more in 800 pages plus than 33 or 30. As well, the years of battling the Catholic hierarchy as well as researching *Fifty Years* undoubtedly gave Chiniquy further insight into the Church. Finally, it is simply wrong to say that there were no charges made by him against the morals of the Roman Catholic clergy in *Life and Labours*. In this work, Reverend Chiniquy stated that while in Illinois:

> we had some discussion with the bishop, and after two years of sharp discussion, I was publicly protesting against what I thought was great iniquity. I publicly protesting against what he had done; and one day, to punish me and my countrymen, we were told that we would be excommunicated.[67]

On the supposedly excommunication, Chiniquy's stated further:

> It was a very warm day and the good priests who came to excommunicate us were thirsty on the way, and had drunk a singularly bad quantity of water, which had an extraordinary effect on their tongues and bodies, so that they could not be understood in what they said.[68]

In other words they were drunk. A couple of pages later, he stated that after leaving the Catholic Church "Then it came into my mind that I had to prepare for a deadly conflict with the Church of Rome-that the bishops and the priests would be against me to put me down, and try to take away my honour, and reputation, and probably my life."

He further details the inhumanity of a wealthy priest who took the food out of the mouths of a poor family to pay for a mass. The mass was performed to get a dead family member out of purgatory. Chiniquy also stated that later in his life, when on a preaching tour of Quebec, Catholic priests got 50 men to swear they would kill or drive him out of the city when they found that threats of excommunication were not keeping Roman Catholics from coming to listen to him. [69]

In *Life and Labours* therefore, Chiniquy accused a bishop of a great iniquity, probably theft, as well as misuse of power. He accused some priests of drunkenness and another of being merciless and greedy. In addition, he also accused members of the Catholic clergy of wanting to slander / libel and possibly murder him. He also accused them of attempting to suppress freedom of speech, of intimidation, as well as counseling to commit murder. So much for a clean moral slate.

Smith's account of Chiniquy's specific allegations against the Church is not correct as well. It is not accurate to say that Chiniquy alleged that "the clergy practically as a whole were drunkards and infidels, whose one interest in their sacred profession was by simony and oppression to make as much money out of it as their opportunities allowed them." When Chiniquy discussed the regular clergy, he quoted a friend as saying that they gave themselves "with more impunity to every kind of debauch and licentiousness than the secular" because they were hidden from the eyes of the public by the walls of their monastery.[70] They were accused of immorality, not of being greedy and wanting to make money by selling positions in the Church and the like.

As well, according to *Fifty Years*, it was not Bishop Panet who acknowledged the immorality of the priests of his diocese, it was Bishop Plessis. In addition, Chiniquy Chiniquy did not say that the sole reason the Bishop of Montreal wanted him to persuade a wealthy lady to join a nunnery was so that her fortune could go to the Catholic Church. In fact he stated the first reason the Bishop gave him for wanting her to join a convent was "the spiritual good which she would receive from her vows of perpetual chastity and poverty in a nunnery."

Next, after a summary of Rev. Chiniquy's general and particular accusations against Church officials found in *Fifty Years*, Rev. Smith gave the reason why Chiniquy should not be believed. In a series of accusations that say far more about him than about Chiniquy, he stated:

> (1) That a book of this kind should deeply impress readers of the Protestant Alliance type is not surprising. But more prudent minds will note (1) that this mass of denunciation was not published till after 1885-that is, after a quarter of a century from the date when, with his apostasy, his experiences of Catholic life from the inside must have ceased. [71]

Fifty Years was first published in 1885, not after that year and while it was a long time after Charles Chiniquy left the Church, as was stated earlier, he said he began to faithfully keep a daily record as a student which he continued afterwards. In declaring what he did, was Rev. Smith asserting that life in the Catholic Church had changed dramatically in the 27 years after Chiniquy had left it? The Apostle of Temperance's criticisms of the Roman Church as an insider concerned only the time he was in the Church, including the disputed "excommunication" period. After this time, he didn't pretend to report the Church's affairs as an insider.

❧

Rev. Smith continued "(2) that all rests on the unsupported testimony of Chiniquy himself." This also is not correct. The ex-priest sharply criticized the actions of the oppressive Bishop O'Regan. If the censure of the prelate rested only on the unsupported words of Chiniquy, how does Rev. Smith explain for example, the January 26, 1857 letter in the *Chicago Tribune* by French Canadian Catholics protesting the actions of the bishop or the articles in the *Tribune* on January 26th, 1857 and March 31st, 1857, detailing his tyranny, as well as the *New York Times* articles in 1856 given earlier. (Figures 13)?[72] In addition, as noted earlier, Catholic sources also detailed the wrongdoings of Bishop O'Regan.

Smith went on:

> (3) that the whole tone of the book is that of a man absolutely egotistic and impracticable, absolutely incapable of seeing any other side but his own, absolutely reckless in his charges against any one who should venture to oppose him, and absolutely exaggerated at all times in his language.

This is an outrageous charge to bring against anyone and a perusal of *Fifty Years* will show that this does not apply to Charles Chiniquy. Why would Rev. Smith accuse another of being reckless in his charges when he, himself, couldn't seem to be bothered to do the research to be sure of his?

Was Chiniquy absolutely egotistic? On the prospect of being the spiritual leader to over a thousand of his parishioners who had followed him out of the Catholic Church, he wrote:

> My joy was, however, suddenly changed into confusion, when I considered the unworthiness of the instrument which God had chosen to do the work…What would become of me, seeing that I was so deficient in knowledge, wisdom and experience!
>
> Many times, during the first night, after the deliverance of my people from the bondage of the Pope, I said to my God in tears:
>
> 'Why hast not thou chosen a more worthy instrument of thy mercies toward my brethren?'[73]

Is this a man who was full of pride? Could Charles Chiniquy only see his side in any disagreement? Rev. Chiniquy praised the character of some Catholic officials he knew, as Rev. Smith acknowledged later in his book. Regarding the first priest he ever confessed to, a man who had asked him questions that deeply offended him, Chiniquy stated:

> I should be misunderstood were it supposed that I mean to convey the idea that this priest was more to blame than others, or that he did more than fulfill the duties of his ministry in asking these questions. Such, however, was my opinion at the time, and I detested that man with all my heart until I knew better. I had been unjust toward him, for this priest had only done his duty.[74]

Was Chiniquy absolutely incapable of seeing any other side but his own? Rev. Smith's ability to himself see any other side but his own has to be questioned when he brushed the ex-priest with the charge of, "being absolutely exaggerated at all times in his language". Smith completed the list of allegations by stating:

> (4) in short, that the author of a story which makes out the Catholic Church of Canada and the United States, at the date of which he writes, to be so essentially different from what unbiased witnesses find it to be within the scope of their own direct observation, is one who paints himself in his own book as destitute of all those qualities which predispose a discerning reader to repose confidence in an author's statements.

The picture of the Catholic Church that has emerged world-wide through the recent crisis of sexual wrongdoing and crimes by priests, bishops and other Church officials, particularly in the United States, is not far off what Charles Chiniquy described more than a hundred years earlier. After Rev. Smith's accusations, which again raise more questions about the Jesuit priest's bias than about Chiniquy's trustworthiness, Smith gave the first detailed example of why Chiniquy shouldn't be believed:

> Thus in the fourth chapter he tells us of a secret meeting in the house of one of his uncles, which was attended by several of the leading inhabitants of Kamouraska. Its object was to discuss the conduct of the clergy in the confessional, and the narrator fills six closely printed pages with a detailed report of the speeches then delivered. He was not invited to the meeting, but was present at it in the character of an eavesdropper, hiding in some unobserved corner, his age at the time being ten. We must suppose, then, that this youthful scribe, with an intelligence beyond his years, took down the speeches in shorthand, in all their grown-up language, and preserved the record for future use; or rather, since we are not credulous enough to believe this, we must suppose that all this account of the meeting was a pure invention of his after-years, and must conclude that the man was capable of such amplifications and inventions, and of palming them off as truths when it happened to suit his purpose. And this point about his method being established, we may surely suspect him of employing it in the similarly detailed stories with which his book abounds, and in which priests and bishops speak just as a fierce anti-Catholic might wish them to speak, but quite unlike the way in which they are found to speak all the world over.[75]

In this statement, Reverend Smith continued to demonstrate that it was he and not Chiniquy that can't be trusted to get the facts right. The meeting Smith said couldn't have been accurately reported, in fact did not take place in the house of Chiniquy's uncle as Rev. Smith stated but at the home of a friend's uncle, according to *Fifty Years*. As well, it took place in the community of St. Thomas, attended by the principal citizens of St. Thomas, not those of Kamouraska. In addition, Chiniquy and his friend listened from an adjoining room, not from an unobserved corner.

Chiniquy introduced the two speakers who addressed this meeting stating, "Dr. Tache presided... He spoke in substance as follows...Next followed a gentleman named Dubord, who in substance spoke as follows".[76] In his book, *The Priest, the Woman, and the Confessional*, Charles Chiniquy stated that the conversations of Dubord he reproduced came from "the old manuscripts of 'my young years' recollections".

Rev. Smith's next problem with Chiniquy's account concerned a sermon he delivered in 1850 at the Cathedral of Montreal. It was on the subject of the Virgin Mary and how Jesus always granted her requests. Chiniquy reported his later conversation with the coadjutor of the Bishop of Montreal, Bishop Prince, who had approved of the sermon. Later that night, Chiniquy read in the Bible of Jesus' view of his relationship with his mother:

> 'While he talked to the people, behold His mother and His brethren, stood without desiring to speak with Him.
>
> 'Then one said unto Him: Behold, thy mother and thy brethren stand without desiring to speak with thee.
>
> 'But he answered, and said unto him that told Him: Who is my mother? Who is my brethren?
>
> 'And he stretched forth His hand toward His disciples, and said: Behold my mother and my brethraen?
>
> 'For whosoever shall do the will of my Father which is in Heaven, the same is my brother, and sister, and mother.'

After reading this and other like passages, he felt God's Word, as well as his conscience, showing him that Jesus didn't always give his mother what she wanted. In fact, once Jesus began his ministry, he never granted one of her public requests. He found himself driven powerfully, though unwillingly, to the conclusion that he had preached an untruth when he had claimed that Jesus always granted his mother's request. In conversation with Chiniquy the next day, Bishop Prince was unable to come up with any arguments against the priest's discovery.[77] Rev. Smith asserted that the conversation Chiniquy reported them having was not believable because no Catholic clergymen would speak this way when debating this point:

> It is a well-known passage, and any Catholic commentary would, if referred to, have explained that our Lord wished to teach a lesson to the apostles and their successors in the ministry, of the devotedness with which they must be prepared to subordinate all earthly ties to the service of their ministry. Yet neither to Chiniquy nor to the bishop does it occur even to consider this explanation, and they talk to one another just as if they were two Protestants.

Chiniquy reported that he had been accused of having Protestant tendencies in the past and he would become a Protestant in less than a decade so it would not have been surprising that he may have spoken like one on this occasion. Rev. Smith stated that these two couldn't have had a debate on whether Jesus always granted his mother's requests.

Of course they could have. The Scripture passage may also teach what Rev. Smith maintained but this is not the point. The question was whether this passage taught that Jesus always granted the requests of his mother and it clearly does not.

Next on Rev. Smith's list of alleged problems with Chiniquy's consistency is that:

> He is continually telling his readers that the Church of Rome forbids the reading of Scripture to the laity, and even to her ecclesiastical students....Yet in the story of his boyhood--in which he tells us how he used as a child to read aloud to the neighing farmers out of a Bible belonging to his family, and how the priest, hearing of this, came one day to take the forbidden book away--he has to acknowledge that this copy had been given to his father as a *seminary prize* in his early days. And--to pass over such insights as he gives us into clerical life in the order of the day observed in the presbytery of his first Cure, where a daily hour was assigned to Bible reading[78] (italics in original)

In *Fifty Years*, Chiniquy said that the Church didn't want Catholics to read the Bible on their own and that included even students of the priesthood. Rev. Smith stated that if Chiniquy's statement is to be taken as absolutely truthful, then Chiniquy would have to acknowledge that the Bible the priest came to take away was given to his father as a seminary prize. Smith does not cite the source for this information so presumably it came from *Fifty Years*. Rev. Smith didn't seem to realize that if this statement is acknowledged to be true, then he would have to admit that the priest indeed had come to take the Chiniquy family Bible away because they were *forbidden to read it.*

Why would it matter if it was a prize? The way Chiniquy reported it, his father received the Bible a very short time before he left the seminary and a career in the priesthood. Amazingly Smith put the words, seminary prize, in italics for emphasis although he apparently was so incompetent, he did not realize that the ex-priest did not say his father received it as such. Chiniquy wrote, "Before leaving the Seminary of Quebec my father had received from one of the Superiors, as a token of his esteem, a beautiful French and Latin Bible."[79] A prize would be an public expression of the esteem of the seminary as a whole, not just one individual.

Smith's point regarding Chiniquy's report of a daily hour of Bible reading during his first Cure doesn't prove Chiniquy wrong. The Bible reading was part of a schedule that Chiniquy and his associate, Reverend Perras, kept as priests, not as members of the lay congregation. As priests, Chiniquy and Perras would read the scriptures to themselves or if any members of the congregation were present, to them as well.

Rev. Smith then brought up a short work, published in 1893, entitled *The Two Chiniquy's*. He described it as a re-publication of a debate in 1851 between Father Chiniquy, who was still in the Catholic Church at the time and a man named Roussy, a Protestant minister. Smith stated:

we may be content to set against his later allegations the statements he made on the occasion of his controversy with Roussy, a Protestant minister, on January 7, 1851. This date, indeed, should be noted, for it means that this controversy took place shortly before his departure from Canada for Illinois, and therefore *after* the many occasions when, according to his *Fifty Years*, he had felt and expressed to personal friends his concern at finding that the Church feared the Bible and sought to hide it from her children. And yet on the platform, on January 7, 1851, he talks just as a Catholic priest would talk, except, indeed, for the repulsive egotism and browbeating which is all his own. Take, for instance, the following passage:

'Certain Protestants still repeat that the Church forbids the reading of the Holy Bible by the people. This is a cowardly and absurd lie, and it is only the ignorant or the silly amongst Protestants who at present believe this ancient fabrication of heresy. Some unscrupulous ministers, however, are constantly bringing it up before the eyes of their dupes to impose upon them and keep them in a holy horror of what they call Popery. Let Protestants make the tour of Europe and America; let them go into the numerous book-stores they will come across at every step: let them, for instance, go to Montreal, to Mr. Fabre's or to Mr. Sadler's; and everywhere they will find on their shelves thousands of Bibles in all modern languages, printed with the permission of the ecclesiastical authorities. I hold in my hand a New Testament, printed less than five years ago, at Quebec. On the first page I read the following approbation of the Archbishop of Quebec: 'We approve and recommend to the faithful of our diocese this translation of the New Testament, with commentaries on the texts and notes at the foot of the pages. Joseph, Archbishop of Quebec.' Every one of those Catholic Bibles, to be found on sale at every bookseller in Europe and America in like manner, bears irrefutable witness to the fact that Protestantism is fed on lies, when day by day it listens with complacency to its ministers and its newspapers, telling it in various strains that we Catholics are enemies of the Bible.' (italics in original)[80]

Charles Chiniquy answered this in the first of his works that Rev. Smith brought up, *The Life And Labours Of The Reverend Father Chiniquy* (1861):

In this Protestant country the Roman Catholics have the privilege of reading the Bible; and if you speak to some of your good Roman Catholic friends, and tell them that they are forbidden to read the Scriptures, they will immediately tell you that you don't know their religion, and that Protestants are always calumniating the Church of Rome. They will tell you with pride that they have a Bible in their own houses, the Douay Bible, and that there are Roman Catholic Bibles sold in all the book shops; and I must tell the Roman Catholics, if there are any here, that I am very glad they look on this as a great privilege to have a Bible in their house. But I must tell them something more. To whom do they owe that privilege? Is it to the Church of Rome? Not at all. It is to their Protestant friends, to the Protestant countries in which they live.

Were they at Rome, they would be put in jail for the same thing allowed to them here. Then, if the Church of Rome permits the reading of the Scriptures, it is not because she likes that, but because she cannot help herself. The light is so near the eyes of the Roman Catholics of this country that it can't be entirely put out from them.[81]

Where Charles Chiniquy lived in his youth, the Church's policy at the time evidently was that the people could not read the Bible. As he said however, the pressure the Church faced in Protestant Canada forced it to change this. Chiniquy stated that although Catholics in Protestant countries were allowed by their Church to have a Bible, it was only on condition that they did not interpret the Scriptures according to their own intelligence. Instead of reading God's Word freely, they were to look to their infallible Church to guide them in all things, including how to obtain salvation. This is why, he asserted, that it was very rare to find a Catholic who had thoroughly read the Bible.

Regarding what he had previously said in debate to Roussy, after his conversion Father Chiniquy clearly indicated that numerous times as a priest, he had said things regarding Christian faith and practices that were misleading or false. On one occasion for example, after confronting the Bishop of Detroit about his hypocrisy regarding temperance, Chiniquy felt as though he was being accused of hypocrisy himself. He heard what seemed to him to be a voice, telling him that he was falsely maintaining that he and other Catholics were following God's Word when they were really following the traditions of man. Charles Chiniquy readily admitted that through his training to be a Catholic priest and afterwards, he held positions contrary to the Bible, as well as his conscience, and this was one of the main reason he finally left the Church of Rome.

Rev. Smith then went on to chastise Chiniquy for downgrading the character of a number of priests with whom he had to do and only reluctantly stating their good points. Again, this has been shown to not be true. To prove the ex-priest was wrong about what he reported regarding the moral shortcomings of various bishops, Rev. Smith introduced Gilmary Shea and his book *The History of the Catholic Church in the United States*. Shea was not an independent scholar however, but evidently a Catholic historian and apologist. Smith quoted Shea as stating regarding O'Regan:

> It may be said of Bishop O'Regan that he was a man in the truest sense, single-minded, firm as rock, and honest as gold, a lover of truth and justice, whom no self-interest could mislead and no corruption could contaminate. He held fast the affection of many and won the esteem of all.[82]

Independent and Catholic accounts pertaining to O'Regan in Chapter 3 show how far off the mark Shea's assessment of this Bishop of Chicago was. Smith then stated:

> So far we have been occupied with the general character of Chiniquy's accusations, the truth or falsehood of which we have sought to estimate by applying tests furnished chiefly by his writings. Probably our readers will agree with us that the result has been to show that this person is not exactly

the kind of witness who can claim to be taken on his own valuation, and, apart from an external confirmation which is not available, can be trusted implicitly. [83]

Certainly one could form an opinion on Charles Chiniquy's character at this point as well as the validity of Rev. Smith's accusation and judgement. Smith then began a chronological critique of Chiniquy's life but unfortunately employed only Catholic documents. One was:

> A copy of a manuscript belonging to the Archives of the College St. Marie, at Montreal, entitled *Manuscrit trouvé dans les papiers de M. le Chanoine Lamarche après sa rnort*. This paper is an account and a criticism of Chiniquy's life, but is defective, the first twenty pages being missing as well as all that followed the forty-four pages preserved. From internal evidence the writer is M. Mailloux, a Grand Vicar of Quebec, who knew Chiniquy very well in his Canadian days, and was afterwards sent to Illinois to undo the evil he had wrought there (Document B).[84] (italics in original)

This paper is undated, it apparently is not the original and as Rev. Smith stated as well, it is defective. This was not just because of the amount of it that is missing. Its author reportedly was M. Mailloux; a man Charles Chiniquy stated was a constant opponent of his. This document therefore has to be rejected as evidence because it is not an original, for the lack of independence of its author and the fact that it is undated. Accusations leveled against Chiniquy by Smith that are only attested to by this document are therefore are not examined.

Rev. Smith brought up allegations of sexual wrongdoings by Chiniquy but each charge has been satisfactorily answered by Richard Lougheed. After this, Smith commented on Chiniquy's mission to Illinois:

> According to his own account (p. 345), he received from Bishop Vandevelde of Chicago a letter dated December 1, 1850, in which, addressing him (? on the envelope) as the 'Apostle of Temperance,' he invited him to abandon Canada and put himself at the head of a vast immigration of Canadians which the Bishop wanted to draw into the as yet uncolonised parts of Illinois, south of Kankakee. In this way they would be preserved from the temptations of the cities and their Protestantism, and would be kept together in communities apart, and so become one day a great political force in the United States. Only, the proposal was to be kept for the present a secret, as the Canadian bishops in their selfishness would oppose a movement, however beneficial in itself, which could not but reduce the population of their own parishes.[85]

Fifty Years reproduced the letter in its entirety. Reverend Smith should have noticed that Chiniquy was addressed as the Apostle of Temperance at its beginning and Richard Lougheed attested to Chiniquy's accuracy when he quoted letters. Smith should have also noticed that Vandeveld said nothing about drawing Canadians to Illinois. Perhaps he did give the letter brief attention because he stated:

Whether Bishop Vandevelde ever wrote such a letter may be doubted, for the style as Chiniquy gives it in his book is suspiciously like his own, nor is it likely that the bishop would have made this discreditable request for secrecy to the prejudice of his episcopal brethren in Canada. Still, it is true that the Bishop of Chicago did wish, not to entice Canadian colonists into his diocese, but to divert those who were streaming in unasked, from the cities to the new lands to the south, and that he wanted some Canadian priests to take the spiritual charge of them.[86]

Rev. Smith apparently managed to successfully refute himself as Chiniquy hadn't said anything about the Bishop wanting to entice large amounts of Canadians to Illinois. According to *Fifty Years*, Vandeveld wanted to direct the already occurring immigration of Catholic Canadians to the state. Smith continued:

> But so far from wishing to keep this desire secret from the Canadian bishops, he had written a letter--the text of which is before us (Doc. E)--on March 4, 1850, to Mgr. Bourget of Montreal. In it he lays his trouble before that prelate, and begs for a Canadian priest or two in most moving terms. Possibly it was as the result of this letter that M. Lebel, of Kamouraska, was sent, and so came to be stationed in Chicago when Chiniquy afterwards arrived.[87]

According to Vandeveld's letter reproduced in *Fifty Years*, the Bishop of Chicago didn't just want his proposal kept from the Canadian bishops, he wanted it kept from everyone. He could have written this March 4, 1850 letter to Bourget and still have written to the Apostle of Temperance the letter Chiniquy said he wrote, for asking for priests is not the same thing as directing immigration toward Illinois and not the same thing as asking Chiniquy to head a colony of Catholic immigrants in rural Illinois. According to the official Catholic historical account, *Notre Dame De Chicago*, Lebel arrived in Chicago from Canada before the year 1850. In fact, he is reported to have arrived in 1848.

Before proceeding to Chiniquy's move to Illinois, Rev. Smith discussed the accusation brought by the girl against the Apostle of Temperance in Montreal which resulted in his suspension in September, 1851. Before introducing this, he attempted to lay the foundation for a successful prosecution of Chiniquy on this charge by reviewing prior allegations to show that the priest had been suspected of sexual wrongdoings before. Most are have been dealt with earlier in this work but he brought up a new allegations against Chiniquy regarding the opposite sex that supposedly had occurred in Detroit:

> Nor can we in this connection leave out of account another thing that may, perhaps, throw a little light on the unpleasantness of his visit to Detroit, which took place just at this time, namely, whilst he was on the way to Chicago. We have already heard his own version (see above, p. 4) of the *contretemps* which caused him to hasten his departure from that neighborhood (p. 349), but an American friend assures us that a version of another kind was given him by the late Very Rev. P. Hermaert, formerly Vicar-General of Detroit. That version is that Chiniquy, who used to visit Detroit on his temperance mission from

time to time, had been complained of to the bishop for his offensive attentions to the daughter of a respectable family. During one of his visits he found that the bishop was going to call him to account for his misconduct, and he hastened away before the bishop could return to the city.[88]

What version of *Fifty Years* did Rev. Smith read? Chiniquy's said nothing about leaving Detroit suddenly. Smith's point was to show that the reason Chiniquy gave for hurrying away from Detroit was not the real reason he did so but Chiniquy did not say he hurried away. He *threatened* to make a quick exit from the city because of the Bishop's hypocrisy by publicly making a temperance pledge and then breaking it in private. However, because Lefevre begged forgiveness and pleaded with him not to go, Chiniquy did not leave earlier than planned.

How could Rev. Smith make such a glaring mistake as this? Could what Richard Lougheed said about another of Chiniquy's critics, Marcel Trudel, be a plausible explanation for Smith's blunders? Lougheed had stated, "Despite his historical rigour in some respects the bias that Trudel shows prevent a balanced evaluation."[89] Was this Reverend Smith's problem too?

Smith did confirm the amount of publicity Chiniquy's letter received encouraging French Canadians already leaving Canada to go to Illinois. Smith stated that the French-Canadian priest:

> published in the Canadian papers a glowing account of the prairies of Illinois, assuring the Canadians that, unless they were quite comfortable at home, their best course was to go there to settle, which they could do with a certainty of immediate comfort if they only had two hundred dollars with them to start with (p. 354). This letter caused a great stir, and induced a great many young men to respond to the advice, but at the same time aroused much indignation among their pastors

Chiniquy said that his letter directing Canadian immigration to Illinois was published in the Canadian press. He added that he would never have published it if he had known the effect it would have on the farmers of Canada, as their farms fell in value dramatically because so many want to sell and go to Illinois. Chiniquy stated "some were praising me to the skies, for having published it, others were cursing me, and calling me a traitor." In his letter reproduced in *Fifty Years*, he did not say that those immigrating from Canada to Illinois could settle there, "with a certainty of immediate comfort if they only had two hundred dollars with them to start with"[90]

Rev. Smith then brought up the accusation of the girl in Montreal that had been used twice against Chiniquy by Bishop Bourget. His report of what Rev. Chiniquy said about this was accurate for the most part although he concluded his guilt in this matter was the real reason he left Canada for the U.S. shortly afterwards. He quoted Chiniquy as stating:

> 'I found,' he says, 'on September 28, 1851, a short letter on my table from Bishop Bourget, telling me that, for a criminal action, which he did not want

to mention, committed with a person he would not name, he had withdrawn all priestly powers and interdicted me' (p. 363). [91]

Chiniquy did not state positively that he was in Montreal on the 28th but it is probable that he was there on either the 28th or 29th. The date, September 28th, was important to Rev. Smith. He reported what Chiniquy said about how he and Father Schneider found and confronted the girl that had accused him:

There, in Father Schneider's presence, and under the influence of Chiniquy's firm cross-examination, she owned that 'he was not guilty,' but that she 'had come to his confessional to tempt him to sin,' and that it was to 'revenge [herself] for his rebuking her that she had made the accusation.' This was on the third day of his retreat, and therefore on October 2nd, a date we may find it convenient to remember. When the retreat was over, he went back to the bishop to whom he had already sent a copy of the girl's retractation. The bishop, he says, fully accepted it as clearing his character, and as proof that he had nothing against him gave him a 'letter expressive of his kindly feelings,' and also a 'chalice from [his] hands with which he might offer the Holy Sacrifice for the rest of his life.' Thus equipped and justified he departed for Illinois, and arrived at Chicago on October 29th.

It must be clearly understood that this is Chiniquy's account of what happened, and that he first gave it, not at the time of the occurrence, but nearly six years later, in a letter dated April 18, 1857, which was addressed to Bishop Bourget from St. Anne's Kankakee, and was published in the Canadian press (p. 526). Until then nothing had been publicly known about the story of this girl.[92]

Yes, this is correct because there was no need for the public to know about this at the time. Chiniquy hadn't been publicly suspended and being a just man, he was not minded to make a public example of Bishop Bourget and the girl. He went to the press only after the Bishop made the affair public. Smith continued on:

The occasion of this letter being written arose out of the schism which by that time Chiniquy had stirred up among the French Canadians in Illinois. We shall understand its character better presently; for the moment it is enough to say that Bishop Bourget had thought it necessary to undeceive these poor French Canadians by revealing to them some of Chiniquy's antecedents. Accordingly, when at the beginning of 1857 some of them, who had renounced their momentary schism, sent him a consoling letter to announce the fact, he replied on March 19, 1857, by a letter (Doc. C) addressed 'to the Canadian Catholics of Bourbonnais' which letter 'was read out in the Bourbonnais Church on Passion Sunday, March 29th' (of that year). We shall have to refer to this letter again afterwards, but must give a long extract from it now.

'M. Chiniquy sets himself on another pedestal to capture admiration, by pretending that God has made him the friend, the father, and the saviour of the emigrants. To judge from these pompous words one would have to believe that he only quitted Canada in obedience to a voice from heaven calling him to the grand work of looking after the thousands of Canadians scattered over all parts of the vast territory of the American Union. But here again I am going to oppose M. Chiniquy to M. Chiniquy, for I suppose that, even if he refuses to believe the words of the bishops, he will at least believe his own. I am going to give an extract from a letter written by this gentleman, but that its nature may be the better understood, I should say that on September 27, 1851, I withdrew from him all the powers I had given him in the diocese, for reasons I gave him in a letter which he ought to have preserved, and which he may publish if he thinks that I have unjustly persecuted him. Under the weight of this terrible blow he wrote to me on October 4th following this letter:--

'Monseigneur, tribulations surround me on all sides. I perceive that I must take the sad road of exile, but who will have pity on a proscribed man on a foreign soil, when he whom he had looked up to as his father has no longer a word of mercy for him? … As soon as my retreat is finished I shall go and embrace my poor brothers and mingle my tears with theirs. Then I shall bid an eternal farewell to my country; and I shall go and hide the disgrace of my position in the obscurest and least known corner of the United States. If, when my retreat is ended, I may hope to receive the word of mercy which you thought it necessary to refuse me yesterday, let me know for the sake of the God of mercy, and gladly will I go to receive it before setting out. It will fall like balm on my wounded soul, and will sweeten the rigours of exile.'

'It was under these distressing sensations and in these painful circumstances that he decided to preach the Canadian emigration.'

Our readers will note several things about this letter. First, it was written from St. Marie's College, while he was still in retreat under Father Schneider, and on October 4th--that is to say, two days after the supposed visit and retractation of the unnamed girl. And yet there is not in it a word of reference to this retractation, nor is what he does say consistent with that story--for Chiniquy certainly does not write as if he felt confident that the bishop would now acknowledge his innocence and reinstate him. Secondly, the letter shows that he was going reluctantly to Illinois, and (so far as he knew then), not to preach, but to hide his disgrace in obscurity. Thirdly, the whole tone of the letter is one of a man who pleads for mercy, not of one who protests his innocence. Fourthly, the circumstances under which it was written imply that he was professing, even if he did not feel, a hearty repentance for an offence committed; since it is evident Bishop Bourget deemed him guilty, and that being so, neither would he have removed the suspension, nor Bishop Vandevelde have accepted him for his diocese, unless he had professed repentance.[93]

In Rev. Smith's account, it is stated twice that Chiniquy's letter was written on October 4th. Rev. Smith apparently didn't thoroughly read the letter because if he had, he would have noticed that this date cannot be the correct one according to the letter's contents. If this correspondence is genuine, Chiniquy is quoted as saying that Bishop Bourget refused him the word of mercy, *yesterday*. That would be October 3rd which would be the wrong date because Chiniquy had his interview with the Bishop on the 28th or 29th of September. If it was written the day after the interview then the correct date for the letter would probably September 29th or 30th. As Rev Smith quoted Bourget as saying that Chiniquy "wrote to me on October 4th" is it not possible that if Chiniquy actually wrote this letter, it was not written on October 4th but received on that date by Bourget?

It should be noted that Rev. Smith did not actually quote from the letter directly but quoted Bourget's rendition of it. Where is the original of this letter? Did it ever exist?

Rev. Smith continued on:

> Fifthly, two other contemporary letters that are before us (Doc. E) point in the same direction. For on October 6th Bishop Bourget wrote to Chiniquy, while still in retreat at St. Marie's, a letter which is apparently the answer to Chiniquy's of October 4th. It breathes the same spirit as all Bishop Bourget's letters, and the reader may judge if it is that of an intolerant despot.
>
> 'Monsieur, I am praying myself and getting others to pray for you, and my heart is not so deaf as you appear to think. My desire is that the most sincere repentance may penetrate down to the very depths and to the innermost parts of your heart. I pray for this with all the fervour of my soul, and if I am not heard it will assuredly be because of my innumerable infidelities. O that I could be free to weep over them, and to bury myself for ever in some Chartreuse, under one of the sons of St. Bruno, whose happy and holy feast the Church keeps to-day.[94]

If genuine, the contents of this letter are very interesting. When Bishop Bourget re-introduced the accusation of this girl in 1857, Charles Chiniquy stated that in doing this, Bourget had done a worse thing than even the tyrannical Bishop O'Regan had ever done. Did Bishop Bourget confirm his own sinfulness? What were his "innumerable infidelities" that would prevent God from hearing his prayer and over which he hoped for freedom to weep over? Smith stated that this letter was apparently the answer to the letter Chiniquy alleged sent on October 4th. Bishop Bourget didn't seem to have taken the time to consider the contents of the Apostle of Temperance's correspondence either.

Of Chiniquy's letter, Smith stated "the whole tone of the letter is one of a man who pleads for mercy" and "the circumstances under which it was written imply that he was professing, even if he did not feel a hearty repentance for an offence committed." If the whole tone of the letter was of a man pleading for mercy and the circumstances implied he was "professing….a hearty repentance for an offence committed" why might Bourget still, "desire the most sincere repentance" from Chiniquy?

Finally, this alleged letter of Bourget would have been sent to Charles Chiniquy. If it was a personal correspondence sent to Chiniquy, concerning a part of his life that he felt would be relevant in the future, wouldn't he have kept it? Charles Chiniquy was to be separated from the Catholic Church in some five years time. If this letter was his own property, how did it end up in the hands of the Church that he struggled against for a significant part of his life? When discussing this part of Chiniquy's account, Richard Lougheed makes no mention of any of these letters. In fact, he wrote,"Chiniquy's written response after this suspension, which is now missing". Again, did this missing letter actually ever exist? Professor Lougheed also stated that Chiniquy appeared to have kept all of his correspondences. If so, why didn't he keep this letter?

Rev. Smith continued:

> In this letter the Bishop makes no reference to Chiniquy going to the United States, probably because that project was not as yet arranged. But M. Brassard, on hearing of the misfortune of his *protégé*, took advantage of Bishop Vandevelde's presence at the time in the neighborhood, and besought that prelate to give him a chance of retrieving himself. A letter from Bishop Vandevelde to Bishop Bourget was a result of this. It is dated 'Troy, October 15, 1851,' and contains the following passage, the only one of interest to us now: 'After all the instances made by M. le Curé de Longeuil (M. Brassard), and the promises of his protégé, I consented to give the latter a trial on condition that he got an *exeat* from Mgr. Bourget exclusively for the diocese of Chicago' (Doc. E).[95]

Much of what Smith stated here, he apparently did without evidence. What proof is there that even if this letter was genuine that Chiniquy was the protégé mentioned in it? At the time, he was the celebrated Apostle of Temperance, traveling in Canada and the United States, preaching against drunkenness with great success. It was to be in this year, 1851, that four years of triumphant service to this cause would be crowned by honours from the city of Montreal and the Parliament of Canada. He was 42 years old and had been a popular and effective priest for some 18 years. He was famous, admired, influential. A protégé, according to Webster's dictionary, is one who is "under the care and protection of another who is interested in his career or future."[96] It is true that earlier in his life, Brassard had been a mentor to Chiniquy but considering the celebrated priest's success, his age and experience, could he really be considered one who still needed care and protection?

According to *Fifty Years*, although he ultimately preferred his Church over the truth, Rev. Brassard undoubtedly was a man whose fatherly instincts caused him to befriended young students and priests, other than Charles Chiniquy. In view of how little Chiniquy needed his help, it appears unlikely that he was the protégé that Brassard was trying to help.

As well, even the small part of the letter quoted by Smith appears to be worded strangely. According to Smith, the communication is supposedly from Bishop Vandeveld to Bourget, yet in the letter Vandeveld states, "on condition that he got an exeat that from Mgr. Bourget" Why, if Vandeveld was writing to Bourget, didn't he say "on condition that he got an exeat from you" instead of referring to Bourget in the third person? Smith continued:

It will be admitted that these various letters throw on the episode of September 25, 1851, a light somewhat different from that in which it appears in Chiniquy's own published account above given, and there will be something further to say on the matter presently. But we have heard Chiniquy appeal to two testimonials of esteem--a letter and a chalice--which the Bishop gave him as a means by which he might always be able to vindicate his character in regard to the charge brought against him by this girl.[97]

What episode of September 25th, 1851 was Smith talking about? The Jesuit priest then reproduced essentially the same October 13th, 1851 letter from Bourget that Chiniquy did, stating:

Chiniquy describes this letter as a 'testimonial of esteem' (p. 528), and again as 'a perfect recantation of all he had said and done against me' (p. 370). Perhaps an undiscerning reader will be disposed to agree in that estimate of its language; but a Catholic acquainted with the style of an *exeat*, or permission to leave one diocese for another, will rather take it as a proof of Chiniquy's insincerity that he should thus represent it

Chiniquy's reproduction of it in *Fifty Years* is as follows:

MONTREAL, Oct. 13th, 1851.

Sir: ---You request me to give you permission to leave my diocese in order to go and offer your services to the Bishop of Chicago. As you still belong to the Diocese of Quebec, I think you ought to address yourself to my lord of Quebec, to get the extract you want. As for me, I cannot but thank you for what you have done in our midst; and in my gratitude towards you, I wish you the most abundant blessing from heaven. Every day of my life, I will remember you. You will always be in my heart, and I hope that on some future day, the providence of God will give me some opportunity of showing you all the feelings of gratitude I feel toward you.

I remain, your most obedient servant,
+ IGNACE,
REV. C. CHINIQUY, Bishop of Montreal. [98]

Rev. Smith stated that, "Chiniquy describes this letter as a, 'testimonial of esteem' " but Smith asserted that it really was an exeat or permission to leave one diocese for another. How could it be an exeat, or permission to leave one diocese for another when no permission was given, as Bourget directed Chiniquy to the Bishop of Quebec to obtain this permission? He continued:

So far these contemporary letters convict Chiniquy of untruthfulness, and this may dispose us to doubt whether it is true that, when suspending him on September 28th, Bishop Bourget refused to tell him either the nature of the crime imputed to him or the name of the accuser. Be it recollected that in Bishop Bourget's *Letter to the Canadians of Bourbonnais* (Doc. C) he says that he suspended Chiniquy 'for reasons stated in a letter which he must have kept and which he may publish if he likes.' Chiniquy's reply to this challenge in his letter to the papers of April 18, 1857, was by bringing forward his story of the girl coming to his confessional, and one would like to know what the Bishop's comment on it may have been. We can have it, for the Bishop, who naturally could not engage in a newspaper controversy with a suspended priest, thought it well that his clergy should know the true facts now that Chiniquy was endeavouring to misrepresent them. Accordingly he drew up the paper we have called Doc. D, and of which we have before us a certified copy taken from the archives of the diocese of Montreal. It is entitled *Explanations of certain Facts misrepresented by Chiniquy in his Letter of April* 18, 1857, and is dated May 6, 1857. It begins with the words, 'These explanations are confided to the wise discretion of the priests, so that each may make such use of them as he thinks desirable.'[99]

If Chiniquy was correct and he was given no letter and no reasons for the suspension, how could he prove this? How could he show he was given no letter or reasons? The bishop had it completely backwards. It is not for his opponents to prove what he says is true, that was for him to do. The prelate's accusations were made public first. They were reproduced in the press and afterwards Charles Chiniquy answered this attack on his reputation, as he surely had the right to do. In so doing, he publicly accused the bishop of great wrongdoing. Bourget however did not answer Chiniquy because Smith says the bishop "could not engage in a newspaper controversy with a suspended priest".

If Reverend Smith had paid attention to what he quoted the bishop as saying, he would have noticed that Bourget invited Chiniquy to *publish* his letter if he felt that he was being unjustly persecuted. Where did the bishop expect Chiniquy to publish the letter? Would it be in the newspapers, perhaps? If this letter indeed existed and Chiniquy had published it and left part of it out or misquoted Bourget, would the bishop have responded publicly to point this out? If he responded, as he undoubtedly would have, would he not have used the same medium as Chiniquy? Wouldn't he then be "engaged in a newspaper controversy with a suspended priests"?

Bourget publicly accused Chiniquy but when the priest fired back, the bishop had no reply. Why did Bourget fail to reply publicly? Wasn't it because in fact, he could not do so, as Chiniquy said?

Did he not receive a tremendous blow from Rev. Chiniquy, an unanswerable rebuke that rendered Bourget dumb? Instead of answering Chiniquy in the public realm, out in the open where the bishop had initially attacked him, Bourget said nothing but privately circulated an answer to his priests. Does anyone except for the truly biased believe that if Bourget could have shown that this well known, "rebellious" priest was wrong in his public accusations against him, he would have done so?

The only acceptable response to a public accusation of great hypocrisy, by such a high profile person as Charles Chiniquy, was a public answer. As Bishop Bourget did not even try to defend himself publicly, it is assumed he couldn't have and his private response that Smith spent several pages discussing is therefore dismissed as unworthy of any further attention.

Rev. Smith accepted Bourget's version of events and concluded:

> We can judge now what were the real motives that caused M. Chiniquy to abandon Canada for Illinois, and whether he has stated them truthfully. Probably our readers will consider that he has not, and that, on the principle 'false in one thing false in all,' he has created a presumption against the truth of any future allegations he may make, those only excepted which are confirmed by independent witnesses.[100]

This also is a good time to use his "false in one thing false in all" principle on Reverend Smith. He continued on with yet more accusations against Chiniquy but through his statements, the Jesuit priest has himself "has created a presumption against the truth of any future allegations he may make" and therefore he is dismissed and left to the backwaters of history, along with his error filled book.

Abraham Lincoln's Beliefs

The beliefs of the great statesman, the 16th President, have been a matter of intense interest for many. Much has been said and written on the subject, some by people who knew Lincoln. John T. Stuart and James H. Matheny, two early associates of Abraham Lincoln, reported that earlier in Lincoln's life, between 1837 and 1840 according to Matheny, Herndon and Lincoln used to speak on the subject of the Bible. According to Herndon, Stuart declared that Lincoln was an unashamed infidel:

> I knew Mr Lincoln when he first came here, and for years afterwards. He was an avowed and open infidel, sometimes bordered on atheism. I have often and often heard Lincoln and one W. D. Herndon, who was a free-thinker, talk over this subject. Lincoln went further against Christian beliefs and doctrines and principles than any man I ever heard: he shocked me. I don't remember the exact line of his argument: suppose it was against the inherent defects, so called, of the Bible, and on grounds of reason. Lincoln always denied that Jesus was the Christ of God,--- denied that Jesus was the Son of God, as understood and maintained by the Christian Church. The Rev. Dr. Smith, who wrote a letter, tried to convert Lincoln from infidelity so late as 1858 and couldn't do it.

According to the Lamon biography, James Matheny reported that Lincoln had disparaged the Scriptures because of their inherent contradictions as well as statements that he believed were opposed to reason. Matheny also stated that Lincoln had written a "little Book on Infidelity". In the biography however, Lamon was forced to acknowledge that Smith had asserted that he had played a role in Abraham Lincoln's conversion to Christianity and although Lincoln had known what Rev. Smith has said, he had not denied it.

Holland answered the Lamon charges regarding Lincoln's beliefs and so did a man named James Reed. At the time, Reverend Reed was the minister of the same First Presbyterian Church of Springfield that Abraham Lincoln and family had once attended. Though he hadn't known Lincoln personally, Reed investigated the allegations and gathered evidence regarding Lincoln's faith that showed Lamon, Black and Herndon were wrong. He delivered this information in an extremely popular lecture that was first given in early 1873 in Springfield. It was later published in written form in the July, 1873 edition of *Scribner's Monthly*, a publication that Josiah Holland had launched in 1870. Included in the lecture was a letter that Reed had received from John Stuart. It concerned what Herndon had quoted Stuart as saying on the subject of Lincoln's beliefs. It read:

SPRINGFIELD, Dec.17th, 1872
Rev. J. A. REED

DEAR SIR--- My attention has been called to a statement in relation to the religious opinions of Mr. Lincoln, purporting to have been made by me and published in Lamon's *Life of Lincoln*. The language of that statement is not mine; it was not written by me, and I did not see it until it was in print.

I was once interviewed on the subject of Mr. Lincoln's religious opinions, and doubtless said that Mr. Lincoln was in the earlier part of his life an infidel. I could not have said that 'Dr. Smith tried to convert Lincoln from infidelity so late as 1858, and couldn't do it.' In relation to that point, I stated, in the same conversation, some facts which are omitted in that statement, and which I will briefly repeat. That Eddie, a child of Mr. Lincoln, died in 1848 or 1849, and that he and his wife were in deep grief on that account. That Dr. Smith, then Pastor of the First Presbyterian Church of Springfield, at the suggestion of a lady friend of theirs, called upon Mr. and Mrs. Lincoln, and that first visit resulted in great intimacy and friendship between them, lasting till the death of Mr. Lincoln, and continuing with Mrs. Lincoln till the death of Dr. Smith. I stated that I had heard, at the time, that Dr. Smith and Mr. Lincoln had much discussion in relation to the truth of the Christian religion, and that Dr. Smith had furnished Mr. Lincoln with books to read on that subject, and among others one which had been written by himself, some time previous, on infidelity; and that Dr. Smith claimed that after this investigation Mr. Lincoln had changed his opinion, and become a believer in the truth of the Christian religion: that Mr. Lincoln and myself never conversed upon that subject, and I had no personal knowledge as to his alleged change of opinion. I stated, however, that it was certainly true, that up to that time Mr. Lincoln had never regularly attended any place of religious worship, but that after that time he rented a pew in the First Presbyterian Church, and with his family constantly attended the worship in that church until he went to Washington as President. This much I said at the time, and can now add that the Hon. Ninian W. Edwards, the brother-in-law of Mr. Lincoln, has, within a few days, informed me that when Mr. Lincoln commenced attending the First Presbyterian Church he admitted to him that his views had undergone the change claimed by Dr. Smith.

I would further say that Dr. Smith was a man of very great ability and on theological and metaphysical subjects had few superiors and not many equals.

Truthfulness was a prominent trait in Mr. Lincoln's character, and it would be impossible for any intimate friend of his to believe that he ever aimed to deceive, either by his words or his conduct.

Yours truly,
John T. Stuart

A letter from James Matheny was also included in Reed's lecture:

Rev. J.A. Reed: SPRINGFIELD Dec. 16, 1872

Dear Sir, --- The language attributed to me in Lamon's book is not from my pen. I did not write it, and it does not express my sentiments of Mr. Lincoln's entire life and character. It is a mere collection of sayings gathered from private conversations that were only true of Mr. Lincoln's earlier life. I would not have allowed such an article to be printed over my signature as covering my opinion of Mr. Lincoln's life and religious sentiments. While I do believe Mr. Lincoln to have been an infidel in his former life, when his mind was as yet unformed, and his associations principally with rough and skeptical men, yet I believe he was a very different man in later life; and that after associating with a different class of men, and investigating the subject, he was a firm believer in the Christian religion. Yours truly,

Jas. H. Matheny

Herndon answered Reed in a Springfield lecture he gave late in 1873. He argued that when Stuart and Matheny denied writing what the Lamon biography attributed to them, they were correct. They hadn't actually written the words, it was Herndon who had written down what they had told them while he interviewed them. As Stuart and Matheny's correspondences shows though, this explanation doesn't pass muster.

Herndon also claimed that James Matheny had stated that Reed had prepared the letter that he, Matheny, had signed. According to Herndon's notes of a December 9th, 1873 interview, Matheny declared that Lincoln was an infidel before he left Springfield in 1860 but after associating with religious people in Washington, he believed that the President became a Christian. As far as the differences between the two versions goes, although this was Herndon's account, it is not too far off what Reed quoted Matheny as saying in the letter to him, the main difference being whether Lincoln had investigated Christianity before he became a convert. As well, even if Herndon was correct in his assertion that Reverend Reed had prepared the letter, by signing it, Matheny had attested to its truth.

Stuart and Matheny denied much of what Herndon had quoted them saying but they evidently did state that Lincoln had been an infidel in his youth. Joshua Speed, who according to Lamon's biography, was a close friend of Lincoln's, also said the 16th President was a skeptic when he was younger. In response to a charge of infidelity made against him when he was running for Congress in 1846, Lincoln had a hand bill published. In the recently discovered document, he stated:

A charge having got into circulation in some of the neighborhoods of this District, in substance that I am an open scoffer at *Christianity*, I have by the advice of some friends concluded to notice the subject in this form. That I am not a member of any Christian Church, is true; but I have never denied the truth of the Scriptures; and I have never spoken with intentional disrespect of religion in general, or of any denomination of Christians in particular

The Lamon biography also commented on the "little Book on Infidelity" that Lincoln was alleged to have written:

> He had made himself thoroughly familiar with the writings of Paine and Volney,--the *Ruins* by one and the *Age of Reason* by another. His mind was full of the subject, and he felt an itching to write. He did write, and the result was a 'little book.' It was probably merely an extended essay, but it was ambitiously spoken of as a 'book' by himself and by the persons who were made acquainted with its contents. In this book he intended to demonstrate,--
>
> 'Firstly that the Bible was not God's revelation; and
>
> 'Secondly that Jesus was not the Son of God."

The little book on infidelity was supposedly taken from Abraham Lincoln's hands and burned by Samuel Hill, his employer in New Salem, because he feared for Lincoln's political future. William Barton explained that if anything like this had happened, what Hill had taken from Lincoln was in all likelihood not a little book but was a letter that Hill had written to his partner, John McNamus. The letter had somehow ended up in Lincoln's hands.

The alleged book has never surfaced. Matheny, apparently the only source of information for its existence, denied what the Lamon biography had attributed to him and said nothing about such a volume. As well, Abraham Lincoln, through the handbill he published, categorically denied writing any such thing.

In any case, it is clear that Herndon could not be trusted to report on the 16th President's beliefs. Firstly, he was essentially ignorant of them for at least a latter part of Lincoln's life, stating that his law partner "never let me know much about his Religious aspiration[s] from 1854 to 1860". Herndon's views on Abraham Lincoln's beliefs evidently had been formed from what he had heard others say.

In addition, even after Lincoln's death, Herndon's opinion of his partner's views on spiritual things apparently shifted over time. In 1866 he declared, "Some men think that Mr. Lincoln did scoff and sneer at the Bible. This is not so; he had no scoff--nor sneer, for even a sacred error; he had charity for all and everything."

Three years later though, he told Lamon "Mr. Lincoln was an infidel--a Deist--wrote a book...in favor of Infidelity &c.--that sometimes...he was an atheist...He held in contempt the Idea of God's Special interference &c. &c."

Finally, he was simply wrong about Lincoln's beliefs. He told Lamont that Lincoln had ridiculed the doctrine of the virgin birth. The Lamon biography, which Herndon played a significant role in creating, asserted that Abraham Lincoln didn't believe in the inspiration of the Scriptures and in his youth if "he went to church at all, he went to mock, and came away to mimic". Yet in his public statements, Abraham Lincoln had flatly denied this.

According to Herndon, Bateman's quote of the President-elect, stating that Christ was God, was false. At this point, Herndon's knowledge of Lincoln's own public pronouncements and the Bible is shown to be questionable. Aside from Lincoln's handbill, words that the President was known to have said addressed this.

In his second inaugural address, President Lincoln stated, "The Almighty has his own purposes. 'Woe unto the world because offences; for it must needs be that offences come; but woe to that man by whom the offence cometh'!" The Almighty that Abraham Lincoln spoke about here undoubtedly was God, as other statements he made shows. He spoke of the Almighty Ruler of nations in his first inaugural address and of Almighty God in his special Thanksgiving Proclamation of April 10th, 1862. As the construction of his statement shows, the words "woe unto the world because of offences" is a quote of Almighty God. Yet it is found in Matthew 18:7 and these are the words of Jesus Christ. Here therefore, Abraham Lincoln evidently affirmed that Jesus Christ is God.

Lamon's *Life of Lincoln* also seemed to try to portray Lincoln as a Unitarian. The biography included a statement regarding the 16th President's beliefs from Jesse Fell, an associate of Lincoln's from Illinois. In 1860, as Secretary of the Illinois Republican State Central Committee, Fell played an important part in Lincoln's candidacy for President and it was for him that Lincoln penned an autobiography that was used to compose campaign biographies.

Fell, a Unitarian, declared that some eight to ten years before President Lincoln's death, he and Lincoln had talked about religion. Finding his friend interested in the views of a leader of the Unitarian Church, Dr W. E. Channing, Fell stated he gave him a copy of Channing's complete works. He also reported that Herndon had given his partner the writings of Theodore Parker, a Unitarian minister, and "though far from believing there was an entire harmony of views on his part with either of those authors, yet they were generally much admired and approved by him." Fell added that in his opinion, Parker was the author whose views on religion was the closest to Mr. Lincoln's and stated that he believed Abraham Lincoln incapable of "professing views on this or any other subject he did not entertain."

Lincoln's statement in his second inaugural address tends to show that he was not a Unitarian, as Unitarian teaching denies that Jesus Christ is God. The Lamon biography also dealt with Bateman's account of his conversation with Lincoln:

> Mr. Bateman does not say so directly, but the inference is plain that Mr. Lincoln had not previously known what were the sentiments of the Christian people who lived with him in Springfield: he had never before taken the trouble to inquire whether they were for him or against him. At all events, when he made the discovery out of the book, he wept, and declared that he 'did not understand it at all.' He drew from his bosom a pocket New Testament, and, ' with a trembling voice and his cheeks wet with tears,' quoted it against his political opponents generally, and especially against Douglas. He professed to believe that the opinions adopted by him and his party were derived from the teachings of Christ; averred that Christ was God; and speaking of the Testament which he carried in his bosom, called it ' this rock, on which I stand. ' When Mr. Bateman expressed surprise, and told him that

his friends generally were ignorant that he entertained such sentiments, he gave this answer quickly: 'I know they are: I am obliged to appear different to them.' Mr. Bateman is a respectable citizen, whose general reputation for truth and veracity is not be impeached; but his story, as reported in Holland's Life, is so inconsistent with Mr. Lincoln's whole character, that it must be rejected as altogether incredible.

In reply to this however, Abraham Lincoln had been running a national campaign for President and it certainly wasn't vital for him to know how the most devout church members of Springfield were going to vote. According to Bateman's account, in the light of the Bible that he had been carefully reading, Abraham Lincoln's emotional statement undoubtedly was the expression of his increasing confusion over the prominent churchgoers' seeming indifference to the injustice of slavery. The Lamon biography asserted that Bateman was wrong because:

> From the time of the Democratic split in the Baltimore Convention, Mr. Lincoln, as well as every other politician of the smallest sagacity, knew that his success was as certain as any future could be. At the end of October, most of the States had clearly voted in a way which left no lingering doubts of the final result in November. If there ever was a time in his life when ambition charmed his whole heart, --- if it could ever be said of him that 'hope elevated and joy brightened his crest,' it was on the eve of that election which he saw was to lift him at last to the high place for which he had sighed and struggled so long. It was not then that he would mourn and weep because he was in danger of not getting the votes of the ministers and members of the churches he had known during many years for his steadfast opponents: he did not need them, and had not expected them.

Bateman did not assert that Abraham Lincoln was unhappy because he feared he wouldn't be elected without the support of the ministers and members of the churches of his hometown. Whether or not the Christian people of Springfield had been his constant opponents, Mr. Lincoln was weeping because if anyone could see the great moral question of slavery, it should have been these, the choicest of God's servants who had the Word of God in their hands to guide them. The Lamon volume also remarked:

> According to this version, which has had considerable currency, he carried a New Testament in his bosom, carefully hidden from his intimate associates: he believed that Christ was God; yet his friends understood him to deny the verity of the gospel: he based his political doctrines on the teachings of the Bible; yet before all men, except Mr. Bateman, he habitually acted the part of an unbeliever and reprobate, because he was 'obliged to appear different to them up.' How obliged? What compulsion required him to deny that Christ was God if he really believed Him to be divine? Or did he put his political necessities above the obligations of truth, and oppose Christianity against his convictions, that he might win the favor of its enemies?

Having declared this, the Lamon account made a very interesting statement about the 16th President's beliefs. In his biography of Lincoln, historian Dwight Anderson commented:

> The Lamon-Black view, largely based upon Herndon's records, was that Lincoln did not change his mind on religious matters, though he did come to recognize the political consequences of infidelity in a highly religious age. As they put it : 'He perceived no reason for changing his convictions, but he did perceive many good and cogent reasons for not making them public.'

Didn't Lamon, Black and Herndon therefore say the same thing about Abraham Lincoln that Bateman was condemned for saying? Did not Lamon and company themselves assert that the President was "obliged to appear different" to others in this case, the general public in this "highly religious age"?

There's been much speculation amongst Lincoln's biographers as to why Herndon, who professed to almost worship his former partner, would have seemingly attempted to diminish his reputation. Herndon complained that Holland and Bateman had made Abraham Lincoln look like a coward and a hypocrite. In a letter to a correspondent, he asked:

> do you for an instant suppose, my dear sir, that if Mr. Lincoln was really a converted man to the faith of three Gods, Revelation, Inspiration, Miraculous Conception, and their necessity, etc., as some of the Christian world pretend to believe of Mr. Lincoln, *that he would not have boldly said so and so acted like a deeply sincere man and an honest one fearlessly of that mob furor?*

According to historian David Donald, Herndon also stated that there was no reason why Abraham Lincoln "should have felt obliged to conceal his change of heart, for to reveal his hidden conversion would have won influential political and social support."

Once again, Herndon's statements were confusing and contradictory. What was Lincoln going to experience if he revealed his conversion, new support or hostile mob furor? The way associates like Herndon, David Davis and others reacted to the report of Lincoln being a Christian, it is easy to see why he might have felt, "obliged to appear different to them".

Herndon also worried that Abraham Lincoln's little infidel book would surface, "when we are dead and gone, and no defence being made--he--L.--will go down all time as a writer on Infidelity--Atheism &c--!"[29] Having Lincoln promote infidelity in a book that might come to light at a later time was apparently worse, according to Herndon's bizarre reasoning, than Lincoln actually being an infidel, which was what he seemingly strenuously tried to convince people he was. It appears he felt it was better that his former partner, "Honest Abe", be thought a liar and an unbeliever than a coward and hypocrite. According to Herndon's criteria, in the end, the Lamon biography portrayed Lincoln to have all those qualities.

Though Stuart and Matheny denied much of what Herndon had quoted them as saying, Stuart, Matheny and another of Lincoln's friends, Joshua Speed, did indicate that Abraham Lincoln was an infidel when he was younger, though.

The solution to the tension between the bona fide words of the 16th President and the testimony of Stuart, Matheny and Speed, may be provided by Lincoln biographer William Barton. Barton had been a preacher in the backwoods of Kentucky and Tennessee during the 1880s, in circumstances he believed would have been similar to what Abraham Lincoln grew up in. He reported that what backwoods preachers called infidelity then would not be accepted as such by evangelical Protestants today:

> If Lincoln was regarded as a infidel, and if he ever was tempted to think himself one, we should not be justified in accepting that judgment as final until we knew and considered what was required in that time and place to constitute a man an infidel.

> In the mind of most if not all of the Baptist preachers whom Lincoln heard while he was at New Salem, a belief that the earth was round was sufficient to brand a man as an infidel.

Regarding his own experiences he stated:

> In this summer of 1881, being then a college student on vacation, I taught school in the mountains of Kentucky far beyond the end of the railroad...... After a few weeks one of my pupils, son of a Baptist minister, was taken out of school. His father being interviewed stated that he was sorry to have the boy lose his education, but could not afford to permit him to be converted to infidelity. What the boy had learned which disturbed his father was that the earth was round.

> The subject provoked widespread discussion, and finally resulted in a joint debate between two school teachers and two Baptist preachers on the question:

According to the Lamon biography, at 17 years old, Lincoln believed the earth was round, something that Baptist preachers in his own community would have called him an infidel for. Barton commented:

> I count it a privilege to have lived with earnest and intelligent people who believed the earth flat, and to whom that belief was an important article of Christian faith. But I saw intelligent young men who had come to another opinion concerning some of these matters who accepted without protest the names that overzealous mountain preachers applied to them, and who, believing themselves to be infidels, in time became so.

It is possible therefore that while in doctrine, Abraham Lincoln was actually not an infidel, he considered himself one and perhaps what he told his associates he was. This could be how the reports of his youthful unbelief came about.

The Lamon biography also inferred that Lincoln would not have carried a pocket New Testament on him but Newton Bateman received support from Francis Carpenter on this point. In a letter to Herndon in late 1866, Carpenter stated that John Jay of New York had told him that on one occasion, during a steamboat trip to Norfolk with Abraham Lincoln, his companion had disappeared. Looking for him in an out of the way place, "he came upon Mr. Lincoln, reading a dog eared *pocket* copy of the New Testament all by himself."

Why did Herndon say what he did about Abraham Lincoln? His statements hurt the President's widow and this may have been part of the reason he said what he did, as he and Mary Lincoln detested each other. Mrs. Lincoln was interviewed by Herndon shortly after husband's death and he reported that she had said that Abraham Lincoln "was not a technical Christian". What did she mean by this? A February 27th, 1861, *New York Times* article sheds some light on the term:

> Mr. Lincoln is not what is technically known as a 'Christian'-- that is, he does not hold fellowship with any particular Church, has not made any public profession of faith, or announced his adherence to any sect or dogma,-- still he is a good man. He does not sit in the seat of the scorner, nor does he walk with the ungodly, or run riot with the pleasures of the world. 'his word,' says his neighbors, ' is as good as his bond, and his note needs no indorser.' He is truthful, regular and temperate. Tobacco and strong drinks are tabooed from his bill of fare. He is generous and open handed--he loves the good and despises the evil--and has never yet been detected in a meanness, a profanity, or a breach of honor. He professes to entertain a profound conviction that this country is in the hands of God, the Maker and Ruler of all men--that all things are ordered by His hand, and that to Him alone can he, as President of this people, look for aid, guidance, and ultimate success.

As it can be seen, though Herndon and other tried to portray Abraham Lincoln as an infidel, the evidence does not bear this out. It is not unreasonable therefore to conclude that Lincoln was what Charles Chiniquy and others said he was, a Christian.

WHO KILLED ABRAHAM LINCOLN?

Part 1 - Page 2

Philomene Schwartz Afidavit, continued from figure 3, with transcription

The Chiniquy Collection

dangerous man, and he is my enemy, having already persuaded several of my congregation to settle in his colony. You must help me to put him down by accusing him of having tried to do a criminal action with you.

Madame Bossey answered: "I can not say such a thing against Mr Chiniquy when I know it is absolutely false".

Rev Mr Lebel replied: If you refuse to comply with my request. I will not give you the 160 acres of land I intended to give you. You will live and die poor."

Madame Bossey answered: "I prefer never to have that land and I like better to live and die poor than to perjure myself to please you."

The Reverend Mr. Lebel several times urged his sister Mrs. Bossey to comply with his desires but she refused. At last, weeping and crying she said:"I prefer never to have an inch of land than to damn my soul by swearing to a falsehood".

The Reverend Mr Lebel then said "Mr Chiniquy will destroy our holy religion and our people if we do not destroy him. If you think that the swearing I ask you to do is a sin, you will come to confess to me and I will pardon it in the absolution I will give you."

"Have you the power to forgive a false oath?" replied Mrs Bossey to her brother, the priest. "Yes" he answered,"I have that power for Christ has said to all his priests,"What you shall bind on earth shall be bound in heaven – and what you shall loose on earth shall be loosed in heaven."

Mrs Bossey then said,"If you promise that you will forgive me that false oath and if you give me the 160 acres of land you promised, I will do what you want"

The Revrd Mr. Lebel then said; "All right."

I could not hear any more of that conversation for in that instant Miss Eugenie Bossey, who had kept still and silent with us, made some noise and shut the door.

Affiant further states that some time later I went to confess to Reverend Mr Lebel, and I told him that I had lost my confidence in him. He asked me why I had lost my confidence in him I answered him. "I lost my confidence in you since I heard your conversation with your sister when you tried to persuade

WHO KILLED ABRAHAM LINCOLN?

her to perjure herself in order to destroy Father Chiniquy.

Affiant further says that in the montht of October AD 1856 the Reverend Mr Chiniquy had to defend himself before the Civil and Criminal Court of Urbana, Illinois in an action brought against him by Peter Spink. Some one wrote from Urbana to a paper of Chicago that Father Chiniquy was probably to be condemned. The paper which published that letter was much read by the Roman Catholics who were glad to hear that that priest was to be finished. Among those who read that paper was Narcisse Terrien: He had lately been married to Miss Sara Chaussy who told him that Father Chiniquy was innocent,- that she was present with me when Reverend Mr Lebel prepared the plot with his sister Mrs Bossey and promised her a large piece of land if she would swear falsely against Father Chiniquy. Mr Narcisse Terrien wanted to go with his wife to the residence of Father Chiniquy, but she was unwell and could not go! He came to ask me if I remembered well the conversation

The Chiniquy Collection

of Reverend Mr Lebel and if I would consent to go to Urbana to expose the whole plot before the Court and I consented.

We started that same evening for Urbana. When we arrived late at night I immediately met Mr Abraham Lincoln one of the lawyers of Father Chiniquy and told him all that I knew about that plot'

That very same night, the Reverend Mr Lebel, having seen my name on the hotel register, came to me much excited and troubled and said,"Philomine, what are you here for?

I answered him: I can not exactly tell you that, but you will probably know it to-morrow at the Court House!"

"Oh wretched girl!" he exclaimed,"You have come to destroy me!"

"I do not come to destroy you." I replied, for you are already destroyed!

Then drawing from his pant - monie book a big bundle of bank notes which he said were worth 100 dollars, he said, "I will give you all this money if you will leave by the morning train and go back to Chicago".

I answered him:"though you

would offer as much gold as this room could contain I can not do what you ask.

He then seemed exceedingly distressed and he disappeared. The next morning Peter Spink requested the Court to allow him to withdraw his accusations against Father Chiniquy and to stop his prosecutions, having he said, found out that he, Father Chiniquy was innocent of the things brought against him, and his request was granted. Then the innocency an honesty of Father Chiniquy was acknowledged by the Court after it had been proclaimed by Abraham Lincoln, who was afterwards elected president of the United States.

Philomine Schwartz

I, Stephen R. Moore, a Notary Public in the County of Kankakee, in the State of Illinois, and duly authorized by law to administer oaths. Do hereby certify that on this 21st day of October AD 1881 Philomine Schwartz personally appeared before me, and made oath that the above affidavit by her subscribed is true, as therein stated. In witness whereto, I have hereunto set my hand and notorial seal

Stephen R. Moore
Notary Public

Part 2

Indictment for Perjury, People vs. Peter Spink, with transcription

Archival
Collections,
Kankakee County
Museum

And afterwards to wit on the 26 day of April 1855 it being one of the regular days of the April term of said court for the year 1855 the following proceedings was had + and entering record by said court as following to wit

"The People & c
vs Indictment for Perjury
"Peter Spink

Comes now the defendant in person and by James L _ _ _ _ _ his attorney also come the people by S. W. B _ _ _ _ _ and thereupon by agreement a jury is being empanelled when the Plaintiffs by B _ _ _ _ enter their whole prosecution herein. Whereupon it is ordered by the Court that the defendant have leave to depart hence without _ _ _ _ _

State of Illinois

Iroquois County J.I Jesse Bennett Clerk of the Iroquois Circuit Court do hereby certify the preceding to be a true full & correct transcript of the Record of the proceedings & of the Indictment in the above entitled cause of the People v Peter Spink In testimony of which & hereunto subscribed and affix the seal of said Court at Middleport this 16th of May AD 1855

Part 3 a
Jury Finding Against Peter Spink Regarding Perjury, with transcription

State of Illinois, Iroquois County, SS.

Of the April Term of the Iroquois County Circuit Court, in the year of our Lord one thousand eight hundred and fifty four

The Grand Jurors, chosen, selected, and sworn, in and for the County of Iroquois in the name and by the authority of the people of the State of Illinois, upon their oaths present that

Peter Spink

late of said County of Iroquois on the 6 day of February in the year of our Lord one thousand eight hundred and fifty four at and within the County of Iroquois in the State of Illinois aforesaid unlawfully, know-ingly & feloniously in a suit tried before James B. Smith who was acting justice of the Peace in and for the County of Iroquois wherein Harmon P. Gundy was plaintiff & Wm Mann was Defendant in an action of Debt the said Peter Spink appeared as a witness on the part of the said Harmon P. Gundy upon the said trial and was sworn & took his corporal oath before the said James B. Smith the justice of the Peace aforesaid to speak the truth the whole truth & nothing but the truth & concerning the matter then depending before the said James B. Smith as a justice of the Peace in & for said County, then & there having then and there having sufficient authority & competent power to administer an oath to the said Peter Spink in that behalf whereupon it then & then became a material inquiry to the issue on the trial of the said issue how many Harmon P. Gundy as a Physician the said ... professional visits in the capacity of Physician the said ... made to the said Wm Mann or his family & said Peter Spink being so sworn as aforesaid then & then before the said James B. Smith the said justice of the Peace upon his oath aforesaid falsely wickedly willfully & corruptly did say dispose and sware to the effect following that is to say that the said Harmon P Gundy in to the said Wm Mann as a physician whereas in truth & in fact the said Harmon P Gundy did not pay a visit ... said Wm Mann six times and so the jurors aforesaid do say that the said Peter Spink did then knowing falsely & feloniously & corruptly ... aforesaid did commit ... & corrupt Perjury

contrary to the form of the Statute in such case made and provided and against the Peace and dignity of the same People of the State of Illinois.

Π. Snapp
States Attorney.
of the Eleventh Judicial Circuit.

Archival Collections, Kankakee County Museum

Part 3 b

Jury Finding Against Peter Spink Regarding Perjury, with transcription

State of Illinois, Iroquois County, SS Of the April Term of the Iroquois County Circuit Court, in the years of our Lord one thousand eight hundred and fifty four

The Grand Jurors, chosen, selected, and sworn, in and for the County of Iroquois in the name and by the authority of the people of the State of Illinois, upon their oaths present that

Peter Spink

late of said County of Iroquois on the 6 day of February in the year of our Lord one thousand eight hundred and fifty four at and with the County of Iroquois in the State of Illinois aforesaid unlawfully knowingly & feloniously in a suit tried before James R Smith who was an acting justice of the Peace in and for the Country of Iroquois wherein Harmon P. Gously was plaintiff & Wm. Manly was Defendant in the action of Debt, the said Peter Spink appeared as a witness on the part of the said Harmon P. Gously upon the said trial and was sworn & took his corporal oath before the said James R. Smith the Justice of the Peace aforesaid to speak the truth the whole truth & nothing but the truth of & concerning the matter then defending before the said James R. Smith as a justice of the Peace in & for said County, then & there having then and there having sufficient authority & competent power to administer an oath to the said Peter Spink in that behalf whereupon it then & there became a material inquiry to the issue on the trial of the said issue how many professional visits in the capacity of Physician the said Harmon P. Gouchy had made to the said Wm Manly or his Family & the said Peter Spink being so sworn as aforesaid then & there before the said James R. Smith the said justice of the Peace upon his oath aforesaid & falsely wickedly willfully & corruptly did say that depose and swear to the effect following that is to say _ _ _ _ _ the said Harmon P. Gously previous to the said trial said the said Wm Manly six professional visits as a Physician, whereas in truth & in fact the said Harmon P. Gously previous to the said trial a said Wm Manly six professional visits as a Physician, whereas in truth & in fact the said Harmon Gously did not pay or visit the said Wm Manly six times and as the jurors aforesaid do say that the said Peter Spink then & there, knowingly falsely & feloniously aforesaid did commit willful & corrupt Perjury contrary to the forms of the Statute in such case mad and provided and against the Peace and dignigy of the same People of the State of Illinois.

Part 4
Chicago Tribune, June 22, 1857

DAILY TRIBUNE.

No. 51 CLARK STREET.

CITY OF CHICAGO.

Monday Morning............June 22, 1857.

The Chiniquy Controversy.

 St. Anne, Kankakee, Co. Illi.,
June 18th, 1857.

EDS. OF TRIBUNE : Will you permit me, through the columns of your independent sheet, to express a few remarks relating to a letter published in the TRIBUNE of the 11th inst., signed " An Eye Witness."

The very enthusiastic description that your correspondent makes of the reception at Kankakee city, of Mr. O'Regan, by the Canadians of Bourbonnais, on *bended knees*, on the 4th of June, is certainly more than we ever anticipated from an " An Eye Witness," and I invite him to write a few more of this specimen, and he may be assured that he will contribute powerfully to promote the cause of intellectual freedom that we defend in Mr. Chiniquy's cause with Bishop O'Regan, before the independent people of the United States of America, and the new generation in Canada.

But an important reason omitted in his letter, perhaps unvoluntarily, when he states that not less than *four thousand* people were present for the reception of Mr. O'Regan at Kankakee, is, the motives why they did so, whether through conviction or molestation.

The demonstration in favour of Mr. O'Regan, the very man who has, to the knowledge of all the community of Bourbonnais, taken away the church from the Canadians of Chicago, their brethren, is not all a triumph for him, should there have been even 20,000 people.

Independence of mind, and more especially, molestation in their private interests, may be accounted for the numerous suit, although less than the enthusiastic figure of *four* thousand, that accompanied Mr. O'Regan from Kankakee to Bourbonnais Grove. The following resolution, amongst a few others, passed at a public meeting, at Kankakee, on the 27th April last, will enable you to see, in its true light, the means employed by these Reverends to insure this long calculated demonstration, and for whom *the end justifies the means* whenever their self esteem and temporal influence is at stake.

Resolved : That our actual sheriff, Mr. Francis Siquin, has, by his integrity and his talents, won the just esteem, not only from his compatriots, but also from the American citizens, who elevated him to one of the highest charges of the county.

Resolved : That the Rev. Mr. Desaulniers has deserved the just reprobation of all honest men in the county, for having announced the infamous design he has conceived, that of destroying Mr. Sequin's commercial business, by using his influence to make him lose the confidence of the merchants in Canada, with whom he is transacting.

Now, that you see one of the leading men, from

A word to Young Men Out of Employment.

(Correspondence of the Daily Chicago Tribune.)

Bourbonnais Grove, Mr. Sequin, surrender under such menaces, made to him in open daylight, one might very reasonably ask what may have done these Reverends through the confessional, in darkness?

Another item upon which your correspondent does not throw light enough, is, the silver sett presented to Mr. Desaulniers, as a token for his eminent services to the congregation, in the present circumstances. He has totally omitted to say that the inhabitants of Bourbonnais did not pay for it, although the priests employed all the means at their disposition to do so ; but that the five-sixths of the sum wanted, was raised among themselves, to purchase it. Honor without profit.

In this circumstance, many inhabitants answered them with indignity, namely : the roofing of their church, which is actually made of painted cotton, and the erection of its steeple, and other public improvements that required their immediate attention.

An " Eye Witness" seems to throw the blame unto Mr. Chiniquy, for the demonstration on the 4th inst. Let me tell you, Messrs. Editors, that Mr. Chiniquy left St. Anne for Chicago on the 1st day of June, and returned the 6th.

Making allusion to the man who held a flag or banner with an inscription on it, your enthusiastic correspondent could find nothing else in his mind but an Irish Orangeman to perpetrate such a deed, and he extends his charitable delicacy so far, as to try and stigmatize a man because he chooses this means to repudiate men into whom he has no confidence. This man, Messrs. Editors, is an American by birth. I was told, by persons who deserve as much, if not more credit than your correspondent, and is married to a Catholic woman. The only crime we can impute him is, that he is a poor, but an honest man, earning his daily bread by the sweat of his brow, for him and his family.

Without constituting myself as a judge in the matter, I may still say, that the first demonstration is not, at my advice, more approvable than the second, and the second was certainly the consequence or the result of the first, for, as remarks your correspondent, the first was calculated to crush the Chiniquy schism, hence a provocation was answered to.

These few facts added to your Correspondent's letter plainly establishes that the difference between these reverends' disciples and us, in our present difficulties with the Bishop of Chicago, stands exclusively on this ground: that we do not personify a principle, and that they do. That we submit to a Supreme Being and to the laws; whilst they submit blindly to men who have substituted themselves to God on earth, and even to the laws.

Although I have never been admirer of monarchical governments, and much less so since I enjoy a share of the protection of the American flag, under which all men are equal, I still entertain the opinion that if the laws of the primitive Church were in strict observance, and that the Clergy should

Part 4
Continuation of article

DAILY TRIBUNE.

No. 51 CLARK STREET.

CITY OF CHICAGO.

Monday Morning............June 22, 1857.

be only the depository of those laws, Catholicism might flourish everywhere in perfect harmony with all other sects, and to the greater satisfaction of the Catholic laity. But since the Clergy has substituted temporal to the spiritual, that he endeavors to make us believe, as in this occasion, that the Pope is the Father, the Bishops, the Son, the priests the Holy Ghost, and the people *nothing*, only good to make them live in a princely style, we cannot sympathize with such an order of things. Hence the Jews and the Samaritans.

Now Mr. "An Eye Witness," I must tell you that I cannot conceive the reason why you strike your blows behind the curtain of the engine, you, the champion of terrific and powerful afterrestrial and

the corn would hardly be worth the gathering. The season is very backward at the best, and it

A word to Young Men Out of Employment.
(Correspondence of the Daily Chicago Tribune.)
CHICAGO, June 17, 1857.

MESSRS. EDITORS :—Knowing that at the present time there are hundreds of good and trustworthy young men in this city out of employment, I deem it the duty of those, who have it in their power, to aid in securing them some reliable means of support. For several years past it has been the chief

celestial a power, while we, the poor Samaritans, in abhorrence to your Synagogue have made it a duty to ourselves and the public to sign our own writings. Come forward, Mr, "An Eye Witness," and give us your name, so that we may know if you are a Christian, the only exception to the rule, who supports by his pen, a man like Bishop O'Regan who has insulted your countrymen, when he said that they could not pay even for the *potatoes and salt* to support their priest; and also Mr. Desaulliers who addressed you this graceful compliment: that you Canadians were all ignorant and unable to sign your own names!

P. GENDRON, Also an eye-witness.

six hours' walk of this city, there could be work obtained for over *one hundred* good, honest and in-

Part 5
Chicago Tribune, August 25th, 1857

DAILY TRIBUNE.

Tuesday Morning.........Aug. 5 1857.

Heavy Failure.

Private dispatches received to the city yesterday announced the...
Insurance and Trust Co...
and Trust Co. was one of...
est corporations in the W...
whole country. The Co...
one in New York and o...
understand that both ha...

The Life and Trust C...
York accounts of most o...
State Bank of Ohio, an...
ber of private institution...
diana. It controlled th...
Cincinnati, and through...
portion of the West, wh...
seriously felt. The disa...
affect our business com...
less lead to many minor...
and Indiana. We have...
and cannot judge of the extent of the failure.
The stock of the company has been quoted lately at 94a94½.

NATIONAL GUARD CADETS.—*Editors Tribune:*— The first moonlight excursion of the season is to be given by this gallant little corps next Friday evening. The magnificent steamer Lady Elgin is chartered for the occasion, and the character of the "Cadets" is sufficiently well known to guarantee

To the Catholics of the Diocese of Chicago.

On the second page of this morning's TRIBUNE we give place to a communication, addressed to the "Catholics of the Diocese of Chicago." It is from the pen of a Catholic Priest, in good standing with his church. It is not written by Father CHINIQUY or any one of his flock, but by a new hand in the controversy. It is a searching criticism on the course of Bishop O'REGAN, and an earnest, manly appeal to the clergy and laity of the Diocese to demand release from an insufferable tyranny.

The following persons were fined for being drunk or disorderly : John Carroll, $3; Felix Randall, $2;

To the Catholics of the Diocese of Chicago.

[For the Chicago Tribune.]

A deep sense of the evils, which have for years past afflicted this portion of the Lord's vineyard, compels the writer to address you, for the two-fold purpose of pointing to the sources, whence arise the difficulties, unfortunately too frequent of late years in the Diocese of Chicago, and already so productive of immense injury to the cause of religion, and the well being of the Church. He does this because his heart has been profoundly afflicted at the evil results of these difficulties, results brought home to him in the daily walks of life, *tangible* and easily seen by those, who, holding the position that he holds, are daily and hourly brought into contact therewith. Another motive for his thus addressing you is, that he may, as he believes, be able to offer you an effective and permanent remedy, which without doing anything inconsistent with the doctrines, or incompatible with the discipline of the Church, may at once relieve the body of the Diocese, and the various congregations thereof, from the evils above referred to. He will therefore proceed to direct your attention to the true sources of the evils, of which there is so general, and he may be permitted to say, *so just* a cause of complaint throughout the Diocese. They arise from various causes, which may be mentioned hereafter, but principally from the tenure, by which the inferior clergy hold their position, and the manner in which the Bishop holds the title to the property of the Catholics of this Diocese, held and used for ecclesiastical purposes. It is not, perhaps, generally known to the Laity, that the United States, notwithstanding the magnificent Cathedrals which adorn many of her chief cities, the superb and palatial residences of many of her Bishops, of which you have an instance in the "Bishop's Palace" in Chicago; her colleges and educational establishments, vieing with those of older countries in the ability and talent concentrated therein, and the numberless other religious establishments, all evidences of a strong and healthy Catholic sentiment; it is not, perhaps, generally known, that with all these advantages, the United States is still held to be only a *Missionary* country, and thus to a certain extent, reduced to a level with the Fejee Islands, or with the barbarous nations of South Africa and Eastern Asia. This, however, is done for certain purposes, chief among which is the retention of powers in the hands of our Bishops, unknown to the Bishops of the Continent of Europe. It produces an absence of restraint on the authority of Bishops over their Clergy, by which the latter are reduced to the level of the slaves of the South, and made the mere instruments of their will, tools in their hands to be used by them with a despotism of authority, not less than that of the Autocrat of all the Russias, or the slave owners of the South. Under this condition of things, the Priest is, to all intents and purposes, the slave of the caprices of his Bishop, for he knows that the Prelate to whom he may be subject, can at any moment and without any reason, by a simple *withdrawal of faculties*, cast him upon the world, to seek a living as best he may, *disgraced* and *degraded* in the eyes of his fellow religionists, and regarded, on account of his religion, with at least disesteem by those, who profess a different faith. He may do this at any moment that he deems fit, without cause or reason, other than his own will. And let it not be said that he will not do so without cause. No reasonable man, we admit, much less a Prelate in the Church of God, should act in such a manner. But when men are elevated to Episcopal dignity, who know nothing of society but what they have learned in the company of the aristocracy of Ireland; who have never labored in the missions, and are *profoundly ignorant* of the duties, trials and troubles, which are the inevitable portion of the pastor of a congregation, and yet more so of one who has various congregations to attend at far distant points; men whose whole life has been spent in the seclusion of colleges and seminaries, *domineering over boys*, and looked up to as oracles; who physically are incapacitated from missionary life, to say nothing of their mental endowments for such duties, and who, to all intents and purposes, know as little of the people of their diocese, their habits, manners, customs and modes of life, as their people wish to know of them on being brought into contact with them; in a word, when men are raised to the Episcopal dignity who are so devoid of common sense and prudence, as on all occasions to express their supercilious contempt for the very people among whom they are required to live, to whom they are expected to give a good example, as well as instruction! men, who, overbearing in manner, domineering in the exercise of their authority, can not permit even a just difference of opinion; what else can be expected of such men exercising Episcopal authority, than that they should act as above referred to. This is no picture of fancy, but a simple and truthful statement of facts, as the writer has the best means of knowing. Else why the murmurs, not loud but deep, of his clergy, at the conduct of the Bishop, murmurs which, like the distant rumbling of thunder, presage the coming storm? Why that feeling of dissatisfaction which the writer has oft and again heard expressed by estimable members of the clerical body in good standing, accompanied by the most contemptuous expressions of feeling toward their Bishop? It is because these men feel that they are worse than slaves, obliged to cringe and crouch at the feet of a despot and autocrat, on whose nod they are compelled to rely for their daily bread; because, like the oppressed to whom there is no other remedy, there is one consolation, that of venting their feelings in expressions of contempt for their oppressor.

Such is not the state of affairs in Continental Europe, despotically ruled as it is, where the Bishops are controlled by Canon Law and immemorial usages. There the pastor is not removable at the nod of his bishop. His faculties cannot be withdrawn without good and sufficient cause, and that cause not only alleged, but proven on a fair and just trial and confrontation of witnesses, as in our own courts of law. There the Bishop is no autocrat, no despot, but a kind father, interposing between the just severity of his courts and the culprit, who, having fallen into errors against the dignity and character of his vocation, truly repents and repairs the errors he has committed.

The evils from which we all suffer, (clergy as well as people,) have their origin in the *non-existence of Canon Law* in the United States, by which the Bishops are vested with uncontrollable power and authority, from which in reality there is no appeal. The remedy is the establishment of Canon Law, and the imposition of those just restraints upon Episcopal power which the wisdom of eighteen centuries has approved. But how is this to be done? Opposition on the part of the Bishops must naturally be looked for, as, like most men, they are but little disposed to resign a power the exercise of which is so sweet. The fact that such opposition will be made is proved in the attempt already made in the first National Council of Baltimore, to introduce the institution of Parish Priests into the cities of the United States, which was indignantly, though naturally, frowned down by the Episcopal body, with only one or two exceptions. Had that attempt proved successful, a very useful restraint would have been imposed on Episcopal power. But it failed from want of unanimity on the part of the clergy most interested therein. Let then the bishops be given distinctly to understand, by the pastors and other clergy, when assembled in synod, they are resolved to be controlled by law and not by the will of man, and let them insist that the Canon Law shall at once be made the law of the Diocese. If the laity will at the same time manifest their determination to support their clergy in procuring their just rights, they will at once remedy one of the worst evils that afflict this Church. The Bishop may recalcitrate, like the donkey which is for the first time put in harness, but he will finally submit, when he finds that the reins are in firm hands, and that further recalcitration is in vain. Not only will he cease to struggle, but as use familiarizes to the gearing, he will be thereafter the first and most willing to draw the load or bear the burthen, until finally he will thank those, who have been the means of imposing it on him, as his benefactors. The laity will no longer see estimable and virtuous ministers of God, men, who were laboring for their spiritual welfare to the best of their abilities, and with acceptance to them, either removed or suspended to gratify the whim or caprice of a despot, without sufficient

cause, but be assured at all times of the ministrations of one, whom they both esteem and love for his virtues. Death or the will of the incumbent will be the only reason, without cause, of removal, and families may hope to grow up under the fostering care of the one pastor, who has been their father in infancy, their guardian in youth, and will be their counsellor in more mature years. Thus, while despotic authority is removed, the reign of law is established, each party observant thereof, will know their respective rights, and thus union, love, respect and obedience will take the places of the discontent and dissatisfaction, which now so generally exist.

The second source of the evils, we complain of, is to be found in the *tenure* by which the Bishop holds the property, devised to him for Ecclesiastical purposes. His predecessors, better conversant with our customs and usages, as a people, from the fact that they were either Americans, or long residents of the country, and therefore, better able to judge of the feelings of the people, which *they respected*, usually took deeds of church property, as "in trust for the use and benefit of the Church" or congregation, deeding it. The present Bishop, with that disregard for all the customs of the people, whom he so utterly *despises*, which is necessary to his regard for consistency, takes deeds in his own name without any "in trust," or other clause, showing the intent or purpose of the devisee. This form of deed, practically, makes him the owner in *fee* of all property deeded to him in this manner, and consequently, irresponsible *in law* for the use to which he may put it. He may take the property of any congregation, held by him as above, and sell it for any purpose he pleases, without restraint or danger of imperilling the validity of the deed, as the purchaser buying from the legal owner in fee, buys in good faith. The proceeds he may apply to such purposes as he pleases, without legal remedy. All such property is therefore virtually lost to the congregations so deeding them. Couple this with the fact, *that the Bishop habitually withdraws his priests from all churches which do not so deed their property to him,* and if he meets with opposition withdraws his faculties from those priests, who do not use all their power and influence to effect his purposes, we have indeed a state of things truly alarming to every Catholic. By this means your property is at his will, to be used by him not for the sole object for which you have given it, but for those purposes to which he may see fit to apply it. If you refuse to allow him to use it as he pleases, or put it into his power to do as he will, he then employs his autocratic authority over his clergy to compel your obedience, by depriving you of the rites of your church, leaving your children unbaptized, your sick unanointed, your children uninstructed in their religion, the sacraments unfrequented, and you, in a Christian country, in a condition, so far as your religion is concerned, but little better than if you were in a pagan land. And why is this done?

Part 6 c
Continuation of article

For a mere worldly object, to compass a mere temporal, mercenary end. Is this not the truth? If any one doubts it, the writer has repeated instances to which he can point, within his own known knowledge. Has he not done this at Peoria with the German congregation, withdrawing the faculties of their pastor until he had compliance with his will? Has he not for the same cause, or a similar one, withdrawn the faculties of the priest, now or lately resident at Galesburg, who who was so unfortunate as to be an American, for which, with that persevering obstinacy usual with him, he has hitherto refused to reinstate him, compelling him to adopt worldly avocations, as his future calling? The writer might refer to other patent instances, well known to the citizens of Chicago, and to almost every congregation in the diocese, did space permit. But suffice it to say that this has been his course, pursued from the day of his elevation to the Episcopal chair. Is there no remedy, or do the Catholics of the Diocese of Chicago wish to be sneered at as the tools of one man, a foreigner by birth, who has the nerve to rule them with a rod of iron, a despot, who seizes upon the title to the property which they have appropriated out of their hard earnings to religious purposes, and holds it with the strong arm? Again I ask, is there no remedy? The writer will suggest one that is both simple and effectual. Let a petition be presented to the next Legislature of the State, asking the enactment of a law, rendering all property held by any person whatever, for church or ecclesiastical uses, subject to the provisions of the law of Trusts, and the holder thereof, whatever his name, or title, or dignity may be, a Trustee, compelling him to render an annual account of the use to which he has applied all moneys derivable from such property. Let such statement be under oath, and a failure to render such statement every twelve months, to be filed in the county records, a misdemeanor punishable by fine and imprisonment. If this be done, as we know will be done, unless satisfaction be given to the different congregations where these property quarrels exist, there will be no further difficulty in regard to church property, no more putting down the screws, to use a common but expressive phrase, on the churches, to secure the title to their property, no more discussions, disputes and schisms about property and titles. To look at us, as matters now are in regard to our real estate difficulties, an outsider would look upon us as a parcel of real estate gamblers quarrelling over the spoil of some unlucky victim. How long this state of things shall last, remains for you to say. You can remedy it if you will, and you have but to give expression to your your will to insure a ready compliance with your wishes. The prelate who rules this diocese is well aware of your discontent, but believes it to be the smouldering embers of a fire nearly quenched.—Manifest to him by one united effort from all parts of his diocese, that such is not the case, that your dissatisfaction is not that of a few, but of all, and the first effective step is taken, and the remedy is applied.

The writer has thus laid before you the sources of the evils which afflict this diocess. In so doing he has spoken distinctly, written freely. To you he would say, weigh well what he has written, ponder well the remedies he has pointed out. Apply them, if you are convinced that they need application, but do so only, as the surgeon does, when removing a cancer, with a firm hand, curing that which needs a cure, touching that which is sound and healthy. If a renovation of the body religious, a cessation of the difficulties so often alluded to, peace and quiet be the result, the writer will have attained the object of his most earnest desires.   TRUTH.

FATHER CHINIQUY TO MGR. LYNCH,

Archbishop of Toronto.

St. Anne, Kankakee County,
Illinois, June 22, 1884.
To His Lordship Lynch, Archbishop of Toronto:

My Lord—The 12th inst. I promised to answer your letter of the 11th, addressed to the Rev. Moderator and to the Ministers of the General Assembly of the Presbyterian Church. I come, today, to fulfil my promise, with the help of God.

I had accused your church to believe and say that she has received from God the power to kill us poor heretics. I said that if you do not slaughter us, today, in Canada and elsewhere, it is only because you are not strong enough to do it. I said, also, that where the Roman Catholics feel strong enough, they do not think it a sin to beat, stone or kill us when they can do it without any danger to their own precious lives.

I said that your best theologians teach that heretics do not deserve to live, and that your great Saint Thomas Acquinas, whom your church has lately put among "the Holy Fathers," positively declares that one of the most sacred rights and duties of your church is to deliver the heretics into the hands of the secular power to be exterminated.

As I expected, you have bravely denied what I said on that subject. In your reply, you complain that the quotations I made of St. Thomas, on that subject, are not correct.

Here is my answer to your denegations. I have the works of St. Thomas just now on my table. I will copy word for word what he says in Latin, and translate it into plain English, respectfully asking your lordship to tell the Canadian people whether or not my translation is correct:

"Quanquam hœretici tolerandi non sunt ipso illorum demerito, usque tamen ad secundam correctionem expectandi sunt ut ad sanam redeant Ecclesiasiæ fidem. Qui vero, post secundam correptionem, suo errore obstinati permanent, non modo excommunicationis sententia, sed etiam sæcularibus principibus exterminandi tradendi sunt."

TRANSLATION.

"Though heretics must not be toler-

property applied to the use of the church in which they officiated. Secular powers of all ranks and degrees are to be warned, induced, and, if necessary, compelled by ecclesiastical censures, to swear that they will exert themselves to the utmost in the defense of the faith, and extirpate all heretics denounced by the church who shall be found in their territories. And whenever any person shall assume government, whether it be spiritual or temporal, he shall be bound to abide by this decree.

"If any temporal lord, after having been admonished and required by the church, shall neglect to clear his territory of heretical depravity, the Metropolitan and Bishop of the province shall unite in excommunicating him. Should he remain contumacious a whole year, the fact shall be signified to the Supreme Pontiff, who shall declare his vassals released from their allegiance from that time, and will bestow his territory on Catholics, to be occupied by them, on the condition of exterminating the heretics and preserving the said territory in the faith.

"Catholics, who shall assume the cross for the extermination of heretics, shall enjoy the same indulgences and be protected by the same privileges as are granted by those who go to the help of the Holy Land. We decree further, that all who may have dealings with heretics, and especially such as receive, defend and encourage them, shall be excommunicated. He shall not be eligible to any public office. He shall not be admitted as a witness. He shall neither have power to bequeath his property by will, nor to succeed to any inheritance. He shall not bring any action against any person, but any one can bring action against him. Should he be a judge, his decision shall have no force, nor shall any cause be brought before him. Should he be an advocate, he shall not be allowed to plead. Should he be a lawyer, no instruments made by him shall be held valid, but shall be condemned with their author.

I could give you thousands of other infallible documents to show the exactness of what I said of the savage, anti-social, anti-Christian, and bloody laws of your Church, in all ages, against the heretics, but the short limits of a letter make it

Columns continue on next page

ated because they deserved it, we must bear with them till, by a second admonition, they may be brought back to the faith of the Church. But those who, after a second admonition, remain obstinate in their errors, must not only be excommunicated, but they must be delivered to the secular power to be exterminated." (St. Thomas Acquinas, 4th v., page 90.)

At the page 91, he says: " Though heretics who repent must always be accepted to penance as often as they have fallen, they must not, in consequence of that, always be permitted to enjoy the benefits of this life. . . . When they fall again, they are admitted to repent. . . . But the sentence of death must not be removed." (St. Thomas, v. 4, page 91.)

You lordship has the just reputation to be an expert man. You then know that, in such solemn questions as are discussed just now, the testimony of only one witness does not suffice—I will then give you another testimony to prove the unpalatable truths which I proclaimed in the presence of the General Assembly of the Presbyterian Church of Canada, viz: That we poor heretics are condemned to death, and are solemnly declared unworthy to live side by side with our Roman Catholic neighbors. That testimony will, no doubt, be accepted as good and sufficient by the people of Canada, if not by you, since it is the testimony of your own infallible church, speaking through the Council of the Lateran, held in 1215:

" We excommunicate and anathematize every heresy that exalts itself against the holy orthodox and Catholic faith, condemning all heretics, by whatever name they may be known—for though their faces differ, they are tied together by their tails. Such as are condemned are to be delivered over to the existing secular powers, to receive due punishment. If laymen, their goods must be confiscated. If priests, they shall be degraded from their respective orders and their

impossible. Those proofs will be fully given in my book, "Fifty Years in the Church of Rome," which (D. V.) will soon come out from the press.

I suppose you will answer me, "Have not heretics also passed such bloody laws!" Yes, they have passed such cruel laws; but they had borrowed them from you. When those nations came out from the dark dungeons of Popery, they could not see the light, at first, in its fulness and in all its beauty. It took some time before they could cure themselves from the putrid leprosy which centuries of life inside the walls of the modern Babylon had engendered everywhere. But you know as well as I do that these remnants of Popery have been repudiated more than a century ago by all the Christian churches. Every year, since it has been my privilege to be a Presbyterian, I have heard a constant and unanimous protest against those laws of blood and persecutions. They are kept in our records only as a memorandum of the bottomless abyss into which the people were living when submitted to the Pope. But you know well, my lord, that all those laws of blood and death have been sanctioned in your last Council of the Vatican by your Church. It was declared, then, that you are forever damned if you have any doubt about the rights and the duty of your Church to punish the heretics by bodily punishments.

But, my lord, let us forget, for a moment, the numberless and undeniable proofs which I might bring to the remembrance of your lordship, to make you blush for having denied what I had said about the unmanly, un-Christian principles which regulate the Roman Catholic Church toward the Protestants, when you have your opportunity. The providence of God has just put me in possession of a fact too public to be ignored or denied even by you.

You know how the Roman Catholics of Quebec have given the lie, with a vengeance, to your denials. You know how more than 2,000 good Roman Catholics came with sticks and stones to kill me, the 17th of this month, because I had preached in a Presbyterian Church on the text, "What must I do to have eternal life?" More than one hundred stones struck me, and if I had not providentially had two heavy cloth overcoats, one to protect my shoulders and the other put around the head to weaken the force and the weight of those stones, I would surely have been killed on the spot. But though I was protected by those overcoats, my head and shoulders are still as a jelly and cause me great suffering. A kind friend, Mr. Zotique Lefebvre, B. C. L., who heroically put himself between my would be murderers and me, to protect my life at the risk of his own, came out from the broken carriage with six bleeding wounds on his face.

The City of Quebec is known to be the most Roman Catholic city in America, and perhaps in the whole world, without excepting Rome itself. Its population has the well-earned reputation to be moral, peaceful, respectable, and religious, as they understand those words among the Roman Catholics. The people who stoned me were not a gathering of a low-bred mob; it was composed of well-dressed men, many with gold spectacles, it was not composed of drunkards; there was not a single drunken man seen by me there; they were not, of course, what is called "liberal Catholics," for those "liberal Catholics," though born in the Church of Rome, have a supreme contempt for the dogmas, practices, and teachings of the priests. Those "liberal Catholics" who, thanks be to God, are fast increasing, are only nominally Catholics—they remain there because their fathers and mothers were so; because, also, they want to attract the people to their stores, sell their pills, or desire to be elected to such and such offices by the influence of the priests. They laugh at your mitre, for they know it is nothing but the old bonnets of the priests of Bacchus, representing the head of a fish. Those liberal Catholics are disgusted with the bloody laws and practices of the Church of Rome; they would not, for anything, molest, insult, or maltreat a heretic. Those liberal Catholics are in favor of liberty and conscience. But the clergy hate and fear them. Had this class of liberal Catholics been numerous in Quebec, I would not have had any trouble. But Quebec is, with a very few exceptions, composed of true, real, sincere, devoted Catholics. They believe sincerely, with your grand St. Thomas, and with

plot, the revocation of the Edict of Nantes, and the deaths of more than half a million of French Huguenots on their way to exile. That stone and that blood will tell you that your church, today, is the same as she was when she lighted the five thousand auto-da-fes, where ten millions of martyrs lost their lives in all the great cities of Europe, before God raised the German giant who gave it the deadly blow you know.

Please, my lord, put that stone and that blood in some of the most conspicuous place of your palace, that you may look at them when the devil will come again to throw you into some ignominious and inextricable slough, as the one into which you fell in your courageous but vain attempt to refute me.

When that father of lies will try again to make use of your pen to deny the bloody laws and bloody deeds of your church, you will tell him, "Get thee hence, Satan, for it is written in our most approved book of theology, St. Thomas, that 'we must exterminate all the heretics.' Get thee hence Satan; for you will not any more induce me to call old Chiniquy insane, for saying that our church is as bloody as ever; for it is written in the Council of Lateran that those who arm themselves for the extermination of heretics are as blessed by God as those who went formally to the rescue of the Holy Land."

Yes, my lord; keep that stone and that blood before your eyes, and when I or somebody else will again warn the disciples of the Gospel against the dangers ahead from Rome, you will not compromise yourself any more by writing things which are not only against all the records of history, but against the public teachings of all your popes, your councils, and your theologians.

With that blood before your eyes, the devil will lose much of his power over you and be forced to give up his old tactics of making you denying, denying, denying, the most evident facts, and the most unimpeachable records of history.

My dear Bishop Lynch, before taking leave of you this day, allow me to ask a favor from your lordship. If you grant it, I will retract what I have said of the anti-social and anti-Christian laws and practices of your church.

Let your lordship say anathemas to the Councils of Constance and Lateran for the decrees of banishment and death, they passed over all those who differed in religion from them. Tell us, in plain and good English, that you condemn those Councils

Columns continue on next page

your Roman Catholic Church, that heretics like Chiniquy have no right to live; that it is a good work to kill them.

This riot of Quebec, seen with the light of the teachings of St. Thomas, the Councils of Lateran, Constance, and the Vatican, show that your letter to the General Assembly of our Presbyterian Church is one of the greatest blunders that your lordship has ever made. The dust you wanted to throw into the eyes of my Presbyterian brethren is all on your face, today, as dark, hideous spots. Your friends sincerely feel for your misfortune.

For, my lord, there is a voice in the stones thrown at me; there is a voice in the bruises which cover my shoulders and my head, there is a voice also in the blood shed by the friend who saved my life at the peril of his own, which speaks louder and more eloquently than you, to say that you have failed in your attempt to defend your church against what I said at the General Assembly.

That you may better understand this, and that you may be a little more modest hereafter on that subject, I send you, by the hands of the Venerable Secretary of our General Assembly, the Reverend Mr. Reid, D. D., one of the hundreds of stones which wounded me, with a part of the handkerchief reddened with the blood of Mr. Zotique Lefebvre, B. C. L., who received six wounds on his face, when heroically standing by me in that hour of supreme danger for my life.

Please look at that stone, look at that blood also; they will teach you a lesson which it is quite time for you and all the priests to learn. They will tell you that your Church of Rome is the same, today, as she was when she slaughtered the hundreds of thousands of Piedmontese with the sword of France; that stone and that blood will tell you what every one knows, among the disciples of the Gospel, that your church of today is the very same church which planned the massacres of St. Bartholomew, the gunpowder for the burning of John Huss, and the blood they caused to be shed all over Europe, under the pretext of religion; tell us that those Councils were the greatest enemies of the Gospel, that instead of being guided by the Spirit of God, they were guided by the spirit of Satan, when they caused so many millions of men, women and children to be slaughtered for refusing to obey the Pope.

And when you will have condemned the action of the depraved men who composed those Councils, you will honestly and bravely declare that your Thomas Acquinas, instead of being a saint, was a bloody monster, when he wrote that the duty of the Church of Christ is to deliver the heretics to the secular power to be exterminated!

Tell us also, that the present Pope Leo XIII., ought to be the object of the execration of the whole world for having lately ordered that that bloody monster's theology should be taught in all the colleges, academies, seminaries, and universities of the Church of Rome, all over the world, as the best, truest, and most reliable exponent of the doctrines of the Church of Christ.

If you grant me the favor I ask, we will believe that your lordship was honest when you denied what I said of the savage, cruel, diabolical laws and practices of the Church of Rome toward the heretics. But if you refuse to grant my request, we will believe that you are still, in heart and will, submitted to those laws and practices, and that you tried to deceive us, after having deceived yourself, when you presented your bloodthirsty church with the rose colors we find in your letter to our General Assembly.

In my next, I will give the proofs of what I said about the idolatry of your church, and, with the help of God, I will refute what you said to defend her practices. Truly yours,

C. CHINIQUY.

1874.]   BISHOP OF CHICAGO *v.* CHINIQUY *et al.*   317

Opinion of the Court.

THE CATHOLIC BISHOP OF CHICAGO

v.

CHARLES CHINIQUY *et al.*

1. CHANCERY JURISDICTION — *enjoining ejectment suit.* A court of equity has no jurisdiction to enjoin the prosecution of an action of ejectment on the ground that the conveyance relied on by the plaintiff is absolutely void for want of delivery and acceptance, or if delivered, it was procured through threats and duress, the defense being complete at law.

2. SAME — *grounds for enjoining suit at law.* The indispensable basis upon which a defendant to an action at law may resort to a court of equity to restrain the prosecution of such action is, that he has some equitable defense, of which a court of law cannot take cognizance, either by reason of want of jurisdiction, or from the infirmity of legal process.

3. INJUNCTION — *of action at law.* An application to enjoin a suit at law concedes the plaintiff's strict legal right to recover, but is based upon the fact that the defendant has equities calling for the interference of the court, as clear as the legal right it seeks to control.

4. Where an action of ejectment is sought to be enjoined on the ground that the plaintiff's deed was never delivered and accepted so as to pass the legal title, a court of equity cannot be invested with jurisdiction to so declare by an allegation that the deed was subject to a trust which the plaintiff is attempting to pervert.

APPEAL from the Circuit Court of Kankakee county; the Hon. CHARLES H. WOOD, Judge, presiding.

Messrs. MOORE & CAULFIELD, for the appellant.

Mr. MELVILLE W. FULLER, for the appellees.

Mr. JUSTICE McALLISTER delivered the opinion of the Court:

This is an appeal from the decree of the circuit court of Kankakee county, perpetually enjoining an action of ejectment pending in that court, which had been brought by appellant, as a corporation sole, having the legal title, against appellees, the defendants therein, to recover the land described in appellees' bill of complaint herein.

The Chiniquy Collection

Kankakee Oct 30, 1883

Dear Father Chiniquy,

I had a successful trip and obtained the affidavit of Horace P. Bennett, who was with Rev. F. A. Conwell, where the assassination of Lincoln was talked of before it had taken place. Mr Bennett is a very responsible man, and his evidence can not be impeached.

I had quite a time to get the statement o f Linneman. He is the person who first told the statement. After I had it prepared, he refused to swear to it, but simply signs it-. He changed his version of the matter considerably, after he learned that I wanted to have him swear to it:

Part 9
Stephen Moore October 30, 1883 letter to Chiniquy, with transcription

The Chiniquy Collection

assassinated but that he was dead: He pretends tho that same woman told him, but he can not remember who – Mr Bennett says he first told them he learned it from a soldier. He corroborates Mr Bennett, and Conwell as to the fact of there being such a conversation. He statement is not the whole truth or else he would have sworn to it. But it is very believable –

I saw myself the large Catholic institution at St. Joseph, where Linneman is. He is a Catholic and was supplying this institution with provision, groceries etc, at the time of this conversation. It was almost wholly settled by Roman Catholics...

and at that time, the community were all Roman Catholics:

It is most remarkable matter that away on the frontier, away from telegraphs and Rail Roads, the assassination was known on Friday Evening, four hours before it took place – nevertheless, here is the clear evidence of this matter.

I have been expecting to go up & see you but am so much engaged, I can not get away. I will see you soon, I enclose you the papers.

Yours truly
Stephen R. Moore

The Chiniquy Collection

WHO KILLED ABRAHAM LINCOLN?

The Chiniquy
Collection

State of Illinois,
Cook County,

Rev F. A. Conwell, being sworn deposes and says, that he is seventy one years old, that he is a resident of North Evanston, in Cook County, State of Illinois, that he has been actively in the ministry for forty-six years and is now one of the Chaplains of the Seamans Bethel Home in Chicago – That he was the Chaplain of the First Minnesota Regiment, in the war of the Rebellion.

That on the 14th day of April AD 1865 he was in St Joseph, Minnesota, and reached there as early as six o'clock in the evening, in company with Mr Bennett, who then and now is a resident of St. Cloud Minnesota. That on this date, there was not telegraph nearer than Minneapolis, which is about 80 miles from St. Joseph, and there was no rail-road communication nearer that Auoka, Minnesota which was about 40 miles distant. That when he reached St. Joseph in the 14th day of April AD1865, one Mr Linneman, who then kept the Hotel at St. Joseph…

The Chiniquy
Collection

told affiant that President Lincoln and Secretary Seward were
assassinated. That it was not later than half past six o'clock Friday
April 14, 1865, when Mr Linneman told me this. Shortly thereafter
Mr Bennett came in the Hotel, and I told him that Mr Linneman said
the President and Secretary Seward were assassinated: and there Mr
Linneman repeated the same conversation to Mr Bennett in my presence!
That during that time Mr Linneman told me that he had the charge
of furnishing the Friary or College for young men under the priests
who were studying for the priesthood at St. Joseph. That there was
a large institution of this kind at St. Joseph at this time. Affiant
says that on Saturday morning April 15 1865 he went to St. Cloud a
distance of about ten miles, and reached there about 8 o'clock in
the morning, that there was no railroad or telegraph communication
to St. Cloud. When he arrived at St. Cloud, he told Mr Haworth, the
Hotelkeeper, that he had been told at St. Joseph that the President
and Secretary Seward had been assassinated, and...

The Chiniquy
Collection

asked if it was true. He further told Henry Clay Wait; Charles Gilman, who was afterwards Lieutenant Governor of Minnesota and Rev Mr Tice, the same things and inquired of them if they had any such news, and they replied that they had not heard anything of the kind. Affiant says that on Sunday morning April 16, 1865 he preached in St. Cloud, and on the way to the Church a copy of the telegram was handed him, stating that the President and Secretary were assassinated on Friday evening at about 9 o'clock. This telegram had been brought to St. Cloud by Mr Gordon, who had reached St Cloud by stage and this was the first intelligence that had reached St. Cloud, of the event. Affiant says further that on Monday morning April 17th 1865 he furnished the Press, a paper of St Paul, a statement that three hours before the event took place, he had been informed at St. Joseph Minnesota, that the President had been assassinated and this was published in the press.

Francis Ashbury Conwell

The Chiniquy Collection

Subscribed by and sworn to by Francis A. Conwell before me, a notary Public of Kankakee County Illinois, at Chicago, Cook County Illinois, this 6th day of Sept. AD1883

Stephen R. Moore
Notary Public

State of Minnesota)
Sterns County) ss
City of St Cloud)

           Horace P Bennett, being
sworn deposes and says that he is
aged Sixty four years old. That he is
a resident of St Cloud. Minnesota &
that resided in this county since the
year 1856. That he is acquainted with
Rev Francis A. Connell. who was chaplain
of the 1st Minnesota Regiment, in the
war of the Rebellion. That on the 14th
day of April A D 1865 he was in St Joseph.
Minnesota. in Company with Mr Francis
A Connell. That they reached St Joseph. about
Sundown of Said April 14th That there was
no rail road or telegraph Communication
with St Joseph at that time. nor nearer than
Anoka. about forty miles distant.
That affiant. on reaching the Hotel. went to
the barn. and Rev Mr Connell went into
the Hotel kept by Mr Zimmerman. and
Shortly afterward Affiant returned to the
Hotel. Mr Connell told him. that
Zimmerman had related to him the
Assassination of President Lincoln. that
Zimmerman was present and Substantiated
the Statement.
That on Saturday morning, April 15th
Affiant and Connell came to St Cloud
and reported what they had been
told at St Joseph, about the assassination

of President Lincoln. That no one at St Cloud
had heard of the event at this time; That
the first news of the event which reached
St Cloud, was on Sunday Morning
April 16th When the news was brought
there by Leander Gorton, Who had just
Come up from Anoka, Minnesota;
That they spoke to several persons at St
Cloud, Concerning the matter, When they reached
there On Saturday Morning, but affiant
does not now remember who the different
persons were.

Mr Zimmerman Said, as affiant now
remembers the transaction that he had
learned of the Presidents assassination
from a Soldier Who was passing
through St Joseph.

And further affiant saith not.

Horace P. Bennett.

Sworn to before me and subscribed in
my presence this 18th day of October
A. D. 1883.

Andrew C Robertson
Notary Public Minn

Part 11 - Transcription
Horace Bennett Affidavit, October, 18, 1883

State of Minnesota,
Stearn County,
City of St. Cloud

Horace P. Bennett, being sworn, deposes and says that
he is aged sixty four years old. That he is a resident
of St. Cloud, Minnesota and has resided in this
county since the year 1856. That he is acquainted with
Rev. Francis A. Conwell who was chaplain of the 1st
Minnesota Regiment in the war of the rebellion. That
on the 14th day of April AD 1865 he was in St. Joseph,
Minnesota, in company with Mr Francis A Conwell.
That they reach St. Joseph about six o'clock of said
April 14th. That there was no rail road or telegraph
communication with St. Joseph at that time nor nearer
than Auoka, about forty miles distant. That affiant,
on reaching the Hotel, went to the barn, and Rev Mr
Conwell went into the Hotel kept by Mr Linneman, and
shortly afterward affiant had returned to the Hotel. Mr
Conwell told him that Linneman had related to him
to him the assassination of President Lincoln, that
Linneman was present and substantiated the statement.

That on Saturday morning, April 15th, affiant and
Conwell came to St Cloud and repeated what they had
been told of St Joseph about the assassination of
President Lincoln. That no one of St Cloud had heard
of the event at this time: That the first news of the
event which reached St Cloud was on Saturday morning,
April 16th. When the news was brought there by Leander
Gordon, who had just come up from Auoka, Minnesota.
That they spoke to several persons of St Cloud,
concerning the matter, when they reached there on
Saturday morning, but affiant does not now remember who
these different persons were:

Mr Linneman said, as affiant now remembers the
transaction, that he had learned of the President's
assassination from a soldier who was passing through
St Joseph, and further affiant saith not,

Horace P. Bennett

Sworn to before me and subscribed in my presence this
18th day of October A.D. 1883
Andrew C. Robertson
Notary Public

State of Illinois
Kankakee County } ss.

Stephen R Moore, of
lawful age, a citizen of Kankakee county
Illinois for thirty five years, and engaged
in the practice of law. That Father
Chiniquy sent me to the village of St Joseph,
and Cloud. Minnesota. to investigate and
report the facts. Concerning the remarkable
Statement of facts. Sworn to by Rev F.A.
Connell. That the Knowledge of the
assassination of the President Abraham
Lincoln. and Secretary of State Seward, were
proclaimed publicly as accomplished
facts. at St Joseph. Minnesota, Several
hours before their occurrence.
Affiant States that he devoted about
Six days. in the investigation of the facts.
by interviews with persons. who heard
it stated publicly that the President
and his Secretary of State were assassinated
Several hours ahead of the time when
the Events took place. in Washington
City. That he talked with Mr
Lemmerman. the same hotel keeper.
mentioned by said Rev. F. A. Connell. that
there. I heard. from Mr Lemmerman himself
that he well remembered having made
that declaration to Mr Bennett and

Rev F. A. Conwell. That Mr Lenneman repeated several times. to me. that it was a public rumour. in the village of St Joseph. that Abraham Lincoln and Secretary Seward were killed. by the hands of an assassin. that day. April 14th 1865. And that that rumour was spread there several hours. before the deed was accomplished in Washington I tried to learn from Mr Lenneman how the rumour was spread. where it originated. and how it was known there that the president was assassinated. hours before the event took place. but he always answered that he did not know: that he had heard it from several persons as a public rumour.

Affiant Says that having fully investigated the facts, he made a report thereof to Father Chiniquy, and when my report was submitted to him, he. Father Chiniquy inquired of me, as a lawyer. if he was not justified from these facts, to believe and publish. that such a public rumour. spread several hours. before the occurrence of the fact, was a sure proof. that that fact was known in that place. only by accomplices. that he. Father Chiniquy had the legal

right to believe and say that some.
of the many priests and monks of that
village. being constantly going to. and
Coming from washington. had learned
that fact from their Co-Conspirators
who were day and night in the house of
Mrs Surratt. where the plot of the
Assassination was prepared:
After having myself spent many days.
in investigating all the facts of that
rumour. I told Father Chiniquy. that he
was perfectly justified. to believe and
publish that the priests and monks
of Rome had learned that fact from their
Co. Conspirators, in washington:
Affiant says that St Joseph was the Center
of a large Catholic population, Containing a
College. for the Education of Priests, and
he repeated this also to Father Chiniquy
and affiant says that it was impossible
for so unnatural and execrable event
to be talked of, in St Joseph. Minnesota
hours before it occurred in washington
Unless the Murderers of Lincoln and
Seward, had accomplices in St Joseph.
And parties to the Crime.
Affiant further States. that he saw
and Conversed with Mr Bennett
who told affiant. that on April 14ᵗʰ

1865. he had heard Mr Lemmeman tell him and Rev F. A. Cecunell that Lincoln and Seward were killed that day, and that declaration was made five or six hours before the act occurred in Washington, I obtained the affidavit of Mr Bennett, to this fact, taken before Judge Robertson, at the City of St Cloud, Sterns County, Minnesota; that said Mr Bennett is a credible and highly respected citizen of St Cloud

Affiant further swears that he learned while at St Joseph, that Mr Lemmeman was the purveyor and confidential man of the many priests and monks of the village of St Joseph. and further affiant saith not.

Stephen R Moore

Subscribed and sworn to before me this 19 day of December A D 1892.

Sid. R. Surfer
clerr,

State of Illinois
Kankakee County

Stephen R. Moore, of lawful age, a citizen of Kankakee County Illinois for thirty-five years, and engaged in the practise of law, that Father Chiniquy sent me to the village of St. Joseph, and St. Cloud Minnesota, to investigate and report the facts, concerning the remarkable statement of facts, sworn to by Rev F. A. Conwell, that the knowledge of the assassination of the President Abraham Lincoln and Secretary of State Seward, were proclaimed publicly as accomplished fact, at St. Joseph, Minnesota, several hours before their occurrence.

Affiant states that he devoted about six days in the investigation of the facts, by interviews with persons, who heard it stated publicly that the President and his secretary of state were assassinated several hours ahead of the time when the events took place in Washington City! That he talked with Mr Linneman, the same hotel keeper mentioned by said Rev. F. A. Conwell, that there, I heard from Mr Linneman himself that he well remembered having made that declaration to Mr Bennett said Rev F. A. Conwell, that Mr Linneman repeated several times to me that it was a public rumour, in the village of St. Joseph, that Abraham Lincoln and Secretary Seward were killed by the hands of an assassin that day April 14, 1865, and that that rumour was spread there several hours before the deed was accomplished in Washington. I tried to learn from Mr Linneman how the rumour was spread, where it originated and how it was known there that the President was assassinated hours before the event took place, but he always answered that he did not know: that he had heard it from several persons as a public rumour.

Affiant says that having fully investigated the facts he made a report thereof to Father Chiniquy, and when my report was submitted to him, he, Father Chiniquy inquired of me, as a lawyer, if he was not justified from these facts, to believe and publish, that such a public rumour, spread several hours , before the occurrence of the fact, was a sure proof, that that fact was known in that place, only by accomplices, that he, Father Chiniquy had the legal right to believe and say that some of the many priests and monks of that village, being constantly going to, and coming from Washington, and learned that fact from their co-conspirators who were day and night in the house of Mrs Surratt, where the plot of the assassination was prepared:

After having myself spent many days in investigating all the facts of that rumour, I told Father Chiniquy that he was perfectly justified to believe and publish that the priests and monks of Rome had learned the fact from their co. conspirators, in Washington:

Stephen R. Moore affidavit, December 19, 1892

Affiant says that St. Joseph was the center of a large Catholic population, containing a College, for the Education of Priests, and he reported this also to Father Chiniquy and affiant says that it was impossible for so unnatural and remarkable event to be talked of, in St. Joseph, Minnesota hours before it occurred in Washington unless the murderers of Lincoln and Seward, had accomplices in St. Joseph, and parties to the crime.

Affiant further states, that he saw and conversed with Mr Bennett who told affiant that on April 14th 1865, he had heard Mr Linneman tell him and Rev F. A. Conwell, that Lincoln and Seward were killed that day, and that declaration was made five or six hours before the Act occurred in Washington, I obtained the affidavit of Mr Bennett, to this fact, taken before Judge Roberson, at the City of St. Cloud, Sterns County, Minnesota, that said Mr Bennett is a credible and highly respected citizen of St. Cloud.

Affiant further swears that he learned while at St. Joseph, that Mr Linneman was the purveyor and confidential man of the many priests and monks of the village of St. Joseph and further affiant saith not.

Stephen R. Moore
Subscribed and sworn to before me this 19th day of December AD1892

Sid R Domfee
clerk

BY THE PIONEER PRINTING CO.,
ELEVEN DOLLARS A YEAR.

Saint Paul Pioneer.

ST. PAUL, SATURDAY, APRIL 29.

From Fort Wadsworth.

Gen. SIBLEY received a private letter yesterday from Fort Wadsworth, dated April 20th. It contains the information that ten lodges of the Sissétons had come

LATE NE[...]

—The Chicago *Tribu[...]* of Mrs. Lincoln to m[...] home. More than a [...] President declared to [...] sonal friends that aft[...]

An Infamous Slander on a Private Citizen.

The *Press* has become notorious for its reckless mendacity and utter disregard of all decency in its attacks upon political opponents, but the public were not prepared for such an exhibition of utter depravity and political rancour as was shown in its columns of Thursday, in attempting to fix upon Mr. LINNEMAN, a respectable German merchant of St. Joseph, the odium of being an accomplice of BOOTH in the assassination of the President, and that, too, upon no other foundation than the most frivolous gossip of a strolling preacher, endorsed by political and perhaps personal enemies of the accused. The *Press* was not even content to retail this gossip, but proceeded to argue at considerable length that "Mr. LINNEMAN has been in close communication with the Knights of the Golden Circle, the Sons of Liberty, or some other secret society of traitors, to whose dark conclaves the fiendish plot was known."

This infamous attack created great indignation among all our principal merchants, who knew that Mr. LINNEMAN was one of the most upright and honorable merchants in the State, of irreproachable private character, and of undoubted patriotism.

Mr. LINNEMAN, who happened to be in the city, waited upon the editor of the *Press*, and backed by several merchants, succeeded in getting the partial retraction and apology which appeared in yesterday's *Press*. But we are assured by prominent citizens that this attempted reparation is not satisfactory to Mr. LINNEMAN or his friends. A state of feeling may have been excited among soldiers and other citizens who will pass through St. Joseph, that before the matter is fully understood, Mr. LINNEMAN's property may be destroyed, and his family abused. The truth is no adequate reparation can be made for an injury of this character.

We trust this event will be a warning to the *Press* for the future. If the editor of that journal cannot be made to realize that a man may differ from him politically without being an assassin, the sooner he is placed in a mad-house the better it will be for the public peace. One would suppose that the libel suit now hanging over the *Press* for most atrocious slanders on a prominent member of its own party (out of which suit it has been trying to wiggle for two years past), might learn the editors a little wisdom. If there is no law to protect people from such assaults as that made upon Mr. LINNEMAN, then our government is very far from what it ought to be.

[...] particularly objection able to any one [...] ardently desires the restoration of peace and Union at the earliest practicable moment. Whether their execution would [...] led to these happy results, it is impossible to say. Time will prove whether

BENJAMIN, [...] of the rebel chiefs, should not be indicted, and tried, and convicted, and punished too, quite as well in Pennsylvania as in any other place. He says:

In Swartwout's case (4 Crauch, 126), Chief Justice Marshall, in his opinion says, speaking

in Stoneham, Mass., ha[...] brothers, and brother-[...] ties of the present rebel[...] killed about four mon[...] called upon to mourn t[...] sous, twins, about three[...]

Mr Lincoln was first nominated for the Presidency, at Chicago, May 1860. He immediately occupied the Executive Chamber, in the State House, as a Reception Room, where he could see & consult with his friends. I was then State Supt of Public Instr. & my office was adjoining the room occupied by Mr Lincoln, with a door opening from one to the other, which was frequently open, so that I could not help hearing much of the conversation between Mr L. & his friends & visitors. I saw him almost hourly during the seven months & more that he remained in the State House, & quite frequently he called to me to come into his room, on various occasions & for various purposes.

A careful canvass had been made of this city (Springfield) and the book, showing the candidate for whom each citizen intended to vote, had been placed in Mr Lincolns hands. Late in the afternoon, towards the close of October 1860, after all had left his room, Mr Lincoln locked the door & requested me to lock mine & come to him. He placed a chair for me close by his side. He had been examining the above-named book, which he still

Josiah G. Holland Papers, Manuscripts and Archives Division,
The New York Public Library, Astor, Lenox and Tilden Foundations

5

the Bible & claim for it a divine character & sanction, and now the cup of iniquity is full, & the vials of wrath will be poured out." He here referred to the attitude of some prominent clergymen in the South, Ross & Palmer among the number, & spoke of the atrociousness & blasphemy of their attempts to defend American Slavery on Bible grounds.

Mr Lincoln's language made a vivid impression upon me, & while I do not claim that the above quotations are absolutely verbatim, I know that they are very nearly so, and the sentiments are exactly as he uttered them.

The conversation was continued a long time, & all that he said was of a peculiarly deep & tender religious tone, tinged with a profound & touching melancholy. He repeatedly referred to his conviction that the day of wrath was at hand, & that he was to be an actor in the terrible drama, wh would issue in the overthrow of Slavery, tho he might not live to see it. . . .

Josiah G. Holland Papers, Manuscripts and Archives Division,
The New York Public Library, Astor, Lenox and Tilden Foundations

7

truth — a conviction that
nothing could ever shake for
a moment. I have heard that
he afterwards claimed to be &
resolved to live the life of a
christian — I do not know if this
was so, but I am firmly persuaded that at the time I speak of
he was not far from the
Kingdom — nearer than he himself
seemed to think.

I remarked, as we were about
to separate, that I had not supposed that he was accustomed to
think so much upon that class
of subjects, & that his friends
generally were ignorant of the
sentiments which he had expressed
to me — He replied quickly: "I know
they are — I am obliged to appear
different to them, but I think
more on these subjects than all
others, & have done so for years
& I am willing that you should
know it."

Mr Lincoln was ambitious,
but his aims were so lofty &
good, & the means he would
use so pure & noble, that it
was not the ambition of other

Josiah G. Holland Papers, Manuscripts and Archives Division,
The New York Public Library, Astor, Lenox and Tilden Foundations

p. 1

Mr Lincoln was first nominated for the Presidency, at Chicago, May 1860. He immediately occupied the Executive Chamber in the State House, as a Reception Room where he could see & consult with his friends. I was then State Supt. of Public Inst. & my office was adjoining the room occupied by Mr Lincoln, with a door opening from one to the other I could not help hearing much of the conversation between Mr L & his friends & visitors. I saw him almost hourly during the seven months & more that he remained in the State House, & quite frequently he called to me to come into his room on various occasions & for various purposes.

A careful canvass had been made of this city (Springfield) and the book, showing the candidate for whom such citizens intended to vote, had been placed in Mr Lincoln's hands. Late in the afternoon, towards the close of October 1860, after all had left his room, Mr Lincoln locked the door & requested me to lock mine & come to him. He place a chair for me close by his side. He had been reviewing the above named book which he still

p. 2

had in his hand. "Let us look over this book", said he, explaining its character "I wish particularly to see how the ministers of Springfield are going to vote." We turned the leaves one by one, each holding it by a hand, he asking me, now & then, if this one or that one were not a minister, or an Elder, or member of such & such a church in the city, and sadly expressing his surprise upon receiving an affirmative answer. In this manner we went through the book, which he then closed & sat for some moments, with his eye upon a pencil memorandum which he had made, in profound silence. At length, turning to me, with a look the saddest I had ever seen, I cannot tell you how touchingly sad it was, he said: "Mr B. here are 23 ministers of different denominations, and all of them are against me but 3 - & here are a great many prominent members of the churches here, a very large majority of whom are against me. Mr B. I am not a christian, God knows I would be one, but I have carefully read the Bible

p. 3

& I do not so understand this book", (drawing from his bosom a pocket testament). "These men well know that I am for freedom in the territories – freedom everywhere as far as the constitution & laws will permit, and that my opponents are for slavery. They know this, & yet with this book in their hands, in the light of which human bondage cannot live a moment, they are going to vote against me. I do not understand it at all".

Here Mr Lincoln paused a good while – then arose & walked back & forth several times, when he sat down & presently said, with deep emotion & many tears, "I know there is a God & that he hates injustice & slavery. I see the storm coming & I know that his hand is in it. If he has a place & work for me, and I think he has, I believe I am ready – I am nothing, but truth is everything – I know that I am right because I know that liberty is right, for Christ teaches it and Christ is God. I have told them that a house divided

p. 4

against itself cannot stand, & Christ & reason say the same, & they will find it so. Douglas don't care whether slavery is voted up or voted down – but God cares, & humanity cares, & I care, and with His help I shall not fail. I may not see the end, but it will come, and I shall be vindicated, and these men will find that they have not read their Bibles aright." Much of this was uttered as if speaking to himself, & with a sad solemnity of manner that I cannot describe. He resumed; Don't it appear strange that christian men can ignore the moral aspects of this contest? A revelation could not make it plainer to me that slavery or the government must be destroyed. The future would be something awful, as I look at it, but for this rock on which I stand, (meaning the Bible, which he held in his hand), especially with the knowledge of how these ministers are going to vote. It seems as if God has borne with this thing (meaning slavery) until the very teachers of religion have come to defend it from

p. 5

the Bible & claim for it a divine character, & sanction, and now the cup of iniquity is full, & the vials of wrath will be poured out" He here referred to the attitude of some prominent clergymen in the South, Ross* and Palmer* among the number, & spoke of the atrociousness & blasphemy of their attempts to defend American slavery on Bible grounds.

Mr Lincoln's language made a vivid impression upon me,& while I do not claim that the above quotations are absolutely verbatim, I know that they are very nearly so, and the sentiments are exactly as he uttered them.

The conversation was continued a long time, & all that he said was of a particularly deep & tender religious tone, tinged with a profound & touching melancholy. He repeatedly referred to his conviction that the day of wrath was at hand, & that he was to be an actor in the terrible drama, wh(ich) would issue in the overthrow of slavery tho(ugh) he might not live to see it.

(*This undoubtably refers to Presbyterian clergyman Frederich Augustus Ross and Benjamin Morgan Palmer.)

p. 6

He repeated many passages of the Bible, in a very reverent & devoted way, & seemed especially impressed with the solemn grandeur of portions of Revelation describing the wrath of Almighty God. In the course of the conversation he dwelt much upon the necessity of faith, faith in God, the christian's God, as an element of successful statesmanship, especially in times like these; said it gave that calmness & tranquility of mind, that assurance of ultimate success, which made one firm & immovable amid the wildest excitements etc. He said he believed in divine providence & recognized God in History. He also stated his belief in the duty, privilege, & efficacy of prayer, & intimated in unmistakable terms that he had sought in that way, the divine guidance & favour. The effect of the interview was to fix in my mind the conviction that Mr Lincoln had, in his quiet way, worked his way up to the christian stand-point; that he had found God, & was anchored upon his

p. 7

truth - a conviction that nothing could ever shake for a moment. I have heard that he afterwards claimed to be & resolved to live the life of a christian - I do not know if this was so, but I am firmly persuaded that at the time I spoke of he was not far from the kingdom - nearer than he himself seemed to think.

I remarked, as we were about to separate, that I had not supposed that he was accustomed to think so much upon that class of subjects,& that his friends generally were ignorant of the sentiments which he had expressed to me - He replied quickly: "I know they are - I am obliged to appear different to them, but I think more on these subjects than all others, & have done so for years, & I am willing that you should know it".

Mr Lincoln was ambitious, but his aims were so lofty & good, & the means he would use so pure & noble, that it was not the ambition of other

p. 8

men - There was something almost Christlike in his aspirations, for I believe he sought peace & power that he might use them to bless the more & not to aggrandize himself - I believe further that he was never even seriously tempted to resort to dishonourable means to gain his ends.

Thus subordinated he not only desired preferment, but keenly enjoyed success. But all the time I believe it was entirely true of him that he "would rather be right than be President"

Dear noble heroic Lincoln - God sends us but one such man in a century, & when their work is done how quickly He translates them.

Part 15

Springfield Address Farewell Address, February 11, 1861

Lincoln (and secretary) version

My friends--No one, not in my situation, can appreciate my feeling of sadness at this parting. To this place, and the kindness of these people, I owe every thing. Here I have lived a quarter of a century, and have passed from a young to an old man. Here my children have been born, and one is buried. I now leave, not knowing when, or whether ever, I may return, with a task before me greater than that which rested upon Washington. Without the assistance of that Divine Being, who ever attended him, I cannot succeed. With that assistance I cannot fail. Trusting in Him, who can go with me, and remain with you and be every where for good, let us confidently hope that all will yet be well. To His care commending you, as I hope in your prayers you will commend me, I bid you an affectionate farewell.

According to The Collected Works of Abraham Lincoln, this version was, "Written down in pencil after the event, as the train leaving Springfield, the manuscript begins in Lincoln's handwriting and concludes in Nicolay's". Roy P. Basler, ed, The Collected Works of Abraham Lincoln, (Rutgers University Press, 1953), Volume 4, p. 190, 191

Illinois State Journal version

Friends,

No one who has never been placed in a like position, can understand my feelings at this hour, nor the oppressive sadness I feel at this parting. For more than a quarter of a century I lived among you, and during all that time I have received nothing but kindness at your hands. Here I have lived from my youth until now I am an old man. Here the most sacred ties of earth were assumed; here all my children were born; and here one of them lies buried. To you, dear friends, I owe all that I have, all that I am. All the strange, chequered past seems to crowd now upon my mind. To-day I leave you; I go to assume a task more difficult than that which devolved upon General Washington. Unless the great God who assisted him, shall be with and aid me, I must fail. But if the same omniscient mind, and same Almighty arm that directed and protected him, shall guide and support me, I shall not fail, I shall succeed. Let us all pray that the God of our fathers may not forsake us now. To him I commend you all---permit me to ask that with equal serenity and faith, you all will invoke His wisdom and guidance for me. With these few words I must leave you--for how long I know not. Friends, one and all, I must now bid you an affectionate farewell.

Illinois State Journal, February 12, 1861

Peter Spink
or
Charles Chiniquy

Champaign Circuit Court
May Term 1856.

Defts Costs.

Clerks fees -

File 73 papers on change of Ven. $3.65
" 2 Par. 10 Dock 11 - 6 Sp. 2.40 . . . . . . 2.60
Call & swear 1st Jury 15 - 29 wit $1.45 . . 1.89
" " 2d " 15 - 29 " $1.45 . . 1.89
Sev. 2 Inter 10 29 aft. wit - $4.35 . . . . . . 4.45
Con 20 20
                                          } $13.68 6.84

Shff Roff 4.80
" Byrne 28.37 33.17

Wit. Amon Bizure 11.20
" Fr. Bechard 11.20
" Paul Latouche 11.50
" J. Labonti Sen 11.20
" S. Goyette 11.20
" G. Letournin 11.50
" Godfroy Lambert 12.30
" M. Martin 12.20
" B. Geffry 12.40
" Maurice Kirby 11.20
" H. L. De Martigny 11.20
" F. Siguin 11.50
" Irome Libonti 11.20
" Wm Manly 11.20
" J. Gagni 11.40
" Gr. M. Howell 11.20
" J. A. Whiteman 9.00 192.60
Interpreter 10.00
" Do 5.00
                                          } $25.00 7.50
                                             $240.11

A true Copy
Attest J. R. Webber Clk

Foto Juan Guzmán

EL OBISPO DAVID G RUESGA, DE LOS PROTESTANTES MEXICANOS

...contra el Evangelio, la iglesia católica practica el genocidio...

(Ver *Religión*)

RELIGION

Los Crímenes de la Intolerancia

Con cristiana serenidad, pero también con grande energía, nos opondremos a que la campaña protestante continúe extendiéndose. Es más, la combatiremos hasta acabar con ella. Tal dijo, a principios de 1944, en ocasión de iniciarse bajo el signo de la intolerancia el *Año Jubilar Guadalupano*, Mons Luis María Martínez, arzobispo de México. Estas palabras fueron, además, una reiteración de la pastoral que el 29 de Oct anterior había dirigido al clero y a la feligresía el propio dignatario: "Conocida es la intensa propaganda que con perfecta organización y poderosos recursos pecuniarios realizan en toda la república las sectas protestantes. Por medio de ella se pretende arrebatar al pueblo mexicano su más rico tesoro, la fe católica que hace 4 siglos nos trajo la Santísima Virgen de Guadalupe... Y así como en la Edad Media, al grito de «¡Dios lo quiere!», todos los cristianos se unieron para conquistar el sepulcro glorioso de Jesucristo; así ahora, con la convicción de que Dios lo quiere y María de Guadalupe lo pide, pongan los católicos sus esfuerzos al servicio de la defensa de la fe".

LUIS MARÍA MARTÍNEZ
"...*El gobierno... tiene guango...*"

La lucha a fondo contra la "serpiente infernal" del protestantismo iba a iniciarse en México. Sería una continuación del infame empeño que el Vaticano había ya logrado poner en obra en el resto de Hispanoamérica. En 1941 el episcopado chileno, en una pastoral colectiva, había condenado las actividades protestantes. En su mensaje de Cuaresma de 1943 hizo otro tanto el obispo de Nueva Pamplona, en Colombia; y le siguieron, en el Ecuador, los arzobispos de Quito y Cuenca. En Costa Rica, el

TIEMPO, 8 de febrero de 1952

Vicario Apostólico de Limón expidió una pastoral semejante; en Nicaragua, el arzobispo de Managua y el obispo de Granada refutaron públicamente a los evangélicos; en Cuba, el arzobispo de La Habana acusó a los luteranos de "herir los sentimientos del pueblo"; y en el Brasil el Card Sebastián Leme de Silveira Cintra, arzobispo de Río de Janeiro, incitó a sus fieles contra las instituciones religiosas de confesión no católica.

Aunque concebida como parte de una campaña general, la persecución contra los protestantes iba a tener en México características peculiares. A una violencia sin precedente, cuyos extremos han sido el asesinato, la violación, el saqueo y el exterminio de breves comunidades, corresponde la indiferencia de la opinión pública y la falta de una acción represiva de parte del estado. Estos hechos coexistentes —el crimen reiterado y la impunidad sistemática— son las notas que califican la historia y los pormenores de tales atrocidades.

Desde Oct de 1944 —fecha en que en nombre de Dios y de la Virgen, Mons Martínez llamó a la violencia— han llegado a conocimiento de las autoridades federales 76 casos perfectamente detallados. He aquí unos cuantos:

◆ *El 25 de Nov de 1944* fueron incendiados el templo evangélico de La Gloria, en el Edo de Veracruz, y las casas de 9 protestantes. Siete personas —entre ellas 5 niños— murieron en el siniestro. Poco más tarde, los católicos expulsaron del pueblo a 60 familias afiliadas a la Iglesia de Dios.

◆ *El 27 de mayo de 1945*, en Santiago Yeche, Edo de México, el sacerdote católico José A Vivas encabezó el asalto a las casas de los pastores protestantes Feliciano Juárez y Vicente Garita. Los predicadores fueron linchados y descuartizados y sus viviendas voladas con dinamita.

◆ *El 1° de Jun de 1945*, el párroco de Caulote, Edo de Michoacán, incendió el templo luterano. Por él incitados, los católicos ultrajaron a las mujeres y golpearon a los hombres. Los evangelistas que lograron salvarse huyeron al monte: 105 llegaron a la ciudad de México en demanda de garantías.

◆ *El 15 de enero de 1946*, en Neblinas, Edo de Hidalgo, varios sinarquistas, encabezados por Cándido Muñoz y Julio Bautista, e incitados por el cura del lugar, asaltaron a los evangelistas ahí reunidos. Hirieron a muchos, expulsaron a los más del pueblo y azotaron y colgaron de un árbol al pastor.

◆ *El 7 de marzo de 1946*, en Actípan de Morelos, Edo de Puebla, los católicos allanaron la casa del ministro evangélico, lo sacaron por la fuerza, lo arrastraron "a cabeza de silla" por todo el pueblo y, ya muerto, quemaron su cadáver en la plaza pública en un auto de fe medieval.

Estas infamias suelen ir acompañadas de terribles impresos. El párroco

DAVID G RUESGA
...*los evangelistas o se van o los matan...*

de San Marcos, en la ciudad de Puebla, distribuyó por aquel tiempo una parodia del Cap XII del *Éxodo*, con una terrible amenaza bíblica a los protestantes: "La 1ª fiesta de Pascua se celebró en las tierras del Faraón y fue esa noche cuando pasó el ángel exterminador; la espada cimbró con golpes decididos las casas que no tenían en la puerta la señal de la sangre del cordero. No había sangre en la puerta donde no se había comido el cordero y allí entró la muerte..."

◆ *El 31 de Jul de 1946*, cuando los agentes de la Policía Judicial Federal, Marcelo Fernández Ocaña y Leopoldo Arenas Díaz llegaron a San Felipe de Santiago, en el Edo de México, a investigar las atrocidades cometidas por los católicos, el sacerdote Pedro Juárez hizo que el populacho los condujera a la alcaldía. A ambos se les dio tormento, pero a Fernández Ocaña le arrancaron el cuero cabelludo con un machete y, vivo aun, le sacaron los ojos con un clavo. Después le cercenaron las orejas, le rompieron los dientes a golpes y lo apalearon hasta fracturarle los huesos. Muerto ya, lo cortaron en pedazos y arrojaron su carne a los perros. Arenas Díaz logró salvarse.

Acaso sea esta la única vez en que la justicia reaccionó en términos de castigar el monstruoso crimen. Algunos de los fanáticos que participaron en el atentado se hallan detenidos en la cárcel de Toluca y es muy posible que se les condene a 18 años de prisión. El cura Pedro Juárez, en cambio, sigue gozando de la misma libertad de incitar a la violencia, según la pastoral del Arz Martínez.

◆ *El 8 de marzo de 1947*, en Ameca, Edo

4C

FAMILIARES DEL PREDICADOR EVANGELISTA
...en nombre de Dios, el arzobispo llamó a la violencia...

de Jalisco, el sacerdote católico, después de una refriega que él mismo provocara, secuestró a varios protestantes, los llevó a su iglesia y usando métodos inquisitoriales los obligó, bajo amenaza de muerte, a bautizarse según el rito de la "Santa Madre".

◆ *El 30 de Jun de 1947*, en Tlanalapa, Edo de Hidalgo, el Dip Leopoldo Badillo y el agente del Ministerio Público Rafael Vargas Rodríguez, arrancaron a los evangelistas el compromiso, según consta en el acta judicial de esa fecha, de no llevar jamás ministros de su culto al pueblo.

◆ *El 17 de abril de 1948*, el presidente municipal de Pala, Edo de Nayarit, prohibió las prácticas evangélicas y dispuso que los protestantes no se visitaran entre sí. A la reclamación que éstos le formularan, repuso: "Es muy sencillo, háganse ustedes católicos y se acabarán los problemas".

◆ *El 7 de Dic de 1948*, en Tabernillas, Edo de México, Aniceto Hernández y Porfirio Velázquez, aconsejados por el cura Luis Reyes, asesinaron al protestante Antonio de la Cruz Carmona. La víctima recibió 3 machetazos en la cabeza, 4 balazos en la espalda y 2 puñaladas en un costado.

El 10 de Oct anterior, al saber que los evangelistas iban a abrir su templo, el sacerdote Reyes dijo en un sermón: "Ustedes, los católicos, no tienen pantalones para acabar con esos malditos protestantes. Si no lo hacen, yo no volveré jamás a impartirles auxilios espirituales". El Gral José María Tapia, en carta del 1° de Nov de ese año al gobernador del estado, reproducía además la siguiente frase del cura de Tabernillas: "El gobierno me viene *guango* (flojo), pues si el gobierno federal interviene se le echarán encima todos los pueblos vecinos, pues al fin en esto tiene su parte el gobierno del estado..."

◆ *El 13 de abril de 1949*, en Río Verde, San Luis Potosí, se halló el cadáver del niño Samuel Juárez, hijo del predicador J Ascensión Juárez, con 85 heridas de arma blanca. El turbio crimen se atribuyó a una venganza del cura José María Rosales, cuyos desmanes habían sido contenidos por el ministro.

◆ *El 27 de Dic de 1949*, entre Tecali y Concepción Cuautla, en el Edo de Puebla, un grupo de católicos, incitados por el cura Antonio Carvajal, asaltaron a los evangélicos Espiridión Pérez y Marcial Escalona. Como en la refriega perdiera la vida Filiberto Hernández, los compañeros de éste incendiaron las casas de los protestantes de Concepción Cuautla y mataron a 6 personas.

◆ *El 13 de Oct de 1950*, en Maguey Blanco, Edo de Hidalgo, Alberto Martín y Teófilo e Isidro Pejay fueron agredidos por un grupo de 25 católicos borrachos. Isidro Pejay fue muerto a golpes con una varilla de hierro. La explicación de que "sentían odio hacia los protestantes" fue suficiente para dejar a los agresores en libertad.

◆ *El 7 de Dic de 1950*, por 2ª vez en el mismo año, los católicos asaltaron el templo de la Iglesia Presbiteriana de Tixtla, en el Edo de Guerrero. Al grito de "¡Viva Cristo Rey!" rompieron los muebles, violaron a las mujeres e hirieron a los hombres, según la exhortación expresa del cura Adalberto J Miranda.

◆ *El 11 de Feb de 1951*, en Coyocala, Edo de Hidalgo, el juez auxiliar Pedro Morales condenó a 11 protestantes a trabajos forzados en obras públicas mientras no renunciaran al Evangelio.

Puestos en libertad el 3 de marzo siguiente, se les expulsó del pueblo, bajo amenaza de muerte.

◆ *El 8 de Jul de 1951*, entre Santa Rita y Tlahuapan, sobre la carretera de Puebla, 2 individuos, montados a caballo, dispararon sobre un grupo de campesinos que se dirigían a una reunión evangélica. La niña María Isabel Suárez, de 5 años de edad, resultó gravemente herida. Unos automovilistas la condujeron hasta el Sanatorio Cruz Celis en la ciudad de Puebla.

La atrocidad más reciente ocurrió el domingo 27 de enero en el pueblo de Mavoró, distante 20 km de Jocotitlán y 40 de Toluca, capital del Edo de México. En ocasión de la visita de algunos predicadores, se habían reunido 21 personas en la casa de Francisco García para dedicarse piadosamente a sus oraciones. Muy poco después empezaron a repicar las campanas del templo católico y minutos más tarde una chusma de fanáticos, armados con palos, machetes, hachas y azadones, cayó sobre los protestantes. Todos recibieron heridas y golpes. El pastor Agustín Corrales fue arrastrado "a cabeza de silla" hasta dejarlo por muerto a la altura del kilómetro 115 de la carretera a Querétaro.

Por vez 1ª en muchos años, la prensa confesional de la capital de la república dio noticia de estos sucesos. *Excélsior*, significado por sus estrechos enlaces con la iglesia católica, informó a 8 columnas, en su edición del martes 29 de enero: "Estuvieron a punto de ser linchados 2 predicadores evangelistas. Los agredió furiosa turba cuando predicaban. Dramática persecución de 10 km, antes de caer, para ser lapidados". Y luego: "Como si se tratara de perros rabiosos, 2 predicadores fueron perseguidos por una enfurecida turba armada con palos y piedras y, al darles alcance, cuando los desventurados habían corrido más de 10 km y estaban exhaustos, los golpearon en forma espantosa hasta dejarlos en estado de coma..." El periódico *Zócalo*, de orientación liberal, publicó un dramático reportaje y varios columnistas, muy a pesar de su confesión católica, condenaron el hecho. Las personas mejor enteradas coincidieron en señalar al cura párroco de Morovó, Fernando Vidal, como el responsable directo del atentado.

Nadie informó, sin embargo, que ese mismo día, a la misma hora, los habitantes de San Pablo Tecalco, en el propio Edo de México, estuvieron en trance de que varios centenares de católicos les arrebataran su templo. En San Pablo Tecalco no hay católicos romanos; todos pertenecen a la rama mexicana fundada en tiempos de la Reforma. Por eso el cura de Santa María Ozumbilla, Antonio Zaizar Torres, quiso aprovechar el 27 de enero, aniversario de la conversión de San Pablo al catolicismo, para reivindicar la memoria del santo en un pueblo de evangelistas puesto bajo su advocación. El audaz sacerdote congregó a los fanáticos de 20 comunidades rurales circunvecinas y

* De Agustín Corrales, predicador evangelista del poblado de Mavoró, Edo de México, fue herido a golpes y arrastrado "a cabeza de silla" por una chusma de fanáticos del lugar.

marchó sobre Tecalco con el ánimo de despojar a los evangelistas de su casa. Estos, sin embargo, advertidos oportunamente, piedieron ayuda a las autoridades y una compañía de soldados se apostó con la orden de impedir cualquier atentado. Zaizar Torres y sus 500 hombres pasaron tranquilamente por San Pablo; pero el cura, ya en las goteras de la población, tornó a renovar su amenaza: "Otra vez será, cuando estén desprevenidos los *juanes*".

Lejos de disminuir en número o en violencia, las atrocidades de esta especie se han ido recrudeciendo. Cada nuevo hecho que acentúa el poder de la jerarquía católica se traduce en una mayor intolerancia hacia las otras confesiones. Primero fue el *Jubileo Guadalupano*, después las ostentosas ceremonias posteriores al 50° aniversario de la coronación de la imagen del Tepeyac; más tarde el entronizamiento de Guadalupe en Roma, París y Madrid; y finalmente la concesión, por el Papa, del título de Primado al arzobispo de México. Este último acontecimiento parece haberse celebrado con las atrocidades más recientes. Aparte las de Morovó y San Pablo Tecalco, en lo que va del año han ocurrido las siguientes:

◆ **En Zacamitla,** municipio de Ixhuatlán, Edo de Veracruz, 2 individuos asesinaron a balazos, hará 4 semanas, al catequista protestante Miguel Martínez. Esto ocurrió 3 días después de que el sacerdote José Pérez había dicho en el púlpito: "Yo les prometo, hijos míos, que voy al frente de ustedes para acabar a palos con los evangelistas".

◆ **En Acazónica,** a 12 km de Fortín de

mente—, o se van o se mueren. Los que vivan aquí tienen que ser católicos".

◆ *En Paso Largo,* Edo de Veracruz, los evangélicos recibieron el 12 de enero pasado un aviso del Director Gral de Caminos ordenándoles la destrucción de su templo. La exigencia se funda en un hecho falso —que la iglesia está en la zona del derecho de vía— y se atribuye a intrigas del párroco.

Estos son los casos —ocurridos en enero— cuyos pormenores se han consignado. De seguro muchos otros se ignoran porque los afectados, escépticos ante la justicia, o temerosos de represalias, sufren en silencio los atropellos. Cuando estos trascienden a la actualidad nacional, el estado se inhibe. Al pedirsele a la procuraduría general una declaración sobre los sucesos de Mavoró, un alto funcionario explicó al reportero de *Zócalo* que pidió la entrevista: "Como se trata de un asunto en el que se han cometido delitos del orden común, no es de nuestra competencia..."

El arzobispo de México trató de salvarse de responsabilidades. Dijo la semana pasada: "Lamentamos los sucesos de Mavoró; pero nosotros no tenemos ningún control sobre el pueblo en ese respecto. Es de sentir que los ministros protestantes se dirijan a pueblos católicos a difundir su fe. Nosotros siempre hemos tratado de evitar estos actos bochornosos; pero el pueblo tiene sus creencias y, buenas o malas, no podemos arrancárselas..."

La declaración del primado, a juicio de un observador, "es insincera, falaz y contradictoria". Precisó:

◆ *"Insincera,* porque no es creíble que el

bien, se enorgullece de los resultados de su cátedra y en ellos se recrea. Las enseñanzas del Dr Martínez en materia de intolerancia se contienen en la pastoral del 29 de Oct de 1944 y son tan claras y brutales como monstruosas y punibles sus consecuencias.

◆ *"Falaz,* porque teniendo el arzobispo suficiente poder para lanzar a los católicos al crimen, lo tiene también para contenerlos; y porque lejos de tratar de «evitar esos actos bochornosos», como dice, los estimula con declaraciones que vienen a justificar, desde su punto de vista, la intolerancia y las atrocidades.

◆ *Y contradictoria,* porque el reproche que lanza a los protestantes, de predicar en pueblos católicos, puede hacérseles a los católicos que difunden su fe en pueblos protestantes, o budistas, o mahometanos, o shintoístas. Y, para ser congruente, el arzobispo debería declarar que de la misma manera que no podrá arrancar su creencia a los católicos, tampoco debe intentar arrebatárseles la suya a los protestantes".

Además, añadió el observador, "...nada tiene que reprochar el arzobispo a nadie que difunda una fe, mientras el Art 24 de la Constitución establezca: «Todo hombre es libre de profesar la creencia religiosa que más le agrade y para practicar las ceremonias, devociones o actos del culto respectivo, en los templos o su domicilio particular, siempre que no constituyan un delito o falta penados por la ley».

Las formas en que se expresa la intolerancia de la iglesia católica en México integran plenamente la figura delictiva de genocidio. Esta palabra, en forma

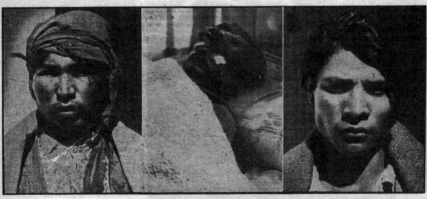

TRES VÍCTIMAS DE LOS FANÁTICOS DEL LUGAR
...las atrocidades se han ido recrudeciendo...

las Flores, Edo de Veracruz, el agente municipal Simitrio Esperilla, decretó a principios de enero que el protestantismo quedaba prohibido. "Les qué quieran seguir siendo evangelistas —dijo oficial-

arzobispo se lamente de que se sigan con puntualidad sus enseñanzas; antes

* De izquierda a derecha: Cesáreo Cruz, Agustín Corrales y Benito Cruz evangelistas heridos en Mavoró.

literal, significa la destrucción de grupos de seres humanos, o su persecución sistemática con propósitos de exterminio. Este "crimen de crímenes", como lo califica el Dr Raphael Lemkin, de la

Universidad de Yale, autor de la palabra *genocidio*, ha sido ya incorporado a la legislación internacional. En 1946, la Asamblea Gral de las NN UU solicitó del Consejo Económico y Social que emprendiera los estudios necesarios para elaborar un proyecto de convención sobre aquel delito. Al cabo de muy engorrosos trámites, el proyecto fue examinado durante la reunión de París por la Comisión Jurídica, y quedó finalmente aprobado por la asamblea general el 9 de Dic de 1948.

En el texto previo al articulado de la convención se declara que el genocidio es un delito de derecho internacional contrario al espíritu y a los fines de las NN UU y que el mundo civilizado condena; que en todos los períodos de la historia el genocidio ha infligido grandes pérdidas a la humanidad; y que precisa la cooperación internacional para liberar al mundo de un flagelo tan odioso. El Art 2º expresa: "Se entiende por genocidio cualquiera de los actos mencionados a continuación, perpetrados con la intención de destruir, total o parcialmente, a un grupo nacional, étnico, racial o religioso, como tal: *a)* matanza de miembros del grupo; *b)* lesión grave a la integridad física o mental de los miembros del grupo; *c)* sometimiento intencional del grupo a condiciones de existencia que hayan de acarrear su destrucción física, total o parcial..."

Según el Art 3º de la propia convención, deberán castigarse, aparte el genocidio en sí mismo, la asociación para cometerlo, la instigación directa y pública, la tentativa y la complicidad. Y considerando que no son los particulares quienes acostumbran perpetrar el genocidio, sino las personas que ejercen cargos de autoridad e influencia, el

Art 4º declara que quienes hayan cometido ese delito, o cualquiera de los otros actos mencionados, serán castigadas, ya se trate de gobernantes, empleados o dignatarios.

El representante de México ante las NN UU, Lic Luis Padilla Nervo, firmó la Convención Sobre Genocidio, el 14 de Dic de 1948. Enviado el documento a la Sría de RR EE, Dn Manuel Tello lo turnó a los licenciados Ernesto P Uruchurtu, SubSrio de Gobernación, y Francisco González, de la Vega, Procurador Gral de la República. El 1º contestó a la cancillería, el 16 de Dic de 1949, expresando que la Sría de Gobernación aprobaba el texto "...por tratarse de contener un crimen que repugna a todas las conciencias". El 2º, a su vez, tampoco formuló objeciones. Dos años más tarde, el 24 de Dic de 1951, el ejecutivo envió la convención a la Cámara de Senadores y ésta, 6 días más tarde, la aprobó sin enmiendas en sesión secreta. Firmaron el decreto respectivo Pedro Guerrero Martínez y Alfonso Corona del Rosal.

Antes de México habían ratificado la Convención Sobre Genocidio los siguientes países: Etiopía, Australia, Noruega, Islandia, Ecuador, Panamá, Guatemala, Israel, Liberia, Filipinas, Yugoslavia, El Salvador, Haití, Francia, Checoslovaquia, Dinamarca, China y Bélgica.

Fundándose en el hecho incontrovertible de que las acciones de la iglesia católica contra los protestantes caen dentro de lo previsto en el Art 2º de la convención, el Comité Nacional de Defensa Evangélica, que encabeza el Obpo David G Ruesga, va a acusar de genocidio a los dignatarios del clero mexicano. La semana pasada, una comisión de abogados estaba entregada a la tarea de formular el documento que se

enviará a las NN UU. En él constan la lista de atrocidades más completa que fue posible obtener y las palabras del Arz Martínez y de otros prelados a cuya influencia es legítimo atribuir la persecución y los crímenes.

"Las iniquidades de la iglesia católica contra el pueblo evangélico mexicano —dijo el Obpo Ruesga— constituyen un verdadero acto de genocidio. Si el Vaticano no es miembro de las NN UU, sí lo es México y este país está obligado a cumplir los compromisos internacionales que ha suscrito, entre ellos la Convención Sobre Genocidio y la Declaración de Derechos del Hombre, en la que se consagran la libertad de creencias y la libertad de expresión del pensamiento".

DGR, vio la luz primera en la ciudad de Morelia el 6 de Jul de 1898. Hizo sus 1os estudios al cuidado de las monjas teresianas y luego pasó al Seminario Tridentino de la capital michoacana. "Asqueado de los métodos y de la vida interna del seminario", según ha dicho, abandonó la enseñanza confesional e ingresó a la Universidad de San Nicolás de Hidalgo. En aquel tiempo —1914— el padre de Dn David, Dn Genaro Ruesga, se lanzó a la Revolución llevado por el ejemplo de su compadre el Gob Miguel Silva. Junto con ellos marchó al cerro el joven estudiante, pero herido a poco en una pierna se trasladó a los EE UU. Tuvo allí contacto con los protestantes y decidió entrar en el Seminario Evangélico de Dallas, en el Edo de Texas. En 1920 regresó a México convertido en predicador: fue el 1er ministro de la iglesia pentecostés y hoy ha llegado a ser el obispo de esa confesión. Controla 280 templos con más de 70 mil feligreses. Vive de su trabajo como comerciante y habla con satisfacción de sus 20 hijos —13 hombres y 7 mujeres—, producto de sus 2 matrimonios.

Ruesga, en su carácter de presidente del Comité Nacional de Defensa Evangélica, ha elevado centenares de quejas ante la Sría de Gobernación. A mediados de 1951, Dn Adolfo Ruiz Cortines, ministro entonces del ramo, pidió al obispo que formulara un proyecto de reformas a la Ley Reglamentaria del Art 130 de la Constitución, con el fin de impedir las atroces rivalidades entre católicos y protestantes. Dn David cumplió con el encargo y entregó, además, un proyecto de ley sobre faltas y delitos en materia de culto religioso y disciplina externa. He aquí algunos artículos del último ordenamiento propuesto:

◆ *"Art 8*" El individuo que, en ejercicio del ministerio o sacerdocio de un culto religioso cualquiera, incite públicamente, o por medio de declaraciones escritas, o prédicas, o sermones, a sus lectores u oyentes, al desconocimiento de las instituciones políticas, o a la desobediencia de las leyes, de las autoridades, o de sus mandatos, será castigado con la pena de 6 años de prisión y multa de $1 mil.

◆ *"Art 9*" Si como resultado directo o inmediato de la incitación a que se refiere el artículo anterior, intervienen

PROTESTANTES DE MAVORÓ, EDO DE MÉXICO
...al grito de ¡Viva Cristo Rey!, violaron a las mujeres...

menos de 10 personas empleando la fuerza, el amago, la amenaza, la violencia física o moral contra la autoridad pública o sus agentes, o hacen uso de armas, cada uno de ellos será castigado con un año de prisión y multa de $1 mil. A los sacerdotes o ministros de culto autores de la incitación, se les impondrá la pena de 6 años de prisión, más las agravantes de 1ª a 4ª clase, a juicio del juez, salvo que del desorden resulte un delito que merezca pena mayor.

◆ "*Art 11ª* Los ministros de cualquier culto que en ejercicio de su ministerio inciten a cometer actos de agresión en contra de una o varias personas que profesan otro credo distinto, sufrirán la pena de 6 años de prisión y multa de $1 mil".

Por razones ajenas del todo a su voluntad, el Obpo Ruesga entregó estos proyectos a la Sría de Gobernación 2 días después de la fecha que se le había señalado. En tal virtud, el Depto Legal y el ministro de esa dependencia no tuvieron tiempo de examinarlos y se perdió la oportunidad de que el Congreso los discutiera en el pasado período ordinario de sesiones. De todas suertes, la reglamentación del Art 130 constitucional sobre nuevas bases y la expedición de la ley sobre faltas y delitos en materia religiosa son necesidades que pronto tendrá que resolver el estado. Tanto más cuanto que el Art 5° de la Convención Sobre Genocidio establece que "... las partes contratantes se comprometen a adoptar, con arreglo a sus constituciones respectivas, las medidas legislativas necesarias para asegurar la aplicación de las disposiciones que contiene y especialmente a establecer sanciones penales eficaces para castigar a las personas culpables de genocidio..."

Historia. No se ha podido precisar quiénes fueron los pioneros del protestantismo en México. Existe, sin embargo, el dato generalmente aceptado de que fue Dn Vicente Rocafuerte, secretario de la legación mexicana en Londres, quien tradujo, en 1824, la *Teología Natural* del Dr W Paley. Este libro —el 1° de su naturaleza que logró llegar al país— fue difundido profusamente en Hispanoamérica. Años más tarde, en 1827, desembarcó en Veracruz el Sr Diego Thompson, representante de la Sociedad Bíblica Británica y Extranjera. Condujo hasta la capital de la joven república 24 mulas cargadas de biblias y otros materiales evangélicos. Logró relacionarse con Dn José María Luis Mora, quien al parecer se convirtió al protestantismo, con Dn José María Alpuche y otros clérigos destacados del tiempo y eso hizo posible que al cabo de 2 años hubieran sido vendidas 2 mil biblias y 5 mil nuevos testamentos. Thompson, además, consiguió que se editara una versión del *Evangelio* de San Lucas en idioma náhuatl. El activo catequista inglés hizo un largo viaje por Suramérica y cuando volvió a México —ya los conservadores en el poder— fue hostilizado a tal punto que se vió precisado a regresar a su patria.

Dn Valentín Gómez Farías facilitó la propaganda protestante en 1833, basándose en el principio de libertad de creencias que iba a consagrar, en 1859, Dn

Benito Juárez. Un poco antes de la Guerra de 3 Años, al promulgarse la Constitución de 1857, se formó la Corporación de Padres Constitucionalistas, en cuyo seno había 3 grupos: el mayoritario, según el cual podía jurarse la Carta Magna Liberal, sin dejar por ello de ser cristiano; otro que propugnaba la organización de la iglesia católica mexicana; y el 3°, francamente minoritario, cuya pretensión era crear una especie de luteranismo nacional.

Vinieron luego los años turbulentos de la guerra, la breve paz del gobierno juarista y la intervención de los franceses. Y en el invierno de 1863 entró a territorio mexicano, por Matamoros, el Sr Santiago Hickey, quien se estableció en Monterrey y logró fundar, el 30 de enero de 1864, la iglesia bautista con el nombre de iglesia cristiana. En esa misma época, Enrique Riley, de la iglesia episcopal, empezó a editar en la ciudad de México el periódico *La Estrella de Belén* y en unión del párroco de la iglesia de Jesús de Azcapotzalco, Pbro Manuel Aguas, introdujo las prácticas evangélicas en los templos de San Francisco y San José de Gracia, que previamente compraron al gobierno. Las demás misiones protestantes llegaron a México durante la década de 1870 a 1880.

El protestantismo en México, desde entonces, está dividido en 2 grandes ramas: los protestantes propiamente dichos y los evangélicos. Estos, a su vez, se subdividen en otras denominaciones: metodistas, presbiterianos, bautistas, nazarenos, congresionales, episcopales y pentecostses. Entre ellos no hay distingos fundamentales de concepto religioso; lo que los diferencia es la forma interna de gobierno, o algunos pequeños detalles, tales como creer en Cristo y no en la Santísima Trinidad. Los protestantes no han llegado a la unidad orgánica en el terreno mundial por el temor de que una vez reunidos —son 400 millones— pueda surgir entre ellos un papa. El organismo que los vertebra es el Concilio Mundial de Iglesias Cristianas, que sesiona cada 4 años.

El Obpo Ruesga calcula que hay en México 2 millones de protestantes de todas las denominaciones. Esta cifra, al parecer exagerada, acaso sea exacta si se considera como protestantes a todos los miembros de una familia cuyo jefe esté afiliado a cualquiera de las denominaciones evangélicas. Lo que es un hecho es que en la república funcionan, con permiso oficial, sólo 300 templos protestantes. Constan, sin embargo, en la Sría de Gobernación 600 solicitudes para abrir al culto otros tantos.

En nombre de los fieles del protestantismo en México, que viven en la zozobra a causa de la persecución, el Obpo Ruesga recordó el sábado 2 las palabras que el delegado de Egipto, Dr Wahid Fikry Raafat, pronunciara ante las NN UU en 1948: "Seguimos creyendo que, para hacer efectiva la sanción del crimen de genocidio, es necesario que el delincuente más peligroso se convenza de antemano de que, aunque pudiese escapar al juicio de un tribunal nacional, no podrá evadir el juicio de un tribunal internacional, que será justiciero".

CIENCIA

Producción de Isotopos Radiactivos

En la reciente edición de la revista *Nucleonics* se inserta un importante estudio que el Prof F W Gilbert, encargado de operaciones de la planta atómica canadiense de Chalk River, hace acerca de la nueva pila *NRX* dedicada exclusivamente a la producción de isotopos radiactivos. Hasta ahora ha quedado ple-

LA PILA ATÓMICA NRX
...sirve de instrumento de investigación...

namente demostrado que los isotopos radiactivos de cobalto son los más eficaces para el tratamiento del cáncer; pero son también los más difíciles de producir.

La pila canadiense *NRX* es la única en el mundo capaz de producir en la actualidad dichos isotopos, y de esa pila sólo hay hasta ahora 2 unidades: la instalada el año pasado en Saskatoon y la montada hace poco en el Hospital Victoria de London, Ontario (Canadá).

Sabido es que para producir isotopos radiactivos cuanto mayor es la corriente neutrónica que bombardea una substancia madre, mayor será la potencia del producto radiactivo producido, y más corto el tiempo necesario para producirlo. Partiendo de esta base, la pila *NRX* goza de una gran corriente neutrónica debido a que su núcleo reactivo es menor en relación con su potencia. La pequeñez del núcleo impone, sin embargo, cierta limitación al uso de la pila en la producción de isotopos ya que la mayor parte del espacio disponible está ocupado por los materiales necesarios para el funcionamiento de la pila.

Como la pila canadiense está diseñada para servir de instrumento de investigación, tiene una capacidad limitada y restringida. Pero cuantas personas tengan interés en conocer sus cualidades pueden obtener un catálogo que contiene todos los detalles relativos a los isotopos radiactivos disponibles y a sus

53

Crimes of Intolerance

With Christian serenity, but also with great energy, we are against the protestant campaign continuing to extend itself And more over, we will fight until we are finished with her. Such was said, in the beginning of 1944, on the occasion of initiating the Year of Jubilee of Guadalupe, under the sign of intolerance, by Monsignor Luis Maria Martinez, archbishop of Mexico. These words were also a reiteration of the pastoral message that he had given the previous October 29 directed to the clergy and the parishioners by the same dignitary. "it is well know the intense propaganda that with perfect organization and powerful financial backing that can be done in the entire republic of Mexico by the protestant cults. Through this she tries to tear away from the Mexican people her richest treasure, her Catholic faith, that has for 4 centuries brought us the most holy Virgin of Guadalupe... And now, as in the middle ages, the cry of "God demands it!", all the Christians united to capture the glorious sepulcher of Jesus Christ; and now we have the same thing, with the conviction that God willing and Maria of Guadalupe praying for it, all Catholics will rise and be strong in the service of the defense of the faith."

photo of Luis Maria Martinez

The fight against the "hellish serpent" of Protestantism is going to begin in Mexico. It would be a continuation of the infamous pledge that the Vatican has already accomplished the rest of Latin America. In 1941 the Chilean bishopric (or episcopate), in a pastoral message they had condemned the activities of Protestants. In his message for lent in 1943 he made a similar message to the bishop of Nueva Pamplona, in Colombia; and he continued in Ecuador, to the archbishops of Quito and Cuenca. In Costa Rica, the Apostolic Vicar of Limon asked for a similar pastoral message; in Nicaragua, the Archbishop of Managua and the bishop of Granada publically refuted the evangelicals; in Cuba, the archbishop of Havana accused the Lutherans of "hurting the feelings of the people"; and in Brazil, Cardinal Sebastian Leme of Silveira Cintra, archbishop of Rio de Janeiro, incited the faithful against any religious institution or confession other than Catholic.

Even though conceived as part of a general campaign, the persecution against Protestants was going to have peculiar characteristics in Mexico. Unprecedented violence, whose extremes included killing, raping, kidnaping, and the destruction of small communities, all corresponding to the indifference in public opinion and a lack of any repressive action on behalf of the state. These coexisting acts - the repeated crime and systematic impunity - are the common notes that describe the history and details of such atrocities.

Since October 1944 - the date in which in the name of God and the Virgin, Monsignor Martinez called for the violence- the federal authorities know about 76 cases, exactly detailed. Here are some of them:

4 Nov. 25, 1944 Burned were the Evangelical Church of Glory in the State of Veracruz, and the homes of 9 Protestants. Seven people, including 5 children, died in this sinister act. A little later, the Catholics expelled 60 families affiliated with the Church of God from their town.

4 May 27, 1945, In Santiago Yeche, in the state of Mexico, the catholic priest Jose A Vivas headed the attack against the homes of protestant pastors Feliciano Juarez and Vicente Garita. The preachers were hung and quartered and their homes blown up with dynamite.

• June 1, 1945, In the parish of Caulote, in the state of Michoacan, a Lutheran Church was burned. The inciters insulted the women and punched the men. The evangelicals that survived fled to the mountains: 105 arrived in Mexico City looking for guarantees of security.

Jan. 15, 1946, In Neblinas, state of Hidalgo, several groups led by Candido Munoz and Julio Bautista, and incited by the local priest, attacks the evangelicals meeting there. They injured many, they expelled everyone from the town, and whipped and hung the pastor from a tree.

March 7, 1946, In Actipan of Morelos, state of Puebla, Catholics flattened the house of an evangelical minister, brought him out by force, they dragged him through the entire town, and now dead, they burned his body in the public square.

These Infamies have been accompanied by terrible printed material. The parish

photo of David G Ruesga

of San Marcos, in the city of Puebla, distributed during that time a parody of Exodus 12, with terrible biblical warning to the Protestants. "The first Passover was celebrated in the land of Pharaoh and it was that night when the destroying angel passed over. The sword rang with decisive blows the homes that did not have the sign of the blood of the lamb on the door. There was no blood in the door where they had not eaten the lamb, and there entered death"

July 31, 1946, When the federal police agents Marcelo Fernandez Ocana and Leopoldo Arenas Diaz arrived at San Felipe of Santiago, in the state of Mexico, to investigate the atrocities committed by the Catholics, the priest Pedro Juarez caused them to drive to the mayor's office. Both men were attacked, but Fernandez Ocana was pulled out by the hair and scalped with a machete, and even though alive, his eyes were gouged out with a nail. Later they cut off his ears, they broke his teeth with punches, and broke many bones in his body. Now dead, they cut him up in pieces, and threw his body to the dogs. Arenas Diaz managed to escape.

Because of the crime, this may be the only time when the judicial authorities reacted to attempt to punish this barbaric crime. Some of the fanatics that participated in the act were detained the a prison in Toluca and it is possible that they will be condemned to 18 years in prison. The priest Pedro Juarez, on the other hand, continues to enjoy his freedom after inciting the violence.

March 8, 1947, In Ameca, state of (page 50 photo of the family of evangelical preacher.)

Jalisco, the catholic priest, after a skirmish that he started, kidnaped various Protestants, took them to his church, and using inquisition methods obligated them, under threat of death, to be baptized according to the rites of the "Holy Mother".

• June 30, 1947, In Tianalapa, state of Hidalgo, the representative of the government Leopoldo Badillo and Police agent Rafael Vargas Rodriguez, received from the evangelicals a promise, according to an official report of this date, that they would never again bring religious ministers to their town.

• April 17, 1948, the mayor of Pala, state of Nayarit, prohibited the practice of Evangelical rites and also prohibited the Protestants to visit in their town. In response to this the Catholics said, "it is very simple, become Catholics, and all the problems will end."

• Dec. 7, 1948, in Tabernillas, state of Mexico, Aniceto Hernandez and Porfirio Velazques, with the counsel of the priest Luis Reyes, killed the Protestant Antonio de la Cruz Carmona. The victim received 3 blows from a machete to the head, and 4 bullets in the pack and two stab wounds in the ribs.

The previous October 10 knowing that the evangelicals were going to open a new building, the priest Reyes said in a sermon, "All of you, Catholics, don't have the pants (guts) to finish off the cursed Protestants. If you don't do it, I will never return to bestow spiritual help." General Jose Maria Tapia, in a letter from Nov. 1 of this year to the governor of the state, also reproduced the following phrase from the priest of Tabernillas, "the government appears soft, and lax to me. If the federal government intervenes they will have to deal with all the neighboring towns, at least in this the state government has its part..."

• April 13, 1949, In Rio Verde, San Luis Potosi, the body of the small boy Samuel Juarez, son of preacher J. Ascension Juarez, was found with 85 knife wounds. This dark crime is attributed the vengeance to the priest Jose Maria Rosales, who had been confronted by the preacher.

• December 27, 1949, between Tecali and Concpcion Cuautla, in the state of Puebla, a group of Catholics, incited by priest Antonio Carvajal, assaulted evangelicals Espiridion Perez and Marcial Escalona. As in the life or death skirmish of Filiberto Hernandez, they set the houses of Protestants on fire, and killed 6 people.

• October 13, 1950, in Maguey Blanco, state of Hidalgo, Alberto Martin and Teofilo and Isidro Pejay were surrounded by a group of 25 drunken Catholics. Isidro Pejay was killed by the blows from a steel bar. The explanation given was "they felt anger against the Protestants" was sufficient to let the group free from jail.

• December 7, 1950, for the second time this year the Catholics attacked the building of the Presbyterian Church of Tixtla, in the state of Guerrero. Under the cry "Christ the King lives" furniture was broken, the women were raped and the men were beaten all through the exhortation of the Priest Adalberto J. Miranda.

• Feb. 11, 1951, in Coyocala, state of Hidalgo, Auxiliary judge Pedro Morales, condemned 11 Protestants to forced labor in public works until they renounced the

Gospel. They were set free on March 3 of the same year, but were expelled from the town under the threat of death.

• June 8, 1951, between Santa Rita and Tlahuapan, on the Puebla State Highway 2 individuals, riding horses, shot into a group of field workers that were directing a gospel meeting. Maria Isabel Suarez, a 5 year old girl was seriously injured. Some motorists drove her to the hospital Sanatorio Cruz Celis in the town of Puebla.

The most recent atrocity happened on January 27 this year in the town of Movoro, 20 km from Jocotitlan and 40 km from Toluca, the capital of the state of Mexico. On the occasion of a visit of several preachers, 21 people were meeting in the home of Francisco Garcia for a special dedication through their prayers. Just after starting the meeting, the church bells of the catholic church started ringing, and a few minutes later a gang of fanatics, armed with sticks and machetes, axes and hoes, fell upon the Protestants. All were beaten and injured. Pastor Agustin Corrales was dragged through the streets and left for dead at km 115 of the Queretaro Highway.

For the first time in many years the Catholic Press from the capital of the Republic gave notice of these events. Excelsior, known for its strong ties with the Catholic Church, reported in 8 columns, in the Tuesday January 29th issue, "they were at the point of hanging 2 gospel preachers. They were furiously attacked while they preached. A dramatic chase ensued for 10 km, before they collapsed, and they were going to be mutilated". And later wrote, "they were treated like dogs with rabies, 2 preachers were chased by the infuriated mob with sticks and rocks, and when they were caught after running 10 km, and were exhausted, they were beaten in a scary fashion, until they were left in a state of coma..." The newspaper Zócalo, a liberal newspaper, published a dramatic report and using various writers, despite their Catholic beliefs, condemned the act. People that were knowledgeable of the incident pointed to the parish priest of Morovó, Fernando Vidal, as the one directly responsible for the attack.

No one published the fact, however that the same day, at the same hour, the inhabitants of San Pablo Tecalco, in their own State of Mexico planned for several hundred Catholics to tear down their church building. In San Pablo Tecalco there are no Roman Catholics; all belong to the Mexican branch founded during the Reformation of Mexico. Because of this the priest from Santa Maria Ozumbilla, Antonio Zaizar Torres, wanted to take advantage of the 23rd of January, the anniversary of the conversion of St. Paul to Catholicism, to reclaim the memory of the saint in a town of evangelicals that was originally dedicated to him. The bold priest brought together the fanatics from 20 rural, outlying communities and marched upon Tecalco with the intention of stripping the evangelicals of their homes. The evangelicals, however, were warned in a timely manner, and asked for help from the authorities and a company of soldiers were given orders to stop any attacks. Zaizar Torres and his 500 men passed by San Pablo peacefully; but the priest, already in the outskirts of the town returned to restate his threat, "there will be another time, when they will not be prepared". (Note: San Pablo means Saint Paul, that the town by its name was dedicated to Paul - translator's addition).

Far from decreasing in number or in violence, the atrocities of this type have been on the increase. Each new act that increasingly accents the power of the Catholic hierarchy results in more intolerance towards other religious beliefs. First it was the Jubileo Guadalupano (year of jubilee of Guadalupe), then the ostentatious ceremonies following the 50th anniversary of the crowing of the image of Tepeyac; later the enthroning of Guadalupe in Rome, Paris and Madrid; and finally the concession, from the Pope, of the title of Primate to the archbishop of Mexico. This last development appears to have been celebrated with the most recent atrocities. Apart from the atrocities in Morovó and San Pablo Tecalco, the following have occurred this year:

• In Zacamitla, municipality of Ixhuatlán, state of Veracruz, 2 individuals shot to death, four weeks before the death of the Protestant Catechist Miguel Martinez. This occurred three days after priest Jose Perez had said from the pulpit, "I promise you all, my children, that I go ahead of you all to finish off the evangelicals with sticks".

• In Zcozonica, 12 km from Fortin de las Flores, state of Veracruz, the city clerk Simitrio Esperilla, decreed in the beginning of January that Protestantism was prohibited. "Those who want to continue to be evangelicals - he said officially - must leave or they will die. Those who live here must be Catholics".

• In Paso Largo, state of Veracruz, the evangelicals received, on the last 2' of January, a notice from the Director General of Highways ordering the destruction of the church building. The notice was based on a false fact - that the church was built on the right of way of the highway - was attributed to the influences of the Catholic parish.

These are the cases - from January - whose details have been officially recorded. Certainly many others have been ignored because the victims, sceptical of the justice system, or afraid of reprisals, suffer their injustices in silence. When these cases become national news, the state suppresses the information. When a high ranking official from the justice department was asked to make a statement about the happenings in Movoro, he explained to a reporter from Zocalo who asked for the interview, "when a crime that is so common everywhere happens, it is not within our jurisdiction..."

The archbishop of Mexico tried to separate himself from any responsibility. He said last week," we lament the happenings in Movoro; but we do not have control over the people in this respect. It is regrettable that Protestant ministers counsel the Catholic people to deny their faith. We have always tried to avoid these drunken acts; but the people have their beliefs, and good or bad we cannot take them away from them..."

The declaration from the Primate, in the judgement of an observer, "is insincere, false and contradictory". Exactly:

• "Insincere, because it isn't believable that the archbishop laments over those who quickly follow his teachings; he actually is proud of the results of his teaching and in those who act upon them. The teachings of Don Martinez on the subject of intolerance are contained in the pastoral lecture of October 29, 1944, and are clearly brutal and monstrous.

• false, because the archbishop has the power to send the Catholics to do the crime, and he has the same power to hold them back according to his own reasoning and instead of that, he motivates them with his declarations that are made to justify, from his point of view, intolerance and the atrocities committed.

• and contradictory, because the reproach against Protestants, preaching in Catholic towns, in such a way to make Catholics deny their faith, could have happened in Protestant or Buddhist or Muslim or Shinto towns. And to be fair, the archbishop should declare that in the same manner that he can't take away the beliefs from a Catholic, neither should he attempt to take it away from the Protestants".

Also, added the observer, "...the archbishop has no grounds to oppose anyone's faith, but article 24 of the constitution establishes "that every man is free to profess the religious beliefs that please him and to practice the ceremonies, devotionals, and religious acts respectively, in religious buildings, or in his home, never that it would constitute a crime or penalty through the law".

The forms that express the intolerance of the Catholic Church in Mexico invoke the complete picture of genocide. This word, in its literal meaning, means the destruction of groups of human beings, or their systematic persecution with the goal to exterminate them. This "crime of crimes", as it is graded by Dr. Raphael Lemkin, from the University of Yale, and author of the word genocide, has been already incorporated into international legislation. In 1946, the General Assembly of the United Nations asked the Economic and Social Counsel that they start the necessary studies to elaborate a project for a Convention about this crime. After much red tape and bureaucracy, the project was examined during a meeting in Paris by the Justice Commission, and finally was accepted by the general assembly December 9, 1948.

The text of the previous article from the congress declared that genocide is a crime against international rights contrary to the spirit and the aims of the United Nations and that the civilized world condemns it; that in all periods of history, genocide has inflicted great loss to humanity; and international cooperation is required to free the world of a hateful scourge . The second article expresses, "we understand genocide to be any of the mentioned acts continued and perpetrated with the intention of destroying, totally or partially, a national group, ethnic, race or religious, such as: a) the killing of the members of a group; b) gravely injuring physically or mentally the members of the group; c) intentionally subjecting the group to conditions that promote their physical destruction, totally or partially...,"

According to Article 3 of the Convention, they ought to punish, apart from genocide itself, the association to commit genocide, the direct and indirect, public instigation of genocide. And considering that they are not particular about those who perpetrate the act of genocide, but the people that hold authority and influence over them, Article 4 declares that those who have committed this crime, or any of the other mentioned acts, shall be punished, whether speaking of governments, employers, or dignitaries.

The representative of Mexico to the United Nations, Luis Padilla Nervo, signed the Convention about genocide, on the 14th of December, 1948. The document was sent to the Secretary of the Republic of the United States of Mexico, Manuel Tello, who turned it over to attorneys Ernesto P Uruchurtu, Sub secretary of the government and Fransisco Gonzalez de la Vega Attorney general of the Republic. The first answered the secretary on the 1 6th of December 1949, expressing that the Secretary of the Government approve the text "...to try to contain a crime that repulses all conscience". The second, in his time, did not raise any objections to the document. Two years later, on the 24th of December 1951, the executive sent the document to the senate, and this, 6 months later, was approved without amendments in secret sessions. The decree was signed by Pedro Guerrero Martinez and Alfonso Corona del Rosal.

Before Mexico had ratified the document about genocide, the following countries: Ethiopia, Australia, Norway, Iceland, Equador, Panama, Guatemala, Israel, Liberia,Philippines, Yugoslavia, El Salvador, Haiti, France, Czechoslovakia, Denmark, China andBelgium had all ratified the agreement.

Founded upon the undisputed fact that actions of the Catholic Church against Protestants fall within the provisions of Article 2 of the convention, the National Committee for evangelical defence, headed by Bishop David G Ruesga, will accuse the dignitaries of Mexican clergy of genocide. Last week, a commission of attorneys was involved in the work of formulating the document that would be sent to the United Nations. They would put in the document, the most complete list of atrocities possible to obtain and the words of archbishop Martinez and of other dignitaries whose influence is legitimate to attribute to persecution and the crimes.

"The iniquities of the Catholic Church against the evangelical population of Mexico - said Bishop Ruesga - constitute a true act of genocide. If the Vatican is not a member of the United Nations, and Mexico is, then this country is obligated to uphold the international treaties that we have subscribed to, and among them is the Convention about Genocide, and the Declaration of Human rights, in which freedom of beliefs, and freedom of expression of thought are included".

DGR (David G. Ruesga) first saw the light in the city of Morelia on July 6, 1898. He did his first studies under the care of the Teresian Nuns, and later went to the Seminary Tridentino in the capital city of the state of Michoacan. "Sickened by the methods and the internal life of the Seminary", according to what he has said, he abandoned the teachings of the confessional and enrolled in the University of San Nicolas of Hidalgo. At that time - 1914 - David's father, David Genaro Ruesga, launched the Revolution using the aid of his good friend, Governor Miguel Silva. Together, they marched the young student over the hills, and even with an injured leg, crossed into the United States. There he had contact with Protestants, and decided to enter into Dallas Evangelical Seminary in the state of Texas. In 1920 he returned to Mexico, converted into a preacher: first he was a minister in the Pentecostal church, and today has become the bishop of that confession. He controls 280 churches with more than 70, 000 faithful members. He supports himself by his work as a business man and speaks with satisfaction of his 20 children - 13 boys, and 7 girls-, the products of 2 marriages.

Ruesga, in his role of president of the National Committee for Evangelical Defense, has raised hundreds of complaints before the Secretary of the Government. In the middle of 1951, Adolfo Ruiz Cortines, then a minister of a government, asked the bishop to formulate a project of reforms to the Regulations Law article 130 of the Constitution, with the goal of impeding atrocities between Catholics and Protestants. Dr. David fulfilled his promise to do so and delivered a reworking of laws containing provisions concerning religious crimes and acts and outside discipline. Here are some of the articles that were put forth:

• "Art 8 the individual that, in exercising of the duties of minister or priest of whatever religious group, in inciting publically, or through written declaration, or sermons, his listeners and readers, against political institutions, or in disobedience to the laws, the authorities or his orders, shall be punished with a penalty of 6 years in prison and a fine of 1000 pesos.

• "Art 9 if as the direct or immediate result of the incitation of what has been previously mentioned in the previous article, less than 10 people use force, threats, physical or moral violence against public authorities or its agents, or the use of arms, each one of them shall be punished with 1 year in prison and a fine of 1000 pesos. The priests or ministers of the religious group who incited the persecution, shall be given punishment of 6 years in prison, but aggravating factors will be taken into consideration by the judge, which may result in a heavier penalty.

• "Art 11 Ministers of any religious groups who exercise from their ministry propaganda to incite others to commit acts of aggression against one or more persons that profess another distinct belief, shall suffer the penalty of 6 years in prison and a fine of 1000 pesos.

For reasons outside of his control, bishop Ruesgo handed over these projects to the Secretary of Government two days after the date that he had indicated. With such virtue, the legal department and this reporter did not have time to examine them and lost the opportunity that the congress discuss this matter during the ordinary passing of its sessions. In all of this, the implementation of Art. 103 of the constitution about the new basis and the expedition of the law against faults and transgressions in religious material are necessities that soon will have to be resolved by the state. Moreover, when Art. 5 of the convention on genocide establishes that, "the contracting (or participating) parties promise to adopt, with changes to their respective constitutions, the legislative means necessary to secure the application of the dispositions that contain and especially to establish sanctions to punish the persons guilty of genocide..."

History. It hasn't been possible to establish exactly who the pioneers of Protestantism in Mexico were. However, it is generally accepted that Vicente Rocafuerte, secretary of the Mexican delegation in London, who translated in 1824, Natural Theology by Dr. W. Paley, was one. This book - the first of this nature that finally arrived in the country - was distributed widely in Latin America. Years later, in 1827, Mr. Diego Thompson got off a boat in Veracruz. He was a representative of the British and Foreign Bible Society. He drove 24 mules laden with Bibles and other evangelical materials to the young Republic's capital. He developed a relationship with Don Jose Maria Luis Mora, who appears to have converted to Protestantism, with Don Jose Maria Alpuch and other notable clergy at that time and this made it possible that in 2 years, they had sold 2000 Bibles and 5000 New Testaments. Thompson, also, made it possible for a version of the gospel of St. Luke translated to the Nahuatl language. The active English evangelist made long trips to South America and when he returned to Mexico (now with conservatives in power) was harassed to such a point, that he saw it necessary to return to his country.

Valentin Gomez Farias facilitated the reintroduction of protestant evangelistic materials in 1833, based on the principle of freedom of beliefs that was going to be established, in 1859, by Don Benito Juarez. A little before the Three Year War, to enact the constitution of 1857, a corporation of Constitutional Fathers was formed in whose bosom were three groups: the majority – who's liberal thought would allow them to consider the Carta Magna, as something that would not interfere with Christianity; another that propagated the organization of the Mexican Catholic church; and the third, frankly the minority, whose pretence was to create some kind of national Lutheran group.

Later came the turbulent years of the war, the brief peace of the Juarez government and then the French intervention, in the winter of 1863, through Matamoros, Santiago Hickey entered into Mexican Territory, who established in Monterrey and founded on the 30th of January 1864, the Baptist Church with the name Christian Church. At this same time, Enrique Riley, from the Episcopal Church, began to edit the newspaper called 'the Bethlehem Star' in Mexico City in union with the leaders of the Church of Jesus the Apostle , Manuel Aguas, introduces the evangelical practices in the times of San Francisco and San Jose de Gracia, who previously bought the government. Other protestant missions arrived in Mexico between 1870 and 1880.

Protestantism in Mexico, since then has been divided into 2 large branches. Protestants strictly speaking, and evangelicals. These are also divided into other denominations: Methodists, Presbyterian, Baptist, Nazarenes, Congregationalist, Episcipalians and Pentecostals. Between them there are no fundamental differences in religious concepts; what is different is the form of internal government, or other small details, such as how to believe in Christ, and not in the Holy Trinity. Protestants have not arrived at an organic unity in the earthly world because of the fear that once united - there are 400 million - there could arise out of them a Pope. The organism that gives them backbone is the World Council of Christian Churches, who meet every 4 years.

Bishop Ruesga calculates that there are 2,000,000 Protestants in Mexico in the different denominations. This number although it appears exaggerated, could be accurate if one considers as Protestants all the family members whose head is affiliated with any evangelical denomination. What is a fact is that there are functioning in the Republic of Mexico with official governmental permission only 300 protestant churches. However in the Secretary of the government there are 600 applications to open other religious meetings.

The name of those faithful to Protestantism in Mexico, that live in the anguish caused by persecution, were remembered by bishop Ruesga when on Saturday the 2nd, he used words that the delegate from Egypt, Dr. Wahid Fikry Raafat, stated before the United Nations in 1948, "We believe that, to make an effective sanction against the crime of genocide, it is necessary that the most dangerous delinquent is convinced beforehand that although he may escape the justice of a national tribunal, he cannot evade the justice of an international tribunal, that will be just".

Notes

Introduction

[1] *World Book Encyclopaedia*, 1978, Volume 12, p. 275-277, Stephen B. Oates, *With Malice Toward None*, (Harper & Row, 1977), p. 5, Charles Chiniquy, *Fifty Years in the Church of Rome*, (Craig and Barlow, 1886, 3rd edition), p. 9, *New York Times*, January 17th, 1899, p. 1, *The Dictionary of Canadian Biography*, (University of Toronto Press, 1990), Volume XII, 1891 to 1900, p. 190, *The Times*, (London), January 17, 1899, p. 10, Jan Noel, "Dry Patriotism: The Chiniquy Crusade", *The Canadian Historical Review*, June 1990, Vol. 71, Issue 2, p. 201, *The United States Biographical Dictionary*, Volume 2, p. 719, *Historical Encyclopedia of Illinois and History of Kankakee County*, 1906, Volume 11, p. 752

[2] Richard Lougheed, "*The Controversial Conversion of Charles Chiniquy*", Diss. Ph.D., University of Montreal, 1993, p. 408, Richard Lougheed, *The Controversial Conversion of Charles Chiniquy*, (Clements Academic, 2008), p. 296, 305, *Dictionary of Canadian Biography*, Volume XII, p. 190, Patricia Godsell, *Enjoying Canadian Painting*, (General Publishing Co., 1976), p. 43, 59, Lucy Maud Montgomery, *Anne Of The Island And Anne's House Of Dreams*, (Courage Books, 1997) p. 369, 370, Pierre Burton, *My Country*, (McClelland and Stewart, 1976), p. 138-154.

In his 2008 book entitled, *The Controversial Conversion of Charles Chiniquy*, Lougheed stated that Krieghoff probably painted a portrait of Charles Chiniquy as well. Later in his book, however he definitely stated that Krieghoff had painted a portrait of Chiniquy. As Chiniquy seems to have been so effectively demonized in Catholic Quebec and other parts of Canada, the comments from the French Canadian politicians, as well as Berton and Montgomery, were generally not positive but even so, they do show his fame and influence.

[3] *New York Times*, January 17th, 1899, p. 1, *Atlanta Constitution*, February 19, 1899, p. 19, "Father Chiniquy Dead", *The Washington Post*, January 17, 1899, p. 9, "Pere Chiniquy's Story", *The Washington Post*, April 23, 1899, p. 18, The Times, January 17, 1899, p. 10

[4] *Kankakee Daily Gazette*, January 17th, 1899, p. 3, Maclean's, July 1, 1998, p. 48

[5] *Kankakee Daily Gazette*, January 17th, 1899, p. 3

[6] *Fifty Years in the Church of Rome*, p. 66-85, 397-403, 603-667, 784-809, *Dictionary of Canadian Biography*, Volume X11, p. 192

[7] *Fifty Years*, p. 663, 664, 718

[8] *The Trial of John Surratt*, (Government Printing Office, 1867), Volume I, p. 133, Roy Z. Chamlee, Jr., *Lincoln's Assassins: A Complete Account of the Capture, Trial, and Punishment*, (McFarland & Company, 1990), p. x, xi, "The Rev. Mr. Chiniquy Makes

Charges", *Chicago Daily Tribune*, March 18, 1893, p. 3. There are four versions of the trial of the conspirators. The best known is the record compiled by Benn Pitman. There also is the Peterson, the Barclay and the Poore version. The proceedings were also given in the Washington newspaper, the *National Intelligencer* and there also is the original military record of the trial in longhand. In *Lincoln's Assassins*, Roy Chamlee stated, "The difference in the words in these various accounts is remarkably slight."

According to the article "The Rev. Mr. Chiniquy Makes Charges", Charles Chiniquy said that his house had been destroyed by fire through arson. He said that this had been threatened if he did not leave St. Anne, Illinois. Two weeks later in a letter to the editor in the *Chicago Daily Tribune*, an anonymous writer declared that Chiniquy was not told to leave St. Anne.

After Chiniquy's death, there reportedly was at least one more instance of loss, due to flooding in the house where his papers were stored. According to Richard Lougheed, the flooding happened in the 1990s when the Chiniquy papers were stored in the home of Samuel Lefebvre: a Chiniquy descendant.

[9] "The Paranoid Style", *Washington Post*, December 29, 1991, p. C7, Lloyd Lewis, *Myths After Lincoln*, (The Readers Club, by permission from Harcourt, Brace and Co., 1941), p. 203, *The Catholics and Mrs. Mary Surratt*, Kenneth J. Zanca, (University Press of America, 2008), p. 75

Stanton is credited with being in charge of the investigation and the trial of the conspirators in Zanca's book. *The Catholics and Mrs. Mary Surratt* states "A Temocratic partisan paper, *The Old Guard*, in September 1867, articulated these sentiments with vitriol for men in the government: 'The trial of young Surratt, the son of that woman of that name who was murdered by Stanton and his satraps...' "

[10] David Balsiger and Charles E. Sellier, Jr., *The Lincoln Conspiracy*, (Schick Sunn Classic Books, 1977), p. 7, Theodore Roscoe, *The Web of Conspiracy*, (Prentice-Hall, 1960), p. 533, Timothy S. Good, ed, *We Saw Lincoln Shot: One Hundred Eyewitness Accounts*, (University Press Of Mississippi, 1995), p. 196, 197, "Civil War widow buried in 1860's style," *Calgary Herald*, June 14, 2004, "Alabama salutes last Dixie widow," *The Province*, (Vancouver, B.C.), July 4, 2004, Deirdre Donahue, "A Troubled Nation Looks to Lincoln", *USA Today*, October 7, 2008, p. D1. In 2008, the curator of the Lincoln Collection at the Abraham Lincoln Presidential Library, Dr. James M. Cornelius, told the author that some 15,000 imprints have been written on the subject of Abraham Lincoln. The October 7th *USA Today* article stated that there are 16,000 books written about Lincoln.

Chapter 1 Chiniquy's Early Life

[1] Charles Chiniquy, *Fifty Years in the Church of Rome*, (Craig and Barlow, 1886, 3rd edition), p. 9 - 163, *The Dictionary of Canadian Biography*, (University of Toronto Press, 1990), Volume XII, 1891 to 1900, p. 189, " 'Personal Anumus' Charged by Watson", *Atlanta Constitution*, November 30, 1915, p. 1, Peter De Rosa, *Vicars of Christ: the Dark Side of the Papacy*, (Bantam Press, 1988), p. 422-424, 426.

Chiniquy's father changed his mind about being a priest however, after witnessing an act of wrong-doing among high-ranking church officials that so shocked him that he abandoned his plans and become a notary instead.

One day, Rev. Morin invited young Charles to give an address at the birthday party of the parish priest, Mr. Varin. Charles did so and was invited to stay for dinner. He stayed and during the evening was shocked by the behavior of the priests that attended who were mostly drunk by the end of the night. According to him, the next morning they celebrated mass as though they had spent the previous evening in prayer and Bible reading.

Once a week, the principal men of St. Thomas, Quebec, quietly met at the home of the father of one of his friends. On these occasions, Charles and his friend were sometimes found eavesdropping from an adjoining room as the topics of the day, including the shortcomings of the priests, were discussed. Not long after his ordeal of auricular confession, he was invited to eavesdrop in on another meeting at his friend's home. His companion told him that the priest Charles had confessed to had been whipped by some men the previous night. The priest had been returning home after visiting the home of two sisters. Though he knew it was wrong, he couldn't resist joining his friend. They overheard that some of the men at the meeting had beaten the priest because they knew why he had been visiting the two women and believed he was a terrible example for the community. The men also discussed the polluting nature of the confessional to children and through it, how many daughters and wives in the village had been seduced by the previous priests in the village.

In his book, *Vicars of Christ: the Dark Side of the Papacy*, former Catholic priest and theological instructor, Peter De Rosa supported Charles Chiniquy regarding the corrupting tendencies of the confessional. He stated, "The Fourth Council of the Lateran in 1215 made it obligatory for lay people to confess annually to their parish priests. This was the same Council at which Innocent III gave celibacy its final form. The combination of these two rules was to prove harmful to the morals of both clergy and laity. It led to the sin known in canon law as 'solicitation', that is, a priest using the confessional for immoral purposes. Of course, penalties were imposed by the church. They became increasingly severe, but there is no evidence that they diminished the number of times priests took advantage of their position to make passes at their penitents.

So widespread was confessional abuse that the laity were told that if their priest was of evil repute they were dispensed from the need to confess their carnal sins to him. The privacy of the confessional provided the clergy with ready access to women at their most vulnerable, that is, when they were obligated by canon law to confess every impure thought, deed and desire. If, say, a woman confessed to fornication or adultery, the priest made matters far worse if he solicited her. But she was not keen to take this outside the seal of confessional. She did not want to risk losing her reputation.

De Rosa also reported, "Some Spanish moralists came to the conclusion that if a woman fainted while confessing and the priest took the opportunity to rape her this did not technically amount to soliciting. The woman was clearly in no condition to respond. Books on moral theology were consulted by priests, not to make them better confessors, but to teach them how to manipulate women in confession without incurring the penalties of canon law."

Again supporting Chiniquy, *Vicars of Christ* stated, "Priests are trained from eighteen and sometimes ten years of age in a seminary, away from all contact with girls and women. They are forbidden to indulge in sex even in their thoughts and imaginings. Every sexual impulse has to be suppressed as a danger to their celibacy. No sooner are they ordained than these young and mostly innocent men are forced to listen, in the secrecy of the confessional, to the most lurid descriptions of sexual activity and deviance. Every sin of sex has to be spoken into their ears, as to number and species. Young women tell them of their innermost thoughts, deeds and longings, sometimes in situations of physical proximity. Through the confessional, a priest with homosexual leanings can discover who are the members of the gay community. From the priest's point of view, the system seems especially cruel. No wonder that too many of them are more absorbed in their own problems than in the problems of their flocks.

As Lea said, in his three-volume work, *A History of the Inquisition in the Middle Ages*:

> No sooner had the Church…succeeded in suppressing the wedlock of its ministers, than we find it everywhere and incessantly busied in the apparently impossible task of compelling their chastity – an effort the futility of which is sufficiently demonstrated by its continuance in modern times. "

The *Atlanta Constitution* reported that in 1915, a Georgia state man who quoted what Charles Chiniquy stated in his book, *The Priest, the Woman and the Confessional*, quoting Roman Catholic theologian, Dens, was actually prosecuted for this. Thomas W. Watson, an editor and author of Thompson, Georgia, was prosecuted for sending obscene material through the mail. In court, Watson stated that the quotations he published, in Latin, came verbatim from *The Priest, the Woman and the Confessional* and in this book, Chiniquy was also quoting verbatim from approved Catholic theologian, Peter Dens' work, *Moral Theology*.

[2] *The United States Biographical Dictionary and Portrait Gallery of Eminent and Self-Made Men*, (American Biographical Publishing Company, 1876), Volume II, p. 718, 719

The United States Biographical Dictionary and Portrait Gallery of Eminent and Self-Made Men also stated of Chiniquy:

> In a sketch of his college life, written by one of his fellow-students, now a member of the Canadian parliament--the Hon. M.J.G. Barth--and cited in a more extended biography written by the Hon. Hector L. Langevin, one of the ministers of the crown and brother to the present Roman Catholic bishop of Ramouski, and published in Montreal in 1849, the following passage occurs:
>
> > 'The piety of Mr. Chiniquy during his studies was such that we were accustomed to consider him as the model of his co-pupils, and his co-disciples used to call him *Le St. Louis Gonzague de Nicholet*.'
>
> He was ordained to the Roman Catholic priesthood in 1833, in the cathedral of Québec, by Bishop Sinaie

[3] *Fifty Years*, p. 183-469

[4] *Fifty Years*, p. 464-466, *New York Times*, January 17, 1899, p. 1, *The United States Biographical Dictionary and Portrait Gallery of Eminent and Self-Made Men*, Volume II, p. 719

Independent sources, including the *New York Times*, confirm what he said. One account reported that an impressive temperance column was erected in Beaufort in recognition of his labors in establishing the first Catholic temperance association in North America there and confirmed that between 1846 and 1851, all distilleries in Quebec were closed except two, thanks to the labors of the crusading priest.

[5] An Act to make better provision for granting Licenses to Keepers of Taverns, and Dealers in Spirituous Liquors in Lower Canada, and for the more effectual repression of Intemperance. Provincial Statues of Canada, VOL. III. 4th Sess. 3rd Parlt, 1851 p. 2078, 2084, 2085, *Fifty Years*, p. 515-518.

Documents from the Canadian Parliament show that it did indeed award Chiniquy 500 pounds sterling and in 1851, it passed a bill for "the more effectual suppression of Intemperance". This Act declared that inn, tavern keepers, etc., who allowed customers to become drunk on the liquor they sold them in their establishments were responsible for their deaths, if it was due to intoxication.

[6] *Fifty Years*, p. 522-534. The priest he knew at the college that helped confront the girl on Chiniquy's third day at the college was named Father Schneider. Chiniquy had four copies of her sworn confession made because he forsaw that the same bishop Bourget, after destroying his own copy, would again try to press this charge against him years later.

[7] Ibid p.186-194, 394-403, 431-449, 470-499, 506-513, 536-561

[8] Ibid p. 507, 537, 538, 555, 558, 561-566.

Lebel was eventually removed from his pastorate when it was discovered he was involved in a sexual relationship with his niece. Lebel was also suspected by Bishop Vandeveld and Chiniquy as being one of those responsible for burning down the church in Bourbonnais, near St. Anne, in May, 1853. Father Chiniquy had served as pastor in Bourbonnais also.

[9] Ibid p. 566-569, 603-623.

As soon as the retreat ended, Chiniquy was summoned to a meeting with the bishop where O'Regan accused him of distributing Bibles amongst his people, which Chiniquy admitted was true, and not teaching the true doctrines of the Roman Catholic Church, which he denied. There was another argument, leaving the bishop furious again.

[10] *New York Times*, January 17, 1899, p. 1, *Kankakee Daily Gazette*, January 17, 1899, p. 3, *Atlas of Kankakee Co*, (J. H. Beers and co., 1883), p.151, *The United States Biographical Dictionary and Portrait Gallery*, p. 719, Catherine Brettell, "From Catholics to Presbyterians: French-Canadian Immigration in Central Illinois," *AMERICAN PRESBYTERIANS, Journal of Presbyterian History*, Volume 63-Number

3, Fall 1985, p.287, John G. Shea, *History of the Catholic Church in the U.S.*, (The Mershon Company Press, 1892), p.614, *The National Cyclopaedia of American Biography*, (J. T. White, 1898), Volume 9, p.79, *Notre Dame de Chicago*, 1887-1937: a history of Notre Dame parish, preceded by an historical sketch of the work of the early French missionaries in the central states--prepared for the occasion of the fiftieth anniversary of the erection of Notre Dame Church, (The Fathers of the Blessed Sacrament, 1937), p. 51, *The National Cyclopaedia of American Biography*, (J. T. White, 1898), Volume 9, p. 79, *Fifty Years*, p. 563, 613, 614, *The National Cyclopaedia of American Biography*, Volume 9, p.79, Bessie L. Pierce, *A History Of Chicago*, (Alfred A. Knopf, 1940), p.360, Fifty Years, p. 623.

According to Catherine Brettell, along with these immigrants, Chiniquy established a colony centered at St. Anne in the early 1850s, (p. 288). Within a few years, other communities such as Bourbonnais, L'Erable and St. Mary were also established through the influx of more than 900 families from Canada.

Regarding Charles Chiniquy statements about his life in Illinois, independent sources support Chiniquy's report that he received an invitation from the bishop of Chicago, Oliv Vandevelt, to establish a colony of French Canadian Catholics on the rich, untamed prairie of Illinois. It is also confirmed that a remarkably effective letter written by Chiniquy was published by the Canadian press, encouraging French Canadians who were already leaving Canada to immigrate to Illinois. It helped to quickly swell the size of the colony he established in the state.

The personalities in the Catholic Church in Illinois and Canada that Charles Chiniquy reported he worked and struggled with were indeed figures in the Church at the time, as Catholic and independent sources confirm. Commenting on the administration of Vandeveld, Catholic historian John G. Shea stated that the bishop:

> felt that there was a steady opposition to him among part of the clergy, neutralizing his efforts for the good of his diocese. He had in vain solicited from the Holy See permission to resign, but when the see of Natchez became vacant he was, at his own request, translated to it.

Another source says essentially the same thing, asserting that Vandeveld was transferred to Natchez after difficulties which included, "troubles arising from disaffections among some of his clergy."

A Catholic account shows that at the time that Chiniquy came to Chicago, in June of 1851, the pastor of the French Canadian Catholics in the city indeed was Father Isadore Le Bel. Chiniquy stated he met Bishop O'Regan on December 11th, 1854. One historical account reported that the Irish born O'Regan was consecrated bishop of Chicago on July 25th, 1854. It added that one of his accomplishments was to erect a "handsome episcopal residence", supporting Chiniquy's statement that O'Regan insisted on building an extravagant palace for his official residence in the young and poor diocese. This same biographical source also stated that the bishop's "administration was, however, not successful. He met considerable opposition from his clergy, and became engaged in certain difficulties with them that discouraged him and made him feel that his usefulness to the diocese was impaired".

Historian Bessie L. Pierce supported Chiniquy's assertion that Bishop O'Regan would have believed he had the right to possess church property. Commenting on O'Regan's predecessor, she stated, "Taking refuge in a law of 1845 investing in the bishop of Chicago and his successors the power to control and convey all church property, Bishop Van de Velde objected to the holding of property for religious purposes by a group of nuns".

Pierce also provided support for Charles Chiniquy's account of his cordial relationship with Bishop Vandeveld, (the bishop's name was spelt several ways) as well as how effective he was in his struggles with the two bishops that followed him. She wrote:

> there were, in addition, vexing administrative problems, particularly in the ministries of Bishop Van de Velde, Bishop O'Regan, and Bishop Duggan. The regimes of the last two priests suffered devastating attacks by Father Chiniquy, a French-Canadian priest, who sometimes preached at St. Louis Church in Chicago

Chapter 2 Lincoln: Childhood to Spink vs. Chiniquy

[1] *World Book Encyclopaedia*, 1978, Volume 12, p. 275-277, *The New Encyclopaedia Britannica*, 2005, Vol. 23, p. 33-35, Charles Chiniquy, *Fifty Years in the Church of Rome*, (Craig and Barlow, 1886, 3rd edition), p. 566, 623-628, Willard L. King, *Lincoln's Manager David Davis*, (Harvard University Press, 1960), p. 301, 302, *Dictionary of American Biography*, (Charles Scribner's Sons, 1959), Volume 3, p. 111, *Biographical Directory of the American Congress: 1774 - 1996*, (CQ Staff Directories, Inc., 1997), p. 211, *World Book Encyclopedia*, 1998, Volume 20, p. 348, 349, Volume 1, p. 754, Figure 1: . Spink vs. Chiniquy, Plaintiff request for change of venue - text added.

Lincoln re-enlisted and stayed in the army a total of 90 days.

Chiniquy's lawyers before Lincoln were Uri Osgood and John Paddock. After he told Chiniquy about Lincoln, his unknown friend paid for the telegram and disappeared without Chiniquy ever learning his name.

Fifty Years reported that David Davis became U.S. Vice-President in 1882, (3rd edition, p. 627). At this time, Davis was a United States Senator (Independent, Illinois). The U.S. Vice-President is the presiding officer of the Senate. In 1881 and through most of 1882, Davis was the elected president pro tempore (temporary president) of the U.S. Senate due to the fact that the former Vice-President, Chester Arthur had become U.S. President after the death of James Garfield. If President Arthur had died while Davis was president pro tempore, Davis would have become the President.

[2] William Baringer, *Lincoln Day by Day, A Chronology*, Volume 2: 1849-1860, (Lincoln Sesquicentennial Commission, 1960), p. 169, *Urbana Union* , May 29, 1856 p. 3

[3] Spink vs. Chiniquy, Plaintiff request to clerk of Circuit Court, Urbana, for subpoenas, April 2, 1856, Plaintiff Costs (list), May Term, 1856, Champaign Circuit Court, case dispositions, May Term, June Term, 1856, Champaign Circuit Court.

Records of the Champaign County Court at Urbana indeed show that in the spring term of 1856, the suit of Spink vs. Chiniquy that had come from Kankakee on a change of venue. The case was not decided and was ordered to continue at the fall term.

[4] *Fifty Years*, p. 654-661. The Sheriff of Kankakee took Chiniquy into custody and transported him, again as a criminal to Urbana. Regarding Lebel, Chiniquy stated that "Not long after the arrival of the trains from Chicago, he came down from his room to see in the book where travelers register their names, if there was any newcomers from Chicago, and what was his dismay when he saw the first name entered was 'Philomene Moffat!' "

[5] *Fifty Years*, p.664-667, Affidavit of Philomene Schwartz, October 21, 1881 (held in the Chiniquy Collection), "Prayer or Prophecy", *Chicago Daily Tribune*, November 1, 1887, p. 9. At the time the article, "Prayer or Prophecy", was published, Moore had evidently become a judge, as he was called Judge Stephen R. Moore.

[6] *Notre Dame de Chicago, 1887-1937: a history of Notre Dame parish, preceded by an historical sketch of the work of the early French missionaries in the central states--prepared for the occasion of the fiftieth anniversary of the erection of Notre Dame Church*, (The Fathers of the Blessed Sacrament, 1937), p. 51-53, Chicago Directory, 1855-1857, p. 81, 84, *Urbana Union*, October 23, 1856, p. 3, *Chicago Daily Democrat*, September 11, 1856, p. 1, October 22, 1856, p. 1.

Efforts to research Narcisse Terrien's life did not yield significant results. Available information showed that he and his wife were French Canadians and about the right age to have been Philonene Schwartz's friends.

According to the U.S. census of 1870, at the time, Narcisse Terrien was living in the French Canadian community of Ganeir in Kankakee County, Illinois. He was listed as a white male, 43 years old, a laborer from Canada. In all probability French, he had apparently acquired some assets by his labors. His wife, listed as Adelle, was a white female age 32, also from Canada. This would have made her close to the same age as Philomene Schwartz, which they probably would have had to have been if they were friends. According to the census, both Narcisse Terrien and his wife were not able to read or write but this may have referred to reading and writing English, French not being counted. Adelle Terrien and Sara Chaussey could have been the same person. Adelle may have been her legal first name and Sara the name she went by, or Adelle could have been his second wife.

Illinois newspaper advertisements proved that there was passenger service between Chicago and Urbana at the time of the trial but it is unlikely that passenger's names were recorded. If they were, this information is probably lost.

[7] Spink vs. Chiniquy, Defence Costs, October Term, 1856, Champaign Circuit Court, Names of Defence Witnesses, October, 1856, Champaign Circuit Court, Plaintiff request to clerk of Circuit Court, Urbana, for subpoenas, April 2, 1856, Plaintiff request to clerk of Kankakee County Circuit Court, for subpoenas, May Term, 1855, Plaintiff Costs, May term, 1856, Champaign Circuit Court

[8] "Prayer or Prophecy", *Chicago Daily Tribune*, November 1, 1887, p. 9, *Chicago Tribune*, July 29, 1893, p. 4, Plat Record, Rosehill Cemetery, Chicago. *Fifty Years* reported that Miss Moffat and Narcisse Terrien gave no testimony in court. As they were responsible for the end of the suit however, it is understandable that they would be included in Chiniquy's expense summary.

[9] *Fifty Years*, p.660, 661, Our Constitution (Urbana, Illinois), October 25, 1856, p. 2, *Urbana Union*, October 23, 1856, p. 3.

The October 23rd *Urbana Union* also reported that, "Mr. Lincoln addressed a large audience at the Court House on Monday evening in usual argumentative style" (Figure 6) and added that Messrs Lincoln, Swett, and Hogg addressed a meeting in West Urbana on Tuesday evening. Chiniquy reported that he and his lawyers arrived at court on Monday, October 20th but he didn't say what day the case was settled. He stated that the court adjourned at ten p.m. on what would seem to have been Monday evening. Does the *Union* story show that Charles Chiniquy was wrong because Lincoln could not have been in court acting for him and also giving a political speech at the same time?

One logical explanation for this apparent tension between what Charles Chiniquy said, backed up in other parts of this drama by Philomene Moffat / Schwartz, and what the newspaper reported, is that Philomene Moffat actually traveled on the evening of Tuesday October 21st, arriving in the early morning of Wednesday, October 22nd, instead of the night earlier. The dismissal of the case would then have happened on Wednesday, October 22nd.

Reading Chiniquy's account, it appears that there was only one day of court testimony, which occurred on the day they arrived. Before the witnesses were called however, he reported that the jury had to be selected and sworn. Although he doesn't specifically mention it, this could have taken a day to accomplish as Chiniquy's defence team would have not wanted to repeat the jury selection mistake that resulted in the deadlock at the first trial at Urbana (see footnote 11 below).

[10] Abraham Lincoln to A. Jonas, Urbana, October 21, 1856, Abraham Lincoln Papers, Library of Congress, Series 4, Box 2, Folder 1855

[11] *Lincoln Day by Day*, Volume 2, p. 181.

If the October 21st Lincoln letter to Jonas refered to Spink vs. Chiniquy, then this would tend to show that the case still hadn't been settled by October 21st.

After a day of wrangling in court Monday regarding the jury, it is possible that Lincoln could have then delivered a speech at the courthouse in the evening. If the day of court testimony was Tuesday, beginning in the morning with Lebel's perjury, Lincoln could have done the cross-examination and the other more difficult work. Leaving some of the evening court labors to Chiniquy's original lawyers, Messrs Osgood and Paddock, he could have spent an hour or two in West Urbana, returning to the hotel that night to take part in the meeting with Chiniquy and the other lawyers. Miss Moffat and Narcisse Terrien would then have arrived early the next morning, Wednesday, to un-hobble Mr. Lincoln.

A book on the daily activities of Abraham Lincoln seems to rule this out however. The entry in *Lincoln Day by Day* for October 20, 1956 reads, "*Urbana*. Lincoln writes court order dismissing Spink *v.* Chiniquy by agreement. DLC-*HW*". There is no date on either document except the year 1856 however, so there is no proof they were written on October 20th from the sources that is cited.

The Court orders dismissing Spink vs. Chiniquy are held at the Herndon Weik Collection, Library of Congress and by the Illinois Historical Survey, University of Illinois at Urbana-Champaign. The two copies are essentially the same with only a slight difference in wording. It is understandable that there would be two copies of the agreement as both parties in the lawsuit would undoubtedly want one.

[12] Albert Woldman, *Lawyer Lincoln*, (Houghton Mifflin Company, 1936), p. 97, *Fifty Years*, p.623, 654-661.

Chiniquy seems to have made a small error regarding the time that Abraham Lincoln was his lawyer. He stated that it was more than a year but according to the dates in his account and other sources, it was between eleven and twelve months from the time he first hired him until the case was dismissed. It was therefore just under a year instead of more than a year. This mistake was found in a number of editions of the autobiography. There also was an obviously typo in the 3rd edition, of *Fifty Years*, 1886, Craig & Barlow, where it stated that David Davis was Vice President of the United States at the time he was the judge of Spink vs. Chiniquy in 1856, p. 654. Interestingly, it was not found in the first or second editions or later editions like the 10th, 13th or 42nd.

[13] Henry Clay Whitney's *Life on the Circuit with Lincoln*, (The Caxton Printers, Ltd, 1940), p. 74

[14] The People vs. Peter Spink, Indictment for perjury, Iroquois Circuit Court, April 26, 1855, The People vs. Peter Spink, Bill for perjury, Iroquois Circuit Court, April 27, 1855, Grand Jury document: specific accusation ofperjury against Peter Spink, February 6, 1854, Alonzo Rothschild, *Honest Abe*, (Houghton Mifflin Company, 1917), p. 155-158, *Life on the Circuit with Lincoln*, p. 74, 75, *Urbana Union*, May 29, 1856, p. 3.

Author Alonzo Rothschild, who also discussed the case in his book, Honest Abe, commented on the attention the case and participants received. He stated that the slander suit was of "wide repute", calling Spink "a prominent citizen of L'Erable" and Chiniquy "the famous priest of St. Anne". No unabashed admirer of the ex-priest, he cautioned that Chiniquy's account of the case differed "materially, at important points, from the official court records". In the general manner of Chiniquy's critics however, he provided no specific examples. Rothschild also called Chiniquy's narrative "overcharged, not to say hysterical" then proceeded to use portions of it, mostly in his own words, as a truthful account of how the legal struggle unfolded.

He disagreed with Chiniquy regarding the result of the trial in the spring of 1856. He stated that the reason the jury was discharged without rendering a verdict was that one juror was dismissed because his child was sick and Spink's side refused to proceed with eleven jurors. He evidently got this version of events from Whitney's

Life on the Circuit with Lincoln. On this point, Whitney is opposed by the Urbana Union, as well as Chiniquy. The May 28th, 1856 edition of this newspaper reported of the trial, "After that much time spent, the jury failed to find a verdict". There was nothing reported about the sick child of a juror.

Alonzo Rothschild did agree with Chiniquy when he said the trial was well under way in the October, 1856 term when the suit was ended by an agreement, written by Lincoln personally. Regarding the agreement dismissing the case, Rothschild stated "By its terms Chiniquy's charges against Spink were withdrawn". A careful reading of the agreement though, shows that Chiniquy did not withdraw any charges, he denied he ever made any. Rothschild acknowledged that Chiniquy believed that Bishop O'Regan was the one behind Spink's prosecution of him but Rothschild evidently was unconvinced of this.

Professor Richard Lougheed agreed with Chiniquy's assertion that a hung jury in the spring court term of 1856 occasioned another trial in the fall. Lougheed also reported that the fall court action again resulted in a deadlock that was solved by agreement. He didn't disclose what evidence showed that there had been a second deadlock. As well, he stated that Chiniquy took back his original accusations as hearsay. The wording of the agreement dismissing the case however, shows this is not what happened.

[15] Richard Lougheed, "The Controversial Conversion of Charles Chiniquy", Diss. Ph.D., University of Montreal, 1993, p. 160-162

[16] Carl Sandburg, *Abraham Lincoln The Prairie Years*, (Harcourt, Brace and Co Ltd, 1926), Volume II, p. 52, 53. Sandburg stated that:

Lincoln, and Leonard Swett took the defence of Father Chiniquy, a French Catholic priest in Kankakee County, who was accused by one of his parishioners, Peter Spink, of falsely accusing Spink of perjury. Father Chiniquy said he could prove his case; he would contest to the last. So a change of venue was taken to Champaign County, where there came to the courthouse in Urbana hundreds of principals, lawyers, witnesses, onlookers, with camp outfits, musicians, parrots, dogs, and changes of clothing. The hotels of Urbana were filled and the overflow slept in tents. The trial dragged on for weeks, and finally the jury went out, and came back unable to agree on a verdict.

> Again, at the next term of court, the case was to be called. Hundreds of people had again arrived with camp outfits, musicians, parrots, dogs, and changes of clothing, to hear the testimony and gossip. Lincoln had between-times been at work on a peaceable settlement, and as the gossips and onlookers were getting ready to hear again all the ins and outs of the scandal, he brought into court a paper that wiped the case off the books. It read: "Peter Spink *vs.* Charles Chiniquy. This day came the parties and the defendant denies that he has ever charged, or believed the plaintiff to be guilty of perjury; that whatever he has said from which such a charge could be inferred, he said on the information of others, protesting his own disbelief in the charge; and that he now disclaims any belief in the truth of said charge against said plaintiff." And they split the court costs and paid their lawyers and everybody went home.

[17] Spink vs. Chiniquy, Defence Costs (list), October Term, 1856, Champaign Circuit Court, Names of Defence Witnesses, October, Champaign Circuit Court, Plaintiff Costs, October Term, 1856, Champaign Circuit Court

[18] *Fifty Years*, p. 661-663. Figure 11 is a reproduction of the promissory note that appeared in *Fifty Years*. *Fifty Years* did not reproduce it exactly but instead, broke up the lines and re-arranged them to fit the page of the book. The original Urbana promissory note, dated May 23, 1856, is held by the Illinois Historical Survey, University of Illinois at Urbana-Champaign.

The agreement that ended the legal struggle specified that each side would pay their own costs. If this agreement had been made before the two sides came to court, then each side would know that they were paying their own costs before they got there. Why then would either party bring the accounts of these costs to be recorded? If each side was paying its own costs, then it would not be the court's business or the business of either party as to what each side's expenses were.

The creation of these lists of costs do make sense if, as Chiniquy said, Spink withdrew his suit after court testimony had been given the day before. Spink's lawyers would have contacted Lincoln, declaring that they wished to settle. Negotiating the agreement would have been expected to take some time and when the parties started negotiations, it wouldn't be known what the final terms would be and who would be paying what. It therefore would make sense for each side to total their costs, either before or at the time of the negotiations.

According to *Fifty Years*, after the trial had ended, a large group of people in Urbana searched the city for the perjured priests in an attempt to punish them for what they had tried to do to Chiniquy, but the priests had escaped. The people blamed Charles Chiniquy for letting them get away but he felt that they had been punished enough by the exposure of their plot.

[19] *Fifty Years*, p. 662-664

[20] *Fifty Years*, p. 667, 3rd edition, 1886, 10th edition, 1887, 13th edition, 1889, *Chicago Tribune*, July 29, 1893, p. 4. American House was also known as the Gere or Champaign House and the Pennsylvania House had been previously known as Urbana House. Unfortunately the whereabouts of either hotel register for this time period is unknown, although the Champaign County Historical Archives holds the register for the American House that contains entries from 1855, that include Lincoln's name.

[21] *The Trial of John Surratt*, p. 1118

Chapter 3 Charles Chiniquy: A Remarkable Life

[1] Charles Chiniquy, *Fifty Years In The Church Of Rome*, (Craig and Barlow, 1886, 3rd edition), p. 630, 631. The Catholic priest of the French Canadian, St. Louis Church of Chicago who was dismissed and sent from the diocese of Chicago for no

reason was Rev. Lemaire. The parsonage was sold for $1,200.00 and the church the French had built was rented for $2,000.00 per year to others.

[2] *Fifty Years*, p. 631-638, Richard Lougheed, "The Controversial Conversion of Charles Chiniquy", Diss. Ph.D., University of Montreal, 1993, p. 161, 162.

Among other things, the delegation asked O'Regan if Chiniquy had been interdicted and if so, why? The bishop replied that he had suspended him on the 19th of August because of insubordination. When questioned further, he admitted that Chiniquy was one of his best priests and that to his knowledge, no accusation of immorality against him had been proven to be true. O'Regan also stated that another reason he wanted the reassignment was to stop the law suit of Peter Spink, although he couldn't promise it would be. He stated that if Chiniquy had said mass since the 19th, then he was irregular and only the Pope could restore him to regular functions as a priest.

Although the delegation told the bishop that their priest had said mass since he was supposedly suspended and therefore would need to go to the Roman Pontiff to be restored, the bishop ordered him to come to Chicago to get his next assignment as priest in the diocese. This showed, according to Charles Chiniquy, that he hadn't been suspended at all. The fact that O'Regan acknowledged that no accusation against Chiniquy had been proved to be true, also showed the priest hadn't been suspended according to *Fifty Years*.

As noted earlier, Chiniquy biographer Richard Lougheed provided support for Charles Chinquy's allegations that O'Regan was secretly backing Spink's lawsuit against him in an attempt to ruin the priest, stating that the bishop, "wanted to relocate Chiniquy, in part, to stop the court case. If the priest had moved the case would likely have been won by Spink."

[3] *Fifty Years*, p. 640-661, 738-743, *Chicago Daily Democrat*, May 1, 1856, p. 3, (this edition is dated Friday morning, May 1, 1856, but this is clearly the wrong date. The internal evidence shows that it undoubtedly was published in the spring of 1857. It in all likelyhood was a May 1st issue as May 1, 1857 was a Friday. A catalog entry note pertaining to this title at the Chicago History Museum, which hold this microfilm reel, noted that there was frequent misdating), "Schism in the Roman Catholic Church of Chicago; Excommunication of Father Chiniquy, The Great Apostle of Temperance", *New York Times*, October 11, 1856, p. 3, "Trouble Among the Catholics in Illinois", *New York Times*, November 1, 1856, p. 3, *The National Era*, (Washington D.C.), June 11, 1857.

The *National Era* reported on a lawsuit between a bishop and Catholic trustees in New York State regarding church property, that it asserted, "bears directly on the point in issue between Bishop O'Regan, of the Chicago diocese, and Father Chiniquy, the good priest of St, Anne's. whom the Bishop has suspended."

Chiniquy's old friends were two Canadian priests: Rev. Isaac Desaulnier, a former schoolmate and Rev. Brassard, one of Chiniquy's teachers and benefactors at the college of Nicolet. Over several days, they worked out a compromise offer for Bishop O'Regan. Brassard would take Rev. Chiniquy's place as pastor of St. Anne and Chiniquy would be his vicar. Chiniquy stated that he and the colonists would accept this agreement, "on that condition the bishop would withdraw his so-called sentence, give back to the French Canadians of Chicago the church he had taken away from them, put a French-speaking priest at the head of the congregation, and forget and forgive what he might consider our irregular conduct towards him"

Desaulnier went to Chicago with the offer but the next day, Brassard and Chiniquy were summoned to the city as well. There they learned that Bishop O'Regan would not agree to the compromise and wanted Desaulnier to take over as pastor at St. Anne. Chiniquy refused to allow this and he returned to the colony.

[4] *Fifty Years*, p. 747-757, *The Chicago Daily Tribune*, January 26,1857, p. 2, December 2, 1858, p. 1, December 3, 1858, p. 1, 2.

The protest of the French Canadian Catholics of Chicago against the bishop's actions, published in the January 26th, 1857 edition of the *Chicago Daily Tribune*, was reproduced essentially word for word in *Fifty Years*.

The *Chicago Tribune* at this time evidently was also known as the *Chicago Daily Tribune* and the *Chicago Press and Tribune*. Charles Chiniquy did receive a good deal of favourable press from the *Chicago Tribune* but the *Tribune* was not an untiring cheerleader of the Apostle of Temperance. The *Tribune* took great issue with Chiniquy on the issue of how the people of Kankakee voted in the fall of 1858, stating that Chiniquy and his people had supported Douglas, slavery and the Democratic ticket. In a letter in his defence, Chiniquy agreed that the Tribune had supported him and expressed his thanks for this. He also denied that he had thrown his support to any party, saying that a preacher of the gospel must not do so. Chiniquy also publicly declared that he was against slavery and its extension.

[5] "Dispute Between Bishop O'Regan and the French", *The Chicago Daily Tribune*, January 27, 1857, p. 2, "The Church Property Question - Father Chiniquy and Bishop O'Regan", *The Chicago Daily Tribune*, March 31, 1857, p. 2, *Notre Dame de Chicago, 1887-1937: a history of Notre Dame parish, preceded by an historical sketch of the work of the early French missionaries in the central states--prepared for the occasion of the fiftieth anniversary of the erection of Notre Dame Church*, (The Fathers of the Blessed Sacrament, 1937), p. 51-55, *The Chicago Daily Tribune*, January 26,1857, p. 2, *The Catholic Church in Chicago*, 1673 – 1871, (Loyola University Press, 1921), p. 149, 150. The *Catholic Church in Chicago* account supports what the *Notre Dame De Chicago* stated regarding the Church of St. Louis.

[6] *Notre Dame De Chicago*, p. 55-57, "French Catholic Meeting in Chicago", *The Chicago Tribune*, January 26, 1857, p. 2, *A History of Chicago from the Earliest Period to the Present Time*, (A. T. Andreas, Publisher, 1884), Volume 1, p. 296, 297, *Fifty Years*, p. 603, 631, 632, "The Church Property Question", *Chicago Daily Tribune*, April 13, 1857, p. 2, (Figure 16), "Who Shall Decide When Doctors Disagree", *Chicago Daily Tribune*, April 15, 1857, p. 1.

"The Church Property Question" included a letter written by Charles Chiniquy in which he detailed the opposition O'Regan had to the clause pertaining to the deed of the colony's church property, "for the use and benefit of the Catholics of St. Anne".

This clause, according to Chiniquy, curtailed O'Regan's ability "to sell our property and go and eat it where he likes (as he has done with the French of Chicago)".

A History of Chicago from the Earliest Period to the Present Time, by A. T. Andreas, closely supports what Chiniquy said in *Fifty Years* as well as the account of the French in the January 26th, 1857 *Chicago Tribune*, though there are some time discrepancies. The account in the *History of Chicago* states that in return for paying for the lot for their church, the French were promised that St. Louis church would "remain a French Catholic Church, and should have a French priest, or the money should be refunded" as the *Tribune* account asserted.

In "Who Shall Decide When Doctors Disagree", the *Tribune* published a letter from Rev. Dillon a couple of days later, disputing what Chiniquy had stated in his letter.

The official Catholic history entitled, *Notre Dame De Chicago*, stated that the St. Louis Church was built on a lot on Clark Street, between Adams and Jackson. It detailed that the French church cost $3,000.00 to build, of which $2,000.00 was donated by P.F. Rofinot. It also reported that he was the chairman of the committee in charge of the financial affairs of the church. P.F. Rofinot undoubtedly was the same man who had presided over the early 1857 meeting of French Canadian Catholics in Chicago, whose vigorous protest about O'Regan's actions were published in the *Chicago Tribune*.

When comparing the official Catholic account of what happened with the one in the *Tribune*, the dates of events in the two versions don't match but the accounts of what transpired are quite similar.

For instance, the *Notre Dame De Chicago* account claimed that the St. Louis Church was moved some time after the month of May, 1858, on the orders of Bishop O'Regan. The account of the French Catholics in the January 26, 1857 edition of the *Tribune* however, stated that the church had already been moved. It seems highly unlikely that a large group of citizens would claim, in a major newspaper of their city, that a particular building in that city had been moved from one lot of the city to another, when it had not been. If this was not true, it would have been very easy to make them all look like they were liars or laboring under delusions. The chronology published in the *Chicago Tribune* therefore has to be preferred at this point.

Notre Dame De Chicago stated that when the pews of the St. Louis Church were sold in May, 1858, there was not enough money to meet expenses. (The sale undoubtedly occurred at an earlier date). The Catholic account reported that the church did not own the lot it was on and the bishop wanted it moved because he didn't wish the church to be on a leased lot. His plan was to install it on a couple of lots he had purchased. At the same time, apparently not knowing about the bishop's designs for the church, a committee made up of a number of men, including the priest and P.F. Rofinot, planned to buy some other city lots to put the church on. The committee collected money from the French congregation to buy the lots. This was done after Bishop O'Regan had promised that the church would continue as a French Catholic Church with a French priest, as was also reported in the January 26th *Tribune* account. The money collected however, was only enough to cover a quarter of the cost of the land. An agreement was made to pay the balance owed for the lots in three annual payments.

Meanwhile, according to *Notre Dame De Chicago*, O'Regan had the church put on rollers so it could be moved to the lots he owned. He also told the French priest that he was silenced. The priest gave the money he had collected to the committee and left Chicago. Discovering the church on rollers, members of the committee went to see the bishop who told them they would not be able to move the church onto their lots until they brought the deed to the land they were buying to him, made out in his name. P.F. Rofinot protested, saying it would be impossible to do this as they only had enough money for the down payment but O'Regan refused to change his mind. Rofinot consulted with his lawyer about suing the bishop but was advised that the prelate would win a court challenge.

According to *Notre Dame De Chicago* account, after dealing with the French Canadian delegation, O'Regan then had the St. Louis Church moved to his lots. The account also stated, "In order to make sure that the French should not occupy the pews for which they had paid on the first Sunday in May, the Bishop had the church raised some four feet from the ground." The same source reported that after about half a year, Rev. John Waldron occupied the church, announcing "that he wanted to establish peace; but he did not succeed."

[7] *A History of the Parishes of the Archdiocese of Chicago*, (Archdiocese of Chicago, 1980), p. 663, *Notre Dame De Chicago*, p. 59, "The Chiniquy Calumnies", *Chicago Tribune*, June 11, 1857, p. 2. The Catholic account, *A History of the Parishes of the Archdiocese of Chicago*, stated:

> Father Waldron, an Irish priest, could not speak French. According to parish legend, he preached sermons in Gaelic, much to the dismay of both French and English-speaking members of St. Louis Church! The French soon withdrew from the parish with the result that St. Louis Church became predominantly Irish.

This is also supported in *Notre Dame De Chicago*. It stated that James A. Dugan, who became Bishop of Chicago in early 1859, tried to help the French:

> Bishop Duggan showed a great sympathy for the French Catholics. He earnestly tried to repair the damage done to the St. Louis congregation; but not able to find a French priest, he sent Father Waldron, an Irish priest unable to speak French to try to gather up the French to their Church. Although Father Waldron was a kind and conciliatory priest he did not succeed to make them forget. The French Canadians unable to converse with their pastor in their own tongue scattered around the west side and were attending the neighboring churches where they happened to roam. In the meantime, business and commerce had invaded the locality where they had been living and they slowly moved west across the river. For a long time they attended Mass at St. Patrick's like exiled wanderers not knowing where to rest.

The public complaints against O'Regan evidently were many and included what the mystery writer called "notorious calumnies" published in Chicago against him.

[8] "The Chiniquy Calumnies", *Chicago Tribune,* June 11, 1857, p. 2, "The Chiniquy Controversy", *Chicago Tribune,* June 22, 1857, p. 2.

The shy correspondent reported on a "magnificent" religious celebration in Bourbonnais Grove, Kankakee County:

> It was designed as a public demonstration by the Canadians, in this State, against the schism of Chiniquy, as a compliment to the Bishop of Chicago, and to the Very Rev. W. Desaulniers, whose zeal and success in putting down that schism, won for him, in union with the Bishop, the love of all good men and the ire of every friend of irreligion.

The author of this letter wrote admiringly of the bishop's speech on Chiniquy, stating that "Now, for the first time, he publicly denounced this miserable noisy schism, and exposed its character and manifold calumnies."

It could be asked though, why there would need to be a demonstration against the schism of Chiniquy, if the Very Rev. W. Desaulniers, along with O'Regan, had already successfully put it down though? Why would the bishop need to publicly denounce the "miserable noisy schism", if Chiniquy and his people had already been crushed? Even hostile biographers agree that the movement that Rev. Chiniquy headed was not successfully "put down".

According to this anonymous pro-O'Regan correspondent, who detailed the prelate's supposed successful visit to Bourbonnais Grove, the bishop of Chicago was a man who could do no wrong and his enemies could do no right. He stated that "His success is certain, for his course is firm and wise, and guarded." The accounts of O'Regan's doings, including official Catholic sources, agree with Chiniquy's statements of the bishop's dictatorial actions. His actions were not wise and he ultimately was not successful. The letter also stated that the man who honored O'Regan with a welcome address on his arrival at the railroad depot at Kankakee was P. Spink of L'Erable. This was Peter Spink, the same man who, according to *Fifty Years*, sued Charles Chiniquy at the bishop's urgings.

According to Gendron's letter, the people of Bourbonnais, who evidently didn't support Rev. Desaulniers, were more concerned about paying for practical things like needed work on public buildings in the community and the like. The gift given to Desaulniers was a silver plate.

[9] "The Chiniquy Calumnies", *Chicago Tribune,* June 11, 1857, p. 2, "The Chiniquy Controversy", *Chicago Tribune,* June 18, 1857, p. 2, *Notre Dame De Chicago*, p. 55, John G. Shea, *History of the Catholic Church in the United States,* (The Mershon Company Press, 1892), p. 617, *The Catholic Church in Chicago*, 1673 – 1871, p. 178.

The name of the writer of this public letter supporting O'Regan was not revealed. Evidently it was because if it had been revealed, it would be clear that this person was not an unbiased eyewitness but someone very close to the bishop. In light of the evidence, the view that O'Regan's actions were only right and proper is clearly a view held only by the author of this letter and the bishop and his few supporters.

Catholic sources did their best to put O'Regan's performance in a positive light but had to admit that his administration was characterized by struggles with his priests. Charles Chiniquy undoubtedly was one of his main opponents. *Notre Dame De Chicago* stated that "Despite the purity of his intentions, Bishop O'Regan was not by nature fitted to the task of taking tactfully in hand and administering with success the delicate affairs of a young and unsettled diocese of western America" It stated that O'Regan was involved in a couple of serious problems, one of which was the "Chiniquy schism", traces of which still remained at the date of writing (1937). Another source stated:

> Bishop O'Regan introduced system into the affairs of the diocese and did much to restore discipline, but his methods excited discontent, which was fostered by many. A number of priests were the nucleus of the trouble, but he firmly delivered his diocese from them.

Richard Lougheed disclosed that O'Regan, the "Irish tyrant", received a steady stream of criticism from both Protestants and Catholics through the *Chicago Tribune*. "As anonymous Catholic priests with inside knowledge publicly decried the lack of accountability and of 'Americanism'on the part of their leader, Bishop O'Regan was, in fact, forced out of office." This agrees with Chiniquy's account, although Lougheed said that O'Regan went to Rome to ask to be relieved of his position and Chiniquy stated that he was ordered there and stripped of his office. As Lougheed said however, O'Regan ultimately was forced from office.

The Catholic Church in Chicago account supports what the *Notre Dame De Chicago* stated regarding Bishop O'Regan's difficulties including the Chiniquy schism although the *Catholic Church in Chicago* declared that the schism was substantially healed through the bishop's earnest efforts.

[10] Richard Lougheed, *The Controversial Conversion of Charles Chiniquy*, (Clements Academic, 2008), p. 53-55, *Fifty Years*, p. 757-763, 776, *Notre Dame De Chicago*, p. 55, *Chicago Tribune*, August 25, 1857, p. 1, 2.

Bishop Bourget stated that he had interdicted the Apostle of Temperance for good reason on Sept. 27th, 1851.

The *Notre Dame De Chicago* account also disclosed that the May 10th, 1900 edition of the Catholic publication, *The New World*, reported that O'Regan had desired to anglicize the St. Louis Church - apparently something he actually succeed at. After the official Catholic reviews of the bishop's performance, is easy to see how it could be concluded that O'Regan's natural disposition made it difficult for him to "tactfully" deal with the affairs of the diocese, despite the "purity of his intentions".

[11] *Fifty Years*, p. 757-763, 776, *The National Cyclopaedia Of American Biography*, (J.T. White, 1898), Volume 9, p. 79, *Chicago Daily Democrat*, May 1, 1856, p. 3, (misdated, correct date likely May 1, 1857), *Chicago Tribune*, Jan 26, 1857, p. 2, Jan 27, 1857, p. 2, Mar. 31, 1857, p. 2, April 13, 1857, p. 2, August 25, 1857, p 1, 2, "Progress

of Liberty of Conscience in the Roman Catholic", *Chicago Daily Tribune*, November 25, 1857, p. 2. The *Chicago Tribune* was also called the *Chicago Daily Tribune*.

O'Regan was made bishop of the extinct diocese of Dora. *The National Cyclopedia of American Biography* reported that when O'Regan died in London, England, he left "quite a fortune". It could be asked where did the humble bishop get this wealth from? Numerous articles in Chicago newspapers show that Charles Chiniquy was telling the truth about this prelate, including the general protest of Catholics against the bishop of Chicago.

In the November 25, 1857, edition of the *Chicago Daily Tribune*, 300 people of St. Anne signed a letter in which they decried the effort by two Catholic priests, Mailloux and Lapointe, to induce a man named Jean Baptiste Belanger to start a lawsuit against Charles Chiniquy and themselves. Belanger said he was offered $3,000.00 to do so.

[12] *Fifty Years* p. 777-785, *Chicago Daily Democrat*, March 31, 1858, p. 1, *Fifty Years*, p. 783. Charles Chiniquy reported that on Palm Sunday, March 27th, Rev. Dunn announced the peace between Chiniquy, his people and the Bishop Smith but he was off by a day, as Sunday was March 28th.

[13] *Fifty Years*, p. 786-803

[14] *The Times*, January 17, 1899, p. 10, *Atlas of Kankakee Co*, (J. H. Beers & Co., 1883), p.151, *United States Biographical Dictionary and Portrait Gallery of Eminent and Self-Made Men*, (American Biographical Publishing Company, 1876), Volume II, p. 721, *Appleton's Cylopedia of American Biography*, (D. Appleton and Company, 1901, republished by Gale Research Company, 1968), Volume 7, p. 58, *Fifty Years* p. 803-817, Bessie L. Pierce, A History Of Chicago, (Alfred A. Knopf, 1940), p.360, *The National Cyclopaedia Of American Biography*, (J.T. White, 1898), Volume IX, p. 80, *History of the Catholic Church in the United States*, p. 623, 624, *A History of the Parishes of the Archdiocese of Chicago*, p. 583. According to *Fifty Years*, French Canadian adults, many of whom were illiterate, began to learn to read so they could study the Scriptures for themselves, often helped by their children who had been educated in the colony's school.

As noted earlier, historian Bessie Pierce confirmed the devastating attacks on Duggan by Chiniquy. Several biographical sources confirm that Bishop Duggan later was institutionalized in St. Louis after going insane.

[15] *Fifty Years*, p. 818-820, *The Dictionary of Canadian Biography*, (University of Toronto Press, 1990), Volume XII, 1891 to 1900, p. 191, 192, *New York Times*, January 17, 1899, p. 1, *The Christian Recorder*, October 26, 1872, "French Canadian Protestants in Chicago", *Chicago Press and Tribune*, August 13, 1860, p. 4.

The *Christian Recorder* reported that Father Gavazzi also visited Charles Chiniquy at St. Anne. According to the *Tribune*, the "semi-editor" of the Boston *Recorder* was in Chicago and reported that since the collision between Chiniquy and the bishop of Chicago, the French in the city, numbering 10,000, are open for Protestant evangelization.

[16] *Fifty Years*, p. 820, 821, *The Times* (London), November 5, 1860, p. 3, Rev. Alexander F. Kemp, The Rev. C. Chiniquy, The Presbytery of Chicago and the Canada Presbyterian Church, (Montreal, 1893), p. 18, "The Chiniquy Mission", *New York Times*, November 12, 1859, p. 1, "The Condition of Father Chiniquy and his Flock", *Chicago Tribune*, September 3, 1859, p. 2.

Chiniquy and his people faced great financial problems with crop failures late in the 1850s and appealed for help from Christians in eastern United States. Help was received although there were critics who said that there were really no hardships in the Kankakee area and Chiniquy and company were exaggerating the problems. Outsiders like J.W. Paillard and T. N. Haskell visited and commented on the conditions that Chiniquy and the colonists were experiencing. Reporting on the front page of the *New York Times* and page two of the *Chicago Tribune*, respectively, they stated that the difficulties were real and help was needed.

An advertisement in the November 5, 1860 issue of the *Times* reported that Charles Chiniquy would be speaking at Exeter-hall, London and stated that more than 6,000 French Canadians had followed Chiniquy out of the Church of Rome. It also stated that he would be accepting donations to fund a college to train French ministers of the gospel.

Kemp stated that he felt that Chiniquy was, "entitled to be regarded as a brother in Christ by the Protestant Churches of Christendom. What the Synod of the Canada Presbyterian Church may do at its approaching meeting it is not for me to say, but I do hope that it will see it to be the path of duty to hold out the hand of fellowship to Pastor Chiniquy and his people."

[17] *Fifty Years*, p. 821-830, *The Dictionary of Canadian Biography*, p. 192, *The Times*, January 17, 1899, p. 10, "A Former French Catholic Priest", *New York Times*, January 19, 1882, p. 2, *The Times*, November 5, 1860, p. 3.

In the article, "A Former French Catholic Priest", the *New York Times* reported that Charles Chiniquy was known as the "Canadian Luther"and an advertisement in the November 5, 1860 issue of the *Times* of London called him the Luther of America. Although in combating Protestants and their beliefs, Charles Chiniquy generally had not used the violent methods Paul had employed in persecuting Christians.

[18] Carl Russell Fish, "Lincoln And Catholicism," *The American Historical Review*, 29, 1924, p. 723, 2 Corinthians 11: 24, 25, *Fifty Years*, p. 823-828, *Forty Years in the Church of Christ*, (Fleming H. Revell Company, 1900), p. 415, Richard Lougheed, *The Controversial Conversion of Charles Chiniquy*, (Clements Academic, 2008), p. 295. In his book, *The Controversial Conversion of Charles Chiniquy*, Lougheed stated "His writings, including tracts, have sold well over one million copies". The Apostle Paul wrote regarding his trials, "Of the Jews five times received I forty stripes save one. Thrice was I beaten with rods, once was I stoned, thrice I suffered shipwreck, a night and a day I have been in the deep".

[19] *The Times*, January 17, 1899, p. 10, "Assault on a Preacher", *New York Times*, August 3, 1873, p. 3

[20] *Fifty Years*, p. 827, 828, "Father Chiniquy Attacked by a Mob", *Chicago Daily Tribune*, June 20, 1884, p. 12, *Chicago Daily Tribune*, August 8, 1891, p. 2, "Lively Riot in Montreal", *New York Times*, February 25, 1875, p. 2, "Excitement in Montreal, the trouble which Mr. Chiniquy's lectures have caused", *New York Times*, November 13, 1884, p. 1, "Canadians Still Excited, Englishmen patrolling the streets of Montreal", *New York Times*, November 21, 1885, p. 1, "Disorderly Students", *New York Times*, November 8, 1884, p. 8, "Father Chiniquy Mobbed, the Roman Catholics of Montreal prevent him for lecturing", *New York Times*, November 7, 1884, p. 5, "Excitement About Religion, a church edifice attacked by a mob - the building partially destroyed – retaliation anticipated – the police on the alert", *Chicago Tribune*, March 2, 1864, p. 2, Father Chiniquy To Mgr. Lynch, Archbishop of Toronto, June 22, 1884, "Refused The Books", *Boston Daily Globe*, February 7, 1892, p. 4.

Rev. Chiniquy reported on attacks made on him in Québec:

The 17th of June, 1884, after I had preached in Quebec, on the text: 'What would I do to have Eternal Life,' a mob of more than 1,500 Roman Catholics, led by two priests, broke the windows of the church, and attacked me with stones, with the evident object to kill me. More than one hundred stones struck me, and I would surely have been killed there, had I not had, providentially, two heavy overcoats which I put, one around my head, and the other around my shoulders. Notwithstanding that protection, I was so much bruised and wounded from head to feet, that I had to spend the three following weeks on a bed of suffering, between life and death. A young friend, Zotque Lefebre, who had heroically put himself between my would-be-assassin and me, escaped only after receiving six bleeding wounds in the face.

The same year, 1884, in the month of November, I was attacked with stones and struck several times, when preaching and in coming out from the church in the city of Montreal. Numbers of policemen and other friends who came to my rescue were wounded, my life was saved only by an organization of a thousand young men, who, under the name of Protestant Guard, wrenched me from the hands of the would-be murderers.

The 1884 *Tribune* account confirmed what Chiniquy said in *Fifty Years* about what happened to him at Antigonish, Nova Scotia. The 1891 *Tribune* account detailed how a mob of Catholics in Escanaba, Michigan forced at least a temporary end to Chiniquy's lectures there, although his supporters asked for troops to protect him.

The *Chicago Tribune* reported on Catholic interference when Chiniquy spoke in Montreal early in 1870, doing so on the front page of the January 11th issue and the January 22nd issue, p. 3. The February 7, 1892 issue of the *Boston Daily Globe* reported how officials of the Haverhill, Massachusetts public library refused to accept a gift from a local donor of books written by Charles Chiniquy, saying that they didn't allow sectarian books in even though the library already held one of Chiniquy's books.

[21] *Fifty Years*, p. 828, "The Controversial Conversion of Charles Chiniquy", Diss. p. 207.

Chiniquy biographer, Richard Lougheed, confirmed the last part of his statement:

"Chiniquy sued an Oblate priest, Father Auguste Brunet, for libel. The visiting missionary had apparently repeated the old accusation that Chiniquy had burned the Bourbonnais church in 1854. A prolonged court case with appeals ran from December 1858 until April 1860. In the end, Brunet lost and was given a long prison sentence, having refused the alternative of paying a fine. After four months, local Catholics, outraged at the injustice, broke into the prison and smuggled him across the Canadian border."

[22] *Atlas of Kankakee County*, Ill., (J.H. Beers & Co., 1883), p. 151, *The Kankakee Daily Gazette*, January 17,1899, p. 3, Charles Chiniquy et al vs. the Catholic Bishop of Chicago, Supreme Court of the State of Illinois, Third Grand Division, April Term, 1866, "Verdict for Father Chiniquy", *Chicago Press and Tribune*, January 23, 1860, p. 4. "Father Chiniquy In Durance", *Chicago Tribune*, April 24, 1867, p. 2.

The *Press and Tribune* evidently misspelled Brunet's name, calling him Burnett. In 1867, the *Chicago Tribune* reproduced a letter by Chiniquy in which he reported that through the efforts of the Church of Rome, he had been brought, as if he was a criminal, to face prosecution before the court at Kankakee.

[24] *Fifty Years*, p. 828, *The Daily Witness*, March 10, 1892, p. 4, "Check To Romanist Aggression", *New York Times*, November 12, 1879, p. 5, "The Limits of Priestly Power", *Brooklyn Eagle*, November 11, 1879, p. 2, *Boston Daily Globe*, May 14, 1888, p. 4, Psalm 90:10, *Dictionary of Canadian Biography*, (University of Toronto Press, 1990), Volume XII, 1891 to 1900, p.192, "Four Score Years Old", *Chicago Daily Tribune*, July 31, 1889, p. 1, *The Christian Recorder*, October 28, 1875.

The *Brooklyn Eagle* also reported the story of the Catholic businessman in Massachusetts who was put out of business because he had attended a lecture by Chiniquy and evidently refused to apologize for doing so. The *Christian Recorder* reported that for publishing Chiniquy's discourses and, apparently, for protesting the spirit of persecution that the ex-priest had to deal with, the Montreal Witness was denounced in Catholic pulpits. As well, Catholics who read it were warned they would be denied the sacraments.

The *Boston Globe* reported that on May 13th, 1888, at age 79, Chiniquy spoke for an hour and a half to an enthusiastic paying audience of 3,000 in Boston. The *Chicago Tribune* also reported of Chiniquy, "at 80 years of age he is one of the most remarkable men of the country, being able to read and write without the aid of spectacles, doing a large amount of work and traveling many miles yearly."

Chapter 4 A Godly President in the White House

[1] *World Book Encyclopaedia*, 1978, Volume 4, p. 478-485, Volume 12, p. 277-285, Volume 13, p. 560, *The New Encyclopaedia Britannica*, 2005, Vol. 23, p. 34-37, William K. Goolrick and eds. *Rebel Resurgent: Fredericksburg to Chancellorsville*, (Time-Life Books, 1985), p.92, 93, Charles Chiniquy, *Fifty Years In The Church Of Rome*, (Craig and Barlow, 1886, 3rd edition), p. 686.

After bidding farewell to his friends and neighbors in Springfield, Lincoln began his trip to Washington on February 11th, 1861.

Lincoln felt he had to suspend *habeas corpus* in the areas where rebel sympathizers were busy helping the South. A few publications advocating sedition were temporarily closed down but most Northern newspapers continued to be printed during the War of the Rebellion and the federal government faced public criticism during the conflict.

The President was criticized vigorously by Supreme Court Chief Justice Roger Taney for the suspension of *habeas corpus* but Lincoln argued that the dissolution of the Union was a much greater evil than the temporary loss of freedom of people seeking the destruction of the country.

Lincoln ended his first inaguaral address with the eloquent and heartwarming words:

> We are not enemies, but friends. We must not be enemies. Though passion may have strained it must not break our bonds of affection. The mystic chords of memory, stretching from every battlefield and patriot grave to every living heart and hearthstone all over this broad land, will yet swell the chorus of the Union, when again touched, as surely they will be, by the better angels of our nature.

Charles Chiniquy pointed out that the man who ordered the first shot of the the civil war to be fired, General P. Gustave Toutant Beauregard, was a Catholic.

[2] *Fifty Years In The Church Of Rome*, p. 626, 627, 657, 662, 706-709, 711

[3] Dr. G. George Fox, *Abraham Lincoln's Religion*, (Exposition Press, 1959), p. 27, *Newsweek*, January 21, 1991, p. 37

[4] Francis Bicknell Carpenter, *The Inner Life of Abraham Lincoln: Six Months In The White House*, (University of Nebraska Press, 1995), p. 192-195., Josiah G. Holland, *Holland's Life of Abraham Lincoln*, (University of Nebraska Press, 1998), Introduction by Allen C. Guelzo, p. xx, *Abraham Lincoln, An Address by Hon. Newton Bateman, LL.D.*, (The Cadmvs Clvb, 1899), p. 5, 6, 21, *The Galesburg Weekly Mail*, October 22, 1897, p. 5.

The political survey that Bateman and Lincoln went through was recorded in book form. *The Inner Life of Abraham Lincoln* was published the year after the President's death. Chiniquy only reproduced part of the Superintendent's statement found in *The Inner Life*.

[5] *The Inner Life of Abraham Lincoln: Six Months In The White House*, p. 191, *Holland's Life of Abraham Lincoln*, p. vii, xii-xv, xx, David Donald, *Lincoln's Herndon*, (Alfred Knoff, 1948), p. 213, *The Galesburg Weekly Mail*, October 22, 1897, p. 5.

Historical records show that Bateman was indeed the Superintendent of Public Instruction for Illinois in the fall of 1860.

[6] *Holland's Life of Abraham Lincoln*, p. xviii - xx, 236-239, *The Galesburg Weekly Mail*, October 22, 1897, p. 5, *Abraham Lincoln, An Address by Hon. Newton Bateman*,

p. 34, 35, *The Inner Life of Abraham Lincoln: Six Months In The White House*, p. 192-195, *Lincoln's Herndon*, p. 214, 215.

Newton Bateman knew Abraham Lincoln and their offices were next to one another in the state capital building. In 1861, when Lincoln left Springfield for Washington to become President, Bateman was notable among those that crowded the railroad station to see him off and was one of the last people to shake his hand. Among Bateman's most prized pieces of Lincoln memorabilia was a rare invitation to accompany the President-elect as far as Indianapolis.

Carpenter did not precisely reproduce Holland's account of Bateman. In addition, Carpenter left out three sentences and one short phrase. The omission of the three sentences does not substantially affect the substance of what Lincoln said. Evidently the same could not be said of the phrase, in the eyes of Lincoln's former law partner, William Herndon. When Holland's biography was published, quoting Bateman, Herndon was angry that the President had been portrayed as a Christian and he felt Holland had made Lincoln look like a hypocrite who hid his beliefs for political reasons. In Holland's volume, in answer to Bateman's remark that Lincoln's friends were ignorant of his beliefs. Lincoln answered, "I know that they are. I am obliged to appear different to them; but I think more on these subjects than upon all others, and I have done so for years; and I am willing that you should know it" Carpenter left out the words, "I am obliged to appear different to them", which Herndon found so offensive.

[7] *World Book Encyclopedia*, 1998, Volume 12, p. 315, *Lincoln's Herndon*, p. 22, Bateman to Holland, June 19, 1865 and statement by Bateman, Holland Papers, *Holland's Life of Abraham Lincoln*, p. xxi, Oscar Fay Adams, *A Dictionary of American Authors*, (Houghton Mifflin Company, 1904), p. 322, *A Dictionary of American Biography*, (Charles Scribner's Sons, 1934), Volume 14, p. 176.

Herndon and Lincoln were law partners for more than 16 years. Although both their names appeared on the sign outside their office, Herndon, who called his partner "Mr. Lincoln", usually did most of the mundane legal research and office work while Lincoln, who called his associate "Billy", did most of the court appearances and dealings with the public. It was the position of the senior partner of Lincoln and Herndon that Abraham Lincoln left to become President.

[8] Douglas L Wilson and Rodney O. Davis, *Herndon's Informants : Letters, Interviews, and Statements about Abraham Lincoln*, (University of Illinois Press, 1998), p. 436, 572, 588, *Holland's Life of Abraham Lincoln*, p. xix, xxiii, *Lincoln's Herndon*, p. 215, William E. Barton, *The Soul Of Abraham Lincoln*, (George H. Duran Company, 1920), p. 303-306, Henry Clay Whitney, *Life on the Circuit with Lincoln*, (The Caxton Printers, 1940), p. 253, Roy P. Basler, ed, *The Collected Works of Abraham Lincoln*, (Rutgers University Press, 1953), Volume 4, p. 190, 191.

After Josiah Holland's book was published, Herndon contacted Newton Bateman and interviewed him about his statements. According to notes Herndon took during the conversation, Bateman told him that he had initially put down in writing only what Abraham Lincoln had said in general terms. Herndon quoted him as saying,

"The question of Religion discussed by Mr. L. and myself was in Oct.-- late in Oct. 1860-- put it down in writing--- at kind of general points-- not precise-- didn't write out in particular and full till after Mr. L. was assassinated."

Bateman's statement, written in his own hand, is preserved in the Papers of Josiah G. Holland, held by the New York Public Library and does indeed show that Holland reproduced his words accurately. (Appendix 3, Part 14) The Massachusetts journalist never retracted what he had written, although being a liberal Congregationalist himself, he would have had no personal reason to portray Lincoln as an evangelical Christian. Newton Bateman did not retract what he said either. In a letter to Herndon, dated March 8th, 1869, he wrote:

> My Dear Sir:
>
> I have yours of the 7th inst. I am too unwell & too busy to write or think to-day -- will try to Speak on the Subject of your note when I can -- *Meanwhile please do not use or refer to our private Conversations or any part of them.* My aversion to publicity in such Matters is intense. The tone Manner &c. of Mr. Lincoln was deeply solemnly *religious* -- it inspired me to awe. He was *applying* the *principles* of moral & *religious truth* to the duties of the hour -- the Condition of the Country & the Conduct of public men -- ministers of the Gospel &c. I had no thought of Orthodoxy or heterodoxy -- unitarianism, trinitarianism or any other ism during the whole Conversation & I don't suppose or *believe he had.* The room was full of God & high truths & the awfulness of Coming Events -- Sects & dogmas in Such a presence! He was alone with the Great God the problem of his Countrys future & his own & I but heard the Communings of his soul --
>
> Truly yours
> Newton Bateman

This appears to be a fairly accurate description of the statements that Abraham Lincoln made in 1860 according to Bateman. The assertion that Christ is God, though a doctrinal statement, flows naturally and logically from Mr. Lincoln's earlier words in his talk with Bateman. Herndon, as the case with most researchers up to more modern times, apparently was unaware that Bateman had sent the eight page account of Lincoln's conversation with him to Josiah Holland.

On December 18th, 1882, Isaac Arnold, an associate of Lincoln, commented on the subject in a letter he wrote to Herndon. He stated in part:

> In regard to Mr. Bateman he does not stand up very squarely. I wrote to him once to ask him if Holland had repeated him correctly & he replied--- as I recollect 'substantially'. His letter was burned in the great fire.
>
> My idea of Mr. Lincoln's settled Views of christianity is about this. He believed in the great fundamental principles of Christianity--- but as to creeds & dogma, he was not strictly *orthodox* [11]

He didn't say why Newton Bateman did not "stand up very squarely" but confirmed that according to Bateman, Holland had substantially reproduced what he said.

[9] *Herndon's Informants : Letters, Interviews, and Statements about Abraham Lincoln,* p. vii-xv, 236, 237, 250-255, 270, 272, 276, 518, 547-550, 576, 577, Dwight G. Anderson, *Abraham Lincoln: The Quest For Immortality,* (Knopf, 1982), p. 62, 64, *Lincoln's Herndon,* p. 214, 223, 224, 236, 237, 250-255, 270, 272, 276, *The Soul Of Abraham Lincoln,* p. 75-77, 162, 163, 320, p. 388, B. Kunhardt, Jr., Philip B. Kunhardt III, Peter W. Kunhardt, Lincoln, (Alfred A. Knopf, 1992) p. 395, *Holland's Life of Abraham Lincoln,* p. xix, xx.

Herndon reported that some of Lincoln's associates he interviewed said Lincoln had been an infidel. One of them, John Stuart, said that a minister, whom he identified as Revd Doct Smith, tried to convert Lincoln and failed.

The Revd Smith he was referring to was Reverend James Smith, who had been the minister of the First Presbyterian Church in Springfield, Illinois in the 1850s. Abraham Lincoln had rented a pew in the church and attended regularly with his family. The idea for the debates with Stephen Douglas that made Abraham Lincoln a national figure may have come from Dr. Smith's own three week long series of debates on the subject of Christianity with well known skeptic and author, C. G. Olmsted. Reverend Smith stated that at the time of the death of one of Mr. Lincoln's sons, in 1849, he had the opportunity to get to know him. To help Abraham Lincoln in this difficult time, Smith lent him a copy of his book, *The Christian Defence.* According to the minister, after reading it, Lincoln was converted and became a Christian.

Lincoln later appointed Reverend Smith to the position of American consul in Scotland.

It was at his post in Dundee that Smith heard about one of the lectures that Herndon had given in Springfield in November, 1866. The subject of the lecture was Ann Rutledge, whom Herndon asserted was the only woman Abraham Lincoln had really loved, his marriage to Mary Todd being essentially a loveless marriage. Ann Rutledge, who died in New Salem when Lincoln was in his twenties, was supposedly his first love. A short time after the lecture, Herndon also wrote a letter to the man who had been the minister of the church that Lincoln had attended, the 1st Presbyterian Church of Springfield. Herndon asked for proof that Mr. Lincoln had become a Christian through his ministry, and having come to the "belief that the Bible was God's *special miraculous revelation.*" If Abraham Lincoln had been converted, he also asked, "why didn't he join your Church, the 1st Presbyterian Church of the city of Springfield?" Angered by the Rutledge lecture and the insulting tone of the letter, Reverend Smith wrote back, rebuking him for his attack on the memory of the 16th President and the injury he had inflicted on Lincoln's widow and sons. Smith declared that Abraham Lincoln, had avowed "his belief in the Divine Authority and Inspiration of the Scriptures". The clergyman also challenged Herndon's contention that he knew Abraham Lincoln well. Asserting that "A law office is by no means the best field for judging the Characters of each other by those who are brought in Contact there" he argued "it is in the family Circle the man exhibits himself as he really is", a circle that Rev. Smith asserted he had been a part of. Herndon did not respond so Smith published his letter in a Dundee newspaper and it was subsequently published in many large American papers.

Chauncey Black was the son of Lamon's law partner, Jeremiah Black. Billy Herndon was also considered to be a joint author of the Lamon biography because he was quoted frequently and because the book was based on records that Black and Lamon purchased from him.

[10] *Lincoln's Herndon*, p. 271.

Within a few weeks of Abraham Lincoln's death, Herndon had begun to collect information about his former partner for a biography he had planned to write and he interviewed a good number of the slain President's associates. The Lamon biography sold only a couple thousand copies.

[11] *The Soul Of Abraham Lincoln*, p. 33, 35, 63-66, 76, 77, 118, 119, 131-133, 146-155, 172-175, 314, 319-321, 331, 341, *Herndon's Informants: Letters, Interviews, and Statements about Abraham Lincoln*, p. 520, 521, 576, 577, 582, 583, 587, *Lincoln's Herndon*, p. 214-216, 237, 238, 256, 257, 269-272, 274-278, 280, 358, *Holland's Life of Abraham Lincoln*, p. xxii, xxiii, Paul M, Zall, *Lincoln on Lincoln*, (The University Press of Kentucky, 2003), p. 70-72, Lord Longford, *Abraham Lincoln*, (Weidenfeld & Nicolson, 1974), p. 46, Roy P. Basler, ed, *The Collected Works of Abraham Lincoln*, (Rutgers University Press, 1953), Volume 4, p. 270, Volume 5, p. 185, Otto Eisenschiml, *Why The Civil War*, (Bobbs-Merrill, 1958), p. 177, *Life on the Circuit with Lincoln*, p. 255, 356, Robert Dale Richardson, *Abraham Lincoln's Autobiography*, (The Beacon Press, 1948), p. 29, *World Book Encyclopedia*, 1978, Volume 3, p. 288, Volume 15, p. 151, *Longman Guide To Living Religions*, (Redwood Books, 1994), p. 256, 28. *Abraham Lincoln: The Quest For Immortality*, p. 64, William H. Herndon, *The Hidden Lincoln*, (Viking Press, 1938), p. 45, *Biographical Directory of the American Congress: 1774 - 1996*, (CQ Staff Directories, Inc., 1997), p. 168, 172, *New York Times*, February 27, 1861, p. 1

[12] Stephen B. Oates, *With Malice Toward None*, (Harper & Row, 1997), p. 150, Michael Burlingame, *The Inner World Of Abraham Lincoln*, (University of Illinois Press, 1994), p. 20-25, World Book Encyclopedia, 1998, Volume 11, p. 243, 244, Volume 12, p. 317, Longford, *Abraham Lincoln*, p. 64, Mario Matthew Cuomo, Harold Holzer, G. S. Boritt, *Lincoln On Democracy*, (Harper & Row, 1990), p. 80. Although Lincoln stated that he had always hated slavery, he remained relatively quiet about it earlier in his political career because he believed it was ultimately doomed. Even after the passage of the Kansas-Nebraska Act, which put the expansion of slavery back on the national stage, he stated, "I confess I hate to see the poor creatures hunted down, and caught, and carried back to their stripes, and unrewarded toils; but I bite my lip and keep quiet."

[13] Otto Eisenschiml, *Why The Civil War*, p. 175, *The Soul Of Abraham Lincoln*, p. 90, 91, 94, 133, 159, 244, 245, *Abraham Lincoln*, p. 46, 47, David Homer Bates, *Lincoln In The Telegraph Office*, (D. Appleton-Century Co., 1939), p. 215.

What many people noticed about one of the President's last major speeches, the second inaugural address, was its religious tone.

A Presbyterian clergyman by the name of Reverend William Roberts stated that when he was a young man, he worked in Washington in the last year and a half of the Civil War. He attended the New York Avenue Presbyterian Church in the capital and said that President Lincoln was a regular and devout worshiper there.

Judge David Davis, an Illinois associate of Abraham Lincoln's, asserted that Lincoln was a very private, shut-mouthed man and doubted he would have discussed his religion beliefs with anyone.

[14] Mark E. Neely, *The Abraham Lincoln Encyclopedia*, (McGraw-Hill, 1982), p. 47, *Herndon's Informants: Letters, Interviews, and Statements about Abraham Lincoln*, p. 521, Herbert Mitgang, *The Fiery Trial*, (Viking Press, 1974), p. 90, 93, Henry Clay Whitney, *Life On The Circuit With Lincoln*, (The Caxton Printers, 1940), p. 248-251, *The Soul Of Abraham Lincoln*, p. 201, 202, *Fifty Years*, p. 713-717, "Who Was More Important: Lincoln or Darwin?", *Newsweek*, July 7/July 14, 2008, p. 33

[15] *Life On The Circuit With Lincoln*, p. 246, *The Abraham Lincoln Encyclopedia*, p. 335, *The Soul Of Abraham Lincoln*, p. 88, 89, Dr. G. George Fox, *Abraham Lincoln's Religion*, (Exposition Press, 1959), p. 28, *The Soul Of Abraham Lincoln*, p. 333, Richard Current, *The Lincoln Nobody Knows*, (McGraw-Hill, 1958), p. 64, 65.

When Abraham Lincoln said he was obligated to appear different to his friends and associates, as Bateman stated, was it because he was afraid of the "mob furor" or because he believed they would not understand his point of view and as General Rusling reported him saying, perhaps laugh about it? He did not have to make any false statements to appear different to most of his friends, he just had to generally say very little or nothing about his beliefs, which according to David Davis, he did.

In his book, *Abraham Lincoln's Religion*, Dr, G. George Fox said of Chiniquy and Lincoln's beliefs,

"When Chiniquy says that during the conversation, Lincoln said, quoting Psalm 19, 'for the judgments of God are true and righteous' -- we are reminded that he made this statement other times. When he quotes him as saying 'is not our Christian religion the highest expression of the wisdom, mercy and love of God,' we know that Lincoln may not have used the exact words, but he had expressed that idea many times. When he made a remark or its equivalent like this: 'It seems to me that the Lord wants today, as he wanted in the days of Moses, another victim--a victim which He Himself had chosen, anointed and prepared for the sacrifice, by raising it above the rest of His people, I cannot conceal from you that my impression is that I am the victim,' we recall from other statements by Lincoln that he looked upon himself as chosen for a divine mission which he felt crystallized itself in the liberation of the slaves."

Henry C. Whitney, who had known Abraham Lincoln since they both had ridden the court circuit in Illinois, attested to his associate's view that God was using him.

In reply to Mrs. Eliza Gurney, widow of Quaker leader Joseph Gurney and a delegation of Quakers, President Lincoln said "being a humble instrument in the hands of our Heavenly Father, as I am, and as we all are, to work out His great purposes, I have desired that all my works and acts may be according to His will, and that it might be so, I have sought His aid".

Henry Whitney stated, "Mr. Lincoln believed himself to be an instrument of God; and that, as God willed, so would the contest be. He also believed in prayer and its efficacy, and that God willed the destruction of slavery through his instrumentality, and he believed in the Church of God as an important auxiliary."

God's Word also comforted Abraham Lincoln, a change that his friend Joshua Speed noticed. Speed stated "The only evidence I have of any change was in the summer before he was assassinated. I was invited out to the Soldier's Home to spend the night. As I entered the room, near night, he was sitting near a window intently reading his Bible. Approaching him, I said: 'I am glad to see you profitably engaged.' 'Yes,' said he, 'I am profitably engaged.' 'Well,' said I, 'if you have recovered from your skepticism, I am sorry to say that I have not!' Looking me earnestly in the face, and placing his hand on my shoulder, he said, 'You are wrong, Speed; take all of this book upon reason that you can, and the balance on faith, and you will live and die a happier and better man'."

[16] *The Lincoln Nobody Knows*, p. 64, "Lincoln, religion and God," *Champaign-Urbana News-Gazette*, February 11, 1993, p. C-4, *The Soul Of Abraham Lincoln*, p. 77, 203, Philip B. Kunhardt, Jr., Philip B. Kunhardt III, Peter W. Kunhardt, Lincoln, (Alfred A. Knopf, 1992) p. 369.

The Kunhardts reported in their book, *Lincoln* that Elizabeth Keckley was Mary Lincoln's seamstress and her best friend after her husband was murdered.

In his first inaugural address Lincoln stated, "If the Almighty Ruler of Nations, with His eternal truth and justice, be on our side of the North, or on yours of the South, that truth and that justice will surely prevail by the judgment of this great tribunal of the American people....Intelligence, patriotism, Christianity, and a firm reliance on Him who has never yet forsaken this favored land, are still competent to adjust in the best way all our present difficulty"

Earlier in his life, in a letter to comfort his dying father in 1851, Lincoln wrote, "our great and good and merciful Maker...notes the fall of a sparrow, and numbers the hairs of our head, and He will not forget the dying man who puts his trust in Him."

Chapter 5 The Catholic Church and the Civil War

[1] Charles Chiniquy, *Fifty Years In The Church of Rome*, (Craig and Barlow, 1886, 3rd edition), p. 691-710, *World Book Encyclopaedia*, 1978, Volume 2, p. 81, Volume 16, p. 378d, *World's Popular Encyclopaedia*, (World Syndicate Publishing Co., 1937), Volume 7, (heading: Jesuits), "Letter From Father Chiniquy", *Chicago Tribune*, August 12, 1864, p. 3, Robert Todd Lincoln to Charles Chiniquy, Sept. 10, 1885. The headline of "Letter From Father Chiniquy" is also on the back cover.

[2] *World Book Encyclopaedia*, 1978, Volume 12, p. 279, Mark E. Neely, *The Abraham Lincoln Encyclopedia*, (McGraw-Hill, 1982), p. 16, 17

[3] Scott Sheads, Daniel Toomey, *Baltimore During The Civil War*, (Toomey Press, 1997), p. 33, 74, Lord Charnwood, *Abraham Lincoln*, (Henry Holt and Co, 1917), p. 239-241, David Herbert Donald, *Lincoln*, (Simon & Schuster, 1995), p. 297-299, James L. Swanson, *Manhunt: The Twelve-Day Chase For Lincoln's Killer*, (HarperCollins, 2006), p. 87, American Federation of Catholic Societies, (corporate author), *Baltimore Historical Book of American Catholic Societies*, 1914, p.55, Mark Neely, *The Abraham Lincoln Encyclopedia*, p. 17, Stephen B. Oates, *With Malice Toward None*, (Harper & Row, 1977), p. 226, 232

[4] *World Book Encyclopaedia*, 1978, Volume 2, p. 50, Baltimore During The Civil War, p. 32, 37, 60, Kenneth C. Davis, *Don't Know Much About The Civil War: Everything You Need To Know About America's Greatest Conflict But Never Learned*, (William Morrow and Co, 1996), p. 182, Baltimore Historical Book of American Catholic Societies, p 67, Kenneth J. Zanca, *The Catholics and Mrs. Mary Surratt*, (University Press of America, 2008), p. 6

[5] Samuel Finley Breese Morse, *Foreign Conspiracy Against The Liberties Of The United States*, (Leavitt, Lord and Co, 1835), p. 90, 91, 118, 119, *Fifty Years*, p. 672, *New York Times*, January 13, 1865, p. 5, March 16, 1865, p. 5, "The Pope's Encyclical. Lecture by Father Chiniquy", *Chicago Tribune*, November 2, 1865, p. 3, "Danger to the Schools", *Chicago Tribune*, April 19, 1859, "Sims Continue Catholic Attack", *Atlanta Constitution*, August 28, 1921, p. 4.

The November 2nd, 1865, edition of the *Chicago Tribune* reported on a lecture that Charles Chiniquy gave in the city, late in 1865, regarding the Pope's 1865 Encyclical. The article stated that Chiniquy,"…prefaced his lecture by reading at some length from the document, and based his subsequent remarks principally on the idea conveyed in that document that the Pope considers it an iniquity that he has not the power to punish heretics; by this fulmination, all the great principles of our own and kindred constitutions are defied." The article also reported, "The speaker considered the Pope to be the most honest man in the whole Catholic Church – he acted from principle, while its minor prelates were influenced by policy, and dared not lay before the world the whole programme. There were three things which the Pope particularly detested – liberty of conscience, the United States, and the people." Charles Chiniquy also was quoted as blaming the Church of Rome for the murder of President Lincoln, saying "Abraham Lincoln was cut down for his love of liberty, not by Booth, but by the church, which was a sworn enemy to his principles."

On the subject of the threat possed by the Catholic hierarchy to American education, the *Chicago Tribune* stated in an editorial, entitled, "Danger to the Schools":

It is understood that the demands of the Hierarchy, speaking through these gentlemen, will be,

1st. The admission of a stated number of Catholic clergymen into the Schools, a certain number of times each week, for the instruction of the children of Catholic parents in their religious duties.

2d. The disuse of the Bible, without note or comment, in all school exercises, lest Catholic children may be cntaiminated by aiving it read, or,

3d. The division of the school money raised by general tax and by the proceeds of the school lands, among the children of Catholics, per capita, that they may have instruction in Catholic schools by the priests, in the Catechism ans other sectarian books.

We are assured that the two first or the last one - will be insisted upon as the "compromise" that the Pope, throught his alien clergy, will be willing to make with the tax-payers of Chicago as the conditions upon which the children of Catholics who are in the main non-taxpayers, may get their education in our Common Schools.

A man writing in the August 28th, 1921, edition of the *Atlanta Constitution* asserted that the Roman Catholic Church was opposed to the American public school system and wished to destroy it. Walter Sims also poined out that in Catholic Mexico and Spain, where the Church of Rome had been in charge of education for centuries, there was much illiteracy and poverty.

[6] *World Book Encyclopedia*, 1978, Vol. 4, p 474, Vol. 5, p. 280, Vol. 14, p. 408, John Hope Franklin, *From Slavery To Freedom: A History Of African Americans*, (McGraw-Hill, 1994), p. 81, 195-197, *Encyclopaedia Britannica*, 1993, Vol. 11, p. 538, *The Abraham Lincoln Encyclopedia*, p. 301, David Herbert Donald, *Lincoln*, p. 199, *Don't Know Much About The Civil War*, p. 123

[7] *Fifty Years*, p. 693, 694

[8] Sidney Kobre, *Development of American Journalism*, (Wm. C. Brown Company Publishers, 1969), p. 323, Oscar and Lilian Handlin, *Abraham Lincoln and the Union*, (Atlantic-Little, Brown Books, 1980), p. 137. In 2008, in an interview with the author, Dr. James M. Cornelius, curator, Lincoln Collection, Abraham Lincoln Presidential Library, reported that some 15,000 imprints have been written on the subject of the 16th President.

[9] Lloyd Lewis, *Myths After Lincoln*, (The Readers Club, by permission from Harcourt, Brace and Co., 1941), p. 337, William E. Barton, The Soul of Abraham Lincoln, (George H. Doran Company, 1920), p. 231, "Lincoln Not A Catholic", *American Catholic Historical Researches*, April, 1905, p. 165,166, Albon P.Man, Jr.,"The Church and the New York Draft Riots of 1863", *Records of the American Catholic Historical Society of Philadelphia*, March, 1951, Vol. LXII, No. 1, p. 35, 36, 42, *Fifty Years*, p. 700-704. Commenting on the Catholic hierchy in the United States during the Civil War, in his paper in the *Records of the American Catholic Historical Society of Philadelphia*, Albon P.Man, Jr.'s declared, "Very few high dignitaries of the Church or prominent laymen publicly denounced slavery in this country". Albon also supported the account in *American Catholic Historical Researches*, stating,"In New York, Brownson alleged, a Catholic found to be anti-slavery was suspected of being shaky in his faith, stigmatized as a Yankee or Puritan—'two of the most opprobrious epithets that can, in the estimate of our New York Catholics, be applied to any man'--, and read out of Catholic circles." Albon also reported, "Protestant ministers were considered obsessed with the slavery problem. While still the official

organ of Archbishop Hughes, the *Metropolitan Record* ridiculed them for supporting the Administration's emancipation policy. Characteristically, the *Irish American* hailed the Catholic clergy of New York for steadily declining 'to preach the nigger from their pulpits...' " Albon stated as well, "The pro-South slant of the *Metropolitan Record* and *Freeman's Journal* and *Catholic Register* of New York City, was typical of the Catholic press in the North. Of the twelve avowedly Catholic newspapers in the English language early in the Civil War, only two were said to be consistently loyal"

[10] *Fifty Years*, p. 700-704, Clement Eaton, *A History of the Southern Confederacy*, (The Macmillan Company, 1954), p. 78, 79, Thomas F. Meehan, "Lincoln's Opinion of Catholics", *Historical Records and Studies*, United States Catholic Historical Society, Volume 16, May, 1924, p. 87, 88.

In his book, *A History of the Southern Confederacy*, historian Clement Eaton commented on the papal recognition of the Confederacy. On the subject of H. Dudley Mann, Confederate commissioner to Belgium, he stated:

> Mann obtained a minor triumph in 1863 in his mission to Pope Pius IX. Catholic Ireland and Belgium had been sending thousands of young men to join the Union armies, stimulated by the huge bounties offered for recruits and by the desire of Irish youth for military training to use later in a fight for Irish freedom. Father John Bannon, chaplain of the Missouri troops, and Lieutenant J. L. Capstom, whom Secretary Benjamin sent to persuade Irishmen not to volunteer for Northern armies, had little success in competition with the lure of a $500 enlistment bounty. Nevertheless, Mann persuaded the Pope to discourage this enlistment of Catholics in Europe. Indeed, the Pope addressed an official letter to Jefferson Davis as 'President of the Confederate States of America,' which Mann unjustifiably interpreted as a recognition of the independence of the Confederacy.

In Eaton's view therefore, the Pope hadn't stooped to recognize the Confederacy in his official letter to Jeff Davis, even if he had discouraged young Catholics in Europe from joining the Union cause and if those Catholics from Ireland and Belgium that did join, did so only for the money and military experience.

Thomas F. Meehan, U. S. Catholic Church historian and apologist, disagreed with Chiniquy as well, stating that the Pope did not recognize the government in Richmond. In his short article, "Lincoln's Opinion of Catholics", Meehan commented that although the Confederate archives in Washington D.C. showed that Bishop Lynch of Charleston, N.C. represented the Confederacy, he was given no support by the Pope. Even if it is accepted that Lynch did not get help from the Pontiff, doesn't this beg the question that if the Pope believed that the Confederacy was unworthy of recognition by the Vatican, why did he allow a Catholic bishop to represent it? As well, why did the Pope allow a Catholic priest to act for the South to try to dissuade Catholics from helping the United States government, as Eaton reported?

[11] Thomas Pressly, *Americans Interpret Their Civil War*, (Free Press Paperback Edition, 1965), p. 56, 57, 142, Roy Z. Chamlee, Jr., *Lincoln's Assassins: A Complete*

Account of the Capture, Trial, and Punishment, (McFarland & Company, 1990), p. 324, *New York Times*, April 29, 1858, p. 8. The April 29th, 1858 issue of the *New York Times* reported that George Bancroft had been elected an honorary member of the Chicago Historical Society.

[12] *Americans Interpret Their Civil War*, p. 142-144, David Chesebrough, *No Sorrow Like Our Sorrow*, (The Kent State University Press, 1994), p. 92-95, Andrew C. A. Jampoler, *The Last Lincoln Conspirator: John Surratt's Flight from the Gallows*, (Naval Institute Press, 2008), p. 122, Pope Pius' IX, letter to Jeff Davis, Dec. 3rd, 1865, *Official Records Of The Union And Confederate Navies In The War Of The Rebellion*, Series II - Volume 3, p. 975, *New York Times*, January 15, 1864, p. 2.

In *The Last Lincoln Conspirator*, Andrew Jampoler stated,"In the North, the Civil War heightened anti-Catholicism because the general view, with some justification, was that the Catholic Church's hierarchy was insufficiently zealous condemning slavery. In fact, few Catholic prelates spoke out against slavery, as did Archbishop John Purcell of Cincinnati. Most saw it as not inconsistent with Scripture and elected instead to represent the economic interests of their generally Irish parishioners (competing with blacks for unskilled jobs) from the pulpit rather than supporting abolition, which they associated with northern Protestants."

[13] "Jeff. Davis and the Pope", *New York Times*, January 15, 1864, p. 2, "Our Paris Correspondence", January 7, 1865, *New York Times*, p. 1, "How The Pope Recognized The Southern Confederacy – His Letter to Jeff Davis", *New York Times*, August 18, 1876, p. 5, "Patriotism as Affected by the Roman System", *Christian Recorder* (Philadelphia, Pa.), April 10, 1890, *The Catholics and Mrs. Mary Surratt*, p. 103, 104, *Fifty Years*, p. 703 704, Thomas F. Meehan, "Lincoln's Opinion of Catholics", p. 87-93.

When *The Catholics and Mrs. Mary Surratt*, was published in 2008, Kenneth J. Zanca was Professor of Religious Studies at Marymount College, Palos Verdes, California, and at the time of writing, he remained on the faculty of this Catholic institution. The founders of this institution were "the Religious of the Sacred Heart of Mary". Zanca received his Ph.D from Fordham, the Jesuit University of New York.

In an 1864 piece the *New York Times* said that in his letter to Jeff Davis, "on the political question", the Pope, "takes care to remain perfectly neutral." It appears, however, that the *Times* editorial staff's eyes had been opened by the year 1876.

Chiniquy related that Abraham Lincoln had told him that the Archbishop of New York, John Hughes, whom the President had sent to Rome during the early part of the war, had treacherously advised the Pope to recognize the Confederate States, instead of acting on the side of the Union. According to Chiniquy, Lincoln also stated that he believed that the Civil War was the work of the Papacy.

In an 1924 article entitled "Lincoln's Opinion of Catholics", Thomas Meehan presented a body of evidence that he believed contradicted *Fifty Years*. He alleged that Hughes and another man, Thurlow Weed, actually prevented England and France from recognizing the Confederacy. To prove this, Meehan reproduced letters, whole and in part, mostly written by Hughes himself. One letter written by Secretary of State William Seward to Bishop Hughes, dated November 2nd, 1861, detailed the scope of Hughes' mission in France and Europe as an assistant to the U.S. Representative Drayton. The other part letters are by Hughes except for a part of a letter by Lincoln.

Among the evidence provided by Meehan, the only person who stated that the Bishop was successful in Europe was Hughes himself. There was no independent confirmation that he and Weed were responsible for keeping England and France from recognizing the Confederacy. The letters from Seward and Lincoln don't clear Hughes. They were written more than a year before the Pope's letter to Davis and at the time of their writing, Hughes may have had a cordial relationship with U.S. government officials such as President Lincoln.

[14] *Fifty Years*, p. 623-627, 664, 700, 701, *The Urbana Union*, May 29, 1856, p. 3, *The Chicago Tribune*, April 5, 1889, p. 1, *Washington Post*, April 4, 1889, p. 1, Thomas F. Meehan, "Lincoln's Opinion of Catholics", p. 87-93.

The *Chicago Tribune* and the *Washington Post* both published the statement of a member of the Canadian Parliament from Quebec. The man, named F. Bechard, said he was the interpreter at Spink vs. Chiniquy. Bechard stated that during the trial, there were no Jesuits seen about the court room and there were none in that part of the country. Chiniquy however, declared that the Jesuits at the court were from Chicago and St. Louis and there certainly were Jesuits in these cities at this time. Bishop Vandeveld of Chicago, a former President of Saint Louis University, was bishop of Chicago until 1854 and he was a Jesuit. Catholic accounts state that there has been a Jesuit presence at the College of St. Louis, (now University of St. Louis), since 1827. They were also visiting and preaching, involved in missions, etc, in Chicago until they got a permanent residence in 1857. Was Bechard the interpreter? A list of defence witnesses in the May term, 1856, shown by Appendix 3, Part 16, appears to list him as a witness instead. The list of defence witnesses in the October term, shown in Figure 5, appear to lists a F. Bechard as a witness too. If he was the interpreter, translating a large amount of the testimony, would he have the opportunity to look around the court room? As well, would he have known all the Jesuits in Chicago and St. Louis at this time and therefore be able to recognize them and thus say whether they were there or not? If he was a witness, he would have been a person living in the Kankakee area, so how would he have known about what Jesuits were or were not in St. Louis and Chicago at the time? As well, as *Fifty Years* describes it, it appears that the Jesuits were present in court on the morning that judgement was to be given. At this time, an interpreter may not have been needed, especially since Chiniquy's side knew that Spink was going to withdrawn his lawsuit, so Bechard may not have even been in court that morning.

[15] *Fifty Years*, p. 656, 662, 702, 787, Encyclopedia Britannica, 1937, Vol. 13, p. 13, David Mitchell, *The Jesuits*, (Macdonald Futura Publishers, 1980), p. [9], *World Book Encyclopaedia*, 1978, Vol. 11, p. 81, William E. Barton, "Abraham Lincoln and the Eucharistic Congress", The Outlook, Volume 143, 1926, p. 375, Mario M. Cuomo and Harold Holzer, eds, Lincoln on Democracy, (A. Cornelia & Michael Bessie Book, 1990), p. xl, Richard Frederick Littledale, Plain Reasons Against Joining The Church Of Rome, (Society For Promoting Christian Knowledge, 1886), p. 177.

Regarding the obedience of the Jesuits, Littledale stated, "…the Jesuits, who, in despite of their own special vow of implicit obedience to the Pope, and their magnifying that as the highest virtue, never once thought of obeying the Brief of Clement XIV. in 1773, which suppressed the Company, declaring it broken up and abolished for ever, but withdrew into the non-Roman dominions of Prussia and Russia, where the Pope's writ did not run".

[16] David Herbert Donald, *Lincoln*, (Simon & Schuster, 1995), p. 446, 447, *World Book Encyclopaedia*, 1978, Vol. 4, p. 485, Thomas M. Harris, *Rome's Responsibility for the Assassination of Abraham Lincoln*, (Heritage Manor, 1960), p. 13

[17] Lenoir Chambers, *Stonewall Jackson*, (William Morrow & Co, 1959), Vol. 1, p. 427, *Archdiocese of St. Louis, Three Centuries of Catholicism, 1700-2000*, (The Archdiocese of St. Louis, 2001), p. 62.

The *Archdiocese of St. Louis*, reported:

> Following the Civil War, the 'Drake Constitution' was adopted in Missouri which fanned anti-Catholic sentiment. The new constitution, among other things, required that priests and ministers should declare that they had always been loyal to the United States against all enemies. The 'test oath' was to be taken by all priests in the archdiocese. Many refused.

[18] *Fifty Years*, p. 696, 703, *The Gangs of New York*, 2002: directed by Martin Scorsese, starring Daniel Day-Lewis, Leonardo DiCaprio, and Cameron Diaz, Joel Tyler Headley, *The Great Riots of New York*, (Bobbs-Merrill Co., 1970, reprint of 1873 edition), p. 136-141, 145, 146, *World Book Encyclopaedia*, 1978, Vol. 4, p. 479

[19] *The Great Riots of New York*, p. 148, 149, 152, 153

[20] *New York Daily Tribune*, July 14, 1863, p. 1, 4, *The Great Riots of New York*, p. 153-253, Albon P.Man, Jr.," The Church and the New York Draft Riots of 1863", *Records of the American Catholic Historical Society of Philadelphia*, March, 1951, Vol. LXII, No. 1, p. 33.

Albon P.Man, Jr.,stated in his paper in the *Records of the American Catholic Historical Society of Philadelphia*, March, 1951 edition, "And if newspapers, eye-witnesses accounts, official records, and other sources agree on any point connected with the disturbances, it is that practically all the rioters were Irish.'…The immediate actors in the late Riots in this city, got up to resist the Draft and create a diversion in favor of the Southern Rebellion were almost exclusively Irishmen and Catholics… ,'wrote Orestes Brownson, and his testimony has ample confirmation".

[21] *The Great Riots of New York*, p. 201, 209, Ray Allen Billington, *The Protestant Crusade 1800-1860*, (Rinehart & Company, Inc., 1952), p. 1, 2, 60, 70-85, 156, 157, 197, 198, 220-227, *The Gangs of New York*.

Authors like Ray Allen Billington have written about the alleged persecution of Catholics by Protestants in America. In his book, *The Protestant Crusade 1800-1860* however, Billington actually provided excellent reasons why American Protestants of Engish stock would be worried about the Roman Catholic Church. He wrote:

Both the Puritans of Massachusetts Bay and the Angicans of Virginia, despite their many differences, shared the fear and hatred of Rome. Their grandfathers had been alive when Henry VIII led the nation away from the Church; their fathers had witnessed wars with Catholic France which threatended to restore the Pope to his former supremacy and had despaired for their faith with the ascension to the throne of Bloody Mary. The settlers themselves had been cradled in an England more bitter against Catholicism then than at any other time. They had seen the constant plot and counterplot of the reigns of Elizabeth and James I when Catholic forces threatened to engulf their land: the Irish uprising at Kerry, the projected attack of the Spanish armies under the Duke of Kent through Scotland, the intrigue of the Jesuits, Campion and Parsons, the efforts to restore Mary Queen of Scots to the throne, the threat of the Armada, and the Gunpowder Plot. This intrique had fastened the conviction in the minds of all loyal subjects that Catholicism was a dangerous and constantly threatening force.

The hatred with which the average Englishman of the early seventeenth century looked upon Popery was due largely to the antinational character of that religion, for Catholicism was feared not only as an antagonistic theology, but also as a force through which the Engish government itself was to be overthrown. From the time of Henry VIII Catholic France and Spain, constantly plotting with the papal party in England to displace the Tutor and Stuart monarchs, had found many Englishmen who were sufficiently loyal to their papal principles to sacrifice national independence as a means of restoring English allegiance to the Pope.

After this review of the history of Romanism in England, it is easy to see why Protestants of the United States would be concerned about Catholicism in America. Billington also disclosed how Protestant speakers in New York and Baltimore were forced from the halls they had rented by Roman Catholic mobs in the early 1830s. Billington wrote:

In 1829 a group of Americans, aroused by the exhortations of a revivalistic preacher, attached the homes of Irish Catholics in Boston and stoned them for three days. Four years later a group of drunken Irishmen beat a native American to death on the streets of Charleston. The next night five hundred natives marched on the Irish section, and troops that were called out stood helplessly by while a number of houses were torn down and burned.

Billington also reported the concerns that Protestants had with the Ursuline Convent school in Charleston, Massachusetts. They did not appreciate the fact that upper class children of Boston where being sent there. According to him, in 1834, a nun named Elizabeth Harrison became temporarily deranged and "escaped" from the institution. She asked for refuge from a resident in the area, but then returned to the convent. Her friends reportedly expected her to leave the convent again in three weeks but when they asked for her, she couldn't be found. This caused great alarm in the area and a large crowd of men from Charleston came to the convent school and ended up burning it down. They evidently were anti-Papists and probably mostly Protestants. There were not injuries reported. The burning caused wide-spread revulsion through the United States.

In 1842, a controversy arose over Bible reading in schools in Philadelphia after the Catholic Bishop protested the fact that Catholic children were being read the Protestant Bible and receiving religious instruction. In the spring of 1844, a group of "natives" met in a part of Philadelphia to hold a public meeting but they were driven from their meeting place by a mob of Irish Catholics. Outraged by the violations of their rights as Americans, they planned to meet again the next day. They met again but as they disbursed, because of a heavy rain, one of the number was shot and killed and a group of Irish forced them to leave. This caused days of riots as "natives" fought the Irish and burned Irish homes and two Catholic Churches. Billington declared of the end of the disturbances:

> The nativistic press and the American Republican party did little to aid the return of peace to the city. Both began a concentrated effort to gloss over the stigma of church burning and remind the people that the trouble had started when Irish laborers had fired on defenseless Americans peaceably going about their business. 'The murderous assault on American citizens,' stated an official proclamation of the native Americans, 'the trampling under foot and tearing into shreds the American flag,…is the cause, the origin of the whole trouble…. Disgraceful as is the burning of the Churches…is it an outrage of a greater character than that which sends the souls of men without a moment's time for preparation, to the bar of God's judgement?

The trouble started when an American man was murdered, exercising his right to freedom of speech, according to Billington's own account and it appears that it is Billington who was engaged in glossing over the murderous examples of Catholic intolerance.

Billington also reported on the violence and lawlessness that Catholic immigrants introduced into America. He stated that violence, which he benevolently termed, "Irish exuberance" was visited on their countrymen and:

> frequently was turned upon natives. In Detroit, Irishmen, having imbibed too deeply of both patriotism and whiskey on July 4, 1835, attacked citizens on the principal street of the city until they were disbanded by mobs of natives. A similar incident occurred in upper New York state two years later when a group of Irish began stopping citizens, asking them if they were Catholics or Protestants and beating the Protestants. In Pennsylvania, drunken foreigners attacked and damaged a Lutheran church.

Billington evidently was able to overcome his own aversion to the "stigma" of people damaging churches, as long as they were not Catholic ones, and he appeared to have no real problem with Romanists committing violent offences against Protestants for the crime of being Protestants. Billington also stated:

Rioting in St. Louis during 1840 was responsible for the death of at least one man, and that city as well as others in the middle west witnessed mob rule when anti-Catholic lectures were attacked by foreign mobs. This rioting and disorder naturally alarmed many Americans. Their country, long quiet and peaceful, now seemed teeming with violence. Mob rule was displacing the ordinary forces of law wherever the foreigners were centered. Popery and slavery, northern nativists agreed, were responsible for this transition, and most of the people agreed with them. 'How is it possible.' one writer asked, 'that foreign turbulence imported by ship loads, that riot and ignorance in hundreds of thousands of human priest-controlled machines, should suddenly be thrown into our society and not produce here turbulenceand excess? Can one throw mud into pure water and not disturb its clearness?' Particularly alarming to many was the fact that in several riots where civil authorities had failed to quell the battling foreigners, priests had accomplished the task easily. This was taken as evidenced of the marshaling of immigrants under priestly control so that they would be ready to strike when the time came to overthrow the government. Nativists were willing to believe that the alien tide had brought not only disorder but political corruption on a scale never before seen in the United States. The immigrants usually voted in a body and normally supported Democratic candidates, a thing which aroused the wrath of the Whigs. This clannish method of voting gave rise to the charge that foreigners cast their ballots as they were told to, and the belief was general that Catholics priests were bartering votes for political favors.

Billington also commented on the Roman Catholic Church's regard for the Word of God:

Further evidence that Rome was hostile to the Scripures was provided in October, 1842, when an overzealous missionary priest in Carbeau, New York, justly angered at the distribution of Protestant Bibles among his parishioners by Bible societies, gathered several copoes of the Scriptures and publicly burned them. This 'Chamlaoin Bible burning,' as it was promptly labeled, immediately was elevated to a national issue by Protestants. Indignation swept the country, fanned particularly by the bold declaration of Hughes' own paper, the *Freeman's Journal*:

To burn or otherwise destroy a spurious or corrupt copy of the Bible, whose circulation would tend to disseminate erroneous principles of faith or morals, we hold to be an act not only justifiable but praiseworthy

[22] *New York Daily Tribune*, July 14, 1863, p. 1, 4, *The Great Riots of New York*, p. 254-257

[23] *New York Times*, July 18, 1863, p. 4, *The Great Riots of New York*, p. 262, Roy Z. *Lincoln's Assassins*, p. 343.

Roy Chamlee stated however, in direct opposition to independant evidence that:

Stanton was well aware of the Catholic hierarchy's support of the Union. During the draft riots in New York City in the summer of 1863, Stanton received invaluable aid from Archbishop John Hughes, McCloskey's predecessor. The Secretary of War invited the influential prelate to Washington to discuss tense situation. On returning to New York, the Archbishop, the most powerful Catholic in America, appealed to both clergy and laity to support the Federal Government. One of the Archbishop's last public appeals supported the Union. He used his great influence to bring order to New York City.

[24] *The Great Riots of New York*, p. 201, Leonard Patrick O'Connor Wibberley, *The Coming of the Green*, (Henry Holt and Co., 1958), p. 82-84

[25] Roy P. Basler, ed, *The Collected Works of Abraham Lincoln*, (Rutgers University Press, 1953), Volume 7, p. 507, *The Abraham Lincoln Encyclopedia*, p. 103, 104, Mario M. Cuomo and Harold Holzer, eds, *Lincoln on Democracy*, (A. Cornelia & Michael Bessie Book, 1990), p. 200, Statement of Abraham Lincoln to Alexander Randall, August 19, 1864, Lincoln Memorial Museum, Washington, D. C., *The Great Riots of New York*, p. 153

[26] *The Great Riots of New York*, p. 155-157, *Rome's Responsibility for the Assassination of Abraham Lincoln*, p. 13, Charles R. Morris, *American Catholic: the saints and sinners who built America's most powerful church*, (Times Books, 1997), p. x, xi, 76, 79. Morris also stated:

> The Civil War reinforced two stereotypes about Irish Catholics. The first was that they were racists, which has served to justify the sometimes sneering condescension of upper-class Protestants toward Catholics ever since. The second was that they were exceptionally patriotic and loyal Americans, who suffered a disproportionate share of casualties in the fight for the Union. If there is a single event that illuminates the roots of both stereotypes, it is the New York City draft riots, the most lethal riot in American history, which stretched over five days in the summer of 1863, leaving 105 dead and thousands injured.

Charles Morris is undoubtedly correct in stating that this event was the most deadly riot in U.S. history but it could be asked, how could this terrible insurrection have possibly shown that the Irish were exceptionally patriotic and loyal to the United States, when it was the Irish, themselves, who were trying to destroy New York? It showed Catholic men that would sooner riot than be drafted to join the fight for their country when they should have been more than willing to take part of on their own free will.

Chapter 6 Stanton Agrees with Chiniquy, the Assassination Heard of Before it Happened

[1] Philip Van Doren Stern, Introduction, *The Assassination of President Lincoln and The Trial Of The Conspirators*, The Courtroom Testimony as Originally Compiled by Benn Pitman, (Greenwood Press, 1976, facsimile edition), p. v-xiii, 28, 29, 78, *World Book Encyclopaedia*, 1978, Volume 4, p. 472, 492, Volume 12, p. 275-286

[2] Edward Steers, *Blood on the Moon: the Assassination of Abraham Lincoln*, (University of Kentucky Press, 2001), p. 211. William Warner, *At Peace With Their Neighbors: Catholics and Catholicism in the National Capital, 1787 - 1860*, (Georgetown University Press, 1994), Charles Chiniquy, *Fifty Years In The Church of Rome*, (Craig and Barlow, 1886, 3rd edition), p. 724-726, "Is the Liberty of the Press in Danger?", *Washington Post*, Febuary 15, 1890, p. 4.

According to the Georgetown University Press, which published his book, *At Peace With Their Neighbors: Catholics and Catholicism in the National Capital, 1787 - 1860*, William Warner, disclosed that Catholics held the main positions of city government in the national capital soon after it moved to Washington from Philadelphia in 1800. Roman Catholics also were important investors, landowners and bankers in the city at this time.

In a letter to the editor in the Febuary 15, 1890 issue of the *Washington Post*, an anonymous writer signed "American" detailed how Charles Chiniquy had been lecturing in Washington, D.C. but the press had not reported on it and the Washington journal, the *Star*, had even refused an advertisement by Chiniquy. The writer stated that "When the Pope of Rome issues an annuncio it is spread broadcast by the press; when a dignatory of the Romish Church delivers an address upon Catholicism or against Protestantism we find it published verbatim; but when aught is said against Catholicism the press is distressingly silent." The writer added that "Surely the Rev. Mr. Chiniquy's lectures are not so insignificant that a few lines cannot be published about them, while many illustrated columns can be given and have been given to the prospectus of the Catholic University in the suburbs of our city". The writer asserted that the Church of Rome would hold the winning hand with the press in her control.

[3] Roy Z. Chamlee, Jr., *Lincoln's Assassins: A Complete Account of the Capture, Trial, and Punishment*, (McFarland & Company, 1990), p. 341-343, Fletcher Pratt, *Stanton, Lincoln's Secretary of War*, (Norton, 1953), front cover, James L. Swanson, *Manhunt: The Twelve-Day Chase For Lincoln's Killer*, (HarperCollins, 2006), p. 96, 97, "The Paranoid Style", *Washington Post*, December 29, 1991, p. C7. Chamlee did not agree with Charles Chiniquy and others regarding the Roman Catholic Church's attitude toward the United States however, stating "Stanton was well aware of the Catholic heirarchy's support of the Union".

[4] Oliver Stone and Zachary Sklar, *JFK The Book of the Film*, (Applause Books, 1992), p.328-331. "The Paranoid Style" was also reproduced in *JFK, The Book of the Film*.

[5] Ben Ames Williams, Jr., *Mr. Secretary*, (The Macmillan Company, 1940), p. 108,109, Erving E. Beauregard, "Edwin McMasters Stanton - Another Look", *Lincoln Herald*, Fall 1995, p. 119

[6] Doris Kearns Goodwin, *Team Of Rivals*, (Simon & Schuster, 2005), p. 567, Donald T. Phillips, *Lincoln On Leadership*, (Warner Books, 1992), p. 30, *Stanton, Lincoln's Secretary of War*, p. ix, Beverly Bone, "Edwin Stanton in the Wake of the Lincoln Assassination", *Lincoln Herald*, Winter 1980, p. 508, 519, "Edwin McMasters Stanton - Another Look", p. 120

[7] Benjamin P. Thomas and Harold M. Hyman, *Stanton The Life and Times of Lincoln's Secretary of War*, (Alfred A. Knopf, 1962), p. 399, Ralph Borreson, *When Lincoln Died*, (Appleton-Century, 1965), p. 43, Stephen B. Oates, *Abraham Lincoln, the Man Behind the Myths*, (Harper and Row, 1984), p. 176.

In his book, Oates stated of Stanton's feeling on Lincoln's death,"Stanton's own grief was inconsolable. Robert recalled that "for more than ten days after my father's death in Washington, he called every morning on me in my room and he spent the first few minutes of his visits weeping without saying a word."

[8] "The Paranoid Style", *Washington Post*, December 29, 1991, p. C7, *Lincoln's Assassins: A Complete Account of the Capture, Trial, and Punishment*, p. 20, 22-26, 35, 36, 39, Erving E. Beauregard, "Edwin McMasters Stanton - Another Look", p. 120, 121, Champ Clark, *The Assassination: Death of the President*, (Time-Life Books, 1987), p. 102, Beverly Bone, "Edwin Stanton in the Wake of Lincoln Assassination", p 509-516, Lloyd Lewis, *Myths After Lincoln*, (Harcourt, Brace and Company, 1929), p. 195, *When Lincoln Died*, p. 40, *Blood on the Moon: the Assassination of Abraham Lincoln*, p. 13, 211, *Lincoln's Assassins: A Complete Account of the Capture, Trial, and Punishment*, 20, 36, 39.

Of the time after the evening of April 14th, Roy Chamlee stated,"Stanton was in absolute control for at least three weeks following the assassination. President Johnson remained, discreetly, in the background."

[9] *World Book Encyclopaedia*, 1998, Vol. 21, p 37, *Myths After Lincoln*, p. 203, Otto Eisenschiml, *Why Was Lincoln Murdered?*, (Little, Brown and Company, 1937), Theodore Roscoe, *The Web of Conspiracy*, (Prentice-Hall, Inc, 1959), William Hanchett, *The Lincoln Murder Conspiracies*, (University of Illinois Press, 1983), p. 196-233, *Lincoln's Assassins: A Complete Account of the Capture, Trial, and Punishment*, p. 166, 533 - 535.

Of Stanton's involvement in the trial, Roy Chamlee reported, "Stanton wanted the conspirators captured, tried and hanged before Lincoln's burial – an unreasonable goal…He wanted the prisoners tried quickly…Stanton ordered them not to bother with insignificant crimes and to concentrate on those directly involvled in the conspiracy." Chamlee also stated, regarding John Surratt's offer to give himself up if offered immunity, "The Government declined his offer. Stanton constantly refused to allow the prime suspects to escape punishment by turning states' evidence."

[10] Mark E. Neely, *The Abraham Lincoln Encyclopedia*, (McGraw-Hill, 1982), p. 288, *Myths After Lincoln*, p. 63, 66, 203, Andrew C. A. Jampoler, *The Last Lincoln Conspirator: John Surratt's Flight from the Gallows*, (Naval Institute Press, 2008), p. 231, *The Assassination of President Lincoln and The Trial Of The Conspirators*, Introduction, p. xx, xxi, 54-57, *Blood on the Moon: the Assassination of Abraham Lincoln*, p. 72, Frank Abial Flower, *Edwin McMasters Stanton: The Autocrat of Rebellion, Emancipation, and Reconstruction*, (The Saalfield Publishing Company, 1905), p. 50, 51

[11] *Fifty Years*, p. 730

[12] Ibid, p. 731, 732

[13] *Fifty Years*, p. 734, 735, (There are small differences between the original affidavit and the version given in *Fifty Years*, undoubtedly either the results of typographical errors in Chiniquy's autobiography or difficulties in reading the text of the affidavit), *Minnesota in the Civil and Indian Wars*, 1861-1865, (prepared and published under the supervision of the board of commissioners, appointed by the act of the legislature of Minnesota of April 16, 1889, Pioneer Press Co., 1890), p. 48, 49, Richard Moe, *The Last Full Measure*, (Henry Holt and Company, 1993), p. 210

[14] Stephen R. Moore to Charles Chiniquy, October 30, 1883, Affidavit of Rev. Francis A. Conwell before Stephen R. Moore, September 6, 1883, Affidavit of Horace P. Bennett before Andrew C. Robertson, Notory Public, October 18, 1883, (see Appendix 3, Part 9 - 11 for original text)

[15] *Saint Cloud Daily Times*, July 10, 1913, p. 1, William Bell Mitchell, *History of Stearns County, Minnesota*, (H. C. Cooper Jr., & Co., 1915), Volume I, p. 415, 436, 576, 626, Volume II, p. 770, 771, E. H. Atwood, *History of Maine Prairie*, (no date of publication, estimated date – 1895) p. 57, Stephen R. Moore to Charles Chiniquy, October 30, 1883

[16] Stephen R. Moore to Charles Chiniquy, October 30, 1883

[17] *History of Stearns County, Minnesota*, Volume I, p. 217, Volume II, p. 1105, 1107, *Saint Cloud Times*, October 1, 1864, p. 3

[18] *Saint Cloud Daily Times*, June 30, 1910, p. 3, *Saint Cloud Times*, November 20, 1912, p. 6

[19] *St. Cloud Daily Times*, November 8, 1926, p. 10

[20] *History of Stearns County*, Volume II, p. 1105-1109

[21] *History of Stearns County*, Volume II, p. 1180, *St. Cloud Journal-Press*, April 10, 1879, p. 3, August 8, 1889, p. 3. Among Leander Gordon's business interests was a flour mill which he operated in partnership with J. E. Hayward. Gordon came from Massachusetts, arriving in St. Cloud with Horace Bennett in 1856.

[22] *St. Cloud Daily Times*, September 5, 1907, p. 3, *History of Stearns County*, Volume II, p. 801, 802, *St. Cloud Journal-Press*, September 5, 1907, p. 3

[23] Stephen R. Moore to Charles Chiniquy, October 30, 1883

[24] *Saint Paul Press*, April 27, 1865, p. 1

[25] *Saint Paul Pioneer*, April 29, 1865, p. 1, (see Appendix 3, Part 13 for original text), *Saint Paul Press*, April 28, 1865, p. 1, *St. Cloud Journal Press*, April 30, 1891, p. 1

[26] *St. Cloud Times*, November 9, 1998, p. 11A

[27] Forrest Wood, *The Era of Reconstruction*, (Thomas Y. Crowell Company Inc., 1975), p. 10, Mario M. Cuomo, *Lincoln On Democracy*, (Harper & Row, 1990), p. xxxviii, *Blood on the Moon: the Assassination of Abraham Lincoln*, p. 282, 283, 287, 293

[28] *St. Cloud Journal Press*, April 30, 1891, p. 1, *Saint Paul Press*, April 28, 1865, p. 1, Affidavit of Stephen R. Moore, made before the clerk of Kankakee Court, December 19, 1892, (see Appendix 3, Part 12 for original text). Why Moore made his affidavit nine years after his trip in 1883 is unclear. It may have been in response to a question arising at the time about the matter or Charles Chiniquy, fearing that the knowledge that Moore had obtained on his trip might be lost at his death, asked him to make a formal sworn statement.

[29] Stephen R. Moore to Charles Chiniquy, October 30, 1883

[30] *Saint Paul Press*, April 28, 1865, p. 1, *St. Cloud Journal Press*, April 30, 1891, p. 1, *Fifty Years*, p. 733-735

THE CONSPIRATORS
Chapter 7 Mary Surratt

[1] Philip Van Doren Stern, Introduction, *The Assassination of President Lincoln and The Trial Of The Conspirators*, The Courtroom Testimony as Originally Compiled by Benn Pitman, (Greenwood Press, 1976, facsimile edition), p. v-xxiii, Mark Neely, *The Abraham Lincoln Encyclopedia*, (McGraw-Hill, 1982), p. 297-299, Edward Steers Jr., *Blood On The Moon: The Assassination of Abraham Lincoln*, (The University Press Of Kentucky, 2001), p. 173-175, Louis J. Weichmann, *A True History of the Assassination of Abraham Lincoln and the Conspiracy of 1865*, (Alfred A. Knopf, 1975), photograph between pages 158 and 159, T. M. Harris, *Assassination of Lincoln: A History of the Great Conspiracy*, (American Citizen Co., 1892), p. 217-219

[2] Introduction, *The Assassination of President Lincoln and The Trial Of The Conspirators*, p. v-xxiii, *Blood On The Moon: The Assassination of Abraham Lincoln*, p. 155-165, *Assassination of Lincoln: A History of the Great Conspiracy*, p. 51-58

[3] Introduction, *The Assassination of President Lincoln and The Trial Of The Conspirators*, p. v -xxiii, *The Abraham Lincoln Encyclopedia*, p. 297, 298

[4] Charles Chiniquy, *Fifty Years In The Church of Rome*, (Craig and Barlow, 1886, 3rd edition), p. 723

[5] *Fifty Years*, p. 719, 720, General L.C. Baker, *History of the United States Secret Service*, (King & Baird, 1868), p. 476, 479, George Alfred Townsend, *The Life, Crime, and Capture of John Wilkes Booth*, (Dick & Fitzgerald, 1865), p. 42. Baker's

quote from *The Life, Crime, and Capture of John Wilkes Booth*, contained a slight typographical error.

[6] *Assassination of Lincoln: A History of the Great Conspiracy*, p. 82-95, *Blood On The Moon: The Assassination of Abraham Lincoln*, p. 94, *World Book Encyclopedia*, 1978, Volume 19, p. 163, William C. Davis, Bell I. Wiley, *Photographic History Of The Civil War*, (Black Dog & Leventhal Publishers, 1983), p. 1218, Introduction, *The Assassination Of President Lincoln And The Trial Of The Conspirators*, p. xviii, James L. Swanson, *Manhunt: The Twelve-Day Chase For Lincoln's Killer*, (HarperCollins, 2006), p. 112

[7] Edward Steers Jr., *His Name Is Still Mudd*, (Thomas Publications, 1997), p. 26, *Fifty Years*, p. 719-723, Roy Z. Chamlee, Jr., *Lincoln's Assassins: A Complete Account of the Capture, Trial, and Punishment*, (McFarland & Company, 1990), p. 164, 175, Edward Steers Jr., *Blood On The Moon: The Assassination of Abraham Lincoln*, (The University Press Of Kentucky, 2001), *The Abraham Lincoln Encyclopedia*, p. 298, The *Assassination Of President Lincoln And The Trial Of The Conspirators*, Introduction, p. vii, *The Catholics and Mrs. Mary Surratt*, p. 20, Kate Clifford Larson, *The Assassin's Accomplice: Mary Surratt and the Plot to Kill Abraham Lincoln*, (Basic Books, 2008), p. xiv.

Kate Larson stated that she began her biography "with the supposition that Mary Surratt was far more innocent of the charges against her than the original trial had determined" but she stated that "the research itself led to an altogether suprising concusion: Mary Surratt was not only guilty, but was far more involved in the plot than many historians have given her credit for."

In his book, *Lincoln's Assassins*, Roy Chamlee said of Mary Surratt's boardinghouse, "The Surratt house, ostensibly proving much-needed income for the widow, was not a boardinghouse in the usual sense. Only trusted friends stayed there. Seldom, if ever, did anyone apply for lodging who was not already known to the family."

In fact, only Catholics lived in this house which President Johnson called "the nest that hatched the egg", being as Chamlee also stated, "the conspirator's principal meeting place". Chamlee also stated, "From the standpoint of economics, there was no reaon for Mary Surratt to move to Washington. Due to scarcity of rooms in the city during the war, the house on H Street could be profitably rented. Also, for a mother protecting her imotional daughter, the farm was less hazardous than the city filled with thousands of undisciplined recruits."

[8] *The Assassination Of President Lincoln And The Trial Of The Conspirators*, p. 85-87

[9] *The Abraham Lincoln Encyclopedia*, p. 329, *The Assassination Of President Lincoln And The Trial Of The Conspirators*, p. 113, 118, 119

[10] *The Assassination Of President Lincoln And The Trial Of The Conspirators*, p. 85-87

[11] *The Assassination Of President Lincoln And The Trial Of The Conspirators*, p. 125-129, *Blood On The Moon*, p. 142.

The six witnesses were Emma Offutt, B. F. Gwynn, Joseph Nott, Mary Surratt's brother J. Z. Jenkins, Richard Sweeney and James Lusby. The two defence witnesses who were drinking were Richard Sweeney and James Lusby. Sweeney testified that he drank on the road with Lloyd and didn't know which one of them drank the most. Lusby stated he had been, "quite smart in liquor" that day, before he had met Lloyd but he didn't think he was as "tight" as Lloyd. He also said that he didn't think he was, "altogether mistaken as to who was drunk that day". Sweeney actually testified that the alcohol didn't seem to affect Lloyd. Evidently self-reporting cases of drinking and driving / riding, he stated that when Lloyd drove from Marlboro to Surrattsville in a buggy, Sweeney accompanied him part way on horseback and Lloyd "kept the road straight, and I did not see him deviate from it."

Lloyd testified that when she was in Surrattsville, Mary Surratt asked him to secure a buggy spring which he apparently also was not too drunk to be able to do.

[12] *The Assassination Of President Lincoln And The Trial Of The Conspirators*, p. 113, 116, 117, 126, *Lincoln's Assassins: A Complete Account of the Capture, Trial, and Punishment*, p. 137, 262, 350.

It appears that Mrs. Surratt's defence lawyers were asserting that it was not possible for witnesses to accurately relate events that occurred when they had been consuming alcohol but two of their own witnesses, Lusby and Sweeney, gave evidence regarding events that happened when they themselves had been drinking. Obviously the defence accepted their testimony as believable, so why wouldn't Lloyd's be also?

Louis Weichmann testified that a man named John Nothe owed Mary Surratt money from a land deal some 13 years before (p. 116). Later testimony gives his name as Nothey. Apparently Mrs. Surratt's late husband had bought some land from George Calvert and had sold it to Nothey. He hadn't paid the Surratts what he owed them and they hadn't paid Calvert. A letter written to John Nothey from Mrs. Surratt on April 14th was introduced by the defence. In the letter, Mrs Surratt stated that she had been ready for two years to settle the land deal with Nothey, and if he did not come in the next 10 days, she would sue him. Her business that brought her to Surrattsville that day was to deliver this letter to a friend, B.F. Gwynn who brought it to Nothey and read it to him. Calvert had apparently died recently and his son, George Calvert Jr., wanted to settle his father's estate as soon as possible. Though he was pressuring her to make arrangements to pay as soon as possible, there is no compelling evidence to show that she couldn't have done her land business the next day or the next week. Roy Chamlee commented on the "abrupt, urgent trip" on April 14th, "to collect a debt about which she had done nothing for thirteen years", reporting in regards to one note written that afternoon, that Mary Surratt actually "penned the letter in Surrattsville, only a short distance from Nothey's house, which seemed absurd". Chamlee also stated that "To the Court, at least, it appeared she had more urgent business to transact in Surrattsville" (than the debt collection - land deal). Chamlee also reported that Gwynn, Calvert and Nothey all knew the Surratts and had done business with them.

[13] *The Assassination Of President Lincoln And The Trial Of The Conspirators*, p. 121, 125, 127, 128. Mary Surratt's brother, J.Z. Jenkins, testified that she had expressed no wish to see Lloyd when Jenkins had talked to her at Surrattsville on the afternoon of the 14th. He said she was at the point of leaving for Washington when Lloyd drove up. Jenkin's impartiality as a witness is questionable however. A member of the military commission questioned him regarding the alleged threats he made against a man who was potentially a strong witness against his sister. Jenkins denied making any threats but admitted that he tried to influence the man's testimony stating "I understood he was a strong witness against my sister, which he ought to be, seeing that she had raised his family of children."

[14] *The Assassination Of President Lincoln And The Trial Of The Conspirators*, p. 116

[15] *The Assassination Of President Lincoln And The Trial Of The Conspirators*, p. 87, 124, John Bakeless, *Spies of the Confederacy*, (J. B. Lippincott Company, 1970), p. 72, 122, *The Abraham Lincoln Encyclopedia*, p. 298.

As Lloyd arrived before she left, she was able to personally give or at least direct him to the package she had brought and request that everything, including the whiskey, be ready for later that evening. Lloyd testified regarding this, "I think I told Mrs. Offutt, after Mrs. Surratt went away, that it was a field-glass she had brought. She did not tell me that Mrs. Surratt gave her a package."

George Cottingham, a special officer of Major O'Beirne's force was called to testify for the defence. After Lloyd was arrested, he was placed in Captain Cottingham's custody. The officer testified that for two days after his arrest, the innkeeper denied knowing anything about the assassination. During this time, Cottingham told Lloyd that he was sure he knew about the conspiracy and should tell all. Cottingham reported that Lloyd said to him, "If I was to make a confession, they would murder me!" Lloyd then told him everything he knew, including the location of the gun that Booth had not taken. It does not seem unreasonable to believe that under the circumstances, Lloyd was initially too frightened to talk. If a group of conspirators could successfully murder a President, then the killing of an ordinary citizen should not pose too much difficulty.

[16] Guy W. Moore, *The Case of Mrs. Surratt*, (University of Oklahoma Press, 1954), p. 4, *Lincoln's Assassins: A Complete Account of the Capture Trial, and Punishment*, p. 165, *The Assassination Of President Lincoln And The Trial Of The Conspirators*, p. 114, 115, *The Trial of John Surratt*, (Government Printing Office, 1867), Volume I, p. 377

[17] *The Assassination Of President Lincoln And The Trial Of The Conspirators*, p. 115, 118, 132, 133, 137, 138.

Witnesses such as Mrs. Eliza Holahan, who also had been a resident of the Surratt boarding house, supported Weichmann. She testified that Payne, who had called himself Wood, had come the boarding-house a couple of times and Atzerodt had also visited the house. Defence witnesses stated that Mrs. Surratt was kind to the sick and hospitable to Union soldiers. She was also hospitable to those sympathetic to the South as well.

[18] *The Assassination of President Lincoln and the Trial of the Conspirators*, p. 113, 114, Andrew C. A. Jampoler, *The Last Lincoln Conspirator: John Surratt's Flight from the Gallows*, (Naval Institute Press, 2008), p. 110. According to Jampoler, born Sarah Antoinette Gilbert, "Sarah Slater was one of the more intriguing Confederate agents". After introductions, Booth, John Surratt, Mudd and Weichmann went to Booth's room in the National Hotel for cigars and wine. Booth called on the Surratt home frequently and the talks with John Surrratt sometimes lasted up to two or three hours.

[19] *The Assassination of President Lincoln and the Trial of the Conspirators*, p. 113, 117

[20] Ibid, p. 113

[21] Ibid, p. 121. According to Louis Weichmann, Mary Surratt was aware that at least one visitor to her house, Sarah Slater, was a Confederate agent.

[22] Ibid, p. 116

[23] Ibid, p. 121,122. When Major Smith first rang the bell, Mrs. Surratt came to the window and said, "Is that you, Mr. Kirby?" Mary Surratt knew William Wallace Kirby, an official of the criminal court in the capital. Kirby was the brother-in-law of John Holohan who, with his wife, lived at the Surratt boardinghouse at the time. Was she expecting this man or another, such as Payne?

[24] *The Assassination Of President Lincoln And The Trial Of The Conspirators*, p. 115, 121-123, 126, 127, 131, 132, *Lincoln's Assassins: A Complete Account of the Capture, Trial, and Punishment*, p. 104, 179, *New York Times*, May 27, 1865, p. 1. Of Mary Surratt and her daughter Anna's non-recognition of Payne, Roy Chamlee stated, "Even those who wanted to believe Anna and her mother had difficulty accepting the Surratts' denial that they recognize Lewis Payne. His distinctive size and shape made him easy to identify, even from a distance. Witnesses who had seen Payne only briefly readily described his features. His face, clean shaven and youthfully handsome, was as readily recognizable as his large muscular form. Detectives wondered how so many strangers could describe Payne accurately and identify him quickly, while those of the Surratt household claimed not to know him." In its coverage of the trial, the New York Times gave the testimony of Rev. Father Young, who stated that had never heard of Mary Surratt having weak eyes and had never been present when she was not able to recognize friends who were a little distance from her. Captain W.M. Wermerskirch, who was with Major Smith at the time, confirmed Mary Surratt's denial.

[25] *The Assassination Of President Lincoln And The Trial Of The Conspirators*, p. 135, 136, *Fifty Years*, p. 722, Andrew C. A. Jampoler, *The Last Lincoln Conspirator: John Surratt's Flight from the Gallows*, (Naval Institute Press, 2008), p. 33. In the *Last Lincoln Conspirator*, Andrew Jampoler stated of Mary Surratt, "Five of the twenty-nine witnesses called to the stand by the defense in May and June testified to Mary's poor eyesight, an attempt to explain away her apparently false statement. 'I assure you,' Mary Surratt has said to Col. Henry Wells during her first

interrogation, 'on the honor of a lady that I would not tell an untruth.' But seemingly in an effort to save herself she had, and been caught at it."

[26] The *Assassination of President Lincoln And The Trial Of The Conspirators*, p. 293, *The Catholics and Mrs. Mary Surratt*, Kenneth J. Zanca, (University Press of America, 2008), p. 24, *The Assassin's Accomplice: Mary Surratt and the Plot to Kill Abraham Lincoln*, p. xvii.

Mary Surratt's defence stated,"The acquaintance with Booth, the message to Lloyd, the non-recognition of Payne, constitute the sum total of her receiving, entertaining, harboring and concealing, aiding and assisting those named as conspirators and their confederates, with knowledge of the murderous and traitorous conspiracy, and with intend to aid, abet, and assist them in the execution thereof, and in escaping from justice. The acts she has done, in and of themselves, are perfectly innocent."

[27] The *Assassination of President Lincoln And The Trial Of The Conspirators*, p. 293

[28] The *Assassination Of President Lincoln And The Trial Of The Conspirators*, p. 114, 294, 295, *The Trial of John Surratt*, (Government Printing Office, 1867), Volume I, p. 377.

On to the subject of Payne's first visit to Mrs. Surratt's house, the defence asserted that Weichmann requested that Payne stay the night, which he did as Weichmann's guest.

The defence stated:

"In the month of March last the prisoner, Payne, according to Weichmann, went to Mrs. Surratt's house and *inquired* for John H. Surratt. 'I myself,' says Weichmann, 'went to open the door, and he inquired for Mr. Surratt. I told him Mr. Surratt was not at home, but I would introduce him to the family, and did introduce him to Mrs. Surratt--under the name of Wood.' What more? By Weichmann's request Payne remained in the house all night. He had supper served to him in the privacy of Weichmann's own room. More than that, Weichmann went down into the kitchen and got the supper and carried it up to him himself, and as nearly as he recollects, it was about eight weeks previous to the assassination. Payne remained as Weichmann's guest until the next morning, when he left in the early train for Baltimore."

According to the court record, what Weichmann actually said before the commission was:

"Some time in March last, I think, a man calling himself Wood came to Mrs. Surratt's and inquired for John H. Surratt. I went to the door and told him Mr. Surratt was not at home; he thereupon expressed a desire to see Mrs. Surratt, and I introduced him, having first asked his name. That is the man [pointing to Lewis Payne, one of the accused.] He stopped at the house all night. He had supper served up to him in my room; I took it to him from the kitchen."

Neither Weichmann or anyone else testified that he had requested that Payne stay the night. Payne had not come to visit him and Weichmann clearly didn't know him, having to ask him his name in order to introduce him to his landlady. After finding out John Surratt wasn't home, Payne asked for Mary Surratt, was introduced to her and undoubtedly spoke to her. It would be logical to suppose it was she who asked him to stay. Weichmann helped Mrs. Surratt on other occasions so helping bringing dinner to Payne in his room wouldn't be out of the ordinary as the "Baptist preacher" probably arrived after the supper hour. He also didn't sleep in Weichmann's room. At John Surratt's trial, Weichmann clearly testified that Payne had never stayed in his room.

The defence stated, "More than that, Weichmann went down into the kitchen and got the supper and carried it up to him himself, and as nearly as he recollects, it was about eight weeks previous to the assassination." Weichmann didn't say this and if Payne had come in March, the most it could have been is some six weeks previous to the assassination.

[29] *Lincoln's Assassins: A Complete Account of the Capture, Trial, and Punishment*, p. 105, 484, 520, 521.

According to McCullough's testimony, the defence was correct in asserting that Weichmann couldn't have come to Booth's room on the 2nd of April. Weichmann however, was just off on the date he had delivered the message, it being a week earlier. McCullough could have categorically denied that Weichmann had appeared to speak to Booth in his hotel room when he was present but he didn't do so.

Chamlee stated of Mudd, "On August 25, 1865, he wrote his wife criticizing the Military Commission and denied that he recognized Booth when he treated him. But again, he admitted that Weichmann's testimony about his meeting with Surratt and Booth was true. Weichmann was wrong about the date, however, which the doctor said was December 23."

[30] *The Assassination Of President Lincoln And The Trial Of The Conspirators*, p. 85, 86.

What Lloyd had testified was. "On the Tuesday before the assassination of the President, I was coming to Washington, and I met Mrs. Surratt, on the road, at Uniontown. When she first broached the subject to me about the articles at my place, I did not know what she had reference to. Then she came out plainer, and asked me about the 'shooting-irons'...When I met Mrs. Surratt on the Tuesday preceding the assassination, I was coming to Washington, and she was going to my place, I supposed. I stopped, and so did she. I then got out and went to her buggy. It had been raining, and was very muddy. I do not know that the word 'carbine' was mentioned. She spoke about those shooting-irons. It was a very quick and hasty conversation. I am confident that she named the shooting-irons on both occasions; not so positive about the first as I am about the last; I know she did on the last occasion".

[31] *The Assassination Of President Lincoln And The Trial Of The Conspirators*, p. 85, 121, 125, 296, *Blood On The Moon*, p.110.

Mrs. Emma Offutt testified that on the day of the assassination, Lloyd came back to Surrattsville from Marlboro where he had been attending court, arriving in the late afternoon with fish and oysters, which is what Lloyd had said. He stated that Mrs. Surratt met him by the woodpile in the yard after he got home. Mrs. Offutt testified that she saw Mrs. Surratt talking to him in the backyard. Mrs. Offutt and Louis

Weichmann both corroborated what Lloyd had reported regarding Mrs. Surratt bringing a package to Surrattsville on that visit and Weichmann confirmed Lloyd's story of meeting Mrs. Surratt at Uniontown on April 11th.

Regarding the April 11th meeting, the defence stated: "In connection with the fact that Lloyd can not swear positively that Mrs. Surratt mentioned 'shooting irons' to him at Uniontown, bear in mind the fact that Weichmann sat in the buggy on the same seat with Mrs Surratt, and he swears he heard nothing about 'shooting irons'. Would not the quick ears of Weichmann have heard the remark had it been made?" What Weichmann actually testified however, was that not only did he not hear about "shooting irons", he stated he heard none of the conversation.

[32] *The Assassination Of President Lincoln And The Trial Of The Conspirators*, p. 115, 118, 119, 294, 298, 299, *The Living Webster Encyclopedic Dictionary of the English Language*, (The English Language Institute of America, 1971), p. 217, *The Trial of John Surratt*, p. 409, *Fifty Years*, p. 724.

According to Webster's Dictionary, a conspiracy is defined as the secret plotting of the two or more persons to do a wrongful act. No person knowledgeable about the Lincoln assassination would argue that Booth and Payne were not working together and just happened, coincidentally, to go about to assassinate a high-ranking U.S. government official, at exactly the same time in the same city on the same night.

It was Major Smith and Captain Wermerskitch who testified of Mrs. Surratt's non-recognition of Lewis Payne, not Weichmann or Lloyd. Regarding Weichmann's knowledge of the conspirators' plans, Weichmann said in court,"I do not know of any conversation that passed between Atzerodt and Booth, or Atzerodt and Payne, having reference to a conspiracy."

Believing that John Lloyd and Louis Weichmann posed the only problem to proving Mary Surratt's innocence, the defence set about to discredit them as witnesses. Beginning with Weichmann, the defence argued that if there was a conspiracy, then he and Lloyd were actually involved in it and testified against the other members to save themselves:

"We may start out with the proposition that a body of men, banded together for the consummation of an unlawful act against the Government, naturally would not disclose their purpose and hold suspicious consultations concerning it in the presence continually of an innocent party. In the light of this fair presumption, let us look at the ACTS OF WEICHMANN, as disclosed by his own testimony. Perhaps the most singular and astonishing fact that is made to appear is his omnipresence and co-action with those declared to be conspirators, and his professed and declared knowledge of all their plans and purposes."

Weichmann did not state that he had knowledge of all of the plans and purposes of the alleged conspirators. He said to the exact opposite a number of times, reporting that members of the conspiracy left his presence to have private conversations amongst themselves.

[33] *New York Times*, May 26, 1865, p. 1, *National Intelligencer*, May 27, 1865, p. 3, *Lincoln's Assassins*, p. 342

Chapter 8 John Surratt

[1] Louis J. Weichmann, *A True History of the Assassination of Abraham Lincoln and the Conspiracy of 1865*, (Alfred A. Knopf, 1975), photograph between pages 158 and 159, Mark Neely, *The Abraham Lincoln Encyclopedia*, (McGraw-Hill, 1982), p. 297, Charles Chiniquy, *Fifty Years In The Church of Rome*, (Craig and Barlow, 1886, 3rd edition), p. 726-729, Andrew C. A. Jampoler, *The Last Lincoln Conspirator: John Surratt's Flight from the Gallows*, (Naval Institute Press, 2008), p. 87 – 89, 131.

The question has been raised as to the alleged slowness of the U.S. authorities to try to apprehend John Surratt in Europe. Commenting on Surratt's flight to Egypt, Andrew Jampoler provides an explanation, "But when he came ashore in Egypt Surratt unknowingly gave up legal protections that had, until then, kept him out of the hands of his pursuers several times. Months earlier the United States had not even approached Great Britian about arresting and extraditing Surratt when he was known to be in Liverpool because of an assumption that Her Majesty's government would never agree to do it."

[2] *The Abraham Lincoln Encyclopedia*, p. 297, *The Assassination of President Lincoln and The Trial Of The Conspirators*, The Courtroom Testimony as Originally Compiled by Benn Pitman, (Greenwood Press, 1976, facsimile edition), p. 115, 131, *History of Saint Charles Borromeo Parish, Pikesville, Maryland, 1849-1949*, (Chandler Print Co., undated), p. 31, Roy Z. Chamlee, Jr., *Lincoln's Assassins: A Complete Account of the Capture, Trial, and Punishment*, p 77, 78, 100, 101, Alfred Isaacson, "John Surratt And The Lincoln Assassination Plot", Maryland Historical Magazine, Volume 52, 1957, p. 316 – 342.

According to Chamlee, there was good reason to believe Surratt was studying for the priesthood but he appeared to make conflicting statements. In *Lincoln's Assassins*, he stated on page 77 that John Surratt was sponsored to study for the priesthood by a priest of Florida, and on page 78 that in July, 1862, Surratt and Weichmann both abandoned St Charles College and their plans for the priesthood. On page 100 he reported that Surratt was a ministerial student at St. Charles and on page 101, that Surratt left school because he felt that the priesthood was not for him. (On page 101, Chamlee also reported that Weichmann related that the school was in favour of the rebellion and the students kept ignorant of Union victories.) On page 340, Chamlee did comment however, that "The term 'student of divinity' could be variously interpreted" and on page 424, he stated that Louis Weichmann "answered a question which came up repeatedly about whether he and Surratt were 'students of divinity'. Weichmann declared that he had been a student of divinity. He admitted that perhaps he should have used the expression 'ecclesiastical student' for Surratt".

[3] *The Last Lincoln Conspirator: John Surratt's Flight from the Gallows*, p. 158 – 161, *The Trial of John Surratt*, (Government Printing Office, 1867), Volume II, p. 1210, 1211

[4] Edward Steers, Jr., *His Name Is Still Mudd*, (Thomas Publications, 1997), p. 50-54, *The Assassination of President Lincoln and The Trial Of The Conspirators*, Introduction, p. xiv, p. 113, Roy Z. Chamlee, Jr., *Lincoln's Assassins: A Complete*

Account of the Capture, Trial, and Punishment, (McFarland & Company, 1990), p. 137, 139, Louis J. Weichmann, *A True History of the Assassination of Abraham Lincoln and the Conspiracy of 1865*, (Alfred A. Knopf, 1975), p. 121. According to Roy Chamlee, Thomas Jones "was the only man in Maryland with whom the Confederate government had an *official* relationship." Samuel Cox was one of a number of friends of the Surratt family who reportedly were arrested during the war.

[5] *His Name Is Still Mudd*, p. 70, *The Trial of John Surratt*, p. 1212, 1230

[6] *The Trial of John Surratt*, p. 1204, Roy Z. Chamlee, Jr., *Lincoln's Assassins: A Complete Account of the Capture, Trial, and Punishment*, (McFarland & Company, 1990), p 142, 439

[7] Edward Steers Jr., *Blood On The Moon: The Assassination of Abraham Lincoln*, (The University Press Of Kentucky, 2001), p. 24, 85-87, *The Assassination of President Lincoln and The Trial Of The Conspirators*, p. 113, 114, 120, *The Trial of John Surratt*, Volume II, p. 791, *A True History of the Assassination of Abraham Lincoln and the Conspiracy of 1865*, p. 30, *The Abraham Lincoln Encyclopedia*, p. 297

[8] *The Trial of John Surratt*, Volume II, p. 1204, 1205, 1230

[9] *The Trial of John Surratt*, Volume I, p. 310, 311. Booth wrote in his diary, in part:

'Te amo.'

APRIL 13, 14, FRIDAY, THE IDES.

Until to-day nothing was ever thought of sacrificing to our country's wrongs. For six months we had worked to capture. But our cause being almost lost, something decisive and great must be done. But its failure was owing to others who did not strike for their country with a heart. I struck boldly, and not as the papers say. I walked with a firm step through a thousand of his friends; was stopped, but pushed on. A colonel was at his side. I shouted Sic semper before I fired. In jumping broke my leg. I passed all his pickets. Rode sixty miles that night, with the bone of my leg tearing the flesh at every jump.

I can never repent it, though we hated to kill. Our country owed all our troubles to him, and God simply made me the instrument of his punishment....

FRIDAY, 21.

After being hunted like a dog through swamps, woods, and last night being chased by gunboats till I was forced to return wet, cold, and starving, with every man's hand against me, I am here in despair. And why? For doing what Brutus was honored for--what made Tell a hero. And yet I, for striking down a greater tyrant than they ever knew, am looked upon as a common cut-throat. My action was purer than either of theirs. One hoped to be great. The other had not only his country's, but his own wrongs to avenge. I hoped for no gain. I knew no private wrong. I struck for my country and that alone. A country that groaned beneath this tyranny, and prayed for this end, and yet now behold the cold hand they extend to me. God cannot pardon me if I have done wrong. Yet I cannot see my wrong, except in serving a degenerate people. The little, the very little, I left behind to clear my name, the government will not allow to be printed. So ends all. For my country I have given up all that makes life sweet and holy, brought misery upon my family, and am sure there is no pardon in the Heaven for me, since man condemns me so. I have only heard of what has been done, (except what I did myself,) and it fills me with horror. God, try and forgive me, and bless my mother. To-night I will once more try the river with the intent to cross. Though I have a greater desire and almost a mind to return to Washington, and in a measure clear my name--which I feel I can do. I do not repent the blow I struck. I may before my God, but not to man. I think I have done well. Though I am abandoned, with the curse of Cain upon me, when, if the world knew my heart, that one blow would have made me great, though I did desire no greatness.

To-night I try to escape these blood-hounds once more. Who, who can read his fate? God's will be done.

I have too great a soul to die like a criminal. 0, may He, may He spare me that, and let me die bravely.

I bless the entire world. Have never hated or wronged any one. This last was not a wrong, unless God deems it so, and it's with Him to damn or bless me. And for this brave boy with me, who often prays (yes, before and since) with a true and sincere heart--was it crime in him? If so, why can he pray the same?

I do not wish to shed a drop of blood, but 'I must fight the course.' ' Tis all that's left me.

[10] *The Trial of John Surratt*, Volume II, p. 1228, 1229

[11] *Blood On The Moon*, p. 80, *The Assassination of President Lincoln and The Trial Of The Conspirators*, p. 4, 307, *The Trial of John Surratt*, Volume I & II, p. 206, 216-218, 220-225, 1190, 1204, 1205, 1230, *The Last Lincoln Conspirator: John Surratt's Flight from the Gallows*, p. 111, 134.

In his diary, Booth stated, "A colonel was at his side". There was no colonel in the box with the Lincolns that night. Major Rathbone was there as a guest of the President and the First Lady. He was certainly not on guard at the time and undoubtedly didn't know Booth was there until the President had been shot. Again, showing his supposed bravery at the time, he recorded that he "struck boldly". What he actually did was shoot a defenceless man in the back of the head who was peacefully watching a play with his wife and friends.

Booth rode to Dr. Samuel Mudd's home during the first night and stayed there. This appears to be some 30 to 40 miles so how did he managed to ride 60 unless he got lost and if lost, how could he be sure how far he went?

In court, R. T. Merrick stated:

"Weichmann says that Dr Mudd introduced him and Surratt to Booth in December, 1864, or January, 1865. That is Surratt's first acquaintance with Booth. There is no proof in the case, not one particle, that Surratt had ever seen Booth before that day. On the 16th of March Weichmann testifies that Booth, Payne, and Surratt came in very much excited and strutted about the room; that Surratt said, 'My prospects are ruined; cannot you get me a clerkship?' The whole thing, whatever it was, was evidently broken up then and there. They were never seen together after that day. The next we hear of Surratt is that he is off with some lady toward Richmond, and then in Canada. For what purpose he was in Canada the court would not let us prove, or we could have shown why he went to Canada. Now, gentlemen, they say Surratt furnished the arms and put them at Surrattsville. Well, now, what is the plain common-sense course of reasoning with regard to all this business? Here were a number of young men, with their minds inflamed upon political topics, sympathizing earnestly with the South, as a great many of our Maryland young men did, desirous of rendering it such assistance as they could, probably helping persons to cross the river, carrying despatches between the United States and the Confederate States, and having arms for the purpose of their common protection; and further than that it is not improbable that there may have been some idea of abducting the President as a measure of war--a thing which was unjustifiable, and for which they might have been taken and executed…

I say again, that at the time of which I have been speaking, there may have been some scheme to take Mr. Lincoln to the south, in order to accomplish an exchange of prisoners, but not to kill him, for that would not have effected their purpose. Killing him would have defeated the object…There may have been among those young men some such wild scheme, but that it was broken up is conclusively established by Weichmann's testimony."

It is interesting that John Surratt's lawyers used Weichmann's testimony to "conclusively" prove that the wild scheme that "may" have existed among the conspirators was broken up. They had called Weichmann among other things, a liar and a perjured person. If they could conclusively establish anything with his testimony then so could the prosecution. The defence continued to try to show that the plot to kidnap was given up well before the assassination:

"But, says my learned brother upon the other side, one of these horses belonged to Surratt, and he bought the horses, and he bought the guns and a rope. What became of those horses? I know that Judge Pierrepont, who is to close this case, will use those horses to caper and prance before you; but what is the fact about them? Cleaver says that Booth brought the horses to his stable; Stabler says Surratt brought the horses to his stable and paid the fare. That after Surratt had paid for their livery for a certain time, Booth paid for the livery. In March, Booth paid for the livery. Surratt told Stabler that they were Booth's horses, and he would pay for them. Booth says to Weichmann, on the 10th of April, the horses are not John Surratt's; they are mine. Booth then says, these horses, although they may have been Surratt's, had become his. What is the conclusion? Isn't it that if Surratt owned these horses, and had been in this conspiracy, he had got tired of the thing and thrown it up. That it had passed from his mind, and he had gone into other matters to which he was devoting his attention, but that Booth, more ardent and determined, still clung to it, and kept the property; and if he wrote Surratt any letter at all, it was in the hope of inducing him to come again under the control of his fascinating and superior mind."

The defence used prosecution witness William Cleaver to help establish their case but they had attacked him on the stand, calling him an accursed man though apparently they needed his testimony at this point. Cleaver also testified that he heard John Surratt say in late January, 1865 "he and Booth had some bloody work to do; that they were going to kill Abe Lincoln, the d----d old scoundrel". Did the defence believe Cleaver here as well?

The aptly named Brooks Stabler stated that Surratt brought his horses to his stable. Surratt paid for them at the beginning and then Booth took over. Stabler did not say that in March Booth paid for the livery. He also did not testify that John Surratt told him the horses were Booth's and he would pay for them. The defence again used Weichmann's testimony as he declared that Booth told him that the horses were his.

The names John Surratt used were: James Sturdy – *The Assassination of President Lincoln and The Trial Of The Conspirators*, p. 118, John Harrison – *The Assassination of President Lincoln and The Trial Of The Conspirators*, p. 117, *A True History of the Assassination of Abraham Lincoln and the Conspiracy of 1865*, p. 331, Henry Sherman – *The Trial of John Surratt*, Volume II, p. 790, 791, Charles Armstrong – *The Trial of John Surratt*, Volume II, p. 905, John Watson – *A True History of the Assassination of Abraham Lincoln and the Conspiracy of 1865*, p. 338, *The Abraham Lincoln Encyclopedia*, p. 297, McCarty – *The Trial of John Surratt*, Volume II, p. 462, Walters – *A True History of the Assassination of Abraham Lincoln and the Conspiracy of 1865*, p. 352, Giovanni Watson – *The Last Lincoln Conspirator: John Surratt's Flight from the Gallows* p.111, John Agostini – *The Last Lincoln Conspirator: John Surratt's Flight from the Gallows* p. 134.

[12] *The Trial of John Surratt*, Volume I, p. 365.

Mrs. McClermont testified that between the 12th and 15th of April, 1864, the three men she overheard, "spoke in an under tone, and the only remark I heard, in speaking to the one who joined them, was 'Jim.' Then I heard the President's name mentioned; one of the men spoke of his coming from the Soldier's Home; then I heard them mention the word 'telescope rifle.' One of these answered and said 'His wife and child will be along.' Another replied, 'It makes no difference; if necessary, they too could be got rid of.' At this I turned, and one of them saw I was looking at them; they ceased conversation and walked on the avenue".

[13] *The Trial of John Surratt*, Volume I, p. 365, 366, *Blood On The Moon*, p. 24. The defence made no attempt to contradict Mrs. McClermont's statement or try to show that she was mistaken or had not told the truth on the stand.

[14] *The Assassination of President Lincoln and The Trial Of The Conspirators*, p. 39, 40, *The Trial of John Surratt*, Volume I, p. 352, 353.

Two years after she testified for the prosecution at the trial of the conspirators, Mary Hudspeth married and gained the last name of Benson. Of one of the men she had observed, Mary Hudspeth testified that, "The man named Johnson was very angry because it had not fallen upon him to do something that he had been sent as a messenger to direct this other man to do". She described the taller man as "gentlemanly-looking" and stated that he appeared to be wearing a disguise of false whiskers and a wig.

[15] *The Trial of John Surratt*, Volume I, p. 353-355

[16] *World Book Encyclopedia*, 1978, Volume 4, p. 830, Volume 13, p. 150, *The Assassination of President Lincoln and The Trial Of The Conspirators*, p. 39, 40, 341, 342.

Mrs. Benson testified that the letters came into her hands the day U. S. Army General Benjamin Butler left New York City. Cox stated that General Butler left the city on either the 14th or 16th of November. Saying that she identified one of the men, presumably the man with the false whiskers, as Booth, Cox asserted she was wrong because Booth arrived in the nation's capital on the 14th and left on the 16th, according to the clerk at the National Hotel in Washington, and therefore couldn't have been in New York in time for her to see him.

The other letter was a correspondence, apparently from the wife of this "Louis", pleading with him to come home. Walter Cox was the lawyer who defended O'Laughlin and Arnold.

[17] *The Trial of John Surratt*, Volume I, p. 352, 405, *The Assassination of President Lincoln and The Trial Of The Conspirators*, p. 341, 342, *A True History of the Assassination of Abraham Lincoln and the Conspiracy of 1865*, p. 42-44, *Saint Paul Pioneer*, April 29, 1865, p. 1, *Lincoln's Assassins: A Complete Account of the Capture, Trial, and Punishment*, p. 45, 46, "The Conspiracy: Trial of the Accused, Testimony Taken on Friday, Additional Testimony Yesterday", *Daily National Intelligencer*, May 16, 1865, Investigation and Trial Papers Relating to the Assassination of President Lincoln, Proceedings of the Court Martial, May 9 – 15, 1865, M599, Roll 8, National Archives, Washington D.C.

In his argument for the two defendants, Cox also stated that six months later, after being shown a photograph of Booth, Mrs. Hudspeth said that one of the men she saw earlier was the actor but according to Cox, Booth couldn't have been in New York at the time. There was a discrepancy between the various records as to what she did say. The Washington newspaper, the *National Intelligencer* reported that she did recognize one of the men as Booth, quoting her saying "The face is the same". The Pitmann record did not record Mary Hudspeth saying anything recognizing one of the men as Booth. The official longhand record of the military commission also reported that she did not. The longhand record stated that she only said that the shape of the face was the same. This would seem more reasonable as according to her testimony, the man was disguised.

As well, Cox declared that she must be mistaken because, among other things, she said that these two men had this conversation "in a car which she represents as crowded". She is recorded as saying nothing of the kind according to the record of the military commission, as well as the *National Intelligencer*, so the arguments of the defence have to be questioned.

The letter from John Surratt read:

'SURRATTSVILLE, *November* 12, 1864.

'DEAR AL.: Sorry I could not get up. Will be up on Sunday Hope you are getting along well. How are times--all the pretty girls? My most pious regards to the latter; as for the former, I have not a continental d--m. Have you been to the fair? If so, what have we now? I'm interested in the ' bedstead.' How's Kennedy? Tight, as usual, I suppose. Opened his office, I hear. Fifty to one 'tis a failure. Am very happy I do not belong to the ' firm.' Been busy all the week taking care of and securing the crops. Next Tuesday, and the jig's up. Good by, Surrattsville. Good by, God forsaken country. Old Abe, the good old soul, may the devil take pity on him.

'SURRATTSVILLE, MD.

'Test: JOHN H. SURRATT.

'To LOUIS J. WEICHMANN, Esq., *Washington city, D. C.'* .

[18] *The Assassination of President Lincoln and The Trial Of The Conspirators*, p. 24, 25, 42, *The Trial of John Surratt*, Volume I, p. 528.

In testimony before the military commission, a man named Richard Montgomery stated that he had carried dispatches from Confederate agents in Canada to the South and back again. Evidently a double agent, he assisted the Union cause by showing the dispatches to the authorities in Washington as he passed through and also informed them on the activities of the rebels. He testified that he knew Confederate leaders in Canada such as George N. Sanders, Jacob Thompson, Clement C. Clay, Beverly Tucker, W. C. Cleary and others. He said that he talked to Thompson in January of 1865 and Thompson said that:

a proposition had been made to him to rid the world of the tyrant Lincoln, Stanton, Grant, and some others. The men who had made the proposition, he said, he knew were bold, daring men, and able to execute any thing they would undertake, without regard to the cost.

He said he was in favor of the proposition, but had determined to defer his answer until he had consulted with his Government at Richmond, and he was then only waiting their approval.

Montgomery reported that he had been in Canada since the assassination and he stated:

I related a portion of the conversation I had had with Mr. Thompson to Mr. W. C. Cleary, who is a sort of confidential secretary to Mr. Thompson, and he told me that Booth was one of the parties to whom Thompson had reference; and he said, in regard to the assassination, that it was too bad that the whole work had not been done; by which I understood him to mean that they intended to assassinate a greater number that they succeeded in killing.

[19] *The Trial of John Surratt*, Volume I, p. 400

[20] *The Trial of John Surratt*, p. 370, 371, 374, 375, *The Assassination of President Lincoln and The Trial Of The Conspirators*, p. 114, 117. Surratt introduced Weichmann to George Atzerodt in the latter part of January, 1865.

[21] *The Trial of John Surratt*, Volume I, p. 376, 399. The day Weichmann went into the attic room, he found John Surratt and Payne playing with spurs, Bowie knives and revolvers.

[22] *Blood On The Moon*, p. 85-87, *The Trial of John Surratt*, Volume I, p. 277, 278, 282, 283, 381, *The Assassination of President Lincoln and The Trial Of The Conspirators*, p. 85-87

[23] *Lincoln's Assassins: A Complete Account of the Capture, Trial, and Punishment*, p. 533, *The Trial of John Surratt*, Volume I & II, p. 381-384, 387, 1105, 1106, 1116, *The Assassination of President Lincoln and The Trial Of The Conspirators*, p. 113, 114. John Surratt and Mrs. Slater, reportedly a Confederate agent, both went to the Southern capital of Richmond, Virginia.

[24] *The Trial of John Surratt*, Volume I, p. 166-168, 217, 387, 388, Volume II, p. 790, 791, 1116. According to Louis Weichmann, John Surratt left that same night for Montreal. The hotel clerk at St. Lawrence Hall confirmed that a man fitting the description of Surratt had stayed in the hotel.

[25] Ibid, Volume I & II, p. 131-159, 162, 176,177, 195-203, 207, 241, 471, 494-498, 500-502, 520-522, 723-745. The four residents of Elmira were Charles Stewart, John Cass, Frank Atkinson and Joseph Carroll. The 11 prosecution witnesses were, Charles Wood, David Reed, Theodore Rhodes, Benjamin Vanderpoel, Scipiano Grillo, William Cleaver, John Lee, Walter Coleman, Frank Heaton, Susan Ann Jackson, Joseph Dye.

[26] *The Trial of John Surratt*, Volume I & II, p. 195, 471, 494-498, 593, 595, 597, 598, 610, 611, 619, 620, 693, 694, 759-761, 778, 779, 924, 925, 935, 936, 999, 1000, 1002, 1003, 1011, 1044, 1045, 1080, 1117, 1121, 1122, 1126-1131, 1143, 1144, 1188, 1189, 1190, 1312-1322, *Lincoln's Assassins: A Complete Account of the Capture, Trial, and Punishment*, p. 525.

Dr. McMillan testified that Surratt mentioned Elmira first when he said where he went after leaving Montreal after being contacted by Booth. John Surratt must have known where he was during those half a dozen days. It was events during this time period that caused him to go into hiding for two years. Surratt's defence reportedly did find another register. This was of the Webster hotel in Canandiagua, New York, where according to Roy Chamlee, the name that John Surratt used to register in the hotel in Montreal, John Harrison, was written in John Surratt's handwriting on the page pertaining to April 15. It reportedly was not allowed as evidence over prosecution objection that no one witnessed Surratt signing the register, if he did indeed sign it.

Early said O'Laughlin's pants were of a conspicuous plaid. Bright, eye catching colours, when compared to black, can be described as light.

The defence challenged some of the prosecution witnesses. The defence pointed out that William Cleaver had been convicted what evidently was the murder of a young girl in Washington. His conviction had been overturned on a technicality and a new trial ordered. The prosecution however, stated that they would not have tried to convict Surratt on Cleaver's testimony alone but his testimony was corroborated by other witnesses. The defence, for all their condemnation of Cleaver, used his testimony as well - *The Trial of John Surratt*, p. 1121, 1122, 1189, 1190.

Two men testified that while carrying out the duties of their regular employment, they saw John Surratt traveling to Washington. One was Ezra Westfall, a train master for the Philadelphia and Erie railroad who said he believed John Surratt to be the man who arrived at Williamsport on a special train from Elmira at 12:30 p.m., April 13th, anxious to continue on to Washington. The other was Morris Drohan, a ferry operator who identified John Surratt as the man he ferried, alone, over the Susquehanna River at Williamsport, also on the 13th. Trains ran from this point to Washington. These men's testimony was not contradicted or challenged by the defence.

The next prosecution witness to see him, barber Charles Wood, gave a detailed narrative, stating he had shaved Booth and Surratt in the company of Michael O'Laughlin and another man in Washington at about nine o'clock in the morning of April 14th. Wood called O'Laughlin: McLaughlin. John Surratt's legal team produced no witnesses to show that Wood's character was such that he shouldn't be believed. The defence instead argued that Surratt could not have arrived in Washington by train until 10:25 a.m. and two of their witnesses, Bernard Early and Edward Murphy, could account for Michael O'Laughlin's whereabouts until about that time or slightly earlier and they said they did not go into Wood's shop. In addition, the defence stated that Wood did not describe the crowd of people that should have been in his shop had it been nine o'clock when he shaved the two men.

Charles Wood did not say definitely it was nine o'clock however. He said "I think it was near about nine o'clock". According to his testimony, after breakfast that morning, he had gone some distance to Secretary of State William Seward's home to shave Seward, who was recovering from a carriage accident. He shaved him in a third floor room in his home, undoubtedly not a straightforward job since the Secretary had a shattered jaw. While he was there, Secretary of War Edwin Stanton came to visit Seward. Meeting national leaders like these was probably not an everyday occurrence for Wood. The extra traveling, going to and from Secretary Seward's home, the natural excitement of being in the presence of these great men, the extra work, undoubtedly made the time fly by. Therefore when he thought the time was around nine o'clock, it easily could have been ten o'clock or later.

The defence argued that the barber shop should have been crowded at nine o'clock, making it unlikely that Wood would have remembered Surratt. In all likelihood though, it was later than that. As well, Booth, whom Wood knew, was with the party. From that night on, the actor was going to become known as the murderer of America's greatest President, an act which undoubtedly would make the barber think back to the last time he had seen John Wilkes Booth and who had been with him.

Wood's statements, in regards to the smaller details, fits with the prosecution's version of events, as well as with other evidence presented. He didn't say that O'Laughlin got a shave because as other testimony showed, he had already been shaved earlier in the day. According to the barber, the group was speaking about Baltimore, which Surratt would have just come from. He declared that Surratt "seemed to be a little dusty, as though he had been travelling some little distance and wanted a little cleaning and dressing up, as I am frequently called upon by gentlemen coming in after a short travel." He added that he "shaved him clean all round the face, with the exception of where his moustache was. He had a slight mustache at the time."

Surratt's defence took exception to this. Showing how poor a grasp his side had on the evidence, defence counsel R. T. Merrick stated "Every witness in the case that testified in regard to him gives him a goatee at the time not so long as he now wears, but one a barber would certainly notice." Actually when they testified about it, prosecution witnesses who placed him in Washington on the day of the assassination said the opposite. John Lee, a former chief of detectives in Washington and a man who knew Surratt by sight, stated that he had no goatee that day. Witnesses Joseph Dye, Scipiano Grillo and Theodore Vanderpoel said the defendant had no beard but did have a moustache the day of the assassination.

Surratt's slightly dusty condition could have been caused by a short trip by horse or a long one by train, possibly with some walking. Though he had been traveling by rail most of the way, Surratt still had gotten a little dirty. Wood reported that the defendant said, "Give me a nice shave and clean me up nicely; I am going away in a day or two." Surratt would indeed soon be back on the road, he would be fleeing for his life that night.

Wood's description of Michael O'Laughlin can be compared with what O'Laughlin's two associates said in court. Early stated that on that morning O'Laughlin "had on a black slouch hat, a black cloth frock coat, and pantaloons and vest of very conspicuous plaid---purple and green." Murphy described him as "dressed in a black cloth frock-coat, I think. He wore a black hat. The pants and vest, I am positive, were of large Scotch plaid." Of O'Laughlin, Wood testified,"He had on a black frockcoat. I think he had a black silk hat, and light pantaloons."

Wood evidently was not far off, the only difference being the pants. As well, the testimony of all the witnesses that saw Surratt in Washington is in agreement with Wood's description of him being clean shaven, except for a moustache.

The defence brought 11 witnesses that said the John Lee had a bad reputation for truth and veracity. They were William Boss (p. 593), Samuel W. Owens (p. 595), T.G. Clayton (p. 597), Joshua Lloyd (p. 598), Colonel James R. O'Brien (p. 610), Samuel K. Brown (p. 611), William O. Baldwin (p. 619), John Wise (p. 620), Patrick McDonough (p. 778), Henry A. Cook (p. 779), and John O'Donnell (p. 779). The prosecution brought seven witnesses who said the opposite. They were Alphonso Donn (p. 1002), George W. Theaker (p. 1003), Alfred G. Hatfield (p. 1011), Margaret A. Fithian (p. 1044), John E. Hatfield (p. 1044), William Parker (p. 1044), and William F. Parker (p. 1045).

Two of the defence's witnesses, William Boss and John Wise, had not heard of Lee's reputation questioned before the trial and therefore were rendered neutral or actually were witnesses for the prosecution. At least two other witnesses, Samuel Owen and William Baldwin said they had heard many people speak of Lee's poor reputation for telling the truth but when asked to name one, could not do so. Another defence witness, Frederick Calvert, said he heard Lee's poor reputation discussed nearly every day when the draft was going on but he could not state the substance of what was said on any of these many occasions. The prosecution therefore questioned the truthfulness of such witnesses. The prosecution also pointed out that as a chief detective in the nation's capital during a civil war, where blockade runners and spies lurked, and were everyone arrested, including those mistakenly, could be denied the writ of habeas corpus, it would be easy for Lee to make enemies (p. 195, 610, 1129, 1130).

Susan Ann Jackson's testimony was challenged by Eliza Hawkins who had been a servant of Mary Surratt for six years and was by her own admission, close to Mary Surratt and her family. Hawkins testified that Susan Ann Jackson had told her that she actually hadn't seen John Surratt in Washington on the day of the assassination. Susan Jackson's testimony was supported by her husband, Samuel L. Jackson, who testified that he had been with his wife and Hawkins the whole time they were held prisoner together by the military and had heard all that had been said and he had not hear his wife say what Hawkins said she did (p. 693, 694, 999-1000).

[27] *The Trial of John Surratt*, Volume I & II, p. 131-137, 1126. Dye and Cooper were sitting on a low platform in front of the theatre which was placed there to assist people to get in or out of carriages. Surratt. Sergeant Cooper also saw the well dressed young man in front of the theatre that Dye said was Surratt but Cooper did not observe his facial features closely enough to be able to identify him later.

[28] *The Trial of John Surratt*, Volume I & II, p. 142-144, 147, 151-153, 147, 570, 571, 1180, 1181, *The Assassination of President Lincoln and The Trial Of The Conspirators*, p. 72, 73.

John Surratt's lawyers called no one to cast doubt on Sergeant Dye's reputation for truthfulness but brought a number of witnesses to the stand to attempt to contradict his testimony.

The defence argued that Dye could not have seen Surratt's face as he turned toward the other men to call out the time to them. In cross-examination however, the defence asked him about this and Dye stated that he could readily see Surratt's face when he looked at the clock. Dye also testified that at one point, Surratt came so close to him, he almost stumbled over the officer's foot.

The defence also alleged that Dye was incorrect as to the three men's size relative to one another but the court record shows they did not properly understand his testimony.

According to the defence, when Dye testified before the military commission, he had said that the man calling the time, John Surratt, was the smallest of them at 5 ft. 7 inches and the other two were much taller. The defence argued that they had proved Surratt to be the largest of the three, evidently meaning the tallest.

According to the record of the military commission, Dye did not state the relative heights of the three men. During cross-examination at the trial of John Surratt, he explained that by small, he meant slightly built so according to that criterion, Surratt was the smallest of the three. He also stated his estimate of Surratt height was not meant to be accurate because it was just that, an estimate made from a sitting position.

At the trial of the conspirators, C. B. Hess was recorded as having the name of C. D. Hess.

[29] *The Trial of John Surratt*, Volume I, p. 557-559, 562, 565-569, 571-576, *The Assassination of President Lincoln and The Trial Of The Conspirators*, p. 79-82.

Along with others, Hess was scheduled to sing a song for the President at the end of the play. He said he went outside of the theatre and joined Carland and Gifford at the front. According to Hess, at the time there was another man in front of the theatre as well, dressed he thought, like a military officer. Hess asked the time, Carland went and looked and told him it was ten minutes past ten. Hess then remarked, "Ten minutes past ten; I will be wanted in a few minutes". He said he left immediately and went inside the theatre. He stated that he didn't think he had been inside for more than two minutes when he heard a pistol shot. Later in his testimony, Hess stated that from the time of the calling of the time until he reached the stage where he heard the pistol shot was 12 to 13 minutes. This 12 to 13 minutes evidently included time for dressing because he said, concerning his request for the time, "I asked it in a kind of very loud tone myself, knowing that I had, at least I supposed I had, about a quarter of an hour in which to dress up---to put on a black dress suit---to appear before the President in."

Adding to the contradictory testimony, Louis Carland said that as he and a group of others went into the restaurant adjoining the theatre, he saw John Wilkes Booth leave the restaurant through a different door. When asked what time this was, he is recorded as saying confusingly, "After the second act; after the curtain had fallen and before it went up on the second act". He testified that after hearing the time, Hess went up the street, turned and as far as he could remember, went into the theatre. He said he and Gifford stood talking outside the theatre for possibly a total of 10 to 15 minutes. He also stated that after telling Hess what the time was, a few minutes later, people came out of the theatre and said the President had been shot. Carland said that between telling Hess the time and the news of the assassination, the street outside the theatre was perfectly quiet, he couldn't remember a soul being on it. He also testified that while he said he could remember the exact words of the calling of the time, he could not remember the identity of any of the people that were talking to Booth in front of the theatre that morning even though he knew them personally.

James Gifford, the stage carpenter at Ford's theatre, testified that he was out in front of the theatre during the first and second act of the play and the beginning of the third. Asked how long he remained in front of the theatre, he said "At the beginning of the third act, about twenty or twenty-five minutes". He saw a number of people in front of the theatre that night but none on the carriage platform. He stated that while he was there with Carland, Hess asked the time. Gifford said after he found out the time, Hess "stood there are awhile and then went into the stage entrance".

These three witnesses were supposedly at the same place at the same time, yet their stories are so different. Hess stated that when he heard Carland call out the time, he left immediately and went into the theatre. Carland said that after he heard the time, Hess went out the street, turned and went into the theatre. Gifford said he stood outside for awhile and then went inside.

Hess testified that while he was talking with Gifford and Carland, there was another man in front of the theatre dressed, he thought, as an officer. Carland said that after telling Hess the time and before the news of the assassination reached them, he couldn't remember a soul being on the street outside the theatre. Gifford stated that he saw a number of people in front of the theatre that night.

Hess first said he didn't think it was more than two minutes after he went into the theatre that he heard a pistol shot. Then he appeared to change his story on the stand, saying it was some 12 or 13 minutes from the time he left the front of the theatre before he heard the shot. Carland testified that a very few minutes after the calling of the time, people came out of the theatre saying the President had been shot. Was this very few minutes, two, five, or ten? It would have taken a short time for the news to be communicated from the theatre to those outside.

It might have been possible for what both sets of witnesses reported, Sergeants Dye and Cooper and the other group, Carland, Gifford and Hess, to have happened, with some time discrepancies

At the trial of the conspirators, two men testified as to what time Lincoln was shot. They were Joseph Stewart, the man that almost caught Booth as he exited the theatre and Dr. Robert Stone, the Lincoln family physician. Stewart said he heard the pistol shot at about 10:30. Dr. Stone said he got to Lincoln at about 10:15, arriving "very few minutes" after he sent for by Mrs. Lincoln. The President's wife had sent for him immediately after the shooting. .

It may have been at one of these times or somewhere between. It is possible therefore that Lincoln could have been shot at perhaps 10:26. If so, then the news might have taken a minute to reach Gifford and Carland outside at 10:27.Carland stated that the two were in front of the theatre for perhaps 10 to 15 minutes. It is possible they could have arrived at the front of the theatre at 10:12. Hess would have come out half a minute later and asked the time. Carland, calling the time could have said it was 12 after 10 or roughly estimating, said 10 after 10. At 10:12, just before Hess and Carland came on the scene, Booth, Surratt and the other man, as well as Dye and Cooper could all have left, departing after the final calling of 10:10 by Surratt.

Putting the picture together chronologically that evening, Dye and Cooper could have arrived at the theatre at 9:30 pm. Approximately four minutes later at 9:34, Booth, Surratt, and the rough-looking man show up at the front of the theatre. They talk and wait for Lincoln to come out of the theatre, but he does not come out. Booth goes into the saloon / restaurant adjoining the theatre. He exits at roughly 9:36, just as Carland, Gifford and company go in. Then at 9:57, Surratt calls the time the first time and then walks up toward H. Street. He returns at 10:05 and calls the time again. He then hurries of up the street again. Returning some five minutes later, he calls the time for the third and final time, 10 past 10.

He then walks rapidly toward H. Street and Booth and the other man leave. Dye and Cooper also leave directly, at perhaps 10:11. Carland and Gifford then exit the restaurant a minute later with Hess arriving out in front almost simultaneously with them. The time is called 10 past 10, inaccurately, or accurately called 12 past 10. Some 14 minutes later Lincoln is assassinated.

[30] *The Assassination of President Lincoln and The Trial Of The Conspirators*, p. 72, 77, 78, 99, 108, 109, *The Trial of John Surratt*, Volume I, p. 576, 816, 1345-1347. Gifford testified four days later on the 19th and again on the 30th. Hess testified on May 31 and Carland testified on June 12th.

[31] *The Trial of John Surratt*, Volume II, p. 816, 818, 819, *The Assassination of President Lincoln and The Trial Of The Conspirators*, p. 108. It is not clear whether Gifford, Hess and Carland knew John Surratt.

[32] *The Assassination of President Lincoln and The Trial Of The Conspirators*, p. 76, 77. Regarding Gifford's questionable patriotism:

> Mr. Gifford is the chief carpenter of the theater, and I understood had full charge of it. I recollect when Richmond was surrendered I said to him, 'Have you not got any flags in the theater?' He replied, 'Yes, I have; I guess there is a flag about.' I said, 'Why do you not run it out on the roof?' He answered, 'There's a rope, isn't that enough?' I said, 'You are a hell of a man, you ought to be in the Old Capitol.'

James Ferguson obviously was wondering why the theater wasn't flying the American flag in celebration of the fall of the rebel capital and felt that because of his attitude, Gifford should have been put in the Old Capital prison in Washington.

[33] *The Abraham Lincoln Encyclopedia*, p. 298, *The Assassination of President Lincoln and The Trial Of The Conspirators*, p. 77, 78, 99, 108, 109, *The Trial of John Surratt*, Volume I & II, p. 127-129, 326-329, 565-576, 814-820, 994.

Carland, Gifford and Hess appeared a combined ten times as witnesses at both the trial of the conspirators and John Surratt's trial. They all testified for the defendants and only one of them, James Gifford, testified on the government side, doing so at both the trial of the conspirators and the Surratt trial. Being the carpenter of Ford's theater, on both occasions he mainly provided information on physical evidence relating to the theater. The defence also attempted to use Carland and Gifford to show Weichmann lied under oath at the trial of John Surratt.

The prosecution alleged that Carland, Gifford and Hess had made up their accounts and in cross-examination, Hess provided some proof for this. In answer to a question from prosecutor Edwards Pierrepont about the calling of the time, Hess stated:

> A. (Speaking in an ordinary conversational tone of voice.) Says I, 'Mr Carland, what time is it?' He walks up in the direction of the click, and then says, 'Ten minutes past ten.' Says I, 'Ten minutes past ten; I am wanted in a few minutes.'
>
> Q. That is exactly what you said?
>
> A. Yes, sir.

A short while later, Hess was asked about the calling of the time and in response, his story changed:

> Q. Did you think there was anything extraordinary in its being ten minutes past ten?
>
> A. No, sir. I did not until they spoke about it.
>
> Q. Then you had to hurry, did you?
>
> A. Yes, sir; I had nothing else to do, and I thought that I had better linger inside than outside.
>
> Q. The play was not then near over when the President was killed?
>
> A. No, sir; I think the second scene was on.
>
> Q. There was no occasion then for you to be in a great hurry?
>
> A. No sir; there was no great hurry.
>
> Q. And you did not hurry?
>
> A. No, sir; I walked on leisurely.

Hess evidently could not make up his mind as to whether he was in a hurry or not. If he had nothing else to do, then he was in no hurry and really was not needed in a few minutes. Perhaps however, Hess and company needed to try to manufacture some excuse to have him enquiring the time to make their story believable.

[34] *The Trial of John Surratt*, Volume I & II, p. 136, 137, 145, 471-473, 661, 662, 1181-1183.

Defence witness Frederika Lambert testified that between 11 p.m. and 12 - midnight, April 14th, two soldiers came past her home on 581 H Street, some distance from Mary Surratt's house at 541 H Street. She asked what the commotion was about and they told her the President had been shot. The evidence she gave indicated that she spoke to different soldiers than Dye and Cooper. Her testimony showed that there was a number of soldiers in the street as the time she spoke to the two soldiers. Dye and Cooper said there was no one else on H Street when they went by, undoubtedly leaving the scene before the large group of soldiers arrived, that Lambert saw. Mrs. Lambert said that the soldiers she talked to said that they were going to Camp Barry. Dye did not say he told the lady he talked to that they were going to Camp Barry though and why would he as he and Cooper were hurrying back to their base? The defence also attempted to show the woman Sergeant Dye talked to on the way to his camp that night was not Mary Surratt. Dye however, did not state positively that it was Mrs. Surratt. He merely said, "she resembled the lady on the trial of the conspirators -- Mrs. Surratt".

[35] *The Trial of John Surratt*, Volume I & II, p. 461, 462, 469, 471-473, 902-908, 910, 941-947, *The Last Lincoln Conspirator: John Surratt's Flight from the Gallows*, p. 108.

At least 11 witnesses testified that the man they positively identified as or said resembled the defendant was in Washington on the day of the assassination. In *The Last Lincoln Conspirator*, Andrew Jampoler stated regarding prosecution witness Henri St. Marie,"What St. Marie said under oath made him the fourteenth prosecution witness to fix Surratt in Washington on the day Lincoln was slain, and the only one to do so purportedly quoting Surratt himself." Lewis McMillen however, did testify that Surratt told him that he started for Washington at the beginning of the week of the assassination on orders from Booth and that he arrived in St. Albans a few days after the assassination, as he fled from U.S. justice.

The priest, Charles Boucher, tried to evade the question of whether he concealed the John Surratt, who went by the name of Charles Armstrong. Boucher helped escort Surratt part of the way to the ship he took to Europe

McMillan testified that on one occasion on board the ship, while holding a revolver in his hand, Surratt stated that he hoped to "serve Andrew Johnson as Abraham Lincoln has been served."

The defence attempted to contradict the doctor's testimony but the only place they showed he erred was an estimate of how overdue one of his bills was. He had treated the sister of the Catholic priest, Boucher, several times in 1864 and Dr. McMillan had said the bill had been overdue for a year or more but it had only been a couple of months.

36. *The Trial of John Surratt*, Volume I & II, p. 134, 135, 151, 152, 166, 167, 169-171, 174, 175, 185, 208, 209, 240-243, 353, 462, 472, 473, 492, 493, 495, 847-859, 895, 897, 908-914, 947-950, 989-991 1021, 1022, 1032, 1193, 1198, 1254, *Fifty Years*, p. 726, 727.

The hotel clerk at St. Lawrence Hall in Montreal testified that a man arrived there on the 18th of April, registered as John Harrison, and then left immediately. The defence agreed that this was the defendant.

Testifying for the defence, Boucher stated that John Surratt came to his parish at St. Liboire, Quebec on about the 22nd of April, 1865 and resided there about three months. Boucher said that in the latter part of July, Surratt went to Montreal to stay in the home of La Pierre's father. He only left the unlit room a few times and those occasions were at night when he went for a walk.

John Surratt was not the only one using an alias. Charles Boucher also admitted that the previous summer he had gone with two other priests to what was apparently a vacation area near Portland (evidently Portland, Maine). He went by the false name of Jary. He did not wear priest's normal clothing and was believed to be a lawyer by the people there. He explained that he gave the false name and did not correct the misconception about his occupation because he was afraid he would be in trouble if it became known he was connected to Surratt's escape. This excuse doesn't pass muster however because at the time, Surratt was still successfully hidden in the papal guard and Boucher's role in his escape was not known by the American public.

The defence brought three witnesses to testify that McMillan's reputation for truthfulness was not good. This group included the lying priest, Boucher, Joseph DuTilley, a close associate of Boucher's, and Sarsfield Nagle, who's testimony was confused and contradictory.

Boucher stated that it was Joseph Du Tilley that brought Surratt to his home. Du Tilley testified that he boarded at Boucher's home for three months in 1864, two and a half months at the beginning of 1865, as well as during several winters after these years. To pay Boucher for his board, Du Tilley said he would drive the priest where he wanted to go in his own carriage. It is theoretically possible that Du Tilley did not know that the man he was transporting was a fugitive from U.S. justice. Nevertheless, even if he did not know and there was no evidence presented that would show he did not, his close association with the lying priest Boucher leads to serious questions about his character.

Regarding Boucher, did he really not know from the beginning who he was harbouring? When he found out who his guest was, why did he continue to harbour this wanted man instead of informing the authorities?

Apart from these two men of dubious character, the defence is left with just Sarafield Nagle questioning Dr. McMillan's reputation for truth. Prosecution witness Alexis Burnette provided some support for the defence at this point, stating that Nagle had a good reputation as a truthful man. Alexis Burnette said that he had heard some people speak against Nagle but he took these to be his enemies. He also reported that Nagle had received $500.00 for his services and expenses as a witness. On the stand, Nagle stated that he felt surprised that McMillan was a witness in the case and said he viewed him, "in the light of an informer ". It could be asked, is it not right and proper for one possessing evidence regarding the guilt of another in a crime as heinous as the assassination of the head of the U.S. government to bring this information forward at the trial of the accused?

In addition, Nagel's statements were contradictory. He said that McMillan was a friend of his who he evidently had met in college, adding that he had the opportunity to get to know the doctor, "more particularly" after their school years ended. He testified that in college, McMillan did not have the reputation of a liar and he had not taken the trouble to inquire if the doctor had acquired such a reputation since.

It could be asked, how would it be possible for Nagle to say that McMillan did not have a reputation as a liar in college, state that he got to know him better after that time and also say he didn't know if he had the reputation of a liar after college, yet maintain that McMillan's general character for truthfulness was bad? Apparently Nagle did not became aware of McMillan's supposed poor character until March of 1867 and that was in connection with the doctor's role in the capture of John Surratt. It appears that Nagle may have been influenced in his view of the doctor by the slurs made about McMillan's character that undoubtedly emanated from Surratt's associates, as well as Confederate sympathizers that were so numerous in Catholic Quebec.

Against the testimony of these men, the prosecution brought six witnesses that testified that they knew that Louis McMillan's reputation for truthfulness was good. The six witnesses who stated that McMillan had a good reputation for truthfulness were Michael Mitchell, Thomas Brawsart, Artemus Stevens, John Erskine, Ernest Racicot and Levi Perkins. Only the three were cross-examined by the defence, with no effect, leaving Louis McMillan as yet another witness to John Surratt's presence in Washington. Dr. McMillan also testified of other treasonous acts that Surratt had confessed to doing.

Rounding out the witnesses whose testimony put John Surratt in Washington on the 14th was Henry St. Marie. He was a member of the Zouaves, in the Papal States. In the spring of 1866, he recognized Surratt, who had also joined the papal guard. St. Marie testified that the defendant told him he was in Washington the night of the assassination and had a difficult time escaping the city afterwards.

The defence did not try to contradict St. Marie's testimony but brought two witnesses to court, Louis Sicotte and Ludgar Labelle, who both said that his reputation for truthfulness was bad. A Roman Catholic, Sicotte, testified that he had told a Catholic curate and others that it was mean and unprincipled for St. Marie to have made the deposition against John Surratt, by which Surratt was arrested. Labelle said he had heard in Montreal many people say it was impossible to believe what St. Marie said but when asked to name some, could not do so. He also stated that he thought it was low for St. Marie to have made the deposition for the consideration of money.

The prosecution introduced three witnesses, Alexis Burnette, Francis Archambeau and Edmund Frechett, who testified that St. Marie's reputation for truthfulness was good. The defence did not produce any evidence that St. Marie had been paid to make the deposition or testify against Surratt. The defence asked why St. Marie would come and witness against his friend. In their view, it seemed, even if Surratt was guilty of helping to kill President Lincoln, St. Marie should not have come to court and told the truth about him because they were friends. Defence lawyer Merrick stated:

> One other witness I have not mentioned---St. Marie; impeached, but vindicated. He says Surratt admitted to him that he was here and escaped from here. I presume there is no member of this jury who would take the word of St. Marie, who would be willing to found his judgment upon it. The learned counsel rests a great deal upon confessions. I shall have something to say of the force of confessions hereafter. I attach no importance to them. He says St. Marie was a friend in the service of the Papal guards. Why is he here? Why should he betray his friend, if it isn't true? Gentlemen, the jingle of yellow earth has been the knell to many a man's honesty. Why was he in the Papal guards? He was pursuing this man. If he was his friend in the Papal guards, why is he here, consenting to come? How could you get him here? Why should he give information to the American consul? Is he so very public-spirited? Does he so love American justice and American glory that he should voluntarily, and without hope of reward or benefit, come forward and inform on his friend to the American consul? Gentlemen, for myself I cannot, without sickening at heart, hear the testimony of any one of these professed informers. In the course of my professional experience I have learned to look upon them with suspicion, with distaste, and hatred. During our civil war, when this land swarmed with petty emissaries of political and private malice, every petty scoundrel in every district had his spy at every table. I have learned to contemn them.

This seems a somewhat strange way of looking at things, setting aside the fact that during the Civil War, his client was an agent for the Confederacy. Defence counsel, R. T. Merrick asked, if Surratt was in Washington that day, why did none of his friends or acquaintances see him and then tell the authorities about it with the exception of David Reed? Maybe they did see him but didn't want to "betray" their friend, no matter who he helped to murder. Two years earlier, this actually happened. At Surratt's trial in 1867, a witness who knew the defendant, William Cleaver, testified that he saw him in the nation's capital on April 14th. He said he didn't tell the military authorities about this in 1865 because he said he was "well acquainted with Surratt and inclined to shield him".

If Surratt was in Washington on the 14th of April, assisting with the planned assassinations, he would want to get out of the capital quickly. He told St. Marie he had a difficult time doing so and left the city disguised as Englishman, wearing a scarf over his shoulders.

Charles Blinn, night watchmen of the passenger section of the Vermont Central depot in Burlington, testified that on the night of April 17th / morning of the 18th, two men, one tall, the other shorter, arrived on the first passenger boat of the season on Lake Champlain. The tall one, who did all the talking, asked Blinn if they could sleep in the depot. The night watchmen gave them permission and woke them at 4 am to catch the train for Montreal. In the morning, when it was light, he found a handkerchief with the lettering J.H. Surratt in the immediate area where the tall man had been lying.

Carrol Hobart, a conductor for the Vermont Central Railroad, ran the train that stopped at Essex Junction, which was a rail connection between Burlington and St. Albans. He stated that on Tuesday morning, April 18th, he took on passengers from the first boat trip up Lake Champlain that landed at Burlington. After the train had left Essex Junction, he found two men on board, one tall, the other short, who said they did not have tickets because they were poor labourers who had been robbed and couldn't afford them. The tall man again did all the talking. Hobart suspected that the two were not who they claimed to be because the tall man's hands were not like those of a labouring man and he was attempting to disguise his accent. Hobart testified, "This tall man tried to use broken English, as if he were a Canuck, but occasionally he would get a little in earnest for fear he was to be put off, and then he would drop the Canuck and speak good square English." Hobart's description of the taller man in the court record reads, "One of them was tall; he was about my height as he stood up in the car; he was rather slim; had on a scull cap---one of these close-fitting caps---and short coat. His vest was opened down low, and his scarf came over under his collar and stuck in his vest."

He testified that John Surratt resembled the tall man very much, though the man he saw at the time had only a moustache and no whiskers on his chin. At the trial, Surratt evidently had a goatee and a moustache. Hobart stated that the tall one whom he said closely resembled the defendant, wore a scarf, supporting St. Marie's statement.

Hobart described the other man as a short, thick-set, "rough-looking man" of sandy complexion who had whiskers around his face and a slouched hat on. He was not positive as to the colour of his whiskers. This could be the same man that the barber Charles Wood said accompanied Surratt, Booth and O'Laughlin when they came into his shop the morning of April 14th. Wood described him as a, "short thick-set man with a full round head; he had on dark clothes which we generally term rebel clothes, and a black slouched hat".

Wood said this man did not speak. The short, thick-set man that Hobart described was also silent. The descriptions seem strikingly similar. Was this the same man that Sergeant Dye saw with John Surratt and Booth in front of Ford's theatre when they were engaged in the final preparations for the murder of Lincoln and other government leaders?

Dye described him as a low, villainous looking person who was the heaviest of the three. Before the military commission he stated, "The ruffianly man I saw was a stout man, with a rough face, and had a bloated appearance; his dress had been worn a considerable time". Dye further described the man he saw. "His moustache was black, and he had on a slouched hat, one that had been worn some time."

Again the slouched hat was mentioned. Sergeant Dye's description sounds very similar to the man seen by others with John Surratt. Of the ruffianly man, Dye also said, "The prisoner, Edward Spangler, has the appearance of the rough-looking man, except that he had a moustache". He was not positive it was Spangler. Sergeant Cooper supported Dye, describing the man as rough-looking and shorter than the man that Dye had identified as Surratt. Benjamin Vanderpool, who said he saw Surratt in Washington on April 14th, also stated that he saw the defendant with a thick-set man and John Wilkes Booth.

This may have been the same man called Johnson that Mary Benson testified seeing in the company of another taller man, in November, 1864 in New York. She used the same method of estimating size as Sergeant Dye which John Surratt's defence team had taken exception to, describing him as large but being shorter and stouter than the other man. She did not describe the other man as large. The letter they dropped concerning the planned assassination of Lincoln mentioned a man named Johnson twice. Johnson was also mentioned in the cipher letter found in North Carolina some two weeks after the assassination. Dated the day after the assassination, April 15, 1865, addressed to John, could it have been for John Surratt?

The five who saw the short, thick-set, rough-looking, silent man were Hobart, Wood, Vanderpoel, Dye and Cooper. Charles Blinn also saw a shorter, silent man with the taller man who had evidently left the handkerchief with Surratt's name on it.

This short, thick-set, rough-looking, silent man, wearing a slouched hat, when seen enough times with Surratt, becomes another way of identifying the defendant, like his physical description, clothing etc. At least six witnesses saw a man who answered to part, if not all of this description, accompanying the man they identified as John Surratt, in Washington or traveling away from the city at the time in question.

[37] *The Trial of John Surratt*, Volume I & II, p. 462, 467, 468, 911, 912.

Surratt had disguised himself when he traveled on the Montreal by wearing glasses and dying his hair. Surratt also said he had been engaged in delivering dispatches for the South during the war as well. As well, he related how he had crossed the Potomac by boat with a group of others one evening, when they were discovered by a Union gunboat, whose crew had thought to have captured them. Surratt and company pretended to surrender but when a smaller boat was sent from the gunboat to pick them up, they fired on it and escaped.

[38] *The Trial of John Surratt*, Volume I, p. 462, Emmett McLoughlin, *An Inquiry Into The Assassination Of Abraham Lincoln*, (The Citadel Press, 1977), p. 137-144, *The Abraham Lincoln Encyclopedia*, p. 297

[39] *The Trial of John Surratt*, Volume I, p. 3, 4, 41, 45-51

[40] *Springfield Daily Republican* (Springfield, Mass.), June 18, 1867, p. 2, *The Last Lincoln Conspirator*, p. 246, *The Trial of John Surratt*, Volume I, p. 4, 5.

There was to be pool of 400 qualified potential jurors from the city of Washington, 80 from Georgetown and 40 from the county of Washington, in the district of Columbia, adjusted as these populations changed in proportion to one another. In *The Last Lincoln Conspirator,* Jampoler stated of District Attorney Edward Carrington at the beginning of John Surratt's trial, "Carrington had been successful at first, but his early legal triumph proved to be temporary. Knowing that the outcome of the trial hinged entirely on the jury, the prosecution had moved swiftly to supplant one, certain to be comprised mostly of Roman Catholics presumed sympathetic to Surratt, with another…"

[41] *The Trial of John Surratt*, Volume I, p. 62, *An Inquiry Into The Assassination Of Abraham Lincoln*, p. 150, 164. *World Book Encyclopedia*, 1998, Volume 4, p. 617, T. M. Harris, *Assassination Of Lincoln, A History Of The Great Conspiracy*, (American Citizen Company, 1992), p. 281, William Warner, *At Peace With Their Neighbors: Catholics and Catholicism in the National Capital 1787 - 1860*, (Georgetown University Press, 1994), p. 192, 1860 United States Federal Census and 1870 United States Federal Census, (Historically, the U.S. census has generally not recorded individual citizen's religious beliefs).

In his 1994 book, *At Peace With Their Neighbors: Catholics and Catholicism in the National Capital 1787 - 1860*, Roman Catholic author William Warner stated that "As mentioned earlier, the rapid growth of the Catholic Church in the Washington area virtually kept pace with that of the nation at large, which saw some 1,600,000 Catholics become the country's single largest denomination by mid-century." The U.S. census reported the American population was 23,191,876 in 1850, so this makes the Catholic population some 6.9% of the American population. Warner also reported that in 1870, there were some 4.5 million Catholics in the United States. As the national census of that year gave the country's population at 38,558,371, this means that Catholics would have made up 11.7% of the U.S. population. In light of this, a reasonable estimate of the population of Catholics in Washington D.C. would be some 11% in 1867. As noted in Chapter 7, there is evidence that the Church of Rome tried to interfere with the process of justice at the trial of the conspirators as well.

[42] *The Trial of John Surratt*, Volume I, p. 117, Thomas Harris, *Rome's Responsibility For The Assassination Of Abraham Lincoln*, (Heritage Manor, 1960 reprint of 1897 book), p.22, *An Inquiry Into The Assassination Of Abraham Lincoln*, p. 147, *Lincoln's Assassins: A Complete Account of the Capture, Trial, and Punishment*, p. 526.

Roy Chamlee Jr. stated "More subtle and effective for the defense was the open display of Catholic support for Surratt. One day, about twenty students from St. Charles College, where Surratt and Weichmann had studied, were present. They made a show of shaking Surratt's hand." Among John Surratt's lawyers, at least one, Merrick, was a Catholic.

Prior to the beginning of court proceedings, the defendant made an application to the court for financial help to plead his case. Despite his pleas of poverty however, Surratt was defended by the distinguished lawyers, Messrs. Joseph Bradley Jr. and Sr., and R.T. Merrick.

[43] *The Trial of John Surratt*, Volume II, p. 1379, *Fifty Years*, p. 627, 628, 729, An *Inquiry Into The Assassination Of Abraham Lincoln*, p. 156, *Blood On The Moon: The Assassination of Abraham Lincoln*, p. 37, 73, Kate Clifford Larson, *The Assassin's Accomplice: Mary Surratt and the Plot to Kill Abraham Lincoln*, (Basic Books, 2008), p. 227

[44] *An Inquiry Into The Assassination Of Abraham Lincoln*, p. 156, 157

Chapter 9 Samuel Mudd, Booth and the Other Conspirators

[1] *The Assassination of President Lincoln and The Trial Of The Conspirators*, The Courtroom Testimony as Originally Compiled by Benn Pitman, (Greenwood Press, 1976, facsimile edition), p. 20, 169, Edward Sears, Jr., *His Name Is Still Mudd*, (Thomas Publications, 1997)

[2] *The Trial of the Conspirators*, p. 71, 178. Gardiner stated that his uncle, who was a neighbor of Dr. Mudd's, sold the horse in the latter part of November. Mudd and Booth traveled together to see the horse and the next day they took delivery of it in Bryantown.

[3] *The Trial of the Conspirators*, p. 206-211. Louis Weichmann had informed the military commission that Samuel Mudd introduced John Surratt and himself to John Wilkes Booth on a street in Washington. They all went to Booth's hotel room later where Mudd, Booth and Surratt spoke privately, supposedly about the sale of Mudd's farm.

[4] Ibid, p. 89, 90

[5] Ibid, p. 88, 89, 169, 330.

Detective William Williams testified that on Monday, April 17th, he asked Mudd: "if any strangers had been that way, and he said there had not....On Friday, the 21st, we went there again for the purpose of arresting Dr. Mudd....I asked him concerning the two men who had been at his house, one of them having a broken leg. He then said that they had been there. I asked him if those men were not Booth and Herold. He said they were not." Colonel H. H. Wells interviewed Mudd about a dozen times after his arrest on Friday, April 21st. According to Wells, Mudd first stated he did not recognize the assassin and only after being shown his photograph and questioned further did he finally admitted that he recognized the wounded man as Booth. Mudd told him:

"He thought there was something strange about these two persons, from the young man coming down shortly after breakfast and asking for a razor, saying his friend wished to shave himself; and when he was up stairs shortly afterward, he saw that the wounded man had shaved off his moustache. The wounded man, he thought, had a long, heavy beard; whether natural or artificial he did not know. He kept a shawl about his neck, seemingly for the purpose of concealing the lower part of his face. He said he first heard of the murder either on Sunday morning or late on Saturday evening."

[6] *The Trial of the Conspirators*, p. 86-88

[7] *The Trial of the Conspirators*, p. 87. A single boot was recovered from the Mudd household which Dr. Mudd said he had cut off the foot of the injured man. It had J. Wilkes written on it, Booth's first initial and middle name but when this was pointed out to Mudd, he denied noticing it before.

[8] *The Trial of the Conspirators*, p. 421, *His Name Is Still Mudd*, p. 44.

Captain George Dutton declared that Mudd made a confession. According to Captain Dutton's sworn statement, while in his custody, Dr. Mudd confessed that he did recognize Booth when the murderer came to his home. The last document in the Pitman record of the testimony at the conspiracy trial is a copy of the affidavit made by Dutton, found in a letter to Judge Advocated General Joseph Holt, head of the military commission. It is easy to see why Mudd would deny knowing that he knew the injured man was Booth but what reason would Dutton have to declare a falsehood? He would have no more reason to lie about this than the other officers who testified that Mudd was nervous, evasive and untruthful.

While in prison, Mudd heard about Dutton's statement and he made an affidavit in response. He denied admitting that he had known it was Booth who had come to his home. In it however, Mudd did admit to meeting John Surratt and Louis Weichmann on a Washington street in the company of Booth and then going into Booth's hotel room for drinks. He said it happened on December 23, 1864 and not January 15, 1865 though, as Weichman had stated.

[9] *The Trial of the Conspirators*, p. 169, 320-324.The meeting of Mudd, Booth, Weichmann, and Surratt had been denied by Mudd's defence. His lawyer, Thomas Ewing Jr. had complained that the other two people that could confirm or deny this meeting couldn't be in court. Booth was dead and Surratt was in hiding.

[10] *His Name Is Still Mudd*, p. 39-45, 47

[11] *The Trial of the Conspirators*, p. 71, 169, *His Name Is Still Mudd*, p. 50, 63.

When Mudd failed to disclose that he had taken part in the meeting with Booth, Surratt and Weichmann in Washington, as well as meeting Booth several times in the neighborhood of Bryantown, he was deliberately trying to mislead the authorities. He clearly lied when he initially denied that two men had passed by his home on April 15th. Saying that he didn't recognize Booth when he came with a broken leg was just another lie.

[12] *The Trial of the Conspirators*, p. 294, 295, 323, 324, *The Trial of John Surratt*, Volume II, p. 1192, 1193, 1244, 1245, *His Name Is Still Mudd*, p. 69.

An important point can be made regarding Mudd's failure to tell the truth about his meeting with Weichmann. The defence teams of Mary Surratt, Dr. Mudd and John Surratt all accused Louis Weichmann of being dishonest. In this one area of testimony however, the thick clouds of defence posturing was lifted by one of the defendants and a clear view of what actually happened appeared. In his affidavit, Mudd confirmed that it was he, one of the conspirators, who was misleading people and it was Weichmann who told the truth, which has implications for other places where defence lawyers and witnesses declared Weichmann was not to be believed.

[13] *The Trial of the Conspirators*, p. 172, 173. William Marshall was the witness who heard Mudd make no objection when Gardiner told the doctor that Stonewall Jackson would soon capture Washington and burn Lincoln in his house.

[14] *His Name Is Still Mudd*, p. vi, 64-66, *The Trial of the Conspirators*, p. 171, 183, 192, Mark Neely, *The Abraham Lincoln Encyclopedia*, (McGraw-Hill, 1982), p. 213

[15] *His Name Is Still Mudd*, p. v-vii, 64, 65, 79, 80, 152, "For Now, His Name's Still Mudd", CBSNews.com, Washington, Nov. 9th, 2002

[16] Charles Chiniquy, *Fifty Years In The Church Of Rome*, (Craig and Barlow, 1886, 3rd edition), p. 723, Constance Head, "Insights On John Wilkes Booth From His Sister Asia's Correspondence", *Lincoln Herald*, Winter 1980, Volume 82, No. 4, p. 542, 543

[17] Asia Booth Clarke, *John Wilkes Booth: A Sister's Memoir,* (University Press of Mississippi, 1996), edited by Terry Alford, originally : Asia Booth Clarke, *The Unlocked Book : A Memoir of John Wilkes Booth by His Sister's Asia Booth Clarke,* (G. P. Putman's Sons, 1938). At the time his book was published, Terry Alford was professor of history at Northern Virginia Community College.

[18] Asia Booth Clarke, *John Wilkes Booth: A Sister's Memoir,* (University Press of Mississippi, 1996), edited by Terry Alford, inner sleeve, "Insights On John Wilkes Booth From His Sister Asia's Correspondence", p. 542, 543

[19] "Insights On John Wilkes Booth From His Sister Asia's Correspondence", p. 543

[20] *History of Saint Charles Borromeo Parish, Pikesville, Maryland, 1849-1949,* (Chandler Print Co., undated), p. 29, 31

[21] *The Trial of John Surratt*, (Government Printing Office, 1867), Volume I, p. 309, *The Trial of the Conspirators*, p. vii, 178, 218, *His Name Is Still Mudd*, p. 40, 69, *The*

Catholics and Mrs. Mary Surratt, Kenneth J. Zanca, (University Press of America, 2008), p. 21

[22] Mark Neely, *The Abraham Lincoln Encyclopedia*, (McGraw-Hill, 1982), p. 227, 228, Clara Laughlin, *The Death of Lincoln*, (Doubleday, Page & Company, 1909), p. 186, Samuel Arnold; edited by Micheal Kauffman, *Memoirs of a Lincoln Conspirator*, (Heritage Books, 1995), p. 175. Michael O'Laughlin was buried by his mother in Green Mount Cemetery, Baltimore.

[23] *The Abraham Lincoln Encyclopedia*, p. 10, 227, Edward Steers, *Blood On The Moon: The Assassination Of Abraham Lincoln*, (The University Press Of Kentucky, 2001), p. 58, *The Trial of the Conspirators*, p. 222, 223, 348

[24] *The Trial of the Conspirators*, p. 42, 43

[25] Ibid., p. 43.

Tom must have gotten drunk, since the letter was postmarked May 8th. Purdy testified,"A charge, such as that alluded to in the letter was made against me, but it was entirely false, and I afterward went to McAleer to get the thing settled. McAleer had a white servant named Tom, a deaf man, who afterward married this girl. I have heard he drinks." Purdy said that he didn't know anyone named Brady living on the South Branch but he had heard of a man named French who lived with a Sue Guthrie. He also stated that "The route through Thornton Gap, crossing by Capon, Romney's, and down the Branch, is an obscure route, of which I never knew till lately. It passes right through by Green's house at Thornton Gap. Green's reputation is that of a very disloyal man."

[26] Ibid., p. 224-230, 346.

An acquaintance of Michael O'Laughlin, Bernard Early, testified about O'Laughlin's actions before the assassination. Early stated that he, O'Laughlin and two other associates, James Henderson and Edward Murphy, came by train to Washington from Baltimore on the evening of April 13th and stayed the night at the Metropolitan Hotel. O'Laughlin had been in Baltimore before this trip. Bernard Early said they had come to Washington see the fireworks scheduled for that evening and generally just to enjoy themselves. Arriving at about 5:30 p.m., Early walked with O'Laughlin to the National Hotel, where according to James Henderson, O'Laughlin went in to see Booth.

Sergeant John Hatter testified that while he was on duty at Secretary of War Stanton's home, at about nine o'clock the evening of the 13th, a man he identified as O'Laughlin came to the house and asked to see General Grant, who was visiting Stanton. The man was refused permission to see the Grant, so he left. Major Kilburn Knox and David Stanton, the Secretary's son, testified that about 10:30 p.m., O'Laughlin came to the Stanton home yet again. This time he asked if the Secretary of War was in. He was told to leave and did so.

[27] *The Trial of the Conspirators*, p. 224, 225, 231, *The Trial of John Surratt*, Volume 1, p. 495-497. Bernard Early, who was called as a witness for both the prosecution and the defence, stated that on the morning of April 14th, after breakfast, he,

O'Laughlin and others went to the National Hotel. O'Laughlin went up to see Booth and then left the hotel without informing his companions, who were waiting downstairs. They did not see him again for almost two hours.

Early stated that the last time he saw O'Laughlin on the night of the 14th, he was going out, apparently for a drink with a man named John Fuller. Fuller testified that he saw O'Laughlin at Rullman's Hotel between 7 and 8 p.m. and then between 10 and 11 p.m. that night. The next afternoon, on April 15th, O'Laughlin and company returned to Baltimore by train.

[28] *The Trial of the Conspirators*, p. 221, 222, 228-232.

No one could directly contradict Wood's testimony that O'Laughlin, Booth and John Surratt were in his shop that morning.

The defence called seven witnesses who testified that they were with or saw O'Laughlin at a time and location in Washington that the defence obviously thought would prove that he could not have been at the Secretary of War's house on the evening of the 13th. Two of them, Henry Purdy, who was the superintendent of Rullman's Hotel and John Giles, the bartender there, stated they saw O'Laughlin that night while they were at work. The time period Purdy and Giles said they saw the defendant at the hotel however, doesn't necessarily rule out O'Laughlin being at Secretary Stanton's home at the time the prosecution witnesses put him there. The seven witnesses were Early, Henderson, Murphy, Daniel Loughran, George Grillet, Henry Purdy and John Giles.

[29] *The Trial of the Conspirators*, p. 226-228, 230, 231.

There was disagreement between what prosecution witnesses and O'Laughlin's associates said he was wearing that evening. David Stanton, Major Knox and Sergeant Hatter all testified that O'Laughlin was wearing dark clothing, a black or dark coat, pants and a slouch hat. Henry Purdy, on duty at Rullman's Hotel, also agreed with them. Purdy stated, "On the Thursday night he had dark clothes on; he generally wore dark clothes". Early, Daniel Loughran and George Grillet all testified that O'Laughlin was wearing plaid pants that night. As with John Surratt, there were two different groups of witnesses who stated they saw the defendant simultaneously at two different places. The prosecution witnesses could have been mistaken or the defence witnesses could have not been telling the truth but what reasons would prosecution witnesses who positively identified O'Laughlin have to lie about it? As well, there is agreement between Purdy and the prosecution witnesses' description as to what O'Laughlin was wearing that night which contradicts his friends' statements.

[30] *The Trial of John Surratt*, Volume 1, p. 209, 228.

It could be asked, where was O'Laughlin on the night of the 13th? Was he at Edwin Stanton's home where three independent witnesses put him, as opposed to where his friends and associates said he was? Was he wearing dark pants, which Stanton, Knox, Hatter and Purdy reported he was clothed with or the plaid pants that his companions said he was wearing? Charles Wood testified he was wearing light pants the next morning. He may have changed from dark pants to plaid ones on the morning of the 14th, thus creating the confusion as what he was wearing.

Early also testified that by ten o'clock, Friday evening, he supposed everyone in the party was under the influence of liquor. O'Laughlin's lawyer, Walter Cox, declared that O'Laughlin, along with along with Early and Murphy, had been invited by Henderson to go to Washington on the 13th of April.

[31] *The Trial of John Surratt*, Volume 1, p. 497, 525, 526, 355, *The Trial of the Conspirators*, p. 228, 229, 344, 345

[32] *The Trial of the Conspirators*, p. xi, xii, 18, 19, 44, 45, 85-87, 118, 144, 145, 223, 234-236, 306, 343, 344, 346, 349, 401, *The Trial of John Surratt*, Volume 1, p. 381, 382, 385, 386.

An examination of the evidence however, does not show that there was no activity among the conspirators from February, 1865 to as late as the evening of April 14th.

Samuel Chester testified that a week before the assassination, Booth told him in conversation "What an excellent chance I had to kill the President, if I had wished, on inauguration day! " Abraham Lincoln took the oath of office on March 4th. John Lloyd had testified of the early March trip of John Surratt, Herold, and Atzerodt to Surrattsville bringing supplies, including guns that Booth was to pick up while fleeing. Samuel Arnold stated that roughly between March 10th and March 24th, there was a meeting of those conspiring to kidnap Lincoln which included himself, Booth, John Surratt, Atzerodt, O'Laughlin and others. Booth's telegraph message telling O'Laughlin, "Don't fear to neglect your business. You had better come at once" was sent on March 13, 1865. His telegraph dispatch urging O'Laughlin to come on, "Wednesday morning. We sell that day sure", came on March 27th. Regarding the March 13th message, did Booth need O'Laughlin immediately in Washington so they could discuss their need to "sell" something in the near future? What were they selling? There was no testimony that O'Laughlin, Arnold and Booth were in any legitimate business together during this time period.

Louis Weichmann testified he received a telegram from Booth which stated, "Tell John to telegraph number and street at once". This message, dated March 23rd, referred to a room in Herndon House, reserved for "a delicate gentleman", who was to have his meals sent up to his room. As noted earlier, this refined person was really the muscular Lewis Payne and Booth wanted to know where he was staying. Why was this young muscular former Confederate soldier hidden away, pretending to be a delicate gentleman? Payne had been banished from Baltimore for viciously attacking a female black servant and he would injure a number of people in Secretary Seward's household in his attempt to kill the Secretary. John Surratt was instructed to immediately get word to Booth where Payne was staying.How could this be part of a plan to kidnap?

On March 27th, Booth sent the coded telegraph message to Michael O'Laughlin and Samuel Arnold, telling them to come to him. It was dated the same day as a letter from Samuel Arnold to Booth that discussed in guarded terms an "undertaking" which was still being pursued that the government was suspicious of. Was this a reference to the conspiracy to capture Lincoln which Arnold admitted he had been part of or another one to kill?

On April 11th, three days before the assassination, Mary Surratt delivered a message to John Lloyd to have the guns at his place ready, as they would soon be needed.

On the morning of April 14th, the scruffy boatman George Atzerodt rented a room in prestigious Kirkwood House where Vice-President Andrew Johnson was staying. Later that afternoon, Mary Surratt brought a field glass to Surrattville, along with another message for John Lloyd to have the guns ready, as well as some whiskey, which Booth and Herold would pick up as they fled.

These people certainly were engaged in a conspiracy at this time. O'Laughlin's associate, Samuel Arnold, admitted to the authorities that they were both part of a plot to capture Lincoln, having met sometime in the middle of March to discuss the plan. In the March 27th letter to Booth, Arnold pleaded with him to desist for a time from the undertaking. Booth apparently was going ahead with what Arnold told the authorities was a plot to kidnap the President, which involved O'Laughlin.

Was he also involved in a parallel plot to kill? O'Laughlin's close association with Booth and other conspirators, the suspicious telegram from Booth talking about their non-existent business activities, not to mention the independent evidence that puts him at Stanton's house, all point to his being a party to a conspiracy. Was it to commit murder? Why did O'Laughlin go to visit Booth in Washington on the night of April 13th and on the morning of the 14th? Why did he go to Stanton's home? His lawyer explained that the trip to the United States capital was an innocent excursion that he was invited on, occasioned by the fireworks display in the city on April 13th. O'Laughlin and company did not go to see the fireworks though and there is no proof he wouldn't have gone to Washington if he hadn't been invited or if there had not been a fireworks display. On the morning of the 14th, why did he leave the National Hotel without telling his friends to be in the company of John Wilkes Booth, John Surratt and probably another member of the conspiracy? He must have surely been aware of their plan to assassinate the leaders of the government.

Earlier that morning, the boatmen Atzerodt poled into the foreign waters of Kirkwood House where Andrew Johnson resided. Hours later, Booth would be at Mary Surratt's house making arrangements for his escape, including the delivery of the field glass to Surrattville. Payne, the powerfully built "Baptist preacher", had been secreted in Herndon House since March 23rd, flexing more than his spiritual muscles. Later that night, their plans would result in the death of the Great Emancipator and almost end Secretary of State William Seward's life. Posing as a Baptist preacher by the name of Wood, Payne had been banished from Baltimore for viciously attacking a female black servant and he would injure a number of people in Secretary Seward's household in his attempt to kill the Secretary. John Surratt was instructed to immediately get word to Booth where Payne was staying.

[33] Clara Laughlin, *The Death of Lincoln*, (Doubleday, Page & Company, 1909), p. 178, Louis J. Weichmann, *A True History Of The Assassination Of Abraham Lincoln And Of The Conspiracy Of 1865*, (Alfred A. Knopf, 1975), p. 9, Lloyd Lewis, *Myths After Lincoln*, (The Press Of The Readers Club, 1941), p. 203

[34] Mark Neely, *The Abraham Lincoln Encyclopedia*, (McGraw-Hill, 1982), p. 10

[35] *The Trial of the Conspirators*, p. 234, 235

[36] Ibid., p. 236, 239, 240, James L. Swanson, *Manhunt: The Twelve-Day Chase For Lincoln's Killer*, (HarperCollins, 2006), p. 87. If any further proof was needed to show who wrote the letter, two witnesses who had seen Arnold's handwriting, U.S. Provost Marshall James McPhail of Baltimore and William McPhail, an associate of the provost marshall, both said that they believed it was his handwriting and the defence did not challenge their statements.

[37] *History of Saint Charles Borromeo Parish*, p. 29, *Memoirs of a Lincoln Conspirator*, p. xiv

[38] *The Abraham Lincoln Encyclopedia*, p. 283, *The Trial of the Conspirators*, p. 74, 75, 248, 249, 281, *The Trial of John Surratt*, Volume 1, p. 570.

Two women who resided behind Ford's theatre, Mary Ann Turner and Mary Jane Anderson, declared that Booth had come to the back of the building that evening and called for Spangler. After the actor had shot the President and escaped, they both saw Spangler outside the theatre and told him that Booth had called for him. According to the two women, he denied that this had happened.

When Spangler ordered Joseph Burroughs, nicknamed "Peanuts" to hold Booth's horse, Burroughs protested, telling Spangler that he was supposed to stand at the stage door to make sure people did not enter the theatre through this entrance. Edward Spangler insisted that he hold the horse and said if he got into trouble, he would take the blame. Joseph Burroughs also went by the name "John Peanut".

[39] *The Trial of the Conspirators*, p. 97, 98

[40] Ibid., p. 75, 102, 103

[41] *The Trial of the Conspirators*, p. 107-109, *The Trial of John Surratt*, Volume 1, p. 589, Volume 2, p. 816.

Carland stated that Ritterspaugh had told him that, "when the man was running past he had said that was Mr. Booth, and Spangler had slapped him in the mouth and said to him, 'You don't know who it is; it may be Mr. Booth, or it may be somebody else'."

This wasn't even close to what Jacob Ritterspaugh testified before the military commission and he should know what happened. He stated that it was after he came back from chasing Booth that he was struck by Spangler and he didn't say anything about identifying the man as Booth. Gifford said that when he and Ritterspaugh had been arrested and imprisoned, Ritterspaugh told him that he wanted to amend what he said to the police in an earlier statement. There was no other evidence presented to support this, however. As noted earlier, it was Gifford, a man of questionable patriotism, who had seemingly attempted to sow confusion as to how and possibly who shot the President at a time when Booth was still at large.

James Lamb testified that Ritterspaugh told him that Spangler had hit him a, "very hard blow" because he had told Spangler that it was Booth that was running across the stage. Like Carland, Lamb has Spangler hitting Ritterspaugh for identifying Booth before he chased him. Both Lamb and Carland's testimony at this point is apparently hearsay as they both testified to what Ritterspaugh reported Spangler saying. Neither of them were present to hear what Spangler actually said and did on this occasion, however. In fact, no one was there to hear this except Ritterspaugh.

Regarding his loyalty, James Lamb testified at the trial of John Surratt that he had expressed sympathy for the South during the Civil War and he also stated that he did not believe that the Confederacy should have been put down by force.

[42] Family tree of Roger Dellinger, RootsWeb.com, 2003, *Blood On The Moon: The Assassination of Abraham Lincoln*, p. 242, *The Sun*, (Baltimore, Maryland), July 25, 1864, p. 2, Maryland 1860 Census, Baltimore City, Sixth Ward, p. 335 (12 June 1860). The record of the burial place of Mary Spangler could not be found. On July 29, 1858, a Baltimore County marriage license was issued for Edward Spangler and Mary Brashears but it did not give the name of the church that they were married in.

[43] *Blood On The Moon*, p. 227, 241, 242, *The Trial of John Surratt*, Volume 2, p. 1181, Edward Steers Jr., *His Name Is Still Mudd*, (Thomas Publications, 1997), p. 31, Record of Internment, Saint Peter's Catholic Church, Feb. 9, 1875. There is some confusion regarding the exact date of Edward Spangler's death. Louis Weichmann reported the date of his death as February 7, 1875 in book, *A True History Of The Assassination Of Abraham Lincoln And Of The Conspiracy Of 1865*, (p. 491) and in *Blood On The Moon: The Assassination Of Abraham Lincoln*, (p. 242), Edward Steers Jr. reported that a grave marker put on Spangler's grave site in 1983 gave the date of his death as February 7th. The Record of Internment of Saint Peter's Catholic Church, Feb. 9, 1875, also gave his date of death as February 7, 1875. The *Baltimore Sun* of February 19, 1875 and February 20, 1875, as well as the *Port Tobacco Times and Charles County Advertiser* of February 19, 1875, all gave the date of his death as February 14, 1875.

[44] Baptismal Register, 1870-1896, p. 1, St. Peter's Catholic Church, Beantown, Maryland

[45] "Insights On John Wilkes Booth From His Sister Asia's Correspondence", p. 543

[46] *The Abraham Lincoln Encyclopedia*, p. 13, 14, *The Trial of the Conspirators*, Introduction, p. viii, *The Trial of the Conspirators*, p. 146. John Greenawalt, proprietor of Pennsylvania House Hotel in Washington, an establishment where Atzerodt often stayed, testified that about two weeks before the assassination he heard the accused state, "I am going away some of these days, and I will return with as much gold as will keep me all my lifetime".

[47] Ibid., p. 144, 145, 147. Robert R. Jones was the clerk who stated that the register showed that Atzerodt checked into room 126.

[48] Roy Z. Chamlee Jr., *Lincoln's Assassins: a complete account of their capture, trial, and punishment*, (McFarland & Company, 1990), p. 20, The Trial of the Conspirators, p. 144, 145. As Atzerodt got on his horse, Fletcher stated that he told him, "I would not like to ride that mare through the city in the night, for she looks so skittish." "Well," he answered, "She's good upon a retreat." Fletcher testified that he then

observed Atzerodt ride to Kirkwood house, go in and then come out again. Atzerodt checked into room 126 in Kirkwood House.

[49] *The Trial of the Conspirators*, p. 146, 147. James Walker was the employee of Pennsylvania House who testified about Atzerodt coming to the hotel between midnight and one o'clock on the night of the assassination.

[50] Ibid., p. 144, 148, 149.

Prosecution witness William Clendenin stated that approximately six o'clock, the morning after the assassination, he was present when a Bowie knife was found in a Washington street gutter. Provost Marshall James McPhail declared that while in custody, Atzerodt admitted throwing in his knife away in the area where the Bowie knife had been found. Why did Atzerodt throw away his knife that night? He was supposed to be only involved in kidnapping and not part of any plan to murder so why would he need to get rid of his weapon?

[51] *The Trial of the Conspirators*, p. 149, 307.

Heziekiah Metz, a resident of Montgomery County, Maryland, testified that a day later, on April 16th, Atzerodt, whom he knew as Andrew Atwood, visited and had dinner at his home, some 22 miles from Washington. During the few hours the defendant was there, the conversation turned to General Grant. It was thought that the general had been shot, evidently on a train car. According to Metz, Atzerodt made the comment, "If the man that was to follow him had followed him, it is likely to be so".

[52] *The Trial of the Conspirators*, p. 153, 302, 306

[53] Ibid., p. 96, 97, 161-165

[54] *Fifty Years In The Church Of Rome*, p. 723, 724

[55] *Lincoln's Assassins: A Complete Account of Their Capture, Trial, and Punishment*, p. 447, *The Abraham Lincoln Encyclopedia*, p. 244, Guy Moore, *The Case of Mrs. Surratt*, (University of Oklahoma Press, 1954), page between 116 and 117, reproduction of the second, extra, edition, Constitutional Union, July 7, 1865, p. 1, *The Death of Lincoln*, p. 191, *The Trial of the Conspirators*, p. 114, 115, 167, Myths After Lincoln, p. 203, *A True History Of The Assassination Of Abraham Lincoln And Of The Conspiracy Of 1865*, p. 9

[56] *The Case of Mrs. Surratt*, page between 116 and 117, reproduction of the second, extra, edition, *Constitutional Union*, July 7, 1865, p. 1, *The Death of Lincoln*, p. 191. *Massachusetts In The Army And Navy During The War Of 1861-65*, (Wright & Potter Printing Co., State Printers, 1895), Vol. 2, p. 455, Andrew E. Ford, *History of the Origin of the Town of Clinton Massachusetts*, 1653-1865, (Press of W. J. Coulter, 1896), p. 456, 457, 459, *The Sun*, (Baltimore), July 8, 1865, p. 1, *The Trial of John Surratt*, Volume 1, p. 386, 437, 438. Reverend Warren Weaver Winchester was appointed Hospital Chaplain, U. S. Volunteers on June 5th, 1862. Rev. Winchester served as chaplain of Finley hospital in Washington. When Atzerodt attended the church service at St. Aloysuis Catholic Church, he was with Louis Weichmann.

[57] *The Case of Mrs Surratt*, (page between 116 and 117), reproduction of the second, extra, edition, *Constitutional Union*, July 7, 1865, p. 1, *The Death of Lincoln*, p. 194, *Memoirs of a Lincoln Conspirator*, p. xiv, *The Trial of John Surratt*, Volume 1, p. 370, 372

[58] *Fifty Years*, p. 718, 721

Chapter 10 The Roman Catholic Church: The Church of God?

[1] "Pope accused of turning back the Catholic clock", *Vancouver Sun*, July 13, 2007, p. A8, James Strong, *The New Strong's Exhaustive Concordance Of The Bible*, (Thomas Nelson Publishers, 1996), p. 1031, 1145 and the New Strong's Concise Dictionary of the Words in the Greek Testament, p. 71, Peter De Rosa, *Vicars of Christ: the Dark Side of the Papacy*, (Bantam Press, 1988), p. 15, 24.

In his book, *Vicars of Christ: the Dark Side of the Papacy*, Peter De Rosa reported, "Then there is this startling fact: in the earliest lists of bishops of Rome, Peter's name never appeared." He also stated of the early church Fathers, "The surprises do not stop there. For the Fathers, it is Peter's faith – or the Lord in whom Peter had faith – which is called the Rock, not Peter. All the Councils of the church from Nicaea in the fourth century to Constance in the fifteenth agree that Christ himself is the only foundation of the church, that is, the Rock on which the Church rests."

[2] *The New Strong's Exhaustive Concordance Of The Bible*, p. 1145 and the New Strong's Concise Dictionary of the Words in the Greek Testament, p. 71. "Vatican restates support for theory of evolution", *Globe and Mail*, January 20, 2006, p. A14, David Yallop, *The Power and the Glory: Inside the Dark Heart of John Paul II's Vatican*, (Carroll & Graf Publishers, 2007), p. 227, George C. Kohn, ed., *The New Encyclopedia of American Scandal*, (Checkmark Books, 2001), p. 72, R. W. Thompson, *The Papacy and the Civil Power*, (Harper & Brothers, Publishers, 1876), p. 244, 245, Richard Frederick Littledale, *Plain Reasons Against Joining The Church Of Rome*, (Society For Promoting Christian Knowledge, 1886), p. 25, 26, Charles Chiniquy, *The Priest,The Woman, And The Confessional*, (The Marshall Press Ltd., undated), p. 159 – 162.

The New Encyclopedia of American Scandal, stated, "In 1990, a Baltimore psychotherapist and former Benedictine monk named A. W. Richard Sipe estimated (and published in *A Secret World: Sexuality and the Search for Celibacy*), on the basis of of extensive interviews conducted over 25 years with 1,000 priests and 500 others (mainly the sexual partners of priests), that half of the 53,000 priests in the Roman Catholic Church were not adhering to their oath of celibacy."

In *Plain Reasons Against Joining The Church Of Rome*, Richard Littledale stated that a great majority of the early church fathers believed that the rock spoken of in Matthew 16:18 was either Christ himself or Peter's confession of Christ. See footnote 30 of this chapter for more division between Catholic doctrine and the Word of God. Though not named, the other disciples besides Peter said they would not deny Christ also.

Of Jesus speaking to his disciples, John 20:22, 23 also reads, "And when he had said said this, he breathed on *them*, and saith unto them, Receive ye the Holy Ghost:

Whose soever sins ye remit, they are remitted unto them; *and* whose soever *sins* ye retain, they are retained.

Of this, Charles Chiniquy explained in his book *The Priest,The Woman, And The Confessional*:

> Both Roman Catholics and Protestants have fallen into very strange errors in reference to the words
>
> of Christ: "Whose soever sins ye remit, they are remitted unto them; and whose soever sins ye retain, they are retained" (St. John XX. 23).
>
> The first have seen, in this text, the inalienable attributes of God of forgiving and retaining sins transferred to sinful men; the second have most unwisely granted their position, even while attempting to refute their errors.
>
> A little more attention to the translation of the 3rd and 6th verses of chapter xiii. of Leviticus by the Septuagint would have prevented the former from falling into their sacrilegious errors, and would have saved the latter from wasting so much time in refuting errors which refute themselves.
>
> Many believe that the Septuagint Bible was the Bible that was generally read and used by Jesus Christ and the Hebrew people in our Saviour's days. Its language was possibly the one spoken at times by Christ and understood by His hearers. When addressing His apostles and disciples on their duties towards the spiritual lepers to whom they were to preach the way of salvation, Christ constantly followed the very expression of the Septuagint. It was the foundation of His doctrine and the testimonial of His divine mission to which He constantly appealed: the book which was the greatest treasure of the nation.
>
> From the beginning to the end of the Old and the New Testaments, the bodily leprosy with which the Jewish priest had to deal is presented as the figure of the spiritual leprosy, sin, the penalty of which our Saviour had taken upon Himself that we might be saved by His death. That spiritual leprosy was the very thing for the cleansing of which He had come to this world, for which He lived, suffered, and died. Yes, the bodily leprosy with which the priests of the Jews had to deal was the figure of the sins which Christ was to take away by shedding His blood, and with which His disciples were to deal till the end of the world.
>
> When speaking of the duties of the Hebrew priests towards the leper, our modern translations say (Lev. xiii. 6): "They will pronounce him clean," or (ver. 3) "They will pronounce him unclean."
>
> But this action of the priests was expressed in a very different way by the Septuagint Bible, used by Christ and the people of His time. Instead of saying, "The priest shall pronounce the leper clean," as we read in our Bible, the Septuagint version says, "The priest shall clean (*katharei*), or shall unclean (*mianez*) the leper."

No one had ever been so foolish, among the Jews, as to believe that because their BibIe said clean (*katharei*), or shall unclean (*mianez*) the leper."

No one had ever been so foolish, among the Jews, as to believe that because their Bible said clean (*katharei*) their priests had the miraculous and supernatural power of taking away and curing the leprosy; and we nowhere see that the Jewish priests ever had the audacity to try to persuade the people that they had ever received any supernatural and divine power to "cleanse" the leprosy: because their God, through the Bible, had said of them, "They will cleanse the leper." Both priest and people were sufficiently intelligent and honest to understand and acknowledge that, by that expression it was only meant that the priest had the legal right to see if the leprosy was gone or not, they had only to look at certains marks indicated by God himself, through Moses, to know whether or not God had cured the leper before he presented himself to his priest. The leper, cured by the mercy and power of God alone, before presenting himself to a priest, was only declared to be clean by that priest. Thus the priest was said, by the Bible, to "clean "the leper, or the leprosy; and in the opposite case to "unclean." (Septuagint, Lev. xiii. 3, 6).

Now, let us put what God has said, through Moses, to the priests of the Old Law, in reference to the bodily leprosy, face to face with what God has said, through His Son Jesus, to His apostles and His whole Church, it reference to the spiritual leprosy from which Christ has delivered us on the Cross.

The analogy of the diseases with which the Hebrew priests and the disciples of Christ had to deal is striking: so the analogy of the expressions prescribing their respective duties is also striking.

When God said to the priests of the Old Law, 'You shall clean the leper," and he shall be "cleaned," or " you shall unclean the leper," and he shall be " uncleaned," He only gave the legal power to see if there were any signs or indications by which they could say that God had cured the leper before he presented himself to the priest. So, when Christ said to His apostles and His whole Church, "Whose soever sins ye shall forgive, shall be forgiven unto them," He only gave them the authority to say when the spiritual lepers, the sinners, had reconciled themselves to God, and received their pardon from Him, and Him alone, previous to the coming to the apostles.

[3] *The Papacy and the Civil Power*, p. 247, 248, *Plain Reasons Against Joining The Church Of Rome*, p. 228

[4] Ibid., p. 288, 289

[5] Ibid., p. 281-284

[6] *The Papacy and the Civil Power*, p. 322-324, *World Book Encyclopedia*, 1998, Volume 15, p. 277, *Vicars of Christ: the Dark Side of the Papacy*, p. 26. The Bible says that Jesus Christ did not have a place to lay his head, (Matthew 8:20). In the *Vicars of Christ: the Dark Side of the Papacy*, Peter De Rosa commented on the wealth of the supposed church of this Jesus, the Church of Rome, stating,"Jesus was born in

a stable. In his ministry, he had nowhere to lay his head. Today, his Vicar inhabits a palace with eleven thousand rooms."

[7] *The Papacy and the Civil Power*, p. 325

[8] Ibid., p. 324

[9] Ibid., p. 325-341

[10] *The Papacy and the Civil Power*, p. 346, 347, Louis Marie De Cormenin, *The Public and Private History of the Popes of Rome*, (T. B. Peterson,1846), Volume 1, p. 204

[11] *The Papacy and the Civil Power*, p. 368, 369

[12] Ibid., p. 369

[13] Ibid., p. 369, 370

[14] Ibid., p. 371, 372, *Vicars of Christ: the Dark Side of the Papacy*, p. 30.

In *Vicars of Christ*, Peter De Rosa stated,"Distortion begins in the lists of the popes where all but one of the first thirty popes are described as martyrs. They probably were martyrs in the sense of 'witnesses of the faith'. There is no evidence that all died for Christ. Further, among the popes were a large number of married men, some of whom gave up their wives and children in exchange for the papal office. Many were sons of priests, bishops and popes; some were bastards; one was a widower, another an ex-slave; several were murderers, some unbelievers; some were hermits, some heretics, sadists and sodomites; many became popes by buying the papacy (simony), and continued their days selling holy things to rake in the money; one at least was a Satan-worshipper; some fathered illegitimate children, some were fornicators and adulterers on a grand scale; some were astonishingly old, some even more astonishingly young; some were poisoned, others strangled; worst of all were those who worshipped a granite God. As well, as these, many were good, holy and selfless popes, and a few martyrs."

[15] *The Papacy and the Civil Power*, 372-377, *A New Ecclesiastical History of the Sixteenth Century*, Du Pin, 1706, Richard Frederick Littledale, *Words For Truth: Replies to Roman Cavils Against the Church of England*, (James Pott & Co., 1889), p. 65

[16] *The Papacy and the Civil Power*, p. 385, 386

[17] Idid., p. 397, 401, 408, 409

[18] Ibid., p. 411, 412

[19] Ibid., p. 412-417, 486

[20] Ibid., p. 485-489.

According to Wikipedia, part of Canon 3 of the Fourth Lateran Council read,"Secular authorities, whatever office they may hold, shall be admonished and induced and if necessary compelled by ecclesiastical censure, that as they wish to be esteemed and numbered among the faithful, so for the defense of the faith they ought publicly to take an oath that they will strive in good faith and to the best of their ability to *exterminate* in the territories subject to their jurisdiction all heretics pointed out by the Church"(emphasis added). Canons 68 and 69 discriminated against Jews by decreeing that Jews were to be distinguished by dress from the "Christians" and that Jews were not to be given public offices.

[21] Peter Kreeft, "Protestants & Catholics, Scripture: our differing perceptions", *National Catholic Register*, November 9, 1986, p. 1, 7, Micheal Baigent and Richard Leigh, *The Inquisition*, (Viking, 1999),

inside front flap, David Cloud, *Way of Life Encyclopedia of the Bible and Christianity*, (Way Of Life Literature, 2002), p. 488-490, Richard Bennett, *Catholicism: East of Eden, Insights into Catholicism for the 21st Century*, (Berean Beacon Press, 2005), p. 74-77, Cecil John Cadoux, *Roman Catholicism And Freedom*, (Independent Press Ltd., 1947), p. 24, 34, Rev. J. Langtry, *Catholic versus Roman: Some of the Fundamental Points of Difference Between the Catholic Church and the Roman Church*, (Hunter, Rose & Company, 1886), p. 102, F. L. Cross, ed., *The Oxford Dictionary of the Christian Church*, (Oxford University Press, 1974), p. 351, *The Encyclopaedia Britannica Dictionary of Arts, Sciences, and General Literature*, (Samuel L. Hall, New York, 1878), Volume VI, p. 512, *New Catholic Encyclopedia*, 2003, Volume 4, p. 301, All Catholic Church Ecumenical Councils – All The Decrees, www.piar.hu/councils/, Heresy: www.newadvent.org, William Shaw Kerr, *A Handbook On The Papacy*, (Marshall Morgan & Scott, 1951), p. 235, *The Papacy and the Civil Power*, p. 445-470, *World Book Encylopedia*, 1998, Volume 13, p. 53, 54, 2005, Volume 16, p. 407, "Early copy of Magna Carta on block", *Prince George Citizen*, December 8, 2007, p. 15.

Regarding tens of millions being murdered through the Inquisition, Richard Bennett quoted John Dowling who quoted Scott's Church History. In *Roman Catholicism And Freedom* Cecil Cadoux reported that in June, 1849, the British Catholic journal, *The Rambler*, stated, "The Catholic has some reason on his side when he calls for the temporal punishment of heretics, for he claims the true title of Christian for himself exclusively…we are prepared to maintain, that it is no more morally wrong to put a man to death for heresy that for murder; that in many cases persecution for religious opinions is not only permissible, but highly advisable and necessary;…" *Roman Catholicism And Freedom* also reported "As late as 1899 there was published a fresh edition of the *Theologia dogmatica et moralis* used in sixty-seven Catholic theological seminaries in France: this edition contained the following words: "The Church has received from God the power to force or repress those who wander from the truth, not only by spiritual penalties, but also by temporal ones….These are prison, flagellation, torture, mutilation, death." In his book, *Catholic versus Roman*, Rev. Langtry stated of the Inquisition, "It is a terrible thing to say, but this conclusion is forced upon the student of history of this dread tribunal that, whatever may have been its object at its first establishment, it was very soon transformed into a vast organized system of murder, carried on mainly for the sake of plunder, under the sanction and direction of the Papal court." On the subject of heresy, the website, New Advent, stated in 2009:

> The Church's legislation on heresy and heretics is often reproached with cruelty and intolerance. Intolerant it is: in fact its raison d'ete is intolerance of doctrines subversive of the faith. But such intolerance is essential to all that is,

or moves, or lives, for tolerance of destructive elements within the organism amounts to suicide...The charge of cruelty is also easy to meet. All repressive mueasures cause suffering or inconvenience of some sort: it is their nature. But they are not therefore cruel. The father who chastises his guilty son is just and may be tender-hearted. Cruelty only comes in where the punishment exceeds the requirements of the case. Opponents say: Precisely; the rigours of the Inquisition violated all humane feelings. We answer: they offend the feelings of later ages in which there is less regard for the purity of faith; but they did not antagonize the feelings of their own time.

The New Advent site evidently obtained its information from the Catholic Encyclopedia. This source also stated,"In proof of which it suffices to remark that the inquisitors only renounced on the guilt of the accused and then handed him over to the secular power to be dealt with according to the laws framed by emoerors and kings." Actually, as the canons of the Fourth Lateran Council stated, it was the Church of Rome who commanded,"that the lords shall be admonished and advised by ecclesiastical censures to take an oath that they will extirpate heretics and excommunicate persons who shall be within their territories"

The article by Peter Kreeft, "Protestants & Catholics, Scripture: our differing perceptions" in the *National Catholic Register* stated, "The classic Protestant suspicion is that Catholics fear the Bible: that the Church forbade the laity to read it for centuries because if that had been allowed, people would have seen how unscriptural Catholic doctrines were. This is simply untrue, of course, but it is still widely believed among Protestants. The belief is declining though, in the face of the strong encouragement by Vatican II and all recent Popes to Catholic laity to read Scripture regularly." The Church certainly did forbid the laity to read it for centuries, as Wikipedia stated on the subject of the Spanish Inquisition, "As one manifestation of the Counter-Reformation, the Spanish Inquisition worked actively to impede the diffusion of heretical ideas in Spain by producing 'Indexes' of prohibited books... The Indexes included an enormous number of books of all types, though special attention was dedicated to religious works, and, particularly, vernacular translations of the bible." If in his statement Peter Kreeft had meant to acknowledge that the Church had indeed forbidden Catholics to read God's Word, he didn't explain why it was acceptable for this supposed Christian Church to have, for centuries, forbidden the words of life to millions of people. Quoting from the book of Deuteronomy, Christ stated,"...It is written, Man shall not live by bread alone, *but by every word* that proceedeth out of the mouth of God" (Matthew. 4:4b, emphasis added). Jesus Christ also said in John 6:63, "It is the spirit that quickeneth; the flesh profiteth nothing: the words that I speak unto you, they are spirit, and they are life." See also Psalm 1:1-3.

[22] *The Papacy and the Civil Power*, p. 471-474, 528-535, Richard P. McBrien, *Lives of the Popes*, (HarperSanFransisco, 1997), p. 252, 253

[23] *The Papacy and the Civil Power*, p. 535, Louis Marie De Cormenin, *The Public and Private History of the Popes of Rome*, (T. B. Peterson,1846), Volume 2, p. 108

[24] *The Papacy and the Civil Power*, p. 477, 478, Louis Marie De Cormenin, *The Public and Private History of the Popes of Rome*, (T. B. Peterson,1846), Volume 2, p. 91, *Words For Truth: Replies to Roman Cavils Against the Church of England*, p. 88, 89

[25] *The Papacy and the Civil Power*, p. 543-553

[26] *World Book Encylopedia*, 1998, Volume 16, p. 408, 196, 197, Vol. 15, p. 834, 463, *World Book Encyclopaedia*, 1978, Volume 4, p. 474, *Fifty Years* p. 699, 700, Roy Z. Chamlee, Jr., *Lincoln's Assassins: A Complete Account of the Capture, Trial, and Punishment*, p. 439, *New York Times*, November 19, 1861, p. 7, 8, *The Catholics and Mrs. Mary Surratt*, p. 56, 83, 106, 107, 137, Andrew C. A. Jampoler, *The Last Lincoln Conspirator: John Surratt's Flight from the Gallows*, (Naval Institute Press, 2008), p. 122, 123, 198, 204, 236, Statement of Surratt Society, "The History of 604 H Street", Surratt boarding-house, 604 H Street, Washington D.C.

Kenneth J. Zanca's book *The Catholics and Mrs. Mary Surratt* is a book offered for sale by the Surratt Society. Based in what used to be Surrattsville, (now Clinton, Maryland), the Surratt Society appears to be involved in a quiet effort to rehabilitate Mary Surratt's image, which still remains a problem to the Roman Catholic Church. Zanca's book helps in this effort in that although he does not rule her guilt out, he contended that "The case against Mrs. Surratt is circumstantial. It will never be known for certain what Mrs. Surratt knew about the kidnapping or assassination plots. We are not privy to the discussions that took place in the various rooms of her boardinghouse on H Street or the in the tete-a-tetes she had with John Wilkes Booth out of the hearing range of others. After so many years of dedicated study and examination by so many rival theorists, her role in the events of 1865 is still an unfinished question. What is left to history, without any ambiguity, is her statement to Gen. Hancock and Father Walter, given the day of her death, just after receiving Last Rites from her priest: "I had no hand in the murder of the president.""

Zanca assertions are ridiculous and he refutes his last statement himself. He wrote,"The three components of the myth are well-known. The first is that Mrs. Surratt, because of her religious values and practice, could never have been involved in a conspiracy to kidnap or murder the president, as if the very fact of her piety demanded that she be innocent. Inherent in this belief is the assumption that external conformity to Christian religious ritual (which is all anyone can ever see) always translates into a moral disposition or a Christ-like heart. Mrs. Surratt had lived, as best as any could tell, a blameless life, they argued.

Did Catholics somehow forget a basic tenet of their own theology – free will? Can anyone assume, given the Catholic teaching on Original Sin, that yesterday's virtue is a guarantee against today's temptation? Yet, the myth persisted in depicting her as a saint, a martyr, an innocent, in the face of the weakness of human nature and the circumstantial evidence against her."

The case against Mary Surratt was not circumstantial. John Lloyd testified directly of her words to him to have the guns ready as well as whiskey for the people that would need them the night of the assassination. It could be asked, were Booth and Herold going to be needing them for a night of drunken duck hunting? Regarding her reported last statement to Hancock and Walter, this is the same "pius" woman who, after kneeling and praying, lied about knowing Payne the night she was arrested, thereby showing her guilt. Roy Chamlee noted, "The conspirators were also ready liars."

An example of Zanca's deficiencies in scholarship is his statement in *The Catholics and Mrs. Mary Surratt* that "In 1861, for example, the *New York Times* said, 'the war has silenced forever the charges against the naturalized citizen and the Catholic as being worthy of citizenship.'" The quote was indeed in the November 19, 1861 issue of the *New York Times*, as the footnote indicated. No page number was given by Zanca, the quote was on page 8. This actually was a statement of a man named William E. Robinson, given in a speech he made on the occasion of a stand of colors presented to the Third Regiment of the Irish Brigade. By the same logic, the *New York Times* then also declared in the same issue that "Humphrey's Homoeopathic Specifics" was able to cure Cholera, Cholera Morbus, Nausea and Vomiting, Asthmatic Breathings as well as the dreaded Salt Rheum and Crusty Eruptions.

Andrew C. A. Jampoler's *The Last Lincoln Conspirator: John Surratt's Flight from the Gallows* was another book on the Lincoln assassination, published in 2008. Jampoler had little use for Charles Chiniquy, calling him "a defrocked Canadian priest who claimed to have been a client of Lincoln's law practice" who, after he left the Church of Rome, "spent the rest of his life libeling the Catholic Church" through his "fables". While Jampoler makes some good points, there are still problems with his volume. He stated that Joseph Dye's testimony was demolished by the testimony of James Gifford, C.B. Hess and Loius Carland. This certainly was not the case. He appeared to an apologist for the Church of Rome when he stated, contrary to the evidence, that Catholics volunteered in great numbers for the Union army. As well, Jampoler concluded that John Surratt was in New York State, not Washington D.C., the night of the assassination, was not involved in the murder and therefore not guilty. He wrote,"Surratt *was* in Elmira when Lincoln was assassinated, and the rest of his life flowed from that single fact (italics in the original)." Earlier in the book however, he stated,"Passing 140 years later, the answer to the key question—where Surratt was the night Lincoln was shot---is not more certain than it was in 1867, although the defense's witnesses from Elmira sound persuasive today." If it was no more certain when his book was published, how could Jampoler stated positively that Surratt was not in Washington the night of the assassination and therefore innocent?

According to *Fifty Years*, Lincoln said the promise of French arms gave Jeff Davis and others the confidence to start the Civil War and interestingly, the *World Book Encyclopaedia* states that "Historians have never reached any general agreement about the causes of the Civil War."

[27] *Fifty Years*, p. 718-725, *The Assassination of Abraham Lincoln and the Trial of the Conspirators*, p. 19, 368, 377, 402

[28] *The Catholics and Mrs. Mary Surratt*, p. 105, 106, 110, Guenter Lewy, *The Catholic Church and Nazi Germany*, (Weidenfeld and Nicolson, 1964). p. 287, 288, 298 - 300, 341, James Carroll, "The Holocaust and the Catholic Church," *The Atlantic*

Monthly, October, 1999, p. 107, Darcy O'Brien, *The Hidden Pope,* (Daybreak Books, 1998), p. 35, 36, Charles R. Morris, "The Worst Thing About My Church", the Atlantic online, January 2001, www.theatlantic.com, Don Lattin, "Pope John Paul II, 1920 – 2005, Beloved, charismatic and controversial, John Paul II transformed the papacy", *San Francisco Chronicle*, April 3, 2005, p. A1, "Pope John Paul II Makes Unprecedented Apology For Sins of Catholic Church", CNN, aired March 12, 2000, Ronald H. Bailey and the editors of Time-Life Books, *Partisans and Guerrillas*, (Time-Life Books Inc., 1978), p. 84, 87, Mark Aarons and John Loftus, *Unholy Trinity: the Vatican, the Nazis, and Soviet intelligence*, (St. Martin's Press, 1991), Preface, p. xi, xii, "Ireland Offered Condolences Over Hitler's Death", *Sudbury Star*, December 31, 2005, [Final Edition], p. C5, "Feudal Gestures", *The Atlantic Monthly*, October 2003, Volume 292, Issue 3, p. 135, David Yallop, *In God's Name*, (Bantam Books, 1984), MEMORANDUM FOR THE OFFICER IN CHARGE,12 September 1947, Case No. 5650-a, Counter Intelligence Corps, Rome Detachment, Zone 5, A.P.O. 512, U.S. Army, www.pavelic-papers.com.

Charles Morris reviewed Catholic author James Carroll's book, *Constantine's Sword; The Church and the Jews*. In the review, entitled "The Worst Thing About My Church", Morris commented on the Catholic Church's actions during the Second World War. Morris, also a Catholic, stated "What is at issue is the Vatican's eyes-averted pattern of accommodating the Nazis. The only possible conclusion from the entire record is that Pacelli, in order to secure the Church's future in Germany and the papacy's institutional interests, was willing to remain largely silent while the Germans murdered millions of Jews." Morris also declared, "Prominent practicing Catholics were salted throughout the Nazi regime, and they were courteously received at the Vatican by the Pope. Hitler's first Vice Chancellor, Franz von Papen, who played a key role in the Nazi subversion of Austria, even received papal honors after the war...There is ample evidence that the murderous activities of the pro-Nazi Ustashe regime in Croatia were well known within the Church hierarchy, yet the Ustashe leader, Ante Pavelic, was sheltered at the Vatican when his rule crumbled..."

According to the Pavelic Papers, a U.S. Army document detailed the incriminating relationship Pavelic had with the Vatican. A September 12th, 1947, document of the Rome Detachment of the U.S. Army Counter Intelligence Corps stated "PAVELIC's contacts are so high and his present position is so compromising to the VATICAN, that any extradition of Subject would deal a staggering blow to the Roman Catholic Church." The Pavelic Papers, according to its website, is a Holocaust education and research project studying the history of the Ustashi movement.

[29] "Sisters of no mercy," *National Post*, August 1, 2003, [National Edition], p. PM. 1. Fr, "The Catholic church's horrifying dirty laundry", *Toronto Star*, August 1, 2003, [Ontario Edition], p. E3, "Vatican newspaper gives thumbs down to film about harsh Catholic convent," *Prince George Citizen*, September 6, 2002, p. 25. In *The Catholics and Mrs. Mary Surratt*, (p. 110), Kenneth Zanca reported that there was no expression of sympathy sent from the Vatican to America regarding the death of President Lincoln but in June, 1865, Pope Pius IX asked about the welfare of Jeff Davis.

[30] Paul Williams, *The Vatican Exposed: money, murder, and the Mafia*, (Prometheus Books, 2003), p. 200, 201, "Ex-Vatican powerbroker living in Sun City," *The Arizona Republic*, May 4, 2003, "Film spotlights 'murky Vatican finances,' " B.B.C. News Online, March 8, 2002, www.news.bbc.co.uk

The Church of Rome evidently has little interest in obeying the Word of God. Instead of commanding "priests" or anyone else not to marry, the scriptures say the opposite. Even the Catholic Bible shows how wrong, actually demonic, the doctrine of celibacy is. In the Saint Joseph "New Catholic Edition" of the Holy Bible, (Catholic Book Publishing Company, 1961), 1 Timothy 4:1-3 reads, "Now the Spirit expressly says that in after times some will depart from the faith, giving heed to deceitful spirits and doctrines of devils, Speaking lies hypocritically, and having their conscience branded. They will forbid marriage, and will enjoin abstinence from foods, which God has created to be partaken of with thanksgiving by the faithful and by those who know the truth",(Imprimatur: Francis Cardinal Spellman, Archbishop of New York).

The Catholic Church forbids marriage to hundreds of thousands of men and the current crisis of sexual abuse, the on-going dark secret of the Church that has finally come to light, shows how foolish it is to repress the natural attractions and needs of men that are satisfied within the bonds of marriage.

As well, the Catholic Church has stated its belief in the theory of evolution.

Chapter 11 America and the Catholic Church Today

[1] 1860 and 1870 United States Federal Census - see footnote 41, Chapter 8, Cathy Lynn Grossman, "Survey: USA's Protestant majority might soon be no more," *USA TODAY*, July 20, 2004, Life section, p. 6d, J. P. Paul Laverdure, "The Religious Invective of Charles Chiniquy: Anti-Catholic Crusader 1875 - 1900", Diss. M. A., McGill University, 1984, p. 17, Charles Chiniquy, *Fifty Years In The Church Of Rome*, (Craig and Barlow, 1886, 3rd edition), p. 668, 669, Paul Blanshard, *American Freedom and Catholic Power*, (The Beacon Press, 1949), p. 4. In his 1949 book, *American Freedom and Catholic Power*, Blanshard stated that the Roman Catholic Church is "an organization that is not only a church but a state within a state, and a state above a state." Of the American Catholic hierarchy, he also stated, "It uses the political power of some twenty-six million official American Catholics to bring American foreign policy into line with Vatican temporal interests."

[2] Catherine Milner, "Church tops lost of Schwarzenegger charity donations," *National Post*, August 25, 2003, p.A10, Karl Rove, "Palin could make the difference in this close race", *The Wall Street Journal*, September 4, 2008, [Eastern edition], p. A17, Thomas Fitzgerald, " 'Scrappy kid' authority on foreign policy; Obama's pick for VP key to white working class", National Post, August 25, 2008, p. A8

[3] Art Moore, "Is Mexico reconquering U.S. southwest?", WorldNetDaily, January 4, 2002, Brenda Walker, "Vatican Promotes Lawless Immigration," www.limitsongrowth.org, A Question Of Amnesty, PBS: Online NewsHour, July 17,

2001, Roberto Suro, "Catholic church alarmed as Hispanics change to Protestant denominations," *The Montreal Gazette*, May 27, 1989, [Final Edition], p. J. 9, Donald L. Barlett, James B. Steele, "Who Left The Door Open?," *Time*, September 20, 2004, p. 50

[4] "Is Mexico reconquering U.S. southwest?", WorldNetDaily, January 4, 2002

[5] *World Book Encyclopedia*, 1978, Volume 19, p. 162,163, Vol. 8, p. 400, Matt Hayes, "Is Mexico Thwarting U.S. Immigration Enforcement?", FOXNews.com, March 18, 2004

[6] Kenneth D. Lewis,"Not In The Cards," *Wall Street Journal*, February 22, 2007, [Eastern edition], p. A15, "Is Mexico reconquering U.S. southwest?," Robert Mahony, "Immigrant Workers Deserve Legal Status and Respect", *Los Angeles Times*, June 8, 2000, [Home Edition], p. 13, Stephen Greenhouse, "Immigrants Rally in City, Seeking Rights," *New York Times*, October 5, 2003, [Late Edition, East Coast], p. 33, section 1, "Vatican Promotes Lawless Immigration", Richard Burke, *The Senator*, (St. Martin's Press, 1992), p. 317, WORLD BRIEFING l AMERICAS; Mexico: Honor For a U.S. Senator, *New York Times*, July 19, 2008, [Late Edition, Final], p. 6. United States Senator Edward Kennedy's immoral behavior has been well publicized. During October, 1991, in a speech at Harvard University, Edward Kennedy stated, "I recognize my own shortcomings -- the faults in the conduct of my private life". Richard Burke, Senator Kennedy's administrative assistant for almost a decade, detailed Kennedy's womanizing and drug use in his 1992 book.

[7] *The Wanderer*, May 28, 1987, p. 1, *National Catholic Register*, November 11, 1986, p. 3

[8] "Religious Tolerance", *The Shepherd of the Valley*, November 22, 1851, "Los Crimes de la Intolerancia", *Tiempo*, February 8, 1952, p. 49 - 53

[9] Russell Watson, "John Paul Goes to War," *Newsweek*, February 12, 1996, p. 39, Michael S. Serrill, "What the Pope Will Find", *Time*, February 12, 1996, p. 45, 46, Evangelicals and Catholics Together: The Christian Mission in the Third Millennium, Michael R. McAteer, "Pope battles for Latin America's Catholic soul", *Anglican Journal*, Volume 125, Issue 3, "Catholicism the one true church: Pope", *Prince George Citizen*, July 11, 2007, p. 14, Chris Woehr, "Protestants Are Not Welcome", *Liberty*, March / April, 1994, p. 24 - 26

[10] "Protestants Escorted Home", *Toronto Star*, August 2, 1998, p.1, "Protestants Are Not Welcome", p. 24 - 26

[11] Reginald Bibby, *Restless Gods*, (Stoddart, 2002), p. 85. Jeffery Simpson, *The Friendly Dictatorship*, (M & S, 2001), p. 4, Stephen Frank, "Where Has Canada Gone? The World's second largest country is being swallowed up by its own irrelevance. Time investigates Canada's disappearance", *Time*, May 26, 2003, p. 16 - 18, Michael Bliss, "Southern Republic, northern dictatorship", *National Post*, September 6, 2002, p. A18. Canadian Prime Ministers wield more power within Canada than any other any other first world leader in their respective democracies.

[12] "Violence Warned of if Quebec separates: Reform party analysis aims to discourage split", Edmonton Journal, December 2, 1995, [Final Edition], p. A8,Graeme Hamilton, "Not For Conformists", National Post, July 20, 2002, p. B3, Dene Moore, "Top Roman Catholic's appeal for forgiveness dismissed by church critics", The Canadian Press, November 21, 2007, William Johnson, "PQ's shock-and-awe plan," The Montreal Gazette, April 18, 2004, p. A.13, Diane Francis, Fighting for Canada, (Key Porter Books, 1996), p. 7, 21, 64, 65, 139-143, 169-175, www.dianefrancis.com.

In the 1950s and before that time, almost all parts of life in Quebec, including politics, were controlled by the Church of Rome. 90% of the population went to church at the time. Today, it is some 20%. The Roman Catholic Church's involvement in Quebec life today may be not as obvious as it was 50 years ago but a large majority of Quebec residents continue to consider themselves Catholics. According a 2002 National Post article, "About 85% of Quebecers still identify themselves as Catholics, even if they rarely attend church, and they still expect to experience key rites of passage in a church. Almost without exception, they reject the idea of converting to a different religious tradition".

[13] William Johnson, "PQ's shock-and-awe plan", The Montreal Gazette, April 18, 2004, p. A.13,

"Ontario: Vatican won't OK priest's bid to run for the Bloc", Ottawa Citizen, November 7, 2006, [Final Edition], p. A12, Sean Gordon, "Gay priest seeks Bloc nomination; But first he needs Vatican's approval Was once rebuked by Pope Benedict", Toronto Star, October 25, 2006, [MET Edition], p. A7, Fighting for Canada, p. 153,154,170, Diane Francis, "What divides our two nations", National Post, December 13, 2003, p. A16, Don Butler, "Pandering to Quebecers hurts nation: historian", National Post, November 1, 2005, p. A1, Martin Patriquin, Philippe Gohier, "Ungodly Union", Maclean's, October 13, 2008, p. 31. Raymond Gravel's superior, Gilles Lussier, the bishop of Joliette, has stated that Gravel did not receive permission from the Vatican to run for Parliament and since winning his seat, he "has been relieved of the exercise of his sacred ministry". The Toronto Star however, has reported that Gravel told Radio-Canada that if Catholic authorities were against it, he would not run. Maclean's reported that Gravel resigned his seat in September, 2008, and also that while he was an member of Parliament, he "was hugely popular with his Catholic base, thanks to his championing of senior's rights- and for being unapologetically sovereignist."

[14] Guy Bertrand, Enough is enough, (ECW Press, 1996), p. 48 - 50, "Quebec fudging French stats?", Prince George Citizen, January 25, 2008, p. 6, Graeme Hamilton, "A party's tongue-tied tactics; PQ leader's plan for the future of sovereignty attracts criticism", National Post, March 15, 2008, p. A13, Don MacPherson, "After starting accommodation debate, ADQ is now silent; Dumont's party is the only one not to submit a brief to the commission", The Montreal Gazette, December 11, 2007, p. A21, Philip Authier, Marianne White, "The big stall: PQ 'under renovation' ", The Montreal Gazette, March 6, 2008, p. A1, Peter Koven, "Quebec separatism seen as spent force", National Post, May 14, 2007, [National Edition], p. FP 2, Jeffrey Simpson, "Harper

bulldozes his way to the brink", *Globe and Mail*, December 2, 2008, p. A1, Jeffrey Simpson, "Spectre of defeat, hasty retreat put party in disarray", *Globe and Mail*, December 2, 2008, p. A1, "A War on our History", *Macleans*, March 2, 2009, p. 4, Caving in to Separatist Demands; We Shouldn't Cancel Re-enactment due to Threats", *Windsor Star*, February 28, 2009, p. A7.

Guy Bertrand is a Quebec lawyer who worked for separatism and was a member of the Parti Quebecois for 25 years, but turned against the cause. Bertrand reported that his own brother has refused to talk to him and a Quebec judge and former colleague told him he was a traitor and should be killed.

The latest accomplishment of the separatists in Quebec has been the cancellation of, at least a significant part of, the official recognition of the 250th anniversary of the most famous battle in Canadian history. Early in 2009, the federal National Battlefield Commission cancelled a re-enactment of the Battle of the Plains of Abraham at Quebec City. The Battle of Quebec, which was won by the British over the French, was the single most important event in America after European contact. Ironically, the victory by the British meant the protection of Quebec's culture, language and religion, ie. Catholicism.

[15] John Clinkard, 'More Canadian Head Offices say "Westward -Ho!" ', *Journal of Commerce*, Vancouver, Issue 78, October 3, 2005, p. 10, "CP Looks West: Companies moving to Calgary from anywhere - including Quebec - are welcome", *Calgary Herald*, [Final Edition], November 16, 1995, p. A18, "Imperial Oil unveils plans to shift 500 employees and head office to Calgary", *Whitehorse Star*, September 29, 2004, p. 19, Martin Patriquin, "A paradise for pedophiles", *Maclean's*, May 28, 2007, p. 20, 21, "Killer saw Quebec as a place to blend in", *Prince George Citizen*, June 6, 2005, p. 6, "Karla Homolka seeks change in latitude; killer setting sail for Caribbean, Quebec TV network reports", *Edmonton Journal*, [Early Edition], December 15, 2007, p. A5

[16] Jan Wong, "Get under the desk", *The Globe and Mail*, September 16, 2006, p. A8, William, Johnson, "If you burn a flag in Quebec, it had better be a Maple Leaf ", *Montreal Gazette*, [Final Edition], October 5, 2006, p. A19, "Keep doors wide open in Canada", *Toronto Star*, [Ontario Edition], December 2, 2007, p. A27, Patrick Toner, "Maybe 'accommodation' is the wrong word", *Saint John Telegraph-Journal*, February 15, 2008, p. A7

[17] "If you burn a flag in Quebec, it had better be a Maple Leaf ", Pat Donnelly, "Jan Wong tries to make it right; Author-journalist atones for her Maoist past in her latest book", *The Ottawa Citizen*, [Final Edition], December 23, 2007, p. C4, Charles Gordon, "Freedom of speech can look after itself ", *The Ottawa Citizen*, [Final Edition], September 24, 2006, p. A10, Andrew Potter, "Thank Harper for an era of gangster separatism", *Maclean's*, Volume 120, Issue 44, November 12, 2007, p. 12, "An abject betrayal of Canadian values", *Canadian Jewish News*, Volume 37, Issue 44, November 1, 2007, p. 8, Jiwani Yasmin, " 'Culture' depends on who's defining it; Anglo culture is dominant and taken for granted; minority cultures are automatically 'different' ", *Vancouver Sun*, [Final Edition], August 8, 2007, p. A11

[18] Graeme Hamilton, "Bon cop, bad cop routine at Quebec hearings; Everyone is a Quebecer, Duceppe says;" *National Post*, December 12, 2007, p. A8, "Thank Harper for an era of gangster separatism", p. 12, Clark Blaise, *I Have a Father*, (HarperCollins Publishers Ltd., 1993), p. 96 - 99, Joseph Varacalli, *The Catholic Experience in America*, (Greenwood Press, 1993), p. 307, Jeet Heer, "America's Hobbits", *National Post*, January 18, 2006, A14, "The French Canadians in New England", *New York Times*, June 6, 1892, p. 4, "The Decline of Protestantism and its Cause", *Freeman's Journal and Catholic Register*, November 23, 1850, p. 2, Richard Frederick Littledale, *Words For Truth: Replies to Roman Cavils Against the Church of England*, (James Pott & Co., 1889), p. 46, 47.

In his book that reproduced the *New York Times* editorial, *I Had a Father*, author Clark Blaise took great exception to the concern articulated by the *Times* to the perceived threat to the United States. In the 1892 editorial, the *Times* expressed unease about the large amount of French-Canadian immigrant who were massed in New England population centers as well as rural areas and their resistance to assimilate into American life and thought. The editorial stated "Mr. Francis Parkman has ably pointed out their singular tenacity as a race and their extreme devotion to their religion, and their transplantations to the manufacturing centers and the rural districts in New England mean that Quebec is transferred bodily to Manchester and Fall River and Lowell". Compare this sentiment to that of prominent Quebec separatist Gilles Duceppe, leader of the Bloc Quebecois party. A 2007 article in the *National Post* quoted him, "He shifted the onus to Quebecers to make it easier for new immigrants to fit into Quebec society. 'Those who come from elsewhere must integrate into our nation. But we have to facilitate that integration,' he said ". If the *Times* editorial is to be condemned for voicing concern for the French Catholic's lack of interest in such things as American democratic institutions, then surely so is the Bloc Quebecois and the sizable portion of Quebec society that supports them more than a hundred years later. In addition, what Catholic academic Joseph Varacalli reported in his book *The Catholic Experience in America* (1993), should be considered. Part of his timeline of the Catholic experience in the United States, under the heading: 1899, (years after the Times editorial), is of interest. There, Varacalli listed: "*Testem benevolent* ('On the Heresy of Americanism') is issued by Pope Leo XIII; debate within the Catholic elite circles ensues over whether or not 'the heresy of Americanism' is real or not". In light of this, was the *Times* far off when it stated of the French Catholics in the same editorial, "This body is ruled by a principle directly opposite to that which has made New-England what it is"?

Quebec is now very secular and this is what Catholicism has done to societies in other locations. On the subject of what Romanism has accomplished in Europe, Richard Littledale stated in his book, *Words For Truth: Replies to Roman Cavils Against the Church of England*, "It was after the whole educational system of France had been for more than a hundred years in the hands of the Jesuits, who were able and accomplished teachers, that the French nation made a public profession of atheism in 1793, and the Christian religion was put under ban for several years, a disaster never yet repaired. And at the last census in 1881 seven millions and a half of Frenchmen (or more than a fifth of the whole nation) returned themselves as of no religion. Of Spain, once the leading power in Europe, a Spaniard has said that the clergy and the Inquisition have made that country "the Turkey of the West;" and in Italy the gulf between the Church and the nation gapes widely with none to bridge it. Moreover, in all these countries a foully immoral literature is current and popular; and political disturbances, aiming at social anarchy, are of incessant occurrence, either in open manifestation or secret plots. It is not we who say so, to make a case for our own side; the witness who has testified most plainly for us is no other than Cardinal Manning himself, who confessed, in an article on 'The Church and Modern Society,' in the *North American Review* of February, 1880, that the most Christian civil society now extant is that of non-Papal England, contrasting with that of France, Italy, and other Roman Catholic countries."

[19] Eduardo Porter, "Protestant Churches Are Learning to Speak Language of Latinos --- Mr Hernandez, Left 'Empty By Catholicism, Preaches Conversion in Parking Lots", *Wall Street Journal*, July 2, 2002, [Eastern edition], p. A. 1, "Catholic church alarmed as Hispanics change to Protestant denominations", *The Montreal Gazette*, "Who Left The Door Open?," Joyce Howard Price, "U.S. Protestant population seen losing majority status," *The Washington Times*, July 21, 2004, p. A1, Don Lattin, "Old-time religion on the decline Fewer Americans identify with Protestant denominations, survey shows", *San Francisco Chronicle*, July21, 2004, p. A2, Cathy Lynn Grossman, "Survey: USA's Protestant majority might soon be no more", *USA TODAY*, July 20, 2004, p. 6d, Life section, Reginald Bibby, Unknown Gods, (Stoddard, 1993), p. 111, 112

Appendix 1

[1] *The Montreal Witness*, March 10, 1892, p. 4, Joseph George Jr., "The Lincoln Writings of Charles P. T. Chiniquy", *Journal of the Illinois Historical Society*, Volume LXIX, Number 1, February, 1976, p. 17-25, Mark E. Neely, *The Abraham Lincoln Encyclopedia*, (McGraw-Hill Inc, 1982), p.57

[2] "The Lincoln Writings of Charles P. T. Chiniquy", p. 17

[3] "The Lincoln Writings of Charles P. T. Chiniquy", p. 20, Thomas P. Meehan, "Lincoln's Opinion of Catholics," *Historical Records and Studies of the United States Catholic Historical Society*, Volume 16 (1924), p. 88, "From Abraham Lincoln's Son", *Columbia*, March, 1922, p. 6, *Fifty Years*, p. 693, 700, 715

[4] Robert Todd Lincoln to Charles Chiniquy, September 10, 1885, The Chiniquy Collection

[5] "The Lincoln Writings of Charles P. T. Chiniquy", p. 18, 22, *Fifty Years*, p. 623-628, 653, 654

[6] "The Lincoln Writings of Charles P. T. Chiniquy", p. 22, *Fifty Years*, p. 658-661

[7] "The Lincoln Writings of Charles P. T. Chiniquy", p. 22, 23

[8] Chapter 3, p. 6, 7, *Notre Dame de Chicago, 1887-193: a history of Notre Dame parish, preceded by an historical sketch of the work of the early French missionaries in the central states--prepared for the occasion of the fiftieth anniversary of the erection of Notre Dame Church*, (The Fathers of the Blessed Sacrament, 1937), p. 55, Richard Lougheed, "The Controversial Conversion of Charles Chiniquy", Diss. Ph. D., University of Montreal, 1993, p. 161-178, Bessie Pierce, *A History Of Chicago*, (Alfred A. Knopf, 1940), p. 360, *Chicago Tribune*, January 26, 27, March 31, April 13, June 11, 1857, *Chicago Daily Democrat*, May 1, 1856, (misdated, actual date likely May 1, 1857), *Historical Encyclopedia of Illinois and History of Kankakee County*, (Middle-West Publishing Company,1906), Volume II, p. 752, John G. Shea, *History Of The Catholic Church In The United States*, (New York, 1892) p. 618, 619

[9] "The Controversial Conversion of Charles Chiniquy", Diss. p. 161, 162, "The Lincoln Writings of Charles P. T. Chiniquy", p. 23

[10] Illinois State Historical Society, Spink vs. Chiniquy file, *Fifty Years* (3rd edition) also reproduced it on p. 663, "The Lincoln Writings of Charles P. T. Chiniquy", p. 23, The original of the bill of Abraham Lincoln to Charles Chiniquy is held by the University of Illinois at Urbana.

[11] Agreement dismissing Spink vs. Chiniquy, Library of Congress, Herndon-Weik Collection, microfilm, 5:2766-2767, Order dismissing Spink vs. Chiniquy, October Term, 1856, Champaign County Circuit Court Record, B, p. 45, photocopy of other copy of agreement dismissing Spink vs. Chiniquy, Illinois State Historical Society, Spink vs. Chiniquy file, Petition of Peter Spink, November 13, 1855, Circuit Court of Kankakee County, see Chapter 2, p.1, *Fifty Years*, p. 623, 624, Defence costs, Champaign County Circuit Court, May Term, 1856

[12] "The Lincoln Writings of Charles P. T. Chiniquy", p. 23

[13] Ibid. p. 24

[14] *The Urbana Union*, May 29,1856, p. 3, *Fifty Years*, p. 663, Albert Woldman, *Lawyer Lincoln*, (Houghton Mifflin Company, 1936), p. 218, 219

[15] Edward Steers, *Lincoln Legends: Myths, Hoaxes, and Confabulations Associated With Our Greatest President*, (The University Press of Kentucky, 2007), p. 62, "The Lincoln Writings of Charles P. T. Chiniquy", p. 21, Carl Russell Fish, "Lincoln And Catholicism," *The American Historical Review*, Volume 29, 1924, p. 723

[16] "The Lincoln Writings of Charles P. T. Chiniquy", p. 24, 25

[17] "The Lincoln Writings of Charles P. T. Chiniquy", p. 24, 25, A. Chester to Abraham Lincoln, June 10, 1864, Robert Todd Lincoln Collection, The Library of Congress, *Fifty Years*, p. 611, Henry Clay Whitney, *Life on the Circuit with Lincoln*, (The Caxton Printers, 1940), p. 74, "The Story Told by an Ex-priest", *Chicago Daily Tribune*, May 31, 1887, p. 2. The *Tribune* article reported on Chiniquy's lecture at a Chicago church and stated that he still, "speaks with a decided French accent, and resorts to the French idiom when heated."

[18] "The Lincoln Writings of Charles P. T. Chiniquy", p. 24, 25, Robert Todd Lincoln to Charles Chiniquy, September 10, 1885, The Chiniquy Collection

[19] "Letter From Father Chiniquy", *Chicago Tribune*, August 12, 1864, p. 3, "Lincoln Memory Honored", *New York Times*, February 13, 1894, p. 5, "The Lincoln Writings of Charles P. T. Chiniquy", p. 25

[20] Richard Lougheed, "The Controversial Conversion of Charles Chiniquy", Diss. Ph.D., University of Montreal, 1993, p. 1, 3, 393, Richard Lougheed, *The Controversial Conversion of Charles Chiniquy*, (Clements Academic, 2008). The book did not become available for sale until 2009.

[21] "The Controversial Conversion of Charles Chiniquy", Diss., p. 232, 406

[22] Ibid p. 217

[23] Ibid p. 217, 222

[24] "The Controversial Conversion of Charles Chiniquy", Diss, p. 109, 226, 227, *Chicago Daily Tribune*, September 16, 1877, p. 2. The *Tribune* account stated, "The Board of French Evangelization have embellished a series of resolutions passed at a meeting held yesterday, expressing regret that the press should have given countenance the statements of Mr. W. B. Court affecting its work. These resolutions approve of Father Chiniquy's work, and the allegations brought against it by Mr. Court are denied. The resolutions are signed by all the Presbyterian ministers in the city."

[25] "The Controversial Conversion of Charles Chiniquy", Diss. p. 218, 219

[26] Charles Chiniquy, *Fifty Years in the Church of Rome*, (Craig and Barlow, 1886, 3rd edition), p 310, 311, 590

[27] The Controversial Conversion, Diss., p. 136, 137, 316

[28] Ibid p. 224, 225

[29] Ibid, p. 118

[30] The Controversial Conversion, Diss., p. 121,122, 147-152, *The Controversial Conversion of Charles Chiniquy*, p. 32, 53, Caroline B. Brettell, "From Catholics to Presbyterians: French-Canadian Immigration to Central Illinois," *American Presbyterians, Journal of Presbyterian History*, Volume 63 - Number 3, Fall 1985, p. 286

[31] The Controversial Conversion, Diss., p. 148, 149, 152, 184, *The Controversial Conversion of Charles Chiniquy*, p. 54, 94.

[32] "From Catholics to Presbyterians: French-Canadian Immigration to Central Illinois", p. 297

[33] The Controversial Conversion, Diss., p. 149-151, *The Controversial Conversion of Charles Chiniquy*, p. 54, 55. The language barrier, (the documents are in French), made it difficult to verify that Chiniquy pleaded innocent instead of an outright denial.

[34] *Fifty Years*, p. 507, 511, 512, 558, 559

[35] The Controversial Conversion, Diss., p. 152, 172, 173, 315, 316

[36] Ibid, p. 173, 325, 406, "From Catholics to Presbyterians: French-Canadian Immigration to Central Illinois", p. 287

[37] The Controversial Conversion, Diss., p. 218, 219, *The Controversial Conversion of Charles Chiniquy*, p. 125-127

[38] *World Book Encyclopaedia*, 1998, Volume 12, p. 315, 327, The Controversial Conversion, Diss., p. 160, 218, Joseph George Jr., "The Lincoln Writings of Charles P. T. Chiniquy", *Journal of the Illinois Historical Society*, Volume LXIX, Number 1, February, 1976, p. 20-23. The sources that do not list a George biography include the American Humanities Index and the catalogue of the Library of Congress.

[39] The Controversial Conversion, Diss., p. 160, 161, 219, 220

[40] *The Controversial Conversion of Charles Chiniquy*, p. 62- 64

[41] Ibid, p. 71, *Fifty Years*, p. 560, 561

[42] *The Controversial Conversion of Charles Chiniquy*, p. 2, 80, 81, *Fifty Years*, p. 632. The quote "He protested that the supension was unjust and therefore null and void" contains, of course, a spelling error.

[43] *Fifty Years*, p. 776-800, 803

[44] *The Controversial Conversion of Charles Chiniquy*, p. 5, 6, *Fifty Years*, p. 227-237, 296. In the original unpublished book manuscript, Lougheed stated of Trudel's biography of Chiniquy," Since publication Trudel apparently regrets the approach and would like to rewrite it".

[45] "From Catholics to Presbyterians: French-Canadian Immigration to Central Illinois", p. 285

[46] *World Book Encyclopaedia*, 1998, Volume 11, p. 358, Mark Neely, *The Abraham Lincoln Encyclopedia*, (McGraw-Hill, 1982), p. 174, 175, "From Catholics to Presbyterians: French-Canadian Immigration to Central Illinois", p. 285

[47] "From Catholics to Presbyterians: French-Canadian Immigration to Central Illinois", p. 285, 286, 297

[48] Brettell to Serup, June 20, 1989

[49] The Controversial Conversion, Diss., p. 134

[50] "From Catholics to Presbyterians: French-Canadian Immigration to Central Illinois", p. 286, 288, 297

[51] The Controversial Conversion, Diss., p. 207, "From Catholics to Presbyterians: French-Canadian Immigration to Central Illinois", p. 289, 290

[52] *Fifty Years*, p. 643-645, 790-803, "From Catholics to Presbyterians: French-Canadian Immigration to Central Illinois", p. 289, 297

[53] "From Catholics to Presbyterians: French-Canadian Immigration to Central Illinois", p. 290

[54] "From Catholics to Presbyterians: French-Canadian Immigration to Central Illinois", p. 292, 297, Armand J. Lottinville, *The Lottinville Family*, (Murray & Heister, 1942), p. 49-51.

Brettell stated that the *Kankakeee Gazette* reported a speech of Chiniquy in which he appeared to be very interested in the money that Presbyterian Church could give his colonists but she did not actually quote the newspaper but from a letter (in French) given in a book. The book is called *The Lottinville Family*. The letter was by a man named Anthony Lottinville, quoting from the *Kankakee Gazette*, evidently in early 1860. It is not apparent however, where there are any holdings of this newspaper and therefore the claim by Lottinville cannot be checked. The Abraham Lincoln Presidential Library has the largest collection of Illinois newspapers of any location but does not have the *Kankakee Gazette* for this time period and neither does the Kankakee Valley Historical Society.

[55] William Hanchett, *The Lincoln Murder Conspiracies*, (University of Illinois Press, 1986), back-flap, p. 234

[56] Ibid., p. 234

[57] George Alfred Townsend, *The Life, Crime, And Capture Of John Wilkes Booth*, (Dick and Fitzgerald, 1865, 1977 limited reprint), p. 42, *The Lincoln Murder Conspiracies*, p. 276

[58] *The Lincoln Murder Conspiracies*, p. 234, 235, 276, 277

[59] *Fifty Years*, p. 776-803, 819, 820

[60] *The Lincoln Murder Conspiracies*, p. 235, 241, *Fifty Years*, p. 456-469

[61] *New York Times*, April 20, 1867, p. 1, *The Lincoln Murder Conspiracies*, p. 241. The *Times* was not always favourable in its coverage of Chiniquy as shown by the April 20th front page article on Chiniquy.

[62] "The Lincoln Writings of Charles P. T. Chiniquy", p. 24

[63] "The Lincoln Writings of Charles P. T. Chiniquy", p. 25, *The Lincoln Murder Conspiracies*, p. 277

[64] The Controversial Conversion, Diss., p. 8, Rev. Sydney Smith, *Pastor Chiniquy*, (Catholic Truth Society), p.1

[65] *Pastor Chiniquy*, p. 2

[66] Ibid., p. 2-5

[67] The Controversial Conversion, Diss., p. 420, Charles Chiniquy, *The Life And Labours Of The Reverend Father Chiniquy*, (Religious Tract & Book Society Of Scotland, 1861), p. 7. *The Life And Labours Of The Reverend Father Chiniquy* is 33 pages. *Why I Left The Church Of Rome*, was published in 1887 by the London Protestant Truth Society and is 30 pages. The 3rd edition of *Fifty Years*, published in 1886 is 832 pages.

[68] *The Life And Labours Of The Reverend Father Chiniquy*, p. 7

[69] Ibid., 9, 23, 24, 27

[70] *Fifty Years*, p. 443

[71] *Fifty Years*, p. 188-192, 515-517, *Pastor Chiniquy*, p. 6

[72] *Pastor Chiniquy*, p. 6, "French Catholic Meeting In Chicago,"January 26, 1857, *Chicago Tribune*, p. 2, "Dispute Between Bishop O'Regan and the French," January 27, 1857, *Chicago Tribune*, p. 2, "The Church Property Question, Father Chiniquy and Bishop O'Regan," March 31, 1857, *Chicago Tribune*, p. 2

[73] *Pastor Chiniquy*, p. 6, *Fifty Years*, p. 801, 802

[74] *Fifty Years*, p. 29

[75] *Pastor Chiniquy*, p. 6, 7

[76] *Fifty Years*, p. 14-16, 31, 33, 37

[77] *Pastor Chiniquy*, p. 8, 9, *Fifty Years*, p. 470-482, Charles Chiniquy, *The Priest, the Woman, and the Confessional*, (The Marshall Press Limited, undated), p. 144, Matthew 12: 46-50, (possibly a Catholic version). A typo is contained in this quote of the Bible from *Fifty Years*. In verse 49, brethren was spelt brethaen.

[78] *Pastor Chiniquy*, p. 8-10, *Fifty Years*, p. 138, 480, 615, 616, 622

[79] *Fifty Years*, p. 9, 12, 81-85, 614-616

[80] *Pastor Chiniquy*, p. 10, 11

[81] *The Life And Labours Of The Reverend Father Chiniquy*, p. 5

[82] *The Life And Labours Of The Reverend Father Chiniquy*, p. 5-7, *Fifty Years*, p. 144-162, 500-503, 778, *Pastor Chiniquy*, p. 11-15

[83] *Pastor Chiniquy*, p. 15, 16

[84] Ibid., p. 16

[85] *Fifty Years*, p. 782, 787, *Pastor Chiniquy*, p. 22

[86] *Fifty Years*, p. 497, 498, *Pastor Chiniquy*, p. 22, 23

[87] *Fifty Years*, p. 497, 498, *Pastor Chiniquy*, p. 23

[88] *Notre Dame de Chicago, 1887-193: a history of Notre Dame parish,* preceded by an historical sketch of the work of the early French missionaries in the central states—prepared for the occasion of the fiftieth anniversary of the erection of Notre Dame Church, (The Fathers of the Blessed Sacrament, 1937), p. 51, Pastor Chiniquy, p. 25

[89] *Fifty Years*, p. 499-505, The Controversial Conversion, Diss., p. 5

[90] *Pastor Chiniquy*, p. 25, 26, *Fifty Years*, p. 508, 512

[91] *Pastor Chiniquy*, p. 26, 27

[92] *Pastor Chiniquy*, p. 27, 28

[93] Ibid., p. 28-30

[94] Ibid., p. 30, 31

[95] *Fifty Years*, p. 728, The Controversial Conversion, Diss., p. 150, *The Controversial Conversion of Charles Chiniquy*, p. 5, *Pastor Chiniquy*, p. 31

[96] *The Living Webster Encyclopedic Dictionary of the English Language*, (The English-Language Institute of America, Inc, 1971), p. 768

[97] *Fifty Years*, p. 763-773, *Pastor Chiniquy*, p. 31, 32

[98] *Pastor Chiniquy*, p. 32, *Fifty Years*, p. 533

[99] *Pastor Chiniquy*, p. 32-35

[100] Ibid., p, 37

Appendix 2

The Soul Of Abraham Lincoln, p. 33, 35, 63-66, 76, 77, 118, 119, 131-133, 146-155, 172-175, 314, 319-321, 331, 341, *Herndon's Informants: Letters, Interviews, and Statements about Abraham Lincoln*, p. 520, 521, 576, 577, 582, 583, 587, *Lincoln's Herndon*, p. 214-216, 237, 238, 256, 257, 269-272, 274-278, 280, 358, *Holland's Life of Abraham Lincoln*, p. xxii, xxiii, Paul M, Zall, *Lincoln on Lincoln*, (The University Press of Kentucky, 2003), p. 70-72, Lord Longford, *Abraham Lincoln*, (Weidenfeld & Nicolson, 1974), p. 46, Roy P. Basler, ed, *The Collected Works of Abraham Lincoln*, (Rutgers University Press, 1953), Volume 4, p. 270, Volume 5, p. 185, Otto Eisenschiml, *Why The Civil War*, (Bobbs-Merill, 1958), p. 177, *Life on the Circuit with Lincoln*, p. 255, 356, Robert Dale Richardson, *Abraham Lincoln's Autobiography*, (The Beacon Press, 1948), p. 29, *World Book Encyclopedia*, 1978, Volume 3, p. 288, Volume 15, p. 151, *Longman Guide To Living Religions*, (Redwood Books, 1994), p. 256, 28. *Abraham Lincoln: The Quest For Immortality*, p. 64, William H. Herndon, *The Hidden Lincoln*, (Viking Press, 1938), p. 45, *Biographical Directory of the American Congress: 1774 - 1996*, (CQ Staff Directories, Inc., 1997), p. 168, 172, *New York Times*, February 27, 1861, p. 1

Index